Economic
Development
ANALYSIS
AND
POLICY

Economic Development

ANALYSIS
AND
POLICY

Loraine Donaldson
Georgia State University

**West
Publishing
Company**

St. Paul
New York
Los Angeles
San Francisco

COPYRIGHT © 1984 By WEST PUBLISHING CO.
      50 West Kellogg Boulevard
      P.O. Box 3526
      St. Paul, Minnesota 55165

Copyeditor: Bernice Lifton
Artwork: Taly Design Group
Composition: Parkwood Composition Service, Inc.
Cover: Relief map of Earth. Photograph courtesy Dr.
      Michael Kobrick, NASA—JPL.

Library of Congress Cataloging in Publication
Data

Donaldson, Loraine.
  Economic Development: Analysis and Policy.

  Bibliography: p.
  Includes index.
  1. Economic development.
  2. Developing countries.
I. Title.
HD82.D614   1984   338.9   83-21924
ISBN 0-314-77898-5

INTERNATIONAL EDITION ISBN: 0-314-80462-5

to Mil
and Joe

Contents

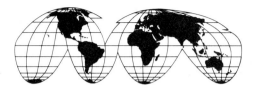

Preface

The study of economic development examines the potential for reducing world poverty and inequality, for improving the health and living conditions of the majority of the world's people, who live in countries that are twenty, fifty, or even a hundred years away from achieving development. The discipline seeks to explain and understand the process of development as it has occurred in earlier and later times and to provide guidance for today's policymaker. The subject's impact upon world events and political stability is far-reaching. Our understanding of development affects economic relations among nation states and global security in a nuclear age. Thus it is extremely important that the study of development be given serious attention in any curriculum.

The subject of economic development has an impressive lineage. The first formal treatises in the discipline of economics dealt with the topic extensively. More currently, most of the specialized areas of modern economics have contributed to the knowledge base. Not only does the study of economic development have a strong base in economics per se, but it has also received an impressive amount of cross-fertilization from diverse disciplines. Many find that the interdisciplinary approach promises the greatest chance for progress in the field, while others note that considerable work must be done before a truly interdisci-plinary analytical framework is forthcoming. Most acknowledge that there is a challenging breadth to the study of economic development that both attracts and intimidates those seeking to understand more about the topic.

Necessarily any book on development must be limited in scope, leaving certain avenues of the discipline underexplored. This work seeks to integrate and simplify advanced material in the economics of development and provide a survey of important principles for the undergraduate and graduate student. As a result of its analytical approach, it is hoped the book will provide the reader with new insights in topical areas. Policy conclusions are derived from the analysis, and illustrations of the topics analyzed drawn from individual countries are presented at the end of pertinent chapters.

The focus is upon analysis of economic development, emphasizing the knowledge base developed in the postwar decades. Some fairly complex analysis has been simplified to make it accessible to a broader audience. A balanced representation of the literature is sought in treatment of topics such as the transfer of technology, resource accumulation and utilization, agricultural transformation, trade and capital flows, industrialization, income inequality, and demographic change. The material is selected and organized so that there is continuity and integration of the subdivisions of development economics. This is achieved in part by the use of graphs as a tool of analysis and an aid to presentation of material. A limited number of graphs are used, and the reader, once familiar with them, can readily relate them to new areas of analysis. The graphs, along with the sequence of topics, facilitate a logical integration of the subject matter into a unified whole. The integration, however, does not preclude selective omission of topics.

The reader must be familiar with basic material taught in principles of economics, but does not need calculus to follow the text. The student with less background can omit sections or chapters giving more in-depth treatment of topics. On the other hand, the material is advanced enough to challenge those who have moved beyond the principles level.

Time constraints may limit the amount of material assigned. Optimally, time permitting, chapters 1 to 5 and 7 to 15 should be thoroughly covered. However, it is possible to select fewer chapters and yet gain a satisfactory cross section of topics. With this in mind, certain comments about some chapters may prove helpful in making a selection.

Chapter 6, "Risk and Uncertainty," is fairly easily omitted, although it is suggested that the instructor abstract important insights of this chapter for students. This is easily done. Also, the instructor may choose to assign the section on international commodity agreements in chapter 6 separately. Chapter 8, "Development Models and Population Growth," may be omitted or only the short section on the Lewis-Fei-Ranis model may be assigned. The other sections of the chapter require more time if the models are covered in detail. Chapter 11, "Trade and Industrialization," is an important one; however, students will need help in mastering its material. If it is omitted, then material in chapters 13 and 18 that draws on certain diagrams will have to be omitted, or else the diagrams used will have to be explained. Chapter 13's in-depth graphic treatment of foreign direct investment may be skipped without loss of continuity. Chapters 16 through 19 are optional, and will generally be assigned when time permits or the focus of

the course demands their coverage. Some of the material of chapter 16 is covered at a lower level in chapter 15.

The text provides the basic background needed to understand the more specialized and diverse literature on economic development. The use of the text, then, can free instructors to choose supplementary readings of interest for the focus of their courses. Once students have gained basic analytical techniques, they can read topical studies with greater understanding.

ACKNOWLEDGMENTS

A book that seeks to present basic knowledge in any area accrues an enormous intellectual debt. In the field of economic development there is an especially large indebtedness to those working in far-flung places and to scholars of many nationalities and diverse intellectual heritage. The richness and variety of the literature make it difficult to select and synthesize the work of those contributing to the field, while the process of condensing and integrating creates an uneasy feeling that the full stature of these contributions will not be adequately brought out. Here I wish to acknowledge this possibility and emphasize that my intention has been otherwise. I can only hope that the book spurs the reader to seek out the original literature and develop a deep interest in further study of economic development. In this respect, I owe a personal debt to Benjamin Higgins for the stimulation provided by his original text on development economics and to John Prior Lewis, Alan Sievers, Stephen Roebuck, George Stolnitz, and the late Robert Turner for their tutorial roles during my years as a student.

This book could not have been written without my students who, over the years, have responded with insight and enthusiasm to development economics and its vital importance to world events. Their response to draft chapters has been a great help in refining my thoughts and presentation. In addition, many details were helpfully checked by my student assistants, Rengia Sonmez, Keith Leggett, and Vernon Sohier.

Portions of the book were read by John Klein, Louis Ederington, Bruce Seaman, Bruce Kaufman, Jorge Martinez, Dennis R. Appleyard, and James H. Cobbe, who made helpful suggestions and comments. Miltos Chacholiades read the entire first draft, and in addition to helpful insights provided unwavering encouragement. The entire manuscript was also reviewed by N. C. Modeste, who pinpointed certain chapters in need of improvement. My editor, Gary Woodruff, has been both helpful and understanding in regard to the book's purpose and scope.

I would also like to thank Dr. George E. Wright and Dr. David T. Watson, both of whom made significant, albeit indirect, contributions to this book.

Finally, I truly doubt the book could have been completed without the work of my secretary, Marilyn King. She painstakingly typed all of the manuscript and, ever alert, caught many oversights on my part. My gratitude to her is very great indeed.

Economic
Development
ANALYSIS
AND
POLICY

Definitions and Measurements of Economic Development

chapter

1

Threstudy of economic development spans centuries and disciplines. There are no simple theories to explain development nor quick routes to achieve it. Yet today there is an urgency about the problems arising from poverty and progress. A world of nation-states that does not provide the basic human needs for its inhabitants cannot be at peace with itself.

The challenge of development economics is to understand the forces at work as a traditional agrarian society is transformed into an economy able to provide higher living standards for all its people. Such understanding sets a framework for designing policies to spur modernization of an economy. Scholars from various disciplines have responded to this challenge; prominent among their contributions are those of economists. In fact, the formal discipline of economics actually originated in the eighteenth century with the study of economic development. This in turn was closely associated with the study of markets and their functions.

Once early insights about the process of development were gained, mainstream economics narrowed its focus and concentrated upon in-depth analysis of the market mechanism, including supply, demand, distribution, market structure, and international trade, all within a static framework. Until the Great Depression economic progress was taken for granted by most economists, although there were exceptions. Among these were economic historians who continued to explore the topic. And many outside mainstream Western economics were influenced by the writings of Karl Marx, whose encompassing but controversial theory of development, put forth in the mid-1800s, was interdisciplinary.

Then, in the aftermath of World War II the importance of the poor countries of the globe in the economic, political, and social structure of the world economy changed. Relative prosperity returned to more developed countries but many less-developed nations were still mired in abject poverty. Where colonial rule lingered national identities demanded independence from foreign political dominance. Acceptance of the idea that development could be accelerated and poverty conquered became widespread. The hopes and problems faced in this milieu claimed international attention, and economists in various specialties joined economic historians to study economic development.

The decades following World War II produced great change in the economies of many less-developed countries. Governments set development goals for their societies and initiated policies to stimulate modernization. The United Nations and The World Bank along with the governments of developed countries added funds and expertise to the effort. This new laboratory for the study of development generated data and other information for exploring and explaining the development process under conditions of the twentieth century. Among those attracted to work in this area are several Nobel laureates in economics.

The rediscovery of and renewed interest in economic development spawned an extensive literature with great diversity of emphasis by specialists of different nationalities. In this book the focus is upon

**The Focus of
the Book**

presenting a core of economic knowledge that analyzes the development process and seeks to explain its underlying causes. Through the presentation, selection, and organization of material, a balanced approach is sought involving increased integration of knowledge about development and an emphasis upon fundamentals. This provides background needed to venture into the vast literature in the area, and a foundation for addressing policy.

The policy analysis is oriented toward development under world conditions as they exist today. In the postwar period the economic systems of most less-developed countries have lacked comprehensive development planning. Traditional and market-type economies coexist with limited planning, as often indirect as direct, decentralized as often as centralized. The policy analysis consequently is geared toward hybrid economic systems where planning controls are used, but are of limited scope. At the same time, less-developed countries have functioned within a world economy where the trading network is heavily influenced by fairly decentralized, market-oriented nations, and where exchange opportunities with the block of centralized economies have been more limited. This too has impact upon the policy analysis.

It is outside the scope of an analytical treatise to delve deeply into the human dimension of poverty. Thus it is important to note here, at the beginning, that the end goal of the study of development is to improve the human condition. The motivating concerns of scholars in this field are human suffering and the denial of human potential inherent in abject poverty.

It would be misleading to imply that the development process is unambiguously positive in its effect upon the lives of those involved. Many voices are raised today against environmental disruption and other costs of growth experienced in developed countries. More people in less-developed countries, however, speak out in support of improved physical and material well-being despite the social and economic costs.

Governments unable to achieve development in less-developed countries often lose political power. The poverty-stricken may well rank economic progress above human rights and may forgo the right to vote in the hope of achieving the right to eat. Their alternatives are stark. Once the West showed it was possible to raise the masses out of poverty—a prospect not contemplated even by the early economists studying the process—development won growing endorsement in the plans and goals of men and nations. This book explores the path, problems, and prospects of an economy seeking to conquer poverty under twentieth century conditions.

The chapter begins with a discussion of definitions and measurements of development. Some statistical profiles and identifying characteristics are presented. The chapter also brings out the limitations of the data base that underlies our study of development. While this base is weak, there is ongoing effort to improve data quality; and empirical work provides useful input into the study of development so long as the limitations of the data base are kept in mind.

Economic development defies concise definition. The student of development is seeking to understand the dynamics of economic change embedded in a historical process that can span a century or more. Following in the footsteps of Adam Smith, the father of modern economics, the study of economic development seeks to explain "the nature and causes of the wealth of nations." To understand development is to understand the process by which nation-states raise the material living and working standards of their people, eliminating the deprivation that characterizes conditions for the masses in most preindustrial states. Development implies transformation of the traditional economic system. The term growth, on the other hand, often refers (sometimes in a theoretical context) to expansion under unchanged economic organization. It is arguable whether or not there is some absolute level beyond which a country grows but without further economic evolution.

Development Is a Historical Process

Development involves the adoption of more efficient technology that benefits from scientific advances and improves resource productivity. The structure of the economy changes, becoming less dependent on agriculture, more industrial, monetized, specialized, and interdependent, while utilizing more physical capital and human skills relative to unskilled labor. The product mix changes as new products and services emerge and the quality of goods and services improves. The government sector grows in importance. The composition of the foreign trade sector shifts to reflect changes in comparative advantage and development needs. Social, political, and economic institutions undergo sharp modification or transformation that can lead to stresses and tensions in the social fabric.

Not surprisingly, development in nation-states with differing historical conditions is not only time-consuming, but also diverse in both pace and character. In fact, some states have not yet begun the process, or show only sporadic evidence of a beginning. Others are accelerating their progress and relative positions, while development in some has slowed. Even with favorable historical circumstances, the process is not a smooth expansion of, economic output accompanied by an untroubled social transition.

As the resource base enlarges and technical change accelerates, resources are employed in new sectors and under new socioeconomic relationships. Traditional economic institutions of the mainly agrarian economy come under stress, and social organizations that flourished in the traditional society are threatened with extinction. The role of the government; the traditional ruling class; the family; extended kinship groups; and mores dictating moral, social, and economic behavior can all suffer disruption, sometimes to the point of crisis.

Inequalities in wealth and income may increase. Certain groups of individuals in various generations suffer declines in their relative and even absolute positions of material well-being. Many gradually find their accustomed work less satisfying or secure as the specialization and discipline of a technically changing society affect their job opportunities and make some human and physical capital obsolete. The disenchantment of unsatisfied expectations spills over into political pressures. When the country cannot calibrate the pace of change in economic areas to that which can be absorbed in social areas, political instability, even upheaval, erupts. Yet seldom does a country that has proceeded past initial modernization retrogress toward predevelopment conditions.

STATISTICAL CLASSIFICATION AND PATTERNS

There is no method for precisely classifying countries according to their development level. All classification schemes are open to criticism. The difficulty of devising a simple, exact scheme stems from the breadth of the development process and its variations among countries. The encompassing nature of the topic is also reflected in the absence of a concise definition of development that would provide clear guidelines for categorizing nations.

More fundamentally, economists do not have a model of the development process that identifies all major variables and specifies how they relate one to the other to effect development. Consequently, a major problem faced in devising an index of development is the selection and weighting of variables. No one set of weighted variables can capture or measure development in a single representative measure. Various indexes that reflect selected development variables are helpful so long as one realizes they are not an exact tool for ranking countries. Indexes that can be used to gain insight into the relative level of development of countries are discussed in a subsequent section in some detail.

Classification of Countries by Development Level

It is common practice to use several indexes and other data reflective of development levels to classify countries into ranked groups or clusters of countries. This circumvents the difficult task of tabbing individual countries as being "just ahead of" or "just behind" another country in their development. It is often stated, for example, that most countries of sub-Sahara Africa are less developed than those of Asia and Latin America, and that some groups of Latin American nations are more advanced than others.

Economists sometimes divide countries with development levels below the most advanced group into two categories—the more-developed group, and the poorer countries, where starvation, malnutrition, and abject poverty are widespread. Over time, of course, the composition of these groups changes. And there is no strict criteria for moving a country from one grouping into another. Most often, however, this broad range of countries below the most-advanced group will be referred to as less-developed countries, or LDCs, in comparison with the more-developed countries, or MDCs.

The term LDC refers to economic, not cultural or social characteristics. Of course the two are interrelated to varying degrees. As mentioned, development creates great pressures for changes in many social institutions. Some changes in social institutions are prerequisite to economic development or conducive to it. They are even used in indexes designed to rank countries according to development levels. The student of development, however, must guard against the idea that economic development standings imply anything about a ranking of social institutions or cultural achievements, or that modernization and material progress necessarily produce social or other changes universally deemed desirable.

Another term oftentimes used for LDCs is "Third World." The first two worlds are the Western-oriented developed countries and the Soviet Union, along with communist countries of Eastern Europe that are oriented toward Russia. It is somewhat misleading to include in the Third World oil-rich LDCs that enjoy high levels of per capita GNP but are not developed. Among these countries is Kuwait, with large oil reserves, few people, and the world's highest per capita GNP.

Before looking at data on countries at various levels of development, it is helpful to identify general characteristics of a traditional economy where little in the way of a modern society has penetrated the economic structure. To some degree these characteristics persist in early stages of development and certain of them are present even in later stages. Following are the characteristics of a hypothetical or composite LDC that has *not begun* development.

Characteristics of a Traditional Economy

The majority of the population works the land. Their productivity is very low and food production per capita in bad harvest years is below nutritional needs. Agricultural methods are traditional and techniques primitive; for centuries there has been little change or innovation. The main food crop is a cereal—rice, wheat, or corn. Tools are simple and are combined with human and animal power. There is little land improvement other than clearing. As much as 40 percent of the harvest is lost to pests and rodents either in the field or in inadequate storage facilities. Food preservation methods are primitive.

The peasant is usually indebted to a landlord, unless he shares tribal land in less densely populated areas. The agricultural sector exchanges goods mainly by barter and most farms are self-sufficient. Market forces affect allocation of productive factors in the rural sector only marginally if at all. The landlord, paid in a portion of crop output, may enter the monetized sector to sell his share. Sometimes peasants, using traditional techniques, produce some small cash crops for export markets.

Minimum necessities of life are produced on the farm. There may be some specialization leading to cottage industries that sell their output to a village merchant. Some itinerant tinkers, blacksmiths, potters, and so forth may sell services and goods to several villages.

When land is scarce, farms are as small as one hectare (2.47 acres) and seldom above five hectares. Landed estates exist in some countries with the peasant in a serflike relation with the landlord. Transportation and mobility are greatly limited and markets small and thin.

Living conditions are primitive. Most often a small mud and thatch hut houses a family of five to seven people. The extended family provides mutual support and security among relatives. Women, in addition to food preparation and child care, provide from 30 to 60 percent of the farm labor when the culture sanctions their participation in the labor force. Work patterns adjust to farming's seasonal swings in labor needs.

The family is illiterate, without health facilities, and suffers from endemic diseases such as amebiasis and other parasitic infections that lower energy levels, work capacity, and resistance to life-taking diseases. Infant and early childhood mortality is high. The average life span is 30 to 40 years. Contaminated water, poor sewerage, and other unhygienic conditions promote illness.

Custom and tradition dictate early marriage, limited individuality, fatalism, and a hierarchical sociopolitical structure. The total system is geared toward survival.

There may be an export sector based on plantation agriculture or raw materials, and owned by foreigners. The technology here is influenced by foreign developed-countries, and the capital initially comes from abroad. There are few links between the export enclave and the rest of the economy. The enclave will be lucrative enough to support an elite group of locals in the same life-style as foreigners.

Pay for laborers in export sectors will be above the subsistence levels in the agricultural sector, and productivity considerably higher. The enclave sector may develop a seaport city that supports a merchant and commercial class and attracts some migrants from the farms for unskilled urban jobs. When a nation-state locates its government in a particular place, urbanization also follows.

Some natives will earn incomes above farm level by joining the militia or the government clerical staff. Usually some minimum education is necessary here. It is often acquired in missionary schools or schools run by foreigners in the export enclave, but increasingly in locally managed educational facilities. Higher government officials are educated predominately abroad, unless the export cities are large enough to establish and maintain a university with support from the foreign community.

The government is usually highly dependent upon the militia in its ability to maintain and exercise power. Its control of the countryside is limited and often ineffective. Law and order may be minimal and interrupted by tribal wars. Customs duties are the government's main source of income.

If world health organizations have penetrated the country to a sufficient degree, death rates may be dropping and population growing. Capital-labor ratios are low and income per capita fluctuates with agricultural output, which is determined mainly by the weather. In a large country, regional disparities in crop harvests can lead to localized famines because of limited communications and transportation.

Such is a brief stereotype or composite picture of a poor and stagnant LDC. For the many LDCs that are developing and have reached various levels of the development process, the topology is varied and many characteristics typical of some are not typical of all. Most, however, have experienced prolonged unevenness in their development such that certain segments or sectors are not responding to or benefiting from development, and exhibit some of the characteristics described.

Countries with ongoing development appear to the inexperienced observer to be a surprising admixture of features common to advanced countries side-by-side with aspects of premodern and early levels of development. Imported modern production methods create a technology gap within the economy. For example, large modern factories exist along with small firms employing low-skill labor and vintage tools or production methods. Home manufacture or cottage industry using centuries-old techniques maintains hold in the countryside. Large farms worked with modern techniques can exist side by side with subsistence plots where peasants have no knowledge of newer methods that can improve yields from small-scale farming. Or, the agricultural sector may remain premodern while the industrial or mining sector has islands of modernity. **Dualism**

Interrelations among the advanced and less-advanced sectors can vary. A strengthening web of linkages creates a broadening base for development. The spread effect, however, may be limited. One impediment to a reduction of sectoral divergence in LDCs is the immobility of resources, a condition that precludes efficient resource allocation. Resources that could contribute more in another sector face economic and social constraints that greatly reduce their mobility, and their contribution to output. (Conceptually, conditions of efficient resource usage require that resources be allocated so that the value of their marginal output is the same in each sector for the last unit of each resource employed in that sector.) Another hindrance can be the lack of linkages between the economic structures of the advanced and less-advanced sectors. The advanced sector does not spread or ignite development in the underdeveloped one. When an LDC perpetuates the dichotomy between sectors for prolonged periods and shows no signs of becoming a more homogeneous, integrated economy, the term *dualism* is applied. Dualism constricts and distorts development because the growth is narrow.

More specifically, the economy is said to be dualistic when over time resource allocation is far removed from efficiency conditions and when the modern sector is capital and skilled-labor intensive compared with the other sectors, has limited production and distribution linkages with the traditional or small-scale sectors, and produces mainly modern products consumed by those working in the sector. The modern sector may also be highly oriented toward trade with advanced countries, and include multinational corporations from those countries. It is not uncommon for the modern sector to be concentrated in one geographic region of the country and be associated with urbanization. When dualism exists, inequality of income tends to be high compared with countries that developed in earlier eras, when technology was not as advanced or as capital-intensive, and the optimum scale of production was not as large.

There are social and political dimensions to dualism. When there are strong contrasts in social patterns between the modernized sector and the rest of the economy, social dualism is said to exist. (Anaylsis of this condition was begun in the work of J. H. Boeke, *Economics and Economic Policy of Dual Societies*, 1953.) Social dualism may involve differences in the role of religion in temporal affairs, the role of the family and extended kinship groups, community relations and accepted economic behavior in labor relations, competition, and so forth. The roots of such differences can be ethnic diversity, differences in national origin, absorption of other cultures through international exposure, and divergent cultural evolution from a common cultural base in different areas of a country over a long historical period. Modernization triggers social changes in the advanced sector and deepens the divisions intensifying social distrust and disunity. When social division is aligned with economically related dualism, the control of dualism becomes more difficult.

Social dualism can increase the likelihood of political instability. Political organizations in the sectors may diverge and reflect social tensions. Because of its economic dominance, the modern sector often attains far-reaching political power. Dominant political groups who do not perceive the limitations that continued dualism places upon further progress in development act in their own short-term self-interest. This can aggravate the inequities of dualism.

Social dualism may reflect the absence of a middle class or the failure of a middle class to develop as rapidly as in growth situations unhindered by dualism. However, skilled labor, such as foremen, mechanics, and electricians, who are in relatively short supply in industrializing LDCs, may constitute a small middle class attached to the modern sector. The vast majority of the population will have income levels well below those of skilled labor, upper-income professionals, and major wealth owners. With population growth the lower-income group enlarges and may even increase relative to the more affluent.

Dualism is often associated with development conditions in Latin America. Asian countries today can be said to exhibit some of its features, and various African countries are manifesting its early symptoms. Even Japan's development process, begun in the later 1880s, is said to have shown a degree of dualism. Some of the analysis developed in this book pays special attention to economic features and problems of dualism and also explores policy options for reducing it.

Some Basic Data   It is helpful at this point to look at some data on underdeveloped countries to get a feel for their diversity as well as their common characteristics. The tables used are based upon data supplied by The World Bank and are presented at the end of the chapter (see pp. 21 to 28). Countries of the world are divided by The World Bank into five groups: Low-Income Countries, Middle-Income Countries, Industrialized Countries, High-Income Oil Exporters, and Nonmarket Industrial Economies. The oil exporters listed in the fourth group are all less-developed countries despite their high income. Countries in the middle-income group have a wide range of income per capita. Those in the top range of the middle-income group are difficult to classify. Most in this group are considered to be less developed compared with the industrialized nations.

In the tables two abbreviations for aggregate production are used, GNP and GDP. GDP stands for gross domestic product, the value of all new goods and services produced during a year by resources, foreign and national, located in the country. The production of new goods and services yields income of equivalent value, some of which is diverted to the government sector as taxes. GNP stands for gross national product, the annual value of all income generated by national resources in the production of new goods and services. Thus, if some national resources earned income while located abroad, the income earned would be part of national income for the home country. Income generated by foreign resources located in the domestic economy are part of the economy's GDP but not its GNP.

Table 1.1 shows the great diversity in size, income per capita and its growth, literacy, and life expectancy among the various countries. It also indicates the large growth in energy consumption per capita associated with development. Many countries in the poorest group had very little growth in their income per capita over the period 1960–80, while most found that their populations continued to expand at a moderate-to-high rate.

The growth rate of GNP per capita is the growth rate of national product less the growth rate of population for the same period.[1] Among the middle-income group, Singapore, the Republic of Korea, Taiwan (not listed), Hong Kong, Yemen, Lesotho, and Romania had growth rates of per capita GNP of 6 percent and more between 1960 and 1980. For many of the poorest LDCs, the rise in per capita income has been only 1 percent per year. One percent of $150 is $1.50; and adjustments for the statistical shortcomings of GNP would still leave the increment to income very small indeed relative to the average annual increment of over $200 in MDCs.

Table 1.2 gives information on the distribution of output among sectors of the economy, and between consumption goods and investment goods. The transformation of an economy's structure is discussed in a subsequent section on patterns of development. Here we note the predominance of agriculture at low levels of development and the high percentage of output that is consumed when incomes are low.

LDCs, as the data illustrate, are a broad range of countries concentrated in Africa, South America, and Asia. Approximately two thirds of the world's people live in these countries and they vary dramatically in their levels of development and incidence of poverty. A majority of these nations are small, with populations below 15 million. Yet the world's two most populous countries, China, with one billion people, and India, with over 600 million, are in this group.

---

1. The reader should not conclude that a reduction in the growth rate of population will raise GNP per capita by the amount of the reduction since the growth rate of GNP is affected by population growth. More is said about this in chapter 7.

LDCs are mainly in the tropical and subtropical areas and a large number experienced foreign rule during the period of Western colonization. In the vast majority population growth is higher than in developed countries. Population density varies greatly in relation to natural resources, however. Even countries such as India are not more densely populated than Japan, the United Kingdom, or Holland today. However, India, China, and certain other LDCs are more densely populated than the countries of Western Europe were in the early eighteenth century, when they were beginning their development process. They are also poorer.

Statistical Patterns of Development

Simon Kuznets pioneered in the development and study of the data pertinent to the historical development process. The problems of interpreting these data and assigning confidence levels to them are large and are discussed in a subsequent section. With the birth of the United Nations, data collection in LDCs was begun, or expanded, and cast into the mold of national income accounting. These additional data have been examined by Hollis Chenery of The World Bank. He carries on in the Kuznets tradition of developing an empirical base for the study of development. With the additional observation periods, he is able to use more sophisticated techniques of statistical analysis in collating and interpreting the data. This approach is narrower, however, than the broad historical one Kuznets used.

Chenery's approach answers an important question about the empirical behavior of development variables. That question is: As income per capita changes, do other variables, social and economic, tend to change systematically so that a set of universal variables can be identified as forming a pattern, changing with development? In other words, of the total set of variables affecting development, is there a subset of variables independent of the individual LDC's special economic and historical conditions that exhibit universal behavior patterns as GNP per capita rises?

Chenery, collaborating with Moises Syrquin, finds that such patterns do exist (Chenery and Syrquin 1975). The authors identify variables that tend to move with GNP per capita and give an example of the magnitude of change for an average economy. They find the variance among countries of those variables, or most of them, is low, and the correlation with specific GNP levels high. Thus they can speak of stylized patterns as the representative country moves along a path of long-term growth. Their statistical patterns for a medium-sized country are shown in table 1.3. The per capita income levels measured are in 1964 dollars and the numbers in the table are derived from cross-country regressions using data from 1950–70. The presumption of a cross-country sample is that different countries can represent an individual one at different levels of per capita GNP, and thus yield the stylized country pattern.

The representative economy's pattern is *not* a norm by which to gauge development performance in the sense that all countries should approximate the pattern shown. Comparisons can be made, but conclusions must be drawn with care by an expert. The usefulness of the data is in the basic information and insights they provide and the questions they pose.

Before discussing table 1.3 we should explain that total value of production of an economy can be subdivided in different ways, each useful. Two common subdivisions of GNP are: (a) *expenditure* categories of private consumption, government consumption, investment (government plus private) and exports-minus-imports; or (b) *income* categories of private consumption, domestic savings, foreign savings inflow, and government revenue. Investment equals domestic savings plus foreign savings.[2]

Production is also broken down into several sectors of origin: primary, industry, utilities, and services. Production attributed to each sector is measured as the value added in this sector, thus eliminating double counting. Two sectors need explanation. The primary share of production includes forestry, fishing, mining of natural resource deposits, and agricultural output. The services sector includes professional services, tourism, household servants, wholesale and retail merchandising, government activities, and transportation. It is sometimes called the tertiary sector and utility services are often included. Industry is then called the secondary sector and includes construction. The data in table 1.3 and additional findings from the study are now discussed to reveal the patterns they establish.

Industrialization   One of the most pronounced and important structural changes that occur with development is the relative growth of industrial output and the relative decline of agriculture's, in most cases the dominant component of the primary sector. Agricultural output grows in absolute terms, but loses its position of dominance to the service sector as development proceeds. The industrial expansion in turn helps to change the character of the enlarged service sector. Specific findings regarding industrial expansion are of interest.

The data patterns lend support to the identification of an acceleration phase in the industrialization process that is closely associated with an upswing in savings and investment. Industrial growth may begin gradually; but it builds momentum before slowing down. The acceleration of industrial output growth is in part related to the low base from which output expands in early development.

The last column, giving the GNP level at which the total change in a variable is half completed, helps to identify this pattern of acceleration. The total increase in savings and investment is half completed at an income level of $200, as is the decline in the primary sector. Rises in industry's share of GNP and the labor force are half completed at $300–$325 income levels, as is the share of utilities. This can vary with size of country among other variables, but the idea behind terms such as "take-off" or "acceleration phase" may have meaning if viewed in relation to changes in specific variables affecting industrialization.

2. When imports exceed exports, there is an inflow of foreign savings. Foreign savings inflows are discussed in detail in chapter 13.

Demand patterns, of course, affect the relative decline of agriculture. At higher income levels there is a relatively greater demand for industrial output. Over the income levels covered, food consumption per capita increases, but only one half as much as per capita income. Thus, at an income of $100 per capita, food consumption is 41 percent of GNP, but drops to 17 percent at an income level of $1,000 per capita. (The percentage of an average family's income spent on food will, of course, be higher than these ratios that show the share of total GNP spent on food.)

Economies of scale also affect structural shifts among sectors. The pattern of industrialization will vary with the size of the country. Table 1.3 gives such a pattern for a representative country of 10 million people, which is considered medium-sized in this study. When countries are compared, a large one will have the same level of industrial output relative to total output at $200 per capita income that the small one has at $400. Certain industries with scale economies such as basic metals, paper, chemicals, and rubber products account for an important portion of the difference at this level of GNP per capita.

Output and labor force shifts among sectors take place at a different rate. Labor force shifts are affected by the technology of production in each sector and its rate of change. At the lowest level of income, the primary sector provides 52 percent of the income but absorbs 71 percent of the labor available. Agriculture's relative share of output falls at a faster rate than its relative share of the labor force.

The relative shares of the labor force in industry and services increase at a faster rate than their relative shares of output. The service sector absorbs more of agriculture's declining share of employment opportunities than industry. The labor force in industry as a percentage of the total labor force exceeds the share in primary production only after an income of $700 per capita is reached.

The slow decline in the relative share of labor in the primary sector is related to the fact that up to an income level of $500 per capita, the growth in labor productivity in industry is larger than that in the primary sector. The primary sector is sometimes viewed as a residual employment sector for those who might otherwise be unemployed.

The Service Sector   Services, including government, retailing, transportation, professional, and other services, increase during early development and then level off as a percentage of GNP. The composition changes greatly in this broad category as growth proceeds. Education and other government service expenditures rise as a proportion of GNP. Utilities, while shown separately here, are often included in the service sector. Their share of GNP doubles over the development process.

Taxes   At lower income levels taxes as a proportion of GNP tend to be low (10 to 12 percent of GNP) even where the government is socialist in outlook. A tax level of 20 percent is not achieved until the country attains an income level of $500 per capita. When a country is poor, most of its output must go to consumption, placing a limit on savings, investment, and government services. As food consumption declines relative to total consumption, indicating that less of total consumption goes toward "necessities," there is more leeway for restricting consumption via taxation for development needs. The transition to lower population growth rates may affect savings and taxation needs for education at higher income levels, slowing down the rise in taxes.

Population The demographic revolution is revealed in the data on birth and death rates. More refined data patterns on these important variables are discussed in chapter 7. Notice, however, that the key to population growth is the difference in the rates of decline in death relative to birth rates.

Urbanization The index of urbanization reflects an early acceleration phase whereby large percentages of the population cluster around cities. LDCs today tend to exhibit more rapid urbanization than Western countries at comparable levels of per capita GNP. They also have experienced higher population growth rates, which can influence the emergence of cities.

Weaker Patterns It is difficult to identify "typical" patterns of trade and capital inflow or income distribution. The variation among countries is broad. The accepted ideology of a country is one variable affecting distribution patterns.

Certain statements, however, can be made regarding foreign savings inflow. As Kuznets first pointed out, savings needed to finance development must come mainly from domestic sources. Foreign capital inflow soon declines from a peak of 24 percent of total savings at the lowest income level for the representative country. And this high rate reflects foreign investment in minerals and metals that have limited impact upon transformation of the domestic economy outside of a contribution to foreign exchange earnings.

When the countries are categorized as large and small, the behavior of trade variables is more uniform. The small countries must be subdivided according to resource endowments to achieve this, however. When discussing trade, 15 million people is the dividing line between large and small size countries.

The large country is more self-sufficient and less specialized in both exports and domestic production. Small countries tend to export 20 to 30 percent of their GNP, more than twice the level for large countries. They are apt to shift toward manufactures exports early when they have few resources. Examples are Israel, Greece, Taiwan, and Tunisia.

The transformation towards manufactures for export lags significantly behind the move toward industrial production for home demand. Manufactured exports equal primary exports at the $500 income level for large countries and between the $600 and $700 income level for small countries. Imports and exports as a proportion of GNP rise with per capita GNP; they rise much more for small than large countries.

PROBLEMS
OF DATA
INTERPRETATION

As various aspects of development are discussed, the meaning and reasons behind these patterns will be explored. The data certainly do not speak for themselves. For example, the relative decline in the share of output generated in the agricultural sector gives no hint of the vital role this sector plays in development. Here, the purpose is mainly to familiarize the reader with the statistical overview.

The Chenery study uses GNP to identify the level of development. It has already been mentioned that the changes are illustrative, not policy targets. Caution is warranted whenever GNP data are used in a study of this type. The following sections explain why.

Limitations of
National Income
Measurements

It is impossible to avoid using GNP (or GDP) per capita, imperfect though it is, as a measurement of affluence, poverty, and development. For one thing, through the postwar efforts of the United Nations, national income accounting measurements expressed in one currency denominator or numeraire are available annually for most countries of the noncommunist world. If there were another, more reliable, yardstick the tendency to depend upon national income measures would not be as compelling. But no more dependable measure exists. By default and by virtue of frequent usage, GNP acquires an aura of acceptability. Misplaced confidence in its reliability creeps into even sophisticated empirical studies. The statistical limitations of national income accounting are reviewed so that subsequent usage of the measures will not be misleading to the reader; and caveats about reliance upon GNP measures will not have to be repeated as various empirical studies are under discussion in subsequent chapters.

Since there are two measures of aggregate economic activity, Gross National Product and Gross Domestic Product, a choice must be made as to which to use. Some factors of production are mobile. Thus, some nationally owned factors earn income abroad while foreign factors earn income in the country of measurement. As a result, Gross Domestic Product, that is, the market value of new goods and services produced within a nation-state, cannot be expected to equal Gross National Product, the market value of income earned by nationally owned factors of production.

Both measures may be cited, or one or the other may be used, depending upon the focus of the research undertaken. Sometimes the difference between the two is striking. Thus when foreign oil firms owned all factor inputs except the oil itself, the national income of some oil-producing countries with few people, and those mainly nomadic, was in large part the royalties paid for the oil. When these countries raised the price of the oil and bought the capital and equipment used in its production, their national income soared. Their gross domestic income also rose, but by less since income from capital was previously a part of GDP. Their physical production of oil at first declined.

In an LDC with large sections of its economy not yet monetized, and with poor or nonexistent records of monetary transactions, methods of estimating GNP or GDP are often predominately indirect and subject to large margins of error. Even basic data that would be helpful to indirect estimates, for example, population or number of businesses in an industry, are poor or unreliable. Often good data collection is a luxury poorer countries cannot afford.

An agrarian economy has many types of economic activity that are not recorded in GNP. The farm is a fairly self-sufficient production unit turning out food, clothing, utensils, housing, weapons, tools, fences, irrigation canals, storage units, water supplies, fuel, and the like. As an economy progresses, division of labor increases and more goods enter the exchange economy. Barter soon gives way to monetary exchange, and trade fairs or local one-day markets yield to permanent businesses located in regional trade centers. Crops are processed off the farm and farms specialize in crops for market. Cottage industries give way to specialized manufacturing firms. Along this route, many goods enter GNP that were formerly omitted, or underreported as part of the agricultural or primary sector's output. It will appear that GNP and industrial output have increased more than they have in actuality when the goods become market transactions and thereby enter GNP. Growth is overstated, some estimates say by as much as one third. Reinforcing overstatement is the identification of many items, for example transportation, power, and communications services, as final goods when in fact in a more complex, interdependent economy they are better designated as intermediate goods. Offsetting this somewhat, however, is the inability to account adequately for improved products and new goods and services.

The main type of investment in agrarian economies will be land improvements such as dikes and irrigation ditches, land clearing, fencing, and terracing. Estimates of this investment, even at cost rather than market value, are statistically weak or nonexistent. Calculations of housing investment, construction, and inventories are also suspect.

The foreign trade sector data are often viewed as more reliable since there are trade records in two countries and entry is at a few ports subject to scrutiny for control and tax reasons. However, there are practices such as over- and underinvoicing to achieve illegal goals, and widespread smuggling, particularly of late in narcotics. Enormous amounts of money are estimated to be involved here. The flow of capital abroad is exceedingly difficult to trace. Currency controls and laws fail to prevent large sums from moving across borders, especially in times of political instability.

Employment in the service sector can be large in LDCs and includes many individuals working for other individuals who keep no records. Children enter this sector as servants, messengers, bootblacks, and such. Employees may be paid partly in upkeep and partly in money in various service jobs. Moreover, around cities there are large numbers of self-employed who do odd jobs, turn scrap materials into cheap products, or resell repaired items. Their income is generally not estimated.

Sometimes statisticians use shortcuts that are conceptually unsound. One LDC estimated GNP as a multiple of its money supply. The multiple used was the one that was frequently given for the United States economy. And usually LDCs use only one estimate of GNP, the final output approach, whereas the MDC's data permit more than one estimate using income data and value-added data. Using more than one approach serves as a check upon accuracy. When GNP is divided by population to calculate per capita GNP, errors in population data, not uncommon in LDCs, can distort this ratio.

Effect of Bias on Growth Rates

Errors in GNP data can distort growth rates. Assume the bias in the data is random in nature, rather than consistent from year to year. The effect of a random error bias of only 5 percent can be astonishingly large. An actual growth rate of 2 percent may be recorded as high as 12.7 percent (Morgan 1975, p. 45). The reason for such high errors in growth rates is that small errors in total GNP are magnified when the change in GNP is relatively small. Thus, even when errors are not large, care must be used when analyzing growth rates of GNP of a normal range of 1 percent to 6 percent. The prayer of the statistician in this case is that errors are not random.

The Index Problem

GNP and GDP are monetary measures of total output that allow aggregation of goods and services. Problems immediately occur in comparing the GNP or GDP of different years when (a) the groups of goods and services produced are not the same, (b) absolute or relative prices differ, or (c) goods' quality changes. There is no way to adjust the data so that the indexes for various years are exactly comparable. In regard to prices, a set of prices can be chosen either from the beginning—or end—period of the index and used for all years. Indexes that cover shorter time spans are more comparable since the index problems have less impact.

An international comparison of GNP-GDP indexes is even more troublesome and less meaningful. The quality of goods can differ greatly. More importantly, there is only a limited range of goods consumed and produced that are the same or equivalent in the MDC and a poor LDC. Moreover, relative prices of the same or similar goods will differ greatly between two such countries, where one has relatively cheap labor and the other relatively cheap capital, or when prices do not reflect competitive market forces. MDC-LDC differences in GNP will be affected by which set of relative prices is used to calculate the value of output.

Most often the problem of which country's relative prices to use is circumvented by taking GNP in national prices and currency and using the foreign exchange rate between the two countries' currencies. This introduces additional bias rather than solving the problem of relative price differences. The foreign exchange rate, while it is influenced by relative price movements, does not measure differences in purchasing power for a representative set of goods composing GNP. It is reflective of supply and demand for exports and imports, capital flows, and government intervention. When exchange rates change continuously, or the government sets multiple rates, the statistician faces a decision as to which exchange rate to use. With the movement to flexible exchange rates among major world traders in the 1970s, international comparison of data became more complicated, and data less comparable between periods before and after the change.

The United Nations International Comparison Project   When GNP or GDP per capita between LDCs and MDCs is compared, ratios as high as 70 to 1 can be found. Yet the meaning of an income per capita of $100 is obscure when considered from the standpoint of managing to survive in America. In an effort to overcome some of the problems mentioned above that produce ratios of this type, a United Nations project selected 10 countries to represent the countries of the world (Kravis et al. 1975). The prices and quantities of different categories of goods purchased in these countries were carefully documented and from these a set of "average international prices" was developed from 1970 data and used for relative prices. Each country's weight in this average was determined by how many countries it was representing. There were 150 categories of goods with detailed items. A representative output sample was taken in each country and per capita GDP was expressed in dollars as a common denominator. This is not the same as using the exchange rate since the international prices were used, and the dollar was simply a convenient numeraire. Where India's GDP per capita was 2 percent of the 1970 United States' GDP per capita and Kenya's 3 percent when using GDP converted by foreign exchange rates, the more sophisticated World Bank measures showed the GDP per capita of India at 7 percent and Kenya at 5.7 percent. Colombia's GDP jumped from 6.85 percent to 15.9 percent of the United States' GDP per capita. Put another way, the United States' income per capita dropped from 50 times that of India and 33 times that of Kenya, to 14 and 17 times, respectively. Notice that India and Kenya reversed their relative positions and Kenya, with a GDP per capita of $275, ranked below India, with $342 per capita.

The latest phase of this project expanded benchmark estimates of GDP final expenditures to cover 34 countries for 1975. The data show in general that use of international exchange rates to compare GDP will grossly understate the relative position of low-income countries. The data also reveal certain interesting facts about the relative composition of spending categories. The share of capital formation in GDP is reduced—sometimes quite sharply—for the lowest-income countries by the use of international prices compared with that derived by using national prices. This is because capital is relatively expensive in LDCs compared with MDCs.

On the other hand, services are relatively cheap in national prices and valuation in international prices raises the level of services to GDP. Comparing all countries, the data show that the share of national income spent upon services remains fairly level as *per capita* GDP rises when services are valued in international prices. The conclusion is that the tendency for historical GDP data to show a rise in the proportion of income spent on services as per capita GDP increases is somewhat misleading: "[I]t is the rise in prices of services, not the rise in quantities, that plays the main role in pushing up service expenditures as income increases." (Kravis, Heston, and Summers 1982, p. 23).

Even with an upward adjustment of GDP per capita provided by the International Comparison Project, a comparison of consumption per   **Consumption Per Capita**

capita and living standards based on such data remains tenuous. Remember that income in LDCs is unevenly divided and a proportion goes to government and investment. For the masses consumption per capita is still a sum so small that a dollar figure is not easily grasped in an MDC environment, where the economy's structure in not geared to barest survival. When GDP or GNP data are used to relate consumption levels of different countries and their growth, the data should be viewed as, at best, rough estimates.

Other Indexes of Development

In another method of comparing economies, a group of national experts who have each closely studied the data and relative progress of his or her LDC compare their respective countries. This method was used by Irma Adelman and Cynthia Taft Morris in a study, which then identified economic, social, and political indicators of development and related them to levels of development (Adelman and Morris 1967).

In a more recent study, the U.N. Research Institute for Social Development devised an index using selected representative variables of socioeconomic progress. The variables used are life expectancy at birth; animal-protein consumption; school enrollment ratio; vocational enrollment ratio; average number of persons per room; newspapers, telephones, and radios per population measure; urbanization; percentage of adult males in agriculture and their output per capita; percentage of economically active population in sectors providing infrastructures and in white collar employment; per capita consumption of energy, electricity, and steel; percentage of GDP in manufacturing; and per capita foreign trade (U.N. Research Institute for Social Development, Report 70.10, 1970).

The index is more stable than GNP and in that sense is superior as a measure of development; it is also broader in scope. Three individual components of the index—electricity consumption per capita, steel consumption per capita, and telephones per 100,000 population—have a correlation of between .85 and .88 with the index and thus are good proxies for development level as defined by the index. GNP per capita is not highly correlated with the index. In part this is because at low levels of development, social and structural indicators are changing more rapidly than strictly economic indicators. The index, then, provides an alternative to GNP; however, it is not as ubiquitously available from period to period. Nor does it have an economic framework of analysis into which it can be readily fitted, as GNP does with Keynesian-type economics.

The Format of the Book

This chapter has talked about the historical dimensions of economic development and the efforts made to identify universal characteristics amidst the historical differences. Problems of definitions and measurements of development were discussed in detail. With this background we can proceed to the analysis of the development process. Chapters that follow present topics in a sequence that promotes an understanding of the interdependent structure of a developing economy. The next two chapters develop a technical base useful in analysis as various areas in the study of development are covered.

TABLE 1.1 Basic Indicators

	Population (millions) mid-1980	Average Annual Growth of Population (%) 1960–70	1970–80	Area (thousand sq. kilometers)	GNP per Capita U.S.$ 1980	GNP per Capita Average Annual Growth (%) 1960–80[a]	Adult Literacy Rate (%) 1977[b]	Life Expectancy at Birth (years) 1980	Per Capita Energy Consumption (kilograms of coal equivalent) 1979
Low-income Economies	2,160.9 t	2.1 w	2.1 w	30,714 t	260 w	1.2 w	50 w	57 w	421 w
China and India	1,649.9 t	2.1 w	1.9 w	12,819 t	270 w		54 w	59 w	514 w
Others	511.0 t	2.1 w	2.6 w	17,895 t	230 w	1.0 w	34 w	48 w	87 w
1 Kampuchea, Dem.	6.9	2.6	−0.2	181					2
2 Loa PDR	3.4	1.9	1.8	237			41	43	98
3 Bhutan	1.3	1.8	2.0	47	80	−0.1		44	
4 Chad	4.5	1.8	2.0	1,284	120	−1.8	15	41	22
5 Bangladesh	88.5	2.4	2.6	144	130	(.)	26	46	40
6 Ethiopia	31.1	2.4	2.0	1,222	140	1.4	15	40	20
7 Nepal	14.6	1.8	2.5	141	140	0.2	19	44	13
8 Somalia	3.9	2.4	2.3	638			60	44	74
9 Burma	34.8	2.3	2.4	677	170	1.2	70	54	67
10 Afghanistan	15.9	2.2	2.5	648			12	37	88
11 Viet Nam	54.2	3.1	2.8	330			87	63	138
12 Mali	7.0	2.4	2.7	1,240	190	1.4	9	43	28
13 Burundi	4.1	1.6	2.0	28	200	2.5	23	42	17
14 Rwanda	5.2	2.6	3.4	26	200	1.5	50	45	28
15 Upper Volta	6.1	2.0	1.8	274	210	0.1	5	39	26
16 Zaire	28.3	2.0	2.7	2,345	220	0.2	58	47	100
17 Malawi	6.1	2.8	2.9	118	230	2.9	25	44	67
18 Mozambique	12.1	2.1	4.0	802	230	−0.1	28	47	121
19 India	673.2	2.3	2.1	3,288	240	1.4	36	52	194
20 Haiti	5.0	1.5	1.7	28	270	0.5	23	53	63
21 Sri Lanka	14.7	2.4	1.6	66	270	2.4	85	66	135
22 Sierra Leone	3.5	2.2	2.6	72	280	(.)		47	84
23 Tanzania	18.7	2.7	3.4	945	280	1.9	66	52	51
24 China	976.7	1.9	1.8	9,561	290		66	64	734
25 Guinea	5.4	2.8	2.9	246	290	0.3	20	45	83
26 Central African Rep.	2.3	1.9	2.1	623	300	0.9	39	44	46
27 Pakistan	82.2	2.8	3.1	804	300	2.8	24	50	209
28 Uganda	12.6	2.9	2.6	236	300	−0.7	48	54	39
29 Benin	3.4	2.5	2.6	113	310	0.4	25	47	65
30 Niger	5.3	3.3	2.8	1,267	330	−1.6	5	43	46

TABLE 1.1   Basic Indicators (continued)

	Population (millions) mid-1980	Average Annual Growth of Population (%) 1960-70	Average Annual Growth of Population (%) 1970-80	Area (thousand sq. kilometers)	GNP per Capita U.S.$ 1980	GNP per Capita Average Annual Growth (%) 1960-80a	Adult Literacy Rate (%) 1977b	Life Expectancy at Birth (years) 1980	Per Capita Energy Consumption (kilograms of coal equivalent) 1979
31 Madagascar	8.7	2.1	2.5	587	350	-0.5	50	47	89
32 Sudan	18.7	2.1	3.0	2,506	410	-0.2	20	46	133
33 Togo	2.5	2.7	2.5	56	410	3.0	18	47	112
Middle-income Economies	1,138.8 t	2.5 w	2.4 w	41,614 t	1,400 w	3.8 w	65 w	60 w	965 w
Oil Exporters	496.8 t	2.5 w	2.6 w	16,135 t	1,160 w	3.3 w	57 w	56 w	658 w
Oil Importers	642.0 t	2.4 w	2.3 w	25,479 t	1,580 w	4.1 w	73 w	63 w	1,204 w
34 Ghana	11.7	2.4	3.0	239	420	-1.0	..	49	258
35 Kenya	15.9	3.2	3.4	583	420	2.7	50	55	172
36 Lesotho	1.3	2.0	2.3	30	420	6.1	52	51	..
37 Yemen, PDR	1.9	2.1	2.4	333	420	12.1	40	45	509
38 Indonesia	146.6	2.0	2.3	1,919	430	4.0	62	53	225
39 Yemen Arab Rep.	7.0	2.3	2.9	195	430	4.5	21	42	58
40 Mauritania	1.5	2.5	2.5	1,031	440	1.6	17	43	196
41 Senegal	5.7	3.3	2.8	196	450	-0.3	10	43	253
42 Angola	7.1	1.5	2.4	1,247	470	-2.3	..	42	200
43 Liberia	1.9	3.1	3.4	111	530	1.5	25	54	425
44 Honduras	3.7	3.1	3.4	112	560	1.1	60	58	238
45 Zambia	5.8	2.8	3.1	753	560	0.2	44	49	832
46 Bolivia	5.6	2.3	2.5	1,099	570	2.1	63	50	447
47 Egypt	39.8	2.2	2.1	1,001	580	3.4	44	57	539
48 Zimbabwe	7.4	3.9	3.3	391	630	0.7	74	55	783
49 El Salvador	4.5	2.9	2.9	21	660	1.6	62	63	338
50 Cameroon	8.4	1.8	2.2	475	670	2.6	..	47	143
51 Thailand	47.0	3.0	2.5	514	670	4.7	84	63	353
52 Philippines	49.0	3.0	2.7	300	690	2.8	75	64	329
53 Nicaragua	2.6	2.6	3.4	130	740	0.9	90	56	446
54 Papua New Guinea	3.0	2.1	2.3	462	780	2.8	32	51	299
55 Congo, People's Rep.	1.6	2.4	2.8	342	900	0.8	..	59	195
56 Morocco	20.2	2.5	3.0	447	900	2.5	28	56	302
57 Mongolia	1.7	2.9	2.9	1,565	..	..	..	64	1,483
58 Albania	2.7	2.8	2.5	29	..	..	..	70	1,118

59 Peru	17.4	2.8	2.6	1,285	930	1.1	80	58	716
60 Nigeria	84.7	2.5	2.5	924	1,010	4.1	30	49	80
61 Jamaica	2.2	1.4	1.5	11	1,040	0.6	90	71	1,326
62 Guatemala	7.3	3.0	3.0	109	1,080	2.8	..	59	229
63 Ivory Coast	8.3	3.7	5.0	322	1,150	2.5	41	47	230
64 Dominican Rep.	5.4	2.7	3.0	49	1,160	3.4	67	61	490
65 Colombia	26.7	3.0	2.3	1,139	1,180	3.0	..	63	914
66 Ecuador	8.0	3.0	3.0	284	1,270	4.5	81	61	640
67 Paraguay	3.2	2.5	3.2	407	1,300	3.2	84	65	234
68 Tunisia	6.4	1.9	2.1	164	1,310	4.8	62	60	590
69 Korea, Dem. Rep.	18.3	2.9	2.6	121			65	65	2,775
70 Syrian Arab Rep.	9.0	3.2	3.6	185	1,340	3.7	58	65	925
71 Jordan	3.2	3.0	3.4	98	1,420	5.7	70	61	522
72 Lebanon	2.7	2.8	0.7	10				66	1,028
73 Turkey	44.9	2.5	2.4	781	1,470	3.6	60	62	771
74 Cuba	9.7	2.0	1.3	115			96	73	1,358
75 Korea, Rep. of	38.2	2.5	1.7	98	1,520	7.0	93	65	1,473
76 Malaysia	13.9	2.8	2.4	330	1,620	4.3		64	713
77 Costa Rica	2.2	3.4	2.5	51	1,730	3.2	90	70	812
78 Panama	1.8	2.9	2.3	77	1,730	3.3		70	895
79 Algeria	18.9	2.4	3.2	2,382	1,870	3.2	35	56	645
80 Brazil	118.7	2.9	2.2	8,512	2,050	5.1	76	63	1,018
81 Mexico	69.8	3.3	3.1	1,973	2,090	2.6	81	65	1,535
82 Chile	11.1	2.1	1.7	757	2,150	1.6		67	1,153
83 South Africa	29.3	2.6	2.7	1,221	2,300	2.3		61	2,895
84 Romania	22.2	1.0	0.9	238	2,340	8.6	98	71	4,659
85 Portugal	9.8	-0.2	1.3	92	2,370	5.0		71	1,433
86 Argentina	27.7	1.4	1.6	2,767	2,390	2.2	93	70	1,965
87 Yugoslavia	22.3	1.0	0.9	256	2,620	5.4	85	70	2,415
88 Uruguay	2.9	1.1	0.3	176	2,810	1.4	94	71	1,219
89 Iran	38.8	2.9	3.1	1,648			50	59	1,141
90 Iraq	13.1	3.1	3.3	435	3,020	5.3		56	664
91 Venezuela	14.9	3.4	3.3	912	3,630	2.6	82	67	2,944
92 Hong Kong	5.1	2.6	2.5	1	4,240	6.8	90	74	1,481
93 Trinidad and Tobago	1.2	2.0	1.3	5	4,370	3.0	95	72	4,872
94 Greece	9.6	0.5	0.9	132	4,380	5.8		74	2,164
95 Singapore	2.4	2.4	1.5	1	4,430	7.5		72	5,784
96 Israel	3.9	3.4	2.6	21	4,500	3.8		72	3,513
High-income Oil Exporters	14.4 t	4.1 w	5.0 w	4,012 t	12,630 w	6.3 w	25 w	57 w	2,609 w
97 Libya	3.0	3.8	4.1	1,760	8,640	5.2		56	2,254
98 Saudia Arabia	9.0	3.4	4.4	2,150	11,260	8.1	16	54	1,984
99 Kuwait	1.4	9.8	6.0	18	19,830	-1.1	60	70	6,159
100 United Arab Emirates	1.0	10.8	13.2	84	26,850	4.3	56	63	4,451

TABLE 1.1 *Basic Indicators (continued)*

	Population (millions) mid-1980	Average Annual Growth of Population (%) 1960–70	Average Annual Growth of Population (%) 1970–80	Area (thousand sq. kilometers)	GNP per Capita U.S.$ 1980	GNP per Capita Average Annual Growth (%) 1960–80[a]	Adult Literacy Rate (%) 1977[b]	Life Expectancy at Birth (years) 1980	Per Capita Energy Consumption (kilograms of coal equivalent) 1979
Industrial Market Economies	714.4 t	1.0 w	0.8 w	30,935 t	10,320 w	3.6 w	99 w	74 w	7,293 w
101 Ireland	3.3	0.4	1.1	70	4,880	3.1	98	73	3,687
102 Spain	37.4	1.1	1.0	505	5,400	4.5	..	73	2,698
103 Italy	56.9	0.6	0.6	301	6,480	3.6	98	73	3,312
104 New Zealand	3.3	1.7	1.5	269	7,090	1.8	99	73	4,706
105 United Kingdom	55.9	0.5	0.1	245	7,920	2.2	99	73	5,272
106 Finland	4.9	0.4	0.5	337	9,720	4.0	100	73	6,001
107 Australia	14.5	2.0	1.4	7,687	9,820	2.7	100	74	6,539
108 Japan	116.8	1.0	1.1	372	9,890	7.1	99	76	4,048
109 Canada	23.9	1.8	1.1	9,976	10,130	3.3	99	74	13,164
110 Austria	7.5	0.6	0.0	84	10,230	4.1	99	72	5,087
111 United States	227.7	1.3	1.0	9,363	11,360	2.3	99	74	11,681
112 Netherlands	14.1	1.3	0.8	41	11,470	3.2	99	75	6,597
113 France	53.5	1.0	0.5	547	11,730	3.9	99	74	4,810
114 Belgium	9.8	0.5	0.2	31	12,180	3.8	99	73	6,513
115 Norway	4.1	0.8	0.5	324	12,650	3.5	99	75	11,749
116 Denmark	5.1	0.7	0.4	43	12,950	3.3	99	75	5,726
117 Sweden	8.3	0.7	0.3	450	13,520	2.3	99	75	8,258
118 Germany, Fed. Rep.	60.9	0.9	(.)	249	13,590	3.3	99	73	6,264
119 Switzerland	6.5	1.6	0.3	41	16,440	1.9	99	75	5,002
Nonmarket Industrial Economies	353.3 t	1.0 w	0.8 w	23,155 t	4,640 w	4.2 w	100 w	71 w	5,822 w
120 Poland	35.8	1.0	0.9	313	3,900	5.3	98	72	5,752
121 Bulgaria	9.0	0.8	0.6	111	4,150	5.6	..	73	5,487
122 Hungary	10.8	0.4	0.4	93	4,180	4.5	99	71	3,797
123 USSR	265.5	1.2	0.9	22,402	4,550	4.0	100	71	5,793
124 Czechoslovakia	15.3	0.5	0.7	128	5,820	4.0	..	71	6,656
125 German Dem. Rep.	16.9	−0.1	−0.1	108	7,180	4.7	..	72	7,136

a. Because data for the early 1960s are not available, figures in italics are for periods other than that specified.
b. Figures in italics are for years other than that specified.

Note: *t* stands for total; *w* stands for population-weighted average.
SOURCE: World Bank, *World Development Report 1982* (New York: Oxford University Press, 1982), Tables 1, 7, 17, pp. 110–11, 122–23, 142–43. Reprinted by permission.

TABLE 1.2 *Structure of Production*

(percentage of GDP)

	Agriculture		Industry		Services		Public Consumption		Private Consumption		Gross Domestic Savings	
	1960[a]	1980[b]	1960[a]	1980[b]	1960[a]	1980[b]	1960[a]	1980[b]	1960[a]	1980[b]	1960[a]	1980[b]
Low-income Economies	50 w	36 w	18 w	35 w	32 w	29 w	8 w	11 w	79 w	68 w	17 w	22 w
China and India		33 w		39 w		28 w		11 w	77 w	63 w	19 w	26 w
Other	49 w	45 w	12 w	17 w	39 w	38 w	10 w	12 w	83 w	84 w	9 w	7 w
1 Kampuchea, Dem.	..	..	..	..	..	..	..	..	..	..	..	..
2 Loa PDR	..	..	..	..	..	..	..	..	..	..	..	..
3 Bhutan	..	..	..	..	..	..	..	..	..	..	..	..
4 Chad	52	57	12	5	36	38	13	18	82	96	5	−14
5 Bangladesh	58	54	7	13	35	33	6	7	86	91	8	2
6 Ethiopia	65	51	12	16	23	33	8	15	81	80	11	5
7 Nepal	..	57	..	13	..	30	..	c	96	93	4	7
8 Somalia	71	60	8	11	21	29	8	19	86	78	6	3
9 Burma	33	46	12	13	55	41	c	c	89	82	11	18
10 Afghanistan	..	..	..	..	..	..	c	c	87	89	13	11
11 Viet Nam	..	..	..	..	..	..	c	c	..	..	..	..
12 Mali	55	42	10	10	35	48	12	22	79	81	9	−3
13 Burundi	..	55	..	16	..	29	3	12	92	86	5	(.)
14 Rwanda	81	48	7	22	12	30	10	12	82	85	8	3
15 Upper Volta	62	40	14	18	24	42	10	16	94	93	−4	−9
16 Zaire	30	32	27	23	43	45	18	12	61	75	21	13
17 Malawi	58	43	11	20	31	37	16	10	88	80	−4	10
18 Mozambique	55	44	9	16	36	40	11	15	81	85	8	(.)
19 India	50	37	20	26	30	37	7	10	79	70	14	20
20 Haiti	..	..	..	..	..	..	c	c	93	91	7	9
21 Sri Lanka	32	28	20	30	48	42	13	8	78	78	9	14
22 Sierra Leone	..	36	..	20	..	44	..	17	..	77	..	6
23 Tanzania	57	54	11	13	32	33	9	14	72	78	19	8
24 China	..	31	..	47	..	22	c	11	77	59	23	30
25 Guinea	..	37	..	33	..	30	..	19	..	67	..	14
26 Central African Rep.	51	37	10	15	39	48	19	c	72	101	9	−1
27 Pakistan	46	31	16	25	38	44	11	11	84	83	5	6
28 Uganda	52	76	12	6	36	18	9	c	75	98	16	2
29 Benin	55	43	8	12	37	45	16	15	75	80	9	5
30 Niger	69	33	9	34	22	33	9	9	79	70	12	21

TABLE 1.2   Structure of Production (continued)

(percentage of GDP)

	Agriculture		Industry		Services		Public Consumption		Private Consumption		Gross Domestic Savings	
	1960a	1980b	1960a	1980b	1960a	1980b	1960a	1980b	1960a	1980b	1960a	1980b
31 Madagascar	37	36	10	18	53	46	20	17	75	74	5	9
32 Sudan	..	38	..	14	..	48	8	12	80	85	12	3
33 Togo	55	26	16	20	29	54	8	16	88	70	4	14
Middle-Income Economies	24 w	15 w	30 w	40 w	46 w	45 w	11 w	14 w	70 w	64 w	19 w	25 w
Oil Exporters	28 w	14 w	24 w	43 w	48 w	43 w	11 w	13 w	70 w	58 w	19 w	30 w
Oil Importers	23 w	15 w	32 w	37 w	45 w	48 w	12 w	14 w	69 w	68 w	19 w	21 w
34 Ghana	..	66	..	21	..	13	10	9	73	86	17	5
35 Kenya	38	34	18	21	44	45	11	20	72	65	17	17
36 Lesotho	..	31	..	21	..	48	17	20	108	158	-25	-78
37 Yemen, PDR	..	13	..	28	..	59	..	..	..	..	..	..
38 Indonesia	54	26	14	42	32	32	12	13	80	57	8	30
39 Yemen Arab Rep.	..	29	..	16	..	55	24	18	..	102	..	-20
40 Mauritania	59	26	24	33	17	41	..	39	79	47	-3	14
41 Senegal	24	29	17	24	59	47	17	14	68	88	15	-2
42 Angola	50	48	8	23	42	29	9	25	77	56	14	19
43 Liberia	..	36	..	31	..	33	7	16	58	55	35	29
44 Honduras	37	31	19	25	44	44	11	13	77	67	12	20
45 Zambia	11	15	63	39	26	46	11	28	48	54	41	18
46 Bolivia	26	18	25	29	49	53	7	10	86	75	7	15
47 Egypt	30	23	24	35	46	42	17	19	71	65	12	16
48 Zimbabwe	18	12	35	39	47	49	11	21	67	63	22	16
49 El Salvador	32	27	19	21	49	52	10	15	79	75	11	10
50 Cameroon	..	32	..	22	..	46	..	11	..	66	..	23
51 Thailand	40	25	19	29	41	46	10	12	76	66	14	22
52 Philippines	26	23	28	37	46	40	8	8	76	67	16	25
53 Nicaragua	24	23	21	31	55	46	9	21	79	80	12	-1
54 Papua New Guinea	53	34	11	30	36	37	26	26	71	59	3	15
55 Congo, People's Rep.	23	12	17	45	60	43	23	13	98	50	-21	37
56 Morocco	23	18	27	32	50	50	12	22	77	67	11	11
57 Mongolia	..	..	..	..	..	..	..	..	..	..	..	..
58 Albania	..	..	..	..	..	..	..	..	..	..	..	..

59 Peru	18	8	33	45	49	47	9	13	64	68	27	19
60 Nigeria	63	20	11	42	26	38	6	10	87	62	7	28
61 Jamaica	10	8	36	37	54	55	7	21	67	67	26	12
62 Guatemala	..	34	..	..	..	..	8	8	84	79	8	13
63 Ivory Coast	43	..	14	22	43	44	10	18	73	59	17	23
64 Dominican Rep.	27	18	23	27	50	55	13	8	68	78	19	14
65 Colombia	34	28	26	30	40	42	6	8	73	67	21	25
66 Ecuador	29	13	19	38	48	49	10	14	75	63	15	23
67 Paraguay	36	30	20	25	44	45	8	6	76	74	16	20
68 Tunisia	24	17	18	35	58	48	17	15	76	60	7	25
69 Korea, Dem. Rep.	..	..	..	..	..	..	..	..	..	..	..	..
70 Syrian Arab Rep.	..	20	..	27	..	53	..	23	..	67	..	10
71 Jordan	..	8	..	32	..	60	..	33	..	94	..	-27
72 Lebanon	12	..	20	..	68	..	10	..	85	..	5	..
73 Turkey	41	23	21	30	38	47	11	13	76	69	13	18
74 Cuba	..	..	..	..	..	..	..	..	..	..	..	..
75 Korea, Rep. of	37	16	20	41	43	43	15	13	84	64	1	23
76 Malaysia	37	24	18	37	45	39	11	17	62	51	27	32
77 Costa Rica	26	17	20	29	54	54	10	18	77	67	13	15
78 Panama	23	..	21	57	56	..	11	15	78	60	11	25
79 Algeria	16	6	35	57	49	37	15	14	60	44	25	42
80 Brazil	16	10	35	37	49	53	12	c	67	80	21	20
81 Mexico	16	10	29	38	55	52	6	12	76	62	18	26
82 Chile	10	7	51	37	39	56	12	12	63	72	25	16
83 South Africa	12	7	40	53	48	40	9	13	64	50	27	37
84 Romania	..	11	..	64	..	25	..	..	..	..	..	..
85 Portugal	25	13	36	46	39	41	11	15	77	74	12	11
86 Argentina	16	..	38	..	46	..	9	..	70	..	21	..
87 Yugoslavia	24	12	45	43	31	45	19	17	49	51	32	32
88 Uruguay	19	10	28	33	53	57	9	14	79	74	12	12
89 Iran	29	..	33	38	38	..	10	..	69	..	21	..
90 Iraq	17	7	52	73	31	19	18	c	48	41	34	59
91 Venezuela	6	6	22	47	72	47	14	13	53	55	33	32
92 Hong Kong	4	1	39	..	57	..	7	7	87	69	6	24
93 Trinidad and Tobago	8	..	46	..	46	..	9	17	61	42	30	41
94 Greece	23	16	26	..	51	52	12	16	77	64	11	20
95 Singapore	4	1	18	37	78	62	8	11	95	59	-3	30
96 Israel	11	5	32	36	57	59	18	35	68	57	14	8
High-income Oil Exporters	..	1 w	..	77 w	..	22 w	..	19 w	..	23 w	..	62 w
97 Libya	..	2	..	72	..	26	..	c	..	41	..	59
98 Saudi Arabia	..	1	..	78	..	21	..	23	..	18	..	59
99 Kuwait	..	( )	..	79	..	21	..	11	..	26	..	63
100 United Arab Emirates	..	1	..	77	..	22	..	10	..	17	..	73

TABLE 1.2 *Structure of Production (continued)*

(percentage of GDP)

	Agriculture		Industry		Services		Public Consumption		Private Consumption		Gross Domestic Savings	
	1960[a]	1980[b]	1960[a]	1980[b]	1960[a]	1980[b]	1960[a]	1980[b]	1960[a]	1980[b]	1960[a]	1980[b]
Industrial Market Economies	6 w	4 w	40 w	37 w	54 w	62 w	15 w	17 w	63 w	60 w	22 w	22 w
101 Ireland	22	..	26	..	52	..	12	21	77	64	11	15
102 Spain	..	8	..	37	..	55	9	12	69	70	22	18
103 Italy	13	6	41	43	46	51	13	16	62	62	25	22
104 New Zealand	..	13	..	32	..	55	13	17	65	61	22	22
105 United Kingdom	4	2	43	35	53	63	17	21	66	60	17	19
106 Finland	18	8	35	35	47	57	13	18	58	55	29	27
107 Australia	12	..	37	..	51	..	10	17	65	61	25	22
108 Japan	13	4	45	41	42	55	9	10	57	59	34	31
109 Canada	6	4	34	33	60	63	14	20	65	56	21	24
110 Austria	11	4	49	41	40	55	13	18	60	55	27	27
111 United States	4	3	38	34	58	63	17	18	64	65	19	17
112 Netherlands	9	4	46	37	45	59	14	18	57	61	29	21
113 France	10	4	38	36	52	60	13	15	62	64	25	21
114 Belgium	6	2	41	37	53	62	13	18	69	64	18	18
115 Norway	9	5	33	41	58	54	12	19	60	47	28	34
116 Denmark	11	..	32	..	57	..	12	27	66	56	22	17
117 Sweden	7	3	40	32	53	65	16	29	60	52	24	19
118 Germany, Fed. Rep.	6	2	53	..	41	..	14	20	57	55	29	25
119 Switzerland	..	..	..	..	..	..	9	13	62	64	29	23
Nonmarket Industrial Economies	21 w	15 w	62 w	63 w	17 w	22 w	3 w	11 w	70 w	73 w	27 w	25 w
120 Poland	26	15	57	64	17	21	8	14	68	73	24	13
121 Bulgaria	32	17	53	58	15	25	3	..	69	..	28	..
122 Hungary	24	14	69	59	7	27	7	9	72	69	21	22
123 USSR	21	16	62	62	17	22	2	c	70	74	28	26
124 Czechoslovakia	16	8	73	75	11	14	6	7	75	66	19	27
125 German Dem. Rep.	..	9	..	70	..	21	..	..	..	..	..	..

a. Figures in italics are for 1961, not 1960.
b. Figures in italics are for 1979, not 1980.

Note: w stands for GDP-weighted average in current dollars for the years in question.
SOURCE: World Bank, *World Development Report 1982* (New York: Oxford University Press, 1982), Tables 3 and 5, pp. 114–15, 118–19. Reprinted by permission.

TABLE 1.3 *Normal Variation in Economic Structure with Level of Development for a Representative Country*

| | Predicted Values at Different Per Capita Income Levels* | | | | | | | | | | |
Process	Mean† Under $100	$100	$200	$300	$400	$500	$800	$1,000	Mean† Over $1,000	Total Change	GNP at Midpoint
	Proportion of GNP (unless indicated otherwise)										
Accumulation Processes											
1. Investment											
a. Saving	.103	.135	.171	.180	.202	.210	.226	.233	.233	.130	200
b. Investment	.136	.158	.188	.203	.213	.220	.234	.240	.234	.098	200
c. Capital inflow	.032	.023	.016	.012	.010	.009	.006	.006	.001	−.031	200
2. Government Revenue											
a. Government revenue	.125	.153	.181	.202	.219	.234	.268	.287	.307	.182	380
b. Tax revenue	.106	.129	.153	.173	.189	.203	.236	.254	.282	.176	440
3. Education											
a. Education expenditure	.026	.033	.033	.034	.035	.037	.041	.043	.039	.013	300
b. School enrollment ratio (of total eligible)	.244	.375	.549	.637	.694	.735	.810	.842	.863	.618	200
Resource Allocation Processes											
4. Structure of domestic demand											
a. Private consumption	.779	.720	.686	.667	.654	.645	.625	.617	.624	−.155	
b. Government consumption	.119	.137	.134	.135	.136	.138	.144	.148	.141	.022	
c. Food consumption	.414	.392	.315	.275	.248	.229	.191	.175	.167	−.247	250
5. Structure of production											
a. Primary share	.522	.452	.327	.266	.228	.202	.156	.138	.127	−.395	200
b. Industry share	.125	.148	.215	.251	.276	.294	.331	.347	.379	.254	300
c. Utilities share	.053	.061	.072	.079	.085	.089	.098	.102	.109	.056	300
d. Service share	.300	.338	.385	.403	.411	.415	.416	.413	.386	.086	
6. Structure of trade											
a. Exports	.172	.195	.218	.230	.238	.244	.255	.260	.248	.077	150
b. Primary exports	.130	.137	.136	.131	.125	.120	.105	.096	.058	−.072	1,000
c. Manufactured exports	.011	.019	.034	.046	.056	.065	.086	.097	.131	.120	600
d. Services exports	.028	.031	.042	.048	.051	.053	.056	.057	.059	.031	250
e. Imports	.205	.218	.234	.243	.249	.254	.263	.267	.250	.045	250

TABLE 1.3 Normal Variation in Economic Structure with Level of Development for a Representative Country (continued)

| | Predicted Values at Different Per Capita Income Levels* | | | | | | | | | | |
Process	Mean† Under $100	$100	$200	$300	$400	$500	$800	$1,000	Mean‡ Over $1,000	Total Change	GNP at Midpoint
	Proportion of GNP (unless indicated otherwise)										
Demographic and Distributional Processes											
7. Labor allocation											
a. Primary share	.712	.658	.557	.489	.438	.395	.300	.252	.159	−.553	400
b. Industry share	.078	.091	.164	.206	.235	.258	.303	.325	.368	.290	325
c. Service share	.210	.251	.279	.304	.327	.347	.396	.423	.473	.263	450
8. Urban share of population	.128	.220	.362	.439	.490	.527	.601	.634	.658	.530	250
9. Demographic transition											
a. Birth rate per 1,000 pop.	45.9	44.6	37.7	33.8	31.1	29.1	24.9	22.9	19.1	−26.8	350
b. Death rate per 1,000 pop.	20.9	18.6	13.5	11.4	10.3	9.7	9.1	9.0	9.7	−11.2	150
10. Income Distribution											
a. Share of highest 20%	.502	.541	.557	.554	.547	.538	.511	.494	.458	−.044	
b. Share of lowest 40%	.158	.140	.129	.127	.128	.130	.138	.143	.153	−.005	

*Per capita GNP in U.S.$ 1964, 10 million population.
†Approximately $70. Mean values of countries with per capita GNP under $100 vary slightly according to composition of the sample.
‡Approximately $1,500. Mean values of countries with per capita GNP over $1,000 vary slightly according to composition of the sample.

SOURCE: From Patterns of Development, 1950–1970 by Hollis Chenery and Moises Syrquin, with the assistance of Hazel Elkington. Copyright © 1975 by International Bank for Reconstruction and Development. Reprinted by permission of Oxford University Press, Inc., London. Table 3, pp. 20–21.

REFERENCES

Adelman, Irma and Morris, Cynthia T. 1967. *Society, Politics, and Economic Development: A Quantitative Approach.* Baltimore, MD: The Johns Hopkins University Press.

Boeke, J. H. 1953. *Economies and Economic Policy of Dual Societies.* New York: New York Institute of Public Relations.

Chenery, Hollis and Syrquin, Moises. 1975. *Patterns of Development, 1950–1970.* London: Oxford University Press.

Kravis, I. B.; Kennessey, Z.; Heston, A.; and Summers, R. 1975. *A System of International Comparisons of Gross Product and Purchasing Power.* Baltimore, MD: The Johns Hopkins University Press.

Kravis, I. B.; Heston, Alan; and Summers, Robert. 1982. *World Product and Income.* Baltimore, MD: The Johns Hopkins University Press.

Morgan, Theodore. 1975. *Economic Development.* New York: Harper and Row.

U. N. Research Institute for Social Development. 1970. *Contents and Measurement of Socio-Economic Development.* Geneva: Report 70.10.

The World Bank. 1982. *World Development Report 1982.* New York: Oxford University Press.

Graphic Presentation of Growth Variables

chapter

2

T his chapter and the following present certain analytical tools and concepts that are readily translated into graphic presentation. Before beginning, however, some general discussion is in order regarding certain methodological questions that have arisen in the area of development economics and the use of theoretical constructs.

Early writers on the subject of economic development such as Adam Smith, David Ricardo, Thomas Malthus, and Karl Marx were political economists, vitally concerned in their writings with the interrelations between policy and development. This orientation toward policy conclusions is very much alive among economic development writers today. The highest standards for policy formulation demand the use of internally consistent theories or models that can aid the policymaker. The scope of development economics has generally presented the policymaker with the quandary of how to formulate policy when the theory tools for this task are inadequate.

Methodology: Models and Their Uses

Theories are extreme simplifications of the real world, maps drawn to guide us through the maze of reality. Theoretical models are helpful abstractions needed to explain and predict phenomena of interest such as prices, employment, investment, or trade patterns. Models must be narrow enough in focus to be tractable. Theories must withstand empirical examination of their predictions and must yield testable hypotheses for falsifying the theory.

The phenomenon of interest here is the encompassing and complex process whereby an economy develops. The scope of this process is vast. To date there is no simple abstraction that satisfactorily captures the vital interrelated links of the development process. One problem is that many of these links are broader than modern economics per se. Development is a social process as much as an economic one. Another problem is that the empirical base for testing hypotheses is weak, especially in the availability of time series data.

There is ongoing debate over whether neoclassical economic theory, which is essentially the theory of modern textbooks using the marginal calculus, is outside its domain of application in the LDC economy. While a full discussion of this question is beyond the scope of this book, consider certain behavioral assumptions of neoclassical economics. One such premise is maximizing behavior by both household and firm, along with perfect information and resource mobility. Firms respond to market prices and other information to maximize firm profits; households respond to these factors to maximize their satisfaction.

Is it misleading to assume firms in LDCs respond to changing price and other market or planners' incentives so that costs are minimized and/or profits maximized; or to assume that households maximize their utility by changing their behavior in response to economic stimuli such as relative prices and job opportunities? If social goals place little emphasis on material conditions or well-being, then maximizing behavior may be a poor assumption. An example is religious beliefs that establish nonmaterialism as an appropriate outlook on life. Another is land use prescribed by status roles assigned to the landlord class.

Is the knowledge base in the LDC so limited that maximizing behavior results in set, established behavior patterns that prevent response to change? If conditions of uncertainty and risk exist, and the economic knowledge base is very limited, then, because decision making is so difficult, rules of thumb may be followed. Custom and tradition dictate the rules to be followed.

Either the absence of behavior that maximizes material goals or a very limited knowledge base combined with high uncertainty will limit the usefulness of adjustment models such as those of neoclassical economics. Instead of adjustment toward efficient resource allocation and maximum output, disequilibrating conditions may exist and persist. Western economic models can fail to predict the outcome in LDCs in the face of such circumstances.

A model can have several uses, however. The neoclassical model in particular can be used to show what ouptut would be under maximizing behavior patterns, with available resources and technology. It establishes limiting conditions for maximum output in an economy. Moreover, to some degree the model's assumptions can be changed. Assumptions such as perfect information can be modified and the results traced through. Interestingly, in some cases maximizing behavior under conditions of uncertainty produces behavior patterns similar to traditional ones.

But such models must be used very carefully in the LDC context. The methodological debate has produced a healthy skepticism about the applicability of the entire tool kit of Western neoclassical economics to the study of all LDCs at all phases of development. Development economists have continued to rely on the theories available, but on the whole have used them selectively and with modification, seeking those that are relevant to the LDC domain. The economists have also reached back to classical economics, which preceded neoclassical economics, in search of helpful analytical frameworks. Moreover, a strong strain of institutional economics (the study of institutional changes that accompany development) and Marxian economics marks writings in the field of development.

The comments of the father of macroeconomics, John Maynard Keynes, are highly relevant to the choice of analytical tools for the policy-oriented field of development economics. Keynes wrote to his colleague Sir Roy Harrod in 1938: "Economics is a science of thinking in terms of models joined to the art of choosing models which are relevant to the contemporary world. . . . Good economists are scarce because the gift for using 'vigilant observation' to choose good models, although it does not require a highly specialized intellectual technique, appears to be a very rare one." (in Moggridge, ed. 1973, pp. 296–97, quoted in Blaug 1980, p. 91).

Any book that is designed to incorporate analysis from work in the development field must draw upon the tool kit of theories used in advanced research. The idea of a production function is basic. And even the concept of an aggregate production function, while highly stylized and open to problems of empirical testing, proves very useful, if mainly as a beginning point for thinking in terms of limits to output, trade-offs in production, and a limited but important set of inputs that influence output. The book uses simplified graphic presentation based on sectoral production functions to emphasize constraints faced by *any* economy and to gain insights into sectoral interrelations in less-developed economies.

Needless to say, as the book proceeds the analysis moves beyond the stylized framework of chapters 2 and 3 to explore more specific conditions that affect production in LDC economies and their capacity for development. And not surprisingly, analysis in topical areas can be unsettled, with conflicting theories or hypotheses contending for dominance. One of the first topical areas to exemplify this is the chapter on the demography of LDC population change. Hypotheses regarding determinants of fertility abound, but none has achieved dominance. Some economists have used the theoretical choice model from the textbook tool kit here, but not without arousing an ongoing debate over its applicability.

Chapter Purposes

The chapter serves two purposes: It introduces important growth determinants, terminology, and concepts; and it provides a simple graphic presentation to help the reader visualize the growth variables introduced.

The graphic approach utilizes a four-quadrant graph simultaneously showing the level of output, the level of capital and labor inputs, the labor-to-capital ratio, and factor productivity ratios. It is designed to reinforce the reader's grasp of specific tautological relations of an aggregate production function by visualizing the interdependence of the variables. The graph is useful in introductory chapters that analyze growth variables. The chapter begins with a discussion of the aggregate production function later visualized in the sets of graphs.

PRODUCTION FUNCTION RELATIONSHIPS

An expanding economy is typically characterized by ongoing changes in growth agents and thus accumulates more workers in the labor force, better trained workers, more equipment and machinery, more efficient equipment or machines, and improved organizational structure. We can classify these causes of expansion into two growth sources: (1) An economy's potential output expands when there is growth of one or more factors of production. (2) An economy's potential output also increases when factors remain constant but average factor productivity, that is average output per unit of factor input, rises. Thus, increases in factor inputs and in factor productivity are the two basic causes of changes in output.

These two forces seldom operate separately. Moreover, where one source of growth is an increase in factors, *and* this increase is not proportionate, individual factor productivity is affected. For example, when output expands due to an increase in capital equipment, each worker has more equipment and labor productivity is higher. Such changes in factor productivity caused by a change in *relative* factor inputs must be separated conceptually from the changes in factor productivity caused by improvements in labor training, equipment, or organization that are also sources of growth. This is done by examining carefully the aggregate production function and the specific assumptions of the function.

The Aggregate Production Function
In discussing the total economy or one of its complete sectors, it is necessary to think of total output and total factor input. However, discussion of a total economy's output of multiple goods and various differentiated factor inputs is intractable, not easily managed. There are too many variables to deal with simultaneously. The tactic used to gain insight into the behavior of important variables affecting growth is to adopt a highly simplified economy—one producing only one good (Q) and using only two factor inputs, land (N) and labor (L), or capital (K) and labor. Each unit of inputs is of the same quality. The production function (f) for such an economy with a given level of technology and using, for example, K and L as inputs, can be written:

$$Q = f(K, L) \tag{1}$$

The assumption is that output is produced as efficiently as possible with given techniques known to the economy so that output from any resource combination is maximized and reduction of either factor input would reduce output. Outputs and inputs are measured in physical units. In one sense it is the production function of a firm or farm writ large. However, since it is an aggregate economy, units of inputs can be conceived of as, for example, services per time period of additional plants (or farms) and labor force units, each of which is identical. These units are small relative to aggregate output and thus the production function has easily divisible units of homogeneous inputs. At a particular time, the amount of labor and capital available for use in production is limited and places a constraint upon total output when there is full employment.

It is helpful in discussing economic growth to be able to express output (Q) in two alternative but slightly different ways. A simple manipulation of equation (1) produces an expression for output in terms of capital inputs *or* in terms of labor inputs. The left-hand side of equation (1) can be multiplied by 1 without changing the equation. First the left-hand side is multiplied by K/K and the terms are arranged as follows:

$$(K \cdot Q/K) = f(K, L) \tag{2}$$

Thus, another expression for output is capital inputs multiplied by average capital productivity, a measure of the average efficiency of a unit of capital. This efficiency measure reflects more than the technology level. It reflects also the amount of labor used per unit of capital. In economic terms this equation says that changes in capital inputs affect output directly through the addition of a productive factor and through the effect the use of more capital has upon average capital productivity. Changes in labor inputs affect output, which in turn changes capital productivity. For example, increased labor inputs raise Q and hence Q/K.

Analogously, output can be expressed as labor inputs times average labor productivity. Multiplying the left-hand side of equation (1) by L/L gives the following equation:

$$(L \cdot Q/L) = f(K, L) \tag{3}$$

Inputs of labor affect output directly and through changes in labor productivity. Changes in capital inputs affect output expressed as $L \cdot Q/L$ through changes in Q, which changes labor productivity. Using these alternate expressions for output, it can be seen that a change in either capital or labor inputs will affect the productivity of the opposite factor, and its own productivity as well.

To simplify notation, let $Q/K = \alpha$ and $Q/L = \beta$. Putting the identities together, we have:

$$Q = \alpha K = \beta L \tag{4}$$

and

$$\alpha/\beta = L/K \tag{5}$$

As L/K changes the ratio α/β will change; relative factor productivity is affected by the relative amounts of factors used. Two economies with identical output and technology but differing relative factor endowments would have different average output per factor input and hence different α/β.

The identities given in equations (4) and (5) hold for any functional form of the equation. These identities can be visualized on a graph if data on output, labor inputs, and capital inputs are known, as in figure 2.1. The axes for all quadrants represent positive measures increasing from the origin. The L/K ratio is the slope of a line originating at the coordinate points for labor and capital inputs in the southwest quadrant and drawn through the origin. The intersection of the α and β coordinates will lie along the L/K line in the northeast quadrant. Output is shown as the area of a rectangle in the northwest quadrant and again as the area of a rectangle in the southeast quadrant. Thus output appears twice on the graph.

The graph also shows that nonproportionate increases in inputs of capital and labor change the slope of the L/K line and thus α/β since the coordinates for α and β must intersect on the L'/K' line in the northeast quadrant. The new level of output will depend upon the new levels of capital, labor, capital productivity, and labor productivity. An equation giving the exact relationship between units of labor and capital inputs and output would have to be known to complete the graph for the new output level associated with the larger inputs of labor and capital. The expression $f(K, L)$ is simply a very general notational form for the production function and thus does not supply the information needed to calculate the new output level.

Generally more properties are given for a production function than those discussed so far. One set of properties is derived by examining

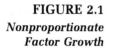

FIGURE 2.1

Nonproportionate
Factor Growth

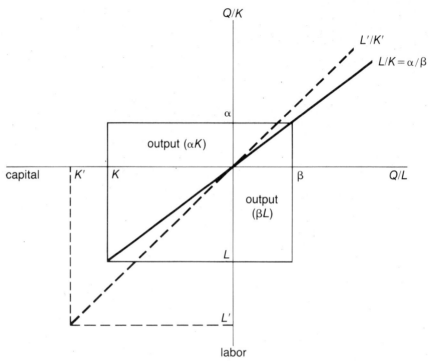

Nonproportionate growth in K and L changes the slope of the line showing L/K to L'/K'.

the technical and engineering limitations that can be expected to affect efficiency measures as factor proportions vary. This is discussed in the following section. After the properties of variable proportions are examined, the subsequent sections explore the effects of scale and technology on production.

Variable Proportions   Generally factors can be substituted for each other so that a given output can be produced with different combinations of labor and capital inputs. For example, an economy that has an out migration of work force members may maintain the same output level if the capital stock is enlarged over the period of out migration. It can be expected, however, that there will be limits to substitution of factors—that a given output level cannot be produced without some minimum input level of capital or labor. Thus there will exist a minimum and maximum L/K.

Assume the production of output Q_o, shown in figure 2.2, using the best technology available, requires a minimum of L_o labor and K_o capital. Point x then gives the most capital-intensive factor combination technically feasible in the production of output Q_o, which is K'_o capital and L_o labor. Output Q_o is shown in the northwest quadrant for

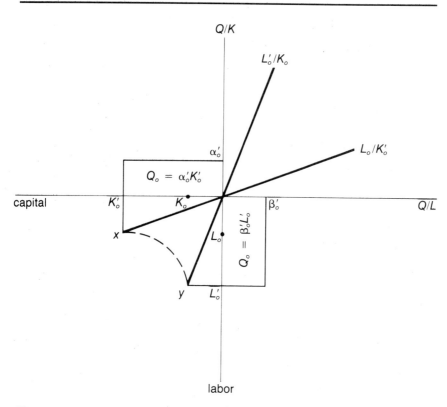

FIGURE 2.2

Isoquant with Factor Proportion Limits

The curve *xy*, called an isoquant, shows all combinations of L and K that will produce output level Q_o. Factor proportions must be in the range between L'_o/K_o and L_o/K'_o.

this factor combination as a rectangle with area $\alpha'_o K'_o$. The most labor-intensive factor combination possible in the production of output Q_o is at a point y with L'_o labor and K_o capital. Output Q_o for this factor combination is shown in the southeast quadrant as a rectangle with area $\beta'_o L'_o$. The factor-combination limits L'_o/K_o and L_o/K'_o reflect the fact that factors are imperfect substitutes for each other.

Extending the idea of imperfect substitution between factors, it is generally assumed that over the range of variation in L/K that is technically possible for a given output level, factors will not substitute for each other in a constant ratio. Rather, when a given amount of one factor substitutes for another, it compensates for fewer and fewer units of the other factor. This is referred to as a *diminishing marginal rate of substitution* between factors. That is, the rate at which capital and labor substitute for each other between x and y (expressed as $-\Delta K/\Delta L$) will not be constant. Instead the substitution path under conditions of infinitely small variations in inputs will trace out a curve convex to the origin as shown by the dashed curve between x and y. As L/K rises, fewer and fewer units of capital are replaced by a unit of labor.

The *rate* at which the substitutability between factors *diminishes* need not be constant. The engineering or technical parameters determine the degree to which resources can replace each other. Economists at times divide the rate of change of the K/L ratio by that of the marginal rate of substitution as a measure of *elasticity of substitution* between factors in the production of a given output level. The less elastic, the more convex the curve.

The alternative combinations of inputs that can be used to produce a given level of output as illustrated by curve xy is called an *isoquant*. Isoquants for higher or lower levels of output than output Q_o in figure 2.2 need not have the same limits or be exactly the same shape as curve xy. Oftentimes analysis is made more manageable by the assumption of the existence of a whole family (or surface) of parallel isoquants lying between the same limits and differing only in output and input levels. In order to draw a family of isoquant curves, technology must be held constant. The effect of technological change upon an isoquant is taken up in a subsequent section. Isoquants are especially useful when a production function is presented for the firm.

The same technical parameters affecting the marginal rate of subsatitution influence the behavior of the production function when one resource is held constant and the other is varied. In this case, of course, output must change. Here the behavior of output can depend upon the initial levels of the constant and variable input. There are three possible cases.

Case 1: Increasing Returns to the Variable Input   Assume capital is the input held constant, and that the initial level of labor inputs is near the minimum limit. As more units of labor are added, it is possible that the labor and capital can be arranged in the production process to achieve greater efficiency once the low initial level of labor inputs is increased. Labor was spread too thin, so to speak, to be as efficiently utilized as it could be with a larger L/K ratio. Under this condition, efficiency gains achieved with movement away from the minimum labor input limit yield increasing returns as labor inputs rise. That is, output rises at an increasing *rate*.

Case 2: Constant Returns to the Variable Input   There may be a range of combinations of labor inputs with capital constant over which the two resources substitute perfectly for each other so that as labor is increased, output increases at a constant rate. Generally, technical constraints prevent this outcome except over limited ranges.

Case 3: Diminishing Returns to the Variable Input   In this case as more and more labor is added to a fixed amount of capital inputs, output increases, but at a decreasing rate. Each additional unit of labor adds less and less to output, and the ratio L/K is moving toward the limits of labor's ability to add to output without an increase in the capital stock.

In thinking about the behavior of output under conditions of variable proportions, it is helpful to assume capital and labor can be sub-

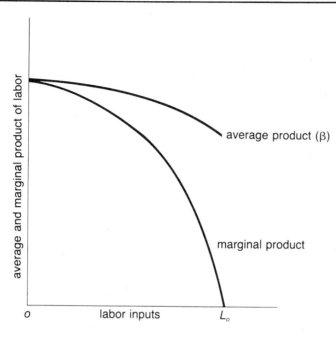

FIGURE 2.3

Average and Marginal Product of Labor

Under conditions of diminishing returns, as labor inputs are added to a constant level of capital inputs, the average and marginal products of labor decline.

stituted or added in infinitely small units so that the function possesses continuity when graphed. Under such conditions the change in output from a change in one unit of a variable input is called the *marginal product.* In case 1 above, the marginal product of labor is rising. In case 2 it is constant and in case 3 it declines.

Assuming continuity so that a smooth curve can be drawn, case 3 is illustrated in figure 2.3. There is some given capital stock that is held constant. As labor is added, the marginal product declines. Output can be measured, as illustrated in the previous graphs, by the area of a rectangle formed by the coordinates for the average product (β) and labor inputs (L) or by the area under the marginal product curve. After L_o, additional units of labor would have a zero or negative marginal product; and thus the marginal product curve traces the labor axis or becomes negative.

The marginal product, then, declines throughout under conditions of diminishing returns.[1] Diminishing returns will also cause the average product (β) to decline as more labor is added. This is shown on the same graph. The two curves are related: as output drops at the margin with additional units of the variable input, it pulls down the average output per unit. Of course, with output rising and capital inputs constant, the average product of capital rises.

1. Sometimes diminishing returns means that the marginal product eventually declines after a range of increasing returns to the marginal input. This usage is omitted here.

From time to time it is important to discuss the rate of decline of
the marginal product curve, that is, the strength of diminishing returns,
the absolute level of the marginal product, and even conditions of
"surplus labor," where the marginal product of labor is zero. Should
surplus labor conditions exist, full employment of labor would violate
the efficiency conditions since the economy can produce the same
output and yet reduce labor input.

Sometimes an LDC is considered to have conditions close to the
limiting case of surplus labor so that the marginal product of labor
(expressed as $\Delta Q/\Delta L$ for discrete changes and dQ/dL for continuous
changes) is approaching zero or is below some reference level, such as
a "subsistence" wage, that is said to equal the average product of labor.
Thus figure 2.3 will be useful for later reference. When we return to
the four-quadrant graph, it is helpful to keep in mind the behavior of
the average product of labor under conditions of diminishing returns.

The simplified scheme developed here for looking at the effect of
factor proportions upon output and productivity is a powerful tool that
has strong empirical foundations. It is often referred to as the *law of
variable proportions* or the *law of diminishing returns*. The firm, an
industry, and a sector, as well as the aggregate economy, can be subject
to the law of variable proportions. Diminishing returns are central to
Malthusian concerns about the effect of population growth upon the
food supply.

Most often when an aggregate production function is used to gain
insight into an ongoing economy, it is assumed that diminishing, but
positive, returns hold throughout the range of factor proportions considered and that there is a continuous, diminishing marginal rate of
substitution between factors. The elasticity of substitution of factors is
then greater than zero. This approach is adopted in this text when there
is a general discussion of an economy. The cases of zero marginal
product, fixed factor combinations and increasing or constant marginal
product are treated as special cases.[2]

**Factor Productivity
and Factor
Proportions:
Summary Equations
and Graph**

Up to this point the possible effect of scale or size of the economy
upon factor efficiency has been ignored. This omission will be rectified
in the next section. *Assume here that scale does not affect factor efficiency.* Continue with the assumptions that factors are divisible, that
diminishing returns hold throughout, and that no resource is surplus.
These premises have important predictive results for the production
function of the aggregate economy where inputs change, but not necessarily in the same proportion. A change in factor proportions affects
average factor productivity in a specific way: The average productivity
of the resource used in growing proportion falls; conversely the average

2. The reader familiar with calculus can recognize that the production function is assumed to be twice differentiable and that $f' > 0$, $f'' < 0$ for capital and labor. Moreover,
subsequent manipulation performed to obtain equations (6) and (7) is possible only
where the function expression is linearly homogeneous.

productivity of the resource used in decreasing proportion rises, other things being equal. Recall that this was the outcome in the example given of diminishing returns with capital inputs constant. These results can be shown to hold generally in the absence of scale effects by dividing equation (1) alternately by K and L:

$$Q/K = f(1, L/K) \tag{6}$$

$$Q/L = f(K/L, 1) \tag{7}$$

Consider equation (6). We divide by K and state that capital productivity is a positive function of the L/K ratio. A rise in labor units per unit of capital makes capital more productive; a fall in labor units per unit of capital lowers the average product of capital. A similar interpretation applies to equation (7).

The lower marginal and average product of a more rapidly expanding resource in the aggregate production function occurs solely because of changed factor proportions, and not because of variations in type or quality of factor inputs. Factor inputs are considered to be homogeneous in order to isolate the effects of factor variations. Quality variations in factor inputs will, of course, affect measures of factor productivity. It is important conceptually, however, to keep the effects of heterogeneity in factor inputs separate from the effects of variations in factor proportions.

As equations (6) and (7) show, an increase in K will lower L/K, lower capital productivity (α), and raise labor productivity (β), given diminishing returns and no scale effects. There are limits to the change in labor and capital productivity resulting from a change in capital inputs and a lower L/K. Figure 2.4 shows that since capital productivity must fall and labor productivity rise, the upper and lower limits of changes in β and α are the coordinate points y and x along L/K'. That is, coordinate points for the new level of labor and capital productivity must lie somewhere between x and y. What values β and α take along the segment $\overline{xy}$ depend upon whether the marginal product of capital is close to the average product or well below the average, and the rate of decline in the marginal product of capital over the range of additions to capital considered. A helpful exercise at this point would be to construct a graph showing the limits for α and β when L/K rises.

An economy that is growing as a result of increases in resource inputs is likely to have a change in the relative supplies of resources since these generally grow at different rates. Their productivity will be affected by the variation in factor proportions. Productivity changes that are referred to as a source of growth, however, are traceable to causes other than changes in relative resources. They are associated with scale and/or technology changes. In a growing economy the effects of scale and technology upon productivity of individual factors can be the opposite of the effect of factor proportions.

Scale

Even though factor proportions are held constant, the productivity of factors can vary with the size of the economy. As the size of the econ-

FIGURE 2.4

*Range for New α, β,
with Increase in K*

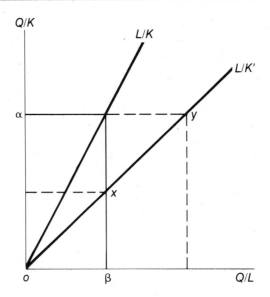

With diminishing returns an Increase in *K* will lower α, raise β. New α, β must lie between *x* and *y*.

omy changes, efficiency of all resources can change because of specialization and technical or social interrelations in organizing production. When proportionate changes in factors do not yield proportionate changes in output, that is, when there are not constant returns to scale, the predictability of factor productivity established in the previous section is lost. When factors double, output does not double. Assume there are increasing returns to scale and, as factors double, output more than doubles. Factor productivity rises even though factor proportions have not changed. Factor productivity is now a function of scale as well as factor proportions.

The problem of prediction can be illustrated by doubling capital inputs and increasing labor inputs by two-thirds. Output increases as a result of increased inputs of resources. The law of variable proportions says that this growth will be characterized by a fall in capital productivity as *L/K* falls. However, with increasing returns to scale, capital productivity is affected positively by the change in size. Scale effects add to the growth in output and it is possible for scale effects to offset completely the effects of variation in factor proportions. Scale effects may, however, simply reduce the impact of diminishing returns. Information about the relative strengths of the effects of scale and diminishing returns upon output and productivity must be known to predict the outcome. Economies of scale are important in LDCs as growth enlarges the economy. There is less occasion to expect diseconomies of scale in the aggregate economy. Scale effects then are one source of growth as they affect factor productivity.

Technological change affects factor productivity. It may increase the productivity of some or all factors. And if factors are growing at different rates, technological change may offset some or all of the effects of diminishing returns to the faster-growing factor. By definition, productivity improvements that are not due to the law of variable proportions or economies of scale must be the result of a change in technology within the framework of the aggregate production function.

Technology

Technological change is a complex and poorly understood process that is interrelated with a large matrix of social, political, economic, and even psychological variables. When the simple aggregate production function with two factor inputs, labor and capital, is used, it is sometimes useful to think of technological change as being "embodied" in the capital and/or the labor. However, because this destroys the fiction of homogeneous inputs as technology changes, the handy, but not too descriptively satisfying, assumption is often made that technology is "disembodied," meaning that it does not change the homogeneous character of capital and labor inputs but is located in the supporting framework of the economy.

The general equation of an aggregate production function with disembodied technology can be represented as:

$$Q = A f(K, L) \tag{8}$$

Embodied technology can be represented as affecting both resources:

$$Q = f(\Phi K, \lambda L) \tag{9}$$

Again, this is a simple notation for the production function, and its exact form is not specified. When Q is expressed as αK or βL, the capital and labor productivity coefficients reflect the specific function that relates inputs to output under given technology. When technology changes, the constants A, λ, or Φ take on a different value. This will cause a change in α and β. As will be discussed in chapter 5, technological change involves changes in both the type and quality of inputs and output as well as the supporting environment within which the economy operates.

In sum, it is common to utilize data on average factor productivity and factor input growth in examining an expanding economy or economic sector. Growth in average factor productivity of an input such as labor can be caused by several conditions: a growth in other factors of production, for example land or capital inputs relative to labor inputs; economies of scale that permit the organization of labor so as to achieve efficiencies as production expands; or changes in technology embodied in the labor, land, or machinery, or in the general economic structure of the society. Factor productivity increases due to economies of scale and technology improvements are a source of growth.

Factor Productivity and Growth: A Review

Factor productivity is affected by the technical limitations of factor substitution. Such limitations effect the degree to which factor expansion contributes to growth. Relatively fast growth of one factor may cause a sharp drop in its marginal product. Technical limitations to factor substitution in the extreme case could cause unemployment of a resource. When the marginal product of, for example, labor falls to zero due, say, to relatively fast population growth on limited farmland, either man hours or workers may be unemployed. The economy lacks enough land to employ the labor fully with the technology in use.

When there are technical limitations to factor absorption, the effect upon the average factor productivity of the relatively abundant factor will vary with the level of technology as well as the limits to factor absorption. High labor density on land farmed using primitive technology will also result in very low average labor productivity for those employed. However, when modern technology is used and technical limitations prevent further labor absorption, the average product (as opposed to the marginal product) of the employed labor may be quite high. The average product is reflective of the level of technology as well as factor proportions. The marginal product reflects to a greater degree the technical limitations to factor substitution. Even with modern technology, the marginal product can be relatively low for a factor when the technical limits to its absorption are approached.

In the simple aggregate production function presented above, we assumed full employment of all resources. Now we turn to a brief discussion of resource employment assumptions for the aggregate production function.

Resource Employment Levels

Aggregate output may be produced under conditions of full employment of all resources or with some unemployment of all or specific resources. Up to this point we have concentrated on the output potential when all resources are employed. This means full and efficient utilization of labor. When the economy responds efficiently to the greater availability of resources, it rearranges factor proportions. The faster-growing resource is combined in greater proportion with the slower-growing one. As will be discussed later, such efficient use of total resources can be achieved by a pricing system that makes it profitable for the operating unit to combine factor inputs according to their relative scarcity, or by planners who are able to calculate opportunity cost of all resources. It should be mentioned that the best efficiency in a poor economy is well below that in a modern economy. The techniques and knowledge used are very different. As we proceed to discuss many topics in development, the assumption of smooth allocation of resources according to their relative abundance is often dropped. We have already mentioned the possibility of technical limitations to full employment.

Labor Productivity, Employment, and Income Per Capita

While employment and productivity of all resources are important, the productivity of labor is particularly significant because it tends to reflect income per capita. Care must be taken, however, when associating rises in labor productivity with gains in per capita income. Specific conditions must be met for a correlation to hold. Output per laborer and income per capita move together, changing by the same percentage, in a growing economy where there is continuous full employment, the same number of labor hours per worker per time period, and a work force that is a constant proportion of the total population. Assume, however, that the labor force employment level or participation rate varies. Then a given percentage change in labor productivity does not yield an equal percentage change in output per capita, and the two can even move in opposite directions. For example, when L changes because of increased hours per workweek or reduced unemployment, and all other factors affecting output are constant, output per laborer falls due to diminishing returns, but output and thus output per capita rises.

In the four-quadrant graph used to illustrate growth, productivity levels and their changes for the two inputs must be known from the production function, and thus will reflect any scale economies, the effects of variable proportions, and technological change. The source of technological change can vary so long as the reader keeps these three effects distinct in his or her mind. The graph is a picture of inputs, output, productivity levels, and factor proportions of the aggregate production function. Growth caused by changes in productivity is reflected in the northeast quadrant. That caused by changes in inputs is reflected in the southwest quadrant. Changes in either quadrant must affect the output quadrants. In order to trace through a change in output, the cause of the change must be identified and the production function relationships understood. Production functions with various properties can be pictured since the graph identities hold for any functional form. For example, the widely known Harrod-Domar production function is explained and related to figure 4.1 of chapter 4 showing growth with L/K, α and β constant.

GRAPHIC PRESENTATIONS OF GROWTH

Often a production function for sectors is used. Growth rates of physical productivity arising from scale and technology can differ among sectors of an economy. And as growth occurs, resource allocation among sectors changes. Sectoral resource allocation can reinforce or offset the effects of scale and technology upon sectoral output. As productivity increases, the same output is produceable with fewer resources. Faster productivity growth in one sector may simply set the stage for transferring resources to another sector that has a high growth rate of demand. Alternatively, the sector with a high productivity growth rate may attract resources, providing additional stimulus to output growth in that sector. We reserve this topic for the next chapter.

This section has three objectives: (1) To illustrate graphically several cases of growth with and without technological change or scale effects and with and without changes in L/K. This reinforces familiarity with the material developed so far. (2) To derive graphically the formula for growth in aggregate output. (3) To define graphically neutral, labor-saving and capital-saving technical change. We begin with a case where inputs of capital and labor grow in the same proportion.

Case 1: Proportionate Growth in Inputs   The economy prior to a change in output has inputs of L labor and K capital and output of $\alpha K = \beta L$, as shown in figure 2.5. Now assume a proportionate growth in labor and capital so that L/K is constant. There are no economies of scale and no change in technology. Output per laborer, β, and output per unit of capital, α, are the same, but output increases by the area $L'Lsv$ or by the area $K'mnK$.

The symbol Δ here means "change in." The change in output for case 1 can be expressed as:

$$\Delta Q_1 = \alpha \Delta K \tag{10}$$

or as:

$$\Delta Q_1 = \beta \Delta L \tag{11}$$

FIGURE 2.5
Growth with L/K Constant

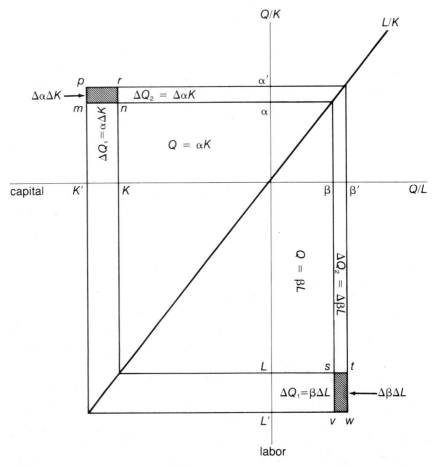

Case 1: Proportionate growth in inputs from K to K' and L to L' raises output by $\Delta Q_1 = \beta \Delta L = \alpha \Delta K$.
Case 2: Technological change raises capital and labor productivity from α to α' and β to β'. Output rises by $\Delta Q_2 = \Delta \alpha K = \Delta \beta L$.

Case 2: A Change in Technology In this case labor inputs are L in figure 2.5 and capital inputs are K. Technological change raises labor productivity from β to β' and capital productivity from α to α'. The growth in output for Case 2 can be expressed as:

$$\Delta Q_2 = \Delta\alpha K \tag{12}$$

$$\Delta Q_2 = \Delta\beta L \tag{13}$$

Case 3: Proportionate Growth in Inputs Accompanied by Technological Change Refer again to figure 2.5. This case combines the first two cases. L/K and α/β remain the same, but all variables are 20 percent larger. Growth exceeds the sum of the output changes in the individual cases, $Q_1 + Q_2$, by the hatched area *stvw* in the southeast quadrant or in the northwest quadrant by the hatched area *mprn*. These two areas are equivalent and can be expressed as $\Delta\alpha \cdot \Delta K$ or as $\Delta\beta \cdot \Delta L$. The expression for growth resulting from an increase in inputs and an increase in productivity becomes:

$$\Delta Q_3 = \alpha\Delta K + \Delta\alpha K + \Delta\alpha\Delta K \tag{14}$$

or:

$$\Delta Q_3 = \beta\Delta L + \Delta\beta L + \Delta\beta\Delta L \tag{15}$$

The last expressions in these two equations (shown by the hatched areas in figure 2.5) become less and less significant as increasingly smaller changes in output are considered, and can be assumed to approximate zero when sufficiently small changes in output are considered. The symbol d is used to represent such a small change and equations (14) and (15) become:

$$dQ = d\alpha K + \alpha dK \tag{16}$$

and

$$dQ = d\beta L + \beta dL \tag{17}$$

The right-hand sides of these last two equations are equivalent general expressions for continuous growth in output, indicating growth is related to changes in inputs and changes in productivity. Changes in productivity can be related to economies of scale as well as to technological change.[3]

Keep in mind here that where L/K changes, diminishing returns are assumed to affect productivity. In the case where productivity increases do not offset diminishing returns, the first expression becomes negative for the relevant resource. Growth is still positive, assuming the marginal product of the resource is not zero. Following up on this point, the next case illustrates that constant capital productivity need not imply an absence of technical change when L/K has changed and diminishing returns exist.

---

3. When the exact equation for the production function expression is known and has certain properties, a growth equation can be derived from the functional equation and ex-expressed in terms of output responses to simultaneous changes in inputs and technology.

Case 4. The Growth Rate of Capital Exceeds That of Labor; and Technological Change Results in Capital Productivity Remaining Constant Starting with an economy using inputs of L labor and K capital in figure 2.6, inputs of these resources grow to K' and L'. The growth rate of capital inputs exceeds that of labor inputs, and L/K falls. Under conditions of diminishing returns to capital, α will decline in the absence of productivity improvements. Here technical advance exactly offsets the effects of diminishing returns upon capital productivity, leaving α unchanged. Labor productivity is affected by more capital per worker *and* improved technology, and rises from β to β'. The change in output is shown by the hatched area in the northwest quadrant and again by the (equivalent) hatched area in the southeast quadrant.

Case 5. The Relative Effect of Technical Change upon Countries with Variation in L/K Consider now a comparison of the effect of technological change upon countries that differ only in their factor ratios.

FIGURE 2.6

Nonproportionate Growth in Labor and Capital Plus Improved Technology

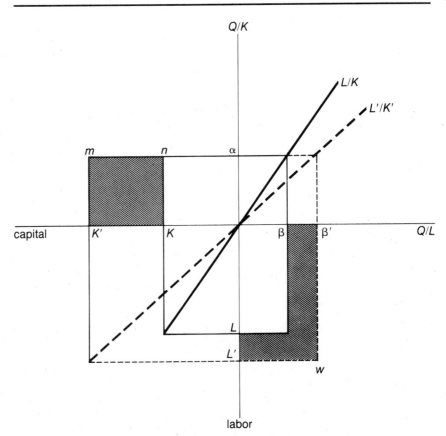

Case 4: The growth rate of capital exceeds that of labor, lowering L/K to L'/K'. Technical change along with more capital per worker raises β to β', and prevents a fall in α as L/K falls. Output rises to αK' or β'L'.

Will technological change be uniform in its effect upon economies with differing L/K ratios? To consider this question we return to the isoquant curve.

Technological improvement affects the position of the isoquant curves since the same output can be produced with less factor inputs. Technological change may affect the L/K limits of some or all curves and the elasticity of substitution. Figure 2.7 shows technological advance that improves factor productivity by 20 percent, reducing the factor inputs needed to produce output Q_o for any L/K ratio between the limits.

The new α and β for the limiting cases are identified by the subscript t. In the output quadrants the curves $q_o q_o'$ and $q''q'''$ are reference curves that show different combinations of K and α or L and β that will produce output Q_o over the relevant range considered here. The output rectangles before and after technological change are shown for the two limiting L/K ratios. After technological change, output Q_o can be produced with K_t' capital and L_t labor or K_t capital and L_t' labor. With technological improvement isoquant curve xy shifts toward the origin since with higher factor productivity for all L/K ratios, less inputs

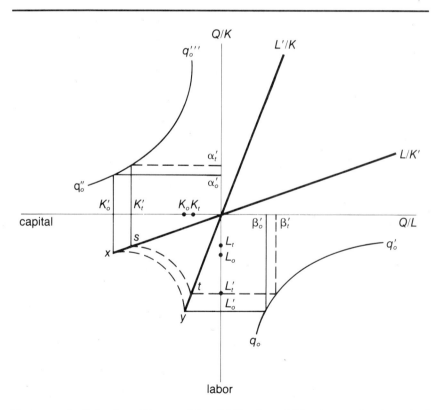

FIGURE 2.7
Neutral Technological Change

Factor productivity rises 20 percent for all L/K ratios, shifting isoquant xy for output Q_o in toward the origin to the position of curve st. Factor inputs needed to produce output Q_o drop for the limiting cases to $K_t'L_t$ and K_tL_t'.

are needed to produce output Q_o. Curve *st* now shows the different factor combinations that will produce output Q_o and curve *xy* will represent an output level 20 percent larger.

Technological change that increases output and factor productivity by the same percentage for any output and *L/K* ratio is called *neutral* technological change. The whole family of isoquants shifts in toward the origin in the same way as illustrated by the shift of isoquant *xy* in figure 2.7.

Technological improvement may vary in its impact so that the percentage change in output and factor productivity is different for different *L/K* ratios. Assume the percentage improvement in factor productivity is 20 percent for the lower ratios of *L/K* in figure 2.7, but less for higher ratios. Isoquant *xy* would shift so that for higher levels of *L/K* it would lie to the left of isoquant *st*. Such a shift is called *capital-saving* technological change. For any *L/K* ratio the marginal rate of substitution of labor for capital would be higher. Economies with lower *L/K* ratios benefit more than economies in the higher *L/K* range. Analogously, technological change that raises productivity by a larger percentage in higher *L/K* ranges is called *labor-saving* technological change.

Technological change may shift the *L/K* limits. Consider the case where technological advance is capital-saving, and shifts the upper *L/K* to a higher level. The less-developed country that is relatively labor-intensive can benefit from such a shift since it may prevent technological unemployment and allow the labor force to shift out of the traditional production methods of early centuries into modern technology even though the capital supply is relatively modest. As will be discussed in chapter 5, technological change that lowers both *L/K* limits, moving the isoquant toward the capital axis, presents problems for the LDC.

Finally, techniques along an isoquant may differ in vintage because of bias in technological change. New processes may apply to only a portion of the isoquant, changing the slope. The vintage of techniques would then differ along the isoquant. Older vintage techniques may then be the ones that remain efficient for some *L/K* ratios, and thus create full employment for some economies.

Conclusions   The terminology and methodology developed in this chapter provide basic background knowledge for the reader. First, in regard to terminology, the alternative expressions for output and changes in output recur throughout the book. It is sometimes helpful in the chapters that follow to express output in terms of labor inputs and labor productivity and at other times denoting output by referring to capital inputs and capital productivity is useful. Moreover, when referring to a production function with land as an input, it can be valuable to refer to output in terms of land and land productivity, the latter sometimes referred to as yield per acre or hectare.

The law of diminishing returns is a fundamental principle, and is considered particularly relevant for the mainly agrarian LDC experiencing population pressures upon the land. The effect of technical change upon factor substitution and factor proportion limits and the role of technological change in the improvement of productivity is central to the analysis of development. Finally, economies of scale and factor growth are recurrent topics requiring fuller discussion and analysis.

The next chapter extends the conceptual and graphic framework, and completes certain background knowledge needed for the study of development. These two chapters develop tools of analysis, and of necessity are relatively technical in nature compared with other chapters of the book.

REFERENCES

Blaug, Mark. 1980. *The Methodology of Economics.* Cambridge: Cambridge University Press.

Moggridge, D., ed. 1973. *The Collected Writings of John Maynard Keynes, vol. XIV, The General Theory and After.* London: Macmillan.

Graphic Analysis
of Development

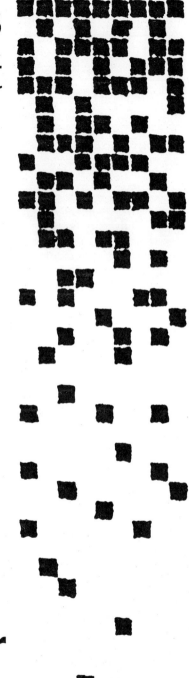

chapter

3

The previous chapter discussed the production function and indicated that it can yield insight into production relationships for the firm, the industry, the sector, or the aggregate economy. In this chapter a graph called the production possibilities curve, or frontier, is developed. Such a graph can show two-sector and three-sector economies. Each good or sector has a production function, with properties drawn from the discussion found in chapter 2.

The relationships among the sectors of a developing economy are central to an understanding of how growth proceeds as a mainly agrarian economy transforms itself into one that is industrially advanced. Thus, a diagram that can picture an economy with more than one sector is highly useful. The graphs developed are extreme simplifications of a complex economy. They are analytical aids that prove valuable in certain later chapters, while focusing attention at this early point upon relationships among sectors that affect growth. Before previewing the topics covered in this chapter, we will examine the general properties of a production possibilities curve and relate them to the institutions of an economy.

Not unlike the graphs developed in chapter 2, the production possibilities curve, or frontier, is a simplified but helpful diagram for conceptualizing the total productive capacity of an economy. However, this second set of graphs illustrates output in a different way. The economy's product mix is represented here by two (or later, three) goods or categories of goods. The production function for each is known. A less restricted production function with more than two inputs can also be handled within this framework.

The economy has a given quantity of each resource—land, labor, and capital. It is assumed to begin with that factor endowments can be fully utilized in the production of either good; that is, the resource endowments are not outside the factor combination limits of either one. The level of technology, whether more or less advanced, is known and constant. The economy, using a specified level of technology and a given endowment of resources, will have a capacity output level in the production of one commodity or category of commodities when all resources are used efficiently. This capacity level for each good is represented in figure 3.1 at points C and A on the axes. If all resources are devoted to good A and none to good C, the capacity output is A units. If good C receives all resources and good A none, then capacity output is C units.

In addition to the extremes of devoting all resources to one or the other good, differing combinations of the two can be produced. Now efficiency conditions require that factor inputs be allocated between the two to maximize output potential of any combination of them. Once an output level for one good is chosen, there is a choice of factor combinations available along the isoquant. The factor combination chosen is the one that allows the highest possible isoquant for the second product to be attained with the remaining resources. Again the

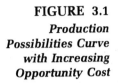

FIGURE 3.1
*Production
Possibilities Curve
with Increasing
Opportunity Cost*

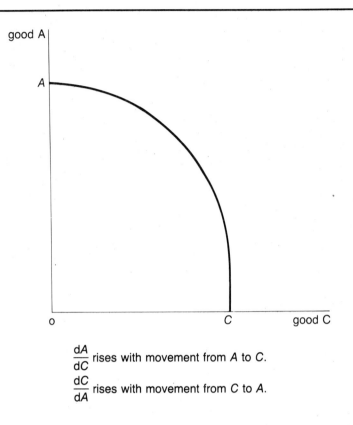

$\dfrac{dA}{dC}$ rises with movement from *A* to *C*.

$\dfrac{dC}{dA}$ rises with movement from *C* to *A*.

idea is that the economy, combining resources in the most efficient manner possible with current techniques and know-how, can produce only so much of the second commodity along with a specified quantity of the first, or vice versa. No recombination of resources will achieve more of the second one without reducing the amount of the first that can be produced. The production possibilities curve, then, traces out the maximum output achievable for different combinations of product mix with full and efficient employment of given resources and constant technology.[1] The shape of the curve is explained subsequently.

**Institutions and
Capacity Output**   A society's organizational features and institutions are important determinants of both its potential productive capacity and actual output. Political, social, and economic institutions affect resource inputs, their growth rate, and the level and growth of productivity. How are institutional characteristics handled in the simple framework of a production possibilities curve?

---

1. The graphic derivation of efficiency conditions in production to maximize each output combination is discussed in chapter 12.

Some organizational features (for example, the assembly line) are treated as technical known-how and subsumed under technology. Such institutions are reflected in the isoquants that show the most efficient production combinations for resource inputs. However, institutions that compose the economic system are to a large degree independent of the isoquant. Countries with the same technology level can have different social structures that affect output.

An established approach that relates the independent institutions to the production possibilities curve is theoretical in nature. The idea is to develop the perfect institutional structure that will ensure operation on the production possibilities curve and thus attainment of the highest insoquant combination. The social organizations of real economic systems can then be described and assessed by how closely they approximate the model of an efficient system.

Given the historical importance of the market system, it is not surprising that a perfected maximization model exists based on market institutions. Western economics since its inception has explored in detail the institutional framework of market systems—systems that are decentralized and allow market-set prices to determine an economy's product mix, factor proportions in production, and income distribution. In the process of examining market systems, economists gradually developed the institutional framework plus other assumptions necessary for the perfectly efficient market economy. This market system model, presented in most books on basic economic principles, is called *perfect competition*. It is a system of perfectly flexible prices, perfect information, completely mobile resources, price-taking small competitors, profit-maximizing firms, and utility-maximizing individuals.

Obviously a real economy organized along market lines deviates to a greater or lesser degree from the model. Such deviations are referred to as distortions. One or more of the assumptions and institutions of perfect competition can be changed to yield insight into inefficiencies the assumed distortions will create. The posited changes in the perfect competition model are drawn from distortions in the real world, for example, a wage rate that is not set by market supply and demand, or a protectionist trade policy. Assuming the distortion itself cannot be eliminated, the question is then asked: Can an institution or policy be introduced that will reduce or correct the inefficiencies resulting from the distortion? In this way we gain insights from the model for improving the functioning of a real economy, thus moving it closer to its production possibilities curve.

Less work has been done on conceptualizing the institutional system of a centrally planned economy that could ensure its operation on the production possibilities curve at a planner-selected point. With the advent of the computer, it is theoretically possible to devise a system that could calculate the efficiency conditions of a total economy, solving for the same type of information we get from prices in perfectly competitive markets. Given the same assumption about human behavior as that of the market economy, that is, that individuals separately and corporately maximize, then planning institutions could be devised that would achieve maximum output. Currently, development of the theoretical planning system that would be perfectly efficient is considered possible, but work is still in its very early stages. Most of the analysis is highly mathematical and thus less accessible than the market model.

Models explaining how an economy with market distortions functions are called models of *imperfect competition*. Considerable work has been done on imperfect markets and their associated institutions—oligopoly, monopoly, Keynesian-type models, and others. Such models help to explain why a market economy falls short of efficiency criteria. They have also been used to design a government-market mixture of institutions that will reduce or correct the imperfections of the market. For example, mixed-market economies have government regulation of industries such as utilities, where competition would be uneconomic, and taxation and spending policies by the central government for countering the business cycle.

The model, or paradigm, referred to for an explanation of inefficiency in premarket or premodern economies is the model of the *traditional* economy. Despite the low income level in such an economy, not all the society's institutions are designed to maximize productive efficiency. In fact, they can impede the maximization of output considerably. For example, religious taboos sometimes dictate an inefficient utilization of resources, prevent the consumption of cheap or nutritious foods, or even ban the eradication of disease-bearing rodents when these animals are deemed sacred. Institutions are valued within society, so a trade-off between efficiency and social organization is not unexpected.

In the simple or naive traditional model, all human behavior related to the economy is dictated by unchanging social institutions, mores, or taboos. The rigid institutions prevent economic improvements. Economic activity is an integral part of social organization, family relations, and religious behavior patterns. Efficiency in resource utilization at given technical levels and/or technical change are precluded because they would demand flexibility and new institutions that would weaken or replace the established order. Impersonal substitution of land or capital for labor, or use of a known production process that casts certain socioeconomic classes into obsolesence or goes against religious beliefs would disrupt the system, its hierarchy and mores, and its stability.

Techniques known in the traditional economy can be very limited and allow very little if any substitution among productive inputs. The unyielding institutions impede technological change that would allow greater substitution among resources and higher potential output levels. The scientific method of problem-solving is unknown; and in fact, education levels are so low as to preclude this approach to technical advance. Institutions change in the traditional paradigm only when a threat to the society looms large, forcing them to bend.

Economies can encompass institutional features of various models, perfect and imperfect. A few LDCs are predominately traditional in their institutional makeup. Most of them display an admixture of modernizing institutions along with the traditional. The majority have areas or sectors of the economy where traditional forces greatly influence efficiency. These are often high-risk sectors of the economy such as weather-dependent agriculture. Thus various models can provide insights into economic performance.

This chapter and the previous one abstract to a great degree from institutional forces at work in order to emphasize certain economic variables central to an economy's performance. The importance of institutional factors was introduced in chapter 1, and discussion of social practices that influence development will recur throughout the book. It is sufficient at this point simply to point out that a society's institutions must be recognized as important determinants of output. Social structures are the product of historical forces both complex and slow to evolve. Outside advisors or leaders of an LDC society may be well aware of institutional changes that would improve economic efficiency but are unable to introduce them because of the social inflexibility. Thus, economies with the same technical potential may differ in the cultural and institutional frameworks that influence the degree to which technical potential is realized.

Chapter Focus

The production possibilities curve for an economy experiencing growth will shift outward. Increased inputs of capital, labor, and land need not affect both goods or sectors uniformly. Scale and technological change can impact one good (sector) or both. Growth influences income per capita and this, in turn, can affect the relative amounts of each good produced. Moreover, the amount of capital goods produced affects growth. We will proceed to explore these growth variables with the aid of the production possibilities curve.

In addition, two other important concepts will be introduced. First, the term "opportunity cost" is explained. This concept is a basic one, vital to understanding efficient resource allocation among sectors and the cost of industrial expansion and import replacement so often supported by LDC governments. Second, problems of achieving full employment of resources will be examined. One cause of idle resources can be a "factor proportions problem." This technical limitation to full employment influences the production possibilities curve. Chapter 2 introduced the nature of the problem by discussing limits to substitution between factors in the production of goods and the idea of a zero marginal product for a factor of production. The production possibilities curve incorporating a factor proportions problems proves useful in subsequent analysis of development.

Before beginning to discuss these topics, we need to glance briefly at the production functions for agriculture and industry. The factor inputs of the production function for the agricultural sector can vary with the level of development. In an agrarian economy with only premodern know-how, the factors of production are basically land and labor when draft animals are not present, as is the case so often in Africa, where endemic disease prevents the use of such animals. Land improvements are minimal, and are included under land inputs. Thus, production is assumed to depend upon only two factor inputs, land

and labor. For economies in later stages of development, it is necessary to consider capital as an input in agriculture.

It is accepted procedure to characterize the production function in industry as having two inputs, labor and capital. Later, capital will be subdivided into human and physical categories. And this sector will also be examined in the case where output is a function of imported inputs such as capital equipment manufactured abroad. In the present chapter, however, trade is only briefly introduced and human capital is omitted.

Production Possibilities Curve for an Agrarian Economy

Figure 3.2 shows a production possibilities curve for an agrarian economy under normal weather conditions. The economy capable of producing along this production possibilities curve has a specified amount of land and labor. Technology is known to be fairly primitive. The farmers can produce two alternative crops, corn and cacao. The subscript c is used to denote corn and the subscript a indicates cacao.

Assume all resources are devoted to corn production. Capacity output of corn, Q_c, can be expressed in terms of land (N) and average yield per acre (μ) or in terms of labor and labor productivity:

$$Q_c = \mu_c N = \beta_c L \qquad (1)$$

Similarly, when all resources are devoted to cacao production, capacity output of cacao can be stated as:

$$Q_a = \mu_a N = \beta_a L \qquad (2)$$

FIGURE 3.2

Production Possibilities Curve for Agrarian Economy

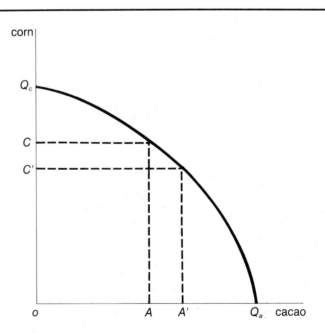

Capacity corn production: $Q_c = \mu_c N = \beta_c L$
Capacity cacao production: $Q_a = \mu_a N = \beta_a L$
The opportunity cost of increasing cacao production from A to A' is a reduction of corn production from C to C'.

The technical level of the economy will be reflected in the land and labor productivity coefficients for capacity output. That is, given L and N, variations in capacity output and hence land and labor productivity will reflect variations in technology.

In addition to growing only corn or only cacao, combinations of corn and cacao, as represented by the curve Q_cQ_a, can be raised. Within the confines of the technology level, each product mix along the curve represents efficiency in production of that output combination. This means farmers allocate resources so that no higher isoquant combination is attainable. The economy can produce more of one crop only by giving up some of the other when it is moving along the production possibilities curve.

The production possibilities curve as explained is a maximum efficiency frontier. However, institutional features of the peasant economy can prevent it from allocating resources efficiently. In the absence of perfect efficiency conditions, farmers operate somewhere inside the curve. The production possibilities curve in such cases identifies the shortfall from potential maximum output. An economy operating inside the production possibilities curve is capable of turning out more of both crops. It is often convenient, however, to postulate that the economy operates at a point on the production possibilities curve when studying the impact of changes in economic variables upon productive capacity.

Movement along the curve in figure 3.2 gives a measure of how much corn must be given up to obtain an additional amount of cacao and vice versa. The cost of more corn is the foregone cacao; and this is also referred to as the *opportunity cost* of corn. As the economy moves from production of C corn and A cacao to C' corn and A' cacao, the opportunity cost of $A' - A$ cacao is $C - C'$ corn. To achieve an equivalent increment of cacao beyond A', more corn must be given up. In fact, the concave shape of the curve indicates that, moving out from the axis, each unit of cacao added requires that a greater amount of corn be given up. The same increasing opportunity cost characterizes movement away from cacao production toward that of corn. More than one cause can be at work here to produce increasing rather than constant or decreasing costs. One force is the law of variable proportions; another is nonhomogeneous resources.

First, the two crops may require different growing conditions in land, temperature, and rainfall. When the land is not homogeneous and lies within different climate ranges, some areas are better suited to one crop and some to the other. As the product mix becomes more concentrated in one or the other, yields per acre decline. Similarly, labor may vary in productive capacity for each crop because of experience, workers' health, or other reasons.

Secondly, assume corn is more labor-intensive than cacao, requiring more weeding and cultivating. (A more precise definition of factor intensity in the comparison of two goods is left to a later chapter.) Assume labor and land are homogeneous. When the two crops are produced, it is possible to allocate the given labor (L) and land (N) so

OPPORTUNITY COST

that the ratio of labor to land used in corn production is greater than the ratio used in the production of cacao. But, as concentration in either crop is approached, full employment requires that the labor/land ratio approach the ratio of resource endowments, L/N. Movement from corn to cacao requires a rising labor/land ratio for cacao as resources are freed from the relatively labor-intensive corn crop. Alternatively, movement from cacao to corn requires a falling labor/land ratio for corn as resources shift from the relatively land-intensive cacao. The marginal rate of substitution between factors affects output response. Output increases, but by less than it would if the ratio of land to labor did not impact factor productivity. In this case the cause of increasing costs with product mix changes between factor-intensive crops is associated with a diminishing marginal rate of substitution as the ratio of labor to land used in producing crops rises or falls.

Recall from chapter 2 that a change in output of corn or cacao can be expressed in terms of either resource as:

$$dQ = d\mu N + \mu dN \qquad\qquad (3)$$

or,

$$dQ = d\beta L + \beta dL \qquad\qquad (4)$$

As explained, at each point along the increasing cost production possibilities curve the economy recombines resources, changing the labor to land ratio in production for each crop in order to achieve the highest combined output level. The productivity coefficients μ and β for each crop change with movement along the concave curve because of shifting factor proportions or the effect of nonhomogeneous factors, not because of change in technology or scale.

Movement along the production possibilities curve involves continuous reductions in one crop's output as output of the other expands. The opportunity cost of cacao, then, can be expressed as $-dQ_c/dQ_a$. The sign is generally dropped. Under conditions of increasing opportunity cost, the absolute value of this ratio rises with movement along the curve from Q_c to Q_a. The ratio for a particular point on the production-possibilities curve can be represented by the slope of a line drawn tangent to the curve at that point. This is done in subsequent graphs.

It is possible (although not highly realistic in most cases) to have a constant cost production possibilities curve. The production frontier is a straight line and dQ_c/dQ_a a constant. At times a constant cost production frontier is drawn to simplify graphic treatment of a topic.

Scale Assume now that one of the crops, cacao, benefits from large-scale farming such that the productivity of land and labor in raising it is a positive function of output levels. When cacao output is large enough for economies of scale to occur, dQ_c/dQ_a falls. Each unit of corn foregone results in greater incremental output of cacao.

Figure 3.3 illustrates the case where a declining opportunity cost of switching from corn to cacao production is encountered once a crit-

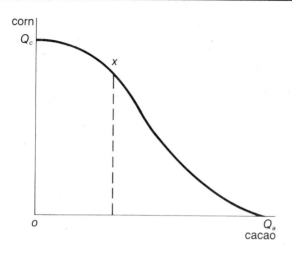

FIGURE 3.3

Production Possibilities Curve with Economies of Scale in Cacao

Up to point x, dQ_c/dQ_a is rising. After point x, economies of scale cause dQ_c/dQ_a to fall.

ical level of cacao output is attained so that scale effects appear. From Q_c to point x, efficiency in production of cacao is falling; after x, it is rising. Should both crops experience economies of scale, the production possibilities curve would be convex to the origin.

Growth in Resources

Growth in resources shifts the production possibilities curve outward and generally changes its slope. Unless all resources expand proportionately, output capacity in both goods does not increase by the same proportion. Assume that labor expands and land remains constant. The increased labor raises output but lowers labor productivity under conditions of diminishing returns. This effect is readily shown by use of the graph of marginal and average product of labor developed in chapter 2.

In figure 3.4 the additional labor, $L' - L$, raises the output of corn. The change in output is represented by the hatched area under the marginal product curve. The average product of labor falls from β_c to β_c'. Thus the new capacity output level is $Q_c' = \beta_c'L'$. The expansion in output, then, is not proportionate to the increase in labor inputs. Similar results could be derived by increasing land (capital) alone.

A graph similar to the one shown for corn could be drawn for cacao, depicting the marginal and average product and change in that crop's output. There is no reason to expect that a growth in labor will raise production of each commodity by the same percentage. Production functions are simply not that similar. When one good is labor-intensive, it can absorb more labor without encountering sharply diminishing returns.

Expansion of factor inputs, then, raises capacity output, shifting the production possibilities curve outward. As explained, without pro-

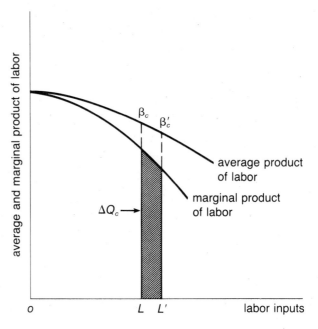

An increase in labor inputs from *L* to *L'* raises corn output by ΔQ_c.
Capacity output for corn is now β'_c times *L'*.

portionate growth of both resources, capacity output in each good cannot expand proportionately. The slope of the production possibilities
curve is modified. A change in that curve's slope changes the opportunity cost of the commodities produced. (Figure 3.11 illustrates such
a shift.)

One insight to be gained here is that countries with differing relative resource endowments will have different slopes to their production possibilities curves even though their technology is the same. This
has implications for the potential for trade between such nations, a
topic explored in later chapters.

**Technological
Change**

Technological change can affect the production function for one or
both crops. Assume first that gains in know-how affect only corn. Capacity output, expressed as $\beta_c L = \mu_c N$, rises because land and labor
productivity do. The production possibilities curve shifts outward, as
shown in figure 3.5, from $Q_c Q_a$ to $Q'_c Q_a$. Any combination of corn and
cacao production is higher due to the increased efficiency of resources
employed in corn production.

Technological change in both corn and cacao would shift capacity
output outward in both corn and cacao. In figure 3.6 it is assumed that
improved technology raises efficiency in production for both crops,
resulting in a parallel shift in the production possibilities curve. Such

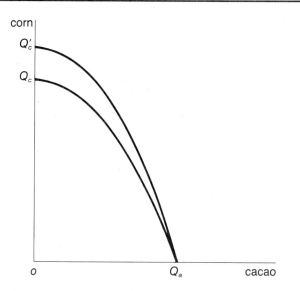

FIGURE 3.5

Technical Advance in Corn Production

Technological change in production of corn shifts the production possibilities curve. Capacity output in corn, $Q_c = \beta_c L = \mu_c N$, rises to $Q'_c = \beta'_c L = \mu'_c N$.

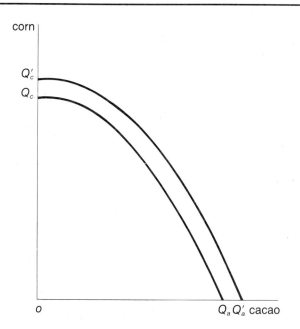

FIGURE 3.6

Technical Advance in Corn and Cacao Production

Technological change shifts the production possibilities curve outward. Capacity output in corn, $Q_c = \beta_c L = \mu_c N$, rises to $Q'_c = \beta'_c L = \mu'_c N$. Capacity output in cacao, $Q_a = \beta_a L = \mu_a N$, rises to $Q'_a = \beta'_a L = \mu'_a N$.

a symmetrical shift is often assumed to occur strictly for convenience in graphic exposition.

In general, technological change cannot be expected to make all goods or sectors of a developing economy respond by the same percentage, and may not affect production of some goods at all. As the economy's relative efficiency in production changes, this influences resource allocation among goods and sectors. Technological progress is also related to the introduction of new goods. An in-depth discussion of technological change is presented in chapter 5.

UNEMPLOYED RESOURCES

Unemployment of resources can arise because of inefficiency or because of technical constraints. The operation of an economy inside its production possibilities curve can indicate unemployed resources. Alternatively, however, technological constraints that cause unemployment affect the curve itself.

Technological Unemployment

Consider the case where there are no economies of scale. Assume that technical limitations are such that as the economy approaches specialization in corn, it cannot absorb increasing amounts of land at the rate by which it is freed from cacao. Some of the acreage is left idle. Additional corn is produced with the minimum labor/land ratio that the limits of technology allow. Thus increased corn production can be achieved at constant cost, assuming all resources are homogeneous. Capacity corn output is lower, of course, than in the case where all land could be brought under cultivation. Analogously, the specialization of the economy in cacao could produce a segment of constant-cost cacao and excess labor that is unemployed.

Figure 3.7 illustrates this, while figure 3.8 helps in visualizing the cause of a constant cost segment on a production frontier and a surplus of one resource. In figure 3.8 total resource endowments are given as N_o land and L_o labor. The minimum and maximum L/N ratios for cacao are shown by the slopes of the designated lines. Assume the dotted curve shows the cumulative combination of labor and land freed from corn production as cacao production is expanded from zero at the origin. Because corn is a labor-intensive crop while cacao is land-intensive, land and labor are not available along the dotted line in the proportion of L_o/N_o. Rather, as corn production first begins to shrink, relatively more land is released for cacao. This means that eventually further declines in corn production will release relatively large amounts of labor to be absorbed in growing cacao.

Prior to point x cacao production can fully employ all resource combinations freed. Past point x, the combination of land and labor freed is outside the L/N limit for cacao, a land-intensive crop relative to corn. Output of cacao must expand along the limit line. Thus each additional unit of corn foregone produces an equal increment of cacao past point x as labor and land are absorbed in constant proportions along xyz.

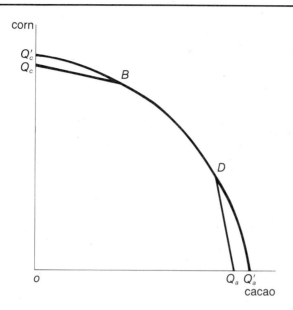

FIGURE 3.7

Factor Proportions Problem Reduces Output Potential

Technical rigidities in the production function cause unemployment of resources outside segment $\overline{BD}$ and lower production potential from $Q'_cBDQ'_a$ to Q_cBDQ_a.

As resource combinations y' and z' are made available, factors used will be y and z, respectively. Thus yy' and zz' depict surplus labor at each output level. The southeast quadrant represents capacity cacao output using L_u labor input with $L_o - L_u$ (or zz') labor unemployed. The northwest quadrant shows that the capacity cacao output utilized all land. Output is lower than in the stiuation where the maximum L/N ratio lies outside curve $xy'z'$. A similar graph could be drawn for the case where surplus land occurs with movement toward complete specialization in corn, the labor-intensive crop.

In figure 3.7 production possibilities curve Q_cBDQ_a with technical rigidities for corn and cacao lies inside a production possibilities curve without technical rigidities ($Q'_cBDQ'_a$). If resources are not homogeneous, the surplus factor segments would be curvilinear and points Q_c and Q_a would lie closer to the origin. Richard Eckaus, who first examined such technical rigidities as they might apply to less-developed countries, refers to unemployment of this type as related to the *factor proportions problem* (Eckaus 1955). It is considered particularly applicable to an industrializing LDC that is adopting modern technology of a capital-intensive, labor-saving nature. For such a situation the production possibilities curve would represent two goods produced with capital and labor, one commodity using capital intensively, the other using labor intensively. Often, since LDCs are relatively capital-shy, there is only a potential for unemployed labor, and the curve would be Q'_cBDQ_a.

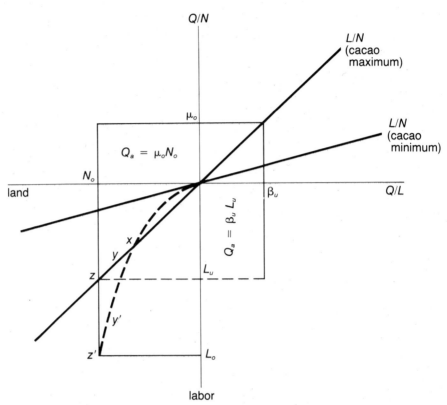

FIGURE 3.8

*Factor Proportions
Problem with Shift to
Cacao Production*

Technological unemployment occurs as, past point *x*, land-labor combinations freed from production of corn along *xy'z'* exceed the maximum *L/N* ratio for cacao as shown. Maximum cacao output uses N_o land and L_u labor, leaving $L_o - L_u$ labor unemployed.

**PRODUCTION-
CONSUMPTION
EQUILIBRIUM**

Up to this point we have been examining supply-side variables. To determine how much of each good will be turned out, demand elements must be known. Demand may reflect the tastes of individuals free to spend their income, or the goals of planners who influence the quantities of each item to be produced. Most often in LDCs it reflects varying combinations of the two. In the absence of foreign trade, only domestic demand for the commodities produced influences their output levels.

Product Mix

In general the relative output levels for a two-good or two-sector economy without trade depend upon relative costs as seen in the shape of the production possibilities curve, individuals' and/or planners' tastes and income level and distribution. The relationship between income and the relative proportions of products consumed is referred to as the *income elasticity of demand.* The income elasticity of demand is defined as:

% change in quantity consumed
———————————————
% change in income

given constant relative prices. When the ratio is greater than one, the demand for the good in question is said to be income-elastic. The growth rate in consumption of the income-elastic product exceeds the growth rate in income so that as income rises, the proportion of it spent on the income-elastic good does too. The demand for the good is income-inelastic when the growth rate in its consumption is below that of income. Food is a category of goods noted for its income inelasticity, as was first observed by Ernst Engel in 1857. Many services are income-elastic. The elasticity of goods with respect to income can change over income ranges.

Because of the relationship between income and the relative amounts of goods consumed, income distribution has an effect upon the product mix. There may also be more subtle effects upon the product mix related to income distribution. People's tastes or consumption levels may be influenced by higher income groups. More is said about this in the chapter on savings.

Growth variables affect both income and the relative costs of production. The production possibilities curve shifts outward and its slope changes. Thus growth affects the product mix. It also creates new products and helps to form new tastes. And trade generally also has a strong influence on the product mix as well as on growth. A simplified graphic representation of changes in the product mix accompanying growth is presented in a subsequent section. In the graphic presentation for any two commodities, if one product or representative category of goods is income-elastic, the other must be income-inelastic, given the two-dimensional nature of the diagram.

Efficiency Conditions

Each sector or industry has an increasing-cost supply curve when the production possibilities curve is characterized by rising opportunity costs. Given consumers' and/or planners' demand curves, prices and quantities can be established that equate supply and demand. Assume that the product mix and relative demand for corn and cacao for production possibilities curve Q_cQ_a in figure 3.9 are C_1 corn and A_1 cacao. The coordinates for C_1A_1 identify the production and consumption point on the curve where supply is equal to demand for both goods. The slope of the production possibilities curve at the output-consumption point represents the opportunity cost of an additional unit of cacao. The inverse of the slope, that is dQ_a/dQ_c, is the opportunity cost of an additional unit of corn.

Under efficiency conditions the supply curves for the industry or sector producing corn and cacao must reflect cost of production as output expands and therefore must reflect the value of the corn (cacao) foregone as an additional unit of cacao (corn) is produced. When supply and demand are in equilibrium, the cost of the last unit produced

FIGURE 3.9

Equilibrium in Production-Consumption

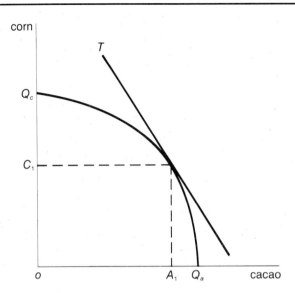

Given a product mix of C_1 corn and A_1 cacao, equilibrium conditions require that $dQ_c/dQ_a = P_a/P_c$ = absolute slope of T.

equals price. With the economy in equilibrium and efficiency conditions prevailing:

$$P_c dQ_c = P_a dQ_a \qquad (5)$$

That is, the value to the economy for the last units produced of both commodities is the same. Otherwise, the economy would desire more production of one and less of the other. Notice that equation (5) can be rearranged as follows:

$$\frac{dQ_c}{dQ_a} = \frac{P_a}{P_c} \qquad (6)$$

This equilibrium statement is summarized by the slope of the *terms-of-trade* line drawn tangent to the production possibilities curve at the production-consumption point. The terms-of-trade line can be read as:

$$\text{opportunity cost of cacao} = \frac{\text{price of cacao}}{\text{price of corn}} = \text{slope of T}$$

Intuitively, this efficiency condition can be thought of as analogous to the equilibrium for a self-sufficient farm where family members allocate labor and land so that they maximize the amount of corn and cacao obtainable from their fields; and they apportion land and labor to corn only up to the point that the satisfaction from the last stalk of corn is equal to that gained from the last pound of cacao beans.

There will be a different set of market-clearing relative prices when the product mix is changed from C_1 corn and A_1 cacao, indicating relative demand and costs have changed. This relationship between equilibrium or scarcity prices and opportunity costs is a fundamental efficiency concept that will be referred to often. And while the graphic representation here is in terms of only two goods or sectors, the simplicity does not detract from its usefulness.

Given relative prices for goods produced (which mirror the production costs and relative demand at full employment output), and the resource endowments of the economy, each resource will have a scarcity or equilibrium price reflecting the strength of demand for that resource, with a specific product mix. Efficiency in resource allocation requires that resources be allocated between goods or sectors so that the value of their marginal products is the same in each good. A variation between goods in the value of the marginal product of a resource means that the transfer of resource units from the lower value use raises the resource's value in use. The value of the marginal product under efficiency conditions in production is the opportunity cost (alternatively called scarcity price or equilibrium price) of the resource. Each product mix creates different relative scarcity prices for resources when goods or sectors making up the product mix use resources in different relative proportions, or when economies of scale affect the productivity of resources.

Resource Equilibrium and Scarcity Prices

These efficiency conditions are relevant benchmarks for any type of economic system. Every economy has a production possibilities curve reflecting opportunity costs. Every economy has a demand function, private and public. When prices reflect opportunity costs and demand, they provide the society with a method of allocating and rationing scarce goods and resources so that neither shortages nor surpluses occur, and maximum output is achieved from limited resources.

Relevance of Efficiency Conditions

Planners can substitute directives for relative prices in order to achieve plan targets. But assuming the planners' goal is to operate on the production possibilities curve at a point they have selected, they need the same information so handily summarized in equilibrium relative prices, that is, efficiency conditions reflective of equilibrium supply and demand in all markets.

In fact, no planned system operates without prices. Individuals receive goods but they also receive money. And prices must appear on goods exchanged for money. Private demand comes into play and planners need knowledge of private demand forces in devising the product mix. Prices are also needed by planners as an accounting aid. Prices are units of account expressed in a common denominator, money. They facilitate handling of data sets, an enormous task for the planner.

When prices do not reflect scarcity value, long lines or production delays develop from shortages and reduce efficiency in production and consumption; or surpluses appear, representing excess investment in warehoused goods. Planners cannot control such forces and black markets emerge to handle the problem of disequilibrium prices set by officials in the planning bureau. Thus planners need knowledge of efficiency conditions and scarcity prices to plan and achieve the maximum output possible from limited resources. Failure to appreciate the subtleties of opportunity cost and market-clearing prices as aids in planning development has led many an overzealous planner astray.

Prices, of course, are central to the functioning of the market economy. They perform many of the tasks handled by planners in a centrally controlled economy. Yet the market does not achieve efficiency pricing unless conditions of perfect competition are present and there are no externalities, that is, costs or benefits not reflected in market prices. Thus, a market-clearing price in the case of imperfectly functioning markets is not the same as the scarcity price reflecting efficiency in production and consumption.[2] However, when markets are not highly imperfect, they perform an enormous information-gathering function in the prices they produce. These prices, while not those of perfect efficiency, will be the least-cost approximation of efficiency prices, and generally yield information the planner cannot readily generate except at prohibitive expense.

How closely market and/or planning institutions in LDCs approximate efficiency conditions in a growth context is difficult to estimate. Undoubtedly it varies among countries. Market institutions in LDCs may be poorly developed and distortions commonplace. Externalities, positive and negative, may be prevalent. It is common for prices of resources in particular to deviate from scarcity value in LDCs; and information needed to calculate scarcity prices is limited. This same information constraint plus problems of implementation can make it difficult for planners to improve market performance or plan better than the market.

Despite these shortcomings, however, the development of markets and the introduction of various degrees of planning in LDCs usually supersede an inflexible traditional economy, which provides only limited institutional apparatus for achieving efficiency under conditions of change and for absorbing technological advance. In fact, one source of growth in LDCs is the closer approximation to efficiency conditions with the demise of the traditional economy and the continuous structural improvements and evolution of new institutions that promote efficiency and growth. (Progress toward efficiency, of course, does not equate with social improvement in its broad meaning, which incorporates value judgments about the "good society." Changes in family relations, religious orientation, community identification, and use of time that arise from economic progress are judged by broader criteria. Thus, full evaluation of the social changes that accompany development is both difficult and controversial.)

A Graphic Summary   Figures 3.10 and 3.11 illustrate changes in equilibrium conditions with growth. In figure 3.10 a parallel shift of the production possibilities

---

2. Where perfect efficiency conditions do not hold, the term opportunity cost is oftentimes used in a more general way in the literature. When, in an economy with given inefficiencies, increased output in one sector must reduce output in another, then the foregone output of the sector giving up resources is said to be the opportunity cost of the expanded one. This understates opportunity cost derived from efficient conditions. Unemployed resources are said to have a zero opportunity cost.

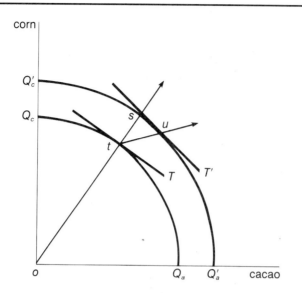

FIGURE 3.10
*Proportionate
Expansion*

A proportionate expansion of the production possibilities curve and an income elasticity of demand of one for both goods move production-consumption from *t* to *s*, with no change in relative prices. When the income elasticity of demand for corn is less than one and for cacao is greater than one, production-consumption moves to *u* and relative prices change to the slope of *T'*.

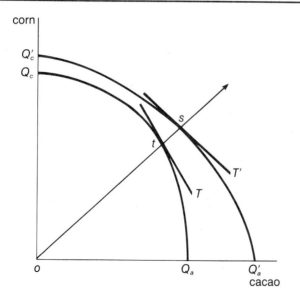

FIGURE 3.11
*Nonproportionate
Expansion*

Relatively greater expansion of cacao productive capacity compared to corn productive capacity lowers P_a/P_c from the slope of *T* to the slope of *T'* when relative quantities of corn and cacao produced and consumed remain the same.

curve leaves the shape unchanged. Expansion of consumption from t to s along the ray from the origin will reflect unchanged proportions in production-consumption of the two goods. Moreover, equilibrium prices will remain as they are since the slopes of the production possibilities curve at t and s are the same. The demand elasticity for both goods in this case is one. Alternatively, expansion of production-consumption from t to u implies that the income elasticity of demand for cacao is greater than one and that for corn is less than one. Relative prices in this case change with growth from the slope of T to the slope of T', indicating corn is relatively less expensive.

Figure 3.11 shows the case where growth modifies the shape of the production possibilities curve and hence the opportunity cost of corn and cacao. The elasticity of demand is assumed to be such that consumption expands along the ray from the origin. However, because supply-side variables have changed, equilibrium prices will do so also to reflect the slope of the production possibilities curve at point s. Relatively speaking, cacao is cheaper and corn more expensive at s compared with t, as shown by the reduced slope of the terms-of-trade line with growth.

CAPITAL GOODS AND GROWTH

We pointed out previously that growth affects the product mix. Conversely, the product mix also affects growth. Consider an economy with resource endowments of L and K, a consumer goods sector (c) and a capital goods sector (k). Both sectors use labor and capital as factors of production. Capacity output in the consumer goods sector can be expressed as $\alpha_c K$, and in the capital goods sector as $\alpha_k K$.

The growth of capital is determined by the production of capital goods. Such goods replace the capital used up in producing output; and when new capital produced exceeds depreciation, the capital stock expands. Here we assume output of capital goods makes a net addition to the capital stock. Capital goods output in a given period then enlarges the production potential for both sectors in the following period since capital is a factor input in the production of both consumer and capital goods.

Figure 3.12 represents alternative combinations for production of consumer and capital goods for an economy. The ray sx, showing the coordinate points for the product mix, is a high-consumption alternative, while the ray rn is a low-consumption alternative choice of product mix. The ray chosen determines the change in the capital stock and thus the expansion of the production possibilities curve.

For simplicity we assume that an increase in the capital stock results in a parallel shift of the production possibilities curve. The high-consumption choice expands the capital stock to K' and the production possibilities curve to $\alpha_c K'$ on the consumer goods axis and $\alpha_k K'$ on the capital goods axis. The product mix on the new curve is at point x. Less consumption allows a higher output of capital, expanding the production possibilities curve to $\alpha_c K''$ on the consumer goods axis and $\alpha_k K''$ on the capital goods axis. The product mix on the expanded production possibilities curve is at point n. Eventually the greater capital formation alternative will allow higher consumption *and* capital goods production than the lower alternative.

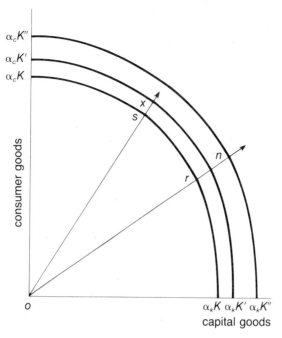

FIGURE 3.12
*Capital Goods
Production and
Growth*

A relatively higher production of capital goods at *r* raises the production possibilities curve from $\alpha_c K\ \alpha_k K$ to $\alpha_c K''\ \alpha_k K''$. A relatively lower production of capital goods results in less growth of productive capacity—from $\alpha_c K\ \alpha_k K$ to $\alpha_c K'\ \alpha_k K'$ with production along ray *sx*.

When an economy cannot produce capital goods needed for growth, then growth depends upon imports of capital. In that case, the division of the product mix between exports and consumption goods affects growth. In the next section we develop a three-sector graph that will be used to illustrate such a case in later chapters.

There is a close interrelation among the agricultural, the export, and the industrial sectors as development takes place. As early as the eighteenth century, treatises on economic development emphasized sectoral interrelations. These writings made certain assumptions about the properties of the production function in agriculture that set a limit upon industrial growth. In fact, we cover this work in a later chapter in order to understand the conditions under which similar limitations upon growth exist today.

**A THREE-
SECTOR
ECONOMY**

In other chapters the relationship of the trade sector to growth will be examined in detail. Perhaps one of the most costly lessons of development experience stems from a failure to take into consideration the close links binding agriculture, exports, and industrial development. Here we expand the two-sector production possibilities curve to incorporate three sectors. The graph, while highly simplified, is useful in the analysis of forces affecting development.

By using a two-quadrant graph, a three-sector economy can be represented in two rather than three dimensions with the help of produc-

tion possibilities curves that incorporate some simplifying assumptions. Assume an LDC devotes resources to food production sufficient
to feed its people. Let this amount of food be point F in figure 3.13. If
all the remaining resources were used to produce a crop for export, E
would represent the level of exports.

Now assume a similar production possibilities curve for food and
industry (not shown). Again let the amount of food needed be F. Then
some maximum amount of industrial goods is produceable with the
resources remaining. This quantity of industrial good is represented at
point B on the industry axis. Output B is expressed in terms of labor
inputs and labor productivity in the industrial good as $\beta_b(L - L_f)$,
where L_f is the labor used in food production when B industrial output
is produced. EB is then derived by allowing varying amounts of exports
and industrial goods production while keeping food output constant.
Note that food output remains constant, but the relative amount of
resources used in growing it will change. This occurs because food,
exports, and industry differ in relative factor intensity. Each new combination of these three goods throws up a new set of resource scarcity
prices and hence optimum input combination of resources.

Some paradigms of developing economies assume structural rigidities in agriculture where there is limited responsiveness to variations in relative demand for resources in other sectors due to imperfect
pricing mechanisms and/or immobile resources. In such cases Q_eQ_f and
EB are reference curves and the economy operates somewhere inside
them. The main use of simplified diagrams is to illustrate the strong
forces affecting the direction of change; the interrelations of the sectors;
and the limitations that total resources, technology, and trade place
upon expansion.

FIGURE 3.13

*Three-Sector
Production
Possibilities Curve*

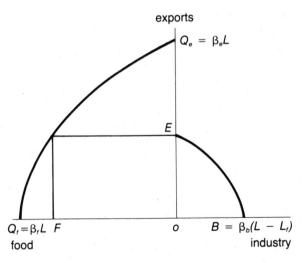

With food needs supplied by production of *F* food, production of export and industrial goods will take place along production possibilities curve *EB*.

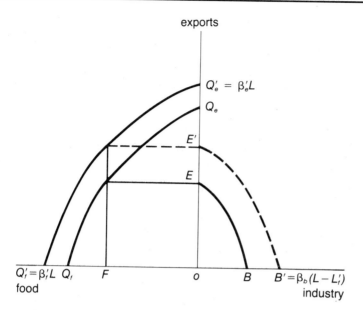

exports

$Q'_e = \beta'_e L$

Q_e

E'

E

$Q'_f = \beta'_f L$ Q_f F   o   B $B' = \beta_b(L - L'_f)$
food   industry

FIGURE 3.14

*Increased
Productivity in
Agriculture*

An increase in productivity in agriculture with food needs unchanged shifts outward the production possibility curves for all sectors as resources are freed from food production.

This diagram is developed further and used in subsequent analyses of trade and development, among other topics. Already, however, it should be obvious that the size of industrial output and export potential are related to the agricultural sector and its efficiency. If the hours worked in agriculture and/or its productivity increase, Q_eQ_f shifts outward, allowing EB a corresponding shift with constant food needs. Figure 3.14 illustrates a change in agricultural productivity. This reduces labor needed to produce F output of food to L'_f so that output potential in industrial output expands to $B' = \beta_b(L - L'_f)$, and output potential in export production to E'. A growth in population can shift Q_eQ_f outward. Its effect upon EB will depend upon the movement of F with population growth.

Saving and Capital Formation

chapter

4

This chapter examines the need in the growth process for saving and the formation of capital, both physical and human, and their relation to technical change. These topics received heavy emphasis in development right after World War II. Arguments for capital-intensive, saving-centered growth plans presented in these writings are reviewed here and the concept of an optimum growth and saving rate evaluated. The saving and investment functions are explored and problems of empirical verification discussed. The chapter provides a perspective for the later discussion of factor intensity in LDCs, development models, financing of development, sectoral investment, risk, and inequality.

CAPITAL FORMATION AND DEVELOPMENT

The Identification and Measurement of Capital

An economy adds to its stock of physical and human capital by forgoing consumption (saving) and using the resources thus freed from turning out consumer goods to form capital above the amount needed to replace that part of the capital stock that wears out each period. Increases in the human and physical capital stock expand an economy's productive capacity over the lifetime of the capital. Present consumption is constrained so that future consumption can be greater when the capital stock grows.

Kuznets (1965, chap. 1) has emphasized the limited fraction of national income necessary to maintain and add to physical capital stock. He found that historically no country devoted more than 20 percent of its income to gross capital formation for periods of two decades or more. This upper limit may have edged higher for post-World War II Japan, communist states, and oil-rich countries. But the point is that 20 percent of GNP or less can maintain a growing, affluent economy.

The physical capital stock accumulated may take on a ratio of between three to seven times annual national output. Variations in the range occur among developed countries and the capital/output ratio is not predictable by level of development according to estimate data. In fact, it is so difficult to measure accurately the stock of capital in a country that even advanced countries do not keep up-to-date series on this.

Replacement of obsolete or worn-out equipment and installations may account for half of new capital formation in MDCs. Capital formation net of capital consumption has varied historically between 5 percent and 15 percent of GNP. And part of this measured capital is residential and related housing and changes in inventories. Kuznets estimates that strictly productive tools that embody modern technology account for a gross capital formation rate of no more than 5 percent to 7 percent of GNP and have a capital/output ratio of close to one.

This is certainly encouraging for LDCs struggling with consumption pressures and brings into question the emphasis upon saving in development economics since at least the time of Adam Smith in the late 1700s. Before downplaying the role of saving, however, consider the importance of human capital to economic development and the need to finance research and development essential to technological change. In the same chapter Kuznets estimates that the inclusion as investment of such growth related expenditures as education, research and development, and health, would widen the respective ratios between MDCs and LDCs for net capital formation proportions from 10 percent to 3 percent to closer to 30 percent and 3 percent! Thus while saving rates as traditionally measured in national income accounting may be a smaller variable in determining growth and income, the financing of human capital, machinery and equipment, and other expenditures needed for technical change is vital to development.

Table 4.1 gives estimates of saving and investment as percentages of GNP for the years 1960 and 1980. Data collected by The World Bank do not show a predictable correlation between saving as a percentage of GNP and the rate of growth of per capita GNP. It has been hypothesized that capital-intensive infrastructure such as transportation, telecommunications, and dams absorb high amounts of savings during certain stages of development, are often built with excess capacity, and yet contribute to growth over a longer period rather than at the time of initial investment. Moreover, with differing rates of population growth, comparable saving rates could produce differing growth rates for per capita GNP. Finally, there is a positive relationship between saving and GNP during early stages of growth. After the achievement of a certain level of development, saving tends to level off. Thus the industrial market economies in table 4.1 do not show the upward trend in saving as a percentage of GNP that is noticeable for lower-income countries between 1960 and 1980.

Capital Formation with and without Technical Change

Growth with or without technical change can require capital formation. Much of technological change cannot be achieved without the formation of both physical and human capital. New machinery, equipment, and tools are needed to effect technical changes and human capital plays a vital role in the development and diffusion of new technology.

Growth without technological change also demands capital. As population expands, there are more young to educate and train in order to maintain the human capital level per capita; and a growing economy usually forms more human capital per capita by educating and training a larger proportion of the inhabitants and raising the education and skill levels of many above their previous levels. Growth without technological change also entails increasing the physical capital available per worker in order to raise labor productivity and offset the effects of diminishing returns to natural resources. Such human and physical capital formation in the latter case calls for no change in known techniques of production, sophistication of machinery, or new skills or knowledge different from those already being taught.

While growth with and without technological change may be conceptualized as distinct, the real growth process embraces both conditions as interrelated contributors. In limited sectors or industries of the economy, technological gains may reduce the physical capital needed per worker or even simplify the process so that the need for human capital in production shrinks. For an economy as a whole to produce continuous technical advance and an expansion of income per capita, however, there is a need for a growing human capital and physical

	Gross Domestic Investment		Gross Domestic Saving		
	1960[a]	1980[b]	1960[a]	1980[b]	
Low-income Economies	19 w	25 w	17 w	22 w	**TABLE 4.1**
China and India	21 w	28 w	19 w	26 w	*Gross Domestic*
Others	11 w	15 w	9 w	7 w	*Saving and*
1 Kampuchea, Dem.	. .	. .	. .	. .	*Investment as a*
2 Lao PDR	. .	. .	. .	. .	*Percentage of Gross*
3 Bhutan	. .	. .	. .	. .	*Domestic Product,*
4 Chad	11	13	5	− 14	*1960 and 1980*
5 Bangladesh	7	17	8	2	
6 Ethiopia	12	10	11	5	
7 Nepal	9	14	4	7	
8 Somalia	10	16	6	3	
9 Burma	12	24	11	18	
10 Afghanistan	16	14	13	11	
11 Viet Nam	. .	. .	. .	. .	
12 Mali	14	15	9	− 3	
13 Burundi	6	14	5	(.)	
14 Rwanda	6	16	8	3	
15 Upper Volta	10	18	− 4	− 9	
16 Zaire	12	11	21	13	
17 Malawi	10	22	− 4	10	
18 Mozambique	10	10	8	(.)	
19 India	17	23	14	20	
20 Haiti	9	18	7	9	
21 Sri Lanka	14	36	9	14	
22 Sierra Leone	. .	15	. .	6	
23 Tanzania	14	22	19	8	
24 China	23	31	23	30	
25 Guinea	. .	11	. .	14	
26 Central African Rep.	20	10	9	− 1	
27 Pakistan	12	18	5	6	
28 Uganda	11	3	16	2	
29 Benin	15	24	9	5	
30 Niger	13	29	12	21	
31 Madagascar	11	21	5	9	
32 Sudan	12	12	12	3	
33 Togo	11	26	4	14	
Middle-income Economies	20 w	27 w	19 w	25 w	
Oil Exporters	18 w	27 w	19 w	30 w	
Oil Importers	21 w	27 w	19 w	21 w	
34 Ghana	24	5	17	5	
35 Kenya	20	22	17	15	
36 Lesotho	2	30	− 25	− 78	
37 Yemen, PDR	. .	. .	. .	. .	
38 Indonesia	8	22	8	30	
39 Yemen Arab Rep.	. .	44	. .	− 20	
40 Mauritania	37	51	− 3	14	
41 Senegal	16	15	15	− 2	
42 Angola	12	9	14	19	
43 Liberia	28	29	35	29	
44 Honduras	14	28	12	20	
45 Zambia	25	23	41	18	
46 Bolivia	14	13	7	15	
47 Egypt	13	31	12	16	
48 Zimbabwe	23	18	22	16	

		Gross Domestic Investment		Gross Domestic Saving	
		1960[a]	1980[b]	1960[a]	1980[b]
49	El Salvador	16	12	11	10
50	Cameroon	. .	25	. .	23
51	Thailand	16	27	14	22
52	Philippines	16	30	16	25
53	Nicaragua	15	20	12	−1
54	Papua New Guinea	15	27	3	15
55	Congo, People's Rep.	45	37	−21	37
56	Morocco	10	21	11	11
57	Mongolia	. .	. .	. .	. .
58	Albania	. .	. .	. .	. .
59	Peru	25	16	27	19
60	Nigeria	13	24	7	28
61	Jamaica	30	16	26	12
62	Guatemala	10	16	8	13
63	Ivory Coast	15	28	17	23
64	Dominican Rep.	12	24	19	14
65	Colombia	21	25	21	25
66	Ecuador	15	25	15	23
67	Paraguay	17	29	16	20
68	Tunisia	17	28	7	25
69	Korea, Dem. Rep.	. .	. .	. .	. .
70	Syrian Arab Rep.	. .	25	. .	10
71	Jordan	. .	48	. .	−27
72	Lebanon	16	. .	5	. .
73	Turkey	16	27	13	18
74	Cuba	. .	. .	. .	. .
75	Korea, Rep. of	11	31	1	23
76	Malaysia	14	29	27	32
77	Costa Rica	18	25	13	15
78	Panama	16	27	11	25
79	Algeria	42	41	25	42
80	Brazil	22	22	21	20
81	Mexico	20	28	18	26
82	Chile	27	18	25	16
83	South Africa	22	29	27	37
84	Romania	. .	34	. .	. .
85	Portugal	19	25	12	11
86	Argentina	22	. .	21	. .
87	Yugoslavia	37	35	32	32
88	Uruguay	18	19	12	12
89	Iran	17	. .	21	. .
90	Iraq	20	33	34	59
91	Venezuela	21	25	33	32
92	Hong Kong	18	29	6	24
93	Trinidad and Tobago	28	28	30	41
94	Greece	19	28	11	20
95	Singapore	11	43	−3	30
96	Israel	27	22	14	8
High-Income Oil Exports		. .	24 w	. .	62 w
97	Libya	. .	25	. .	59
98	Saudi Arabia	. .	26	. .	59
99	Kuwait	. .	11	. .	63
100	United Arab Emirates	. .	30	. .	73

TABLE 4.1
Gross Domestic Saving and Investment as a Percentage of Gross Domestic Product, 1960 and 1980 (continued)

	Gross Domestic Investment		Gross Domestic Saving		TABLE 4.1
	1960[a]	1980[b]	1960[a]	1980[b]	*(continued)*
Industrial Market Economies	21 *w*	23 *w*	22 *w*	22 *w*	
101 Ireland	16	28	11	15	
102 Spain	19	21	22	18	
103 Italy	25	25	25	22	
104 New Zealand	24	23	22	22	
105 United Kingdom	19	16	17	19	
106 Finland	30	28	29	27	
107 Australia	29	24	25	22	
108 Japan	34	32	34	31	
109 Canada	23	22	21	24	
110 Austria	28	29	27	27	
111 United States	18	18	19	17	
112 Netherlands	27	22	29	21	
113 France	23	23	25	21	
114 Belgium	19	21	18	18	
115 Norway	30	28	28	34	
116 Denmark	23	18	22	17	
117 Sweden	25	21	24	19	
118 Germany, Fed. Rep.	27	25	29	25	
119 Switzerland	29	27	29	23	
Nonmarket Industrial Economies	25 *w*	24 *w*	27 *w*	25 *w*	
120 Poland	24	19	24	13	
121 Bulgaria	27	. .	28	. .	
122 Hungary	24	23	21	22	
123 USSR	26	24	28	26	
124 Czechoslovakia	17	25	19	27	
125 German Dem. Rep.	. .	. .	. .	. .	

a. Figures in italics are for 1961, not 1960.
b. Figures in italics are for 1979, not 1980.
Note: *w* stands for a GDP-weighted average.
SOURCE: World Bank, *World Development Report 1982* (New York: Oxford University Press, 1982), Table 5, pp. 118–19. Reprinted by permission.

capital stock. Thus savings are needed to finance technical change and capital formation, two interrelated and very important elements of economic development.

Consider how the simple model developed in chapter 2 can be used to trace the relationship between physical capital formation and growth. Figure 4.1 shows a steady-state gain in output with full employment, where the labor force and capital stock both grow at a rate of 10 percent for each of three periods. Technology is constant and there are constant returns to scale. Thus L/K, α and β are unchanged.

The economy with K_0 capital stock has output (Q_0) represented by the areas αK_0 or βL_0. These variables can be expressed in value terms. Generally the capital stock value divided by the value of annual output

Physical Capital Formation and Growth in a Production Function Framework

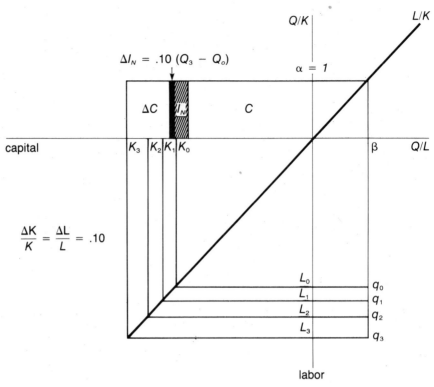

FIGURE 4.1

Steady State Growth

Growth of capital and labor of 10 percent per period, with technology constant and constant returns to scale, increases output 10 percent per period, leaving α and β unchanged.

has a range above one and, thus, Q/K is less than one. However, as Kuznets noted, a value of one is representative for strictly productive tools. For simplicity of graphic illustration here, α is given a value of one, and thus when the area of the graph marked I_N is 10 percent of Q, this increases the capital stock by same percentage.

Total saving from Q_0 output is shown by the hatched area. This also represents total investment, I_N. It is assumed no new capital is needed to replace worn-out capital stock. I_N, then, is the net increase in the capital stock. I_N raises K_0 to K_1 in the first growth period, an increase of 10 percent. Since L also grows by 10 percent in this period and α and β are constant, output rises by 10 percent. Saving must rise by 10 percent of the change in output from Q_0 to Q_1 if I_N in the next period is to grow by 10 percent. Thus the marginal propensity to save out of increased income ($\Delta S/\Delta Q$) must equal the average propensity to save (S/Q) out of income. And since saving equals I_N along an equilibrium growth path, $\Delta I_N/\Delta Q = I_N/Q_0 = .10$. The graph shows the change in saving, or ΔI_N, by the end of the third period of growth, as well as ΔC. Thus ΔK in each period is 10 percent larger than ΔK in the previous period due to compound growth. The labor force grows at a similar compound rate.

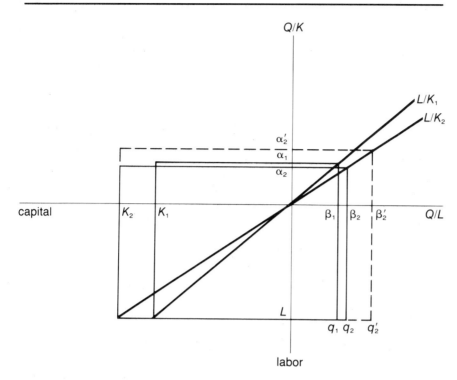

FIGURE 4.2
Capital Growth with Lower and Higher α

Capital formation without technological change: Output increases from $\beta_1 L$ to $\beta_2 L$.
Capital formation with technological change: Output increases from $\beta_1 L$ to $\beta_2' L$.

By period three, then, saving has grown by the area marked ΔI_N and the remaining incremental output, ΔC, is spent on consumption, so that consumption expenditures per laborer remain constant. The economy has expanded but, assuming a constant proportion of labor force to population, income has remained constant on a per capita basis. A growth in saving and investment is important in this case because it prevents a *decline* in per capital output.

The effects of physical capital growth in excess of expansion of labor force, with and without technical change, can be illustrated with the diagram in figure 4.2. For simplicity labor, L, is held constant. The results are the same as those where both capital, K, and L grow but K grows faster. Full employment is another simplifying assumption. As K increases from K_1 to K_2, L/K falls, lowering α somewhat due to diminishing returns. Capital formation of the same technical vintage raises output per laborer from β_1 to β_2.

Now assume technological improvements are embodied in the new capital and the same amount of resources are devoted to capital formation so that K_1 increases to K_2. When this new capital has a higher efficiency ratio (α_2') than capital of the old vintage (α_2), labor productivity will rise further (to β_2'). Note that the new, technically more efficient capital need not have increased α above α_1 in order to raise β above β_1 and β_2. Thus growth accompanied by more technically efficient capital may exhibit a falling α when capital accumulation is more rapid than labor force growth.

The alert reader will have noticed that technological change that raises α above α_1 can raise β without an increase in K, and with L/K unchanged. This can occur when the existing capital stock is replaced with more advanced stock as old equipment wears out. Recall that initially this possibility was assumed away.

Suppose, however, that to improve capital equipment, resources allocated to consumption must be used instead for research and development and other inputs required for the acquisition and absorption of more productive capital. This will reduce consumption per capita for a time until the resulting improved productivity raises output sufficiently to restore consumption to its original levels. Even then, ongoing growth could require increasing such expenditures preparatory to technological change. When economies cannot raise GNP per capita because they cannot tighten their belts and accummulate the saving necessary for capital formation plus technical change, they are said to suffer from a *saving gap*.

A society free of this gap can raise per capita output by saving more and lowering L/K, thus raising β. In other words, for such an economy the growth rate of capital would exceed the growth rate of the labor force. This economy could also raise β by devoting resources to technical change as well as capital accumulation in excess of labor force growth. Thus a saving constraint affects growth by affecting both the amount and productivity of capital acquisition.

Capital-Intensive Development

The assumption of full employment can now be dropped and the impact upon growth of (physical) capital-intensive processes examined. The contribution of technical change is ignored. There are two reasons set forth in the literature for using capital-intensive processes even though they may entail unemployed labor. One cites profit levels, the other "consumption wages."

An early argument for high capital intensity was set forth by G. Galenson and H. Leibenstein (1955, pp. 343–70). They argued that capital-intensive processes increased profits as a ratio to GNP and that the main source of savings in an LDC economy is profits. In their model it is uncertain whether or not the capital-intensive process is more efficient, or whether the product mix should be designed to increase capital intensity. The main emphasis is upon how quickly K (as opposed to α) rises. In the long run, more rapid accumulation of capital per worker would raise labor productivity by a greater amount.

This thinking is not unlike the actual approach of the Soviet planners. Capital productivity was virtually ignored in early years. They were able to achieve such high capital formation by using the state-controlled profits to produce more capital rather than increase living standards under Stalin. For any type of economy this demands high savings from the people.

P. C. Mahalanobis, an Indian statistician, influenced Indian planning along those lines by diverting capital to the most capital-intensive areas of industry, such as transportation, to the neglect of agriculture. The plan was not a success because of the inability of a country with such low per capita income as India's to ignore efficiency criteria in the allocation of capital and to forgo consumption, especially that of food. Foreign exchange problems associated with the approach are discussed in chapter 12. Unfortunately, many LDCs assume the most capital-intensive project is the most modern and thus the best one for development.

Sen (1975) and Marglin (1976) are both concerned with the saving rate as it is related to unemployment in an economy where the most efficient production process choice creates technological unemployment at the going wage rate—an institutionally-set rather than a market-set wage rate. Following Sen and Marglin, assume that most products and processes must be relatively capital intensive because of the absence of efficient, less capital-intensive technology. Assume that past some employment level labor, particularly if unskilled, added to the production process has a very low marginal product. Labor will actually be unemployed rather than added at this low productivity level when wages do not drop to the level of the marginal product. Such a case can exist in LDCs where wages are influenced by political and institutional factors.

Figure 4.3 illustrates the Sen-Marglin case. The subscripts u and f refer to the unemployment and full-employment cases, respectively. Full employment will add to output so long as the marginal product

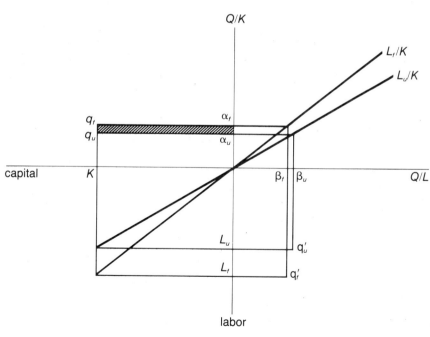

FIGURE 4.3
Output with and without Full Employment of Labor

Full employment output $= \alpha_f K = \beta_f L_f$.
Output with $L_f - L_u$ unemployed labor $= \alpha_u K = \beta_u L_u$.

of labor is not zero. But the low marginal product will reduce the average product of labor β_f, below the unemployment level β_u.

Assume that the additional output gained by employing all labor, represented in the northwest quadrant by the hatched area, is small and exceeded by the wages paid to the formerly jobless. Then, assume the propensity to spend from wages of the worker is one, that is, the worker does not save. In such a case consumption spending rises by more than the additional product provided; and saving-investment is assumed to adjust downward to allow real consumption to rise.

When saving falls, capital formation and technological progress, and thus development, are slowed. There is, then, a short-run trade-off between full employment and growth. But, according to Sen and Marglin, employment in the longer-term will be higher because there will be more capital available to employ workers efficiently at the institutional wage. The best policy then, should such conditions exist, is to leave workers unemployed when their subsidized income is below the wage rate. It should be mentioned that lowering the minimum wage or taxing wages of workers to control their consumption is considered to be politically impossible. Even in today's communist regimes, controls are far from total and workers in Eastern Europe particularly have resisted government efforts to reduce their consumption levels.

Human Capital Formation

Human capital formation refers to an increase in skills, knowledge, and health that results in higher productivity as a worker acquires more capability and as organizational arrangements and technical absorptive capacity respond to this enhanced proficiency. Formal schooling, although important, is only one way of acquiring human capital. Other methods are on-the-job training, or apprenticeships; adult training through government extension services; short courses; public television; and improved health services.

Formation of human capital influences the age when people enter the work force, and this can affect total output. A very poor economy generally has a largely illiterate population. Some who manage to learn to read and write lose these skills by not using them. The very poor rural economy is essentially an oral one, unable to provide opportunities to read and write. Children may enter the informal work force at an early age. By the time they are 15 they usually put in the same workday as an adult, although their productivity is generally lower than that of their elders. Some studies, however, show children under 15 contribute little to output in LDCs, even in rural areas (Mueller 1976). In cases where children under 15 are productive, their working need not compete with their education when school sessions are coordinated with the economy's use of child labor. A typical example is where school is not in session at planting and harvesting time. Schooling for the young, therefore, need not result in a reduction in output due to the loss of child labor. However, extension of education into the mid-to-late teens and early twenties will reduce the size of the labor force.

Expenditures on human capital must compete with those for physical capital for the limited savings achievable in a poor economy. Assume planners want an equivalent return on human and physical capital. Human capital has a longer gestation period than physical capital and thus for each dollar spent must return more in increased output to compensate for the delayed return. When human and physical capital are joint inputs in the sense that more technically advanced physical capital requires a minimum input of complementary human capital, savings must be apportioned between the two forms of capital.

The saving constraint limits the ability of a poorer LDC to increase dramatically its people's general education level. A discontinuous jump in, for example, formal schooling would demand more resources, and thus reduce those available for consumption and physical capital goods. It is generally important to its develoment for a very poor economy to select areas for increasing education that will have a high payoff and a low cost. Sometimes literacy is improved by educating older children because they can learn more quickly than younger ones. There is a large literature concerned with optimum education expenditures and planning. Here, however, concentration is upon the need for saving to finance such expenditure.

The growth of human capital can be expected to raise the productive capacity of both capital and labor. Thus, as the human capital stock rises, output, α, and β, rise. This impact of human capital upon productivity in part helps to explain how growth can be accompanied by a falling L/K ratio and a constant α. The human capital per unit of physical capital usually increases with growth and forestalls diminishing returns as physical capital per laborer rises.

Figure 4.4 illustrates that growth in human capital along with physical capital $(L_H + I_P)$ can require a large allocation of output away from consumption. In the case illustrated, human capital formation raises α above the old level, despite a growth in the capital stock. Output rises from the double impact of two types of capital formation.

As the human capital stock grows, it must be maintained or output per capita will decline. That is, new entrants in the labor force must be provided at the minimum with the level of human capital of those already working. The gradual enhancement of human capital provides the greater productivity that enables the economy to maintain and increase its human capital stock. These productivity gains must be high enough to allow the labor force/population ratio to decline as the years of schooling are extended.

High rates of population growth can make it more difficult to maintain and increase the human capital stock since a larger proportion of the population is in the younger age groups. The labor force is a smaller percentage of the population and yet must provide resources for investing in the education of many young people.

More advanced education in an LDC demands not only savings from the economy, but also generally means sending the student abroad and thus requires savings in the form of foreign exchange. As will be discussed in a later chapter, foreign exchange may be a greater con-

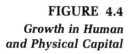

FIGURE 4.4

Growth in Human
and Physical Capital

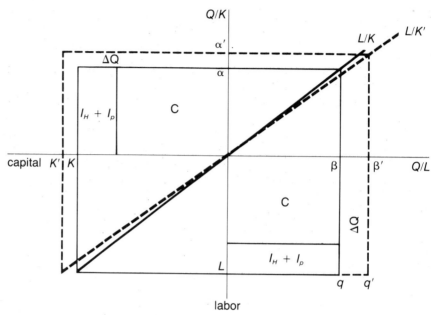

Growth in human and physical capital both raise β. Growth in human capital raises
α, and in this case more than offsets diminishing returns.

straint than the saving capacity. The point should be clear, however,
that there is a community sacrifice in the form of consumption forgone
when the young are educated. Inevitably many of those who are sent
abroad from LDCs to study remain on foreign soil, and never return to
raise the income and productivity of the poor society.

SAVING AND
DEVELOPMENT

It is not surprising that when saving alone is seen as a mechanism for
raising per capita income, to the exclusion of other changes such as
technological advance, economies of scale, and sectoral shift, and the
need for both physical and human capital is considered, the task of
development appears overwhelming. Such single-minded focus upon
saving as a source of growth gave rise to the pessimism of vicious cycle
theories. These theories imply that poverty is self-perpetuating, that
there is a poverty trap, especially when population growth rates are
high. The hypothesis states that labor productivity is low because there
is little capital per laborer; yet savings for capital formation cannot be
increased to provide more capital per worker because consumption
needs are inflexible at such low living standards, especially when population increase is unchecked. The failure to lower L/K by raising K is
then the key to poverty, for it keeps output per capita low.

Even within the confines of a saving-centered paradigm of growth,
the constraints on increasing saving are not always as great as assumed.

As other writers have noted, poor societies have built pyramids, raised cathedrals and fought wars with savings from the populace. An increase in workdays per year is one form of additional output that can provide savings. This usually occurs as self-sufficient farms become more specialized and move to cash crops and multiple crops. Industrial activity also raises the annual number of workdays compared with farm activity. And to some degree, foreign savings may be available to a poor country. As Kuznets early noted, however, the preponderance of savings must arise from internal sources throughout the long development process.

Technological change in early periods of development may not appropriate large amounts of resources since, when judiciously pursued, the experience of other countries can be borrowed at relatively low cost. Moreover it sets the stage for cumulative productivity gains that can break the poverty trap. And it shortens the period of extreme self-denial since it can lower the capital inputs per unit of output, at least for physical capital inputs if not for those of human capital.

The capital constraint also was overestimated as a result of policies that promoted waste of capital. The idea that savings shortages or limits were the key to poverty of stagnant LDCs found seeming confirmation as data from growing LDCs appeared to establish the need for much higher saving rates than those achieved by the poorest countries. Further examination, however, reveals that many of the policies designed to promote industrialization in more advanced LDCs encouraged to a certain degree a more capital-intensive development process than necessary. Further discussion of this is found in chapter 12 on the promotion of industry.

The Harrod-Domar Growth Model

The emphasis upon saving as the central determinant of growth rates arose in part from the tendency of planners to use a simple growth model such as that illustrated in figure 4.1. They concentrated upon the saving rate necessary to ensure a certain growth rate of the physical capital stock that would in turn achieve a growth target for output, given population expansion. Estimates of capital productivity were made from data on the economy taken from recent years and, by assuming this ratio would not change perceptibly with additions to the physical capital stock, the saving-investment target for a given growth rate could be specified. This target rate was influenced by the projected gains in the labor force as population grew. This, in a rough way, guided planners on the need to tax or otherwise influence saving so that growth targets assumedly could be fulfilled. Its attractiveness lay in part, at least, in its simplicity. Saving targets are much more amenable to policy formulations and implementation than technological change.

This simple model, which in its barest form states that the growth rate is equal to $\Delta I_N/\Delta Q \times \alpha$, is known as the Harrod-Domar model after the originators, R. F. Harrod and E. Domar, who derived it as an extension of the Keynesian static system (Harrod 1939, and Domar 1946). Alternatively, the growth rate can be expressed as the marginal propensity to save ($\Delta S/\Delta Q$) times α.

This growth equation results from the set of growth relations illustrated in figure 4.1 and thus can be constructed from the graph. The graph shows a growth each period in K, L, and Q of 10 percent. In the graph K increases by 10 percent of K_0, 10 percent of K_1, and 10 percent of K_2 in steps and, thus, there is a compound growth effect with ΔK (or I_N) increasing 10 percent each period. This means ΔI_N, the net *change* in the capital stock *increment* per period, is 10 percent of ΔK per period. Said another way, the growth rate of investment, $\Delta I_N/I_N$, and hence saving is 10 percent.

Now note that this last result can be derived from the original equation:

$$\text{Growth Rate} = \frac{\Delta I_N}{\Delta Q} \cdot \alpha = \frac{\Delta I_N}{\Delta K \alpha} \cdot \alpha = \frac{\Delta I_N}{\Delta K} = 10\%$$

Thus with α constant, the growth rate depends upon the growth rate of saving and investment.

With the use of the model in LDCs, the emphasis shifted from the Keynesian world of underconsumption, where saving rates lowered aggregate demand, resulting in unrealized output and idle resources, to a world of low savings capacity rooted in poverty. The presumption was that investment, private and/or public, would be higher next period if saving/output would rise. That is, the investment function was presumed to be very responsive to the availability and cost of funds. Thus there was no problem of savings not being used for investment spending and thereby causing a drop in income levels. Later models have paid more attention to an optimum growth in consumption and saving in the context of LDC development. This remains, however, an underexplored topic.

The model also focused planners' attention upon the possibility that, at the margin as new capital was formed, capital productivity could be improved if α were higher for new capital. This could lead to an emphasis upon technological change. In practical use, however, it often became a misleading criteria for project selection as opposed to an emphasis upon improvement of technical efficiency. Projects with the highest capital productivity were chosen without regard to how wasteful they were of other resources or their interdependence with capital formation in areas of low α.

Recent work in development has tended to emphasize technological change and human capital formation in conjunction with saving and physical capital as vital keys to successful economic evolution. As mentioned, they are interrelated, as are so many variables of LDC growth. The saving rate remains important, but it does not occupy the pinnacle it once did as the single explanatory variable in growth. The relationship between population growth rates and saving has also transcended the simple, vicious cycle concept where the function was negative throughout. Much more is said on this topic in the chapters on population. Finally, education of a growing population constricts consumption, but when geared to the development requirements, it contributes to gains in productivity.

What determines the level in LDCs of saving out of income (*the average propensity to save*, or *APS*) and the change in saving with a change in income (*the marginal propensity to save*, or *MPS*)? As important as these questions are, we do not have definitive answers. The main impediment to finding answers is the poor quality and limited quantity of data. In a survey article, Raymond Mikesell and James Zinser (1973, p. 1) note: "A number of alternative hypotheses (derived mainly from the literature relating to developed economies) have been advanced, but the paucity of data has made it difficult to test these hypotheses and obtain results which warrant a reasonable degree of confidence."

The Saving Function in LDCs*

It will be helpful to review a few key ideas touched on elsewhere. An economy saves when it forgoes consumption so that resources otherwise used for consumer commodities are freed to produce capital goods instead. The value of the investment spending for a given period of income and production is then the equivalent of the value of saving. This assumes a money value can be given to any nonmonetized production and income that would be the equivalent of its market value.

The process by which resources are freed for investment differs in various economies. In a mixed market economy private allocation decisions exercise command over resource use outside a limited public sector. Both market and nonmarket forces affect income distribution, the distribution of savings to finance investment, and the preference for consumer goods as compared with investment goods. The public sector, through taxation, direct command over resources, or even via inflation that can arise out of government decisions to spend and create new money, can affect the level of consumption relative to investment in the economy. In a centrally planned state the government, theoretically at least, can determine investment and saving levels consistent with its plans by issuing directives for resource allocation. Where, as in most LDCs, decentralized planning exists, the government generally cannot determine the overall saving level. Rather it tries to influence it via direct and indirect measures that affect resource allocation to a lesser degree than does central planning.

In the economy without central controls, then, it is important to know the determinants of saving. The majority of the research has been devoted to identifying the factors that shape private saving. As mentioned, the data base is insufficient to warrant confidence in the results of the studies to date. However, it is informative to think about the different specifications of saving functions that have been tested to date. Not unexpectedly, these have been variations for the main part of saving functions applied to MDCs.

The majority of the studies use a cross-sectional (more aptly called cross-country) approach in their statistical testing of the saving function. This means that, in the absence of adequate time series data from individual LDCs, savings data and data on the determinants of saving

---

*This and the following four sections treat the saving function in some detail. The reader may advance to the summary section following these four sections without loss of continuity.

are from many countries. The presumption is that the saving function derived is a representative one for all LDCs. This supposition is a precarious one since the data are not comparable from one country to another. Also, countries may have various conditions, social and otherwise, that affect the average propensity to consume with some degree of consistency within an individual country, but the effect of such variables can differ among states. Before summarizing the results of the studies, the variables tested are discussed. The reader interested in the exact functional form of the equation is referred to the Mikesell-Zinser article and its bibliography.

The simplest function is Keynesian in form and relates saving to current income or per capita income. The general presumption is that the MPS is larger than the APS and thus the APS rises with income. Studies indicate the median and average values for the MPS are between 10 percent and 15 percent for periods of more than 10 years and that the MPS is not uniformly greater than the APS. However, when per capita income rises (as opposed to aggregate income), there is generally an increase in the MPS, and thus the MPS exceeds the APS. The change is not dramatic, however, if Singh's cross-sectional study is reliable. With a growth rate of 2 percent in per capita GNP, it would take 50 years to raise the APS by 3 percent (Singh mimeo, April 1971, p. 32, quoted in Mikesell and Zinser 1973, p. 7).

As mentioned in chapter 1, Chenery and Syrquin find evidence that the MPS is not constant over the growth path, giving an elongated S-shape to the long-run saving function. As income per capita rises, the MPS increases and then declines; the APS rises, then levels off. In the last part of this chapter, the saving pattern of Japan is examined and turns out to be an exception to the general case.

Government saving and private saving can be determined by different variables, and thus are examined separately. Various studies have looked at private saving and broken it down into subgroups. Houthakker (1965), and Williamson (1968), both find that saving out of nonlabor income greatly exceeds that put aside out of labor income. There is evidence of proportionality between income and saving in each group, that is, MPS = APS. There is little knowledge about the behavior of private corporate saving.

While current income undoubtedly influences aggregate and household saving heavily, often some modification of this simple function is used in an effort to achieve a better explanation of current saving. The permanent income hypothesis developed by Milton Friedman has been a popular choice in regard to household saving. This theory assumes a long-run planning horizon (three years) and a desire to achieve a planned level of saving out of permanent or expected income over that planning horizon. Actual income in any period can differ from permanent income, and the difference is called transitory income. The presumption is that when transitory income occurs, the consumer will save the total amount or at least a larger percentage than from permanent income. Empirical specification of permanent income varies. The studies for many countries show a divergent MPS for permanent and transitory income (Mikesell and Zinser 1973, p. 9).

There is a general presumption that wealth affects saving negatively, that is, households or groups with similar income levels but different accumulated wealth or assets will show a different saving propensity: Those with higher wealth save less. This effect is not necessarily strong. Thus higher-income groups with more wealth will generally save more than low-income groups. Measurement and data problems are particularly acute in relation to wealth.

Theoretically, a higher interest rate would induce savers to put aside more since the return is higher. In Korea and Taiwan increases in the real rate of interest (that is, the monetary rate adjusted for inflation) appeared to affect some savers. However, empirical studies fail to detect a role for interest rates in increasing the saving propensity.

Do higher child dependency ratios, and hence population growth, reduce saving, as has been presumed by many writers on development? The thinking is that households with fewer children would not use the extra income to purchase other goods but would save part or all of it. In terms of aggregate income and consumption, education expenditures are arbitrarily considered consumption rather than investment expenditures.

For the aggregate saving rate the attention is upon child dependency as it affects consumption relative to productive capacity. Important as this topic is, it has not been explored statistically to the point where any conclusions can be stated with confidence. A cross-country study by Leff (1969) and some studies of Latin American urban households indicate that dependency ratios have a negative effect upon saving (Musgrave 1978). Where it is negative, the impact of children on saving may be slight, if the latter study is indicative of the true picture. This study refers to urban households, however. The chapter on population discusses this topic further, specifically in relation to rural saving.

Income Distribution and Saving: Occupation

When households are equalized for such determinants of saving as income and wealth, do certain groups—the self-employed, the entrepreneurs, the urban groups, the wage earners, the farmers—differ in their tendencies to save?

When certain groups save more per unit of total income, then income distribution affects aggregate saving. When income groups vary in their MPS out of increments to income, then redistribution of income at the margin will affect saving.

There is a long presumption in economic literature since at least the days of the Classical economists that entrepreneurs have the highest saving propensities in an economy. Even Karl Marx subscribed to this thesis. A study by A. C. Kelley and J. G. Williamson for Indonesia (1968) supports this presumption. And, as mentioned earlier, cross-section studies find saving from nonlabor income is higher than that from labor income.

Relative Income and the Saving Function

Sociologists, and some economists, have contended that the aggregate saving function is influenced by relative income. For example, in an economy at a given level of national income, the aggregate APS and

MPS would differ, depending upon whether income and wealth were more or less equally divided.[1] And, the satisfaction level from a given bundle of consumption is said to be a function of the consumption levels of others. These influences of relative income, if they exist, have important implications for LDCs. They affect the viability of policies of income redistribution and the psychic costs of growth as they are related to self-denial.

When saving is a function of relative income, then saving functions for aggregate and group behavior become more complicated than the simple Keynesian-type function. Information would be needed about how the propensity to save is affected by redistribution of income.

Perhaps the effect of redistribution upon aggregate saving is best understood by first looking at a hypothetical household saving function based on income alone. Assume, as in figure 4.5, the APS and MPS vary with income and thus the function is curvilinear, with the MPS and APS rising. The range of income distribution is from 10 to 100 units of income. Redistribution would narrow the range to, let us say, between 20 and 60 units. Saving would rise slightly for the lower-income group that formerly put by little or nothing. However, this increase in income goes to a group that is still in an income range where the MPS and APS are lower than those of the more affluent group that lost the income. Aggregate saving for the economy declines.

Now introduce a wealth effect upon saving and let it be negative. Redistribution of wealth will increase saving if those receiving additional assets lower their saving by less than those losing wealth raise theirs. The wealth effect is the opposite of the income effect when inequality levels are changed. The saving function that includes wealth as an independent variable would give an estimate of which effect would prevail, given the degree of redistribution of wealth relative to income.

The above predictions based upon the idea that saving is a function of income and wealth alone will not hold if relative income levels affect saving. In such a case, as income is redistributed, the APS and MPS of the economy would change. For example, those receiving income at the lower income levels would have a different MPS than the graphic presentation; and even those not receiving redistributed income but who now stand in a different *relative* position will show a different MPS and APS. The whole saving function takes on a new position and slope as the inequality range changes. In order to predict the effects of income distribution upon saving, with or without income growth, we would have to know how income distribution affects the

---

1. Relative income can also apply to incomes in one country compared with those in more-advanced countries or to some previous peak income experienced, as for example, over a business cycle. The effect of more-advanced countries upon the saving rate of LDCs is referred to as the "demonstration effect." (Nurkse 1953). The idea that saving is related to previous peak income levels (the Duesenberry function) has led to the hypothesis that countries with high growth *rates* of income will save more. Hagen (1975, p. 344) connects this to the high Japanese saving rate. As a generality, however, the data do not support this hypothesis.

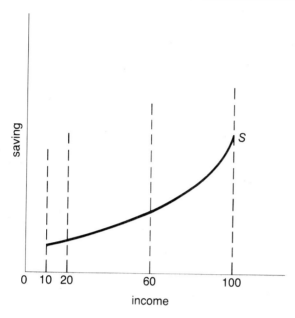

FIGURE 4.5

Households' Saving Function

Saving function with increasing slope or *MPS*.

saving function. The relative income effect could reinforce or offset the simple income effect accompanying redistribution.

Common in the literature is the implicit assumption that the income effect dominates the offsetting effects of income distribution, should there be any, and thus greater equality is presumed to lower aggregate savings.[2] The effect of wealth redistribution (particularly that of land) is often said to have a positive effect upon aggregate saving when the historic distribution is highly skewed. At this time, however, such assumptions are not empirically verified.

Another presumption often found is that if redistribution results in lower aggregate saving by households, government taxation can offset this and help channel the resources freed by taxes into investment. The outcome, of course, can vary with the political organization, political pressures, and effectiveness of government taxation programs. Communist countries have been very effective in ensuring saving and investment amidst more equal income distribution. This is related to their direct control over resources. Every government, however, faces a limit to its ability to restrict aggregate consumption. These limits

2. Surjit S. Bhalla, for example, using data from India, finds that a permanent income hypothesis is supported by the data, but that higher-income households had a higher MPS out of permanent income than lower-income households. He concludes that the observed increase in the MPS as income rises means that income redistribution would have a negative impact on the supply of household savings and consequently on growth when there is a savings constraint (Bhalla 1979).

vary, depending upon the country's political structure and historical influences. Where relative income influences the psychic satisfaction from consumption, so that gratification is enhanced as inequality is moderated, the limits to government-induced saving will be lessened.

The Foreign Sector and Savings

LDCs may borrow the monetary savings of MDCs, thus gaining purchasing power for additional investment goods. Foreign savings enter a domestic economy by an excess in the value of imports over exports. The savings can be in the form of investment goods or consumer goods. However, when consumption is satisfied in part from foreign imports not paid for with exports, domestic resources are freed from consumer goods production.

One way to view foreign savings is as an increase in permanent domestic income that will affect domestic saving through raising income. It can be expected that part of the income will increase saving, how much depending upon the MPS. Another hypothesis, for which there is some statistical support, is that an inflow of foreign savings tends to lower domestic saving by the government sector and thus reduces the national average saving rate.[3] The presumption is that the government feels less pressure to obtain savings from the domestic economy (Rahman 1968).

The permanent income hypothesis has been applied with some success to the foreign trade sector. The idea is that because income fluctuates greatly in this sector, a larger portion of it will be considered transitory and the saving rate will be higher than that for the country as a whole.

A cross-section study by Knudsen and Parnes (1975, p.121), however, finds a stronger relation between instability and consumption in the domestic than in the export sector. However, there is some evidence that *countries* with greater instability in export earnings, in accordance with the permanent-income hypothesis, consider a larger proportion of their income to be transitory because it is subject to greater uncertainty, and thus save a higher percentage of it (Yotopoulos and Nugent 1976, pp. 335–36; Knudsen and Parnes 1975, p. 121). Government taxation can also vary with the export sector income where the government relies heavily upon customs duties and export taxes. This variation in taxes can affect saving and investment by this sector. Mikesell and Zinser, however, criticize studies that purport to show a positive relationship between exports and savings and a higher propensity to save in the export than in other sectors, indicating the methodology used does not support the hypothesis (Mikesell and Zinser 1973, pp. 18–19).

Investment Opportunities and Saving

In LDCs the saver and investor are often the same person or entity. Some economists have posited a saving function that is influenced by the opportunity to invest. This is said to apply, for example, in agri-

---

3. As Nugent and Yotopoulos (1976, p. 176) note, if the foreign inflow is considered transitory income, it should raise the APS.

culture, where the low-income peasant will consume more when he does not perceive an outlet for his saving with a relatively secure return. When he has the opportunity, however, to invest on the farm and receive a safe return he will save more, perhaps foregoing leisure rather than consumption to form capital goods such as irrigation ditches with his own labor. R. I. McKinnon (1974, p. 64) argues that improved savings institutions that ensure a safe return adjusted for inflation can raise the level of saving of such groups.

Chenery and Eckstein (1970) suggest that a shortage of foreign exchange can prevent saving because investment cannot take place unless capital can be imported. When at the margin the foreign exchange available falls short of the unconstrained MPS, that propensity drops. Saving is higher in certain periods not because of transitory income, but because the foreign exchange is available for capital imports, a prerequisite for investment.

Note that the uncertainty of investment return is said to affect saving in the opposite way that, according to the permanent-income hypothesis, uncertainty of income affects saving. A greater degree of uncertainty in income receipts raised the saving propensity, but in the case of investment returns, the propensity to save presumably falls because secure investment outlets for savings are either not available or not perceived by the saver. The effect of uncertainty upon investment decisions, and hence capital formation, is discussed in chapter 6.

In summary, the most important single determinant of aggregate saving is national income or per capita income. Better empirical studies based on more reliable data are not expected to contradict this general result, at least for the economy that is not centrally planned. However, better data could establish the degree to which the APS and MPS diverge, if at all, in LDCs at different periods of development. The saving function can differ among LDCs. Some variables that are currently being examined to determine if they affect differences are the stability of income, the distribution of income and wealth, child dependency ratios, the development of integrated financial markets responsive to all potential savers, government taxation policies, government response to foreign saving inflow, and the foreign exchange constraint. Better data are needed to establish the importance of such variables to the aggregate and/or household saving functions.

Summary: Determinants of LDC Saving Functions

Saving is a necessary enabling factor for investment to take place since it frees the necessary resources. However, saving may or may not constrain investment, depending upon the demand for resources to form investment goods. Generally it is presumed that there are enough potentially profitable investment projects in the aggregate economy to more than exhaust the resources freed by saving in LDCs. This is particulary true where the government sector is influencing investment strongly for development purposes and there are many socially prof-

DETERMINANTS OF INVESTMENT

itable projects whose benefits to the total economy exceed their costs. The implication is that an increase in the saving rate is helpful to investment and growth and will not result in resources idle because of inadequate investment expenditures.

Such is the general presumption. By no means, however, do all LDCs possess a buoyant investment function, both private and public. And slow growth or stagnation may be the outcome. We turn, then, to a discussion of the major variables affecting the aggregate investment level in an LDC, remembering that the saving constraint can place a limit upon investment.

The Aggregate Investment Function

When considering the variables dominating investment decisions in the context of developing economies, preconceptions about the institutional framework for executing investment, based upon developed country conditions, should be set aside. One cannot automatically assume that there is a private sector replete with entrepreneurship, institutional support responsive to investment decision-making needs, human capital to carry out the investment, and a banking system through which the government monetary authorities can make new money available to supplement saving and thereby the funding of investment.

Models used for MDC economies assume the decision-maker calculates the expected profits, discounting them to accommodate for the expected time flow of monetary receipts and payments. Accounting records accurately pinpoint past results and form a basis for future expectations, enabling the firm to identify its optimum capital stock and plan its investment outlays. The cost of information, which reduces uncertainty, is low. And once a decision is made to invest, the result is a smooth multiplier effect rippling through an economic machinery responsive in all sectors to increments to spending. The saving constraint is de-emphasized for MDCs because people save more at higher-income levels; and emphasis in such nations is upon ensuring that resources left idle by the high savings are utilized. Aggregate investment in MDCs is positively related to aggregate demand, and is spurred by bank credit over and above current saving that allows idle resources to be acquired for investment. A large capital stock varies in age and replacement needs, generating internal depreciation funds used for maintaining and adding to it as profitability dictates. Market prices reflect scarcity—supply and demand—and signal with approximate accuracy the profitable outlets for new investment funds.

While this vignette is the background for models of MDC economies, it does not picture conditions in LDCs. The investment environment in LDCs can be very rudimentary and distorted. Risk levels are often relatively high. Lack of information means great uncertainty about the viability of new investment. And LDCs may have greater risk aversion than MDCs because of their lower income levels. Partly as a result of the different conditions that prevail in LDCs, the determinants of investment identified as major vary from those in MDCs.

The approach in looking at aggregate investment is to identify major variables at work, particularly those amenable to policy manipulation. The complexity and multiplicity of variables affecting investment directly and indirectly mean no one variable is a dominant determinant of investment in the way that income relates to saving. It is common to divide the variables affecting investment in the private economy into cost-side and revenue-side. And in addition to considering the static, or short-run, aggregate investment function, it is useful to weigh factors influencing the dynamics of investment over time, that is, the secular, or long-run, investment function. We begin by discussing revenue or demand-side variables discussed in the literature.

Consider a closed economy, one without foreign trade, that is growing as a result of increased productivity, and thus experiences reductions in the saving constraint. Now think about the income elasticity of demand for each sector and industry as income grows. Some categories of goods are income-inelastic, that is, as income increases by a given percentage, demand for those goods rises by a smaller percentage. Other items are income-elastic and demand expands by a greater percentage than income does. We will assume perfect information and investment decision-making. The capital stock would expand to satisfy the change in the demand matrix. If the product mix favored more capital-intensive industries with growth, aggregate investment as a proportion of GNP would rise. This very simple description captures the essence of *balanced growth*. Applied to reality it is a growth path dominated by changes in domestic demand, with limitations upon specialization and trade.

Demand-Side Variables

Let us examine now another simple scenario. The economy is open, highly specialized, and dependent upon foreign demand. When the demand matrix is dominated by foreign demand and its growth rate, then investment is determined in large degree by demand changes in that sector. In this case, then, the foreign sector is a *leading sector* when the rate of growth of foreign demand exceeds the domestic.

Historically, discussion centered upon the dynamics of demand, domestic and foreign, as a determinant of shifts in the investment function in LDCs has vacillated between stressing the adequacy and inadequacy of domestic and foreign demand as spurs to growth of investment. As early as Adam Smith (1776), the size of the domestic market as a determinant of investment entered the literature. Smith emphasized cost-side variables, however, declaring that division of labor leads to productivity gains and is limited by the extent of the market. Ragnar Nurkse (1953) emphasized that in poor economies the market size is a function of income per capita, which in turn depends upon the capital stock. With a limited domestic market there is little inducement to increase the capital stock; yet that is the main way, according to Nurkse, to raise per capita income, which can spur investment. The cycle of low investment and low income persists when the domestic market is small.

Nurkse looked at the historical setting in nineteenth-century LDCs and said that foreign demand had been a major escape route for these countries from the limited domestic market. Trade had served as an "engine of growth" in this period, according to some economic historians (Robertson 1940, p. 214). When Nurkse addressed twentieth-century conditions, he concluded that trade and foreign demand would not play the role of "leading sector." His reason was the low income elasticity of demand for raw materials needed for growth patterns in the more advanced technical society of the twentieth century, plus the increased supply in the first half of the century of many raw materials for which there were no adequate subsitutes.

Nurkse's solution was similar to an idea presented as relevant to Eastern Europe after World War II and set out in Rosenstein-Rodan (1961). There must be a "big push" whereby many investment projects are undertaken simultaneously. Scale and other economies of such a coordinated push will lower firms' internal costs, generating additional income. Supply will create its own demand where the push is adequate to increase efficiency and aggregate income. Investment ahead of unplanned market growth creates the income that justifies the investment when enough projects are undertaken at one time. Such a joint investment scheme would allow the government sector to invest in "lumpy" capital infrastructure projects not justified by marginal growth in small markets, where the absence of such projects contributes to slow or low growth in private investment. When there is a saving constraint, the big push depends upon foreign saving in the form of foreign aid.

The big push was a concept of accelerated balanced growth for countries unable to export anything but raw materials, for which there was only limited demand. Stimulus to investment was to be created in the home market. It presumed the human capital and other resources needed were available so that investment of this scope could be coordinated and executed.

The role of foreign demand in spurring domestic investment has also been associated with economies possessing surplus resources. The foreign markets stimulate discovery and exploration of new resources that would not be profitable with only limited domestic markets as an outlet. This creates investment for export sales when foreign demand grows. Depending upon the type of resource discovered and exploited, the spillover effects upon domestic income and investment can be high or low. Such investment in resource discovery and exports, however, usually presumes a large role for foreign investment in LDC exports of raw materials to satisfy the overseas demand. Resource discovery and exports have quickened investment growth in countries such as Canada and the United States in earlier periods as well as in many of today's LDCs.

Chenery and Strout (1966) prefer to view foreign demand as producing a constraint similar to the saving constraint that can limit aggregate investment. The constraint comes into play when foreign exchange earnings are inadequate for capital and other imports affecting the level of investment spending. For some countries the foreign exchange constraint may be more binding than the saving constraint. These ideas are discussed in detail in chapter 13.

When an LDC approaches a certain market size, scale effects begin to operate in some industries. They also affect infrastructure such as transportation, communications, and utilities. Productivity rises, as do profits, and investment is positively affected. Additional growth means that new areas encounter scale economies that further lower costs. Scale effects, then, may play a role in creating an acceleration phase of investment and saving. Population growth may also have a part in affecting scale and thereby investment.

Before turning to supply-side variables, we will look briefly at the effect of government activity upon investment. Most writers on development assume that government policies and decisions will have a strong influence upon an LDC's investment function. Certainly government has a great impact on the investment function in agriculture. The reasons for this are discussed in chapter 9, on agricultural transformation. Infrastructure, including both social and financial, is often characterized by direct government decisions on allocation. Investment in industry and the foreign trade sector are commonly influenced both directly and indirectly by government policies.

Government work programs for the unemployed and seasonally underemployed can mobilize idle resources for capital formation projects such as roads, irrigation projects and community sewer and water improvement. Better organization and deployment of resources can lessen the saving constraint at certain phases of development and may contribute to a higher level of investment to GNP.

Cost or supply-side elements have entered as dominant variables into many conceptualizations of the investment function in LDCs. As discussed in chapter 8, the Classical economists made aggregate investment a function of changing labor costs, which were determined mainly by changes in food costs with development. Food costs, according to this school, inevitably rose due to population pressures on limited land available for food production.

Supply-Side Variables

The secular investment function conceived by Karl Marx, while focusing on demand, domestic and foreign, also emphasized certain costs. Marx assumed growth was accompanied by ever-increasing capital intensity and a factor proportions problem so that labor could not be substituted for capital even though wages fell as unemployment swelled. This adversely affected profits as domestic demand dropped with unemployment, except when foreign demand substituted. Moreover the burgeoning capital stock exerted cost pressures that reduced profit rates as maintenance and replacement cost rose and firms operated below capacity. In both the Classical and Marxian systems, the investment level stagnates when costs reduce profits or profit rates. This halts growth under capitalist organization where government does not play a role in investment.

Surplus labor models emphasize low wages for labor transferred from heavily populated agriculture as the cause of profits and expansion in industry. In the latter sector, profits and growth strongly influence the investment function. The improved efficiency in labor utilization creates the profits from which savings take place, and applies the spur to industrial investment. Unlike the Marxian model, low wages here do not adversely affect demand and thereby investment. The saving constraint is circumvented by redeploying the surplus labor. These models are discussed in chapter 8.

Hagen (1975) argues for an investment function that is affected mainly by technological improvement and thereby lower cost. As with the Classical model, the entrepreneurs are the key to the investment function. They create the saving simultaneously with investment through increased technical competence and elimination of less efficient processes. Small markets do not limit investment for the purpose of cost-cutting, and increased efficiency expands the market so that new products can be introduced. Hagen generally downplays the need to commit resources to set the stage for technological change. The entrepreneur is a seemingly costless agent of investment and technical advance. Chapter 5 is devoted to technological change and its importance to development.

Summary
Summing up, we can say that two constraints operate upon investment: those of saving and of foreign exchange. Whether one or both of them are binding varies among LDCs according to specific conditions in each country and its level of development.

The investment function is influenced by multiple variables, including noneconomic ones. Generally the literature supports examination of the following economic variables as possibly exerting major impact upon investment in LDCs: demand, domestic and foreign; labor costs; capital costs; scale effects; technological change; government sector activity that affects investment; the size of the industrial sector relative to the total economy; and the level of risk. There is no simple relationship between these and investment. Other chapters of the book deal more specifically with some of the variables and their effects on investment and development.

Finally it should be noted that models of growth and development often divide income into profits and wages. This is called the functional distribution of income. Profits are the income of the entrepreneurial class, and are assumed to be invested automatically. Clear distinction between a saving and an investment function is then lost. Investment and saving are functions of the proportion of income going to profit. The discussion of the complexities of the investment and saving functions points up the need to keep in mind the extent of simplification of these functions in the models discussed in chapter 8.

OPTIMUM GROWTH AND SAVING
Saving must be encouraged, if not forced, in LDCs because at low levels of income consumption needs preempt resources. Any government or society, whether ideologically of the left or right or somewhere between, that wishes to develop must divert resources from consumption to investment spending. And as output increases, how much goes to raising living standards and how much to form capital will help determine further growth. The fact that very poor economies have few free resources once fairly rudimentary living needs are met means that

the capacity for improving consumption levels for early generations is quite modest. In recognition of the sacrifices of early generations, it is sometimes said the development comes "off the back of the peasant."

There have been various institutional arrangements whereby consumption has been maintained within a range that was compatible with growth. Laissez-faire capitalism of the nineteenth century produced an income distribution conducive to growth and a capitalist class that used the savings for that purpose. After the communist revolution, the Soviet system controlled resources directly and government planners used the savings for growth. The Japanese economy, examined in the next section, has produced a mixture of government taxes, savings from profits, and frugality by the public in general that has been conducive to historically steady and increasing levels of savings.

Two elements can make the diversion of resources from consumption to growth needs difficult in today's more advanced LDCs. The demonstration effect can induce those with the income to consume at levels comparable with MDCs and much above the levels these latter countries attained at their earlier ranges of per capita GNP. This includes consumption of modern military hardware. And in mixed economies the spread of ideas about income redistribution can lead to demand at early stages that the government establish minimum wages and provide social security, housing, and other benefits with tax money. In some cases, the product mix can be tilted toward consumption and/or military priorities that halt further improvements in living standards or even lead to their deterioration as the capital stock fails to keep up with population growth. However, even with the threat of these forces, some LDCs have attained historically high growth rates in the postwar years (see table 1.1). In a number of cases, part of the savings for this growth came from abroad, enabling the LDC to use foreign resources for development.

Given the potential for conflict between consumption levels and growth, the question arises: What is the optimum rate of growth for an LDC? What rate of savings does this require? Keep an open mind that the optimum rate of growth could be zero or negative. And because this is a normative question involving value judgments, we must ask if there is any accepted method for defining optimality as it relates to growth.

Today, growth is most often evaluated in terms of human welfare, not by national prestige. However, two insurmountable problems involving measurement and aggregation prevent an objective determination of a socially optimum growth rate.

First, there is no unit in which to measure satisfaction or welfare arising from growth. An ordering of preferences in regard to growth rates is all that can be accomplished. But even this ordering is difficult because it is hard to predict the far-reaching social as well as economic changes that accompany development related to a chosen growth rate. The social and human dimensions of changing conditions of, for example, employment, family and religious ties, tenancy and land rights, technology requirements, and government controls are difficult to assess in advance.

Second, even assuming that an ordering of growth-rate preferences by individuals is possible, and each individual can state categorically that he or she ranks a particular growth rate first, another second, and so on, this does not ensure that an optimal growth rate can be identified. Development affects the welfare of individuals in the current generation differently and also has a different impact upon individuals in future generations. Is the welfare of those yet unborn to be given weight in the choice of growth rates? How? When today's individuals differ in their choice of a preferred growth rate, how are their preferences to be weighted and aggregated?

Inevitably the forces and groups determining the type and pace of growth are without a calibrating mechanism to achieve an optimum.[4] Value judgments must enter into planners' target growth and savings rates, and valuations of present versus future consumption. Future consumption may be worth less than present, especially to the very poor. But there is no scientific way to identify a "social interest or discount rate" for the community.

Nevertheless, it is common to refer to a community or social discount or interest rate identified by the few that has some legitimacy with the many. If the growth rate equals the social interest rate, then the community theoretically will be compensated for restricting current consumption and any other costs of development by the extra future consumption and other benefits. The greater the uncertainty of such an outcome, the higher the social discount rate should be. But such a general statement is suspect, as explained, and incomplete because it ignores value judgments about the distribution of costs and gains while assuming they are measurable.

The reader should not leave this chapter without realizing there is no scientific approach to identifying an optimum growth rate and its accompanying savings rate for an LDC. A feasible growth rate is another matter, amenable to scientific analysis, if not satisfying precision. In the absence of criteria for sanctioning a certain growth rate for a given LDC, the overwhelming temptation is to succumb to the recent Western dictum that more is better. This is especially true since, with rapid population increases, higher growth is required to avoid declining GNP per capita. Development as a goal involves far-reaching value judgments, however, and recently arguments have surfaced against the highest feasible growth rate when it carries growing dualism and inequality.

Japan is an example of a country that by historical comparison enjoys a high growth rate. The concluding sections of this chapter describe salient characteristics of the Japanese saving-investment performance and their impact upon that nation's development. Since this is the first of a number of country-specific illustrations that appear at the end of chapters, it is appropriate at this point to explain their scope and function.

---

4. In welfare economics the optimum is most often defined along the lines set forth by Vilfredo Pareto, where increased welfare is the change from an initial situation for which the income distribution is given. If no one is worse off and at least one person is better off, then welfare is said to have increased.

Country-specific illustrations are designed to reinforce selected concepts or chapter points by drawing upon historical experience. Each vignette is limited in scope and time so as to sharpen the chapter features under scrutiny. The cases used are not necessarily free from alternative interpretations. Scholars often differ over historical cause and effect. Information sets are inevitably incomplete in country studies and data available can support more than one explanation of events. The laboratory of the real world is different from a controlled experiment. And the judgments needed to make conclusions can be affected by what model is applied and even by the researcher's own policy predilections. Given the complexities of the real world there is always room for disagreement. Not surprisingly history is continually being rewritten.

SCOPE AND PURPOSE OF COUNTRY VIGNETTES

REFERENCES

Bhalla, Surjit S. 1979. Measurement Errors and the Permanent Income Hypothesis: Evidence from Rural India. *American Economic Review* (June): 295–307.

Chenery, H. B. and Eckstein, P. 1970. Development Alternatives for Latin America. *Journal of Political Economy* 78 (July): 966–1006.

Chenery, H. B. and Strout, A. M. 1966. Foreign Assistance and Economic Development. *American Economic Review* 56 (September): 680–733.

Domar, E. 1946. Capital Expansion, Rate of Growth and Employment. *Econometrica* 14 (January): 137–47.

Galenson, G. and Leibenstein, H. 1955. Investment Criteria, Productivity and Economic Development. *Quarterly Journal of Economics* 69 (August): 343–70.

Hagen, Everett E. 1975. *The Economics of Development.* Homewood, Illinois: Richard D. Irwin.

Harrod, R. F. 1939. An Essay in Dynamic Theory, *Economic Journal* 49 (March): 14–33.

Houthakker, H. S. 1965. On Some Determinants of Saving in Developed and Undeveloped Countries. In *Problems in Economic Development,* edited by E. A. Robinson. New York: Macmillan and Co.

Kelley, A. C. and Williamson, J. G. 1968. Household Saving Behavior in the Developing Economies: The Indonesian Case. *Economic Development and Cultural Change* vol. 16, no. 3, pp. 385–403.

Knudson, O. and Parnes, A. 1975. *Trade Instability and Economic Development.* Lexington, Mass.: Lexington Books, D. C. Heath and Co.

Kuznets, S. 1965. *Economic Growth and Structure.* New York: W. W. Norton and Co.

Leff, N. H. 1969. Dependency Rates and Savings Rates. *American Economic Review* 59 (December): 886–96.

Marglin, S. A. 1976. *Value and Price in the Labour-Surplus Economy.* Oxford: Clarendon Press.

McKinnon, R. I. 1974. *Money and Capital in Economic Development.* Washington, D.C.: The Brookings Institution.

Mikesell, Raymond F. and Zinser, James E. 1973. The Nature of the Savings Function in Developing Countries: A Survey of the Theoretical and Empirical Literature. *Journal of Economic Literature* 11 (March): 1–26.

Mizaguchi, Toshiyuki. 1970. *Personal Savings and Consumption in Postwar Japan.* Tokyo: Kinokuniya Bookstore Co.

Mueller, Eva. 1976. The Economic Value of Children in Peasant Agriculture, in *Population and Development*, edited by R. G. Ridker. Baltimore, MD: Johns Hopkins University Press: 98–153.

Musgrave, Philip. 1978. Determinants of Urban Household Consumption in Latin America: A Summary of Evidence from the ECIEL Surveys. *Economic Development and Cultural Change* 26 (April): 139–53.

Nurkse, Ragnar. 1953. *Problems of Capital Formation in Underdeveloped Countries*. New York: Oxford University Press.

Ohkawa, Kazushi, and Rosovsky, Henry. 1965. A Century of Japanese Growth, in *The State and Economic Enterprise in Japan*, edited by W. W. Lockwood. Princeton: Princeton University Press.

Rahman, M. A. 1968. Foreign Capital and Domestic Savings: A Test of Haavelmo's Hypothesis with Cross-Country Data. *Review of Economics and Statistics* 50 (February): 137–38.

Robertson, D. H. 1940. The Future of International Trade in *Essays in Monetary Theory*, edited by D. Holme. London: P. S. King and Son Ltd.

Rosenstein-Rodan, P. N. 1961. Notes on the Theory of the Big Push, in *Economic Development for Latin America*, edited by H. S. Ellis and H. C. Wallich. New York: St. Martin's Press.

Rosovsky, Henry. 1961. *Capital Formation in Japan 1868–1940*. New York: The Free Press of Glencoe.

Sen, Amartya. 1975. *Employment, Technology and Development*. Oxford: Clarendon Press.

Singh, S. K. 1971. The Determinants of Aggregate Savings. *World Bank*, mimeo 32 (April). Quoted in Mikesell-Zinser, p. 7.

Williamson, J. G. 1968. Personal Saving in Developing Nations: An Inter-temporal Cross Section from Asia. *Economic Record* 44 (June): 194–210.

Yotopoulos, P. A. and Nugent, J. B. 1976. *Economics of Development*. New York: Harper and Row.

Characteristics of the Japanese Saving-Investment Process

Japan today, following a century of economic development, is the giant of Asia and a leading world economy. The pace of her evolution is outstanding despite handicaps of dense population and scarce resources. During her development she faced most of the problems experienced by LDCs struggling in today's environment. In particular relative to Western nations she was a latecomer to development and she started from a per capita income base not much higher than poorer LDCs have today. Kazushi Ohkawa and Henry Rosovsky (1965) identify 10 key characteristics of Japan's century of development, begun after the political transition in 1868 from Tokugawa to Meiji rule.

1. A relatively high rate of overall growth in output and per capita income, with some spurts and some slackening;

2. A pattern of population expansion which, in rates of natural increase, is reminiscent of Europe's historical experience rather than that of currently underdeveloped areas, and which did not include substantial emigration or immigration while retaining a highly flexible labor supply;

3. For the given level of per capita income, a relatively high proportion of domestic investment (and saving) accompanied by several upward movements of the investment (saving) ratio;

4. For the given level of per capita income, a relatively low percentage of personal consumption, accompanied by several downward shifts of the consumption ratio;

5. A sustained low capital-output ratio, showing, however, an upward drift in the Post-World War II period;

6. Modern economic growth taking place, in general, in an inflationary setting, the only exception to this being the 1920s;

7. Recurring balance-of-payments crises such that one may almost speak of a chronic deficit in foreign payments;

8. The general coexistence of traditional and modern economic sectors, partly reflected in the bimodal (large-scale/small-scale) distribution of enterprises;

9. The important role played by government in furthering economic modernization, especially in mobilizing and spending investment funds;

10. A specifically created group of financial institutions that greatly enhanced the supply of capital.

Of particular interest here is the saving-investment process that has helped to transform Japan into a modern state from a nation that had 80 percent of its people employed in primary production in the 1860s. The data base for a confident analysis of the saving function and investment magnitudes by sectors is lacking. However, diligent research has provided figures that allow many insights into the accumulation process in Japan from its early inception. And several distinguishing features emerge.

The saving-investment levels of Japan prior to World War II were moderately high by comparison with today's developing countries. They were also steady, with two spurts to higher levels. Gross domestic capital formation as a percentage of gross domestic product averaged about 12 percent from the late 1800s until 1907–16. There was a surge in capital formation to 18 percent in the period around World War I, as Japan benefited from new trade in war-distorted markets. Investment ratios stayed on a plateau until the internal military buildup of the 1930s. It was mainly the period following World War II that saw Japan emerge as a high-saving country. Again this was a remarkably steady rate at high levels. Interestingly, the rise in the postwar saving ratio coincided with a decline in inequality from prewar levels.

THE SAVING FUNCTION

From both pre- and post-World War II data on saving-investment ratios, it is clear that there is a differential saving ratio among income classes. The Japanese entrepreneurial saving propensity can easily rival that of the parsimonious Scotsman idealized by Adam Smith. The conspicuous consumption so often found today in LDCs was for the most part absent in prewar Japan. Nonproductive absorption of income in areas such as landed estates, lavish housing, or consumer durables and luxury goods was limited among the entrepreneurs. The high saving among this class continued in the postwar years.

Profits from which saving could be set aside were kept high relative to wages in Japan as a result of the abundance of labor and the failure of Western-style union organization to take hold. Moderate inflation, averaging 8 percent, favored profits over wages.

Workers may have received only modest wage increments, but they were supplied with growing amounts of affordable, traditional labor-intensive consumer goods. Their expenditures, then, supported the labor-intensive sectors. Workers in the modern sector, which began to employ a considerable proportion of the populace in the 1920s, were paid bonuses linked to profits. A study of this bonus scheme in postwar Japan by Toshiyuki Mizaguchi (1970) concludes that the transitory nature of the income tended to increase workers' saving ratio and thereby the aggregate average propensity to save. He also feels the rapid growth rate of GNP may have increased postwar saving ratios. The failure of consumer credit to develop in Japan also plays a role in worker saving. Workers must save enough to purchase an item rather than obtain credit and pay on time.

Several other variables invite speculation about their influence upon saving. Commentators on Japan's consumption patterns note that the centuries of isolation from Western influence limited the demonstration effect and produced ingrained, traditional consumption habits throughout the population. Japan is also a culturally homogeneous society, a fact that may have limited consumption differentials between income groups. And in the absence of a liberal social security system, family obligations that lay claim to future income could moderate present consumption from wages.

Population growth of about 1 percent was modest by comparison with current LDC rates, and probably had little if any negative effect upon household saving. By keeping laborers plentiful and profits up, its impact may have been positive.

Finally, foreign saving did not make a notable contribution to Japanese development. She essentially financed her own development with only occasional periods of limited foreign borrowing prior to World War II. On occasion she borrowed abroad for disaster relief needs.

INVESTMENT PATTERNS

The distinguishing feature of early Japanese investment patterns is their concentration in the traditional sector—in labor-intensive production processes, including agriculture. Rosovsky (1961) estimates that 68 percent of investment was in the traditional sector in 1890, 44 percent in 1900, and 32 percent as late as 1917. Much of this was labor-absorbing such as structures and irrigation, as opposed to nontraditional projects like public utilities, railroads, and equipment, which were import-intensive. Except for the military and some infrastructure, however, nontraditional investment was in light industry—in consumer goods such as modern textiles, plate glass, and light electrical machinery. The shift to capital-intensive heavy industry like iron and steel, heavy machinery, nonferrous metals, and transportation equipment, did not occur until after World War II.

This composition of investment as well as consumption allowed Japan to utilize her factor proportions efficiently and conserve on imports, resulting in high capital productivity. Moderate, steady levels of saving-investment financed a relatively strong growth rate while consumption also grew. Japan did not rank with the heavy investors until the last phases of her modernization.

The government played a particularly large part in early industrialization. Its role extended beyond such measurable areas as investment ratios into a myriad of nonquantifiable avenues of influence, some direct, some indirect. The state built infrasturcture and pilot factories, subsidized new industries and the military. It is estimated that government investment as a share of gross domestic fixed capital formation exceeded 50 percent from the late 1800s to World War II. The land tax and later a more diversified tax base financed this public sector investment. The government promoted development of a banking system that helped finance private sector investment and also invested in human capital following the Meiji Restoration. However, premodern Japan at the end of the Tokugawa era already enjoyed an impressive literacy rate for its income level, so that the government of modernizing Japan could build upon the ex-

isting human capital stock. In fact this stock of human capital is considered to have played an important role in the dynamism of the country's early growth. Even the peasantry was in part literate.

The infrastructure developed by the government enlarged the domestic market, allowing scale economies. Japan also successfully sought out foreign markets, first in exports of tea and raw silk, later in textiles. This allowed raw materials, capital, and technology to be imported. Modern industries were not able to achieve continuous growth in domestic markets sufficient for their expansion due to the population's low purchasing power. By 1905, however, some of the new industries had expanded into export markets, achieving their scale efficiencies and growth impetus from external sales. And the expansion of foreign trade during World War I helped to lift the investment level to a new plateau.

Finally, the government played a key role in investment supporting research and development. It introduced new technology, starting up pilot factories in new industries, invested in technical training needed for new technology, and in general absorbed a good proportion of the risk associated with the transfer of technology from the West.

In sum, Japan lightened the sacrifices of growth by maximizing the efficiency of expenditures on consumption and investment through the production of relatively labor-intensive goods in both sectors. This allowed moderate saving to produce steady growth adequate to raise income levels in a densely populated country. Her choice of commodities for trade also reflected this appropriate product mix for her resource base. And the high postwar saving-investment ratios helped Japan recover from the decline in living levels and destruction of capital wrought by World War II. In this period she regained her prewar status and then moved on to become a dominant world economy. Throughout the growth process she borrowed Western technology and adapted it to her economic structure. This too lightened the investment needs for growth.

Technology and
Development

chapter

5.

An African woman, bent over a simple handmade hoe cultivating plants from native seeds on burned land leached of topsoil, without fertilizer or irrigation, is farming with techniques used for centuries. Her ways of drying, preparing, and storing her crops are also extremely primitive. The agricultural technology in sub-Sahara Africa is less advanced than the time-tested methods followed by traditional Asian peasants who practice contour farming and simple irrigation, harness bullocks for plowing, and process their food with mechanized milling and other similar techniques. And both are less advanced than the modernized Taiwanese farmer who cultivates up to three crops a year using hybrid seeds, fertilizers and pesticides, tractor services, irrigation pumps, and modern food processing techniques, combined with farm labor of greater skill and education levels. Dependency upon the contributions of nature decreases with more advanced technology.

Modern technology advances at an historically rapid pace today in affluent countries, and technology gaps have widened between the advanced countries and the least developed ones. A primitive economy cannot make use of a great proportion of advanced technology due to its complexity and resource needs. And while technical change in LDCs has been rapid in many cases, it has also been uneven. The apparently simple task of improving the African woman's way of farming is deceivingly difficult. Yet more and more, technology is emphasized as central to the development process. In this chapter we explore the complexities of this topic. Treatment of the subject is, typically, fairly broad. Yet to some degree the topic lends itself to the use of analytical techniques introduced earlier.

Technology and Technological Change: Scope of the Concept

There exists no theory to explain or predict either the rate of discovery of new technology or of its diffusion throughout an economy. And for an LDC that will be borrowing methods already in use in MDCs, there is no adequate understanding of the determinants of the rate of absorption of known technology. Yet some statistical studies indicate that technological change has been the most significant factor in per capita growth in MDCs, more so than increased inputs of resources, or economies of scale. The attempt to determine statistically the relative importance to growth of its components is open to criticism. But all students of economic development pay homage to technological change as a vital force in that process. Thus it is important to explore current understanding of the role of such change historically in MDCs, and currently in LDCs, despite the limitations of such knowledge.

The concept of technology and technological change is a broad and encompassing one. Technology refers to the uitlized pool of knowledge and know-how in the industrial arts that is embodied in human skills, social organization, equipment and infrastructure, and reflected in the type and quality of output of the economy. Technological change, often referred to as innovation, in some way improves the efficiency or productivity of the economy by advances in knowledge applied in the production of goods and services like those already in use, or to new

113

ones. Discoveries in the pure sciences may eventually lead to technological change if they can be incorporated into applied industrial arts. However, technological change can be unrelated to pure science as in the introduction of the assembly line, modern accounting, or the inventor who comes up with a better machine by tinkering with the old one. The rate of technological change refers to how fast technology is changing over time. In general the more sectors in an economy that are affected by technological advances, the greater the rate of change for the total society.

Technological change is pervasive in its effects upon an economy. In previous treatment we understated its ramifications by assuming it affected production processes and thereby the productivity only of existing resources. But technology can create new resources and new products, improve the quality of those already in use, and can even affect the growth rate of inputs. It does not just shift old production functions; it also creates new ones. All these areas need some further elaboration.

First consider how technology affects output per unit of input in the production process. A new machine may be the vehicle for greater productivity. Alternatively new managerial or other human skills may be the conduit for better productivity. Man and machine may combine as channels of change. The machine may reduce the human physical exertion demanded and thereby raise worker productivity. Technical change that raises productivity can be embedded in organizational innovations and may be prerequisite to the achievement of economies of scale. It may increase the elasticity of substitution among natural resources, resulting in greater efficiency. And it can enhance efficiency in the production of factor inputs—physical and human capital.

New resources may be created as more advanced technology makes accessible natural wealth that formerly could not be extracted, or creates new resources out of other inputs, or finds a use for a mineral or metal previously considered worthless. It improves the quality of resources by changing them in ways that upgrade their performance. New commodities and changes in the quality of old ones are among the important outcomes of technological progress. The consumer has a greater range of goods of varying quality from which to choose.

Technological change also affects growth of inputs. That it has impact upon the discovery and creation of new resources has already been mentioned. Inasmuch as technological change raises productivity, it has a feedback effect upon the growth of capital, since as output grows an economy can form more capital. It also has a similar effect upon itself, in financing new technology and enlarging the technical base from which further improvements can emerge. Such are the positive effects of technology upon growth.

The adoption of modern technology in LDCs can also have negative repercussions. Here we emphasize that technological change renders obsolete some of an economy's human and physical capital stock, and thereby imposes a faster depreciation rate upon this stock. It is assumed that the technically changed stock is more productive and/or better able to satisfy consumer wants than that existing prior to the innovation, or it would not have been profitable for the economy to invest in technical change. Yet individual dislocations for people who lose their jobs or whose assets become obsolete present shorter-term adjustment problems that are intensified when the pace of change is rapid. Arnold Heertje surveyed the works of economists writing during early phases of development in the West and found that most of them assumed technological changes were digestible with only very short-term business and employment dislocations because such changes were *gradual* (Heertje 1977, p. 36). Efforts to impose a very rapid rate of technical progress by importing advanced technology and human skills into today's LDCs have induced dislocation of indigestible proportions in some cases such that the attempted changes are inefficient.

Further, rapid technical change generally imposes greater demand upon the economy for savings to form new investment, to finance research, and to provide sectors and individuals distressed by the innovation with human and physical capital so that their earning capacity does not drop permanently. When an LDC fails to ameliorate human dislocation brought on by rapidly changing technology, social and political instability can erupt.

As will be discussed later in the chapter, moden technology often uses intensively resources that are relatively scarce in LDCs, and is apt to be characterized by a low elasticity of substitution between capital and labor. For these reasons some economists feel it must be modified prior to being adopted by LDCs. Even slower rates of importation of modern technology have created problems associated with dualism, a topic exlored later.

Finally, the rapid introduction of new methods and equipment carries with it costs of social dislocation and change when the family, the community, and the individual find relationships severed, anxieties raised, and freedoms sacrificed. And as historians have noted, modern economic development has bred a high incidence of social strife in the form of internal revolution and international wars.

Optimal Rate of Technological Change

Obviously a variable as pervasive as technological change creates effects in the economy that are not necessarily reflected in prices and costs, especially when markets are imperfect and information costs high, as in LDCs. As a result governments are generally involved in decisions about technical change—decisions more encompassing than just financing research and development. Examples are laws governing patents, the environment, and technically created monopoly, along with policies dealing with the dislocation of technical unemployment. Most importantly, governments interested in growth generally incorporate policies in their development plans to promote and accelerate technical transfer and innovation.

Once government's role as guide for the pace and type of technical change has been established, then the question arises: What is the most desirable rate of such change? As with an optimum saving rate associated with an optimum growth rate, there are any number of complex issues involved that undermine our ability to establish optimality.

Problems arise from the qualitative changes within the total economy brought on by technological change. Such problems must be added to those associated with establishing a community welfare function at a point in, and over, time. It is difficult to conceive of or to identify a social consensus on an optimum rate of change that weights the social costs and benefits, especially when many who suffer these costs will not be rewarded by the economic changes in their lifetime. Moreover, with technological change maximization of consumption can no longer be the simple or single objective function. The planners may organize their approach to the problem by thinking of costs and benefits, but the weighting of each factor as it affects different groups, individuals, and generations invariably leads to the incorporation of values, of judgments that must be salable in the political arena.

The presumption is widespread that technological change in LDCs should be accelerated, that it lags behind the ill-defined optimum in situations of low per capita GNP. The increased productivity flowing from technical progress in the West has produced the miracle of affluence for the masses, a miracle never contemplated up to the modern industrial age. Its environmental fallout may even be controllable by further advances in technology. Without technical advance in LDCs, there is no hope of eradicating the world's remaining poverty. Those interested in eliminating the extremes of deprivation in the world generally rest their hopes on technological change, even if that hope is misplaced.

NEW TECHNOLOGY AND ITS SPREAD

What determines the rate of discovery of new technology and its diffusion throughout an economy? Why has technological change accelerated in modern Western economies and what determines variations in the pace of acceleration? What determines the rate of transfer of technology to LDCs? As admitted already, our understanding of this process is woefully inadequate. The search for paradigms explaining technological change and identifying the interrelated variables has proven fertile ground for scholars in various disciplines including historians, sociologists, physical scientists, and economists. Not unlike the phenomenon of development with which it is closely interrelated, technological change may be a complex process that varies in its causal network through time and among historical situations, defying simple generalization. Here we introduce some insights into this broad topic.

Innovation, Entrepreneurship, and the Socioeconomic Framework

Some explanations of technological change have focused on the entrepreneur as the innovator and central variable in the paradigm. A socioeconomic structure that allows or fosters entrepreneurship is identified as crucial to development. Generally this socioeconomic structure is some form of capitalism as it has evolved in Western economies.

The Classical economists of the late eighteenth and early nineteenth centuries assumed technological change was possible in the industrial sector as long as there were capitalist entrepreneurs with profits to use in acquiring the resources for technological change, and as long as competition kept them on their toes. The inability of technological change to overcome diminishing returns to labor in agriculture with the growth in population would raise food prices, the main component of wage costs. Higher wages in industry would reduce profits and, hence, technological change. Continued population growth would bring about stagnation, since profits would be eaten up by wage costs. The stationary state was one of low income for the masses and population growth checked by the poverty.

Marx, like the Classical economists, treated technology as exogenous, that is, arising outside the economic structure, readily available according to the economy's needs and dependent upon the competitive entrepreneur-capitalist and profits for its application. He assumed technological change would increase the capital intensity of the firm, replacing labor, and that it depended upon large profits to finance the necessary investment. Both agriculture and industry were capable of technological advance so long as profits were available. As unemployment from the labor-replacing capital arose, consumption would fall and affect profits. Moreover, costs of capital and the growing amount of it needed would lower the rate of profit, expressed as a ratio affected by capital costs in the denominator. Bankruptcies and reduced competition would shrink entrepreneurial activity in the economy. However, prior to its social and economic deterioration, the capitalist system and the entrepreneur would produce vast advances in technology and labor productivity.

Increased poverty and unemployment of the masses would lead finally to a revolution that would replace capitalism with the next historical epoch, socialism. The masses then would benefit from the technological advances achieved under capitalism. In the Marxian model technology could overcome population pressures. Moreover, the timing of abrupt social change was influenced by a fundamental shift in the "technostructure." Technology for Marx had a pervasive influence on social organization. It was subject to changes that over historical periods created new identifying characteristics, and thereby sequential stages, of historical development.

Capitalism and the role of the entrepreneur in achieving technical progress were central also to the writings of Werner Sombart (1927), Max Weber (1930), and R. H. Tawney (1926). The latter two explain the rise of capitalism as an historical epoch based on the Reformation and emergence of the "Protestant ethic," which legitimized the pursuit of profit for reinvestment and progress. While Protestant groups might have been rejected because of their beliefs, economic success was the mark of being among God's elect. Entrepreneurship associated with group behavior, ethics, and social repression has also been utilized in studies of the role of the Jews, Chinese, Indians, and other alien and indigenous minority groups as carriers of technology, sometimes through migration. Their part in technical transfer and its spread is limited, however, when they do not achieve a minimum of integration into the society, but remain islands unto themselves.

Schumpeter (1942) idealized the entrepreneur as the innovator in a capitalist environment of monopolistic competition. He separated profits and the entrepreneur, emphasizing that with a banking system the latter could use other people's savings in introducing technological change. The innovator's motivating force, however, was still profits, and as the first to introduce a new idea or product, he would enjoy monopoly profits for a period of time. However, in the Schumpeterian capitalism there was ease of entry into new areas and technological change was rapidly diffused through imitation by managers in other firms. The technological change is embodied in or enabled by new, or autonomous, investment; it is followed by the induced investment of the imitators. New money created by the banking system can help to finance this investment in larger amounts than those possible with only current savings.

Schumpter said the entrepreneur was a product of smaller-scale capitalism that created the right social climate for the pursuit of profits, the introduction of new ideas, and the untaxed legacy of the family firm. This type of capitalism, according to him, died with the corporate form of routinized research and development carried out in laboratories by teams of technocrats. Thus as with Marx, the death of capitalism provided for a successor system that could continue technological change. But both Marx and Schumpeter were so engrossed in explaining capitalism and its death that they did not discuss in depth how technological change would proceed without the entrepreneur of capitalism.

Emphasis upon the innovative, individual entrepreneur as the sine qua non of development for today's less-developed economies characterizes the work of E. E. Hagen. He finds such an individual just as indispensable in the task of developing an LDC, where much of the technical change will come from imitating and adapting known techniques, as in the case where the innovator acts in the orthodox sense of creating de novo. Changes in productivity are the main sources of a dynamic development process for Hagen. His definition of innovation is all-inclusive. He realizes the tautology of an explanation that in an oversimplified form says development occurs because there are agents who increase productivity or do something new. To add profundity to his analysis, he seeks to explain the origins of entrepreneurship. In doing so, he transcends his discipline of economics, delving into the psychological and social behavior of the individual.

Hagen's book, *On the Theory of Social Change*, offers an explanation of the development of entrepreneurial behavior in a previously traditional economy governed by customs and mores where an authoritarian hierarchy resists change. According to Hagen, a deep-seated disturbance originating outside the social organization must disrupt its stability and change the child-parent relationship in order for entrepreneurship to arise in the next generation. Without such a shock to the perpetuating custom-bound authoritarian society, the child will be trained to avoid anxiety by awaiting directions rather than exerting any initiative. But when some historical accident (typically, an ascension of a new group to power) disturbs the status of lower- or middle-level elite groups, the resulting social tensions will bring about two important changes: First, the group whose status is upset will, over several generations, in turn reject the behavior patterns of the top elite and their traditional values. Second, the anxieties and rejection of traditional views and mores of an authoritarian society destroy the pattern of inculcating the youth of the rejected groups with the traditional behavior patterns. Over several generations there is the possibility for the children without role models to develop more initiative and innovative behavior patterns. If their attention turns to the economic sphere as a path to status shunned by the top elite, then entrepreneurship and economic development can follow. Obviously in the Hagen frame of reference, entrepreneurship is not something one is taught in school or on-the-job training.

In the 1975 edition of his text on development, Hagen briefly explores the logical implications of his ideas for the type of economic system that can support entrepreneurship and hence development. He concludes that socialist, communist, and capitalist systems (with family firm or corporate structure) can all yield a supporting social network to allow innovation. He breaks the connection between private profit motives and the motivation necessary for entrepreneurship. Service to the state or community is an equally positive motivation he concludes, as the Soviet Union in its more than half century of communist growth illustrates.

The role of government in technological change is emphasized by many current writers, who find that the financing of technical progress has become an increasingly important factor in explaining the rate of such change. Today's highly sophisticated, complex technology can require large sums of venture capital. The riskiness of the investment, the long payback period, and the possibility of externalities that create returns not for the firm but for the economy as a whole, have all fostered a large role for government financing of research and development. And team research replaces the stress upon the individual as catalyst in the process. Some writers cite national defense as the main variable establishing the legitimacy of taxation for research and development. Government is central to the process; but it is difficult to identify just what type of role it should assume to "optimize" technological change and what organizational structure is most conducive to innovation research and development.

In countries without private ownership of firms, technology is seldom restricted by patents. This should accelerate technological change because all firms can have access to new knowledge. Innovation, in theory at least, can be fostered and encouraged by state rewards at a cost to the economy below that of the patent; and technological diffusion would not be inhibited. Along these same lines, but assuming private ownership of firms in LDCs, it could be beneficial for the government of a less-advanced nation to pay licensing and royalty fees on importable technology they need that is controlled by private firms abroad and then let the knowledge be used by all domestic firms. This would discourage monopoly and promote diffusion. The snag is that foreign firms often will not agree to this arrangement.

Interestingly (and contrary to the Hagen conclusion), the literature on technical change in the Soviet Union reports a relatively poor performance in the modern arena of technical advance (as opposed to technology absorption), at least outside of a few defense-related areas. The development of new and better consumer products has been almost completely neglected. This was in part a deliberate policy. In an economy technically less advanced it served to increase the absorption rate of Western technology in the process area. Engineering advances could be assimilated more quickly despite limitations in human skills and other factors, and greater output achieved, when quality standards were low and the product mix was limited. Another reason for limited innovation is that central planning does not eliminate the risks and uncertainty of technical change, and the Russian bureaucrat at the firm level proved averse to risk. The bureaucrats responded to a reward system tied to attainment of output targets.

Large corporate firms also can finance the research and development needed to keep their relative share of a market or provide growth for the firm. The dynamism of technological competition rather than atomistic competition is emphasized when an economy replaces the family firm with the large corporation. The large enterprise as an agent of technological change has focused attention upon the variables affecting the profitability to the company of financing technological change. Patent laws are one variable. Supply factors are often mentioned, but elements of demand also play a role in encouraging technological advances. Jacob Schmookler (1966), for example, assumes technological change is achievable in most any area to which MDCs care to commit their large supply of scientific and technical skills, and without much cost differential among areas. In such a world it is demand forces that direct inventive activity to various areas of the economy with a given supply of technical skills. The technical team capable of innovating is seen as readily assembled should management generate the funds and corporate support for their performance. They are a product of investment in education.

Managerial behavior patterns affect innovation in oligopolistic market structures. Managerial conduct varies historically among different industries (Bain 1968). There is no strong evidence to support the assumption that the largest firms with the greatest market power excel in technical advance. In fact it would appear that less-dominant companies originate more of the important new developments. Yet there is undoubtedly a size below which research and development are not viable (Kennedy and Thirwall 1972, p. 49; and Bain 1968, p. 460).

Inasmuch as technological change is related to individual creativity, and incidence of ingenuity if not genius, some writers feel that advances in knowledge, and thus technological change, are a function of population growth and/or size, at least in MDCs (Simon 1977). Also, population growth in preindustrial, seminomadic societies is said to induce the adoption in many instances of more advanced techniques of agricultural production (Boserup 1965).

Nathan Rosenberg (1976, chaps. 5, 6, 11) contends that a main source of technological change is programmed in the complex web of industrial machine technology that creates the need for and points toward the next innovation. Such technology also helps to form the type of human capital essential to accomplishing the job. Technological change begets technological change when there is a capital goods sector. The rate of invention of new methods, or variation in that rate, according to Rosenberg, may be traceable to unusually strong historical forces. Such forces disturb a weaker innovative effort when they threaten the firm's existence. Examples are war-born disruptions of main supply sources or unusual labor unrest that threatens the supply of workers.

The Diffusion of Technology

More is known about the diffusion of technology than about the causes of its rate of change. This is somewhat encouraging to the development economist since the LDC will usually borrow, adopt, and adapt known techniques. And this process should have some kinship to the diffusion of technology in advanced economies.

Schumpeter thought the business cycle and availability of low-interest bank credit affected the timing of innovation and its diffusion. In his view the diffusion process took less time than the business cycle and competitive forces ensured this relatively rapid spread. Historically, this does not appear to have been the case; the process is usually more time-consuming.

In a pioneering study, W. Salter (1960) found that economic conditions influence the timing and diffusion of technology, but that determining variables differ among firms. Factors leading to the rapid adoption of a new technique in the industry as a whole were expected profitability, short payoff period, less concentration in the industry, low ancillary costs of adopting the new techniques, and lower age of the existing capital stock.

Edwin Mansfield (1971, p. 88) notes that dissemination is a learning process both formal and informal in nature. He identifies four principal factors determining the diffusion rate of new technology: (1) the extent of the economic advantage of the innovation over older methods or products, (2) the degree of uncertainty associated with using the innovation when it first appears, (3) the extent of the commitment required to try out the innovation, and (4) the rate of reduction of the initial uncertainty regarding the innovation's performance. Technological diffusion will be more rapid when in relation to others the new methods and/or equipment are expected to be relatively profitable yet require relatively less investment financing, and the anticipated risk associated with adopting them is relatively low.

An industry's propensity to assume risk also affects the rate of adoption. "For equally profitable innovations requiring the same investment, the rate of adoption in one industry might be higher than in another because firms in that industry are more inclined to take risks, the industry's markets are more keenly competitive, or the industry is healthier financially." (Mansfield 1971, p. 90). Diffusion is more likely to be prolonged when the adopter must acquire new knowledge, change behavior patterns, or coordinate the efforts of a number of organizations. Moreover the amount of supportive and complementary economic activity necessary to prevent bottlenecks in production can affect adoption. And even for advanced Western economies, which are the focus of these studies, innovation is found to spread more rapidly where it ". . . requires few changes in sociocultural values and behavior patterns . . ." (p. 91).

Turning to the firm, Mansfield identifies characteristics that can set the pace of adoption of new techniques. He finds the firm's size and profit expectations from the new technology are two variables that often influence diffusion (pp. 93–94). In relation to LDCs, Rosenberg (1976, chap. 11) identifies the sophistication of the machine tools sector as affecting diffusion.

Some Generalizations

The threads of analysis pertaining to technological change under different levels of development, economic organization, and historical periods yield persistently similar patterns that vary more in coloration than overall design. Like the proverbial carrot and stick, profits and losses are closely associated with the creation of technological advances and their diffusion. This is true under both historical conditions of atomistic competition and less competitive conditions, where the behavior patterns of large firms and the entry of new firms help determine competitive pressures. Because there are externalities associated with technological change, the government has a role in ensuring that the appropriate amount of resources are devoted to research and development. In completely planned economies such as the Soviet Union where market pressures are largely absent, and profits and losses redound to the state, bureaucratic directives have been substituted for competitive profit and loss. International competition is a spur to state action. The system, according to Western analysts, has been more successful to date in borrowing technology than creating it anew or modifying it.

The financing of new technology, especially capital goods, whether by private profits and savings, new money and inflation, or public savings from taxes or profits of government-owned firms, is integral to technological change and can limit the rate of change. The attitudes toward risk of the individual, the firm, and the government affect behavior patterns under the inevitable uncertainty that marks technological change. The sophistication of the machine-goods industry in earlier periods of development played a historical role in diffusion. And last, but perhaps most important for technological evolution in LDCs, the reluctance to change sociocultural values and behavior patterns to accommodate technological advance can prevent, impede, or slow such change. Education aimed at transforming sociocultural networks incompatible with development is costly and time-consuming. Moreover, formal education can be the captive of the forces inhibiting change and thus, according to Hagen, cannot inculcate behavior patterns necessary for innovation.

The Transfer of Technology

Among the vast stock of technology worldwide, some will be economic for absorption by LDCs. In borrowing methods currently used in modern nations, LDCs will be changing from very primitive technology in many cases and thus attempting to overleap a technology gap that is wide by historical standards. Countries such as Japan and the Soviet Union faced lesser gaps in their early stages of development.

At first blush, this stock of technology appears to be a great advantage to a latecomer. Such LDCs will not have to await many technological breakthroughs unavailable at comparable levels of development for MDCs. The costs of financing new technology has been borne mainly by others. Of course technology is not free-floating. It resides somewhere in machinery and equipment, in human skills and human capital, and in the organization and institutions of a society. These complementary resources must be available or the technology cannot be absorbed. Moreover the most efficient technology may not be of value to a poor country if it applies only to goods or services not used at lower-income levels, or requires economies of scale not attainable in low-income markets. And absorption calls for human attitudes toward risk and change that, while not necessarily as creative as those required for de novo innovation, are at least responsive to opportunities for economic improvement.

Hagen has divided the development process into stages that describe the evolution of technical absorptive capacity in industry (1975, chap. 6).

Stage 1: Advance in Self-Contained Processes In this phase exposure to advanced processes used abroad can lead to the adoption of simple machinery and techniques for producing familiar goods widely used such as rice or wheat flour, footwear, lumber or other building materials, and textiles. The production process at this stage must be straight-lined and self-contained. It does not require feed-ins or vital linkages with other sectors or suppliers, other than raw materials readily available and storable. A technically more subdivided input-output matrix is beyond the organization and scale capacities of the economy at this stage. Foremanship and worker discipline must develop.

Stage 2: Increases in Interrelationships In this stage specialization of production will occur in items common to many firms, such as industrial chemicals and packaging materials or cement. Mechanical and metalworking skills within the country develop so that simple tools and machines, formerly imported, can be produced, repaired, and maintained locally. Capital intensity and scale increase along with linkages, and there may be some outside financing.

Stage 3: Expansion of Light Engineering In this phase the manufacture of light engineering goods such as bicycles and metal casings for consumer durables expands more rapidly than industry in general. The products must not require too exacting specifications.

Stage 4: Control of Quality and Tolerances By this stage the strands of the input-output matrix have woven themselves into a net as the country produces simple machines, transport vehicles, and fairly complex metal products. The industrial complex is capable of handling quality and size tolerances of the more complex techniques used in production of these goods. The need to diversify and limit individual risk arises. This can be accomplished by the corporation, and leads to a more complex legal framework for the firm. Some professional management appears along with depersonalization of business relationships formerly dominated by family interconnections.

These stages lead up to the last one, the industrial complexity of advanced countries. It take several generations at the minimum before the country can turn out goods meeting exacting quality tolerances and demanding high human skills. At a point in time, some sectors of a country can be in different stages, especially where technical dualism has resulted from government planning policies that affect sectors unevenly. A country cannot bypass a developmental stage but can accelerate it, according to Hagen, if its people have the technical ingenuity and entrepreneurial resourcefulness that characterized, for example, Japan.[1] Moreover, foreign firms do not play a role until stage four and cannot accomplish technical leaps for an LDC as a whole.

Industrial Concentration and Technology Transfer

There is some support for the idea that concentrated market structures in LDCs have facilitated the *transfer* of technology and economized on the level of entrepreneurship or decision-making needed for the transfer. In LDCs many large firms are integrated vertically to a greater degree than their counterparts in advanced countries. There is less specialization and subdivision of functions in nascent market economies, in part because of a need to mobilize and ensure supplies of various inputs. Sometimes the functions of firms are extended when they enter areas that are complementary, either technically or economically, or when such expansion allows them to internalize gains that otherwise might be absorbed by other firms or redound to the general economy. Such conglomerate organization easily emerges in economies that do not control monopolizing activity, and in centrally planned economies. When capital markets are underdeveloped such firms will internalize that function, often seeking out wealthy families as sources of financing. A relatively small number of firms and families, then, may dominate the economy. Their orientation is towards imitation within their enclave of the advanced technology and products of affluent industrialized economies at relatively early stages of development.

Nathaniel Leff (1979) argues that such organization by firms, which he refers to as "The Group," has aided development by overcoming bottlenecks, particularly shortages of entrepreneurship, and high risks in LDCs that would otherwise have prevented absorption of Western technology. Others are critical and say such organization severely distorts the economy, creating dualism, so that continued technical evolution is stymied.

---

1. The government in Japan played an important role in the transfer process in providing innovative leadership, financing of investment, and reduction of uncertainty and risk connected with new technology.

Since The Group creates new distortions in the process of overcoming original ones, it cannot be viewed as a best solution. As discussed in chapter 6, uncertainties and risk arising from characteristics of underdevelopment can be reduced in ways that attack the problems more directly with government help or participation while avoiding new distortions. In the absence of well-designed government policies, islands of hierarchical control such as The Group's operations are historically common. In Japan in earlier periods The Group, known as the *zaibatsu*, was important to technical transfer. The government was effectual in overseeing the development role of member firms. Today The Group in LDCs may control the government. And in reaction to this power, dominant firms are often the object of nationalization attempts. In Mexico The Group has been very powerful, despite the leftist ideology prominent within factions of the ruling Institutional Revolutionary Party. The government in Mexico, however, controls many sectors of the economy.

The Multinational Firm and Technology Transfer

At earlier stages the LDC imports managerial and technical services that may have some impact on transplanting technology or lead to transfers at later stages. The multinational or transnational corporation does not locate in LDCs in areas other than raw material production to any great degree until industrial development is more advanced. However, in such later phases the multinational firm can be a conduit for the transfer of technology. Because of its size, knowledge, and power, countries that have experienced colonial domination commonly view such a firm with grave reservations.

Most LDCs consider the multinational firm a mixed blessing as far as technology transfer is concerned. Not unlike The Group, with which it may construct a partnership (oftentimes due to government edict precluding complete foreign ownership), it can internalize gains from its technical monopoly and limit positive spillover for the LDC. There is evidence that in some cases a relatively high price via royalties and profits is paid for the technology. Skill development may be helped or harmed. The foreign manufacturing firm in LDCs has the potential for replacing budding entrepreneurship and usurping scarce local inputs. Generally it has been necessary to pass laws compelling the multinational firm to train and employ local labor in higher-level skill areas before the firm would do so, preferring to import its own personnel for more skilled jobs. Yet there is no doubt that the foreign firm can raise the technical level in an LDC and the absorption rate for modern technology. The Republic of Ireland is a case in point. Chapter 13 explains how Ireland's export capacity picked up when multinationals moved in. As mentioned, foreign firms will not begin the industrialization process in predominately agrarian settings, however. The LDC must accomplish the technical transformation associated with the beginning of industrial activity through its own channels of technical transfer.

Various multinational corporations have broken down the production process so that the more labor-intensive segments can be produced in LDCs. Some Western economists view this as a rationalizing of global production, with efficiency effects upon world income. LDCs have been quick to note, however, that this transfers less technology and trains the domestic work force only in simpler techniques. They also point out that internal pricing policies of the multinational may appropriate the efficiency gains for countries other than the LDC.

Product and process adaptation in response to conditions in a particular LDC are generally not economic for the large multinational corporation that centralizes its research and development and duplicates its operation processes worldwide to achieve scale effects. Such corporations have the ability to raise cheap capital in world financial markets. They have little incentive to reduce greatly their capital intensity and absorb labor when the total operation is located in the LDC, as opposed to a labor-intensive segment of the operation.

All in all, the multinational corporation as an instrument of technical transfer has some drawbacks in regard to timing and other LDC needs. Yet in many cases it has made strong contributions to technical absorption. And individual multinational corporations have undoubtedly contributed to technical transfer while avoiding the disadvantages mentioned. The multinational firms' potential for creating economic distortions means that governments in LDCs generally circumscribe their operations. The multinational corporation is also a source of savings, and affects the balance of payments of LDCs. These topics are discussed in chapter 13, which develops a graphical analysis of the impact of the foreign firm upon the LDC.

The Institutional Component of Technology Transfer

Modernization of institutions that influence the economy can take varying forms. Institution-building for development does not require rigid adherence to specified blueprints. Various combinations of social organizations can support modernization. Yet, the process of establishing new institutions or modifying existing ones is slow and sometimes socially disruptive. The need for changes in human organization limits the pace of technological advance, preventing rapid transformation. The human element—the rate at which individuals and groups will modify their behavior patterns—determines the rate at which new techniques of production can be absorbed. Innovative transformation of institutions is an important component of development, and of technology transfer in particular.

At early stages of development 80 percent or more of the population is engaged in near-subsistence agriculture. Technological absorption in farming is extremely difficult despite technology that transplants well into small-scale production units without demanding relatively large amounts of scarce capital and skilled labor. The clues to the absorption problems of this sector lie in the need to change sociocultural behavior patterns plus a production function characterized by high risk, in part rooted in the vagaries of weather.

In traditional agriculture the custom-bound social and economic institutions along with the ancient technology have ensured survival, albeit rather precarious survival, through history. Customs and mores, passed through illiterate generations, are the conduits for transmitting knowledge and establishing authority. Acceptance of new education sources is slow. Vested interests reside in the systems of land ownership and village authority. Many of the behavior patterns, social relations, vested interests, socioeconomic organizations, and farming practices must change with the absorption of modern agricultural techniques.

While market forces can play a constructive role, innovative leadership and financing for technical change must depend in some measure upon government policies. The orientation of the government bureaucracy frequently requires institutional reform before needed agricultural policies are emphasized. Institutional balance is not easily achieved when bureaucrats denigrate agriculture. Also, enlightened government leadership often requires breaking the hold over policies and resources of an agricultural elite or an industry-oriented political structure.

The Green Revolution in agriculture is a social phenomenon as much as an economic one. In India, a country with a cadre of sophisticated government planning personnel and more advanced agricultural techniques than most African countries, it took over 15 years to change wheat farming from its traditional patterns. Rice farming has not yet been transformed. Problems arose in developing institutions needed for meaningful tenancy reform; for storage and marketing of crops; for distribution of irrigation water, seed, fertilizer and fuel; for absorption of surplus labor (including the breakup of the illegal caste system); and for production incentives, including reduction of risk and prices. Methods of a more authoritarian and collective nature used by communist governments such as China or Albania to speed agricultural transformation have not yielded superior results, and in some cases have yielded declines in productivity. They have avoided extremes of dualism in the changeover period and distributed the output more equally, however.

In contrast to the change-resistant rural sector, the more urban commercial or industrial sectors have more literacy, flexibility, and exposure to modern techniques; and individuals' attitudes toward risk are not conditioned by weather disasters. Moreover, this minority of the population has usually attracted some of the younger, more innovative, and venturesome farm people, reducing somewhat the incidence of these traits in the agricultural sector. Yet for any sector, the absorption of modern technology or its adaptation is a time-consuming process, demanding social conditioning and careful selection of the technology to be transferred if the transplant is to produce development instead of an alien modern graft subject to rejection in all but small enclave areas of the economy. A country such as Israel, made up of social institutions and human capital imported from advanced economies, can overcome the shortage of natural resources and achieve modernity in a quarter of a century when financing from outside sources is available. Similar change could take a century for countries with few human skills and lacking modern social institutions, even if they are relatively favorably endowed with natural resources.

SELECTION AND   The previous section concluded a broad-based discussion of techno-
ADAPTATION OF   logical change. It is helpful at this point to pinpoint economic effi-
TECHNOLOGY   ciency conditions for selection and adaptation of technology.

Factor Intensive   The production isoquant of the textbook reflects the state of technology.
Isoquants   It can be constructed without knowledge of relative factor prices. An
isoquant is a technical efficiency frontier that identifies for a selected
output level all the techniques that are most efficient in producing that
amount of output with varying quantities of two factor inputs. Thus
output q_1 may be producible with relatively more or fewer capital inputs, but some other resources must vary inversely with those inputs.
The isoquant includes only techniques that minimize the amount of
the replacement resource needed, say labor, for a given reduction in
the amount of capital. The other techniques are less efficient and thus
excluded. Neither resource can be decreased beyond some limit. At
some point, further reductions in capital are not technically feasible,
that is, there is no known technique that would allow output q_1 to be
produced with less capital. This holds analogously for labor.

When there are two goods produced with the same two resources,
say capital and labor, and relative factor prices are given, the factor
intensity of the two can be compared. It is possible that for any quantity
produced of these commodities where costs are minimized, one item
will always have a higher K/L ratio. When for *any set* of relative factor
prices selected, one good is always more capital intensive, this good
is identified as the relatively capital-intensive one. The other is then
classified as relatively labor-intensive.

It should be noted that the production function of a good characterized as relatively capital-intensive need not exhibit a constant K/L
ratio at all output levels, given a set of relative factor prices. All that
is required is that the capital-intensive item be more capital-intensive
when compared with the labor-intensive one under all conditions.
Economies of scale in the production of some goods can lower K/L
ratios as output becomes larger, given the same relative factor prices.
On the other hand, some studies show a range of increasing K/L ratios
as output expands. Since LDCs have small markets and limited capacity for capital formation, goods that are relatively labor-intensive or
that use relatively less capital at small output levels will conserve on
scarcer resources.

LDCs and MDCs will have different relative factor prices, with
capital (physical and human) being relatively cheaper in MDCs. As a
result, when producing the same good as MDCs, LDCs will use techniques that are more labor-intensive in order to minimize costs, assuming low-skill labor is priced to reflect its scarcity value relative to capital. Thus for production of both capital-intensive and labor-intensive
goods, LDCs will choose techniques that allow conservation of scarce
human and physical capital when these factors reflect their scarcity
value. However, when production functions are technically limited
there may be little leeway for substituting labor for capital. And LDCs

are then forced to adopt techniques similar to those used in MDCs if they choose to produce such goods.

Technological change affecting processes renders methods previously used obsolete, in other words, inefficient. The new technology may supersede the old completely or just replace old techniques for some output and K/L ranges. Thus the most modern equipment may be efficient only at MDC relative factor costs, while vintage equipment remains efficient at relative factor costs found in LDCs. Technological change can reduce the amount of labor and/or capital needed for output and thus change the degree of factor intensity. Modern technology of more recent vintage is in some cases so efficient, especially at high output levels, that it uses both less capital and less of other resources than much older production processes that are relatively labor-intensive. This is especially true when the current technology replaces techniques of cottage industries where one or two people use ancient skills to make simple goods like cloth, utensils, shoes, and other items of daily use.

Isoquants from real-world data seldom reflect the total relative factor intensities for a production function that is fully integrated, one where there are no purchased inputs such as electricity and other utilities, raw materials and semifinished intermediate goods, wholesaling and retailing. Only knowledge such as this, however, would enable us to identify the true relative factor intensities of different goods or techniques. The capital intensity ratios for manufactured goods found in statistical data usually relate just to the value-added portion, and do not reflect the capital-intensive nature of the communications, transportation, power, and other elements of the economic infrastructure required by modern technology. This point is more than academic since many LDCs have been advised to develop and subsidize modern capital-intensive infrastructure as a prerequisite to modernization and industrialization. Once such infrastructure is in place, then the latest techniques of production in industry that utilize such inputs will often be the most efficient, even when labor's wage is relatively low. A provocative question is whether or not this superiority in efficiency over more labor-intensive techniques is for some goods the outgrowth of the government subsidized infrastructure. Vintage techniques often needed less capital-intensive infrastructure, one possible reason being that transportation and energy costs were relatively higher at the time these techniques were developed.

The textbook isoquant, illustrated in figure 5.1, is certainly naive in its assumption of numerous alternative techniques that, over a given range, allow for continuous factor substitution. Moreover, unused techniques may not be *operational* ones in the real world. The former require expenditure when not in use to make them operational. Such costs must be compared with potential savings from the technique. Thus, relative and absolute factor prices become in part determinants of operational techniques. And technical change in MDCs affects the value of vintage equipment and hence its attractiveness to LDCs. It can also have an effect upon the price and availability of spare parts for this equipment when MDCs are the main suppliers.

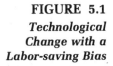

FIGURE 5.1

Technological Change with a Labor-saving Bias

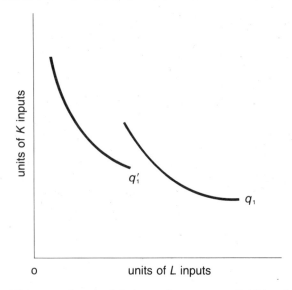

Isoquant q_1 shifts upward to the left, becoming more capital-intensive.

Biased Technological Change

This discussion flows easily into the causes of the suspected bias in modern technological change. Data appear to support a trend over time for scientific advances applied to industry to be labor-saving in that they decrease the amount of labor used per unit of physical capital. That is, technological change causes production functions to become more physical capital intensive. It is believed that the data supporting this do not just reflect the cheapening of capital relative to aggregate labor costs with the accumulation of capital stock over time, and the consequent tendency for capital to be substituted for labor. Instead the isoquant is said to have shifted inward, as shown in figure 5.1, from q_1 to q_1' in a nonneutral fashion, being skewed toward the capital axis with technological advance. The effect is said to be pervasive enough that economies with relatively high L/K ratios are at a disadvantage.

The idea that this capital intensity bias is not a "natural drift" determined entirely by outside variables such as the laws of physics, but is partly determined from within by economic variables has been put forth by several writers. S. Ahmad (1966), W. Fellner (1970), and J. R. Hicks (1964), consider the idea that rising labor prices can induce innovation with a capital-intensive bias designed to save on the relatively expensive factor. Habakkuk (1962) and Rosenberg (1972) have compared the historical sequence of inventions in early America with that in Europe, arguing that relatively cheap capital and expensive labor induced a higher incidence of labor-saving inventions in the United States. Critics have pointed out that the reduction of any factor input can increase profits, and dispute the stimulus of relative factor costs to technological bias.

Less attention has been paid to identifying a historical bias in skilled-labor intensity with modern technology, particularly by industry breakdowns. When modern capital requires labor with longer periods of training and education, it can be said to be more human-capital intensive. However, where modern machinery simplifies the task so that less skilled labor is needed, the opposite bias can occur. The presumption is that for the total economy, there is a bias of modern technology toward higher skilled-labor intensity not connected with the greater abundance and hence relatively lower price in MDCs of skilled labor.

In an LDC, the ability to forgo consumption so as to invest, and to forgo earnings in order to acquire education, is limited because of low incomes. Thus inputs that can be devoted to capital formation, both human and physical, are limited. Consequently these resources are in relatively short supply. LDCs will thus be restricted in their ability to absorp modern technology when it is biased toward this type of resource intensity since poor nations will have less of the necessary complementary resources.

Intermediate Technology, Product Adaptation

Are modern techniques less flexible in their range of factor substitutability than obsolete ones? That is, have the isoquants over time become not only more skewed toward human or physical capital intensity, but are they also more L-shaped, indicating a lower elasticity of substitution of unskilled labor for these factors? The thinking is that this indeed may be the case, again striking a blow at the simple idea that technology is easily transferred.

The LDC faced with these limitations can minimize the severity of their impact by policies that affect the product mix and by innovative adaptations of product and process. Consider first the effect of variations in product mix upon the absorption of modern technology. If through specialization and trade and/or influence of demand factors, the LDC can concentrate more on turning out goods that use less of the country's relatively scarce resources, this can offset somewhat the effects of factor intensity bias.

The product mix, especially when income inequality is high, can be shaped by the "demonstration effect," the demand for modern goods as prestige symbols or simply as a means to attain the living standards of advanced nations. Such goods include consumer durables, government subsidized airlines, and defense weaponry. These commodities are introduced by trade and then imports are replaced by home production. Rigid imitation of the quality and type of foreign product desired leaves little leeway for flexibility in factor substitution.

Japan offers an outstanding historical example of an LDC that avoided a large demonstration effect upon her product mix except in circumscribed areas like the military. Even though income inequality was not historically low, the controls over consumer imports and the strong traditionalism in Japanese tastes shaped her product mix so that consumption favored time-honored products that utilized relatively simple labor skills intensively and so conserved on capital. Even when foreign goods introduced new tastes, the Japanese were quick to adapt the manufacture of these to their land's more available resources.

Sometimes this changed the product's quality or nature and gave it a more national flavor.

The Japanese also shine as innovators in the area of process adaptation. They were adept at making use of older machinery bought cheaply abroad, and changing the production method and equipment to conserve on their scarce resources. For today's LDCs, however, the technology gap is wider and there is a felt need, according to some development economists, for an international effort to devise technology that is less intensive in human and physical capital. This technology would be closer to the labor-intensity ratios of primitive or early vintage know-how but more efficient, and thereby competitive with modern technology; hence the name "intermediate" or "appropriate" technology. Research centers for the development of such innovations now exist.

In the development of intermediate technology some economists emphasize the production process as the appropriate focus, others stress capital equipment, and others the final product. The late E. F. Schumacher (1973) was a proponent of a technology and product change that would be smaller scale and less environmentally destructive. Frances Stewart (1977) describes the characteristics of appropriate technology and the changes it would bring in an LDC with a backward sector and a sector using inappropriate modern technology. Suitable technology would yield goods that use locally produced inputs and are standardized to fulfill basic needs of the total population as opposed to a rich elite. The production process is preferably small scale and labor intensive compared with modern technology, and uses machinery that is simple to make, operate, and maintain.

Actually the technology of the Green Revolution and some equipment developed for agriculture are examples of successful intermediate technology, except perhaps in their environmental impact. The breakthroughs were developed in agricultural research centers staffed by personnel from advanced and LDC countries and financed in great part by funds from MDCs. LDC governments are participating in the ongoing research necessary to stay abreast of new diseases, pests, and genetic mutations that can hamper their progress.

The development of intermediate technology for industry would be particularly helpful for countries such as many African nations, where both physical and human capital are well below the demands of modern technology. Be allowing small-scale, labor-intensive manufacturing, intermediate technology could avoid the sharp dualism of a very small manufacturing sector trying unsuccessfully to match the quality and efficiency standards of modern technology, and absorbing the limited capital in a few, government-favored projects. Poor, labor-surplus economies would also be potential beneficiaries.

Rosenberg and others are exploring the idea that the development of a domestic capital goods industry is a prerequisite to innovation leading to intermediate technology. The experimental research whose breakthroughs in plant hybrids made possible the Green Revolution were unique in that MDCs assumed a leadership role; their scientists devised a highly applicable process for various conditions of world agriculture that yielded dramatic improvements in yield per acre. In industry, the argument goes, nothing so spectacular will develop. Rather, on-the-scene feed-in and feedback from day-to-day operations must, with the stimulus of profits, generate small innovations in response to local conditions. Those who emphasize capital equipment as the locus of technological change argue that the existence of a domestic capital goods industry, even if small and limited in scope, is vital to the development of intermediate technology responsive to locally appropriate technological change. Feed-in or feedback networks or profits are not significant enough to induce the development of intermediate technology by the capital goods industry in MDCs that are the main suppliers of capital goods to LDCs. Nor has the on-the-scene multinational firm responded to local conditions in a manner that would foster intermediate technology.

Inasmuch as small LDCs with limited GNP per capita cannot readily support a capital goods industry, the possible contributions of specialization and trade among LDCs in capital goods is being explored. Frances Stewart also foresees beneficial potential in increased trade among LDCs in appropriate goods of all types. India now exports some machinery that might be classified as intermediate technology.

The financing of the development of intermediate technology has not been examined intensively. Yet, the importance to technological change of financing sources has already been emphasized. A U.S. Department of Commerce study (1967) finds that research and development costs consist primarily of tooling and manufacturing engineering expenses, while the costs of the basic invention and subsequent engineering design compose at most 30 percent of costs and may go as low as 15 percent. Thus costs at the firm level for new ideas from research centers can be high. Would private profits in LDCs be an adequate spur? Would not foreign aid and national government subsidies be a prerequisite? If the greatest applicability for intermediate technology is in the least-developed LDCs, would their risk function, innovational talents, and institutions be sufficient for the task at hand? If not, can an international framework conducive to the development of intermediate technology on a scale adequate for the task be designed and instituted? These are questions pertinent but as yet unanswered.

The implications of intermediate technology for labor absorption and employment, capital needs, and the productivity of both can be illustrated with the graph shown in figure 5.2. Modern technology requires moving from $\bar{L}/K_1$ with low capital and labor productivity α_{t_1}, β_{t_1}, to L_u/K_3 with high labor productivity, β_{t_3}, but some unemployed labor and the importation of large amounts of capital, K_3. The economy using intermediate technology has a more moderate need for capital formation, K_2, and yet has the ability to employ her people fully with equally high output ($\beta_{t_2}\bar{L} = \beta_{t_3}L_u$). Capital productivity of intermediate technology, α_{t_2}, is greater than α_{t_3}, and the L/K ratio is higher. With continuous technological change, the growth in capital productivity relative to that in labor productivity will be higher for intermediate than modern technology. In this example, then, the emphasis is upon raising capital efficiency. Analogously, the emphasis might also be upon

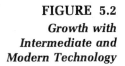

FIGURE 5.2
Growth with
Intermediate and
Modern Technology

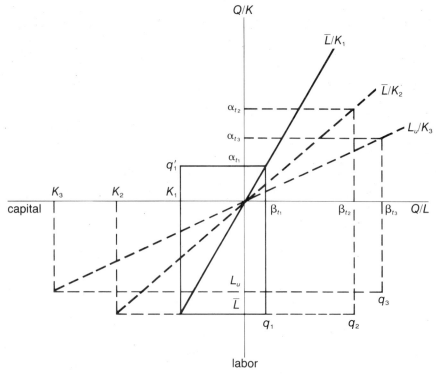

Growth with intermediate technology and full employment expands output to $\beta_{t_2}\bar{L}$, using K_2 capital stock. Growth with modern technology and unemployment expands output to $\beta_{t_3}L_u$ and requires K_3 capital stock. Total output is the same.

increasing human capital efficiency and decreasing the need for as much human capital inputs.

TECHNOLOGICAL CHANGE AND LIMITS TO GROWTH

Throughout the study of economic development, economists have worried about the effects of diminishing returns related to the slowest growth factor, which is judged to be natural resources. Population growth can mean each laborer has fewer resources to work with when natural resources and capital do not keep up; and, all else being equal, such a condition reduces labor productivity, the determinant of income per capita. Even when capital growth exceeds that of population, unless there is (1) a favorable elasticity of substitution between capital and natural resources so that capital can efficiently replace natural resources of increasing scarcity, and (2) capital growth is adequate to fulfill substitution needs and population growth needs, then per capita income will decline because of diminishing returns.

In a less aggregate sense, when some sectors are strongly affected by diminishing returns, the question becomes: Will they be bottleneck sectors for growth? Or, can the effect of diminishing returns be minimized or avoided altogether by changing the product mix so that this sector's products are not limiting to growth? The Classical economists concentrated on food production as a potential bottleneck sector sufficiently important to halt further growth in per capita income or population. The major portion of the world's diet is wheat, rice and, to a lesser degree, corn, a very basic diet that does not present potential for greater food consumption efficiency. Thus there has been concern for the effect of growing population upon world food supply. Similarly, fuel plays a fundamental role in the MDC economy. Its growing scarcity and the lack of substitute sources of energy create the potential for a bottleneck sector.

Less attention has been given to the effect upon growth that diminishing returns to capital have, although Lord Keynes considered the matter. In a process of growth, capital tends to increase relative to both labor and natural resources. As mentioned, this works to mitigate the drop in labor productivity that can come with a relatively slow growth in natural resources. However, when this expansion in capital leads to a lower marginal product for capital and, under competitive conditions, a lower rate of return, capital accumulation will be affected. Profits have been identified as an important, even vital, element in the motivation of further capital accumulation. Theoretically a level of profits could be reached where there was no incentive for further capital growth.

In summary, population growth without technological change, eventually will lead to a decline in per capita output and income. Simon Kuznets suspects that in some Asian countries this has indeed happened. In MDCs technological progress has improved the efficiency of all factors, overcoming diminishing returns. Its specific impact on each factor is worth noting.

The effect of technological change upon capital has been to offset some, if not all, of the effects of diminishing returns to capital accumulation. This in turn has maintained a level of profits consistent with further capital accumulation and technological change.

As for natural resources, technological change has conserved natural resource input needs per unit of output, increased the substitutability among resources, created new ones, and devised methods to recycle and renew natural resources, and has also improved the ability to locate and extract new stores of them. A leading example of dramatic strides in technology is the Green Revolution in agriculture, which increased output per acre many times over. And new techniques in genetic engineering hold promises of further inportant changes in agriculture.

The effect of technological progress upon labor has been to raise human productivity and create new services and products to absorb people displaced by technology. Technological breakthroughs in health have contributed to the large increase in population, while those in other areas such as petrochemicals have offset in part positive health effects by blighting the human environment.

Advances in technology have not just affected the supply side of natural resources. Through their effect upon productivity, they have helped to raise productive capacity and income, leading to higher levels of demand. Growth in demand pressures natural resources that are limited in quantity and have few substitutes. Yet in many cases such demand upswings have undoubtedly stimulated technological change on the supply side to alleviate shortages. The more rapidly demand levels expand, the more likely there will be short-run bottlenecks before technological responses can be developed on the supply side. But with technological responsiveness, some diminishing return effects have undoubtedly been held to the short-run.

The Case of LDCs Today

A major problem faces LDCs today, one that was not present in its current intensity for MDCs at similar stages of development, except perhaps Japan. That problem is the relatively high ratio of population to natural resources for many nation-states along with the absence of geographic areas open to and suitable for out-migration. During the historical periods of discovery and colonization of the Americas and other "new lands" with very low indigenous populations relative to land and other resources, these new countries had increasing returns to population growth. That is, there were so few people to begin with that resources lay idle in large quantities and more inhabitants resulted in the existing resources being used more efficiently. Thus the marginal product of labor was rising rather than falling, labor was in great demand, and a widow with 10 children could quickly remarry. Moreover, the mother countries of Europe did not know the population pressures of China, Taiwan, Java Island in Indonesia, or Korea today. Even Japan's present-day densities are high relative to the beginning of its development 100 years ago.

The point is, some of today's LDCs have already encountered sharply diminishing returns because of limited natural resources even prior to development. This means their development effort must produce a higher rate of capital formation, and/or their technological development and product mix must be more conservative of resources than better-endowed countries. All three conditions held for Japanese development. She has had historically high capital formation over certain periods, her patterns of consumption and her trade specialization have helped her conserve on less abundant natural resource inputs, and she has pioneered in technological innovation that conserves on her relatively scarce factors.

Needless to say, diminishing returns due to limited natural resources are more easily forestalled during a successful growth process with technological momentum than under conditions of very low per capita income in a country that has yet to establish a development push. One can feel optimistic when contemplating the success of Taiwan and Korea in the postwar period. However, their achievement, not unlike that of Israel, is associated with a very high rate of inflow per capita of aid and foreign capital during strategic periods, and with a successful foreign trade effort not easily duplicated in today's trade situation. Also, they have brought their population growth under control, as did Japan in its historical development.

Some LDCs today are relatively well endowed with resources, and many do not suffer from the high population densities of Asian countries. Those less densely inhabited countries with low per capita income levels are poor because of primitive technology, not diminishing returns to labor. Their inability to control their birth rate as health conditions improve, however, could lead to pressures on resources. Diminishing returns related to natural resources is not the ogre the doomsayers would have us believe. But it is a formidable force where technological change is absent and population pressures are intense. The technical expertise of the West is effective in overcoming diminishing returns, but, with exceptions such as agriculture, it is often a very capital-intensive technology. Thus intermediate technology that conserves on capital, should it be developed, must work within the confines of resource scarcities if it is to be appropriate for labor-surplus LDCs. This difficult task is more easily accomplished if the product as well as the production process can be adapted.

The last secton of this chapter discusses the early development of the machine tools industry of Taiwan, a densely populated country. In this industry we find product adaptation, small-scale operations with specialized production runs, a lack of linkages or supplier specialization within the industry, a lack of exacting quality tolerances or standardized parts, and little external financing by family-run firms. Efficiency in the Taiwanese machine tools industry depended on three factors: First, the production process was suited to the technical capacity levels of the country at the time, in part because of product adaptation. Second, the manufacturing process economized on scarce human and physical capital. And third, the industry's market structure met the needs of small-scale customers.

REFERENCES

Ahmad, S. 1966. On the Theory of Induced Invention. *Economic Journal* 76 (June): 344–57.

Amsden, Alice. 1977. The Division of Labor Is Limited by the Type of Market: The Case of the Taiwanese Machine Tool Industry. *World Development* vol. 5, no. 3: 217–33.

Bain, Joe S. 1968. *Industrial Organization.* New York: John Wiley and Sons.

Boserup, Ester. 1965. *The Conditions of Agricultural Growth.* Chicago: Aldine Publishing Co.

The Economist. 31 July 1982. Taiwan, A Survey. p. 9.

Fellner, W. 1970. Trends in the Activities Generating Technological Progress. *American Economic Review* 60 (March): 1–29.

Habakkuk, H. 1962. *American and British Technology in the Nineteenth Century.* Cambridge: Cambridge University Press.

Hagen, Everett E. 1962. *On the Theory of Social Change.* Homewood, Illinois: The Dorsey Press.

———1975. *The Economics of Development.* Rev. ed. Homewood, Illinois: Richard D. Irwin.

Heertje, Arnold. 1977. *Economics and Technological Change.* New York: John Wiley and Sons.

Hicks, J. R. 1964. *The Theory of Wages.* London: Macmillan and Co.

Kennedy, C. and Thirwall, A. T. 1972. Surveys in Applied Economics: Technical Progress. *Economic Journal* 82 (March): 11–72.

Leff, Nathaniel, H. 1979. Entrepreneurship and Economic Development: The Problem Revisited. *Journal of Economic Literature* 13 (March): 46–64.

Mansfield, Edwin. 1971. *Technological Change*. New York: W. W. Norton and Co.

————1972. *Technology and American Growth*. New York: Harper and Row Publishers.

Rosenberg, Nathan. 1976. *Prospectives on Technology*. New York: Cambridge University Press.

Salter, W. 1960. *Productivity and Technological Change*. London: Cambridge University Press.

Schumacher, E. F. 1973. *Small Is Beautiful: A Study of Economics as if People Mattered*. London: Blond and Briggs.

Schmookler, Jacob. 1966. *Invention and Economic Growth*. Cambridge, MA: Harvard University Press.

Schumpeter, J. A. 1942. *Capitalism, Socialism and Democracy*. New York: Harper and Brothers.

Simon, Julian. 1977. *The Economics of Population Growth*. Princeton, NJ: Princeton University Press.

Sombart, Werner. 1927. *Der Moderne Kapitalismus: Historisch Systematische Darstellung des Gesanteuropäischen*. Munich: Duncer and Humblot.

Stewart, Frances. 1977. *Technology and Underdevelopment*. Boulder, Colorado: Westview Press.

Tawney, R. H. 1926. *Religion and the Rise of Capitalism: A Historical Study*. New York: Harcourt, Brace and Company.

U.S. Department of Commerce. 1967. *Technological Innovation*. Washington, D.C. (January).

Weber, Max. 1930. *The Protestant Ethic and the Spirit of Capitalism*. New York: Charles Scribner's Sons.

Product Adaptation and Technology in the Taiwan Machine Tool Industry

Taiwan in the postwar period has made impressive strides toward development, in part with the help of foreign aid. Yet by any standards her internal dynamism has been outstanding. And she accomplished this with a rapid population growth rate of almost 3 percent until the 1970s. She lacked a natural resource base to support her industrial development past a certain stage and thus moved fairly early to the export of manufactures. Success in industrial development demanded technical absorption, adaptation, entrepreneurship, and labor skills. Here we look at an industry that without direct government subsidies or attention, developed during the import substitution period, then made the transition to export success under favorable external stimuli. The industry chosen, machine tools, has an integral link to successful technical development.

Taiwan has an official policy designed to foster technology absorption and development. Part of that policy is to attract foreign firms that will import the more advanced technology and allow the country to be competitive in exports in labor-intensive areas. The government also sets policies that encourage domestic firms to modernize and vie with foreign firms. Domestic corporations have succeeded in acquiring the technology for manufacturing products like sewing machines and electronics in competition with multinationals.

The government plays a catalyst role in certain fields in introducing new technology. Recently it set up a pilot plant and trained technicians in microelectronics. The plant incorporates advanced technology bought abroad from RCA and for which royalties must be paid. The private sector holds shares in the firm along with state-owned banks. The government has also sought contracts with foreign firms to undertake research particularly suited to Taiwan development potential. Manpower for modern technology is subsidized by public education. By international standards Taiwan educates a high proportion of engineers.

To date Taiwan's expenditure upon technology has not been large relative to GNP when compared with modern countries that are industrial leaders. A 1981 study showed that .6 percent of GNP was spent on science and technology. The private sector accounted for only 20 percent of such expenditures. Most firms in Taiwan are too small to undertake research and development on an efficient scale (*The Economist*, July 1982). The family firm is the rule in Taiwan and most businesses operate on a small capital base, borrowing from unorganized sources such as family and loan sharks. The machine tools industry typifies such organization.

The development of the machine tools industry in Taiwan in the period following World War II provides an example of growing technical capacity and also of technical limitations. Outside of the government-sponsored military area, machine tools capacity grew without direct subsidy in response to internal and then external market stimuli, catering to the lower end of the price-quality spectrum of the market. Certain characteristics of this market dictated industrial organization, and limited both specialization and the level of technical sophistication. Alice Amsden (1977) provides an interesting historical assessment of this important sector of Taiwan development from the period following World War II up to 1975.

Machine tool shops first arose to provide repair or reconditioning services to small local firms. From there they branched out into the manufacture of lathes, drill presses, punching machines, and other power tools. The industry even in its more modern form is not highly capital intensive. Skills are needed and the technical know-how as a whole was acquired relatively slowly and, to a great extent, in learning while doing. Some machine tools builders acquired their mechanical knowledge in the prewar period from the Japanese—either by being employed in that country or in Manchuria under Japanese occupation. A typical channel of technology diffusion was to copy pre-World War II models of simpler machine tools. Needless to say, techniques varied in the industry and there was very little standardization of processes or product. Most firms did not invest in formal training to upgrade their workers' skills. They could not afford such expenditures.

The industry and the market it served during this period were dominated by the family firm. The manufacture of machine tools combined a nucleus of progressive firms along with a majority using more primitive production techniques. In 1966, 80 percent of all machine tools firms had fewer than 20 employees. This dropped to somewhat more than half by 1973.

Yet at that time, only a handful of firms employed more than 100 workers (Amsden 1977, p. 223). The early period saw a competitive shakedown and by the early 1970s about 40 firms could be considered to be of fairly high standard. Eight firms accounted for almost half of all lathes built in 1972, and two large firms with 400 to 600 workers dominated the export trade.

The machine tools industry typically served family-run firms repairing and, to a lesser degree, producing metal and machine products. Shops repairing bicycles, taxis, rice-milling equipment, and agricultural implements were typical customers. Producers of spare parts for these types of repair services, as well as manufacturers of shoemaking machinery, sewing machines, and agricultural equipment bought domestic machine tools.

The distinguishing features of the tools themselves were that they were simpler types and cost-competitive with more technically sophisticated imports, in part due to a cost-quality tradeoff. The distinguishing feature of the industry's organization was its vertical integration. That is, each firm tended to be fairly self-sufficient, completing a whole range of processes such as iron casting, welding, heat treatment, electroplating, and making tools and dies. The industry was not large enough for further specialization until the 1970s. Thus its products were individualized for customers. The close tolerances of modern machine tools and interchangeability of parts could not be achieved. Even leading toolmakers, as late as the 1970s, produced roughly 90 percent of their parts internally (Amsden 1977, p. 223). Thus specialization and division of labor has been limited by the size and character of the market. This in turn has hampered to some degree further technical progress.

The strong desire to maintain the family-controlled business may also have played a part in firms' vertical integration and self-sufficiency. The industry would have needed outside capital to become more specialized, and a decline in the number of small firms. In many cases greater technical absorption and more sophistication was beyond the reach of the family group. The resistance to moving away from the family type of business organization has been described as follows:

> The relationship between family and business in Taiwan is very close; the head of the family wants to be boss of his own business too. Most of the big companies are still run and partly owned by their founders, while family members take many of the top positions. That is a strong incentive for men who would have become professional managers to go and found their own companies (The Economist, July 1982, p. 9).

Taiwan's machine tools industry did not have a symbiotic relationship with large manufacturers where new technical needs were transmitted from firm to tools producer. This contrasts with historical conditions, for example, in America. Rather, in Taiwan the most enterprising firms of the industry groped their way toward a standardized product to win orders from large manufacturers for less-sophisticated tools. More-sophisticated tools were imported.

As the domestic market began to limit the growth of the industry, there was a fortuitous increase in foreign demand during the Vietnam War and the prosperous period of the early 1970s. The cheap labor and simpler design of Taiwanese machine tools kept cost low and yielded a product that was attractive to export markets in other less-developed Asian countries and even in some more advanced countries such as Japan, Australia, and New Zealand. This brought efficiencies of scale not achieved in domestic production. By the 1970s between 25 percent and 40 percent of Taiwan's machine tools output was exported (Amsden 1977, p. 225). As mentioned, the more progressive large companies dominated the export picture. These firms were able to upgrade the quality of their product somewhat and standardize their parts more. Foreign buyers demanded standardized, interchangeable parts that could be ordered by catalogue. They were attracted to the technically simple version of the product that required less capital investment than higher quality tools.

Labor costs have been rising in Taiwan. This will eventually force her to the higher end of the quality spectrum if she is to remain competitive internationally. However, competition here means the industry must invest more in close tolerance equipment and technology. To raise the capital for this and institute the degree of flexibility needed in management, the family firm may have to fade.

Risk, Uncertainty, and Development*

chapter

6

The terms risk and uncertainty are often used interchangeably. They denote a state of limited and questionable knowledge in the world of economic activity. Uncertainty is common in the economic arena because information about variables affecting economic activity is imperfect. Action without a perfect information set requires risk assumption; the degree of risk varies with the characteristics of the information set.

LDCs are often classified as high-risk economies. Many times it is political uncertainties that are dominant among the risk variables identified. However, a combination of causes, both endogenous and exogenous to the economic system, contribute to conditions that make many if not most LDCs high-risk economies. Agriculture dominates the society at low levels of income, and weather and pests create great unpredictability there. The vicissitudes of foreign trade, especially for a country exporting only a few kinds of products, add to instability and uncertainty. Limited ability to respond technically, lack of accurate information, structural rigidities, inflation, and a host of other problems common to poorer economies contribute to uncertainty.

It is true that many types of risk are reduced with development. Yet development entails social and economic change; and such change cannot take place without its own uncertainty and risk. An economy that avoids risk where it is integral to economic advance will remain stagnant. Thus there is an interplay between risk assumption and development. There can be a reluctance in poorer economies to assume the risks accompanying development because of the high risks already prevalent. Consequently it is important for an LDC to recognize and deal with existing risk elements as well as the additional ones inherent in capital formation, technological change, agricultural transformation, and so on. Here a simple analysis of risk and risk assumption explores approaches to policymaking under risk. Then selected areas important to the development of the economy are considered from this standpoint.

Behavior Patterns Toward Risk

In addition to the degree of risk, the behavioral response to it by the populace engaged in economic activity is of major relevance. The entrepreneur's behavior toward risk was discussed in the last chapter. Attitudes toward it may vary among societies and groups within a society. Many institutionally shaped behavior patterns reflect group response to uncertainty.

When information is sparse, as it is in very poor economies, the people cling, to a technique of production that worked for their ancestors. This ancient method acquires religious sanctification and the potential for success in their folklore if the spirits or gods are appeased. Scholars examining the traditional society emphasize that behavior patterns passed down through generations have attributes that ensure

---

*This chapter is designed to deepen the reader's awareness and understanding of the effects of risk and uncertainty on economic responses, and thereby policy success, in LDCs. The chapter may be omitted without loss of continuity.

survival. This kind of society attempts to minimize risk by avoiding the uncertainty of experimentation. The unknowns of new activity are viewed as holding the potential for disaster. The outside observer often fails to grasp the role of established custom in dealing with risk and uncertainty. And the traditional society has no way to certify the reliability of outside experts and does not want to gamble that those bringing new methods have better knowledge than their ancestors. They are sometimes right, since the ouside experts may also be entering a new environment having uncertainties for them.

As the information set of the LDC enlarges and education improves, unswerving adherence to economic custom gives way to a willingness to use the improved information available to estimate the outcome of activity in more areas, that is, to form expectations about new behavior and compare them with the outcome expected from the old ways. Traditional practices are gradually opened to evaluation. As this occurs, custom dictates behavior in fewer areas of activity. The analysis developed in this chapter assumes the economic agent calculates and compares the risks of alternate economic behavior, at least in some areas, choosing the action that suits the agent's attitudes toward risk. Calculations of this type are necessary if economic performance is to improve since economies function efficiently only where the agents respond to changing information by adjusting their activity.

Admittedly, behavioral theories of risk analysis are not well developed beyond a few simple assumptions or observations, as we shall see. In the models used, individuals and groups acting under conditions of uncertainty are said to form expectations from limited information about the consequences of economic activity undertaken and the value of those consequences to them. Activities are pursued under conditions of uncertainty because the *expected utility* from the results of the action is ranked higher than that from alternative enterprises.

Risk Assumption by Individuals: The State Preference Approach[1]

When risk is associated with variation in states of nature affecting economic activity, a probability can often be assigned to the outcome. For example, over repeated annual observations it is established that a flood occurs an average of every other year. For any one year there is a 50 percent chance that there will be a flood. On the other hand, risk associated with, say, political instability is not connected to natural phenomena and does not afford an opportunity for repeated observations. Political instability is subject to greater knowledge limitations in most situations, as are many other conditions affecting economic activity. Herein, however, an illustration is developed in the context of states of nature with established probabilities about their outcome.

First consider variance in income around the mean value for a farmer with no wealth except human capital, and no way to insure

---

1. This section draws in part upon material in chapter 13 of P. R. G. Layard and A. A. Walters, *Microeconomics*, McGraw-Hill Book Co., 1978, which in turn draws upon work by J. Hirshleifer, *Quarterly Journal of Economics*, November 1965, pp. 509–36, and May 1966, pp. 252–77.

against fluctuations in farming income. Assume the variance in income is a function of rainfall and that for simplicity there are two possible states: it either rains or it does not. Further assume that in each growing period there is a 50-50 chance of each state. Assume net income is as follows in each state, depending upon whether or not the farmer uses fertilizer:

Farmer's Net Income in Two States of World			Average Over Many Crops
Technique	Rain	No Rain	
(a) No fertilizer	40	20	30
(b) Uses fertilizer	50	10	30

Over many growing periods the probability is that both methods produce the same average income. However, income varies more when fertilizer is used and thus technique (b) is said to be characterized by more risk.

The farmer may have incomplete or inaccurate information, and make his decision based on subjective probability. When the subjective probability differs from the probability derived from experience, this influences both the expected average return or income and the perceived risk, which is affected by the dispersion around the mean. Here, however, we assume the farmer is aware of the correct probabilities.

In figure 6.1 all income combinations that would produce an average income of 30, given a probability of 50-50 for each income possibility, are shown along the line connecting income levels of zero and 60 on each axis. When rain does not affect the outcome, income does not vary. Such a case is shown as point e on the 45-degree certainty line where income is 30 with or without rain. In the case considered, only points a and b are possibilities. Cases could be posited, however, where various techniques would produce income combinations with variances that lie on both sides of the certainty line, and produce the same average income over a period of repeated harvests.

The question arises: What would be the preference of the individual if any combination along the income line could be chosen? The answer is that most people would prefer certainty of income compared with variance, that is, they eschew risk. They must be given the probability of earning more on the average before they will assume risk. How much more may depend in part upon their income level. Even in higher-income economies, however, people in general display some risk aversion.[2]

The simple example ignores, among other things, the mechanism whereby income distributed unevenly over several periods is made available for spending on a more even basis. Any costs or rewards

---

2. An explanation given for risk aversion by an eithteenth-century Swiss mathematician, Daniel Bernoulli, was that the marginal utility of income decreases as income increases. Thus, losses are felt more keenly than gains since income falls.

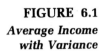

FIGURE 6.1

*Average Income
with Variance*

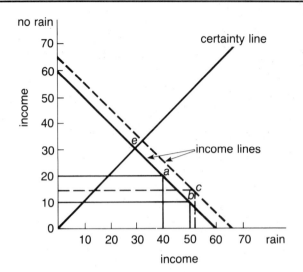

With a 50-50 chance of rain, income averages 30 anywhere along the 60-60 line.
Income does not depend upon rain along the certainty line.

attached internally to redistribution of riskier income must be included
in the computation of net income. Assume now the extreme case where
income (that is, the crop) in a subsistence, nonmonetized agriculture
cannot be redistributed and that the income level of 20 per period is
a subsistence level. Then the farmer will not consider technique *b*, or
a technique such as *c* that raises income but leaves it below subsistence
in growing periods with no rain.

Just what combination of higher-income, higher-risk/lower-
income, lower-risk will represent an equivalent trade-off for the farmer?
Figure 6.2 shows a series of trade-off or risk-income indifference curves
that vary with income level as they move out from the origin. Indifference curve I_1 shows that so long as income is no lower than 20 in
one state, there are several combinations of state-variance that are equally
acceptable to the individual, that is, among which the individual is
indifferent. Note, however, that the greater the variance of income, in
other words, the further the state-variance combination is from the
certainty line, the higher income must be to yield the same satisfaction
as a sure income of 30. At point *e* on curve, I_1, for example, expected
income is .5(20) + .5(58) = 39, and yields the same satisfaction as a
certain income of 30.

As average income from an activity is higher, the income line shifts
out from the origin. There will usually be more than one state-variance
combination to choose from along a given income line. The producer
picks the income-producing activity with a combination that is on the
highest indifference curve.

Note that at higher income levels there is a greater range over which
income can vary before reaching the limits established by subsistence

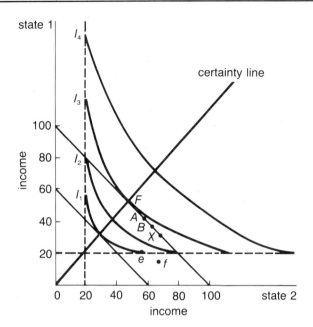

FIGURE 6.2
Individual's Risk-Income Indifference Curves

Income varies between states 1 and 2, except along the certainty line. There is a 50-50 chance of each state occurring. Average income is the same along any line connecting equal income points on each axis. There is a whole surface of indifference curves showing the trade-off of certainty for income that leaves the individual equally well-off.

income. It is assumed the individual enjoying higher income is willing to tolerate greater variance in income or risk that is possible at higher income levels. Moreover, as drawn here, the higher-income individual requires less trade-off in income to induce higher risk assumption, as indicated by the decrease in convexity of the I curves as they move further from the origin.

Indifference curves showing an individual's trade-off of income for reduced risk are based on subjective perferences. The level of expected utility of income or satisfaction is the same along any one indifference curve although income varies. In other words, the expected satisfaction derivable from income in the simple case shown depends upon its stability. An indifference curve with low curvature would represent low risk aversion; risk aversion increases with curvature. Here, as mentioned, it is assumed risk aversion varies with the income level so that the convexity of indifference curves is greater in lower income ranges.

In high-risk economies many individuals may be in higher-risk situations because circumstances do not offer them a choice. Individuals at point e on their indifference curve would resist a movement to point f off their indifference curve if they could effectively do so, even though such a shift would produce a higher average income. They would, in fact, prefer an income level of 30 to f if the income of 30 were certain. This demonstrates the reason resistance to change can be expected in low-income sectors of LDCs when the change raises income but increases its variance. Discussion along these lines is presented later in the chapter.

The diagram can be useful in analyzing response to investments with varying risk. The income line can be changed to represent instead the net return earned on equal investment outlays when there are two possible states of the domestic economy that affect the returns on each investment. There is a 50-50 probability that each state will occur. Examples of two such states might be high and low terms of trade for exports that affect investment returns in most sectors, or good-harvest and bad-harvest years that reverberate throughout the total economy.

Let point F on the certainty line, representing an average income of 50, be the net return earnable when money is invested abroad in a "riskless" investment. Points A, B, and X represent differing variance or risk but the same average return of 50 expected from investment in agriculture, industry, and the export sectors, respectively, of the LDC. Because A, B, and X lie on lower investor risk-indifference curves (not drawn), the investor chooses to invest abroad. But when higher-risk domestic investment yields commensurately higher returns than riskless foreign investment, so that A, B, and X are located along I_3, then the investor would find home investment in all sectors equally as attractive as foreign ventures. Put another way, when there is competitive bidding for investment funds, more risky investment will have to pay a higher return to attract funds. On the other hand, should there be a method by which the risk could be reduced in one or all sectors of the domestic economy, investment would take place at a lower return. This is the principle upon which insurance is based: Income will be exchanged for a reduction of risk.

Two Categories of Risk   In reality projects are more complicated in regard to their risk characteristics and the forces producing risk than the simple two-state illustration used. Some risky projects involve losses. Investors may not be able to play the law of averages when there is a loss potential, but rather must take a "one-shot" chance. Their eggs are all in one basket so to speak. On the other hand, there is the possibility that the investor can diversify investments and affect total risk exposure favorably.

The many causes of risk are sometimes divided into two categories: *event uncertainty* and *endogenous uncertainty* (Hirshleifer and Riley 1979). Event uncertainty is related to the unknowns of events exogenous to the economic system, as example, certain components of technological change, the weather, political factors, or attributes of the economic structure that reflect the country's level of development. Endogenous uncertainty arises from imperfections of the economic system itself. This type of risk reflects the cost of information, or stems from poor policies or economic organization. It can sometimes be eliminated or reduced at a cost below benefits for growth. The classification is helpful in later discussion relating risk to development and policy responses.

Risk and growth are interrelated in several ways. Risk affects the amount of investment allocated to various areas of the economy when investors are risk-averse. Funds will flow to more secure areas so that the return at the margin is lower than for more insecure areas. This can affect growth when higher-risk investment projects are important to development, and funds attracted to such projects are limited. Moreover, a reduction of risk would result in a shifting of funds from lower- to higher-return investment, raising total output.

The Effect of Risk upon Growth

Risk and uncertainty in the economy are related to the hold that tradition has upon the populace. Tradition often inhibits technical change. Such change is avoided since it means increased uncertainty in an already highly chancy environment. This means some higher-return, higher-risk projects that could bring needed new technologies are not undertaken. The importance of this kind of progress to development was explored thoroughly in chapter 5. Not surprisingly, historical literature traced in that chapter paid close attention to innovators strongly inclined to assume risk as compared with the timorousness of the general populace. Their pioneering activities reduce the risk level for technology imitators.

The aggregate investment and saving functions can be affected negatively by risk. For example, the level of risk in an LDC may climb relatively high by historical standards in conditions of political instability. In LDCs without well-developed financial systems to allow diversification of investment, the saver and investor (often the same person) cannot find investment opportunities with returns acceptable for the level of risk. Relatively savings from income are low and consumption is high as investors shun risky domestic ventures. Less investment means slower income growth and thereby less savings *and* consumption. Or, savings go abroad, despite controls, as investors seek safer outlets for funds and diversify their portfolios away from the high level of risk in the domestic enonomy. Controls cannot contain determined investors seeking safe havens for their savings.

Another common example is the case where the propensity to save is affected by inflation risks. Unpredictable inflation (a not uncommon occurrence in LDCs), combined with an interest rate too low to offset the expected erosion of future purchasing power from savings, can lower saving from income. People spend rather than save in order to minimize the inflation tax. High consumption reduces the resources available for investment or needed government services. And, as discussed in chapter 17, inflation in some cases can distort investment allocation so that growth is retarded.

Population growth can be affected by risk. Chapter 7 discusses the complexity of identifying determinants of population growth. The chapter examines the possible effects of risk upon family size. It is hypothesized that risks related to old age, ill health, or employment uncertainties can influence the demand for children. Population growth in turn affects economic development, as shown in chapters 7 and 8.

In sum, risk aversion affects some major growth variables: technological change and innovation, saving rates and the level of investment, efficiency in allocation of investment, and to some degree population increase. Remember that attitudes toward risk are subjective and LDCs may differ in their composite private-plus-public risk assumption so that one LDC undertakes relatively high-risk, high-return projects supportive of development, while another does not. For any given activity or project, whether or not it is carried out can depend on its expected utility (given the hoped-for benefits from other activities) and hence its risk, and the risk-assumption profile of the population. The reward for risk, its level, and the attitudes toward it can all be affected by policy, although the last is least tractable. We turn now to a discussion of policies designed to deal with risk exposure and the reward for risk assumption.

POLICY IMPLICATIONS

The government sector by its very nature affects risk since it pools and spreads the uncertainties of projects undertaken among the populace. In a communist society risks are shared very widely. Market systems can also reallocate risks efficiently through devices for pooling and sharing them. Fuller discussion of the relationship between the type of economic system and risk is deferred to a later section. Here we note that LDCs most often have mixed economies, with some activities greatly influenced or controlled by government and some taken on by the private sector.

Policymaking Under Conditions of Risk: The Mixed Economy

In mixed economies when a risk-averse private sector does not undertake higher-risk projects conducive to growth, and when the government is risk-indifferent or less risk-averse than private enterprise, the government can carry out the projects directly, or subsidize them so that they fall within the risk-assumption range of the private sector. The number and income levels of investors in LDCs can be too low to provide private funding for larger, longer-term projects that have considerable risk elements and are needed for LDC development. Projects such as land reclamation or large-scale mineral exploration come to mind. The government generally assumes full responsibility for funding larger, riskier projects. For smaller projects subsidies may be adequate. For example, a government development bank may invest in a private firm to provide more venture capital for development and thus absorb some of the risk.

It should be noted that the theoretical discussion as to whether government subsidy or government investment is preferable requires specification of the exact risk conditions and remains unsettled in that no general conclusion has been reached. Another difficult question because of its normative nature is whether planners ought to be indifferent to risk in selecting projects when the people are not (Arrow and Lind 1970; Mayshar 1977 and 1979; Hirshleifer 1966).

Development strategists seeking to reduce uncertainty in LDCs can concentrate upon areas of the market economy where the marginal benefit greatly exceeds the marginal cost of risk reduction or risk subsidy. Consider first policies to affect investment when there is event uncertainty. The insurance principle of pooling risk can be called upon to reduce risk. Farm cooperatives, through group purchasing, marketing, storage, insurance, and loans, can pool some risks and affect the variance of income experienced by individual members. Laws that provide for business and personal limited liability and risk-sharing result in a more widely distributed burden of risk. Government sponsorship of financial institutions such as stock and bond markets and development banks at the appropriate time can allow diversification and thereby spread the risk of investment. Financial development is discussed in chapter 17. Here a simple example illustrates the relation to risk reduction.

Suppose one firm in five fails in its first years of operation, creating losses for the owner. If the investor is liable only up to the amount he or she has sunk in the enterprise, creditors, suppliers, and others share in losses in the event of complete failure. The investor who can diversify by buying stock in many firms can expect a lower variance in income than when investing in only one firm. When investing in risky projects he or she can choose a group to invest in whose members complement each other in that one varies above the mean as the other varies below it. The investment portfolio would then exhibit lower variance in income than the individual projects and thus less risk for a given mean income level.

The effects of diversification can be shown by reference to the risk/income indifference curve for the simple-case diagram used previously and redrawn in figure 6.3. Assume the investor is initially at point A on indifference curve I_1. Now assume that instead of investing only in project A, the risk-averse investor splits the investment between projects B and C, earning an average income between the average for B and C. The investor's new income and variance will be at point E midway

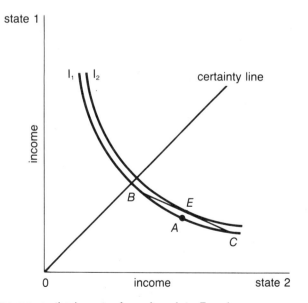

FIGURE 6.3

Higher Welfare with Diverse Income Sources

Diversification moves the investor from A on I_1 to E on I_2.

on a line drawn between points B and C. Point E is tangent to a higher indifference curve, I_2. The investor could also select projects beyond the limits of his or her indifference curves with higher returns and risk, combining them with lower-return, lower-risk projects. Total income variance is reduced, and the investor is in a preferred position. Notice also that when state 2 is not always the state in which the higher income occurs, but some projects produce higher income in state 1 while others are more profitable in state 2, then diversification yields greater certainty of income since the projects offset each other. A higher indifference curve is achievable by combining income projects with favorable covariance of income in preference to an individual project on a given indifference curve.

Again an example from agriculture can illustrate. Assume there is a crop that thrives in drought and one that thrives in rain, producing equal income in the favored state; but both produce no income in the unfavored state. There is a 50-50 chance of each state. Total income now becomes certain when the farmer divides acreage between crops or joins a cooperative where total acreage is divided between crops and income is shared. Such a division would be preferable to either crop alone or a lower-yield one that produces less average income from total acreage but has smaller variation in alternate states than the other crops. The reader can show this by drawing a line between projects located on the same indifference curve that have higher income in opposite states, finding the midpoint of the line, and the indifference curve tangent to that point. An illustration could also be developed where investment in firms with favorable covariance places the investor on a higher indifference curve. Stock markets, as mentioned, are a vehicle for such diversification.

The government in the LDC may be able to lessen the curvature of the populace's indifference curves at lower-income levels by the provision of social insurance. To varying degrees social insurance protects against loss of income from old age and ill health and provides for health-related expenses. The result may be a greater willingness to assume investment-related risk once individual uncertainties about one's future well-being are lowered. The financing needed for social security varies with the degree of protection sought. Lowering income levels among the higher-income groups to finance social insurance can have some offsetting effects since higher-income groups may have less risk aversion.

The tax system is also a vehicle for affecting risk. The variance in income can be changed by cushioning losses when risk assumption brings positive externalities for the economy. Tax deduction of losses is one method of lowering risk. It should be noted that a progressive or proportionate tax that fails to make adjustment for variance in income and losses will penalize riskier activities.

Assume, for example, two projects: One brings an income of 20 every year. The other regularly yields an income of 100 one year and a loss of 50 the next. Average income is 25 from this project. Now assume a tax rate on annual income of 10 percent, but no adjustment for loss. Taxes are 2 for the low-risk project; and they average 5 per year for the high-risk project, but must be paid as a tax of 10 every other year. This is in effect a tax rate of 20 percent on the riskier enterprise.

Progressive taxes penalize riskier projects more than proportional taxes since the tax rate rises with income. Thus, for a tax system to remain neutral vis-à-vis risk there must be adjustment for losses. And for a progressive tax system there must be adjustment for variation in income.

When the tax system penalizes risk assumption, then the market return will have to be higher to induce investment in riskier projects. There are qualifications to a full tax adjustment, however. Full absorption by the government of losses could encourage waste. Moreover, some riskier projects bring windfall gains that the government wishes to tax more heavily. An example might be high income from the discovery of natural resource deposits.

The government has an important role in alleviating employment risks faced by the work force in a mixed-market economy. Development requires growing specialization by the labor force, their susceptibility to obsolescence as technology changes, and their willingness to participate in labor markets subject to changes in demand. The risks associated with market uncertainties can be shared by the general populace when the government subsidizes worker training and retraining and when unemployment problems associated with poor economic organization are minimized. More is said about policies affecting labor force utilization in chapter 15.

The government's approach to technology transfer can affect the risk levels associated with technological change. The last chapter discussed material relevant to this point. The Japanese approach is interesting in retrospect. The Japanese maintained a strong, semifeudal role for government in technology transfer, a role that spread the risks, yet encouraged innovation and rewards within the private sector. The government heavily subsidized the acquisition of information and knowledge, and there was joint private-government participation in new technology areas. The labor force's resistance to technical change was minimized since, by adapting technology from the West, they were able to avoid high rates of obsolescence of their human capital. Even the absorption of feudal-type relations into the corporate structure so that there were mutual obligations between government, corporate owners, and workers was a method of reducing social change and the attendant risks of the impersonal labor market. An interesting question today is whether the development of intermediate technology would reduce the risks inherent in technology transfer and change.

TWO HIGH-RISK SECTORS

The previous section outlined in a general way the approach to policymaking under conditions of risk in the typical case of a mixed economy. At this point it is helpful to utilize the analysis of risk developed in the chapter to gain more specific understanding of ways in which it can affect development. This will give the reader a feel for the importance of the topic. Along these lines, the next two sections discuss risk as it relates to the agricultural and foreign trade sectors. Following the overall discussion of the trade sector, a special section treats international commodity agreements designed to reduce the risk of price fluctuations. In the next two sections the relationship between government organization and risk is discussed, along with the implications of risk for inequality. The chapter then concludes with a section relating risk to the performance of the planned economy of communist China.

Agriculture   The uncertainties of weather plague agriculture, as do the threats of heavy pest infestation and blight. The organizational structure for spreading risk in traditional agriculture can be poorly developed and heavily dominated by rigid historical institutions. Thus the allocation of risk in agriculture among landlord, moneylender, middleman, peasant, and day laborer is generally not characterized by broad choices and free bargaining so that each achieves the highest possible indifference curve, willingly trading off income for security. Historically sanctioned conditions imposed by the landlord or moneylender on the peasants can be particularly harsh. The peasants must pay a high price to avoid risk or have a heavy portion of risk forced upon them because of their limited bargaining power and low social position.

Because the risk level is high in agriculture, any change that would add uncertainty can meet with resistance. Referring back to figure 6.2, changed farming practices that raise average income but at the same time raise the variance in income can place the farmer on a *lower* indifference curve. Or, the peasant may be at a point such as *f*, which he would avoid in a situation of more varied alternatives and freer choice. Even though average income is higher with change, the additional uncertainties result in the farmer's preferring a more certain, if lower, income.

Government policies aimed at modernizing agriculture must be designed to deal with the distribution of risk and the risk aversion of the low-income peasant. And it is not uncommon for the landlord class to be relatively risk-averse. The institutional structure may have to be overhauled so that there are tenancy or land reform, marketing cooperatives, credit cooperatives, greater incentives to the farmer for risk assumption, and greatly improved information. Policies must ensure reward for the risks of technical change. Successful government policies will raise income and lower uncertainty. The farm sector not only receives higher income, the income it receives brings greater satisfaction because of its reduced variance. This enables the government to tax the agricultural sector more readily without loss of incentives, covering any costs it incurs in reducing risks, and generating money for development.

The handling of risk and uncertainty in agriculture is a great challenge to any LDC. Not surprisingly, where risk has been ignored as a component of an agricultural strategy, failures have followed. The peasant is often better off with his old seed than the new miracle seed of the Green Revolution if there is a chance he cannot obtain water, fertilizer, and pesticides in sufficient quantities and at the necessary times. Farmers with few acres know that when there is a water shortage, irrigation water is allocated to those with large holdings. Experience with the new seed, information, and market acceptance are absent or uncertain. The peasant must specialize more to attain the largest cost reductions and yield gains; and this increases the risk of crop failure or price fluctuations when the supportive framework does not spread risk. Often the peasant's share or return from increased yields after taxes, rent, and so on, is low or uncertain. With increased profits from new hybrid seeds, some landlords have rescinded tenancy and evicted peasants from the land. It is not surprising that a low-income peasant already enduring the high risks inherent to agriculture will not change to new hybrid seeds when the risk is higher and the return for assuming it unpredictable or relatively low.

Failure to consider the risks faced by the poor peasant led some observers to the erroneous generalization that the peasant did not respond to market forces. Frustrated planners have often indicted recalcitrant farmers for being extreme risk avoiders. A statement closer to the truth is that poor peasants can prudently assume only modest additional risk, receive little if any compensation for imposed risks, and will accept some additional risk where the return is commensurate. In sum, a poor institutional framework and an absence of government policies for dealing with risk and return have been instrumental in the peasant's resistance to agricultural transformation, a topic explored in chapter 9.

Intriguingly where the state assumes the risk by taking over agriculture and paying the peasant a set wage, inevitably low in a poor society, transformation can proceed rather rapidly, but work motivation and efficiency suffer. Communists have had trouble "liberating" the peasant. There are generally enough freedoms under the landlord system to yield some psychic income, especially in more prosperous· countries such as those of Eastern Europe. And this loss of freedom is sorely resisted by the farmer. Moreover, when work effort is not rewarded in communal farming, motivation suffers. There have also been problems of neglect and extremely poor administration in the planned agriculture of communism. Policies adopted in the People's Republic of China actually raised risk, as explained in the last part of this chapter. Agricultural support systems for private farming and cooperatives are in many situations more versatile than centralized government planning, and can pool risks while stopping short of state-run agriculture.

Foreign Trade

In addition to agriculture, foreign trade can hold relatively high risk for an LDC, and the two sectors often overlap. Trade is a vital component of the development effort; thus its hazards cannot be avoided. And as in agriculture, many risks cannot be reduced because the LDC has no control over them.

Specialization is necessary to trade. Most often the LDC has a comparative advantage in the export of raw materials such as metals, min-

erals, agricultural raw materials, and forest products. When manufactured goods are exported, comparative advantage is usually in those
using relatively large amounts of unskilled labor, indigenous raw materials, and simple technology. Such specialization means the LDCs
are tied to the fortunes of one or two export items. Poor countries are
generally too small and technically unsophisticated to have a more
diversified array of export industries such as larger MDCs exhibit. And
being underdeveloped, they find it harder to respond to changes in
competition, demand or supply, technical change, and discriminatory
practices. Even markets for exports are often concentrated geographically.

Reducing these risks is not easy. LDCs generally try to industrialize
and lessen their dependency upon imports. Usually, however, industrialization does not achieve this. It merely changes the type of imports
upon which the economy depends, as explained in chapter 11. Industrialization can help, however, in diversifying exports into manufactured goods areas. The cost of reduced specialization must be weighed
against the advantages of reduced risk.

Risk impinges upon the inflow of foreign savings and the outflow
of domestic savings for LDCs. Foreign capitalists can acquire funds
more cheaply in MDC economies and, often being large and diversified,
can commit larger amounts to a risky project. Thus investment in LDCs
may appear attractive to foreigners despite risks, if the return is high
enough. But the high risk tends to offset the potential for an LDC to
acquire relatively low-cost savings from abroad, and to limit the total
amount of foreign savings available. Moreover, unexpected increases
in the level of risk can lead to capital flight from LDCs and cause a
foreign exchange crisis.

Domestic money may also leave the LDC in response to risk. Wealthy
domestic investors with international business know-how will seek to
reduce risk by investing some of their capital abroad. They can attain
a higher indifference curve by having an international investment portfolio with risk characteristics that vary from their domestic holdings.
Unfortunately, such diversification is detrimental to development of
the LDC because it diverts abroad the country's savings badly needed
for the domestic economy. For this reason LDCs typically restrict the
outflow of savings abroad.

The ever-present schemes to circumvent international investment
restrictions upon locals, however, underline the importance of developing a capacity within the domestic economy enabling the investor
to achieve diversification of risk. The problem of capital outflows is
related in part to large fortunes and inequality within an LDC. The
small businessperson who does not deal in the foreign trade sector is
not part of the LDC's international portfolio problem.

INTERNATIONAL COMMODITY AGREEMENTS AND RISK

The intense interest of LDCs in international commodity agreements
is in part traceable to their need to reduce risk. When demand and
supply for exports are fairly inelastic, as is often the case with commodities, relatively small changes in demand result in relatively large
changes in price and earnings. The hope is that international com-

modity agreements would reduce fluctuations in earnings by stabilizing prices.

Commodity agreements are designed to stabilize prices over the
cycle by responding to cyclical supply and demand shifts. For example, when an increase in demand or a supply shortfall threatens to
send prices up, the price rise would be dampened by release of stores
from stockpiles. In cases where supply is enlarged or demand drops,
price declines would be limited by stockpiling the additional supply.
A technical complication is that cycles can be irregular in nature and
it can be difficult to separate cyclical fluctuations from secular trends
in prices. It is much too costly and inefficient to try to offset secular
trends.

Even where secular forces are absent, problems remain. Cycles can
be related to supply and/or demand. Stabilization of prices for supply
related cycles does not stabilize export earnings except for large exporters when the large exporting country handles the commodities fund
internally. To understand this, we begin with the example of external
financing of the commodities fund.

Consider the case where stockpile adjustments are financed outside
the country exporting the commodity so that monetary variations from
the stockpile sales or purchases do not affect the income of exporters
or producers. The impact upon the exporters' income of stockpile adjustments that stabilize prices will depend upon whether the source of
the fluctuations is a shift in demand or supply or both.

The Case of an External Fund

It is helpful to consider shifts of demand and supply separately to
illustrate how each affects stability of earnings. Let us examine first
the case where demand shifts cause instability in world price and there
is no commodity agreement that steadies prices. Figure 6.4(a) shows
the instance where world price shifts due to changes in world demand

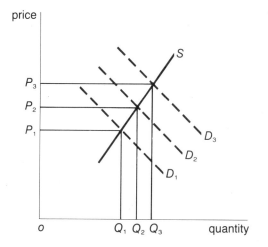

FIGURE 6.4(a)
Demand-side Shifts

Changes in price due to change in demand: earnings ($P \times Q$) change. A stable
price would stabilize earnings when supply is constant.

FIGURE 6.4(b)

Supply-side Shifts

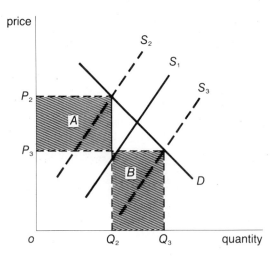

Changes in price due to changes in supply, demand being constant: With supply shift from S_2 to S_3, earnings change from $P_2 \times Q_2$ to $P_3 \times Q_3$. The difference in earnings can be small when the area A and the area B are approximately equal. This result is possible for a large exporter that influences price. For the small exporter the outcome of a shift in supply is the same as in diagram (c).

and the LDC's supply is stable. Earnings, which are the area $P \times Q$, fluctuate with movements in price, and a commodity agreement that stabilized price would have a similar effect on earnings. To stabilize price the world commodities stockpile would be built up through purchases as demand fell, and reduced through sales as demand rose.

FIGURE 6.4(c)

Supply Shifts with Price Constant

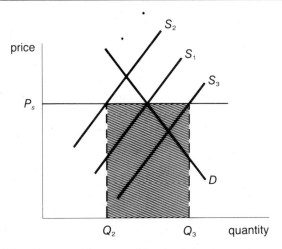

With price stabilized by a world commodities fund, foreign exchange earnings can vary from low to high supply years by the area $P_s \times Q_3$ less the area $P_s \times Q_2$.

Now assume the instability originates from supply shifts. The international stockpile adjustments can modify these supply shifts. However, the exporters' incomes will vary since the quantity sold has changed. The important question, then, is whether income variation is higher or lower than it would be without stockpile adjustments. In fact, stabilization of price causes earnings to fluctuate more than in the case where price and quantity sold both change. The difference depends upon the shifts of the curves and on the elasticities.

Figures 6.4(b) and (c) illustrate the case of supply shifts without and with price stabilization. In diagram (b) price fluctuates as supply shifts in a country that is a large exporter. A shift in supply from S_2 to S_3 causes earnings to change from the area $P_2 \times Q_2$ to the area $P_3 \times Q_3$. When the area A is equal to the area B, then earnings do not change. This occurs when the price elasticity of demand (defined as percentage change in quantity sold divided by the percentage change in price) is equal to one. When demand is price-inelastic, earnings fall when price drops, but rise when price rises. When demand is price-elastic a fall in price raises earnings, a rise lowers them. Yet because price and quantity provide offsetting impact upon earnings, the price change has a stabilizing effect upon earnings.

Figure 6.4(c) shows the results of a stabilized price, P_s, as supply fluctuates. A shift in supply from S_2 to S_3 causes earnings to fluctuate by the hatched area. Thus, for the large producer a commodities agreement destabilizes rather than stabilizes earnings compared with a free market, where there are offsetting price changes when supply shifts. For the small exporter who does not influence world price, there are no offsetting effects to supply shifts of the type illustrated in diagram (b). The difference between a commodities agreement and no agreement depends solely upon whether flexible world prices, when compared with a stable world price, happen to offset or reinforce the effect upon earnings of the small exporter's supply shifts.

Jere Behrman in his study of commodity agreements notes that "for many of the relevant commodities, existing estimates indicate that short-run nonprice shifts in the supply curves tend to be larger than those in the demand curves . . ." (1978, p. 34). Because steady prices do not stabilize earnings when supply-side shifts occur, the proponents of commodity agreements have related supply-side stability to price stability. It is argued that risk reduction from more predictable prices improves supply-side stability. Greater price stability under certain cost-side conditions can lead to reduced business failures even where earnings are not stabilized since producers can plan their output more efficiently. Situations of speculative overinvestment in response to boom prices and fallout from such investment are moderated or eliminated. Stability of prices can ensure a higher level of stable investment since risk is reduced. In addition, fluctuating export prices can affect the general price level in a country, and thereby risk, when exports are an important component of total output. There is substance to these points. It must be concluded, however, that many supply-side shifts are independent of price so that the risk of fluctuating earnings can intensify with commodity agreements, especially for large exporters.

In some cases commodity agreements have been formed by countries that produce a major portion of world output. Stockpiling is then handled by the exporting countries and not by an external common fund encompassing all producers and consumers. The nation's foreign exchange earnings and the individual producers' incomes from exports are not the same because of stockpile sales and purchases. In such cases the country's foreign exchange is stabilized by stockpile adjustments when the source of instability is supply shifts, but destabilized by demand shifts. The earnings of individual producers will vary as explained above, however. The cost of stockpiling is lower, of course, when consumers participate in financing.

If undertaken, commodity agreements should encompass both buyers and sellers. Consumers as well as producers are affected by reduced movements in price, and consumers benefit from stockpile supply releases in periods of shortages. The price stabilization can affect the general price level in both consumer and producer countries, which in turn impinges on risks associated with economic activity. Some commodity agreements have included consumers, and those proposed by the United Nations would be a cooperative endeavor.

Historically international commodity agreements have had limited acceptance and success. The problems surrounding management and financing of the stockpile have inhibited implementation of the pacts. These require control of supply for certain types of commodities in order to minimize stockpiling. For example, if tin prices weaken, its production may be reduced rather than letting large stockpiles accumulate. Allocation and monitoring of quotas have typically been difficult to administer successfully. Where producers finance the stockpile and the main exporters are poorer countries, financial shortfalls easily arise. The United Nations approach would pool the funds of multiple commodities in the hope of overcoming the financial limitations.

Cartels such as the Organization of Petroleum Exporting Countries are designed to improve the rate of return as well as reduce the risks of trade for the producer. In a cartel monopoly control of supply must be established. Only a few commodities lend themselves to successful cartelization of this type, however, so this is not an avenue of general applicability for dealing with foreign trade risks.

ECONOMIC SYSTEMS AND RISK

Trade and agriculture are singled out because of their strategic importance to a developing economy. Risks in these areas contribute to development problems and are not easily reduced. Moreover they are typically areas of intensive planning controls and efforts. For their plans to succeed, planners must deal with the risk elements. Where the private sector's risk-assumption propensity is low and risk reduction is not feasible, projects important to development may require the government to absorb the risk. However, acceptable levels of risk associated with a commensurate return can elicit participation by the private sector, and may have a positive influence upon efficiency, capital accumulation, and work effort when the risk is not beyond the private sector's capacity. And as the next section notes, governments may raise rather than reduce the level of risk in an economy, even though their goal is to do otherwise.

The centrally planned economy will generally, at equivalent development levels, have different patterns of endogenous risks when compared with the mixed or more market-oriented economy. Neither operates with perfect knowledge, but the planned economy has a more complete information set. Both distribute the risks of event uncertainty and endogenous uncertainty. The planned economy spreads risk over more people and is generally presumed to have less incidence of risk per person. **Government**

Even MDC market economies with highly developed markets for both capital and insurance cannot perform the risk redistribution function perfectly, either because of high contractual costs for some types of complex risks and/or fraud (Arrow and Lind, 1970). The greater dispersion of uncertainty can allow the planned economy to undertake higher-risk, higher-return projects more readily than market economies, where the risk is more concentrated and the possibility of spreading it is more limited. However, the mixed economy, through the government sector, can undertake various development projects carrying higher risk but promising greater return and spread the risk, while allowing the market to reward and redistribute risk for surer projects.

Risk assumption must occur in all economic systems. When individuals differ in their risk preferences, and choice is allowed in trade-offs between risk assumption and return, those who are less risk-averse will take more chances. Well-functioning market economies provide individual investors and workers with a wide choice about taking risks. When decisions on risk for the economy are centralized, risk assumption will reflect the preferences of the planners, a more limited, more homogeneous group. In calculating risks, the planners generally add to the economic uncertainties the political ones implied in project failure. The tendency is for planners to be a somewhat cautious group; they are not indifferent to risk despite being able to spread it over the populace.

It is a misconception to think that the centrally planned economy is riskless. Event uncertainty arises from such variables outside the system as weather and level of development. But a complex planning structure can create endogenous risks stemming from the planning organization, especially when shortages of human capital lead to poorly conceived and executed projects. Most importantly, the process of development is not understood well enough to blueprint it successfully through all its levels and in all circumstances. This means the attempt to do so carries risk. In fact, in large countries at low levels of development, a comprehensive hierarchical network like the Soviet planning apparatus can be unattainable, as the Chinese have discovered. Consequently planning in China has taken on a more loose-knit regional organization with greater concentration of risk than the Soviet-type system.

While experience has shown many kinds of risk are lessened in a centrally planned economy, reduction of risk, of course, can promote but does not ensure technical change. The matrix of projects designed by the planners can be a less efficient set than the one generated in more decentralized systems, well organized to spur innovation. Finally, reward for the assumption of the risks of technological change and innovation vital to development must be built into the centrally controlled economy as well as the market-influenced one since individuals in both types of societies can be expected to be, on the whole, risk-averse. This has ramifications for income inequality, a topic pursued in the following section.

As mentioned, the government sector in mixed economies can spread the risk for projects entailing high event uncertainty. Yet the mixed economy shares with the planned the possibility of creating endogenous risks via the planning process. That is, there is not always a drop in risk in the mixed economy as a result of government activity. In actuality the experience of mixed economies with planning for development is checkered and difficult to gauge in regard to endogenous risks. Well-meaning political leaders in LDCs intent upon fostering industrialization in high-risk market environments have at times added uncertainty factors of their own making. Government control of foreign exchange, import licenses, commodities supplies, the money supply, and credit allocation have oftimes been so administered that uncertainties and risks are exacerbated. The effect is then counterproductive to industrial development.

Investors must not only gauge private sector risks, they must also anticipate the probability of government actions in areas that would adversely affect the project's rate of return. When foreign exchange is allocated by the government on the basis of shifting or uncertain criteria, projects can become riskier in case of expected shortfalls in foreign exchange. When inflation caused by government management of the money supply distorts credit allocation, the risk of interrupted financing of credit needs can deter investments. If rules and regulations are always changing, it is difficult for the investor to plan. Thus, to avoid adding unnecessarily to the uncertainties inherent in the underdeveloped economy, the government must develop expertise, exhibit consistency in its policies, and build confidence in its competence in the investing community. Often this is a task too large for the fledgling planners to achieve in the milieu of LDC politics.

The reader may have realized by now that no particular economic organization is free of event uncertainty or endogenous uncertainty, or handles risk perfectly. Market, centrally planned, and mixed economies are subject to risks related to their structure and the LDC experiences risks inherent in the level of development. Whatever the system, an awareness of the interrelation of risk and development is important to the advancement effort. Government policies that work directly or that work indirectly through the framework of a market system can fail when the individual's risk aversion is ignored.

We have mentioned the presumption that the willingness to assume risk varies positively with income level and the return for risk assumption, and the fact that technological change involves risk assumption. The question arises: In a poor, private economy with low average per capital income, is high inequality of income a prerequisite to risk assumption needed for development? Is the alternative a pooling or sharing of risk via public projects to reduce or eliminate uncertainty?

Income Inequality and Risk

Income inequality is clearly not a sufficient condition for risk assumption. Subjective variables affect risk assumption. There are many economies where great income inequality has been accompanied by wealthy people's aversion to risk. The rich class avoids risk and attempts to maintain the status quo. This ensures the upper class a dominant social position that would be threatened by technical progress. The landlord class in various historical settings of underdevelopment has been notorious in its risk aversion and sociopolitical dominance. In contrast, wealthy families involved in industrialization in LDCs (often referred to as the Group), assume risk, although they seek to control risk levels through their cohesion and government influence.

But the question persists: If relatively high income inequality is not a sufficient condition for risk assumption at low levels of average per capita income, is it a necessary condition? It is conceivable for there to be a group that does not demand a trade-off of income for risk assumption and that undertakes chancy projects despite a low present income. But the nagging suspicion recurs that high inequality may be a necessary condition for adequate risk assumption related to development in very poor economies *unless* there are successful government policies to reduce and spread risk.

The other side of the coin is the impact of risk on income inequality. Schumpeter assumed that risk assumption by the entrepreneur was a route to the building of family empires based on the family-owned firm. He considered this a positive motivating factor for innovation in society. The literature on inequality in developing economies has not examined closely the relationship between inequality and risk. Undoubtedly, though, the wealth of the Group can be to some degree related to risk assumption.

Consider an LDC with on-going risk assumption and differing individual risk-assumption preferences. Assume there is a set of possible economic activities that differ rather markedly in return because of a broad risk range. Failure in risky ventures yields a lower income than success in surer ones, while success in unpredictable projects will bring a higher income than either. These conditions can yield unequal income to projects and to risk assumers participating in the income from projects according to their willingness to take risks. Thus risk assumption could, along with other variables, play a part in income inequality. This income inequality, in turn, can affect risk assumption.

It should be remembered, however, that there is no presumption that the higher the risk, the greater a project's contribution to economic advance, or that all risky projects promote development. The illegal international transfer of cocaine is a risky activity that has earned foreign exchange for individuals in LDCs, who often keep these funds abroad. There are many less risky uses of these resources that would contribute more to development.

Conclusions   It is hypothesized that risk aversion is greater in low-income than in higher-income countries due to their poverty; and yet their economies are in most cases high-risk ones. Risk is connected to the technological change vital to development. Thus, the failure to assume certain types of risks can deter development. Risk factors can lead to lower savings and income. When lower-risk, lower-return projects are substituted for those with higher returns, and greater risks, or when saving is adversely affected by risk avoidance, growth is lower.

Risk is inherent in less-developed countries no matter what their type of economic system or organization. Many types of market institutions and government planning or participation can help reduce risks inimical to development. Unfortunately, given skill shortages and the reality of politics, the government often contributes risks that impede development.

Since there is no way to eliminate all uncertainty, this presents the need to reward the assumption of risks conducive to development. We do not know enough about the relationship between risk assumption and income to say high inequality is a prerequisite to risk assumption in LDCs. The presumption is that when mechanisms for risk sharing are developed in LDCs with low per capita income, and policies and structural organizations that contribute to uncertainty are avoided, the chance-taking needed for growth will be adequate without high inequality.

Risks inherent to agriculture such as weather-related harvest failures must be assumed. Often institutional arrangements and/or government policies impose losses associated with risks upon the rural poor, contributing to their straits. High imposed risk among such groups, given their poverty, can create resistance to the uncertainties of change connected with development.

The foreign trade sector has long been a focus of LDCs' attention and efforts to reduce the risks faced there. Commodities agreements have been proposed as a way to mitigate risks arising from export price fluctuations. Price stability for exports does not stabilize export earnings, however, unless all price fluctuations are due to demand shifts and prices are stabilized through a world commodities fund rather than an LDC exporter's commodities fund.

REFERENCES   Arrow, K. J. and Lind, R. C. 1970. Uncertainty and the Evaluation of Public Investment Decisions. *American Economic Review* (June): 364–78.

Behrman, Jere R. 1978. *Development, the International Economic Order and Commodity Agreements.* Reading, MA: Addison-Wesley Publishing Co.

Cheng, Chu-yuan. 1982. *China's Economic Development.* Boulder, CO: Westview Press.

Hirshleifer, J. 1965. Investment Decision under Uncertainty: Choice-Theoretic Approaches. *Quarterly Journal of Economics* (November): 509–36.

———1966. Investment Decision under Uncertainty: Applications of the State-Preference Approach. *Quarterly Journal of Economics* (May): 252–77.

———and Riley, John. 1979. The Analysis of Uncertainty and Information—An Expository Survey. *Journal of Economic Literature* (December): 1375–1421.

Layard, P. R. G. and Walters, A. A. 1978. *Microeconomics*. New York: McGraw-Hill Book Co.

Mayshar, J. 1977. Should Government Subsidize Risky Private Projects? *American Economic Review* (March): 20–28.

———1979. Should Government Subsidize Risky Private Projects? Reply. *American Economic Review* (June): 462–63.

Endogenous Risks in Communist Agriculture: The Case of China

A billion people—roughly one fourth of the world's population—live in the People's Republic of China, an Asian country about the size of the United States with a climate that ranges from frigid to equatorial. While well-endowed with certain natural resources, including coal and oil, China has limited arable land per capita, much of it leached of fertility from centuries of intensive cultivation. Diminishing returns in agriculture have limited the country's economic development. Following a long, costly civil war, China emerged after World War II a poverty-stricken agrarian economy committed to communist transformation.

Chinese strategies for development under communist leadership have been ambitious and bold. From 1953 to 1957 the country's leaders tried to copy the Stalinist model of Soviet development, concentrating on heavy industry while extracting a surplus from a reorganized agriculture. Such a policy was not suited to the Chinese economy with its population pressures upon land, technical backwardness, and limited saving capacity. This unbalanced growth strategy resulted in agricultural bottlenecks with shortages of food for the people and of raw materials for industry. The high capital intensity of the investment sector was not suited to China's labor/capital ratio.

Rather than retreat to more modest goals, Chairman Mao Zedong, the revolutionary leader of China's Communist Party, designed a new strategy in 1958–60 called the Great Leap Forward. While the capital-intensive modern sector would still absorb some resources, the focus would shift to less capital-intensive, small-scale production in the countryside (including "backyard" steel production), and to the mobilization of surplus manhours for such projects as irrigation, road building, and flood control. Thus, technological dualism was introduced to limit industry's investment needs and provide capital-forming projects for agriculture. Despite some remarkable results in 1958, the economy soon collapsed from poor organization and overly ambitious goals.

The 1961–65 strategy retreated from communist transformation of the agricultural sector, backyard steel furnaces, and grandiose goals. A revised assessment of China's potential led to a more gradual movement toward communal farming and an admission that a balanced approach to agriculture and industry was a prerequisite to success. The economy turned inward as a result of a split with Russia and the withdrawal of Soviet aid in 1960. And rather than extolling the growing Chinese population as the nation's greatest asset, the leaders enacted strategies to curtail fertility. Material rewards and incentives abolished during the Great Leap Forward were reinstated.

The pragmatism of the early 1960s ended with Mao's move to resume more radical programs and perpetuate this strategy after his death through determining his successor. There was a power struggle between Mao's radical followers and the more moderate party leaders who opposed taking the riskier route laid out by the party chairman. This contest lasted from 1966 to 1976. There were periods when Mao reintroduced measures followed in the years of the Great Leap Forward. The small-scale industries established during this later period, however, proved more efficient than those of the Great Leap era, and agriculture was not destabilized as much. In general, however, the period was marked by extensive political dislocations and even chaos. It is referred to as the Cultural Revolution.

Following Mao's death and the strife over the succession moderate forces gained control. Technocrats and intelligentsia were reinstated. The political struggle to establish communism took a backseat to economic pragmatism. China was opened to Western influence and trade, one of the bolder changes of this period. Strategies of the deceased Mao were criticized and his cult destroyed in a move to prevent a return to more radical policies.

Vacillations in economic policies created endogenous risks in the Chinese economy. China has had fluctuations in GNP related to both endogenous risks and event (weather) risks. The agricultural sector of the economy well illustrates these two types of risks and their links to overall economic performance.

UNCERTAINTY IN THE COUNTRYSIDE AND ECONOMIC PERFORMANCE

When the communists took over in 1949, at least 80 percent of the Chinese people were peasants. Traditional agriculture was the mainstay of the economy. One of the leadership's first tasks was to begin the transformation of the agricultural economy from one based on private property to a state-owned and organized sector. A major uncertainty facing the regime was how fast communist agriculture could be established without arousing peasant resistance that could cause a major setback on the road to communism in the countryside. Mao's ambitious goal in this respect was to have peasants who worked according to their abilities and consumed only according to modest needs. Mao was very anxious to accelerate the transformation. He was a risk assumer. Other party leaders held back. And disagreement over the timing of the collectivization of farming persisted for years, causing a serious split within the party leadership.

By 1951 the Central Committee issued its first directive on agricultural reorganization. There were to be three sequential phases in the process of collectivizing agriculture that would gradually eliminate private farming. These steps were to be the formation of mutual aid teams to coordinate labor use in peak labor periods, the organization of cooperatives where pay was related to land and work claims, and the formation of advanced collective farms where private property was completely abolished and socialist labor received rewards set by the state.

According to the First Five Year Plan (1953–57) one-third of farm households were to be brought into cooperatives by 1957. Mao, however, intervened to accelerate the movement and by 1956, 92 percent of peasant households had been recruited into cooperatives and collectives. This haste created grave problems of organization, management, and incentive. Peasant resistance flared. This is not surprising given the extraordinarily short period of eight years (1949–57) within which the work situation, social relations, and income claims of millions of peasants were dramatically changed.

Rather than pausing to regroup and reform the cooperatives and collectives, Mao proceeded with his design for rapid industrialization and further advancement of agriculture along communist lines. Rural communes were formed with a goal of integrating all rural economic and political control into enlarged collectives or communes. Private plots for farming allowed under collectivization were abolished. All income was distributed by the commune and cooking and other tasks were shared in collective living styles. Women joined the farm work teams in increased numbers. The strong traditional family obligations of the Chinese were to be broken down in order to create uncompromising loyalty to a communist system of fellow workers. Such drastic socioeconomic experimentation was part of a campaign for development described above as the Great Leap Forward.

Turmoil and sabotage of the communes followed. The leadership had to retreat. By 1959 there were major concessions to the protesting peasants, including the return of private plots for raising vegetables and pigs. Peasants returned to family cooking. Smaller units of control emerged, with local teams having more freedom to manage work. And there was a retreat from egalitarian income distribution and a return to reward for work effort.

Output had dropped so much by 1961 that there was a proposal to assign land to individual households with a production quota to go to the state. This idea spawned a bitter party division that culminated in the Cultural Revolution of 1966. Again Mao and the more radical wing of the party won out. There was a return to ideological purity and a ruthless system set up for implementing the return. Agriculture stagnated. Chu-yuan Cheng writes of this period: ". . . under the concepts of continuous revolution and class struggle, there was no security for any member of the society. The ordinary individual in China—the worker, peasant, student, or cadre member—could not visualize his future with any certainty or plot a rational course toward it" (Cheng 1982).

By 1972 moderates again gained a leadership role in agricultural policies. Gradually the rural commune system reverted to the approach taken in the 1962–65 period, with substantial retreat from more ambitious communist goals. But during the height of the political turmoil of the Cultural Revolution, fear ran so high that decision-making at lower and middle levels became a slow, torturous process of group meetings.

As these brief summary paragraphs suggest, the peasant has faced great uncertainty under state-controlled agriculture in China. To the hazards of weather, pests, and natural disasters has been added the unsettled organizational structure of socialist agriculture. The peasant cannot predict with confidence the security of the private plot, a correspondence between work and pay, a certain share of the collective income, or the efficiency of the system once weather is accounted for. And while the lowest-income peasants are more secure than they were prior to socialist organization since they are assured a minimum income level, middle- and upper-income peasants are less secure since their land and capital wealth, such as livestock and tools, are gone and from time to time they have been declared "enemies of the state" upon which they depend for a livelihood. Not surprisingly this affected work incentive and, combined with organizational inefficiencies, brought a fall in output. Output declined despite the increased number of labor hours demanded of the peasant. In fact, on the basis of pay per hour worked, most peasants saw their income shrink. Group pressure and ideological persuasion were substituted for economic reward. For the peasant the marginal hour on the private plot, when it was permitted, promised a more certain and higher return than the marginal hour worked for the state to finance economic growth. The regime thus had a running battle trying to achieve optimum allocation of peasant labor hours under a system of unequal rewards for private plot and state farm work.

AGRICULTURE'S EFFECT UPON AGGREGATE ECONOMIC PERFORMANCE

Study of aggregate economic performance in the Chinese economy shows that the dramatic changes in policy created instability. China's development effort is greatly affected by her agriculture's performance. The effects of weather plus policy upon farming have caused major fluctuations in economic activity. These cycles have been no less marked than those found in economies without centralized planning (Cheng 1982, p. 293).

Between 1950–76 there were three major cycles and several smaller ones. The trough of the first cycle in 1961 came with the collapse of the Mao-inspired Great Leap Forward and resulted in a 27 percent drop in GNP. The widespread dislocations evoked by the Cultural Revolution produced a 13 percent fall in industrial output in 1967. The struggle over Mao's continued influence and successors to this role between 1974 and 1976 also disrupted growth but on a lesser scale than previous policy-related declines (ibid., pp. 308–312).

Dislocations in agriculture, whether policy or weather related, resulted in an induced investment cycle. In some cases, the benefits of good weather were more than offset by negative policy effects. Cheng concludes that the "erratic twists and turns" of policy played a more important role than other forces in economic fluctuations (ibid., p. 323). Such policies reflected the fact that Mao was a risk assumer. When he dominated party action, he proceeded with strategies that were highly risky. These sprang from a drive to establish communism in the countryside at a rapid pace. They proved to be destabilizing and thus costly. But the system rebounded and, while agriculture has not performed up to standards found in Taiwan and certain other Asian countries, the economy as a whole has performed better than, for example, the economies of India or Indonesia. And Mao's agricultural policies succeeded in mobilizing labor hours on a large scale for irrigation and other capital-forming rural projects. China had to retreat from Mao's radical policies, however. And certainly Mao could not remove the peasant from the security of the family unit when the state system of security was a poor substitute.

The Demography of LDC Population Changes

chapter

7

Dating from the earliest studies, population has been viewed as integrally related to economic development. Modern insights into population growth and changes are relevant for the developing LDC seeking to predict or affect population growth. Yet the determinants of human reproduction have proven to be very difficult to identify, perhaps because of the many shifting variables that coalesce to affect childbearing. Death rates exhibit more predictable patterns today than birth rates. As a result, much of the writing on demographics concentrates on identifying the determinants of fertility.

Here we select from the literature some of the current ideas about population determinants and the economics of population growth to give the reader insight into this important topic. Caution is advised in assessing policies concerning control of population increase for two reasons. First, knowledge about the causes of population change is very tentative, consisting of many hypotheses, some of which are not mutually consistent; and there is insufficient statistical data for culling hypotheses. Second, the effects of population change upon development are complex and multifaceted. Thus programs aimed at controlling population can easily turn out to be ineffective or, in some cases, even detrimental to economic goals.

The chapter begins by examining ideas about the determinants of fertility and mortality that are most relevant to LDCs; it proceeds to explore in a very simplified way the implications of variations in population growth for economic performance. More sophisticated models relating population changes to development are treated separately in the chapter following this one.

Mortality Rates

Mortality rates are a function of advances in medical science and care as well as nutrition and age. Before the Industrial Revolution in Western countries, death rates were around 35 per thousand, or 3.5 percent of total population. Today in the West, death rates are 9 per thousand. The decrease in infant and young children's mortality contributed greatly to this decline. The fall in death rates was gradual inasmuch as scientific progress in disease control and public hygiene was in its pioneering stages.

In contrast to the West, the drop in death rates in Asia, Africa, and Latin America has been precipitous. In these countries death rates had been as high as 45 per thousand. Accumulated technology in public health was applied in the twentieth century. Concentrated attacks after World War II on such killers as tuberculosis, malaria, smallpox, cholera, and typhoid fever resulted in dramatic drops in mortality. More gradual declines have come with improvements in nutrition, preventive medicine, and health care for the populace as incomes have risen, reducing deaths from respiratory and other diseases common to all countries. Crude death rates in LDCs are now between 10 and 18 per thousand. Life expectancy has shot up since the drop in mortality is concentrated in the younger age groups. The trend in mortality is still down for many countries as improvements in food supplies, water systems, public hygiene, and health facilities continue. African countries particularly will see further declines in their mortality rates. This dramatic drop in deaths in a relatively short historical period lies behind the demographic revolution in LDCs today.

The Demographic Revolution   Birth rates minus death rates determine the rate of population growth. In Western Europe and Japan, for reasons not fully understood, birth rates in the 1700s and 1800s did not approach the biological maximum as they do in many of today's LDCs. Instead of reaching 45 to 50 per thousand, birth rates were closer to 35 per thousand or even lower when today's MDCs began their industrial development. Population growth has a compound element built in as children grow up and beget children. As a result, a 1 percent differential in birth rates can have a great impact upon population size.

Today birth rates in most African countries are above 40 per thousand. Such high rates are also found in many countries of Latin America and Asia. The most populous countries of the world, India and the People's Republic of China, whose population increase weights heavily in world population changes, have birth rates between 26 and 36 per thousand. In contrast, those of MDCs are under 20 per thousand. In the more advanced countries, birth rates are only slightly above death rates, and exhibit a downward trend.

Figure 7.1 contrasts the stages of population transition from high birth and death rates to lower rates for the post-1800 period in MDCs and LDCs. The graph gives a simplified view of population expansion in different centuries. It is based on a sample of countries since census data were not taken for many countries in the two groups, and for others the data were incomplete or inaccurate. Moreover, fertility and mortality differences in individual countries are obscured by aggregation. For example, the demographic transition for individual countries typically involves a movement from high, *fluctuating* birth rates to low, fluctuating rates.

Notice that around 1800 the growth rate of population was actually higher in MDCs than LDCs (.55 percent versus .45 percent) even though birth rates were lower. This was due to a somewhat higher death rate in LDCs. The graph clearly shows that the transition to lower death rates in MDCs was more gradual than that in LDCs, and the changes in the population growth rates much lower. After the death rate began its continuous gradual decline in MDCs, the birth rate followed. As the MDCs developed in the mid-1800s, there was a modest bulge in population because of the lag in the decline in birth rates.

By comparison, the 2.35 percent growth rate after 1950 in the LDC population is so large that it is called the demographic revolution. Death rates in LDCs began to fall in the late 1800s while birth rates remained high. The plummeting in death rates after World War II was followed, with a lag, by falling birth rates. In sum, the demographic transition period in the West from high to low rates of population growth produced a much smaller bulge, or stage two, in population growth than that currently being experienced in LDCs. Because two

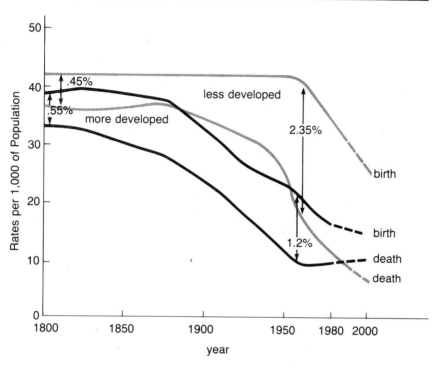

FIGURE 7.1

The Demographic Transition in LDCs and MDCs

Birth and death rates for LDCs (gray) and MDCs (black). In the last century both LDCs and MDCs had small natural increases in population due to high death rates. In LDCs the more precipitous drop in death rates and delayed drop in birth rates generated a natural increase in population of 2.35 percent in the late 1950s. LDC birth rates, while falling, remain relatively high.

thirds of the world's population lives in LDCs, the demographic revolution in these countries has produced historically unprecedented growth rates of the world's population. And many of these countries are still in stage two of demographic transition.

In today's LDCs the concentration of mortality reductions in younger age groups combined with the high birth rates has resulted in relatively high numbers of younger, dependent people. Looking at LDCs in contrast to MDCs, the work force, composed of those between 15 and 65, is a smaller percentage of total population. The differential averages about 12 percentage points, but individual cases vary either side of this average. Countries such as India and China, with population growth rates close to 2 percent and birth rates below maximum rates, will have a lower dependency ratio than more prolific countries with population increase running at 3.5 percent. *Changes* in population growth rates also affect the dependency ratio. It is only in cases where the age-specific birth and death rates remain steady for a prolonged period that

Dependency Groups and Population Growth

the percentage of the population in each age group does not change. (Thus, when economists build models with labor force inputs as a constant equal to the rate of population growth, they are assuming very special, stable population conditions that approximate only very roughly the real world.)

Recent Trends in Population Growth

At this time it is believed that the world has already seen its highest population growth rates arising from the demographic revolution. Fertility rates eventually drop in LDCs with social modernization and/or economic development. In fact, there is at present evidence of dramatic declines in some LDCs. Between the mid-1960s and 1970s, estimates show fertility rates fell 10 points or more in some 30 LDCs. And significant contractions have taken place in backward economic settings in seeming response to policy efforts. As such evidence accumulates, some feel it points to potential success for government programs aimed at accelerating the rate of reductions in fertility in today's LDCs. If China succeeds in her recently announced goal of trimming population growth rates below 1 percent, that will mean a reduction of 10 million per year in the growth of world population. Table 7.1 shows the drop in birth and death rates by regions.

Determinants of Fertility Rates

Both morally and economically declines in mortality rates are highly desirable. From an economic standpoint the young supported during their dependent years are not lost prior to their years of participation in the labor force. Also, losses among workers are lower. Where control of population is desired, attention must be paid to curbing fertility. The question of great interest is: What determines fertility rates and their changes. Can the methodology of economics provide insight into

TABLE 7.1
Changes in World Birth and Death Rates by Regions 1950–77

	1950	1960	1970	1977
Birth Rates				
MDCs	23	21	18	16
China	40	37	30	26
Other Asian LDCs	44	43	41	36
Latin American LDCs	42	41	39	34
African LDCs	48	48	47	46
Death Rates				
MDCs	10	9	9	9
China	23	16	11	10
Other Asian LDCs	27	20	18	16
Latin American LDCs	15	12	10	8
African LDCs	28	24	20	18

SOURCE: Reprinted with permission from *World Development*, Vol. 8, Table 2, p. 40 and primary sources listed there, Nick Eberstadt, "Recent Declines in Fertility in Less Developed Countries, and What 'Population Planners' May Learn From Them," copyright © 1980, Pergamon Press, Ltd.

fertility? Or is its study mainly a province of sociology, psychology, or medical science?

A general theory of the determinants of fertility has yet to be developed. The fact that we cannot predict this kind of behavior or explain past trends reflects the limited success of all disciplines in analyzing this challenging subject. Moreover, the knowledge base is not notable for the cross-fertilization of ideas arising within social science boundaries. For example, Charles Tilly complains that the economists' contributions have severe shortcomings and as a result have had little impact upon historical studies (1978, p. 39). And Richard Easterlin writes:

> . . . there is a notable scarcity in the economic analysis of fertility of references to physiological or biological factors that may influence fertility. There is also inadequate consideration of the nature of and evidence on the ways in which fertility is actually regulated. . . . In contrast, sociologists start with what might be called the production side of fertility. The analysis typically proceeds from discussion of frequency of intercourse and the reproductive capacity of a population to specific methods of fertility regulation, such as abstinence, contraception, and abortion, by which births are kept below the biological maximum. Beyond this, the discussion moves on to motivational and other factors, but the framework becomes much less uniform from one writer to another (in Tilly, ed. 1978, p. 59).

Steven Beaver sums up in a general way the other components that sociologists examine. He notes that the cluster of social factors affecting fertility rates identified in various studies includes the relaxation of sex-role restrictions on women, the weakening of extended kinship systems, and the reduced status value of children, especially male heirs (1975, pp. 8–9). Psychological factors mentioned as affecting fertility include nonfatalism, materialism, rationality, and secularism. Beaver and others caution against assuming family size is a planned, conscious decision. Everett Hagen cites the lack of knowledge by the social sciences to identify and test statistically theories of subconscious behavior affecting family size. Examples of subconscious behavior given are "manliness and mastery on the part of the man, . . . relieving the emptiness of life on the part of the woman and . . . many factors in the complex tensions between husband and wife." (1975, p. 56).

The best we can do at this time is point out that social, economic, and psychological factors combine to affect fertility rates; and the technology of birth control is a facilitator in the decline of procreativity. Economic factors have been identified and measured in some detail, perhaps because they are easily quantified for empirical work. Also economic as compared with social factors may be more readily manipulated or changed by policymakers attempting to curb the birth rate. Yet, identification of the noneconomic variables and their susceptibility to short-run change can be invaluable in development policy. They are so intertwined with economic conditions that it is difficult to ignore them without chancing policy failure. Some examples can help illustrate this point.

The social elements that determine marriage age in various LDCs affect fertility. Later marriages tend to reduce fertility when natural fertility within a given environment is below what is desired. Also, younger women married to younger men conceive more readily. Europe's birth rate during early development was affected by later marriages. Moreover, historians present evidence that the preindustrial European peasantry closely matched marriage and fertility to the support capacity of the land (Tilly 1978, p. 22).

The age of marriage is influenced by family and social pressures. Teenage marriages are usually influenced or arranged by the family; and such marriage is the norm in today's LDCs. Interestingly, though, social and economic elements affecting marriage age have been changing in these countries so that the age at which a woman weds has been rising. Some governments have enacted laws setting a minimum marriage age; yet these laws are not always correlated with a rising age of marriage for teenagers. Laws that do not reflect social norms regarding wedlock tend to go unenforced.

The government of China has set a relatively high legal marriage age. China is looking towards additional methods of birth control to supplement this policy. Yet Mao himself acknowledged that in the countryside the Chinese peasant was obsessed with having sons to the point that legal sanctions were not effective.

India provides a dramatic example of problems faced by the policymaker bent upon restraining fertility. Demographers usually point out that modern advancements in birth control methods can increase their acceptability and frequency of use. Yet the Indian government in the 1970s found out that acceleration of the use of certain modern methods of birth control was impossible because of the lack of social and psychological acceptance of such technology. The government's attempt to force vasectomies on men helped to topple the party in power.

Statistical Findings   The identification of economic and other variables that have a statistically significant coefficient when regressed upon fertility rates for samples including today's LDCs has generally been limited to cross-country studies because of the absence of time series data for individual countries over long enough periods. Generalizations from such studies are necessarily tentative since the statistician must make the specific assumption that fertility rates within a country over time are represented by a group of countries at different levels of development as measured by GNP, per capita GNP, or some other index.[1] Moreover, the data used may be subject to error rates as high as 20 percent in some cases.

---

1. For a critique of cross-country studies related to the fundamental methodology, see David H. Heer, "Economic Development and Fertility," *Demography* 3:423–44, 1966.

Statistical studies that differ in their methodology, their definition of the variables or proxies, and treatment of the data groupings can produce contradictory results. A consistent, significantly negative relationship has generally emerged, however, in studies relating education, urbanization, and economic development proxies such as steel consumption, newspaper circulation, or radios per thousand, to fertility. And recent statistical work has linked duality and inequality to high fertility. There is no generally accepted set of hypotheses explaining the exact relationship between these variables and fertility.

Infant or child mortality has been found in some studies to be positively related to fertility. The hypothesis is that women have more babies when they believe each child's chances of survival are poor. Despite the empirical difficulties in establishing cause and effect, some writers feel a decline in mortality is one of the most important factors in fertility decline (Cassen 1976, pp. 785–830). Simon Kuznets notes: "If it is the surviving children that are planned for, the difference in death rates alone would account for more than half of the observed differences in crude birth rates." (1973, p. 100). Of course, since mortality is highest among the young and old, declining mortality reduces the proportion of the population made up of women of childbearing age. This can lower the birth rate even if age-specific fertility holds constant (Anker 1978).

In addition to the variables mentioned, the statistical relationship between growth (defined as rising income per capita) and fertility has been closely examined. Fertility for a country varies over time with the level of income, tracing out an inverted u shape as shown by the solid line in figure 7.2. As income per capita rises from low levels, we see a small positive increase in fertility. There is an interim range of income over which fertility may fluctuate some but does not show a trend. Eventually as income continues to rise, procreativity declines (Mueller and Cohn, January 1977, pp. 325–47; Easterlin, Pollak, and Wachter, in Easterlin, ed. 1980, chap. 2).

Fertility and Income

This behavior pattern is a composite, and can reflect variations among subgroups in society. The early increase is often traced to improved nutrition and health and the greater ability of a family to support children. Inequality in the distribution of income can influence the duration of this effect, extending it into higher levels of income. Moreover, the height of the curve varies in different societies.

It is difficult to know if income itself or some of the many variables that change as it does are related to the decline in fertility. The rate of decline varies among socioeconomic groups. It drops more slowly at first for agricultural and mining households and those more recently migrating from rural settings. Eventually the pace of decline slows for groups with low fertility and rates among groups converge after a period of divergence. A fertility rate declining as per capita income rises, then, can be associated with both changing fertility within socioeconomic groups and shifts in the relative importance of socioeconomic groups (Haines 1979; Repetto 1979).

Easterlin, Pollak, and Wachter suggest that *desired* fertility is constant and then drops as modernization emerges. They explain the observed relationship between income and fertility as follows: First they assume the taste for having children varies according to socioeconomic status. Thus they divide the populace into differing socioeconomic strata and consider the effect this has upon aggregate behavior. Second, it is assumed that at low-income levels there is a shortfall between desired and actual fertility. As a result fertility rises with income because of health improvements for low socioeconomic groups. For other socioeconomic groups it will be falling due to taste factors as income rises. When low socioeconomic groups predominate, actual fertility rises. Eventually with modernization higher socioeconomic groups are more numerous and fertility declines. When fertility does not vary with income, this reflects offsetting influences between groups (Easterlin, Pollak, and Wachter, in Easterlin, ed. 1980).

THE ECONOMICS OF FERTILITY

The question has been asked; What economic impact do children in LDCs have upon their parents? Is such impact important enough to affect fertility, or is it of minor consequence? Generally it is felt a complex set of social, psychological, and historical variables determine fertility. Yet economic influences have a subtle way of creating structural rigidities that impose limitations upon human behavior. And as Karl Marx pointed out, the technical limitations of a society interact with and influence social organization and ideas. Where elements of the economic undergirding that helped form historical attitudes about family size remain intact, they must be considered in order to attain successful population policies.

The Economic Value and Cost of Children to Parents

With such thoughts in mind, population experts have examined whether or not children, before they marry, contribute enough to family income to offset what they consume, and possibly add to family income. It appears that even in rural areas in LDCs children from birth to their marriage consume more than they produce, although male children more closely approximate paying for their consumption (Mueller, in Ridker, ed. 1976, pp. 98–153; Lindert, in Easterlin, ed. 1980, chap. 1). This means parents give income to children that could otherwise go to consumption or savings.

Once children are preceived to have a cost and thus to compete with other uses for income in the family budget, and even for parents' time that has an opportunity cost, then the question arises as to whether a change in the cost of children would affect the number a family has. The government, through taxation, variation in charges for services, or laws, can change the cost of children to parents. To the degree that the cost of children is important in the matrix of variables determining fertility in LDCs, there is scope for influencing fertility rates.

A static, constrained *economic choice model* is sometimes used to predict fertility response to cost changes.[2] In this approach the parents have a time and an income constraint. Noneconomic factors determining the taste for children are taken as given, just as with tastes for goods, services, and leisure. Given wages, prices, and the opportunity cost of time, the family tries to maximize satisfaction so that the last units of time and money spent on children provide the same satisfaction as the last units spent on other consumption and leisure activities. The indivisibility of children and uncertainties in rearing them, of course, render the equilibrium approximate rather than exact.

In the economic choice model, then, children, as other activities that absorb time and income, are assumed to be subject to a choice response as their relative price changes. However, there are two possible reactions when the relative price of children changes: Fertility may be affected as couples fit family size to its cost; or expenditures per child may be adjusted. Thus the tie-in between fertility and the cost of children is complicated by the adjustment possible for the household in outlays per child as opposed to a change in fertility. In the aggregate, however, it is predicted that some adjustment in fertility will occur as relative prices change.

In addition to a substitution effect with a shift in relative prices, the model predicts an income effect as wages or the income-generating wealth of parents change. Higher income from work raises the opportunity cost of time spent on children, and thus the income effect is not straightforward as it is in the simple consumer choice model. When income rises the effect will be positive in that parents will want more children and/or will spend more on each child. However, the rise in earning power raises the cost of time spent on children, who are time-intensive. Thus there will be a negative substitution effect when wages rise. Again, this negative substitution effect can be expressed in lower fertility and/or reduced expenditure per child. The relationship between income and fertility, then, is difficult to predict.

The model has been used to predict reduced fertility in cases where the woman's paid job opportunities and wages rise. On the other hand, an increase in the man's income will not raise the opportunity cost of children so much because he is apt to devote less time to children. Here the positive income effect may dominate. Moreover, whether or not the woman tends to be active in the job market varies according to her education and age and the number and ages of her children, her migrant status, her marital status, and her health (International Labor Organization 1976, p. 41). Religion can play a role too. Some Moslem countries have more limited labor force participation by women.

When the methodology of economics is applied to planning family size, children are often treated as if similar to consumer durables in

Economic Methodology Applied to Fertility

Children as Consumer Durables

---

2. The first article along these lines was that by Gary S. Becker in *Demographic and Economic Change in Developed Countries*, National Bureau of Economic Research, Princeton University Press, 1960. The approach is now referred to as the Chicago-Columbia approach.

that they provide satisfaction over an extended period of time and have certain attributes of an investment good. In such a framework the emphasis is upon expected returns and costs of children to parents, and to methods of financing their rearing. A decision to invest in children means that alternative uses for time, income, and credit are forgone.

In very poor societies the child may be affordable because of ease of financing. Children are purchased on a "pay as they grow" basis. For a small down payment and monthly installments a poor family can acquire on time a highly valued child. A family may be unable to finance anything else of comparable value on credit. Where land is densely populated, farmland is seldom placed on the market in agrarian societies, and its cost and financing are dear. Each child is a different combination of changing characteristics producing a potential kaleidoscope of pleasures and even retirement support. Despite the high uncertainty of these returns and the costs of having children, their expected value is relatively high in a preindustrial setting with limited exposure to modern goods.

While this treatment of decisions to have children is engaging to a degree, there are distinct limitations to the parallels between the decision to raise a family and the purchase of consumer durables. Seeking other economic analogies, economists often point out that children provide security for parents. Such security may be related to the youngsters' sex and/or number. The next section examines this idea.

Children as
Social Insurance

Children as Social Insurance

A fruitful economic framework for understanding the economic forces interacting with social institutions and mores affecting the demand for children, and hence fertility, in LDCs is the framework dealing with economic response to uncertainity and risk. The family, and more particularly the extended family, is the main or only form of social insurance attainable in poor societies. The extended family provides health and life insurance, income maintenance insurance in case a member cannot work, and a retirement annuity adjusted for inflation. Thus children reflect a rational trade-off of income in exchange for, among other satisfactions, lowered risk. The very low earnings make reduction of uncertainty in income of prime importance.

While the nuclear family could have higher savings for eventualities like old age with fewer children, it could not provide the pooling of risk that the large clan does. Moreover, insurance policies affording the degree and diversity of security provided by the clan would generally be difficult for the family to finance if they were available. Savings usually take some other form—gold, bank accounts, land—none of them risk-free. In fact, a large choice of forms for saving is generally not available in LDCs. A logical alternative is a minimum of three sons and this easily leads to a family of six children. And one of these sons could hit the jackpot in the genetic lottery, catapulting the family out of poverty. Not surprisingly, clan or tribal allegiance persists until substitutes emerge and incomes rise. And, of course, important noneconomic aspects come into play, affecting group cohesion along family lines. In fact, as emphasized earlier, it is difficult to speak of separable economic factors independent in their explanation of variables such as fertility and family relations.

There is empirical work bearing on the topic. Surveys indicate old-age support is considered an important advantage of having children. Moreover, there is evidence that fertility is significantly lower in countries with social security benefits for the elderly (Lindert in Easterlin, ed. 1980, p. 50; Hohm 1975).

The risk and uncertainty framework is consistent with an increase and then a decline in fertility as income rises. As development proceeds and incomes exceed subsistence, families can afford additional children, who raise the level of insurance coverage for old age and other contingencies. In the long-run, incomes rise sufficiently to reduce risk aversion; in addition, income tends to become more secure with development. Less comprehensive insurance than that provided by the large extended family can suffice, or new kinds of protection can substitute. Thus the desired family size drops.

Some Applications and Caveats

Again, the framework of the extended family and its role of reducing risk and uncertainty can be used to explain a direct relationship between fertility and mortality. Contrary to social insurance provided by a government or a large and stable insurance company, the family is an insurance policy with less certain benefits. Declines in mortality reduce the number of children needed to achieve coverage of a given probability. On the other hand, should the reduction in cost increase the level of coverage sought, then fertility need not be lower. This is likely to occur at lower income levels. Recall that this type of analysis assumes that the family is in equilibrium so that the marginal utility of security and other satisfactions provided by the last child relative to its cost is equal to the marginal utility of other items relative to their costs. Only in such a case could a change over a limited range in the cost of children lead to adjustments to family fertility.

Job opportunities for women can be viewed within the framework of economic choice or of risk and uncertainty. Some time is diverted from home production to raise children, who also consume some home production. Market work may yield higher income than home production, and children curtail access to the job market. The income lost when the mother stays home with a family is part of the cost of children. Better job opportunities and wages raise this cost.

A woman with a job and work experience also increases the security of total family income since in the case of the man's illness or death, she has proven marketable skills. And when earnings vary with the weather, business conditions, or the like, two sources of income moderate such variance. Not surprisingly, then, increasing attention is being paid to job opportunities and wages for women as they may relate to family size. T. Paul Shultz has found some evidence of a connection in LDCs between fertility and opportunities for women's employment outside the home (January 1974).

Given the limited state of knowledge at this time, policy implications of economic theorizing should be weighed carefully. Certainly well-designed programs of population control must take into account the broad social determinants of family size embedded in historically evolved mores and institutions. The framework explaining economic forces at work simply emphasizes variables that are part of a socioeconomic composite. Among these variables, the role of children and the extended family as social security and insurance are important considerations in the design of successful programs encouraging reduction of fertility.

The economic choice model may also provide insights. On the other hand, the recent trend toward increasing the cost of children as a policy to reduce fertility is open to serious criticism, and illustrates a misuse of the model. The result can be less expenditure per child and reduced formation of human capital.

Income Elasticity of the Demand for Children

Can we say anything about how the desired family size varies in the long run with increases in income? Empirically it is difficult if not impossible to answer this question categorically if the question refers to a pure income effect. To isolate the effect of income alone upon desired family size, all other determinants of fertility must be known and accounted for, including effects from all price changes. Such determinants of fertility could change over time with adjustments in the societal network that accompany development and a rise in income.

From the evidence available, it appears that income is a good proxy for some important variables at work that affect fertility, at least at certain stages of development. There is evidence, referred to previously, of an increase and eventual decline in fertility as income per capita climbs from very low levels. Yet the specific level of fertility per income level can be affected by country-specific variables, and is not the same in all historical settings.

Here a graph is drawn reflecting the pattern of rising and eventually falling fertility with development. Assume it shows the behavior of the secular demand for children as income changes from subsistence levels to those in the crossover range from LDC to MDC.

Two constraints limit the number of children per family: the biological maximum and the minimum nutritional requirements. The biological maximum constraint is operative only where the society sanctions marriage of the female in her early teens and birth control is not prevalent. These two limitations are shown by the two dotted lines in figure 7.2 The line representing the biological maximum is horizontal. The subsistence line varies with income. Thus at some income level (y) the parents could maintain only themselves. As income increases by enough, they can support one child. Each additional child is assumed to need the same minimum increment of income. Thus the subsistence line for a family is given along yx. The solid line D_c shows the typical behavior pattern as income rises from low levels that curtail family size. The D_c curve merges with the subsistence line at low levels of income. The discrete points showing number of children have been joined to better outline the pattern of demand. The graph can then be translated to represent the aggregate demand for children as income varies.

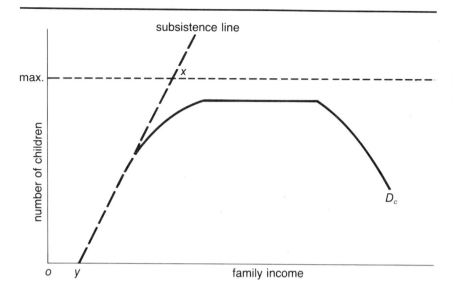

FIGURE 7.2
Fertility and Income

The number of children desired shown as a function of income.

At very low income levels parents may realize they cannot feed an additional mouth. This can affect mores about sex and reproduction. As incomes rise the nutritional constraint dissolves and the demand for children becomes less income-elastic. In this range the effect of income may be more subtle. Parents and society may define the "necessary" goods needed per child so that more additional income is needed per child than under constraint conditions. Then, over a range of increasing income the number of children wanted does not vary with income. And as the society becomes more affluent, the number of children desired declines. The level of the curve varies among societies, and is affected by the variables discussed previously.

Nutritional subsistence income is directly related to the number of children desired only where density is high or land available to the poor is restricted. Where land is relatively abundant in situations of primitive agriculture with limited knowledge about farming, restricting the number of children does not raise the amount of food available for each child. In such cases labor, along with a few rudimentary tools, is combined with land to produce crops. Storage of crops is very limited. Food supply per capita in any one year is a function of the weather. In most years there is enough food, although nutritional balance may be lacking. Parents are unable to predict or control fluctuations in output so survival of children is a function of their age and health in bad harvest years. Parents in such situations will conclude that the gods control their standard of living, not their own actions or family size.

Will a change in the relative price or cost of children shift the demand curve? If so, will it do so in all income ranges considered here? Empirically these questions have not been answered. Recall that the graph omits levels of income associated with MDC classification at the very high income ranges.[3] As constructed here, a change in the price of children or the goods perceived as "necessary" for each child in the lower-income range on the graph would shift a portion of the demand curve. A rise in either of these would shift the upward-sloping section of the curve at lower-income levels. As the slope falls for this section of the curve, the income level at which the curve becomes horizontal is higher and the horizontal section of the curve is shortened. The number of children supportable at lower income ranges has dropped with their increased cost. It seems plausible, however, that in income ranges above those close to subsistence, fertility will not respond to limited cost changes amidst the life-style and orientation of parents in poorer economies.

Assume this curve represents the demand for children in Ruratania. Assume conditions are such that some reduction in fertility rates is deemed beneficial for raising per capita GNP. When the economy is on the upward-sloping section of the D_c curve, taxation on children lowers income and can force some families to have fewer children. It is very difficult both politically and economically, however, for LDCs to pursue a policy of heavy taxation that reduces income already at or near subsistence levels. Moreover, poor, uneducated parents may not estimate correctly how many children they can maintain. Income reductions often lead to starvation or malnutrition, endangering the health of the populace.

Over a range of higher-income levels taxation of children does little if anything to change family size; rather policies that set charges for health care or education according to the number of children in a family using the service can deter the consumption of services that promote development at low-income levels. The price elasticity of children is zero, but the income effect forces a reduction in expenditure per child. The lesson here is obvious. Taxation to finance human capital expenditures necessary for development should be independent of access to the services it funds in order to minimize the income effect upon human capital formation.

Another approach suggests itself by the shape of the curve at low income levels. If parents could be convinced that the "necessary" food and clothing needed per child was greater than the actual or established subsistence level, the number of children would drop as income rises in the short run. This short-run fertility decline would allow policymakers time to work on long-term determinants of demand and shift the curve downward. Moreover, this is an acceptable approach to lowering the slope of yx contrary to certain taxation approaches. A similar short-run effect on fertility would result from an upward shift in the minimum acceptable standard of living of the parents, and thereby of their children. Such a shift may accompany migration and help explain

---

3. The literature using the Chicago-Columbia approach generally supports a price elasticity for children in very affluent economies where much more is spent on children, raising their cost, and where the value of the parents' time has risen. Here this higher-income range is not represented.

some evidence of differences in rural and urban fertility in a transition situation. The minimum living standards are often higher in urban areas, partly because of social amenities, and there is a greater range of income to measure living standards by.

When the LDC is in the horizontal range of D_c, the focus for a policy of fertility reduction must be upon the social and other factors related to desired family size that could be changed so as to shift the demand curve for children downward. Education of women is attracting attention as a possibly potent variable for influencing fertility levels.

When fertility rates approximate the biological maximum, delayed marriage will help even when only a portion of the marriages produce the maximum number of offspring. Communist China is currently pursuing this policy. Historically, Irish birth rates were affected by late marriage.

Job opportunities for the female outside of agriculture and home production as development reduces the dominance of agricultural employment can affect attitudes and economic variables bearing upon fertility. And, while a reduction in mortality rates by itself will boost population in the short-run, the longer-run effects upon fertility can be positive. Because changing attitudes about children can have the greatest impact upon fertility, and because these attitudes reflect behavior patterns and mores embedded in cultural identities and moral beliefs, downward shifts of the curve can require extended time periods even with well-developed policy approaches.

Children as Investment: The Economy

While children are a net cost to parents as well as to siblings, who have lower income because they are members of larger families, a child is a produced resource to the economy. The economy forgoes consumption to form children, who then become productive inputs over a protracted period of time, thus maintaining or adding to the labor force. Just as with physical capital goods, the initial cost and ongoing costs over time must be weighed against the increments to output. The resources invested in children could alternately be put into essentials like capital equipment and infrastructure.

Assume the planners, reflecting a community consensus in a poorer LDC, have instituted policies ensuring that 12 percent of income is saved and invested for growth. Assume that investors, competing for the savings, have bid the interest rate to 15 percent. Now calculate the net present value of an additional child as the present value of an infant's expected lifetime stream of consumption $(-)$ and production $(+)$, adjusted for mortality and other risks, using a discount rate of 15 percent.[4] If this present value is negative, then resources allocated in-

---

4. Present value is calculated for years other than year zero and added to the unadjusted value for year zero. The production value minus consumption value for each year is divided by $(1+i)^n$ where i is the discount rate of 15 percent and n is the cumulative years from one to n, the normal life span of a child. The formula is more complex when mortality probabilities are introduced. In general, the adjustment for death preceding the normal life span reduces the present value. A present value of zero indicates the child earns enough over a lifetime to cover his or her consumption and pay the 15 percent return earnable in alternative investments.

stead to investment areas that will earn the 15 percent return or more will be more conducive to growth.

Placed in a framework of productive wealth, a negative present value of a child indicates the additional person is a poor investment to the economy, not because over a lifetime the child would not produce an excess over what he or she consumes, but because the child would not be as productive as other types of investment that could earn the scarcity return on the savings invested. Notice that since a child requires initial outlays and often is not productive for 15 years, any present value with other than a very low discount rate is likely to yield a negative present value for children when their productive earnings are low in their early work years.

We have already noted that in LDCs children have high value to parents and the society is oriented toward large families. It is highly unlikely that population will grow at the rate that maximizes growth in per capita GNP when decisions on family size are strictly private. The conclusions drawn from the present-value approach are that society prefers more children to a greater growth of income, even or especially in situations of poverty; and it adds to the supply of labor when additions to capital are preferable economically from an investment-growth standpoint. In addition, since the cost of preventing an additional birth is low, the benefits of birth control for economic development in densely populated LDCs exceed its cost.

The present-value approach is a partial-equilibrium approach, however, and ignores repercussions upon the total economy of population size and its growth. Population growth may affect scale, technology, or investment, and may also exhibit externalities as growth proceeds. Such impacts are generally not captured in the present-value approach. And since growth is a long-run concept, it is unclear how the benefits and costs for different generations should be weighted one against the other. The rate of discount is generally chosen arbitrarily because there is no consensus on the appropriate saving rate for current and future generations. Simon notes a sharp drop in population can have an important growth impact later on as the labor force/dependents ratio falls with aging of the populace (Simon 1977, p. 431). Moreover, the present-value framework has inherent problems in treatment of the additional individual's own consumption and interrelated family utilities (Blandy 1974).

Before assuming a decline in fertility as judged by the present-value approach is desirable for the LDC economy, it is necessary to explore the impact upon economic development and growth of differing rates of population expansion. A beginning is made in the concluding section of this chapter and more sophisticated models are discussed in the next one.

POPULATION GROWTH AND DEVELOPMENT

Growth in aggregate output occurs when an economy increases inputs of capital, skilled and unskilled labor, and natural resources, and when it experiences productivity gains from technological change, economies of scale, and sectoral shifts. A rise in population is generally assumed to affect growth variables other than just that of the labor force. Many economists feel that models of development must treat population as an important endogenous variable affecting, and affected by, economic dynamics. Current understanding of how population growth impacts development suffers from the lack of a general theory of economic development. Ad hoc speculating about how population growth can influence particular development variables is less than satisfactory, and empirical work cannot proceed with a high degree of confidence in the absence of a theory.

The following sections survey current ideas about the effects population expansion can have on variables important to growth and development. Using a three-sector production possibilities curve graph of an LDC, with food needs treated as a constraint, the impact of different population growth rates is analyzed. The reader with preconceived ideas gained from the popular press will find the conclusions rather mild and highly qualified. The approach omits the relationship between the environment and population growth as hypothesized by the science of ecology.

The effect of population upon saving and investment varies among sectors. Here we consider agriculture, industry, and infrastructure in turn.

Population Effects upon Saving and Investment

Agriculture In LDC agriculture the saver, investor, and producer of capital are often the same unit—the family farm. In the off-season the family clears new land; irrigates; builds fences and barns; constructs roads, dikes, and wells. This type of investment is very difficult to estimate for purposes of national income accounting. Consequently much of it, particularly land reclamation and improvement, does not show up in GNP.

Julian Simon argues that with higher population growth, the farmer and his family will put in more hours on this type of capital formation increasing the agricultural capital stock (1977). For farming oriented LDCs this is a dominant part of their capital stock inasmuch as the capital/output ratio in agriculture is about 4/1 compared with 2/1 or 1 for manufacturing.[5] Since the work hours in agriculture are variable with underemployed labor, both consumption and savings can rise. Food consumption will usually rise, and may comprise a larger proportion of total consumption. Per capita income may remain the same.

Whether or not consumption rises more than investment may depend upon economies of scale for the household. An additional child does not imply proportionally increased outlays to attain the same consumption level per child. Also, expenditure on additional children can reduce other types of consumption. When consumption consists only of necessities, however, substitution between goods and children will not be by choice.

---

5. A larger K/O ratio in agriculture does *not* imply a higher K/L ratio.

In sum, output, investment, and consumption may all rise in agriculture with population growth and it is difficult to say whether the saving and investment rates vary with the rate of population growth. Population density can affect the results.

Industry   In the urban and industrial sectors, household savings will be cut when children are not a substitute for consumption only, and where the wealthier class does not increase their savings to provide for their children's future needs such as education. (Recall from chapter 4 that the effect of children upon the saving level in urban areas of some LDCs in Latin America is thought to be slight, although negative.)

The saver and investor are often the same person in industry, and the level of profits affects savings. With a greater number of people, and hence a larger labor force, wages are usually lower relative to profits. This tends to raise investment and savings as a percentage of GNP. When population growth does not greatly lower income per capita, then the market size varies directly with population growth. This may stimulate industrial expansion because of scale economies. However, as explained below, the short-run capacity to import capital goods used in the industrial sector shrinks when an increase in population reduces agricultural exports.

Infrastructure   Government funds will have to be diverted from transportation, communications, and utilities to education, health, and housing investment. The gestation period of the three former services is shorter, and the investment is more directly productive. Even with the diversion of tax funds, it may not be possible to increase or even maintain the economy's level of human capital with rapid population growth. Moreover, a decline in infrastructure can affect other investment negatively since this sector complements capital formation in agriculture and industry. Infrastructure also has its investment potential crimped when population growth diverts foreign exchange away from capital imports. Yet, as noted below, scale effects are important to this sector.

Economies of Scale   Some infrastructure is only profitable with minimum density levels. Examples are roads, dams, ports, and irrigation systems. Industrial output in many areas is subject to strong economy-of-scale effects. Where division of labor and scale economies are limited by small populations, an increase in the number of people can have a positive scale effect that raises productivity and investment. Economies of scale constitute one of the most important positive elements arising from population growth.

Labor-Force Size, Participation, and Diminishing Returns   Higher dependency ratios accompany climbing rates of population growth. This may affect labor force participation in terms of hours worked, entry and retirement age, and women's employment outside the home. It has already been mentioned that hours worked for capital formation in agriculture can increase. An increase in urban children can lead to more women and children joining the labor force, and can prevent earlier retirement, swelling the work force. Such increased participation will not be large enough, however, to overcome the tendency of the employed population to dwindle as a percentage of the total population because of the higher dependency of younger age groups.

In addition to its effects on labor force participation, a rising population results in a growing pool of workers. However, an expanding population, especially one with a high rate of growth, can experience diminishing returns to labor force growth that result in lower output per worker. This is particularly true when the percentage of unskilled workers increases because of a decline in human capital formation.

Foreign Trade and Population Growth

In the Heckscher-Ohlin model of trade, where a country specializes and exports goods that embody relatively large amounts of its abundant factors, a high growth rate in one factor (labor) would enable the country to specialize in goods using that factor intensively. Assuming the nation is already exporting labor-intensive goods, it would simply specialize more and trade more. This presupposes foreign demand and the terms of trade do not decline. The burgeoning labor supply enables the country to participate more in trade, and the gains it receives help to offset diminishing returns. J. E. Meade warns, however, that as more and more LDCs export manufactured goods using great amounts of unskilled labor because of generally high population growth and the need it creates for food and other imports, the terms of trade will turn against labor-oriented commodities (Meade, June 1967).

As illustrated in the last section of this chapter, in the short run crops for export tend to diminish when scarce land is diverted to domestic food crops in countries with structural rigidities. Even where agriculture does not provide exports, expanded food needs can funnel foreign exchange away from imports of capital goods to imports of food. Only in areas of surplus land is population growth likely to expand crops for export. This impact of the need for more food upon exports is immediate, while any positive labor force impact upon manufactures exports is delayed.

Technological Change and Population Growth

Little attention has been given to the connection between technological change and population growth or density. Boserup, taking a historical approach, points out that many nomadic or seminomadic peoples in sparsely populated areas have been forced into a technically more advanced form of sedentary farming by population pressures on food needs. Many of these peoples knew of the technology previously but refused to adopt it when population pressures did not require it (Boserup 1965). In a cross-country study Thirwall found statistical support for the conclusion that population growth has a negative effect upon LDC capital accumulation but influences total productivity growth positively (Thirwall 1972).

The pace of technological change may pick up the larger the talent pool from which to draw people for work on various frontiers of science. There are probably some economies of scale to technological change, and size effects upon markets may encourage competition, forcing the more rapid spread of technical know-how. The financing of technology may suffer, however, from the pressures of population upon savings and investment.

When population growth increases the number of unskilled workers as a proportion of the work force, technology tranfer becomes more difficult. Modern techniques tend to need a certain minimum proportion of skilled workers. Population growth can also reduce the economy's K/L ratio, which will make technology transfer harder since the elasticity of substitution of labor for capital is not high in many modern industries.

Unemployment and Population Growth

While population growth generally increases the labor force size, it may also contribute to a higher rate of unemployment. One reason is a tendency for more rapid population growth to make it more difficult to attain comparable growth rates in physical and human capital. Complementary inputs necessary to provide jobs are then lacking. Assimilation of large numbers of younger workers into the work force is generally marked by higher unemployment rates among them.

Inequality and Population Growth

Differentials in fertility rates among various income classes are under examination as a possible cause of growing inequality. Parents with less wealth and income have higher fertility rates, with the exception of very low income levels where the mother's health is affected by poverty. Wealth, income, and time are divided among more children in larger families. The education, health, and economic choices of children in larger families can place them at a disadvantage vis-a-vis children from smaller families.

In an aggregate sense, the differential rate of population growth between the poorer and richer groups makes it more difficult to reduce relative inequality and the absolute gap in incomes between rich and poor (Adelman, Morris, Robinson 1976, pp. 561–82). Higher population growth occurs in the rural sector, making it more difficult to reduce relative employment in agriculture by providing enough jobs in industry. Chapter 14 discusses the variables that can affect inequality in LDCs. At present many variables in addition to fertility are thought to contribute to the relatively high inequality in many LDCs. Here we simply point out that population growth is thought to make it more difficult to reduce the number mired in absolute poverty.

IDEAS ABOUT "OPTIMAL" POPULATIONS

Economists have examined the concept of "optimal" population and found that it is highly subjective and involves value judgments. Such ideas as expressed by modern population alarmists that the world is overcrowded, or should maintain higher living standards and open space as opposed to more people reflect personal choice and values, and implicitly assume an optimum population identified somehow, usually by personal preferences. Such a concept may become more objective if ecologists are able to prove that certain population levels are the maximum sustainable without disastrous results. Currently, ecology is a very young discipline without conclusive findings and the economics of population growth does not support the alarmists who speak of disastrous results from "overpopulation."

Value judgments, openly expressed, about population have generally been more readily accepted as a part of economic assessments applied to heavily populated LDCs with levels of income so low that vital needs cannot be met. For such countries, economic analysis points to a high probability of increased abject poverty with continued population growth. The misconception in the general literature has been that such conditions characterize large numbers of LDCs and the additional, unfounded supposition that control of population will yield development in all LDCs.

When dealing with absolute population, it is also interesting to inquire if there is a minimum population and area that will allow a country economic development. The vast majority of LDCs have less than 20 million people each. Many have fewer than 4 million. These very small countries do not have a wide complement of resources. Many are cut off from trade and economic cooperation with neighboring states and nations with similar market structures. Their main export earnings are perforce from raw materials sent to MDC markets. Unless there are highly favorable terms of trade from exports, incomes are not easily raised. Economists generally conclude that industrial development in such countries requires greater interdependence through trade and cooperative efforts with neighboring states. Of course, a superior economic arrangement would be economic union brought about by political union. It may not be judged a superior political arrangement, however, especially by those involved.

Graphical analysis can be helpful in studying some implications of population growth. Assume the following age distribution for an LDC with high and low population growth rates ($\dot{P}$). These figures approximate real-world differences and they reflect variations in the stage or intensity of the demographic revolution.

A Production Possibilities Graph with Population Growth

	Young Dependents 0–15	Work Force 16–65	Elderly Dependents Over 65	Total
	(millions of people)			
Small LDCs				
Low $\dot{P}$	5	12.5	2.5	20
High $\dot{P}$	9	10	1	20
Large LDC				
Low $\dot{P}$	10	25	5	40
High $\dot{P}$	18	20	2	40

FIGURE 7.3 *Population Growth Rate, Size, and Output Potential*

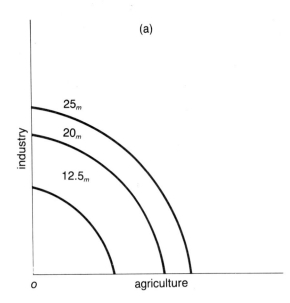 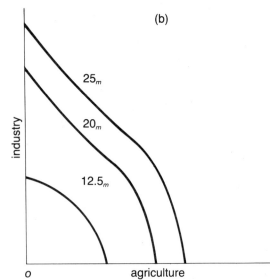

Workforce differences and output potential
FIGURE 7.3(a) without scale effects
FIGURE 7.3(b) with scale effects in industry

Consider two LDCs with the same low population growth rate, same K/L and N/L ratios, same human capital ratio and technology. There are no scale effects, and the only difference between the two countries is that one has twice the resources of the other. Their production possibilities curves would have the same shape, with the smaller country's being one half the larger's, as shown in figure 7.3(a) by the curves marked 12.5m and 25m.

By contrast, a country with 40 million people compared with the country with only 20 million, but with a higher growth rate of population, would have a work force 20 percent smaller than the large country with a low population growth rate. If this country had the same capital, technology, and other resource complements as countries with low population growth rates, it would have a lower *per capita* GNP than the countries with less fertile inhabitants. Its production possibilities curve would lie below that of the large country with 25 million people of work-force age since it would have only 20 million people in that age group. This is shown in figure 7.3(a) with the work-force size beside the production possibilities curve.

Now assume economies of scale exist.[6] Generally scale effects are more important in industry than agriculture. This would push out both production possiblities curves for the large LDCs and change their shapes,

---

6. Scale effects can arise from higher income per capita as well as from higher total population. Here the latter is emphasized.

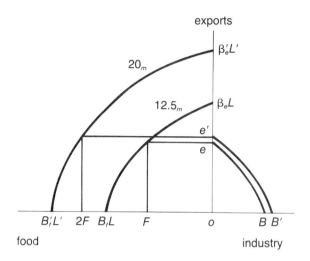

FIGURE 7.4 (a)

Higher/Lower Population Size, Growth Rate with Diminishing Returns in Agriculture

Higher population growth rate and higher L/N give diminishing returns in agriculture. Capacity output in the food and export crops and in the industrial sector are less than proportionate to the labor force differential between the large and small country. Food needs in this situation greatly limit industrial capacity for the large country relative to the small country.

as shown in figure 7.3(b). The size of the scale effects would have to be known in order to say anything about per capita GNP in the country with 20 million people in its work force compared with that in the country with 12.5 million. If large enough, scale effects could equalize income per capita in the two countries despite the smaller work force per capita in the nation with high population growth. Note, however, that the large country with the lower rate of population growth would have higher per capita GNP than either of the other two.

The assumption that each country has the same ratio of natural resources to population can be dropped and the effects of diminishing returns studied. Suppose the larger countries have less land per labor input. Agricultural output cannot be proportionately higher. The effects of this can be shown using the three-sector diagram in figure 7.4(a) depicting the countries with work forces of 12.5 million and 20 million, respectively.

The nation with 20 million workers has twice the population of one with 12.5 million. Its agricultural output is less than twice as high because of (a) diminishing returns to land, and (b) a work force less than double that of the smaller LDC. (The effects of diminishing returns upon the food and export crops will generally not give a parallel shift of the curve. For simplicity, however, we show the shift in figure 7.4 as parallel.) As figure 7.4(a) indicates, food needs are double those of the small country (2F versus F). Even assuming constant returns in industry, this makes the export and industrial potentials of the small country almost equal to those of the larger country for the case illustrated.

FIGURE 7.4 (b)

*Higher/Lower
Population Size,
Growth Rate with
Diminishing Returns
in Industry*

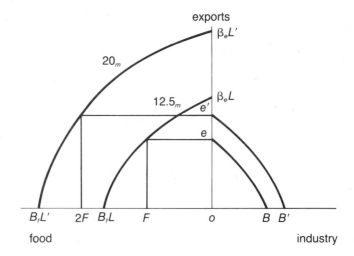

Higher population growth rate and higher *L/K* give diminishing returns in industry. Capacity output in the food and export crops for the large country are proportionate to labor force differentials but less than proportionate to population and food needs. Industrial capacity is limited relative to the small country by food needs and diminishing returns to labor in industry.

Now assume the large country with the higher population growth rate has the same labor/land ratio but less physical capital per work force member than the small country with the low population growth rate. Assume further that this affects output in industry but not in agriculture. Capacity food output, $\beta_f L'$ for the larger country, then is 1⅗ as large as capacity food output for the smaller country, $\beta_f L$; but food needs are double those of the smaller country since the larger country has a population of 25 million. Even without diminishing returns to land, the work force effects, food needs, and a lower complement of capital resources result in a relatively smaller export and industrial potential for the larger country, and of course lower output per capita. Note that if the need for food with high population growth meant that the agricultural work force in the larger country had to put in more hours, this could offset some, if not all, of the effects of smaller work force numbers.

A more populous country that has developed industrially to the point where it has a potential for manufactures exports might have labor-intensive exports that enable it to trade to meet its food needs, avoiding some of the effects of diminishing returns to increased food production. Internal scale economies can be helpful in beginning manufacturing industries that can, once domestic experience has been gained, work into the export markets. Notice also that a country that was able to tighten its belt and save more would tend to have a higher physical and human capital stock in relation to its work force. While it is harder to save more with a higher population growth rate, a country that did so could offset the effects of a smaller labor force. And, of course, when technology differs among countries with different population growth rates, this can override any of the effects considered above.

The preceding analysis helps to explain why poorer LDCs that have both high density ratios and rapidly growing populations will tend to experience lower per capita GNPs. Diminishing returns, consumption pressure on capital formation, and export bottlenecks will tend to inhibit industrialization and technical advance. These nations have more rapidly growing labor forces, but the work force/dependency ratio is lower. Scale advantages are unlikely to offset these conditions. On the other hand, it is harder to generalize about more moderate rates of population growth, especially where density levels are not excessive, and the LDC has developed a capacity for exports of manufactures along with high rates of capital formation. In some of the more advanced LDCs, high consumption levels with faster population growth could have a positive feedback, or accelerator effect, upon investment in industry.

Empirical studies have not established a strong relationship, either positive or negative, between population growth rates and per capita output. Nor does there appear to be an inverse relationship between growth rates of per capita income and population density. (See Hagen 1975, p. 189; Kuznets 1967, pp. 170–93; Conlisk and Huddle 1969, pp. 245–51.) Certainly this is consistent with the above analysis, which indicates that the interaction of population growth with other variables affects the outcome. The rate of technological change is especially important to the end result.

In concluding this chapter we examine the case of Brazil to illustrate the relationship between population and economic development in a less densely populated country that has had historically high population growth rates.

REFERENCES

Adelman, I., Morris, Cynthia T.; and Robinson, S. 1976. Policies for Equitable Growth, *World Development*, vol. 4, no. 7: pp. 561–82.

Anker, Richard. 1978. An Analysis of Fertility Differentials in Developing Countries. *Review of Economics and Statistics* February: 58–69.

Beaver, Steven E. 1975. *Demographic Transition Theory Reinterpreted: An Application to Recent Natality Trends in Latin America.* Lexington, MA: Lexington Books.

Becker, Gary S. 1960. *Demographic and Economic Change in Developed Countries.* National Bureau of Economic Research. Princeton, NJ: Princeton University Press.

Blandy, Richard J. 1974. The Welfare Analysis of Fertility Reduction. *Economic Journal* 84 (March): 109–29.

Boserup, E. 1965. *The Conditions of Agricultural Growth.* London: Allen and Unwin.

Cassen, Robert H. 1976. Population and Development: A Survey. *World Development* 4 (October-November): 785–830.

Conlisk, John, and Huddle, Donald. 1969. Allocating Foreign Aid: An Appraisal of a Self-Help Model. *Journal of Development Studies* 5 (July): 245–51.

Easterlin, Richard A. 1976. Population Change and Farm Settlement in the Northern United States. *Journal of Economic History* 36 (March): 45–75.

———1978. The Economics and Sociology of Fertility: A Synthesis. In *Historical Studies of Changing Fertility*, edited by C. Tilly. Princeton, NJ: Princeton University Press.

Easterlin, R. A.; Pollak, R. A.; and Wachter, M. L. 1980. Toward a More General Model of Fertility Determination: Endogenous Preferences and Natural Fertility. In *Population and Economic Change in Developing Countries*, edited by R. A. Easterlin, chap. 2. Chicago: The University of Chicago Press.

Eberstadt, Nick. 1980. Recent Declines in Fertility in Less Developed Countries and What Population Planners May Learn from Them. *World Development* (January): 40.

Hagen, E. E. 1975. *The Economics of Development*. Homewood, IL: Richard D. Irwin.

Haines, Michael. 1979. *Fertility and Occupation: Population Patterns in Industrialization*. New York: Academic Press.

Heer, David M. 1966. Economic Development and Fertility. *Demography* 3: 423–44.

Hohm, C. F. 1975. Social Security and Fertility: An International Perspective. *Demography* 12 (November): 629–44.

International Labor Organization. 1976. *World Employment Programme: Research in Retrospect and Prospect*. Geneva: International Labor Organization.

Kuznets, Simon. 1967. Population and Economic Growth. *Proceedings of the American Philosophical Society* 3 (June): 170–93.

———1973. Economic Aspects of Fertility Trends in the Less Developed Countries. In *Population, Capital and Growth*. New York: W.W. Norton and Co.

Lindert, P. H. 1980. Child Costs and Economic Development. In *Population and Economic Change in Developing Countries*, edited by R. A. Easterlin, chap. 1. Chicago: The University of Chicago Press.

Meade, J. E. 1967. Mauritius: A Case Study in Malthusian Economics. *The Economic Journal* June: 233–55.

Merrick, Thomas W. and Graham, Douglas H. 1979. *Population and Economic Development in Brazil: 1800 to the Present*. Baltimore, MD: The Johns Hopkins University Press.

Mueller, Eva. 1976. The Economic Value of Children in Peasant Agriculture. In *Population and Development: The Search for Selective Interventions*, edited by R. G. Ridker, pp. 98–153. Baltimore, MD: The Johns Hopkins Press.

Mueller, Eva, and Cohn, Richard. 1977. The Relation of Income to Fertility Decisions in Taiwan. *Economic Development and Cultural Change* 25 (January): 325–47.

Repetto, Robert. 1979. *Economic Equality and Fertility in Developing Countries*. Baltimore, MD: The Johns Hopkins University Press.

Simon, Julian L. 1977. *The Economics of Population and Growth*. Princeton, NJ: Princeton University Press.

Shultz, T. Paul. 1974. *Fertility Determinants: A Theory, Evidence and Application to Policy Evaluation*. Santa Monica, CA: Rand Corporation.

Thirwall, A. P. 1972. A Cross Section Study of Population Growth and the Growth of Output and Per Capita Income in a Production Function

Framework. *The Manchester School of Economic and Social Sciences* 4 (December): 339–56.

Tilly, Charles. 1978. The Historical Study of Vital Processes. In *Historical Studies of Changing Fertility*, edited by C. Tilly. Princeton, NJ: Princeton University Press.

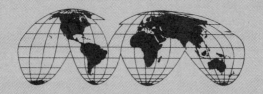

Demographic Patterns and Growth in Brazil

Brazil occupies a large tropical expanse on the continent of South America. She has sizable uninhabited areas in the interior. Starting with a population of roughly 3 million in 1800, Brazil today is a nation with over 100 million people. Moreover, along with the United States, she is one of the few countries to have experienced comparatively high population growth for a century or more with the help of immigrants. There have been periods of great growth in per capita GNP linked to a rapidly rising population. Because of low density relative to its natural resources, Brazil has typically sought more people, including slaves as well as free immigrants. Despite a comparatively high natural rate of increase in her population, she has not tried to reduce fertility rates via government policies. The desire for more people reflects a spirit of nationalism more than religious opposition to birth control.

Population growth has not been without some negative effects—in particular upon income inequality. But overall, population growth in Brazil has been associated with, first, export booms and, then, scale economies related to industrialization and infrastructure formation. It has provided the impetus for expansion into the internal frontier lands of tropical rain forests and great geophysical wealth. The demographic history of Brazil is one of unusual scope and interest. It has been chronicled in some detail by Thomas Merrick and Douglas Graham in their book, *Population and Economic Development in Brazil: 1800 to the Present* (1979). Some of their many insights are summarized here.

Merrick and Graham identify five broad phases of population growth in Brazil that since 1800 have been integrally related to her economic performance. The phases represent distinct demographic composites, and each covers roughly a doubling of the population; the earlier ones, however, are longer because of slower rates of population growth.

Phase 1 was from 1800 to 1850. Population grew at approximately 1.56 percent a year to about 7.2 million in 1850. During this phase slaves from Africa and some European immigrants contributed to the population increase. The major source of growth, however, was from the natural increase of nonslave population. This population was dominated by ex-slaves and their progeny. Historically Brazil allowed slaves to buy their freedom. She also experienced high rates of miscegenation so that there is a large colored population traceable to intermarriage between Africans or their descendants with Europeans.

Slavery was directly related to the export trade of the 1800s. Slaves were imported by the Portuguese to produce sugar and cotton in the northeast and sold to coffee barons in the southeast as coffee replaced sugar and cotton as the dominant export crop. They also worked in urban areas as artisans. Because of high mortality rates among both adults and children at the time, and the freeing of slaves, the slave population failed to reproduce itself. Thus Brazil imported new Africans until the slave trade ended in 1851. She finally freed all slaves in 1888, peacefully.

Phase 2, from 1850 to 1890, saw population double again, growing at 1.7 percent per year. Again the natural population growth dominated the increase, and there were no slave imports. European immigrants, mainly Portuguese, also contributed to the rise. However, it was phase 3, from 1890 to 1930, when free immigrants made their greatest contribution. The stimulus for this immigration was the growing strength of coffee exports.

The European immigration in total exceeded the slave imports. It was more concentrated, geographically, clustering in the coffee region of São Paulo and in urban areas. Brazil needed labor on the coffee plantations so badly that she subsidized migrants during this period. By the late 1800s migrants from northern Italy dominated the inflow, with Portuguese coming in a distant second. Spain and Germany, along with other European countries, rounded out the list of countries providing labor imports into Brazil up to this time.

Many immigrants to the coffee regions became small landholders, their income as laborers providing the saving for this. They received a fixed wage for weeding and caring for a given number of trees, a share of the harvest, rent-free housing, and land for garden crops and livestock, plus occasional income from day labor. This was in stark contrast to ex-slaves in the northeast who became subsistence sharecroppers on arid land. European migrants arrived as often as not with as much human capital as Brazilian natives in the settlement regions. They were assimilated quickly and provided entrepreneurial skills for the industrial sector. In contrast, ex-slaves who were not sharecroppers typically became urban servants. Both sources of labor, however, were gained by Brazil at the beginning of their productive years and did not have to be supported during their childhood.

Phase 4, from 1930 to 1955, saw the most rapid population growth in Brazil's demographic history. Immigration gradually tapered off, but the decline in mortality, with fairly steady, high fertility rates, led to a doubling in population in three decades. The momentum for population growth in this period was internal to a relatively greater degree than during the stages of slave imports and higher immigration. The high fertility rate persisted despite substantial urbanization and industrialization. At this time demographers wondered if Brazil would experience a demographic transition phase.

The last phase, still ongoing, does show evidence of demographic transition. Fertility has moderated somewhat, from 44 births per thousand to 40 per thousand in 1960–70, with subsequent drops in the 1970s. The country's population growth rate remains high, however, in the range of 2.2 percent. It should be noted, moreover, that the trend toward lower fertility was under way in the south and southeast of Brazil before 1950. This points to an important aspect of the demography of Brazil—the sharp regional differences, particularly between the low-income northeast and the affluent southeast. In fact, there appears to be little, if any, decline in fertility in the northeast (Merrick and Graham 1979, p. 255).

FERTILITY/MORTALITY PATTERNS

We turn now to certain fertility/mortality patterns established by Merrick and Graham, using data from the 1970 census, and some possible explanations for these patterns. This summary draws heavily from chapter 10 of their book.

Rural/Urban Fertility

Total fertility is 56 percent higher in rural than urban areas. The differential is much less in the low-income northeast—24 percent—than in the southeast—62 percent. Fertility in the central western states of the frontier receiving rural migrants also shows high rates for the rural areas and lower urban rates in urban settings.

Marriage Age

The high fertility in Brazil compared with her overall development level is related in some degree to the marriage age. Brazilians typically marry in their early twenties, later than the age common in some Asian societies where teenage marriage is typical. Even rural areas in Brazil show an average marriage age of 21.6 years. Brazil on the other hand does not duplicate the European pattern of late marriage and a comparatively high proportion of women who stay single. The relatively late age for rural marriage no doubt reflects the high mobility of the population. Migration between regions as industrial and geographic frontiers have opened up has produced imbalances between males and females of similar age. For example, there is a relatively high proportion of women remaining single in the northeast, the area of greatest out-migration.

Contraception

Modern methods of birth control have become increasingly available to urban women in high socioeconomic groups. The government has never supported a policy of widespread dissemination of contraceptives to the poor.

Income Per Capita

Brazil, as mentioned, has a high fertility rate relative to other countries at similar income levels. Not surprisingly this reflects to a great degree her economic and social dualism. The differential in fertility rates between areas of higher and lower per capita income is greater than that for mortality rates. Life expectancy at birth in the low-income northeast is 20 percent lower than in the south. Both rural and urban fertility rates are higher in the northeast.

Urban Assimilation

Socioeconomic status and length of residence both appear to affect the prolificness of migrants to Brazil's cities. As they are assimi-lated into urban socioeconomic groups, the migrants' fertility rates change to approximate those of the new social groups to which they belong. The growing security of urban income compared with rural income may also lower fertility.

Female Education and Labor Force Participation

Women's education and their participation in the labor force as industrialization proceeded have changed their social status both at home and at work. A modern outlook on the role of women and the optimum family size may have lowered fertility. A woman participates to a greater degree in the decisions about her life, including child-bearing. And educated mothers can easily work in Brazil as a result of job opportunities for skilled labor and an abundance of cheap household servants who migrate to the cities from the northeast. Job opportunities, then, may make a contribution to lower fertility among the educated women.

Infant Mortality

There is still deep poverty in Brazil. Even in urban areas, poverty is abysmal. Factors such as nutrition, safe water and other health essentials affect infant mortality levels. Studies show infant deaths increased in the late 1960s, when real wages were declining for urban workers (Merrick and Graham 1979, p. 268). The level of infant mortality may be one cause of higher fertility among the rural and urban poor.

Land Abundance

High levels of land per capita on frontiers like those that existed earlier in the United States are currently found in Brazil and have been identified as a possible cause of higher fertility. Richard Easterlin proposed a link in the United States between land available for children to inherit and fertility (1976). Merrick and Graham document studies for Brazil showing that fertility in rural areas varies with land-density pressures (1979, p. 272). In general the frontier areas have lower density. However, many seeking a new life on the frontier have no chance to acquire land because of the socioeconomic variables at work in Brazil. Many of the newly opened lands in the center of the country are large tracts used for cattle farming or other land-intensive uses. As a result, the frontier cannot affect fertility to the degree it once could in the United States.

CONCLUSIONS

Brazil's population growth, unusually high for a semiindustrialized country, can be examined with greater insight when two of its characteristics are kept in mind. First, the dual nature of the nation's economy and the immigrant sources of her population have produced a relatively sharp demographic dichotomy between regions and between rural and urban populations. The poorer segments of the populace, including recent migrants to the cities from rural areas, have relatively high fertility, while more prosperous, educated individuals of European ancestry are less prolific.

Second, Brazil is a frontier country with large geographic areas unsettled. This has meant that even with very unequal access to new lands and other wealth, the sharply diminishing returns common to heavily inhabited regions are absent. And there are still economies of scale to be gained from having more people. New settlements are able to accommodate some proportion of the population growth so that

land shortages are not acute. Moreover, Brazil has a sizable, highly modernized industrial sector that absorbs population from the land. Employment in service areas linked to industry is relatively high. The affluence of the industrial sector supports more government and private service employment than is possible in poorer economies, even if some of the jobs are for low-paid servants and petty services.

Unlike Brazil, poorer agrarian countries that are densely populated do not have a safety-valve for population pressures on the land. India, for example, cannot provide large new settlement areas for her rural population. And there are no scale economies to be gained from further population growth. Moreover, the industrial base of a poorer country such as India is not able to generate the many service-linked jobs for migrants that Brazil's prosperous industrial sector does. Thus, Brazil's official policy has been to encourage or simply ignore her high population growth rates, particularly since there is no indication that this growth hinders overall gains in GNP. One reason for this is that Brazil has had sufficient savings to improve the overall education level of the rapidly expanding population, although access to education is uneven.

Unfortunately, the dual pattern of population growth intensifies the inequality present in Brazil. But, as discussed in chapter 14, the country's inequality has many other sources.

Development Models and Population Growth

chapter

8

In discussing economic development models it is common to refer to the earliest, the Classical model. It is actually a composite model drawing on the ideas of Adam Smith, Thomas Malthus, David Ricardo, and John Stuart Mill, economists writing during the development of the West in the late eighteenth and early nineteenth centuries. In the attempt to combine their ideas and cast them in a thought framework of the current day, their original concepts and contributions are somewhat distorted.

The Classical model inspired W. A. Lewis's model of surplus labor in the 1950s and a school of thought known as neo-Malthusians, which subscribes to the tenets of the model today. This durability attests to its sophistication, and it remains after 175 years perhaps the most satisfying paradigm of development that introduces population as an endogenous variable. It has been described as a model of the race between technological progress and population growth. Yet it produced no hypothesis of technological progress, and its theory of population change emphasized mainly a rising death rate as a check upon population growth *after* industrialization succeeded, with fertility rates remaining constant. Its haunting conclusion is that development allows population to expand, but prosperity and growth end because of the population expansion.

The Classical model looks at the development path over the long run as inputs of capital (K), labor (L), natural resources (N), technology (T), and entrepreneurship (E) change. The production function for agriculture is characterized by diminishing returns to labor because land is in limited supply. For the industrial sector the production function features some scale economies in early industrialization from division of labor and its accompanying specialization. And let us assume conditions of perfect competition, since economies of scale were not large enough to produce monopoly or noncompetitive markets under the state of technology of the time.

A Stylized Presentation

The entrepreneur is the "hero" of the model in that he is the saver-investor and innovator. Despite the importance of this role, the Classical economists simply assumed there were many to fill it so long as market capitalism was allowed to operate freely, relieved of the intervention of mercantilist policies. Inputs of entrepreneurship are assumed to rise with the growth of the industrial sector. The landlord class does not innovate and is essentially nonproductive.

The knowledge base for technological change is also a given, exogenous to the model. The ingredients for technical advance were assumed plentiful for industry while there was an adequate flow of capital for new investment. A competitive environment populated by aggressive entrepreneurs promoted technical change. Thus technological change required, among other things, net investment above depreciation, competition, and entrepreneurs. Because technical advance calls for resources, we treat it as a produced input rather than a parameter.

As used today, the Classical model of development has two sectors, although the original writers did not ignore foreign trade. The production functions in agriculture (denoted by subscript f) and industry (subscript b) are different. Taking agriculture first, output is a function of labor inputs, land, and technology:

$$Q_f = g(L_f, \overline{N}, \overline{T}_f) \qquad\qquad (1)$$

Technology in agriculture, T_f, does not change over the development process. Its level was that of England at the time. And interestingly, the level of technology had risen in the years leading up to the industrial revolution, but the Classical economists chose to ignore agriculture's potential for continuous technological change. The missing components were an innovating landlord class and technology embodied in capital inputs.

The bars over $\overline{N}$ and $\overline{T}_f$ indicate they are constants. $\overline{N}$ will be settled and all land utilized as population grows. $\overline{N}$ is not homogeneous in quality. Labor will be added to the best land until its marginal product of labor (MP_{L_f}) is the same as for the next best land, which is then put under cultivation. Thus there are no increasing or constant returns to labor in agriculture, only diminishing returns. Capital is not viewed as a substitute for land.

Labor inputs in agriculture increase in some proportion to population growth. Such growth eventually brings the marginal product of labor in agriculture down to a level where, assuming laborers are paid the value of their marginal product, wages are at a subsistence level. The landlord captures the scarcity value of the land. The agricultural sector shows declining labor efficiency over time as the work force grows and land is fixed. Food output per capita declines, and food prices will rise with mounting demand.

Malthus supplied the theory of population growth. He assumed that the fertility rate is constant; the death rate varies with economic conditions. As food becomes short, the death rate rises until it finally equals the birth rate. Population growth then halts as death, disease, pestilence, and even wars take their toll. Prior to this state, a constant rate of population expansion means absolute numbers are rising exponentially as in figure 8.1.

Full employment is assumed in the model. A portion of labor force growth must go into agriculture as food needs rise, and the industrial sector also absorbs some of the labor growth. But the work force in industry is limited by the availability of funds from cash flow and profits saved to hire workers. The industrial sector is more complex and, while the purpose here is not to build a mathematical model, it is helpful to relate the variables to each other in notational form as well as words. Additional variables are as follows:

Q_b = industrial output per time period
R = profits and rent per time period
W = total wages per time period
w = wages per worker
$\overline{w}$ = subsistence wage
I = investment = dK per time period
S = savings per time period

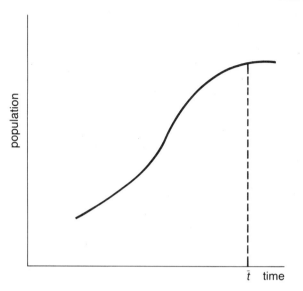

FIGURE 8.1

Malthusian
Population Growth

Population rises until subsistence food production is reached at time $\bar{t}$.

The terms of trade between industrial and agricultural output as development proceeds, P_b/P_f, are known, and the above variables can be denominated in equivalent food units. Output in industry varies with inputs of labor (L_b), capital (K), entrepreneurship (E), and technological change (T_b), a resource-absorbing input that draws from a stock of available technical knowledge:

$$Q_b = g(L_b, K, T_b, E) \qquad (2)$$

As output expands there are first increasing and then constant returns to scale as the effects of the division of labor are exhausted. The ability of the industrial sector to utilize entrepreneurial labor and assimilate better technology, two exogenous variables, depends upon its growth and profitability. Technological change is related to capital formation and profits, and to organization such as specialization of tasks and competition. For simplicity, we emphasize the importance of profits (R) and investment (I):

$$T = g(R, I) \qquad (3)$$

As mentioned, the amount of labor hired depends on a wages fund coming from cash flow and savings channeled into investment:

$$L_b = g(W_b) \qquad (4)$$

Thus the industrial work force is related to the size of the industrial sector and the growth of its capital stock. Modern versions of the Classical model drop this idea of a wages fund and relate the size of the labor force in industry to the marginal product of labor and the wage rate.

The Classical model emphasized supply-side limits to investment as opposed to demand-side variables. Investment tended to be buoyant so long as resources were available. The freeing of resources for investment depended upon savings and hence upon profits, the only source of savings. The saver and investor were the same person, the entrepreneur. Therefore, we note that investment depends upon profits and savings from profits:

$$I = g(R_b, S) \tag{5}$$

In turn, savings is a function of profits and entrepreneurs' propensity to save from profits—an assumed constant propensity:

$$S = g(R_b, E) \tag{6}$$

Notice that profits are pivotal in the system. They are designated R_b, the return to entrepreneurial innovation and capital inputs. Profits are equal to the value of industrial output minus industrial wages:

$$R_b = P_b Q_b - W_b \tag{7}$$

Equation (7) holds the key to the secular decline of profits and eventual stagnation when certain arguments of the Classical economists are accepted. To see this more clearly, we need to substitute equivalent expressions for output and total wages. Total industrial wages can be broken down into the wage rate times the number of workers employed in industry, and output can be alternately expressed as average labor productivity (β) times labor inputs in industry:

$$W_b = wL_b \tag{8}$$

$$Q_b = \beta_b L_b \tag{9}$$

Substituting these two alternative expressions for industrial wages and output into equation (7) gives:

$$R_b = P_b (\beta_b L_b) - wL_b \tag{10}$$

The importance of this equation can be understood when it is noted that a decrease in profits relative to the value of output in industry reduces saving and investment relative to the value of industrial output and thereby limits technological change. Thus profits affect technical change as well as react to it. We now follow the arguments of the Classical economists regarding the eventual decline of profits and the limits to grow.

The determinants of Q_b, here expressed as $\beta_b L_b$, are known from the production function. Labor productivity is related to capital inputs and embodied technical change, both of which depend upon savings and investment. Savings and investment both depend upon profits. Thus improvement in labor productivity is tied to the growth of profits. Furthermore a secular fall in profits will reduce labor productivity unless technical change is capital-saving, thereby requiring less capital per unit of output. The Classical economists did not assume biased technical change. In fact, they tended to argue for proportionality of labor to capital in industry.

Anything that increases the wage rate can reduce profits. The determinant of the lower limit of the wage rate is the cost of food. The plot sickens! Diminishing returns in agriculture must raise food prices, boosting wages in the industrial sector. If labor productivity in the industrial sector (β) and/or the price of the industrial good (P_b) cannot climb enough to offset rising wages caused by higher food costs, then $P_bQ_b - W_b$ declines and profits are squeezed. The outcome, then, is linked to the price of food relative to the price of industrial output. Thus, in order to follow the arguments further, it is helpful to make another change in the way the profits equation is expressed. We express profits in food units by dividing through by P_f, and rearrange the equation as follows:

$$R_b/P_f = L_b(P_b/P_f \cdot \beta - w/P_f) \tag{11}$$

With population growth, w approaches $\overline{w}$, subsistence wages. When $\overline{w}$ is reached, the increase in food prices will push the wage rate up by the same percentage, so that w/P_f is a constant. The term $P_b/P_f \cdot \beta$ is not likely to be constant. With food prices rising, profits will fall unless P_b or β_b offsets the increase of P_f. However, labor productivity does not tend to rise unless profits do, enabling capital formation and technical change to take place. This leaves the outcome dependent upon the terms of trade between industry and agriculture, P_b/P_f. The terms of trade between industrial goods and food depend upon the relevant supply and demand curves. The shift in the supply and demand conditions in agriculture compared with industry as growth proceeds determines how the terms of trade change.

The supply of industrial output, Q_b, changes with increases in inputs of labor, capital, and entrepreneurship; with advances in technology, and scale effects. The shift in demand for industrial output is predominately a function of the change in income of the growing middle class, and the income of the landlord class. It is, then, a function of the growth in profits and rents (ΔR). The workers were not large consumers of the industrial good.

The supply of agricultural output, Q_f, depends upon increases in labor, and land of declining fertility. Diminishing returns prevail and accelerate when all land is cultivated, and changes in output are based on changes in labor alone. On the other hand, the demand for food rises as population swells; and population is growing exponentially. With these conditions in mind, the Classical economists assumed the terms of trade eventually would move in favor of agriculture as food prices rose relative to the price of industrial output. Thus P_b/P_f falls in later stages of growth.

A Graphic Review of the Classical Model

Graphs of the supply and demand curves for labor with population growth, of industrial sector output and its division into wages and profits, and of the economy's two-sector production possibilities curve and terms of trade help to sum up our discussion of the Classical model. Consider first the labor market in this model. The short-run supply curve of labor is a function of population size and the disutility of work. There is some level of pay, called subsistence wages ($\overline{w}$), below which labor's earnings cannot fall because death rates increase and reduce the supply of workers. When wages are at subsistence and the pool of workers stabilized, the supply curve of labor is a horizontal line up to the point of full employment. At wage rates above subsistence, workers will put in additional hours or some additional people will take jobs; and thus the supply curve of labor slopes upward.

Figure 8.2(a) pictures this curve for three different population sizes; it shifts outward as population increases. It shifts upward with a rise in food prices since subsistence wages are determined by a minimum amount of food purchasable with the wages. That is, $\overline{w}$ is a minimum wage expressed in food purchasing power as:

$$\overline{w} = \frac{w}{P_f}\bigg|_{minimum} \tag{12}$$

We assume P_f rises with population growth. Hence $\overline{w}$ denominated in food prices corresponds to a rising nominal wage rate along the vertical axis.

The demand curve for labor in agriculture is downward sloping because of diminishing returns. The corresponding curve for industrial labor is also downward sloping. The Classical economists thought of the short-run demand curve as being related to a "wages fund" coming from the firm's internally generated cash flows, and particularly from profits. Thus, the lower wages were, the more laborers or their hours the fund could purchase. Today we would emphasize the effect of diminishing returns to additional labor in the short-run, with the capital stock fixed and technology constant, that would be reflected in the downward-sloping demand curve. With growth of the industrial sector's capital stock, its number of entrepreneurs, and the effects of technological change and economies of scale, the demand curve for labor

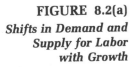

FIGURE 8.2(a)

Shifts in Demand and Supply for Labor with Growth

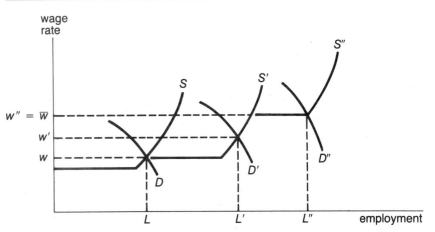

Nominal wages rise from *w* to *w″* as *L* grows from *L* to *L″*. Real wages fall from *w′* to $\overline{w}$ as *L* grows from *L′* to *L″*.

in industry shifts outward. When scale effects are exhausted, and the other variables no longer increase, the demand curve remains stationary. Figure 8.2(a) shows shifts in the economy's total demand curve for labor with growth and increasing money wages, but variation in real wages, in other words, the wage rate divided by the cost of food. The real wage rate is reflected by how close w is to the horizontal segment of the supply curve, which indicates subsistence wages.

Given rising wage rates, the short-run demand curves for labor in industry (MP_{L_b}) handily sum up the progress of industry. Figure 8.2(b) illustrates progression toward a stationary-state economy. The variables that shift demand are directly related to profits. When the latter rise slowly, the change in demand for labor slackens, reflecting a slower growth rate in industrial output. As mentioned, an important variable affecting profits (R) is the wage rate, since $R_b = P_b Q_b - w L_b$. The Classical economists assumed rises in real wages, that is, wages divided by the price of food, with population growth in periods prior to exhaustion of land in agriculture. Early growth allowed improved living standards for the masses plus a rapid expansion of the industrial sector as Q_b denominated in food grew at a faster rate than W_b denominated in food.

Continuation of population growth, however, brings on sharply diminishing returns in agriculture, raising food prices relative to industrial prices. The supply curve of labor shifts upward more sharply as food prices climb, pulling money wages with them, but lowering workers' real wages. Rising money wages diminish the increase of profits upon which further gains in industrial output depend. The continuing shrinkage of profits relative to the value of output slows investment. Labor productivity gains are affected by the dwindling profits and investment that slow technological change.

FIGURE 8.2(b)   *Industrial Wages, Profits, and Employment in the Classical Model*

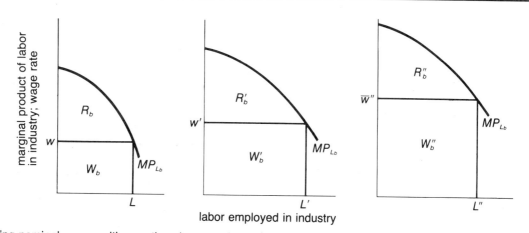

Rising nominal wages with growth reduces profits/output in the industrial sector. The MP_{L_b} curve eventually becomes stationary as profits are insufficient for capital formation and technical change. Profits R_b'' finance replacement of the existing capital stock.

Real wages are declining but they cannot fall below subsistence or the worker will not have enought to eat. As population grows, the demand for food grows exponentially while output of food per capita approaches the subsistence level ($\overline{w}$). When wages reach $\overline{w}$, nominal wages must rise in proportion to increases in the cost of food. The terms of trade between agriculture and industry have turned in favor of agriculture. Profits are squeezed as Q_b (denominated in food) rises at a slower rate than W_b (also denominated in food).

With wages continuing to move up because of higher food prices brought on by population growth and no potential for technical advance in agriculture, technological progress in industry grinds to a halt and investment in just equal to capital consumption. A stationary state has been reached. No resources are available to improve technology, so old machines are replaced without modification. Wages are at subsistence level, $\overline{w}$, and population is constant.

The total economy can be seen graphically in figure 8.3. The production possibilities curve shifts outward with capital accumulation, labor force growth, and the effects of scale and technology. Output potential for agriculture shifts outward relatively less than that for industry since once all land is utilized, only increases in labor raise agricultural output potential. And this potential grows relatively slowly because of diminishing returns. The production possibilities curve's outward shifts reach an end when population growth is halted by the constraint of subsistence wages, and profits are too low to finance further growth in capital. The economy in the stationary state remains on a set production possibilities curve, replacing worn-out capital and maintaining population. Technology does not change once capital falls to replacement levels.

Because population growth raises the demand for food relative to that for industrial goods, D_f/D_b, the community consumption point or product mix changes to reflect this. Its loci on various expanding pos-

FIGURE 8.3

Growth in the Classical Model

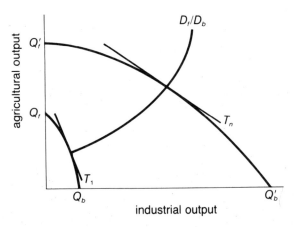

The terms of trade turn in favor of agriculture as the demand for food relative to the demand for manufactured goods (D_f/D_b) rises with population growth.

sibilities curves (not shown) are traced along the D_f/D_b line. The terms of trade change, as a result, from the slope of T_1 to the slope of T_n, indicating relatively higher food prices.

The stationary state, according to the Classical economists, was the end result of a long-run development process. Incomes could be above subsistence prior to this state; and during development income as well as the exact timing of the stationary state could be affected by the benefits of specialization and trade. In the long run, though, world population would pressure land resources and halt progress. No country could supply others with cheap food when all were densely populated. The confines of the British Isles certainly colored the Classical economists' reading of the future behavior of development variables.

The Classical model's outcome hinges upon certain key assumptions that, given the hindsight of 175 years, do not seem valid. Fertility rates have not been constant. Capital can be an important input in agriculture and substitute for land. Inputs of capital and technological advances in agriculture have more than offset diminishing returns to land; and the terms of trade with growth do not tend to turn against industry. Technical progress in industry appears to be related to savings and investment, but not in such a rigid fashion as assumed in the model.

Relevance of the Classical Model

However, the model still provides insights of current worth. It identifies a strong interrelation between industrial growth and agricultural performance. It points to key variables of development that must be included in any theory of the process, and analyzes their interdependence. The Classical model can be viewed as a model of dualism. In the absence of investment in agriculture, productivity gains are limited to the industrial sector and aggregate growth is affected by relationships between the sectors. Labor productivity in agriculture declines and the landlord class receives rising economic rents as population increases. Note that dualism in not characterized by a factor-proportions problem arising from capital intensity of modern technology in the industrial sector. Nor is it related to monopoly in the industrial sector, with differentials in bargaining strengths in favor of industry. Trade in the stylized version presented here is not a factor, and the marginal product of labor and wages are the same in both sectors. Rather the dualism is traceable to a noninnovating landlord class and a high, constant fertility rate, and, of course, the law of diminishing returns. The manufacturing sector must pay higher nominal wages, and as a result, the spread effects of industry are reduced or limited. The Classical model, then, gives us a fairly limited set of sufficient conditions for dualism.

Notice that industrialization in the Classical model succeeds despite impoverishing population growth. According to neo-Malthusians this is an impossible outcome under conditions where population density in agricultural economies is high because of modern science's effects

THE LEWIS-FEI-RANIS MODEL

on death rates. Such economies are viewed as unable to raise savings, and hence investment and productivity, and thus are said to be caught in a Malthusian population trap.

W. A. Lewis has studied such an economy from a Classical viewpoint. He emphasizes savings and profits as a source of savings. Rather than concentrating on technological change, he focuses on surplus agricultural labor with low marginal product and on other low-productivity "make-work" jobs. He forms a model whereby the excess labor is transformed into savings. Fei-Ranis refined and further specified the Lewis model, and it is now known as the Lewis-Fei-Ranis model (Fei and Ranis 1964; Lewis 1954).

The model concentrates on the absorption of surplus labor, with negligible contribution to agricultural output, into a nascent industrial sector. This industrial sector is assumed to be supplied with entrepreneurs who can innovate in making use of labor-intensive techniques.

A basic assumption of a surplus-labor model is that labor can be removed from the agricultural sector without a drop in farm output. This means either (a) the marginal product of labor in agriculture is zero, or (b) the marginal product of labor in agriculture is negligible so that with less laborers but more hours worked, the output of the agricultural sector does not fall.

Obviously with such a low marginal product of labor in agriculture, the wage cannot be equal to it. The assumption is that members of the family farm share the output, each receiving the average product of labor, which is low but at or above subsistence. When labor is attracted to industry from agriculture the wage will be low, but somewhat above the agricultural level—enough to compensate for slightly higher living costs. So long as the marginal product of labor in agriculture is below this industrial wage level, the value of the output lost in agriculture from migrant laborers is less than their industrial wage. Agriculture will not compete with industry for labor until redundant workers are removed and their marginal product rises above the institutional wage. A low marginal product of labor in agriculture means industry can attract workers at a constant cost. The constant wage rate, then, is an institutionally, as opposed to a market set wage rate, and is related to a subsistence income.

The industrial sector hires laborers up to the point where the institutional wage equals their marginal product in industry (MP_{L_b}). As figure 8.4 shows, when profits (R_b) are plowed back into investment, the MP_{L_b} curve shifts outward, increasing labor absorption. If it shifts so as to increase the L/K ratio, industrial expansion and labor absorption accelerate.

As industrialization proceeds, agriculture must feed its own labor force, now putting in longer hours, and also supply food for the growing number of industrial workers who are working longer hours than when on the farm. Fei-Ranis emphasize that when redundant labor is exhausted, a continued supply of constant-cost labor will require technological change in agriculture so that agricultural output can be increased with less labor per unit of output. This agricultural surplus provides raw materials for industry, export earnings to buy capital

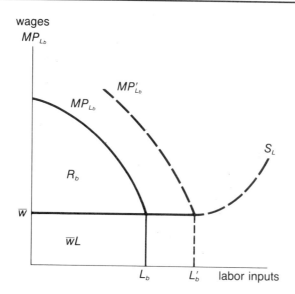

FIGURE 8.4

Industrial Sector Growth, Lewis-Fei-Ranis Model

Reinvested profits, R_b, increase the capital in industry. This raises the marginal product of labor curve and employment in industry, (L_b).

imports, and food for industry at prices low enough to keep wages from rising. Obviously the peasants must be prevented from consuming the surplus.

Industry takes the agricultural surplus, in the form of labor, food, imports, and raw materials, and turns it into industrial growth. Savings as a proportion of income rise because the growing manufacturing sector has constant labor costs, and saves from profits. Technological progress can further enhance profits. The terms of trade do not move against industry in the labor-surplus model. With a growing population, innovation that is capital-saving or "capital shallowing," and thus absorbs high amounts of labor to capital, will help move the economy's center of gravity to the industrial sector.

In sum, the industrial sector will rely on increased inputs of low-cost labor as a source of beginning savings accumulation to set the stage for capital growth and innovation. As growth continues, there is a period where innovation results in a shift toward higher L/K along with higher labor and capital productivity. With capital becoming relatively more plentiful, L/K will begin to drop and labor productivity will rise at a faster rate. Figure 8.5 illustrates early growth with more inputs and no change in technology from $\alpha_1 K$ to $\alpha_1 K'$ in the northwest quadrant and $\beta_1 L$ to $\beta_1 L'$ in the southeast quadrant. Growth with innovation toward capital shallowing absorbs more labor per unit of capital while increasing productivity. Output expands to $\alpha_2 K''$ or $\beta_2 L''$. Notice that capital productivity must grow relative to labor productivity in this type of technological change; that is, as L/K rises so does α/β. The reader can construct the next stage.

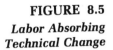

FIGURE 8.5

Labor Absorbing
Technical Change

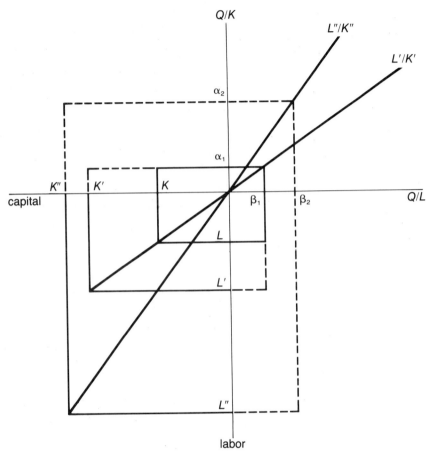

Industrial sector growth with capital shallowing: L/K and α/β rise.

Fei-Ranis define balanced growth as an industrialization process facilitated by stability in the terms of trade. Shifts in the demand and supply curves of labor are synchronized so that once redundant agricultural labor is gone, industry absorbs additional labor at the rate at which changes in agricultural productivity release it. Figure 8.6 illustrates growth with constant wages.

The importance of the foreign trade sector to a labor-surplus economy's development is downplayed. However, in a later work, Fei-Paauw consider the growing importance, after earlier industrialization, of labor-intensive export growth (Paauw and Fei 1973).

The closed-economy concept of balanced growth can be graphed showing constant terms of trade as the demand for food relative to industrial goods (D_f/D_b) declines with rising income and slowing population (figure 8.7). There may be a period of increasing D_f/D_b in early growth. Productivity gains are important in both sectors to achieve this balanced development. In early expansion there is a movement from

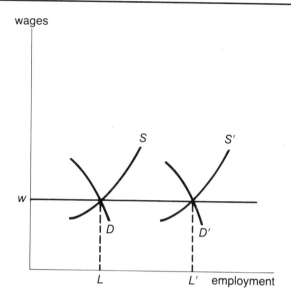

FIGURE 8.6
Growth with Constant Wages

As the supply of labor rises from S to S', the demand for labor rises from D to D', leaving equilibrium wages unchanged.

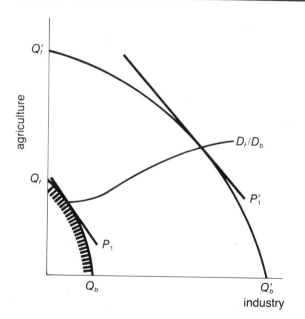

FIGURE 8.7
Balanced Growth

The terms of trade (P_1) are unchanged as relative supply (Q_f/Q_b) responds to the growth path in relative demand (D_f/D_b).

inside the production possibilities curve with underemployed labor to a position on the production possibilities curve with labor fully employed. The production possibilities curve can continue to move outward with population growth. There is no stationary state.

Relevance of the Model

This is a truly optimistic scenario, starting from Malthusian conditions. Yet Fei-Ranis claim Japan and Taiwan fit this model. Others have argued that the data for surplus-labor economies do not support the model. Capital shallowing may not have existed historically so much as periods of growth without capital deepening, followed later by the usual rise in K/L ratios. Foreign trade has generally been more important than Fei-Ranis allow. And much attention has been focused on whether surplus labor is empirically significant in densely populated countries. If it is not, then surplus labor is not a source of early savings increases.

The literature in the 1960s attacked the empirical significance of surplus labor (Jorgensen, in Adelman and Thorbecke, eds. 1967; Kao, Anschel, and Eicher 1964, pp. 129–44; Schultz, T. W. 1964). It soon became clear that the seasonality of farm labor influenced the conclusion that there were idle labor hours in agriculture. Yet, during planting and harvesting even heavily populated farm communities were short of labor, despite the fact that most family members worked in the fields at that time. Removal of laborers might be partly overcome by the remaining farm members working longer hours during the year. But without at least a minimum of reorganization, farm output would drop.

Developing countries generally devise methods for handling peak period needs as farm laborers transfer to other sectors. Schoolchildren from nonfarm areas may be brought in to help, along with migrant farmhands who follow the crops around the country. Cooperative tractor services can meet peak-period needs. The existence of surplus labor hours during the year will influence the appropriate approach to reorganization and technical change in agriculture. The opportunity cost of moving surplus workers to another sector is the output forgone in agriculture. This will usually be above zero, but in surplus-labor situations will be below the value of the laborer's output in another sector.

Finally, current technical and other conditions in LDCs with high population growth have not been conducive to the rapid absorption of labor into the industrial sector. These circumstances have prevented a convergence of the marginal products of labor in industry and agriculture and have led to persistent dualism rather than a smooth shift of gravity toward the industrial sector. As the following models illustrate, more attention is now given to the ramifications of different rates of population growth upon development than to the static neo-Malthusian emphasis upon density levels.

KELLEY-WILLIAMSON-CHEETHAM MODEL

In a book entitled *Dualistic Economic Development, Theory and History* (1972), the joint authors, Allen Kelley, Jeffrey Williamson, and Russell Cheetham (K-W-C hereafter) develop a mathematical simulation model reflective of structural conditions in LDCs today. The model emphasizes savings and capital formation, technological progress, and population growth as the pivotal variables affecting changes in per capita GNP in a dual economy. Unemployment is excluded from the model, along with the institutional wage. The paradigm is too complex to be explained here in its entirety. Rather, we discuss only some of its assumptions and some of the results as they pertain to population's impact upon development.

The book presents no theory of population growth. The initial rate of population expansion in the first time period is an exogenous variable, a given. This rate can be changed to trace through the effect of different population growth rates in various simulations. An initial rate is a composite of those stipulated for the agricultural and industrial sectors. However, population growth is assumed to vary consistently between sectors—it is always higher in the agricultural sector and lower in the industrial. Thus the rate of population growth over the development path is a weighted function of the rate of growth in the two sectors. When the model generates a sectoral shift, the population growth rate changes. As the economy industrializes, the rate declines.

Technological change in the K-W-C model is more important to savings and capital formation than an increase in savings is to output, in contrast to the early stage of the Lewis-Fei-Ranis model. There are three important areas where technical progress has impact upon development. Such progress can affect (1) the K/L ratio and hence savings needed for growth, (2) the level of output and profits and hence savings and capital formation, and (3) the sectoral shift toward industry, which in turn lowers population growth. Technological improvement affects the sectoral shift through effect (2). Industry is benefited relatively more by increased capital formation since the production function in the industrial sector is more capital-intensive than that in the agricultural sector. Not surprisingly, the authors conclude that the importance of technological progress has been underestimated in the development literature. However, they do not explain the causes of technical change, which is an exogenous variable in their model.

The saving function is similar to that of the Classical model. K-W-C make the simplifying assumption that saving is a constant proportion of income from profits and other capital assets. Savings to GNP rise as profits to GNP do. The savings needed for growth is inversely related to a rising efficiency ratio (α) for capital. The rising capital efficiency reflects the assumption of a constant rate of technical improvement that overcomes the tendency for diminishing returns to cause α to drop as growth proceeds and K/L rises.

Contrary to the Classical model, a higher rate of population growth raises the rate of profit and savings. Considering the case where labor grows faster than capital, K-W-C note that there will be a drop in the marginal product of labor and a rise in that of capital. Under scarcity pricing, profits relative to total wages rise, leading to a faster rate of capital accumulation. Again we encounter the idea that lower wages accompany larger populations and that this enables savings/income to be higher. But here the result does not depend upon surplus labor in agriculture.

A higher rate of population growth, however, slows the growth of industrialization, a result related to specific arguments of the agricultural production function. The model contains an agricultural production function where capital is included and is a perfect substitute for land. Moreover, in agriculture labor is assumed to have an elasticity of substitution for capital greater than or equal to one. This is in stark contrast to the assumptions of the Classical model. The authors argue that most land is augmentable, but that little data exist to estimate a land-expansion equation. The elasticity of substitution between labor and capital is based on empirical evidence.

Agricultural employment as a proportion of total employment rises as labor grows relative to capital, restricting industrialization. This occurs because the production function in agriculture is assumed to call for the farmer to substitute a greater amount of labor for capital with a given drop in the price of labor vis-à-vis capital. And additional laborers are needed to feed a growing population. Thus, even without technological change, the impact of population growth upon per capita output is uncertain. It depends upon the relative magnitudes of the positive and negative effects upon per capita GNP. The lower labor productivity and the sectoral shift toward agriculture are negative; the increase in capital formation is positive.

The K-W-C model can be shown graphically in a simplified form. Viewed graphically in figure 8.8, the industrial sector growth of the K-W-C model differs from that of the Lewis-Fei-Ranis model mainly in the labor supply curve. The short-run supply curve (S) slopes upward throughout since there is no surplus labor. The marginal product of labor in agriculture is positive, above subsistence, and rises as labor is withdrawn from that sector.

With population growth that slows with industrialization, the short-run supply curve of labor shifts outward from S to S' and then to S" in figure 8.8(a). The long-run supply curve of labor (S_L) slopes gently upward as the number of inhabitants expands. The agricultural sector

FIGURE 8.8(a)

Kelley-Williamson-Cheetham Model: Labor Market

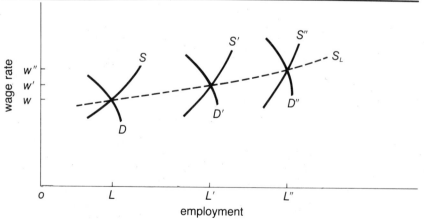

Population growth determines slope of long-run supply curve of labor (S_L) and rate of rise in the wage rate (w).

absorbs workers readily without sharply diminishing returns since capital substitutes for land. Wages rise in the long run with population growth, but not precipitously as in the Classical model. Real wage increases are related to labor productivity growth and thus to capital accumulation and technological change.

Profits/wages in figure 8.8(b) increase with expansion of the industrial sector. When population grows more slowly, real wages rise faster. Yet *relatively* more labor is absorbed in the industrial sector when this is the case. This follows from the assumption that the marginal product of labor (MP_L) falls faster in industry than in agriculture. Thus, when population growth is rapid, relatively more labor remains in agriculture and L/N and L/K rise in this sector.

In figure 8.9 a higher population growth produces a larger pool of workers and wages of w' rather than w. Each sector hires labor up to the point where the value of labor's marginal product equals the wage rate. When population growth is higher, wages are w' and L_a'/L_b' is larger than L_a/L_b. Higher wages do not stymie industrialization even though profits/wages are lower so long as technical change can shift out the MP_L curves. Remember that the Classical conditions that cause food prices to rise rapidly are excluded here. Economies of scale could also effect the level of MP_L as population grows, raising profits/wages.

K-W-C perform a sensitivity analysis with assumed labor force parameters, *no* technological change, and a 50-year growth period. Several generalizations emerge:

Results of K-W-C Simulations

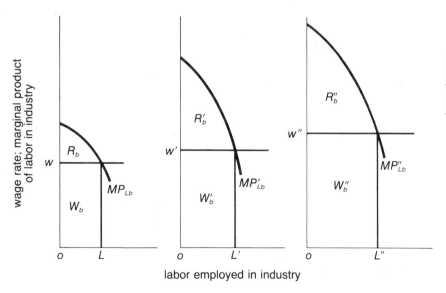

FIGURE 8.8(b)

Kelley-Williamson-Cheetham Model: Industry Growth

In industry capital accumulation and technological change shift the marginal product of labor (MP_L), allowing the ratio of profits to wages in industry (R_b/W_b) to rise with a moderate rise in w.

FIGURE 8.9   *Sectoral Employment with Larger/Smaller Labor Force*

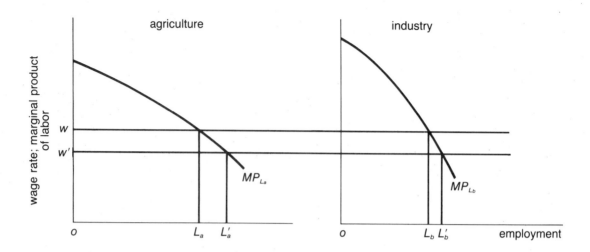

A larger population results in a greater proportion of the labor force in agriculture (L_a'/L_b' vs. L_a/L_b) relative to industry because there are more sharply diminishing returns to labor in industry. This slows industrialization.

1. An increase in labor force growth tends to exert its influence mainly in the first two or three decades.

2. GNP per capita will decline but the negative influence will be attenuated through time as capital accumulation effects brought on by population growth offset in part the impact of diminishing returns to labor growth.

3. The rate of industrialization is sharply curtailed in the first two decades because of the technical difference in the labor absorption potentials of agriculture and industry.

4. Even at a slower rate, industrialization continues, decreasing the growth rate of population. This will in turn diminish the adverse effect of population growth on per capita GNP.

5. The magnitude of the rate of population growth is important because of the model's sensitivity to changes in this parameter. Both Japan and Southeast Asia's data, when used in the model, perform well. Japan's rate of labor force growth during development was one half that of Southeast Asia's today. Given the sensitivity of the model to such large differences in labor force growth, the conclusion is that Japan's outstanding growth performance is in great part due to a low rate of population increase.

6. The long-run severity of the problem of population growth is not as great as often implied, provided it does give rise to increased rates of capital accumulation. This conclusion does not presume technological change which, of course, can prevent a decline in per capita output with population growth.

There is no allowance in the model for the need for an agricultural surplus for export, raw material, and urban food needs. Moreover the terms of trade, that is, the price of industrial goods in terms of agricultural goods, is a decreasing function of wages when capital intensity in industry is greater than that in agirculture. In other words, reduced wage costs shift the supply curve outward in agriculture proportionately more than in industry. This affects relative prices. With high population growth then, the terms of trade turn in favor of *industry* as wage reductions reduce costs by a greater extent in agriculture than in industry. This contrasts with the Classical and Lewis-Fei-Ranis models, which lay more emphasize on increasing demand for agricultural output rather than increasing efficiency and reduced costs in agriculture with population growth.

The model reveals a capital shallowing period for agriculture in early phases, but industry shows a consistently rising *K/L*. Not unlike the Lewis-Fei-Ranis model, there is a connection between population, wages, profits, and investment whereby abundant labor can lower wages, raise profits, and thereby increase investment. In the K-W-C model, however, abundant labor does not speed industrialization because of technical rigidities in the industrial production function, where the elasticity of substitution of labor for capital is less than one.

Probably the most optimistic assessment of the impact of population upon development is presented by Julian L. Simon (1977). He too develops a simulation model, but he extends the time frame beyond the K-W-C model. His conclusion regarding the relationship between population growth and development is:

SIMON MODEL

> The answer provided by the empirical explorations together with the simulations is that in the short-run a very low population growth rate is rather advantageous. But in the long-run—say after 75–150 years—moderate population growth does better than either a stationary population or very fast population growth.

Simon explores in considerable depth how population growth will affect all the growth variables; and some of his findings were included in the earlier discussion of this. He particularly emphasizes the impact of population on parents' work-leisure decision and the substitution effects upon consumption. He argues that more children may be a substitute for other consumption rather than for saving. He also includes stronger economy of scale effects than those of the Classical model. And he attaches them to agriculture as well as industry since they affect agricultural infrastructure such as roads, marketing networks, and dams. And, as in the K-W-C model, aggregate demand, which is related to population, affects capital formation and output positively; and land is understood to be augmentable by capital. The model assumes that involuntary unemployment does not vary with the population growth rate. And it omits the foreign trade sector.

Output in both sectors is determined by the following production function:

$$Q = f(K, M, T, J) \tag{12}$$

where M is man-hours, a variable that is positively related to population growth in the agricultural sector. J is infrastructure and is a function of the population density in previous years. Productivity gains from J effects are emphasized more than exogenous changes in technology—the variable of such importance in the K-W-C model.

The effects of population growth upon industrialization are qualified:

> An additional child is likely to increase the amount of work supplied by his parents. But at the same time he alters the shape of their indifference functions among industrial goods, food and leisure. The net result will probably be less demand for industrial goods, especially in relatively poor countries, which will slow down the industrialization process.
>
> After he enters the work force, the additional person may have a positive effect upon total and industrial demand. If the increase in total demand over the entire life cycle of an incremental person is large enough, and if the accelerator and other investment effects, plus economies-of-scale effects are great enough, an incremental person can have a net positive effect upon the proportion of the work force in industry. But if the parameters are not appropriate for it, the proportion of people working in industry will be less than otherwise (p. 156).

Key elements that affect the outcome in the Simon model are the substitution of work for leisure with the arrival of additional children, a positive but diminishing marginal product of labor in agriculture so long as capital formation accompanies (or is the result of) increased labor hours, the substitution of food for industrial goods in the allocation of income with population growth, economies of scale, and an acceleration effect upon industrial investment from expansion of output.

A different set of values chosen for parameters could yield a more negative or strictly positive impact of population growth. They would simply be less defensible parameters, according to Simon.

Conclusions   The reader has now explored enough models to have a feel for the variables and the two-sector general equilibrium approach. What can be said about the construction of the population models? First, they are more complete than partial equilibrium analysis such as the cost-benefit approach. They force the analyst to consider all important variables, their interrelations, and their determinants.

Given the complexity of the development process, it is not surprising that different authors stress different variables and different functional relations. Models must be viewed at this stage as exploratory frameworks of unsettled design. There is no theory of economic development or population growth to guide the selection of variables, and models must perforce have limited variables and equations in order to remain tractable. The empirical data needed to identify the functional relationships and their magnitudes are inadequate.

As work continues, models may converge in a more universal, homogeneous design. Even with more confidence in the model, the task assigned it in relation to population growth is formidable since the forecasting time period is so long. Reliability in projecting far into the future is limited because the parameters used are based on historical data that also stretch back many decades.

In concluding, one generalization made by Kuznets in the 1960s should be kept in mind: Low per capita income in today's LDCs is not traceable to differences in population growth rates; causes are multifaceted and include the broad spectrum of social and economic variables set out and discussed in earlier chapters. Productivity differences associated with variables other than diminishing returns hold the answer to why incomes in Tanzania and Japan differ.

Finally, recent studies are looking into the relationship of population to dualism and high inequality of income. Thus work continues along the lines begun almost two centuries ago by the Classical economists. In contrast to the Classical approach, however, much more attention is being given to the effect of population growth upon unemployment. The presumption of the two-sector models that industry can readily absorb large transfers of labor out of agriculture has proven to be misleading. We return to these topics in future chapters.

REFERENCES

Fei, John C. H. and Ranis, Gustav. 1964. *Development of the Labor Surplus Economy.* Homewood, Yale University Press.

Jorgenson, D. W. 1967. Testing Alternative Theories of the Development of a Dual Economy. In *The Theory and Design of Economic Development,* edited by J. Adelman and E. Thorbecke. Baltimore, MD: The *Johns Hopkins Press.*

Kao, C. H. C.; Anschel, K. R; and Eicher, C. K. 1964. Disguised Unemployment in Agriculture: A Survey. *Agriculture in Economic Development.* New York: McGraw-Hill: pp. 129–44.

Kelly, Allen; Williamson, Jeffrey; and Cheetham, Russell. 1972. *Dualistic Economic Development: Theory and History.* Chicago: The University of Chicago Press.

Lewis, W. A. 1954. Economic Development with Unlimited Supplies of Labor. *The Manchester School of Economics and Social Sciences* 22 (May): 139–91.

Paauw, Douglas and Fei, John C. H. *The Transition in Open Dualistic Economies.* New Haven, CT: Yale University Press.

Schultz, T. W. 1964. *Transforming Traditional Agriculture.* New Haven, CT: Yale University Press.

Simon, Julian L. 1977. *The Economics of Population Growth.* Princeton, NJ: Princeton University Press.

The Importance of Agricultural Transformation

chapter

9

T he economy of countries at very low levels of development is centered around food production. The ebb and flow of their economic activity conform to centuries-old patterns ruled by the rhythm of the seasons. Weather is the overpowering force determining economic output. Even when a foreign enclave exports some of a country's commodities, its activities do not penetrate the economic life of the vast majority. The people's main preoccupation is how to keep from starving. For development to occur, this centrality of agriculture must yield to a changing pattern of resource distribution that allows the emergence of other economic sectors.

However, the agricultural sector is essential to the development process that diminishes its own importance. It must provide food for the people and raw materials for industry. It is the source of commodity exports to be traded for capital and other imports vital to development. Development means that increasing percentages of the population are diverted to nonagricultural pursuits. Thus, agriculture must feed more people while employing a relatively smaller number of them to do so. The inability to do this can raise food prices and industrial wages, cutting profits and savings. This was explored in the chapter on population models.

When the majority of people are in agriculture, and its output dominates GNP, the sector is a natural base of taxation and a source of savings to help finance development expenditures. The resources freed when consumption is kept under control, particularly consumption from rent on land, are referred to as an agricultural surplus, usable in industrialization and in the development of agriculture that sets the stage for industrialization. Forms that the surplus can take have been mentioned above.

There is a balance between agriculture and the other sectors that must be carefully nurtured, a balance involving variables of demand as well as supply. Extraction of too large a surplus can destroy the balance. The rural sector must be allowed to grow as a market for other sectors. This is especially true in large countries where trade demand cannot compensate for low domestic purchasing power. Agriculture's purchases of investment inputs from other sectors raise agricultural productivity, providing markets that can stimulate off-farm inputs.

Bruce Johnston and Herman Southworth highlight the interdependence of agriculture with other sectors in successful development as it fulfills the various roles, and point to the importance of technological advance in agriculture:

> For these roles to be fulfilled, however, agricultural productivity must be increased. This requires a variety of off-farm inputs; providing them can be a stimulus to the industrial sector. It also requires incentives to farmers to invest in these inputs, in the form of attractive markets for their increased output; this also the growing nonfarm sector can provide. For incentive income to be meaningful to farmers, there must be goods that they can buy with it; the development of this rural market can also provide stimulus to nonagricultural industries. Thus growth in

*the two sectors interact, each supporting and stimulating the
other (Southworth and Johnston 1967, p. 4).*

THREE PHASES OF AGRICULTURAL DEVELOPMENT

Not unlike the process of economic evolution of which it is so much
a part, agricultural development can differ in various historical settings. The common underpinnings of technology, population growth,
factor substitution, and income per capita, however, place limits on
variations so that certain characteristics are shared to some degree.
Moreover these characteristics form three fairly distinct phases wherein
the agricultural sector conforms to a greater or lesser degree to the
stereotype description. The development of the stylized phases helps
pinpoint the important variables of change in agriculture at various
stages of an LDC's development.

Phase 1 Agriculture

Phase 1 agriculture in its most primitive state is characterized by underutilized land and technology below levels that provide support for
a high density of population. It is predominately a subsistence, nonmonetized agriculture without market crops. There is geographic and
even farm self-sufficiency in the absence of a developed network of
transportation and marketing. Cottage industry produces the necessities available and the simple tools used.

Exports may come from foreign enclaves. These use modern production techniques, thus creating a dual or bimodal agriculture. The
main contact of the foreign sector with the domestic is through the
labor supply the former hires.

The tools used and the improvements made to land by the unskilled labor are rudimentary. Slash and burn agirculture may be followed because, under conditions of low technology, it uses fewer man-
hours. In this type agriculture farmers continuously move onto new
land as the old, cultivated without attention to maintenance of topsoil,
becomes infertile. Such procedures cannot be used where portions of
land available cannot be left idle for 10 or 20 years. In rainy areas the
burned field provides only two or three years of harvests before it
rapidly loses minimum fertility. Risks arising from vagaries in the
weather are very high and can only be reduced with changes in institutions and technology.

In phase 1 capital (tools, land improvement), labor, and land are
joint inputs used in fairly fixed proportions. The determining variable
is the low level of technology. Without a change in the farmers' capacity to absorb technical improvements, more sophisticated inputs
are useless. Technological advance is extremely slow in the traditional
social structure of preindustrial society. Moreover a foreign enclave is
of little help in achieving such transformation. Foreign capital and
skills are combined with unskilled domestic labor to produce export
crops that do not influence domestic agriculture. Only limited amounts
of foreign aid can be utilized efficiently. More sophisticated tools and
other inputs cannot be used without technical change that identifies
the type of investment needed, and creates conditions that will make
it effective.

An increase in population brings underutilized land under cultivation. There must be a technology leap to reach phase 2. However, limited changes in technology in phase 1 bring small increases in productivity, often increasing the land a farm production unit can till, and reducing crop loss. The growing of small-cash crops can arise when transportation improves. Many areas of sub-Sahara Africa are in this phase.

A graph helps pinpoint the production function relationships. Phase 1 agriculture, where labor productivity (β) is not far from subsistence and output per acre (μ) is also low, is represented in the diagram shown in frame (a) of figure 9.1. When L and N expand in the same proportion (not shown), supportable population can rise even though labor and land productivity remain the same. Simple technical advances in this stage may raise worker productivity and even expand the land a laborer can farm, lowering L/N somewhat. This latter case is illustrated with the move to L'/N' as technology advances accompany labor force growth, raising β and μ to β' and μ'.

The introduction of conservation practices can allow a greater density of population in this phase, particularly in areas with sufficient rainfall and soil of high fertility. Such practices emphasize replacing and conserving soil nutrients with the help of manures as well as by terracing and other antierosion techniques, all involving increasingly complex, labor-intensive practices to use land and water resources more efficiently. Historically such improvements, according to Yujiro Hay-

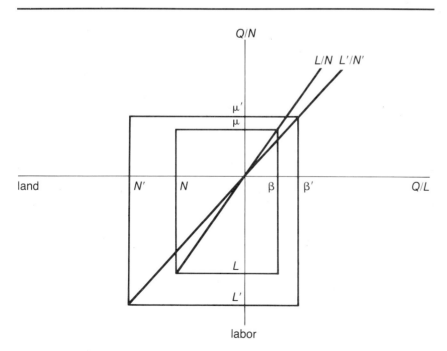

FIGURE 9.1(a)
Phase 1 Agriculture

With technological change, β rises as improved techniques allow workers to farm more land; with proportionately less growth in the labor force, L/N and μ/β fall.

FIGURE 9.1(b)
Phase 2 Agriculture

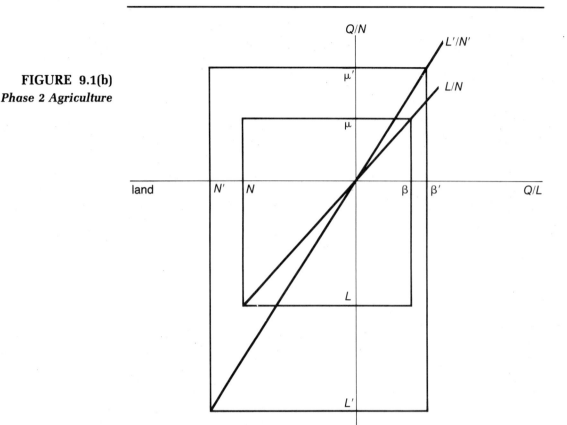

L/N rises over phase 1. Technical change offsets diminishing returns, raising β and μ/β. The main sources of growth in output are increased labor inputs and increased productivity from land.

·ami and Vernon Ruttan, allowed growth rates in agricultural output in the range of 1 percent per annum over relatively long periods (1971, p. 34). These authors emphasize that "agricultural growth rates in this range are not compatible, however, with the requirements of less-developed countries today for modernization and economic development under conditions of explosive population growth and rising per capita incomes." (*ibid*). Output in phase 2 agriculture, on the other hand, is capable of annual growth rates of 4 percent or more.

Phase 2 Agriculture   The density of population to arable land in this phase may be well above that of phase 1 so that only limited increments to land farmed can be made. The most efficient approach to growth in food supply under such conditions requires increased yields from land already being cultivated. There is mixed subsistence and market agriculture, with a greater proportion of farm output flowing into cash crops as a result of specialization. Commercial sale of crops allows farmers to purchase inputs needed to improve productivity and to increase yields through concentration on specific crops. The labor force in agriculture continues to grow with population; however, the *proportion* of the labor force in agriculture is below that in phase 1. Changes in the relative distribution of labor helps increase output in other sectors, particularly the industrial. Yet where population growth is strong, productivity, while rising dramatically, cannot increase fast enough to enlarge the average acreage per farm.[1]

The overcoming of the technology bottleneck distinguishes phase 2 from phase 1. The institutional framework has been transformed to accommodate continuous innovation and its diffusion. As John Mellor writes: "Agricultural development in phase 2 is a dynamic process providing a continuing rate of increase. It is not just a process of introducing a given set of innovations and reaping a once-for-all benefit. It is a phase in which a stream of innovation is generated by the process itself." (Mellor 1966, p. 225). As a result of continuous technological change plus the low initial level of efficiency, the growth rate of productivity in agriculture tends to be higher than the rates in other sectors (Kilby and Johnston 1975, p. 62).

The scientific approach to agriculture involving ongoing experimentation and adaptation of high-yielding staple food crops was first developed and introduced in temperate regions. In the 1950s Nobel laureate Norman E. Borlaug, undertaking research at the International Center for Corn and Wheat Improvement in Mexico, began experimenting with a hybrid wheat developed from a cross between seeds produced in the United States and those of a Japanese dwarf variety. Continuous crossings ultimately produced a much higher-yield, more disease-resistant wheat. The new hybrid seeds were distributed in Mexico, and following successful use there, were released for global commercial use in the 1960s. This semidwarf, high-yield Mexican wheat variety was introduced into tropical Asia, and set the stage for the Green Revolution of the late 1960s.

Experimentation with corn and rice hybrids followed. Advances here came more slowly and produced less spectacular yield increases. Research on staple crops oriented toward feeding the world's population is now an ongoing effort, and experiment centers located in various climatic areas of the globe are now furthering the development of higher-yield hybrids in other grains and staple crops used in arid regions and subtropic climates. Advances in genetic engineering promise

---

1. The rate at which labor can be transferred to the industrial sector is a function of the percentage of the labor force in agriculture, the rate of growth of the total labor force, and the rate of growth of nonfarm demand for labor. When the nonfarm sector is small, say 20 percent of the labor force is located there, and population grows at 3 percent, the nonfarm sector's growth rate must be above 3 percent to allow a growth in nonfarm/farm employment. A 5 percent growth rate in nonfarm employment could absorb one third of the *change* in population growth when the population increase is 3 percent. The same growth rate in nonfarm employment could absorb one half the change in the population when population growth is 2 percent. Unless population growth affects favorably the growth rate in the demand for labor in the nonfarm sector, then high population growth will mean slower gains in the percentage of labor employed outside of agriculture.

to bring important new breakthroughs. Yet the hybrid seeds are only one component of the technical package of phase 2 agriculture.

The technology used in cultivating staple grains calls for a complex of inputs to achieve large yield increases, Capital is a joint input of almost fixed proportion with certain inputs that lead to technological change. Agriculture's capital needs rise with the need for fertilizer; pesticides; irrigation facilities; energy; marketing, storage, and transportation infrastructure; and ongoing research to stay ahead of rust, blight, and pests, to raise yields, and to improve livestock. However, this does not mean that modern agriculture requires large, capital-intensive farms. The technology is scale neutral in respect to the farm size. It is subject to factor intensity reversal in that efficiency is achievable with highly labor-intensive methods on the farm when labor costs are relatively low and with highly capital-intensive methods when capital costs are relatively low.

The LDC at this phase is comparatively labor abundant, making it inefficient to utilize labor-saving capital equipment on the farm. However, since the Green Revolution has also opened possibilities for multiple cropping, tractor services supplied by cooperatives can allow for harvesting and field preparation at peak labor-use periods. The cooperative reduces the need for wide-scale, intensive use of farm machinery and allows fuller utilization of labor with multiple crops. Traditional forms of farm capital created by labor inputs such as irrigation ditches, hand-dug wells, and land clearing remain a relatively abundant form of capital not subject to the conservation rules for modern capital.

The labor-intensive farm must acquire water, seeds, fertilizer, and pesticides in fairly fixed proportion or the "miracle" hybrid seeds lose their power to raise yields four to five times traditional levels. Without adequate complements the farmer may realize crop yields below his centuries-proven methods. When the new technology is ineptly supported, the farmer will reject the new methods because of increased risk. Many new supporting institutions and organizational patterns are needed for technological transformation to occur. Investment in education applicable to agricultural progress is vital. Government orientation must be toward agricultural improvement or the many supportive public services needed will not be forthcoming. Land reform, credit availability, and institutions that provide incentive for the farmer to produce more while reducing risk all play an enabling role.

While agriculture accounts for a large proportion of total employment and output in this phase, there is a growing industrial sector with which agriculture is becoming increasingly interdependent and with which it must vie for capital. When the capital available to agriculture goes into capital-intensive farming rather than supportive inputs for labor-intensive farming, transformation is blocked for large segments and dualism develops. Farms receiving the capital are large and have high yields per worker while the traditional farming sector cannot raise yields per worker or per acre. Inequality increases and poverty for some deepens.

Some large capital-intensive farms may be associated with foreign plantations formed when land was more plentiful. Insofar as financial capital is raised abroad, it may be cost-efficient for the foreign managers to farm in this way. The economic rent from this type operation can flow mainly overseas unless taxes extract it for domestic development. Failure to do so loses sorely needed foreign exchange for the LDC, an important form of the agricultural surplus.

Once population density is high, the economic value of land is enhanced. Underutilized land such as exists when an elite controls large tracts they do not farm efficiently is costly to the economy. Even when foreign plantations are run efficiently, it is important for the economy to receive a rent equivalent to the scarcity value of the land reflective of a nation's need to feed its people adequately. This can conflict with private property rights acquired during periods when land was cheap. Poor land utilization, however, affects the potential for development.

Where the LDC has large deposits of ore of high export value, the pressure for agricultural modernization is not as great. In the absence of such largesse, however, there is a delicate balance between agricultural and industrial growth. Poor land utilization or the excessive protection and expansion of industry will deny needed resources to agriculture. This in turn will slow further expansion of industry and development.

The description of phase 2 is easy, but the achievement of it is demanding and time-consuming. Development economists concerned with the worsening poverty in the rural sector when transformation is uneven and incomplete are suggesting a rethinking of development strategies and the devising of more decentralized, mass-oriented policies with restrictions on capital-intensive production in both industry and agriculture when it creates dualism, underemployment, and poverty. More is said about this later.

Again it is helpful to summarize production function relationships and illustrate them graphically. Frame (b) in figure 9.1 represents phase 2 agriculture and offers a contrast to phase 1 illustrated in frame (a). In phase 2 agriculture land surpluses have been exhausted and land expansion (N to N') is slower than population growth (L to L'). Moreover, some land additions may be of poorer quality. Without technological change, diminishing returns would cause labor productivity to fall back toward subsistence and below.

Notice that technical improvement must raise land productivity (μ) relative to labor productivity (β) in order for L/N to rise without lowering output per laborer. More labor per land unit in and of itself increases μ/β; however, as mentioned, this lowers β. The importance of technological change that raises the productivity of both labor *and* land is evident at this stage.

A third factor of production such as fertilizer or labor-intensive capital goods, either domestic or imported, can be introduced into the analysis. These factors substitute for land and help boost output per acre, offsetting in part the effects of diminishing returns to labor. Their use is part of the technical change that raises land and labor productivity.

In sum, with technological gains and population growth in phase 2, the proportion, but not the absolute size, of the labor force in agriculture declines. A higher output per unit of labor input frees relatively more workers for other sectors without a fall in food supplies. The Green Revolution is accompanied by a dramatic rise in yields per acre for staple crops. Economies of scale are not important since the technology is scale neutral. The land can be relatively heavily populated yet absorb the technology. In the latter case μ/β must rise above levels with lower population density.

Phase 3 Agriculture

Growth in phase 3 involves a leap in the capital-labor ratio as agriculture is mechanized. There is much more technological continuity between phases 2 and 3 than between phases 1 and 2. Technological change has now developed its own momentum. The labor force in agriculture begins to decline absolutely and labor-saving machinery raises worker productivity to allow this decline.

In this stage, agriculture has been surpassed in growth and expansion by other sectors, and its contribution to GNP is diminished as a percentage of the total. Thus, while growing amounts of capital inputs are needed, the farming sector is now relatively small. Supplying its capital needs without denying other sectors is feasible when capital formation is adequate.

Farms get larger and self-sufficient agriculture disappears. Crop specialization leads to greater interdependence and subdivision of the farm-to-market transfer. Externally supplied inputs into the agricultural production function such as farm machinery, chemicals, transportation and storage costs, veterinarian services, and credit costs dominate value added in the agricultural sector. Livestock, especially beef, absorbs increasing amounts of available grain.

In the context of the familiar growth variables, phase 3 agriculture requires large amounts of capital to raise labor productivity, and substitute for labor. The labor force in agriculture begins to dwindle, supplying workers to other sectors and lowering L/N and μ/β. The capital is necessary to maintain and increase food production. Countries in this phase can vary greatly in yield per acre depending upon their L/N ratios, and thus the degree of labor intensity of their agriculture. Holland and Denmark boast higher yields per acre in general than the United States or Canada and use more labor per acre. In 1975, for example, wheat yields measured in hundred kilograms per hectare were approximately 50 for Holland and Denmark, but only 17 for North America.

Thus the process of agricultural development involves rising labor productivity in each phase, and this allows structural transformation toward industrial expansion. Increases in labor inputs are a relatively important source of growth in phase 2, while in phase 3 gains in capital inputs become important. Technical change is a major contributor to growth, raising yields per acre in phases 2 and 3 well above those of phase 1. And finally, changes in the institutions of the traditional economy are important contributors to growth in agricultural productivity. The risks related to weather and pests decline when the new technology is properly supported by well-designed institutional change.

It is helpful to look at historical agricultural data for selected countries for 1955 and 1965 in order to get an idea of the progress made in transforming agriculture. Table 9.1 shows productivities of land and labor, the ratio of these two, and the direction of change in labor and land inputs between 1955 and 1965. Hayami and Ruttan calculated productivity ratios using an index of output composites expressed in equivalent wheat units. The data were adjusted to exclude inputs of capital, seed, and fertilizer. The adjustments were approximate and did not, for example, eliminate the effect of the Aswan Dam upon land productivity in Egypt. This way of estimating aggregate output allows international comparison of efficiency ratios but inevitably incorporates index problems that affect data precision.

The sample of countries is limited by data availability. Many of the nations included had not made the full technical transition to phase 2, although the period covered was one where the groundwork was being laid for such a transition. Taiwan stands out as a country that had indeed completed the technical leap to stage 2.

Countries experiencing improvements in labor and land productivity with little if any change in μ/β are Argentina, Brazil, Ceylon, Greece, Peru, and Portugal. All except Argentina, Greece, and Portugal increased both land and labor inputs over the period. Four relatively labor-abundant countries—India, Taiwan, Turkey, and Egypt—experienced a rise in μ/β over the period.

STATISTICS ON AGRICULTURAL TRANSFORMATION

TABLE 9.1 *Estimated Land and Labor Productivities in Agriculture, 1955 and 1965*

	Output per Hectare in Wheat Units		Output per Male Worker		Land Productivity ÷ Labor Productivity		Change in Inputs (u=up, d=down, s=approx. same)	
	1955	1965	1955	1965	1955	1965	Labor	Land
Argentina	.36	.45	34.7	42.9	.010	.010	d	d
Brazil	.48	.63	8.1	10.4	.059	.061	u	u
Ceylon	2.49	3.02	3.8	4.5	.655	.671	u	u
Chile	.45	.49	11.7	13.4	.038	.037	u	u
Colombia	.80	.81	8.3	9.0	.096	.098	u	u
Greece	.99	1.53	7.9	12.1	.125	.126	s	s
India	.94	1.13	2.4	2.2	.392	.514	u	u
Ireland	1.37	1.63	16.4	24.3	.084	.067	d	u
Israel	2.36	2.54	14.8	38.9	.159	.065	d	u
Italy	2.64	3.31	10.8	20.1	.244	.165	d	d
Japan	7.02	7.54	7.7	13.1	.912	.576	d	u
Mexico	.21	.29	4.1	5.5	.051	.053	u	u
Peru	.47	.60	9.1	11.1	.052	.054	u	u
Philippines	1.63	1.39	3.7	4.1	.441	.339	u	u
Portugal	1.59	1.83	7.3	8.6	.218	.213	s	u
Spain	1.10	1.21	8.5	12.2	.129	.099	u	u
Syria	.38	.43	9.4	11.2	.040	.038	u	u
Taiwan	7.85	11.92	6.7	8.1	1.172	1.472	u	d
Turkey	.48	.68	6.3	7.6	.076	.089	u	u
Egypt	.56	7.75	3.7	4.6	.151	1.685	u	s
Venezuela	.24	.29	6.9	10.6	.035	.027	u	u

SOURCE: Y. Hayami and Vernon Ruttan, *Agricultural Development: An International Perspective*, Baltimore, MD: The Johns Hopkins University Press, 1971, p. 73. Reprinted by permission.

Countries in phase 3 that had declines in labor inputs over the period were: Ireland, Argentina, Israel, Italy, Japan, and Spain. The ratio μ/β fell for all except Argentina, where it remained unchanged. Nations evidencing limited if any improvement in output per hectare over the period gauged by aggregate data are: the Philippines, Venezuela, Colombia, Chile, Mexico, and Syria. All increased land and labor inputs into agriculture in order to feed their growing populations. For some of these states progress was uneven or dual so that the aggregate figures reflect a failure to progress toward transforming all of agriculture. Mexico, which had benefited from the Green Revolution at this time, is a case in point. Only one country in the table, India, is without improvement in labor productivity for the period. The effects of the Green Revolution occurred there in the late 1960s and 1970s.

Changes in Regional Food Grain Consumption 1961–79

The spread of improved technology in farming has been uneven among LDCs and this has affected food grain consumption per capita in various regions of the globe. Data for changes in consumption of this group of basic foods appear in table 9.2. Figures are presented for three-year averages in order to adjust for harvest and price fluctuations. Sub-Saharan Africa is a notable problem area. There food grain production has failed to keep up with population growth. South Asia also suffered a drop in consumption of these grains, but to a lesser degree than sub-Saharan Africa. Recall that much of sub-Saharan Africa is still in phase 1 agriculture. The growth rate of food grain consumption per capita for developing countries as a whole increased in the 1970 period from .3 percent to .7 percent, despite poor performances in the above regions.

GRAPHIC ANALYSIS AND REVIEW

The role of agriculture in providing food and exports and in freeing labor for industrial expansion is illustrated with the help of a three-sector diagram. The diagram for phase 1 will be somewhat different from the diagram for phase 2, which was introduced previously.

TABLE 9.2 *Food Grain Consumption Per Capita, 1961–79*

Country Group and Region	Kilograms per Capita			Average Annual Growth Rates (percentage)	
	1961–64	1970–73	1976–79	1961–64; 1970–73	1970–73; 1976–79
World Total	312.1	342.8	362.1	1.0	0.9
Developing Countries	223.0	229.7	239.9	0.3	0.7
Low-income Countries	207.1	202.7	202.4	−0.2	0.0
Sub-Saharan Africa	159.5	151.9	141.3	−0.5	−1.2
South Asia	215.6	211.8	213.5	−0.2	0.2
Middle-income Countries	238.1	255.6	275.7	0.8	1.3
Sub-Saharan Africa	140.7	150.0	148.5	0.7	−0.2
East Asia	257.2	271.2	282.7	0.6	0.7
Latin America	235.7	244.0	249.1	0.4	0.3
Southern Europe, Northern Africa, Middle East	390.6	441.0	495.8	1.4	2.0

SOURCE: World Bank, *World Bank Development Report 1982* (New York: Oxford University Press, 1982), Table 7.2, p. 102, from data by Food and Agricultural Organization. Reprinted by permission.

When land is available for clearing and equally suited to food or export **Phase 1** crops, then labor is the limiting resource. Workers make additions or improvements to the land and simple tools in the off-season. It is homogeneous, unskilled labor and can transfer between crops at some constant opportunity cost. Thus the production possibilities frontier is a straight line. Capacity output for the food crop can be expressed as $\beta_f L$. Similarly the output potential on the export crop axis is $\beta_e L$. The slope of the constant-cost production frontier ($\beta_e L/\beta_f L$) is determined by labor's productivity in the export crop relative to its productivity in raising food. In this example, control of the export sector is in domestic, not foreign, hands.

If the food and export crops are one and the same, then the food axis and the export axis will show equal potential output. A common situation, however, is where land and other resources can be used in raising a food crop or an export crop that has a comparative advantage in trade for needed, nonproduceable imports, but not for food imports. In international trade potential, then, food is a nontraded good. Its nontradable status and terms of trade reflect supply and demand variables, including transportation, marketing and storage conditions, and protectionism abroad.

Unless noted otherwise, the two-crop case is assumed in order to provide analysis of greater insight, and the export crop remains the crop of comparative advantage for export. That is, changes in the export crop's terms of trade vis-à-vis nonproduceable imports does not bestow an export advantage on the food crop. However, it is possible for the LDC to specialize completely in the export crop, importing food as well as nonproduceable imports. Conditions necessary for complete specialization are noted below. This too, however, is not considered to be the typical case.

Figure 9.2 shows the peasant economy engaged mainly in food production at point F because of low labor productivity. The terms of trade between the export crop and imports are shown by the slope of T. With production of e exports, imports can equal m. Assume the imports are manufactured goods. The economy is too poor to specialize and import more, at least at the given terms of trade. An increase in population raises L, which spreads onto additional land, leaving β_f and β_e constant. The production possibilities frontier would shift outward in such a case, raising food production and imports proportionately so that income per capita would remain constant.

Some economies of this type specialize completely in the export crop, trading for food and imports of manufactures. To do this, the terms of trade for exports/food must be higher than the domestic opportunity cost as shown by the slope of the production possibilities line. If the terms of trade were lower than the domestic opportunity cost, there would be a food shortage as exports would fail to earn imports equal to previous levels of food production. Thus, in figure 9.2 complete specialization is beneficial when Ee exports exchange for more than ef food.

It is necessary to improve labor productivity in agriculture before workers can be freed to move to an industrial sector. First consider a gain in productivity in the export crop. As technology in the export

FIGURE 9.2

*Phase 1 Agriculture
with an Export and
Food Crop*

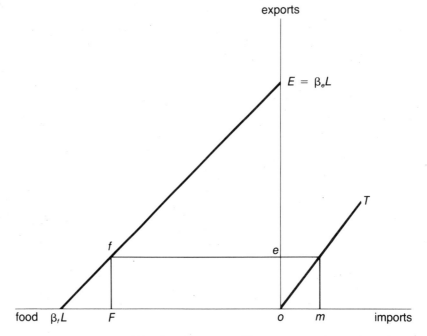

The economy produces *F* food and *e* exports. The exports exchange for *m* imports
along the terms of trade line *T*.

crop improves, labor productivity rises; as β_e in figure 9.3 increases,
capacity export production ($\beta_e L$) rises to $\beta'_e L$. Export potential is now
e'. This allows new imports or the transfer of labor to nonagricultural
pursuits.

More dramatic results can be achieved if labor productivity in the
food crop rises, boosting $\beta_f L$ to $\beta'_f L$ and e to e''. An increase in productivity in the food crop that raises output potential is more advantageous
than a similar percentage gain in productivity in export production so
long as production is concentrated in food. Of course, the country
specializing completely in exports and importing its food will benefit
from increased productivity in the export crop since it can export and
import the same amount without using the total labor supply, freeing
workers for nonagricultural pursuits. The case shown, however, illustrates why technical change in a small export enclave that does not
affect efficiency in food production has limited impact upon development.

Phase 2   The graph of a more advanced economy possessing an industrial sector,
and here assumed to be in phase 2 of its agricultural development, was
explained in chapter 3. Such a graph is shown again in figure 9.4,
where it is used to discuss technical change. Capacity food output
when all resources are used in that sector can be expressed as $\beta_f L$.

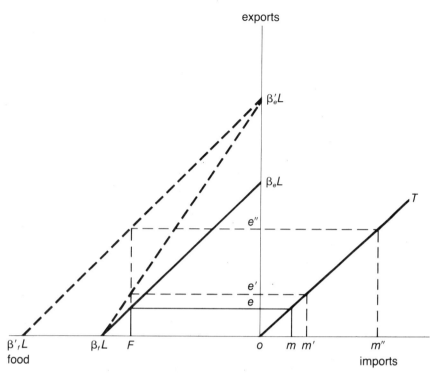

FIGURE 9.3

Phase 1 Agriculture: Technological Change in Food Compared with Exports

When labor productivity in export production rises from β_e to β_e', exports rise from e to e' and imports from m to m', with food production at F. When labor productivity in food production rises from β_f to β_f', exports rise from e' to e'' and imports from m' to m'' with food production at F.

However, this measure of labor productivity only applies to the capacity point since labor productivity changes along an increasing cost production possibilities curve as resource inputs are divided in the most efficient manner between food and exports. For the same reason the notation for labor productivity in exports (β_e) and in industrial goods (β_b) refers to the specific axis output level only. An improvement in technology changes labor productivity at each output point along a production possibilities curve, shifting the curve.

Industrial capacity along the axis in the northeast quadrant is the maximum industrial output possible with the simultaneous output of F food, the food needs or constraints of the economy. This industrial output capacity can be expressed in terms of labor inputs as $\beta_b(L - L_f)$, where L_f is the labor inputs used in producing F food. Export capacity assuming food production of F (point e) is similarly determined; but the labor force division would not be identical because there is a different production function involved.

Before discussing the case of phase 2 agriculture with ongoing technological change, it would be helpful to review the case of population growth without technological change in agriculture. This situation was illustrated in figure 7.4 in Chapter 7.

Population Pressures in Phase 2 Agriculture   Once a large proportion of arable land is occupied, the growth of population is accompanied by a less than proportionate increase in land brought under cultivation. As L/N rises, labor productivity drops in the absence of technological change. Capacity output in the export and food sectors increases by less proportionately than does the labor force. Thus the change in potential output will be:

$$dQ_f = \beta_f dL - d\beta_f L \quad \text{for food, and}$$

$$dQ_e = \beta_e dL - d\beta_e L \quad \text{for the export sector.}$$

This means per capita output potential in agriculture declines. One farm worker can feed fewer people. Yet food needs rise in proportion to the increase in population. To keep food supplies per capita constant, more workers must be occupied in food production (L_f') and thus fewer members of the expanded labor pool (L') are available for non-food production. That is $(L' - L_f')/L'$ is less than $(L - L_f)/L$. As a result, industrial output per capita is smaller after population growth.

Suppose now that each worker in agriculture puts in a longer day or week. In this way it is possible for agriculture's labor needs to grow no more than proportionately to population increase. The additional hours lower β_f and β_e further as labor input rises; but so long as the marginal product of labor hours is positive, output could rise proportionately with the number of workers. There is a time limit to this type of adjustment, however. Other modifications could also influence the outcome. Consumption of food per capita affects the size of the industrial sector. Any inefficiency by the household in food processing, storage, or consumption can retard industrialization.

Technological Change in Phase 2 Agriculture   Technological change, as in phase 1, is highly important to a rise in income per capita and, in phase 2, to industrial growth. Figure 9.4(a) shows technological change in agriculture with population constant. Labor productivity rises, increasing capacity output along the food and export axes to $\beta_f'L$ and $\beta_e'L$, respectively, and moving the production possibilities curve outward. Food production at F can now be produced with less labor (L_f'). This allows a large rise in potential industrial output even though there has been no technological improvement in industry. As L_f declines to L_f', potential industrial output rises from $\beta_b(L - L_f)$ to $\beta_b(L - L_f')$ along the industry axis.

Consider now the same technical gains for food production as the case above, but with no change in export sector productivity. As figure 9.4(b) shows, industry capacity along the industry axis, $\beta_b(L - L_f)$, shifts by the same amount as L_f falls to L_f'. However, export capacity output along the export axis, $\beta_e L$, remains the same. Maximum export production, assuming production of F food, expands from e to e', less

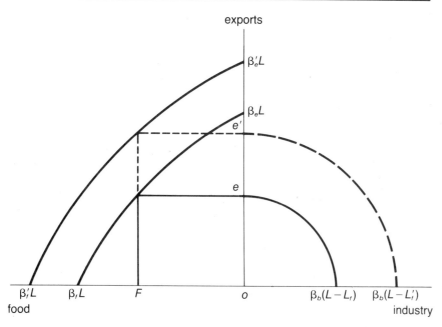

FIGURE 9.4(a)

Technical Progress in Food and Export Crops

Technological change in agriculture raises β_f and β_e, allowing a more than proportionate shift in export and industry output potential when food production does not change.

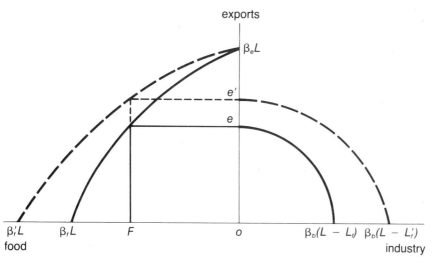

FIGURE 9.4(b)

Technical Progress in Food Crop

Technological change in food production raises β_f and lowers L_f, allowing expansion of export and industry output potential with constant food production.

than the case where export productivity rose. Moreover, combination levels of export and industry production potential do not increase by as much as in figure 9.4(a). Industrialization, then, can be helped by productivity growth in exports based on agriculture. Much more is said about the interrelation between export potential and industrialization in later chapters treating trade. Note, however, that increased productivity in the export sector *only* would not raise industrial potential beyond point $\beta_b(L - L_f)$, although the production possibilities for combinations of export and industrial production would increase.

Industrialization and Agricultural Transformation   Can industrialization proceed without progress in agriculture so long as there is increased efficiency in industry? Technological change in industry alone would raise β_b, shifting out point $\beta_b(L - L_f)$ on the industry axis, while leaving capacity food output, $\beta_f L$, and points $\beta_e L$ and e on the export axis unchanged. This allows industrial output to rise relative to total output, assuming food needs do not expand. Recall, though, that when diminishing returns occur as population rises, technological progress in agriculture as well is necessary to prevent a decline in the *proportion* of labor in industry. Thus, even though there is technical advance in industry, its absence in agriculture means there may be a decline in the industrial sector's relative output with population growth. This occurs when $(L - L_f)/L$ falls and β_b cannot rise enough to offset the effects of a lower percentage of the labor force being available to industry. There is a limit, then, to industrialization via increased labor productivity in the industrial sector and low labor allocation to that sector due to a stagnant agriculture with diminishing returns. In fact, this is reminiscent of the Classical model.

Capital and Phase 2 Agricultural Transformation   Capital goods, often imported, are important to expansion of agricultural and industrial output in phase 2 once technical advance over phase 1 creates capacity to absorb capital equipment. The accumulation of capital raises labor productivity in agriculture and industry, shifting the production possibilities curves outward. It substitutes for relatively scarce land in agriculture and is integral to the growth of output in industry. Technological change can be in part embodied in the capital. As will be discussed in a later chapter, the ability to diversify exports is directly connected to capital imports prior to the development of a domestic capital goods industry.

The increased level of formation of human capital also distinguishes phase 2 from phase 1 agriculture. It is integrally associated with technological change. The same examples used to illustrate the effects of improved know-how apply to changes in human capital as it affects simultaneously or alternately β_e, β_f and β_b. And the same conclusions follow: A neglect of education and other forms of human capital formation in agriculture can stymie industrial development.

The graphs are extreme in their simplification, yet they point to some strong conclusions that have been underlined by agricultural experts analyzing the development process. The more important of these are:

Conclusions

1. At early stages of development, a continuous growth in labor productivity in agriculture is a necessary condition for industrialization.
2. When a large majority of the people work in food production, increased labor productivity in this sector is more conducive to industrialization than increased labor productivity in export production.
3. With population growth, improved labor productivity in agriculture must offset diminishing returns or the proportion of the labor force in industry will decline.
4. As land becomes heavily populated, technical change must be of the type that raises yield per acre. Technical progress that is not highly capital-intensive is needed to allow the limited capital available to support widespread agricultural transformation and industrialization.
5. New and changed social institutions are important contributors to improved agricultural productivity in early development.

The analysis used here abstracts from the structural immobility problems that plague LDCs with frustrating tenacity, and the tendency for the economy to operate somewhere inside its production possibilities curve. Some of the greatest difficulties of development reside in the area of resource allocation. The model used so far is a beginning point in that it analyzes enabling changes that allow reallocation within a framework of resource limitations. Now we are ready to discuss aspects of dualism that arise when inefficient allocation and slow response to reallocation needs retard economic progress.

DEVELOPMENT WITH AND WITHOUT DUALISM

The term dualism has a long history in development literature, but an imprecise definition. The end result of dualism is that the set of economic activities under study has bimodal characteristics that persist for periods of time considered long in the light of history. Most often it is hypothesized that the advanced or prosperous sector's activities to some degree affect the lack of progress or prosperity in the less advanced sector.

Dualism

The causes and types of dualism differ. It is found in both MDCs and LDCs. Its depth and longevity are greater in LDCs, partly because of the international technology gap and the LDC's limited capacity to assimilate foreign technology. Certain sectors, subsectors, or geographic areas of the LDC become modernized, adopting advanced methods of production acquired from MDCs. The ownership of wealth—that is, income-producing assets—is highly skewed. The limited capital, land, human skills, and foreign exchange are disproportionately appropriated by the modernized sector. Employment in this sector does not spread rapidly enough relative to the growth of population in the backward sector to avoid growing disparities and continuing bimodal characteristics. According to Gunnar Myrdal (1968), the prosperous sector exerts negative "backwash" effects, social and economic, upon the backward sector, subsector, or region. These conclusions come from field study of developing countries in Asia. Such dualism is affected by and affects inequality in the economy.

Dualism is generally accompanied by technical dualism, the condition where firms or farms differ greatly in the vintage of their technology yet coexist in the same economy, albeit with limited interchange in some cases. This is explained by the technology gap and the absence of intermediate techniques, and by factor proportions rigidities and indivisibilities in modern technology. It is increasingly clear, however, that technical dualism can be fostered by policies that accentuate the impact of rigidities as opposed to policies that minimize such effects. As mentioned, the factor proportions problem is not inherent to the technology of agriculture.

Dualism can be related to foreign trade and foreign investment. When an export enclave dominated by firms from abroad produces mainly for export and has few if any linkages with the domestic society, there can be, in essence, two economies existing side by side—the modern enclave, foreign dominated, and the agrarian domestic economy. The unsophisticated domestic economy cannot take over the production for export when the technical requirements are complex. The technical potential of an LDC evolves only gradually, as discussed in the chapter on technology.

The export enclave may, over time, spawn a limited domestic industrial sector oriented towards the higher incomes of this sector. Generally dualism of this type arises from policies favorable to the emerging domestic industries. Protectionist policies and subsidies like favorable foreign exchange rates or financing are so designed that it is profitable for this sector to be capital-intensive and technically advanced in its production processes and product mix. Government policies may also lead to high wages in the protected sector in the face of a low opportunity cost for labor and a backward agriculture. The subsidies affect factor proportions so that technical dualism is intensified. Vested interests control the political network that could change the policies contributing to dualism. Similar policies can also encourage dualism in agriculture. This type of distorting policy is examined in some detail in chapter 12.

Sometimes it is the failure to devise or execute needed programs that promotes dualism. The failure to form human capital can contribute to structural unemployment when labor is immobile without such improvements in its skills. Instead of migrating to industry, workers remain underemployed on the land. When capital formation and technological change reduce the need for farmhands, this can be offset in part by cutting man-hours per worker, a work-sharing device. The industrial sector in such a case substitutes physical capital for human capital. Businesses can secure the returns from investment in physical capital. In contrast, labor training may not pay other than for family firms as corporate workers may leave to join other companies before the costs are recouped. The marginal products of labor in agriculture and industry diverge and output is below capacity. Dualism emerges.

Market imperfections may mean that investment is not highly mobile among sectors. When increases in savings available for investment are channeled mainly into the advanced sectors, then capital intensity in these sectors rises relative to others. The return to new investment will differ among sectors, and growth potential will be diminished. The modern, large-scale agricultural and industrial sectors are the usual beneficiaries of funds for investment, at the expense of their small-scale counterparts. Chapter 17 discusses how the lack of adequate financial infrastructure can contribute to such market imperfections, and thus to dualism.

Foreign control of land can result in dualism within agriculture. LDC borrowers usually lack access to world financial markets. The foreign-owned operation, on the other hand, typically raises money in a low-cost world capital market. When it maximizes profits, it will not be as labor-intensive as the domestic unit that faces relatively high capital costs and substitutes labor for capital. With more capital and possibly more advanced technology, the average product of labor and its marginal product are higher in the foreign sector.

In the absence of the foreign plantation, labor would spread onto the foreign-held land, and with more land per worker, labor's marginal and average products would rise above their previous levels in domestic agriculture. The rent would now be a source of domestic income. The loss incurred from lower wages for those formerly employed in the foreign sector would have to be deducted from these gains, as would any taxes previously paid from foreign profits. The proportion of domestic output being exported might change, affecting foreign exchange earnings accruing to the domestic economy. They could rise or fall.

Savings arising in the foreign trade sector can now be diverted to other sectors with a higher growth return, whereas when they were foreign income they were less easily shifted and often went abroad. However, when the export crop is grown on land ill-suited to other crops and requires large amounts of capital for its cultivation—capital that must be imported—there is little gain and probably loss from excluding foreign agriculture. Or, where land is not relatively scarce but underutilized, it is doubtful gains would arise from taking over foreign agriculture.

Inasmuch as an LDC cannot shed its economic skin and emerge modernized overnight, there will be some bimodal features in LDCs not characterized by dualism as it is described here. An economy in the historical sequences of modernization in which technology is imported and very advanced relative to local methods is likely to experience transitional divergences, if history is any guide. The transitional contrasts are generally perceived as lesser in depth or in bimodal divergence and duration than when dualism per se prevails. Not surprisingly there is often disagreement in the literature as to whether a country is experiencing transitional bimodal characteristics or dualism, and whether or not dualism is avoidable in that particular economy and at what cost to whom. The questions become more complex when the social concepts and consequences of dualism are included.

Development without Dualism: A Strategy
Peter Kilby and Bruce Johnston ask the question: Is there a development strategy for latecomers that can avoid dualism and high levels of inequality in both agricultural and nonagricultural sectors without sacrificing growth? Their answer is yes, and they ask more specifically: On the supply side, what type of industrial sector will absorb relatively unskilled workers, with minimum transferable skills, from agriculture at an optimum rate? And what type of agricultural transformation allows labor transfer while providing adequate food and raw materials, and avoids poverty endemic to high inequality and underemployment? On the demand side what types of agricultural and industrial development provide demand linkages that are mutually reinforcing as transition from agricultural dominance begins, thereby providing growing mass markets rather than independent, narrow ones serving mainly the industrial higher-income group?

The type of agricultural and industrial transformation that achieves supply and demand requirements for development without dualism for latecomers in early phases of development is outlined by Kilby and Johnston in their book *Agriculture and Structural Transformation, Economic Strategies in Late Developing Countries* (1975). The following paragraphs summarize their strategy.

As latecomers, LDCs have an advantage in their agricultural development and thereby in acceleration of their growth paths. They can borrow modern agricultural technology yet avoid dualism because fortunately this technology at the operational unit level is consistent with factor intensity reversal, from the highly capital-intensive agriculture of the United States to the highly labor-intensive agriculture of Taiwan, without loss of efficiency. Moreover, the operational unit can be small-scale without loss of efficiency so long as there is crop specialization.

Development of agriculture can proceed by concentrating resources and technology modernization in a small proportion of larger farms or it can move to modernize the total sector, more or less, in what Kilby and Johnston call a "unimodal" strategy. Both will raise productivity in agriculture, a needed ingredient of development. However, these authors contend a unimodal strategy is superior to a bimodal in its contribution toward other important growth variables and development goals, which are: (1) advancing structural transformation from agricultural to industrial and related sectors, (2) raising the welfare of the farm population, and (3) modernizing rural attitudes and behavior patterns so that change and labor transfer are facilitated on a broad front instead of just within islands of modernization (Kilby and Johnston 1975, p. 128).

While a unimodal strategy conserves on capital inputs at the farm level, both approaches require commitment of resources to off-farm inputs in the areas of labor-training, government programs including ongoing research and development, infrastructure development, and improved marketing and distribution of output and inputs. A unimodal strategy requires an even distribution of these inputs so that they affect all farms rather than an absorption of the inputs by larger farmers with political and economic bargaining power.

The strategy is facilitated by making use of market forces and decentralizing decision-making to the farm level when such decentralization is buttressed by appropriate government orientation toward pricing, taxation, and land tenure. The Green Revolution can increase income and demand for unskilled farm labor since it allows multiple cropping, closer planting, and other advantages that call for more labor input for careful cultivation, weeding, and feeding of the two to three plantings it allows. Former government policies of subsidizing capital input costs must be dropped to allow demand for labor to rise. Also government rural work programs can contribute marginally to labor demand and can supply useful infrastructure such as roads and irrigation facilities. This type of policy can help the very poorest when labor demand in general for farm work is high because of labor-intensive farming.

Thus scarcity pricing in agriculture leads to less inequality because it is an improvement over poorly designed subsidies and institutions affecting farm income distribution that typify the bimodal strategy. Longer-run mitigation of inequality can occur when growing prosperity and better education of the small-plot cultivator reduce family size. Moreover, market forces will more successfully redistribute income in the political milieu of early development than will taxation of a minority group of prosperous farmers for transfer to low-income groups.

The purchasing power to acquire off-farm inputs and the type of off-farm inputs (tractors versus simpler tools of a more labor-intensive type) vary between unimodal and bimodal patterns. Income from cash crops and demand patterns associated with small, labor-intensive modernizing farms will not be the same as demand patterns associated with capital-intensive large farms. Kilby and Johnston argue it is more probable that agricultural modernization will be associated with optimal demand growth relative to supply growth with a unimodal strategy. When increase in food output is high but the purchasing power to improve diets is limited, balanced growth is less likely. And depressed agricultural prices under such situations in early transformation limit further expansion, since agriculture dominates the economy and must affect its own market as well as provide a market for off-farm products. A restraint on agricultural purchasing power due to subsistence farming amidst modernized, large farms is thus a deterrent to growth. A broadened purchase base associated with cash crops for all farms will lead to optimal demand and supply conditions. Such a base develops purchasing power adequate to encourage crop expansion plus consumer market growth.

The product mix induced by a unimodal strategy will reflect a demand for simple, mass-consumed items. The manufacture of such items is more easily undertaken in an economy in early transition since they require fewer scarce resources, particularly skilled workers and imported inputs, and utilize relatively more inputs of unskilled or semiskilled labor. This allows a unimodal production function in the industrial sector. Rather than a product mix reflecting demand for modern goods by a small, affluent minority, demand is for mass-consumed items of cheaper quality and shorter durability. The production function in industry uses relatively simple technology. This sector can utilize or adapt older machinery and produce some capital goods it needs domestically, thereby becoming less capital intensive. This reduces the differential between rural and urban incomes since demand for skilled relative to unskilled labor drops.

In the nonagricultural sectors, too, subsidies to capital-intensive production are removed. Savings and capital formation can actually be larger with a unimodal industrial sector. This is because a higher (equilibrium) interest rate may elicit increased savings, and with an equilibrium foreign exchange rate, as opposed to an overvalued one, there is greater incentive to export. Both savings and foreign exchange earnings affect capital formation capacity.

The strategy minimizes the capital requirements for farm equipment and for industry. Islands with low capital productivity relative to labor productivity, and hence low L/K, no longer exist. Limited capital is spread among more producer units. The attack on poverty proceeds on a broad front. While this approach presents procedural and institutional challenges, especially for the government that must oversee the framework yet is dominated by special interest groups, the experience of Japan and Taiwan bears witness to its feasibility.

A Graphic Comparison   Figure 5.2 in chapter 5 showed the impact of intermediate technology on L/K, capital productivity, and labor productivity as compared with growth stimulated by the use of modern, more capital-intensive technology. Here a somewhat different diagram helps us compare the unimodal and dual approaches. In figure 9.5, frame (a), the total labor supply is represented by the length of the horizontal axis. The capital stock is sector-specific. Each sector has a curve showing diminishing marginal product of labor drawn from its respective axis. Labor absorbed in the traditional sector is L_t, measured by the distance O_tX. The remaining labor supply, L_m, is absorbed in the modern sector.

The human and physical capital committed to the traditional sectors in industry and agriculture is minimal and not the inputs requisite for intermediate or modern methods of production. Average and marginal product of the labor serving this sector are low. In contrast, larger amounts of human and physical capital relative to labor are used in modern farming and industry. The curve showing the marginal product of labor for the modern sector in figure 9.5(a) is very high up to the point where it drops to zero. Technical limitations of the modern industrial production function prevent further absorption of labor at a relatively high K/L ratio; and thus additional labor inputs would add nothing to output.

The wage rate in the traditional sector is equal to the institutional wage, which is affected by the productivity of labor and institutionally determined division of the output. The wage rate in the modern sector

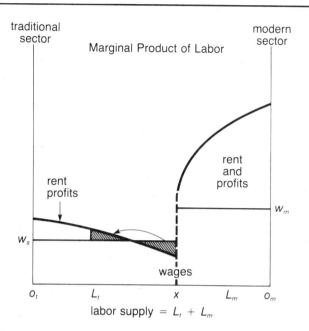

FIGURE 9.5(a)
Dualistic Development

Modern technology that is capital intensive limits the absorption of labor in the modern sector to L_m. The marginal product of labor differs between the traditional and the modern sectors. Wages and profits are institutionally set.

reflects the institutionalized bargaining power of modern workers and the large amount of human and physical capital per worker that makes their marginal product relatively high. Profits and rents in both traditional and modern sectors are identified in figure 9.5(a) in the areas under the curves depicting the marginal product of labor above the wage rate. Total wages are the areas below the wage rates plus the wages, shown by the hatched area, that encroach upon profits and rents in the traditional sector.

Unimodal development is illustrated in frame (b) of figure 9.5. Intermediate technology is used in all sectors. The capital supply, both human and physical, is allocated to all sectors so that its contribution at the margin is equalized. Small-scale units absorb divisible physical capital and produce simple goods of lower unit value than more sophisticated modern merchandise with the same function. The two sectors now represented are agriculture and nonagriculture. The intersection of the curves representing sectoral marginal product of labor simultaneously determines labor allocation and the wage rate. There is no unemployed labor in either dual or unimodal strategies by assumption.

Notice that wages relative to profits and rent are higher with intermediate technology. The product mix can affect the price of labor relative to the price of capital. And with intermediate technology, labor is in greater demand than with dual technology. Both factors cause the higher wage rate relative to profits and rents. Growth requires less

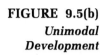

FIGURE 9.5(b)
Unimodal
Development

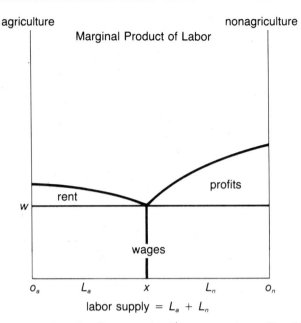

Intermediate technology in all sectors leads to sectoral equality of the marginal product of labor and of wages when they reflect scarcity value. Wages are above subsistence levels. They are higher relative to profits than in dualistic development because of the absence of high capital intensity in both products and processes.

capital formation since L/K is higher with intermediate technology for a given output. The masses in agriculture with incomes above subsistence produce cash crops and provide markets for the small but growing industrial sector.

With dualism a large proportion of the labor force works in the traditional sector, which produces only a small percentage of total output, however. The modern sector tends to supply its own purchasing power since wages and income in the traditional sector are low. There is limited transfer of income generated in the modern sector to the traditional one, especially the agricultural subsistence sector. The dualism described can persist for long periods of time. This persistence distinguishes it from historical experiences with dualism most currently developed countries have had, as does the degree of inequality and contrast in life-style.

Tanzania's development strategy, initiated in the 1960s and 1970s, was designed to prevent high inequality and dualism in a country still in phase 1 agriculture. However, unlike the Kilby-Johnston approach, Tanzania introduced planning that relied upon a state bureaucracy for administration rather than upon market forces. The political ideology and scope of Tanzania's African style of socialism has created widespread interest. The next section examines the plan to improve phase 1 agricultural performance and the problems encountered during the formative decades of planning.

REFERENCES

Aldington, T. J. 1975. Tanzanian Agriculture: A Decade of Progress in Crop Production. *Tanzania Notes and Records* 76: 57–66.

Fraser-Smith, S. W. 1965. Agricultural Transformation Through the Village Settlement Scheme. *Agricultural Development in Tanzania*, edited by Hadley E. Smith. Dar es Salaam: Tanzanian Institute of Public Administration.

Hayami, Y. and Ruttan, V. W. 1971. *Agricultural Development: An International Perspective*. Baltimore, MD: The Johns Hopkins University Press.

Kilby, P. and Johnston, B. F. 1975. *Agriculture and Structural Transformation, Economic Strategies in Late Developing Countries*. New York: Oxford University Press.

Lofchie, Michael F. 1976. Agrarian Socialism in the Third World: The Tanzanian Case. *Comparative Politics*, vol. 8, no. 3, pp. 479–99.

———— 1978. Agrarian Crisis and Economic Liberalization in Tanzania. *The Journal of Modern African Studies*, vol. 16, no. 3, pp. 451–75.

Mellor, John W. 1966. *The Economics of Agricultural Development*. Ithaca, NY: Cornell University Press.

Myrdal, G. 1968. *Asian Drama*. New York: Pantheon.

Southworth, Herman M. and Johnston, Bruce F. 1967. *Agricultural Development and Economic Growth*. Ithaca, NY: Cornell University Press.

Weaver, James H. and Kronemer, Alexander. 1981. Tanzanian and African Socialism. *World Development*, vol. 9, no. 9/10, pp. 839–49.

Changes in Phase 1
Agriculture of Postcolonial
Tanzania: 1961–80

Tanzania is one of the poorest nations of the world. She is a fairly large African country of 18 million people located on the east coast of the continent. Colonized first by the Germans, then after World War I by the British, she gained independence peacefully in 1961. The legacy of colonialism left little changed among the traditional rural population. The main impact of foreign control was upon export crops and the infrastructure needed to market products such as sisal, cotton, and cashew nuts.

Tanzanian agriculture in the 1960s and 1970s supported over 90 percent of the population, a population growing at 3.4 percent per year in the 1970s. With the exception of some large plantation crops and progressive export farmers, agriculture was mainly subsistence, phase 1 agriculture. Corn or maize and, to a lesser degree, rice and wheat were the food crops. Export crops included sisal, cotton, coffee, cashew nuts, tea, and tobacco. Eighty percent of export earnings was from agricultural commodities, with the remaining income from mining or tourism. Prices for export commodities fluctuated widely. New export crops were introduced after independence to diversify export earnings and reduce foreign sector risks.

Phase 1 agriculture is rain-fed. Tanzania is subject to droughts; in particular the drought of 1973 had a devastating effect upon her economy. Moreover, infestations of the tsetse fly restrict the land area that can be inhabited and farmed. Prior to "villagization," begun under development planning, most farmers practiced shifting cultivation in order to leave old land fallow once soil nutrients were depleted. Much of the soil of Tanzania was leached. Farmers did not practice soil conservation, and soil erosion was widespread. Traditional seeds were saved from each crop and the main tools used for hand cultivation were the hoe, the machete, and the axe. At the time of independence, oxen were not used to any degree. Simple carts and oxen-drawn farm implements were lacking. There was widespread illiteracy, a high death rate, and poor health linked to water contamination and other conditions of poverty. Thus the efficiency of labor inputs, the main productive resource in addition to land, was affected by physical deficiencies caused by food shortages during droughts and a lack of basic health maintenance.

GOALS OF AFRICAN SOCIALISM

After independence, and under the guidance of Julius Nyerere, a charismatic leader educated by missionaries, Tanzania chose a socialist (but non-Marxist) path to development based on "familyhood," or the traditional mutual social support system common to rural Africa. A key component of the Tanzanian model for African socialism is sharing within the village and cooperative. The plan called for "villagization" of the populace, which, under the security of colonial rule, had dispersed fairly widely throughout the land. Instead of a small group of extended family members farming in scattered locations of this low-density country, villages of 100–800 people were to be formed.

All land was nationalized. Except for private plots alloted each household, farming under the plan was to be communal or block farming. Block farming allows peasants to cultivate their own sections of contiguous, single-crop plantings, often of a marketable crop. The farmer receives income from marketed crops, after taxes to support local subsidies and national needs. The price paid for the crop is set by government marketing firms that sell it either domestically or abroad. Communal farming, by contrast, requires joint labor input on all land, with the farmer remunerated by number of workdays according to government-set pay scales. It is the visionary goal of *ujamaa*, the familyhood ideal of social sharing. Socialist organization of this type is the instrument for controlling dualism within agriculture and between agriculture and an emerging, very small industrial sector.

The goal of egalitarian distribution of income is of prime importance; consequently, methods for improving income must be compatible with this goal. In addition, it is envisioned that as development proceeds, the villages will produce, with some degree of specialization, simple consumer goods. This would disperse industry and orient production toward incentive goods for the masses, as suggested by Kilby and Johnston. Thus the farmer would be spurred to produce for the market (albeit for state-dominated markets), and not just for subsistence. To accomplish this, however, the self-sufficient peasantry must be enticed into relocation. This is no small task. The problem here is succinctly put by a member of the rural settlement commission:

No one appreciates better than I do the difficulty in persuading the average rural Tanzanian to move from his present environment into a new settlement in which he will be expected to live in a concentrated village. In the first place, good agricultural land in Tanzania is, for the most part, in scattered pockets. The average farmer, therefore, lives in a small hamlet, where he has a small shamba on which, in most years, he grows enough for his and his family's needs, just outside his front door. To do this he does not have to exert himself very much; he is subject to no strict discipline and is not particularly concerned if the source of the water he uses lies some distance from his home because this is not his worry—his wife has to get it for him (Fraser-Smith 1965).

The specific goals of the five-year plans starting in 1967 were to raise the education level of the rural populace, provide a source of potable water, establish village health clinics, and increase agricultural output so that the people would raise enough food for their own needs. By 1980 there had been dramatic changes in these areas. Adult literacy and school enrollment rose sharply, life expectancy soared to 50 years from ranges in the 30s, and at least a portion of the villages were provided with health clinics and clean tap water. The success in food production was promising but less dramatic.

IMPACT OF AFRICAN SOCIALISM UPON AGRICULTURE

The weather still determines crop production in Tanzania. The droughts of 1973–74 and 1979–80 greatly reduced agricultural output and brought the threat of starvation. Foreign aid helped meet the country's food needs and balance-of-payment crises. Other adversities experienced in the 1970s were the breakup of the East African Community, a common market arrangement, and war with Uganda. These dislocations make it hard to assess the achievements of increased "villagization" and socialization of the rural sector during this period. Nevertheless, it appears that with some pragmatic changes such as a retreat from communal agriculture, food production capacity improved. Tanzania, however, illustrates the slow technical change that marks phase 1 agriculture. Technical capacity in farming, planning, and administration is very limited.

It is useful to examine the costs, benefits, and mistakes of the agricultural reorganization. First, it is important to note that the technical changes introduced for farming per se were very limited. Some improved techniques (seeds, planting practices) were possible under dry farming for maize. These were introduced in some regions with success. Most gains were to be achieved through increasing the amount of land a farmer could till, thus utilizing surplus land; through modest scale economies achievable with population clusters; through taking advantage of surplus labor hours off-season to improve simple tools or to construct village storage facilities; and through improved infrastructure, especially education. A few villages were supplied with tractor services for heavy tasks like preparing the soil, but this was very limited, being both import and capital intensive. Thus the main costs of the program were the skilled labor costs associated with administration and the building of infrastructure.

The gains hoped for as a result of these changes in farming were

■ Increased food supply per capita,
■ Improved human capital and technical absorption as a result of both rural education and the demonstration effect of village farming,
■ An agricultural surplus to finance national and local projects,
■ Control of dualism and,
■ A growth in national identity among tribal people.

Not surprisingly success was partial, and mistakes were made. "Villagization" was resisted. Most fundamentally, the mistake of trying to collectivize an independent peasantry was costly in that it led to a greatly reduced work effort. This is typical of communist experience with collectivization. Tanzania retreated from this goal after the effects were evident, and emphasized block farming instead.

The second major mistake was in the area of price incentives. The urban elite succeeded for a while in getting administered food prices that were below world price levels. However, as rural/urban inequality worsened and incentives in agriculture suffered, there was a move in 1973–74 to reverse the terms of trade back toward their equilibrium level.

Third, orthodox economists have pointed out that administering the controlled economy is very expensive and that a greater role for the market could lessen the need for scarce, costly administrative skills and reduce bureaucratic mistakes. They point out that nationalization of truck transportation reduced rather than improved transport efficiency; that state farms (some set up jointly with foreign interests) using hired labor were unsuccessful; that nationalization of retail trade, or the threat of it, led to a lack of consumer goods needed as an incentive to farmers to produce for the market; and that low interest rates discouraged saving and wasted capital.

Fourth, the plan emphasized raising food at the expense of producing for export. The emphasis upon subsistence farming was well placed. And the effort to diversify agricultural crops exported was a success. However, unnecessary disincentives penalized export production and created a foreign exchange bottleneck detrimental to development goals. The progressive export farmers were wealthier and, being technically more advanced, could cultivate greater areas. Their landholdings were reduced, their use of hired labor was condemned, and they were penalized by prices and input costs administered by the state. The result was a decline in export production as land and labor was switched to food production.

Figure 9.6 shows how the expansion of food production capacity from $\beta_f L$ to $\beta_f' L'$ created the potential for both more food and more exports. This was accomplished by improved organization and infrastructure that allowed use of surplus land and labor hours combined with simple technical improvements in subsistence agriculture. However, the transfer of too many resources to food production at F' created a balance of payments shortfall $(m - m')$. Unfortunately at the very same time this was happening, the terms of trade deteriorated because of higher

FIGURE 9.6 *Imbalance in Tanzanian Resource Allocation*

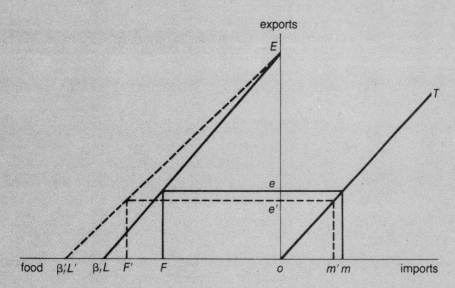

Reorganization improved agricultural productivity, labor hour inputs, and farmable land, shifting food capacity output from $\beta_f L$ to $\beta_f' L'$. Excessive allocation of resources to food production relative to export production created a shortfall of imports: $(m - m')$.

prices for imported goods, in particular oil, creating even greater import shortfalls. Moreover, in the years of drought, β_f dropped sharply, shifting the production possibilities curve inward below its original level, drawn to reflect normal rainfall.

Finally, there were other miscellaneous shortcomings that have been noted such as oversized villages creating diseconomies of scale under present technical capacity, inadequate soil conservation practices for continuous farming, and waste of fertilizer dispensed by the state without charge. The government tried to correct overcentralization of decision-making after the problem was recognized. Resistance to "villagization" continued.

The experience with rural socialism has been disappointing for some observers since it involved retreat from the ideal of *ujamaa*, and did not produce dramatic progress over two decades. However, rapid advances amidst the conditions of phase 1 agriculture that prevailed in Tanzania after colonial rule would have surprised most agricultural economists and classified Tanzania as a historical exception. She illustrates vividly how difficult the engineering of institutional change in traditional agriculture can be (Aldington 1975; Weaver and Kronemer 1981; Lofchie 1976 and 1978).

Inequality:
Global

chapter

10

T his chapter deals with the unprecedented divergence in per capita GNP and living standards among countries today. The topic is an especially sensitive one in international forums. Its importance is tied to political as well as economic interrelations. Because the scope of the subject is so broad, it is not possible in one chapter to present an exhaustive treatment.

Questions such as the following recur with predictable frequency: Why has income inequality between the richest and poorest nations increased? Will this trend be reversed or intensified? Can a world with widening ranges of inequality maintain political stability? Is the poverty of the poorest related to the growing affluence of the rich? Do market mechanisms, national and international, inevitably aggravate inequality? Such broad questions covering widely diverse countries and their interrelations are difficult to answer definitively, and remain topics of heated debate at the current time.

Much of the forward-looking thinking in this area by reformers seeking to reduce global inequality is centered upon international trade relations. Much of the backward-looking discussion concentrates on the impact of the colonial era upon inequality and current growth potential. We only mention the latter briefly and move on to analyze trade and inequality.

INEQUALITY IN AN INTER-DEPENDENT WORLD

Implications of National Growth Base Differentials

The thesis recurs, especially among LDC investigators, that the growth base has been stunted for some LDCs by colonial interference in earlier periods.[1] The colonial era reached its zenith under the far-flung British empire of the 1800s, and was characterized by trade specialization between the mother country and her colonies. The latter were for the most part suppliers of commodities and importers of final goods. Legal and financial arrangements enforced by military power enabled the mother country to determine trade flow patterns both directly, and indirectly through markets. Political control by the mother country and the absence of free trade shaped the development paths of the colonies.

The net impact of colonization upon the LDCs' potential for development in the postcolonial era and upon the growing inequality among nations is difficult to assess with finality. Each country, of course, has its own historical context that affects its growth base. Political instabilities and wars following the demise of colonialism must be considered when examining the fact that the postwar growth period has seen a widening of income differences between many poor and rich nations. Bangladesh, for example, was carved out of the poorest agricultural region of Pakistan after civil war; and Pakistan itself was an outgrowth of civil war in postcolonial India. The history of Africa following World War II is noted for its breakup of former colonial empires into geographic units of varying economic potential and resource balance. And the list could go on. The point is that a nation's growth base is related to social, political, and historical conditions as

---

1. For a dissenting view, see P.T. Bauer, "The Vicious Circle of Poverty," *Weltwirtschaftliches Archiv*, vol. 95, no. 2, 1965, pp. 4–20.

well as economic; and the postwar growth experience has been colored by a broad spectrum of country-specific circumstances, many of which reflect prewar colonial status.

Since 1945 the matrix of country inequality has been a shifting one. What is noteworthy is that the living standards in MDCs (and among the rich elite in LDCs), as compared with those for the poverty-stricken masses in LDCs, exhibit extremes historically unparalleled among nations. And with the breakup of the old colonial empires and intensified nationalism, the burden of dealing with this destitution rests upon the nation-state—often newly formed—wherein it exists. The alleviation of world poverty is not acknowledged generally as an MDC responsibility in and of itself, standing solely on humanitarian grounds, without consideration of national goals of both donor and beneficiary. Yet the very extent of the poverty is overwhelming. The World Bank has estimated that nearly 800 million individuals are denied basic human necessities and live under conditions of chronic disease, illiteracy, malnutrition, and squalor. In the poorest countries, resources for dealing with their poverty are woefully inadequate (Chenery et al. 1974, p. 12.).

This world of inequality is intertwined and interdependent as never before. Large volumes of trade flow between developing and developed countries, along with financial capital and human assets; and resources vital to continuing world prosperity are located in large proportion in LDCs. Moreover, the political stability and orientation of many strategically located LDCs is considered vital to MDC national defense. Table 10.1 indicates the magnitude of trade among richer and poorer economies for 1960 compared with 1980. Table 10.2 shows the flow of loans and private investment in 1970 and 1980.

The New International Economic Order

LDC members of the United Nations, through their work on its commissions and in its forums, have supported the proposition that the international trade network contributes to global inequality. At their request global inequality was considered at a special session of the United Nations General Assembly convened in 1974. The timing of this meeting in part reflected the unprecedented redistribution of world income to oil-exporting LDCs that occurred when the international oil cartel, OPEC, raised world oil prices dramatically in the early 1970s. The economic and political repercussions of the cartel's actions focused the attention of both MDCs and LDCs upon the international economic system and its organization.

The special session set the stage for the adoption of a resolution by the United Nations General Assembly in 1974 in favor of a "New International Economic Order" founded on a more equitable basis. This resolution reflects three broad areas of Third World concerns or goals: (1) obtaining needed foreign exchange, (2) acquiring better terms for and types of technology transfer, and (3) increasing the decision-making power of LDCs in the international system. The New Order would include commodity agreements to affect the terms of trade, reduced protectionism in MDCs toward LDC exports, foreign aid issued in the form of Special Drawing Rights on the International Monetary System, the recognition of each nation's sovereignty over its own resources, and rules and regulations governing the multinational corporations. Many of the changes called for in the resolution had been put forth before other forums within and outside the United Nations.

While individual components of the New Order were not new, the conceptual framework was. And the MDCs' qualified acceptance of—or acquiescence in—this framework and its general goal of a new economic order constituted a change from their previous position. The assembly's resolution emphasized the need for coordinated effort to achieve change. United Nations members agreed to work toward an international system that reduces inequality and is more responsive to LDC development needs and world interdependence. Work is now going on to achieve change, but to date its pace has been slow. Commitment to various reforms differs greatly among the more developed countries. The discussions relating to topical changes are referred to as the "North-South dialogue."

Chapter Focus

As mentioned, the whole topic of international inequality is exceedingly broad and complex. In this chapter certain basic aspects of this vast subject are treated in some detail. We begin by noting that once a sizable income gap develops, it tends to widen because growth is cumulative. A brief explanation is given of why foreign aid has not prevented a growing range of global inequality. International trade is examined both as a possible contributor to the disparities and at the same time an indispensable aid to development. As is often the case in a book of this type, we seek to generalize with some degree of simplification. It is important to point out at this point that the chapter does not treat the special situations that deviate from the general case for each topic. And the political arguments for withdrawal from trade are left for the interested reader to pursue elsewhere.

International Inequality—The Compound Growth Effect

Not unlike the concept of compound interest, growth builds upon itself. An economy accumulates a capital stock over time incrementally, updating it when old components wear out, changing its composition, and adding net new capital. Human capital stock also tends to grow cumulatively, being replaced, changed, and augmented. And there is some evidence that the more advanced an economy, the more technology contributes in increasing measure to the growth process. Technology, too, then appears to build upon itself so that its impact upon an economy accelerates with development. An economy's current income level depends upon this base generated by a historical development process.

MDCs derive a certain momentum from their broad base. They tend to exhibit ongoing growth and productivity increases that raise GNP per capita when savings rates are adequate, aggregate demand and employment well managed, and the workweek maintained, and in the absence of wars or dislocations such as followed formation of OPEC.

The LDCs must outpace this growth performance in order to catch up. In the big-growth era of the 1960s, rates of growth of per capita GNP for MDCs in real terms reached as high as 4.5 percent. This is double long-run historical rates, however. The 1970s saw a sharp decline in the growth rate of per capita income in some MDCs.

Japan and Russia began development facing a smaller gap between their own and the advanced Western economies than that separating LDCs and MDCs today. With very high savings rates to their credit, they narrowed the difference in income per capita between their countries and more advanced Western economies, despite war losses, over a modernization period beginning in the late 1800s. They enjoyed continued gains in the 1930s, when the Western world stagnated or grew very little.

The process of "catching up," or narrowing the gap, for an LDC tends to come during a period of accelerated growth when savings rise more rapidly, surplus or underemployed labor is more fully utilized, the resource allocation process is improved, economies of scale spur efficiency, and technological change gains a momentum from a more technically sophisticated base. For per capita GNP in some LDCs to gain relative to MDCs, population growth must be under control. These conditions all bespeak an LDC past the beginning stages of development and high dependence upon agriculture. For less advanced LDCs (and any low-growth LDC), the gap can easily widen relative to MDCs.

The income gap can also widen between more advanced LDCs with higher per capita GNP and those with lower income per capita. And this indeed has happened in the postwar years. Mexico and Brazil are examples of pull-away LDCs in Latin America, while Greece, Turkey, Taiwan, and South Korea are LDCs outside Latin America that are also further along the development path. They have accelerated their growth relative to other LDCs, and have also narrowed the difference between themselves and MDCs. And, of course, OPEC, by a flick of the pricing pen, launched some of its member countries onto a per capita income level above that of the richest MDC. But our emphasis here is upon the growth base and its compound effect over time for countries without an oil bonanza.

The impact of the compound growth effect upon income gaps can be illustrated as follows: Assume a 10 percent growth rate in per capita GNP in an MDC over a five-year period. Assume income per capita is $4,500 in the MDC in period 1. At the end of five years, this figure will have increased $450 to $4,950. Assume income per capita is $100 in the LDC in period 1. The gap between the two is $4,400 in this period. For this gap to be the same five years later, income per capita must rise by 450 percent in the LDC (that is, by $450) since in the MDC it grew by $450 in five years. This is not possible under ordinary circumstances. The larger the discrepancy in per capita income, the higher the growth rate differential must be to maintain a *constant* gap.

The same effect is at work between very poor and more advanced LDCs. At a compound growth rate of 3 percent per annum, a $100 per capita GNP will increase to $438 in 50 years, while a $1,000 per capita income will rise to $4,384. The lower-income country still has an income one tenth that of the wealthier one, but the gap will have widened from $900 to $3,946 in 50 years. It is not hard to predict, then, that less advanced LDCs are the ones that have the least chance to narrow the gap between themselves and more developed countries in a decade or two, and that the inequality between the richer countries and the poorest will tend to increase. MDC efforts to reduce the gap have centered around foreign aid, but the programs have been inadequate to overcome the compound growth effect.

A full discussion of the economic impact of aid is deferred until chapter 13. Here the topic is introduced briefly within the context of inequality. Foreign aid can alleviate conditions of poverty and provide resources for development. It cannot catapult a country into modernity. The ability to absorb and use aid resources productively varies from country to country.

Foreign Aid and Inequality

The supply of aid resources is limited by the willingness of MDC countries to give grants and concessionary loans, either directly or through international agencies. In affluent countries there are many claims upon the public purse, and foreign aid must compete with other claims for the tax revenues available. Foreign aid is not always supported by the populace in MDCs and this influences the politicians. Not surprisingly the demands for foreign assistance exceed aid monies. Except in individual cases deemed vital to national defense at one time or another, aid to LDCs has not been large enough to prevent growing inequality.[2]

Over the postwar period, foreign aid has served an admixture of defense, economic, and humanitarian goals of the affluent nation-states. The dominant variable affecting the bilateral allocation of aid has been the clash between Western and communist ideology as it affects global defense. Much of the assistance has been in military and economic areas supportive of defense strategy. Thus, the needs of the poorest countries are not necessarily given priority. Such aid has even exacerbated inequality and poverty when competing MDCs supply arms to LDCs, enabling small military skirmishes to flare into wider conflicts. Another influence upon economic aid allocation has been economic interests inherited from the colonial period.

Not only can aid fail to reach the countries in greatest need, it also may not reach those in the worst straits within a country. It can be difficult in some cases to earmark assistance for projects affecting the poorest people in an LDC since loans and grants must be channeled through national governments. Such governments tend to be controlled or influenced greatly by an upper-income elite. They too are a factor affecting the division between military and nonmilitary aid and the orientation of projects toward areas that can help the neediest.

Even though it may not have been of the right kind, in the most needed place, or in the amount necessary to hold back the widening

2. Postwar Marshall Plan aid to war-torn Europe was extensive and helped greatly to reconstitute the economic capital destroyed. Even with the war's destruction, the technical, physical, and human capital base to rebuild upon was above LDC levels.

income inequality, foreign aid in many cases has made a significant contribution to the alleviation of poverty. And recently there has been a swing among bilateral and multilateral aid dispensers, particularly the World Bank, toward meeting the needs of the poorest. Aid by the rich Arab oil countries appears to be assuming the familiar defense-related pattern, however, instead of one geared only to relieving poverty. The potentially positive role of foreign aid in development is analyzed in chapter 13.

Table 10.3 gives data on aid flows over the period of 1960–80 for OECD noncommunist, OPEC, and communist countries. OECD aid fell over the period from an average of .5 percent of GNP in 1960 to .38 percent of GNP in 1980. In constant dollars (1978 = 100) OECD aid rose from $13.1 billion in 1960 to $22.7 billion in 1980. OPEC aid vaired between $4.6 billion and $6.9 billion in current prices. As a percentage of OECD aid, OPEC's was highest in 1975–76. Economic aid from communist countries to LDCs is small when compared with OECD aid, amounting to $3.3 billion in 1980.

TRADE THEORIES AND INEQUALITY

Having mentioned the cumulative effect of growth on inequality and the effect of foreign aid upon narrowing the gap, we turn now to specific questions about the relation of the world trade network to income disparities. Do the economic and political interrelations between the richest and poorest economies, with the attendant technology gap, contribute to growing inequality? Does the trade network that is central to these interrelations create growth that distributes the gains more than proportionately toward MDCs; or does its resulting growth favor MDCs at the expense of LDCs—a zero-sum game?

Before assessing the arguments that more of the gains from trade have accrued to MDCs than LDCs in the postwar period, when income gaps have become historically high, the question of whether trade is a zero-sum game (in other words, one country benefits because the other loses) must be addressed. Dating from the birth of modern economic analysis, there has been a long history of theoretical and empirical analysis of trade. The analysis strongly supports the conclusion that, overall, trade benefits a country even though certain groups within its economy may suffer short-run harm. Undoubtedly there have been historical cases under imperialism where trade imposed upon the LDC by the colonial power was detrimental to the weaker country's development. And in chapter 13 cases are discussed where trade involving foreign direct investment can retard industrialization. Yet, the conclusion for the general case is that trade creates potential gains for freely participating countries, that is, all nations can benefit from an increase in total goods attainable.

In the next section a brief discussion of the basic reasons for trade and a summary of its potential benefits as explained by the theory of comparative advantage are presented. This is followed by comments upon the broader but less cohesive literature that argues foreign commerce is detrimental to "dependent" countries, especially LDCs. In the antitrade tracts the current trade network, populated by multinational corporations, is viewed as an extension of that prevailing under colonialism. Reflecting Marxist roots, "detrimental" in some of these writings refers not just to material losses, but includes sociopolitical costs as well.

Specialization and trade characterize all but the most primitive economic structures. This commerce can be regional, national, and international. It can flourish when transportation accommodates it at small cost. The process of development provides increased scope for intra- and interregional markets to emerge and become increasingly interdependent, with accompanying mobility of goods and resources. A natural extension of national specialization is international specialization. International trade provides a means of paying for capital goods, technology, and other resources vital to the development of an LDC. Experience shows that the LDC has little chance of avoiding interdependence with more advanced countries if it wishes to develop. And, as was documented in the statistical patterns of development, countries successful in lifting their economic levels have realized increases in exports and imports as a percentage of GNP. Small countries exhibit particularly high ratios since they have less potential for internal trade.

The Potential for Gains from Trade

   The advantages of foreign trade were first worked out by the Classical economists, writing during the early growth period of the Western world. Among them it was David Ricardo who worked out the analysis showing that trade is not a zero-sum game even where an LDC is less efficient in general than an MDC trading partner. In fact, according to Ricardo's analysis, LDCs and MDCs should have large potential for gains when they trade with each other since their production possibilities curves are often more dissimilar than the curves of counterpart countries at similar development levels. But before Ricardo, Adam Smith and others had emphasized the case of absolute advantage. Since this too carries weight where the trade of LDCs is concerned, and represents the simplest argument for foreign commerce, it is helpful to begin with a discussion of absolute advantage.

LDCs have absolute advantages, that is, they are able to produce certain products with fewer resources than other countries, when they have superior climate and growing conditions for crops; when they possess rare, superior, or readily accessible extractive resources; and in products making intense use of crafts not well-developed elsewhere such as needle skills, deep-sea diving, oriental carpet-making, or jade-carving. The advantages of trade emerge when each country specializes in its areas of absolute advantage, trading for goods it cannot produce as cheaply and/or cannot produce at all.

Absolute Advantage

But suppose an LDC can produce nothing more efficiently than other countries. Is it foreclosed from foreign commerce? Must its inefficiency be reflected in high export prices that preclude exchanges? The answer

Comparative Advantage

is no. As Ricardo showed, the country must only be able to trade at a
rate of exchange of exports for imports that is better than its domestic
terms of trade in isolation. So long as the autarky, or domestic terms
of trade differ from the world terms of trade, *one* good will exchange
at a ratio better than the domestic ratio, and be competitive in world
markets.

This point is not obvious and to demonstrate its truth it is helpful
to assume a world composed of two countries, one MDC and one LDC
not too dissimilar in total productive capacity, although they may differ strikingly in per capita output. For simplicity, assume a constant-
cost production possibilities frontier for both countries as shown in
figure 10.1. Factors of production are assumed to be mobile nationally,
but immobile between countries. The line representing the full employment output combinations of wheat and cloth also gives the domestic opportunity costs (a constant) and, hence, the domestic terms
of trade. The two countries have different opportunity costs, and hence
different slopes to their production possibilities frontiers. This establishes different domestic terms of trade, as explained in chapter 3.

The LDC is known to be less efficient in both goods and therefore
must be *relatively* less inefficient in one of the two goods that both
countries can produce. Figure 10.1 shows that the LDC has a comparative advantage, that is, it is relatively less inefficient in wheat, and
the MDC has a comparative advantage in cloth. Comparative advantage
is determined by comparing each country's opportunity cost of wheat
and cloth. The LDC must give up 1¼ units of wheat to obtain one unit
of cloth, whereas the MDC obtains one unit of cloth by giving up only
¾ of a unit of wheat. However, for one unit of cloth the LDC obtains

FIGURE 10.1

Comparative
Advantage

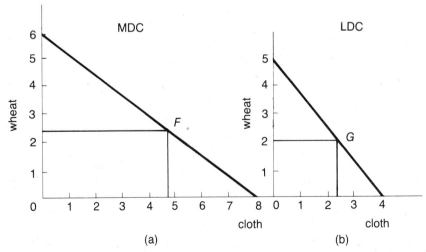

Pretrade production and consumption is at *F* for the MDC and at *G* for the LDC.
Based on opportunity cost, the LDC has a comparative advantage in wheat, the
MDC in cloth.

1¼ units of wheat because it is less inefficient in the production of wheat. Said another way, $(dQ_w/dQ_c)_{MDC} < (dQ_w/dQ_c)_{LDC}$. Both countries are limited to production and consumption somewhere on their production possibilities frontiers such as points F and G.

Now, by rotating the LDC diagram counterclockwise and the MDC diagram clockwise, they can be juxtaposed with the maximum output in their good of comparative advantage located at C in figure 10.2. When there are constant costs as output of one good expands, each country will specialize completely in order to trade at more favorable export (import) terms of trade. Total output of both goods has increased with trade and is now AC of cloth and EC of wheat.

Assume the countries agree, via bargaining, upon international terms of trade between their respective domestic opportunity costs and hence domestic terms of trade. The slope of line T is the international terms of trade. And assume the quantity of trade is at point H, with the MDC exporting CB of cloth in exchange for CD of wheat sold by the LDC. At point H both countries are outside their domestic consumption capacity of F and G, consuming more of both goods. This is true despite the fact that relative prices change with trade so that the export good

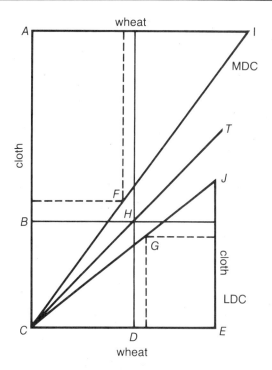

FIGURE 10.2
Gains from Trade

With specialization and trade, production moves from G and F to C, and the terms of trade equal the slope of CT. The LDC exports CD wheat in exchange for DH cloth, increasing consumption. The MDC exports CB cloth in exchange for BH wheat, increasing consumption.

in each country rises in price, that is to say, it exchanges for more of the other good, now imported.[3]

So long as dQ_w/dQ_c as reflected in *relative* prices differ, that is, the domestic terms of trade in autarky differ, there are advantages to trade in the form of higher combinations of goods than domestic production can supply. These gains can be maximized by specialization in production so long as relative costs continue to reflect a comparative advantage as production expands. This is the doctrine of comparative advantage. And the more the pretrade terms of trade differ, the greater potential there is for gains from specialization and trade. The LDC is not precluded from foreign commerce even though the MDC has an absolute advantage in both goods. The doctrine is generally unaffected by increasing or even decreasing costs, although there can be less than complete specialization as relative costs change so that the trading countries produce some of the imported commodity.

The LDC often trades for items it cannot produce or resources it does not have. If it can produce more than one good that is demanded in world markets, however, then the domestic terms of trade for those goods compared with the world terms of trade will identify the commodity for export. If it can export only one good, then it must use that one to obtain the imports not produceable within its borders. Exchange and hence trade will take place when the imported goods are preferred (either by consumers or planners) to the export good or to the domestic items produceable with the resources used to turn out exports.

Determinants of Differences in Relative Costs The opportunity cost differences that give rise to gains from trade are traceable to various possible causes. The technology gap between the LDC and MDC may be larger for one good than another and hence yield differing relative efficiencies. LDCs often specialize in products that have established markets and technology, and are said to be in later stages of the "product life cycle." Such goods may be relatively labor-intensive. Recall from chapter 3 that resource endowments affect an increasing-cost production possibilities curve when the goods made differ in the relative intensity with which they use resources. The LDC may have a comparative cost advantage in the relatively labor-intensive good as a result of a larger ratio of labor to other resources than the MDC. Economies of scale can affect relative efficiency and cost ratios, and trade allows greater access to efficiencies of scale by enlarging total demand.

Transportation costs create regional trading advantages; and some countries export goods they can produce at a relatively low cost because there is limited home demand for those items relative to other domestic goods. The extreme form of demand skewness for a good or exportable resource is the case of trade as a "vent for surplus," where

---

3. Depending upon demand conditions, it is possible that countries prefer to consume somewhat less of the export good and consume relatively more of the now-cheaper import good. This will depend upon private sector demand and hence price elasticity and income elasticity of the two goods, or upon planners' preferences.

without foreign commerce some resources would be underutilized. Finally, when the trade network operates with restrictions such as subsidies, tariffs, and quotas, this can affect comparative costs, as well as the gains from trade.

Conclusions of the Modern Model

The Ricardo model has been refined and expanded into a more sophisticated exploration of the gains from trade. This modern theory of international trade shows us that a country maintaining a posture of free trade without tariffs, quotas, subsidies, or other distortions maximizes its national welfare so long as world trade is characterized by competitive markets without distortions or externalities, and so long as the national income distribution effects are deemed acceptable. Free trade may not maximize a country's welfare when these conditions do not hold. Yet even where there are distortions, externalities, undesirable distribution effects, and dynamic growth considerations, analysis shows there are usually a set of policies that, when pursued, allow a country to achieve gains from constrained trade.

Factor Prices and Trade

Competitive models also show that the returns to factors of production are affected by trade. The gains from trade ultimately become income to factor owners. When trade is based only on relative factor proportions (the Heckscher-Ohlin-Samuelson model), the model shows conditions under which it is possible for factor prices to be equalized for trading partners. When this occurs, labor and capital each reflects a global scarcity price. This need not reduce global inequality, however, since factors are distributed unevenly among countries. In fact, if poorer countries possess relatively large amounts of resources with a lower scarcity price worldwide, such as labor, while richer countries have relatively abundant resources with a higher world scarcity price, such as capital, inequality among nations may increase with trade. The advantage of trade is that the nation-state has higher income than when it is not trading, not that it necessarily has an income level that is closer to that of the trading partners. Trade in this model raises the price of the relatively abundant resource in each country, generally reducing *national* inequality. It may, but need not, reduce international inequality.

The essence of the Heckscher-Ohlin-Samuelson model is that a good will be cheaper prior to trade in the country possessing relatively more of the resource used intensively in its production—either labor or capital. Countries are assumed to exhibit similar demand patterns and the same technology that is characterized by constant returns to scale. When trade occurs, each country specializes in the commodity intensively using its relatively abundant resource. As foreign demand is added to domestic demand for the export good, the price of each nation's export good rises. This stimulates transfer of resources to the export sector. One world price is established for goods traded. The resources used in relative abundance in the export good are in greater demand, and the resource price rises in the exporting country. This increases income for the factor owners. Demand and supply conditions determine how much incomes grow in each country. When capital-intensive goods are in relatively great demand, richer, capital-intensive countries may benefit more from trade than poorer, labor-intensive countries. Capital-intensive goods may refer to goods calling for human plus physical capital.

Limitations of the Modern Model

It would be misleading to leave the impression that modern trade theory is without weaker links. The model is static in nature and must be adjusted to take into account dynamic features of specialization and trade. Some aspects of the dynamics of trade are discussed in a subsequent section. Protrade economists point to the empirical evidence as support for the positive dynamics of trade. They emphasize the experience of Western developed nations, noting how trade has increased technology transfers, innovation, and competition. They also point to studies showing a strong correlation between trade and LDC growth rates (for example, Kravis 1970, 850–72; Michaely 1977, 49–73; Cohen 1968, 334–43). Yet critics say there is no acceptable treatment of the dynamics of trade from a theoretical viewpoint.

Another weaker link of modern trade theory is the use of a community or national welfare function. For example, the communities consuming at H in figure 10.2 are said to be in a preferable position to their pretrade consumption points, G and F, because they obtain more goods. The pretrade and posttrade distribution of goods among individuals is ignored, despite the fact that trade demands the reallocation of resources and can affect some individuals or groups negatively.

More precisely, the idea of a community welfare function is an extreme simplification or fiction since it is not possible to aggregate individual preferences into a community preference function that represents the welfare of the nation, in other words, of all its citizens as a unit. Such a function by its very nature encounters aggregation problems, and does not deal with distribution effects within a country. Typically, whenever trade analysts consider national distribution effects, they assume the national political structure can rectify any unsatisfactory results so that anyone made worse off by trade will be compensated. Compensatory distribution payments are assumed to be feasible within but not between nation-states. In fact, the model fails to emphasize directly the impact of trade upon international inequality, the topic under discussion.

Not surprisingly, the case against trade is often built on welfare considerations of income distribution. Yet the constructs that replace the community welfare function can be equally weak. Moreover, those seeking to refute the theoretical analysis supporting trade have not developed a literature of comparable rigor showing trade to be potentially detrimental. Arguments over the actual effects of trade, then, become case-specific, relying upon empirical documentation. Most development economists conclude that it is highly unlikely an LDC seeking development today would be better off economically without trade.

The reader should be aware, however, that arguments over the benefits of foreign commerce (particularly the relative benefits) are ongoing. The trade economist tends to emphasize the loss of the potential gains from trade because of inability to solve the political-economic problem of distribution. Some political activists tend to ignore the economic losses of forgone trade so long as the personal or perceived national welfare function they operate under is maximized. The discussion over the benefits of trade for LDCs sometimes encounters emotional minefields that destroy dialogue among parties seeking to establish routes to development for the LDC.

Here we readily acknowledge that *free* trade (that is, trade that is carried on without LDC government intervention of any kind) for a developing LDC in the real world situation is only rarely the optimal policy. We emphasize that development without trade is improbable. And we leave open for future discussion just what policies LDCs can best pursue in the interest of economic evolution and welfare in the area of trade. We further acknowledge that world inequality may be increased by trade, and will return to this point later in the chapter. Now we turn to a brief summary of the arguments for withdrawal from trade.

There is a diverse set of writings, mostly Latin American, that stress the disadvantages of dependency in trade relations when the trading partner is economically more advanced. While the literature and ideas are not cohesive, they are sometimes referred to as the "dependency school of thought." A unifying theme of their studies is that the levels of development in LDCs and MDCs are highly interrelated through a trade network dominated by MDCs. Some writings in this group, particularly those supporting the ideas presented by the United Nations Economic Commission for Latin America (ECLA), contain mainly economic arguments about the relative advantages of the world trade network to MDCs that are at the center of bargaining strength and economic control, and the weak bargaining positions of the LDC periphery countries. These ideas are presented later. Here we consider the literature sympathetic to the idea that LDCs are better off withdrawing from trade.

The Dependency School

The radical dependency writers follow Karl Marx in assuming that social institutions are directly related in a fairly rigid way to the economic structure and its technology. Modern capitalism is viewed as a class society with workers exploited by the capitalist class. Once capitalist relationships establish a highly dualistic economy and a capitalist class structure tied to advanced countries through trade, the historical conditions cannot be changed without a revolution. Capitalist countries that are less ripe for a revolution are simply in earlier stages of a methodical march toward deteriorating and intensifying dualism.

The dependency school writings arguing that trade between more-developed capitalist nations and LDCs is a zero-sum game are couched in socialist and Marxist terminology (Griffin 1978, and Frank 1967, are two examples). It is often asserted that the trade network is exploitive, and has, via the capitalist system and the multinational companies, historically spread exploitation into LDCs with harmful social and political ramifications. In this school's examples, a local elite, remnant of colonial ties and oftentimes linked to foreign capitalists, is identified as the carrier of modernization within the LDC. The group's focus is on imitation of MDC technology and integration of a small modern enclave with the MDC trade network. The group and its MDC associates benefit at the expense of the LDC economy outside the enclave area by using political and economic power to exploit the backward sector. The net socioeconomic effect is said to be negative for the LDC and positive for the MDC. It is sometimes claimed that a country must withdraw from trade to rid itself of capitalism, as Cuba did, and then perhaps reenter the international commercial network on its own terms. Trade could be allowed during the political transition with countries of acceptable political persuasion, such as Cuba's trade with Russia.

Dependency school writers are not alone in noting that trade and dualism are related. Development literature outlines the difficulties or disadvantages today's LDCs face in absorbing modern foreign technology into their socioeconomic milieu, and the costs of such absorption— not just in payment of monopoly rents on the technology, but in the distortions that can readily arise. The literature documents the frequency of dualism and the problems LDCs face under its yoke. Yet the forms and implications of dualism in the less radical literature are different. Protrade advocates, implicitly if not explicitly, assume that dualism and other distortions can vary in intensity among countries over both earlier and later stages of industrialization. These distortions can be the result of avoidable policies and conditions that can be controlled if not eliminated entirely. Less radical writers do not blame as many domestic distortions, social and economic, upon advanced capitalist influence through trade as the radical wing of the dependency school does. Supporters of trade concentrate on methods of benefiting from modern technology and trade while avoiding indiscriminate technical transfer. Generally those who argue trade is vital to development do not deny the existence of historical cases where specific colonial, postcolonial, or other trade arrangements have had negative impact. Rather, they emphasize that, despite incidences of unequal bargaining power, LDCs can gain from trade in today's Western trade network.

Some of the domestic policies that underpin distortions associated with trade are discussed in chapter 12, on promotion of industry. Here we simply report the view, held particularly by some members of the dependency school, that technical transfer and trade inevitably lead to costs and distortions that benefit the MDC but weaken socioeconomic conditions in the LDC. As mentioned, the rationale given in the dependency school literature for rejecting trade is both political and economic in nature. And the welfare function used gives no weight to capitalist income.

Certain shortcomings of the dependency school writings should be noted. Their empirical content is generally inadequate to support the generalization that due to exposure to colonialism and postcolonial trade with capitalist MDCs, an LDC must develop a form of dualism that retards its growth and is socially disruptive. Theoretical aspects of the arguments are underdeveloped, and there is no careful calculation of the economic cost of trade withdrawal. In the role of critics, however, this group of writers has forced development economists in the protrade ranks to consider carefully the policy strategies relating to trade, and to acknowledge that there is a quantum leap between economic theory and the application of such theory to real world problems and plans.[4] But in regard to their overall antitrade theme, Paul Streeten notes: "The interesting question then is not 'Do the developing countries benefit or lose from their coexistence with developed countries?' but, 'How can they pursue selective policies that permit them to derive the benefits of the positive forces, without simultaneously exposing themselves to the harm of the detrimental forces?' " (1979, p. 30).

We turn now to the traditional literature that supports the conclusion that from an economic standpoint trade is a positive-sum, not a zero-sum game. As mentioned, to date there is no adequate analysis of trade as a zero-sum game explaining why LDCs that freely participate in exchange will suffer economic losses. If trade contributes to global inequality, then, the probable route of its doing so would be through the distribution of its gains. The following discussion considers the main arguments presented in the literature about forces at work that would produce terms of trade more favorable to one of the trading countries. It is followed by a brief discussion of the impact of the dynamics of trade upon differential growth rates, with specific reference to the empirical data bearing upon this subject.

THE TERMS OF TRADE AND INEQUALITY

Commodity Terms of Trade   The new set of relative prices faced by a country engaged in trade is called the commodity or barter terms of trade. While the commodity terms of trade are simplified here to refer to two goods, one exported and one imported, these terms of trade actually refer to an index of the prices received for export goods relative to an index of the prices paid for imports, using a selected base year equal to 100. If this ratio rises, and autarky relative prices remain constant, a country can be said to receive a greater proportion of the gains accruing from increased world efficiency with specialization and trade. Of course, there is no index for autarky prices, a deficiency that complicates measurement of the gains from trade. Table 10.4 gives the terms of trade for all but the centrally planned economies for 1960 and 1978, using 1970 as the base year. Changes during this period, of course, are affected by the large jump in energy costs in the 1970s.

It is helpful to represent the terms of trade graphically again. Figure 10.3 shows the commodity terms of trade for two goods or sets of goods as represented by the slope of line T_W. Assume the slope of T_M represents the pretrade domestic price ratio for all MDCs and the slope of T_L depicts the autarky price ratio for all LDCs. A T_W closer to T_M would

---

4. The reader interested in this group of writings is referred to a survey article by Gabriel Palma, "Dependency: A Formal Theory of Underdevelopment or a Methodology for Analysis of Concrete Situations of Underdevelopment," *World Development* 6 (July/August 1978): 881–924.

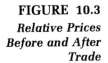

FIGURE 10.3
*Relative Prices
Before and After
Trade*

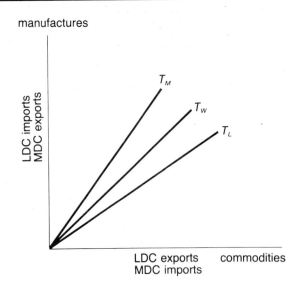

Autarky terms of trade for MDCs (exports/imports) are the slope of T_M. Autarky terms of trade for LDCs (imports/exports) are the slope of T_L. With trade, commodity terms of trade (manufactures/commodities) for LDCs and MDCs are the slope of T_W.

give MDCs greater gains from trade; one closer to T_L would give LDCs greater gains. Here T_W is arbitrarily drawn midway between T_M and T_L.

Division of Gains The theory of comparative advantage explained that gains from trade exist because with specialization world output is larger. Here we emphasize that the terms of trade, T_W, determine how the additional units of goods are shared among traders. Yet the exact effects of the shared gains on income inequality between the two countries are not readily measured since trade changes relative prices, production, and the relative quantities of goods consumed in each country.

The more ambitious goal of determining the change in economic well-being resulting from trade-related income shifts and then comparing the pretrade and posttrade welfare of two countries or groups of countries presents an even more complex measurement problem. This problem centers upon the fact that "welfare" cannot be measured for comparison purposes. We say a country is better off materially when it has more goods, and this is conceptually accurate; but we cannot measure how much better, even if each country receives the exact same increment of goods as its share of the gains from trade. Countries with different income levels, tastes, and population will not obtain the same improvement in well-being from equivalent goods increments resulting from trade gains. Just as it is impossible to measure individual well-being and make interpersonal comparisons of welfare positions, it is impossible to make intercountry comparisons. There is no yardstick for such comparisons. Nevertheless, the statement made above holds that the further the T_W line lies from a country's autarky terms of trade line, the greater the gains from foreign commerce for *that* country.

The arguments that surface in world forums over the terms of trade are concerned with the division of the gains from trade on the grounds that a *normative* position can and should be taken. The general posture of LDCs, and those concerned about global inequality (measured by an index of goods available), is that trade ought to reduce it and should never increase it between poorer and wealthier countries. There has been a tendency to gauge changes in the relative division of the gains from trade by examining changes in the index of the commodity terms of trade over time. Commodity terms of trade that move in favor of the LDC serve as a rough indicator of trade conditions favorable to reducing income disparity between MDCs and LDCs. As the next section makes clear, this is a misleading gauge unless autarky prices are constant.

Changes in Autarky Prices   Both the terms of trade (T_W) and autarky relative prices change over time, and thus affect the gains from trade. Before examining the determinants of the commodity terms of trade, it is important to note that changes in relative demand and supply conditions in a country will affect its autarky relative prices, and hence its potential benefits from trade.

First consider a proportionate expansion in the production possibilities frontier with constant relative demand for both import and export items, as indicated by the consumption line in figure 10.4. The domestic terms of trade (T) remain constant, as shown by a movement from A_1A_1' to A_2A_2'. Now let expansion be greater in the export good, with a shift to A_3A_3'. With no change in the relative amounts of each item demanded, consumption will remain in the same proportion, shown by the slope of its line. Because relative costs are now different, the slope of T must increase, indicating cheaper autarky prices for export goods. The effect of such a change upon figure 10.3, with T_W constant, would be to increase the gains from trade for the country. Note that changes in relative demand will also change autarky relative prices.

Growth in both the MDC and LDC country geared toward the export good, with a movement such as that from T_1 to T_2 in figure 10.4, would increase the slope of T_M in figure 10.3 and reduce that of T_L as the export good in each country becomes relatively cheaper. A growth oriented toward the import good in each country would move T_M and T_L closer to each other in the absence of offsetting demand effects. The countries' production possibilities curves become more similar, reducing the gains possible with trade. Under changing conditions, then, a constant T_W does not ensure that a country's share of the gains from trade is unchanged.

Consider two examples. Assume the exports of LDCs are all agricultural commodities and those of MDCs are manufactured goods. Productivity and supply increases in both agriculture and manufacturers have been high. However, the income elasticity of demand in MDCs is low for agricultural goods. Referring back to figure 10.3 again, this means the slope of T_M falls. In LDCs assume population growth is high

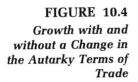

FIGURE 10.4

Growth with and without a Change in the Autarky Terms of Trade

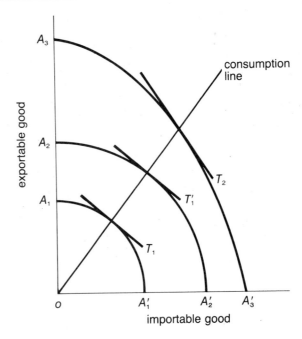

A parallel shift in the production possibilities curve from A_1A_1' to A_2A_2', with relative consumption unchanged, leaves relative prices the same. A movement to A_3A_3' changes relative costs and autarky relative prices. Exportables are relatively cheaper, as shown by the slope of T_2.

and the demand for food has an income elasticity close to one. The terms of trade in autarky (T_L) are assumed to change little. In this scenario, a not too unrealistic one, the slope of the world terms of trade line (T_W), if unchanged, will lie closer to T_M than T_L in figure 10.3, meaning MDC gains from trade are less.

Consider a second example, where LDC exports are scarce minerals and metals whose extraction costs are rising worldwide relative to prices of manufactures. T_M and T_L in figure 10.3 would both move counterclockwise toward the manufactures axis. A constant T_W in this example would mean less equally divided gains from trade, that is to say, the LDC would experience reduced gains with T_W constant.

Even though data on the terms of trade are not sufficient to determine gains from international exchange, the commodity terms of trade are an important variable in the equation for such gains. And literature on development pays special attention to this variable since a swing in it has impact upon LDC development. Moreover, the fact that reductions in the gains from trade can lead to hardship as income declines has political as well as economic importance. The next section looks closely at the factors determining T_W.

Determinants of the Commodity Terms of Trade   What determines the level of the terms of trade, T_W? "Supply and demand in world markets" is a facile answer. However, supply and demand may work through either competitive or noncompetitive markets. Various economists studying world commerce have emphasized specific determinants of supply and demand and market structure.

In the competitive model trade can increase inequality since the terms of trade as determined by competitive demand and supply conditions can favor one country more than another. Changes in technology, the relative supply of factors of production, and relative demand can lead to changes in the gains from trade under competitive conditions. A technological bias that is capital-using or augments labor would help to keep the demand for capital goods high despite an increase in supply of capital, as would a rise in demand for capital-intensive goods relative to labor-intensive goods. While there has been growth in demand for labor-intensive goods in the postwar period, increases in labor supply in some LDCs and in labor-intensive goods exported have been large. Both trends may have affected the terms of trade for manufactured goods between individual MDCs and LDCs to the advantage of MDCs that export capital-intensive goods.

The Competitive Model

Ragnar Nurkse emphasized the effect of a low income elasticity of demand for raw materials as a reason for trade not serving as an "engine of growth" for LDCs. This low income elasticity is connected to technological change that has created new resources, greater substitutability for all resources, and reduced raw materials needed per unit of output (in Haberler and Stern, eds. 1961). The terms of trade are affected by the relatively slow rise in demand for LDC commodity exports compared with MDC exports with income growth. Trade, then, does not reduce the gap in income between MDCs and LDCs, and may help to increase it. Nurkse suggested a development policy that looks inward for its growth thrust.

Benjamin Higgins postulates a "Giffon" good effect upon export prices of certain food items (1968, p. 288). He notes that with productivity gains and greater rice output prices can fall not only because the supply of rice expands, but because cheaper rice is tantamount to an increase in income for the mass of poor people. When their income rises from this price effect, they will switch some of their purchases from rice to other foodstuffs they consider superior (the Giffon effect). Cheap rice is then exported, and Higgins concludes: "Thus improvements in rice culture benefit the rest of the world more than they do the rice-growing rural sector itself" (ibid., p. 288).

Trade models that assume perfect competition, then, can explain a declining terms of trade trend for a country by using supply and demand analysis and without reference to noncompetitive conditions or situations of unequal bargaining strength. Literature on the topic, however, often relies on models of imperfect competition to analyze the potential for unfavorable trends for LDCs, and considers the effect of differing technical advantages upon trade gains.

Raul Prebisch, a Latin American economist associated with the United Nations Economic Commission for Latin America, was one of the first to argue that the gains from trade reflected in the commodity terms of

Models of Imperfect Competition

trade are distributed in greater proportion to MDCs. His data applied to historical periods before the Great Depression, but his arguments are considered applicable to postwar trade and data. His position was buttressed by Hans Singer, Gunner Myrdal, and others. Essentially they argue as follows: LDCs import from MDCs differentiated manufactured goods that are priced in oligopoly fashion, with part of the gains in productivity distributed to organized labor in MDCs, part to oligopoly profits, and little to consumers in lower prices. It is assumed that improvements in product and quality do not compensate for the downward rigidity of relative prices that characterizes oligopoly.

LDCs, in contrast, sell their products either in competitive markets or markets dominated by large purchasers with superior bargaining positions. They export mainly raw materials and have little control over price. Over time demand for MDC exports has remained strong relative to supply, supporting the oligopoly pricing rigidity and enabling relative prices for these goods to rise. The weak demand relative to supply of raw materials produces unfavorable terms of trade for LDCs that worsen as supply grows faster than demand. The outcome is that MDCs have captured the greater part of the gains from trade, and their share is increasing. This is not proved empirically, but evidence is offered on the secular terms of trade. While such data on T_W alone do not prove the gains are going in greater proportion to MDCs (as shown earlier), a continuous trend in one direction—downward for LDCs—was presumed to reflect a less favorable position than one without this trend.

As it turns out the data used by Prebisch were not robust. But the basic hypothesis remains that with growth in the world economy, productivity gains of LDCs exporting raw materials are passed on in great part in lower prices to their foreign customers while the same is not true of MDCs because of the noncompetitive structure of world markets for their exports. W. Arthur Lewis added the idea that surplus labor in LDCs kept costs and export prices low (1955).

The idea that factor prices are not determined exclusively by market forces and can be influenced by employment levels in both LDCs and MDCs has been emphasized by the neo-Ricardian school in Cambridge, England (Metcalfe and Steedman 1974, pp. 581–95). Distorted factor prices affect goods prices that must reflect cost of production. With imperfections in the markets for capital and labor, specialization need not occur in products that are the relatively more efficient products of trading countries. This will affect the relative gains from trade and could even lead to losses. Planned economies are particularly subject to the problem of specializing in the wrong good because of a lack of efficiency prices. Arguments by the neo-Ricardians extend this distortion to market economies, advanced as well as less advanced. Chapter 12 presents the neoclassical approach, theorizing that distortions in factor prices can be offset by subsidies or taxes. In LDCs with large proportions of laborers receiving a wage that does not reflect their scarcity value at the margin, offsetting policy actions may be mechanically difficult to execute simply because of the scope of the problem relative to government policy options. Neo-Ricardians argue, moreover, that when such distortions are embedded in an institutional framework that determines income distribution, compensating corrections can be politically impossible to achieve in the real world.

The control of export prices by multinational corporations (MNCs) has been pinpointed as a reason for LDCs' relatively poor gains from trade. Prices paid for raw materials by bargaining agents such as the large oil corporations prior to the formation of OPEC were, it was argued, monopsony prices that reflected the superior negotiating position of the large producers. And even the accounting transfer prices within MNCs for their branches located in LDCs have been documented as creating trade terms favorable to the multinationals (Vaitsos 1974). These internal accounting prices are influenced by company strategy geared to tax advantages for global operations, transfer of profits among countries, and other company and country-specific variables.

Terms of trade have also been affected by protectionist policies in MDCs, which buy most LDC exports. These exports are highly concentrated in primary goods. Raw materials are among the least protected commodities when they are to be used as an input for manufactured goods. However, MDC tariffs are deliberately set on processed raw materials, intermediate goods, and final goods. This can prevent the LDC from exporting final and intermediate goods even though in the absence of protection it may have a comparative advantage in them. In many cases the prices of processed, intermediate, or final goods would be more likely to avoid unfavorable trends in their commodity and/or income terms of trade, and the extra value added could earn additional foreign exchange for LDCs. On the other hand, all categories of food exports face relatively high protectionist policies because MDCs tend to protect their domestic agriculture from foreign competition, adversely affecting the demand and price of LDC food exports, raw or processed.

Tariffs, quotas, and pressures upon LDCs to enforce "voluntary" export restrictions are all protectionist policies employed by MDCs against LDCs' export of labor-intensive manufactures. This tends to keep LDC export prices lower than they would be under conditions of unrestricted demand, since the bulk of LDC world market sales are to MDCs. On the other hand, restriction by LDCs on their imports from MDCs place less downward pressure on MDC prices because the restrictions affect mainly the type of imports (capital goods versus consumer goods) and not spending for imports.

As more LDCs industrialize and add to the world supply of manufactures exports of the same goods such as labor-intensive textile goods, shoes, toys, and certain household items, this will increase competitive pressures on prices and intensify demands for protection from MDC producers and laborers. In the short run, at least, this does not promise greatly improving terms of trade to LDCs switching from dependence on raw commodities to labor-intensive manufactures exports. Increasing competition is likely to lead to price cutting by countries anxious to maintain and increase their foreign exchange earnings on price elastic manufactured goods.

For some LDC export goods, shipping charges are a substantial proportion of their prices. World ocean shipping charges reflect government intervention and the activities of cartels formed to "stabilize" prices for various routes. LDCs have little if any influence over shipping charges or availability of cargo space. Moreover, LDC trade tends to be greatly dependent upon ocean shipping. Because of high fixed costs, shippers often give lower rates on bulk items. This favors some LDC exports of raw materials, but has a less favorable impact on less bulky processed goods (Yeats 1979, chap. 7).

Charles Kindleberger argues (1956) quite plausibly that compared with MDCs, LDCs are less able to respond to shifting prices and demand by changing supplies and products exported, and that this can affect their commodity terms of trade. One hallmark of LDCs is a structural rigidity that impedes their response to change. Concentration in a few goods and even a few overseas markets typifies trade patterns of many LDCs. When the terms of trade deteriorate for a given major export good, the LDC may not be able to shift resources readily to other exports with a better terms of trade.

The trading block of communist countries with planned economies bargains over trade terms bilaterally. They sometimes use an average of Western prices over a business cycle. In other cases the terms of trade are related to political goals. The planned economies take less advantage of the gains to be attained from an open-trade posture, and their exports and imports make up only a small proportion of world trade (see table 10.1). Their markets are not open to trade on the basis of competitive pricing. Thus, while most of the comments here apply to the noncommunist trade network, the communist trading block does not afford favorable opportunities for LDCs to improve their terms of trade. There are certain exceptions such as Cuba, where political considerations dominate.

International Commodity Agreements

LDCs have asked for commodity agreements that besides making prices more stable, would transfer more of the gains from trade to them by raising their export prices above current levels. Many LDCs indicate they would find this preferable to foreign aid as a redistributive device. They view it as correcting the forces working against improvement in their gains from trade.

MDCs tend to concentrate on the alternative efficiency criteria of aid versus higher commodity prices and assume current prices reflect free market competitive forces. They conclude that aid is more flexible, and more efficient, and in the long run more beneficial since high prices would encourage technological substitutes and would impose poor terms of trade upon LDCs that import commodities. It is usually assumed that the volume of aid would be no higher or more automatic under commodity agreements than with loans and grants, a contention LDCs doubt. In general LDCs would like a price support system that works much as the United States farm price support program has worked to distribute income toward the farmer. MDCs point out how this overcommits resources to agriculture and is administratively expensive, requiring purchases, storage, and control of crops, and has saddled the consumer with high prices.

Empirical research has not attempted to measure the division of the gains from trade—a formidable if not impossible task. It has concentrated instead on *changes* in the terms of trade, cyclical and secular. Such studies show, as might be expected, that changes in the terms of trade for LDCs vary for individual countries and according to periods selected for examination. LDCs with downward secular trends in their terms of trade tend to be highly specialized in the export of primary goods with low income elasticity of demand.

PROBLEMS OF MEASURING THE GAINS FROM TRADE

It should be noted that empirical studies are affected by statistical limitations; it is impossible to surmount the "index problem." Indexes cannot take account of product and quality changes. This may not pose a problem for export indexes when LDCs sell abroad a staple crop or a mineral or metal that has not changed over the period covered. On the import side, however, it is quite likely capital goods and other imports have undergone modifications that cannot be adjusted for satisfactorily when calculating the import index. Moreover, quality improvements, when they reduce choice, are not necessarily helpful to the LDC. As mentioned in chapter 5, sometimes vintage machines are a better buy for the LDC that is relatively labor intensive. And other complications exist. Reliable statistics may not be available. The data are sensitive to the choice of a base period and historical data are lacking for most LDCs. Transportation costs affect imports and exports differently so that when such costs are included, they can cause a change in the terms of trade. Data limitations may mean that export prices do not include customs, insurance, and freight, while import prices do. Thus, in addition to the conceptual limitations of the commodity terms of trade as an indicator of the gains from trade, statistical weaknesses can affect their usefulness.

After this survey of arguments on why the gains from international commerce as affected by the commodity terms of trade have been appropriated in larger proportion by MDCs, to a greater or lesser degree, it is still uncertain that trade over time has increased the inequality between the LDC and its trading partners. Development economists have long noted (and Japan early discovered) that the *income terms of trade* can be more important to economic development than the commodity terms of trade. The income terms of trade are calculated by multiplying the commodity terms of trade index times an index of the quantity of exports sold. They give a measure of changes over time in total imports available as a result of rising or falling foreign exchange earnings. In other words, a country needing foreign exchange earnings for imports vital to its development could benefit by lowered export prices when the demand curve is price elastic. Even with import prices unchanged, foreign exchange earnings will increase and allow imports to rise. Figure 10.5 illustrates this. Prices fall from P_W to P'_W and exports rise from Q to Q'. Foreign exchange earnings rise by area B minus area A.

The Income Terms of Trade

The shape of each country's demand curve will depend upon the shape of the world demand curve and the country's share of the market.

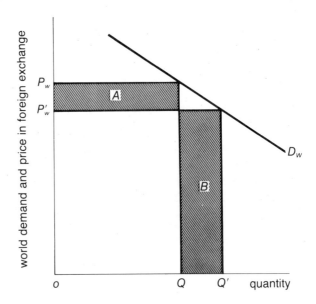

FIGURE 10.5

*Decline in World
Price, Elastic
Demand*

A fall in world price from P_w to P'_w with elastic demand raises foreign exchange earnings from exports by area *B* — area *A*.

Elasticity of demand is higher for an individual country than for the market as a whole. An LDC that is not a sizable exporter of a product with inelastic world demand can lower its price and benefit from increased earnings at the expense of world competitors. However, the income terms of trade argument does not apply to large exporters of price-inelastic goods when price declines. Many LDCs are concentrated in products that are price-inelastic and lose foreign exchange when export prices drop.

Of course a preferable situation for the LDC to that shown in figure 10.5 would be an outward shift in its demand curve so that it reaps additional export earnings at the same or higher price. This entails growing demand for LDC products greater than supply increases and explains LDCs' concern over protectionist policies in MDCs that affect demand expansion. Planned economies, as mentioned, restrict trade even more than those of the West, and offer LDCs no promising alternatives to interdependence with the Western trading network.

**The Dynamics
of Trade**
Development may be affected by the growth rate of foreign trade. An expanding trade sector can accelerate the rate of technical change and capital accumulation, and thus the growth rate of productivity. Many imports needed for economic improvement are not produceable by the LDC. Imported capital and technology connected with trade shift the production possibilities curve outward.

Development can be positively affected by linkage effects from foreign commerce. When the trade sector draws on other sectors for inputs or creates new economic activity from its income effects, there is economic stimulation in affected areas beyond the trade sector. Efficiency gains from increased domestic competition or scale effects can stimulate growth in situations where the trade sector enlarges rapidly.

Thus, the full gains from trade cannot be measured in the exact fashion represented previously in figure 10.2, but must reflect the impact of dynamic growth. Growth effects from trade can offset a movement in the commodity terms of trade that favors the MDC, and the total gains may favor the LDC over the period considered. This can occur when MDCs receive less stimulus to growth from trade than LDCs do.

It should be noted, however, that the stimulus from trade can vary with the type of product exported as well as imported. For example, some studies indicate that certain types of mining and other forms of mineral extraction in LDCs have little spillover or linkage effects upon important development variables. It is incumbent upon the LDC to use royalties and tax monies from such operations to kindle development.

Cyclical fluctuations in export earnings have been studied because of the possibility that they will reduce the beneficial development linkages of trade. Swings in export earnings presumably interfere with full employment of resources, create dislocations and risk costs, and generally render planning, direct or indirect, more difficult. Chapter 11 examines such effects in more detail.

In sum, then, stable foreign exchange earnings and a secular growth rate of trade greater than the average of all sectors would tend to affect growth positively. Should MDCs' trade exhibit higher growth rates than that of LDCs, and should their export earnings have greater stability, then trade may have facilitated or contributed to growth in MDCs more than to LDCs and thus widened the gap in their incomes. Measurement problems prevent a definitive assessment of the relative growth impetus from trade. We mention here some evidence bearing on the topic.

Studies show that instability of export earnings is greater for LDCs than for MDCs (Coppock, 1962; Erb and Schiavo-Campo 1969; Mac-Bean 1966; Glezakos 1973, pp. 670–79). When supply and demand curves for LDC exports are inelastic, small shifts in the curves can result in large price changes. Price inelasticities of supply and demand combined with cyclical fluctuations in demand have had an effect upon fluctuations in LDC export earnings. It is suspected that greater concentration of LDC exports in both commodities and regions contributes to relative instability since there is less opportunity for offsetting changes. Also contributing are supply-side fluctuations due to imponderables like weather failure, political instability, inept government marketing boards, and immobility of resources.

In regard to the secular growth rate in trade, trade in manufactures since World War II has had a growth rate higher than that of world manufacturing output. Other categories of traded commodities, with exceptions such as oil, have not had as high a growth rate as manufactured goods. With higher manufactures output per capita, MDCs have outstripped most LDCs in export growth performance over the past 35 years. However, some LDCs have participated in the expansion of manufactures exports, especially South Korea, Taiwan, Hong Kong, Spain, and Greece. The World Bank finds that in addition to the slow rise in postwar global demand for agricultural goods, a large share of which LDCs supply, population growth and inadequate attention to improving agricultural production also affected export growth of LDCs (The World Bank 1978, p. 9).

The causal nexus between the dynamics of trade, development, and growth is complex, imperfectly specified from our theories about trade and development, and therefore extremely difficult to quantify. Export instability and income elasticity of demand for exports are only two variables that weigh upon the outcome. And surprisingly, empirical studies have been unable to establish that instability in export earnings necessarily curbs LDC growth rates (Glezakos 1973; Yotopoulos and Nugent 1976, p. 336).

There is evidence, however, that countries with slow growth of export earnings, especially but not exclusively smaller countries, suffer in their development progress from the shortfall in foreign exchange. A sluggish export growth rate for LDCs could enlarge the income gap between them and the MDCs. And Glezakos offers evidence that the growth rate of exports is a more important factor in the economic growth of MDCs than LDCs (1973, pp. 670–79). At least such evidence lends support to the argument that differential growth rates in LDC and MDC trade can contribute to a divergence in the incomes of trading partners. The effect of export earnings growth on development is examined more closely in chapter 11. The analysis, there brings out the interrelations between development and changes in the income and commodity terms of trade.

Conclusions

What conclusions can be reached? In the absence of trade relations with more advanced countries, the lowest-income LDCs would remain poor for a longer time. Active trade relations can provide economic gains for both LDCs and MDCs. There is no reason to expect that supply and demand forces under competitive conditions will yield an equal division of the gains from trade. Moreover, the trade network is characterized by pursuit of state and private interests and by uneven economic power, and thus trade can favor the economic unit with stronger bargaining power. Trade flows are also characterized by cyclical swings and other elements of instability that can have impact upon differential growth rates.

When the gains from trade favor MDCs, inequality is heightened. The variables contributing to disparity need not intensify to exacerbate inequality between rich and poor nations. Simply by widening the gap, trade can contribute to a further widening of absolute income differences, as explained earlier in connection with the compound growth effect. However, the gains from trade stem from a complex network of interrelated factors, and cannot be measured by a movement in the terms of trade, whether commodity or income.

It is very difficult, if not impossible, to determine that there is a systematic bias in the world trade network in favor of all MDCs and against all LDCs. Even assuming trade intensifies global inequality, such a statement does not imply that trade has not contributed to development in LDCs and does not justify a policy of withdrawal from trade. Trade is not a zero-sum game.

Within more advanced nation-states with mixed market-government economies, the distribution of the gains from specialization and division of labor, extraction of depletable raw materials, and returns to accumulated capital and technical stocks do not depend exclusively upon market forces as they affect income. Such a distribution would create large inequalities deemed socially unacceptable. Supply and demand are relied upon to achieve efficiency, and redistribution is accepted on the grounds of social justice. Among nation-states trade relations undertaken for self-interest can create uneven gains related to market forces and/or bargaining power. There is no accepted social responsibility among nation-states in regard to redistribution of income affected by trade to the countries or individuals around the globe with the lowest earnings.

Foreign aid has provided only limited redistribution, and has not always reached the poorest within national boundaries. Critics of the international economic system note this shortfall of aid and point out that nationalism facilitates the disinheritance of the world's poor by the wealthy states; yet trade relations with nation-states harboring the poor raise incomes of the affluent states. Widespread dissatisfaction among the LDC members of the system is so strong that they have called for a New International Economic Order.

When a few individuals within poorer LDCs reap gains from trade without redistributing them, the trade network invites condemnation by those concerned with income distribution. Radical critics advocate withdrawal from the system. The topic of national inequality is explored in chapter 14. Suffice it to say here that from an analytical standpoint trade may, but does not necessarily, contribute to national inequality. Trade can moderate inequality within LDCs by influencing the product mix and hence the relative demand for abundant labor. It can intensify such inequality when it contributes to unemployment and conditions leading to dualism, or generates income from natural resources that is distributed unevenly.

TABLE 10.1 *Destination of Merchandise Exports, 1960 and 1980*

	Destination of Merchandise Exports (percentage of total)							
	Industrial Market Economies		Nonmarket Industrial Economies		High-income Oil Exporters		Developing Economies	
Origin	1960	1980	1960	1980	1960	1980	1960	1980
Low-income Economies	51 w	51 w	21 w	4 w	1 w	5 w	27 w	40 w
China and India	39 w	49 w	36 w	5 w	(.) w	5 w	25 w	41 w
Others	66 w	56 w	3 w	4 w	2 w	5 w	29 w	35 w
1 Kampuchea, Dem.	..	..	..	..	..	..	..	..
2 Lao, PDR	..	41	..	0	..	10	..	49
3 Bhutan	..	..	..	..	..	..	..	..
4 Chad	73	32	0	0	0	5	27	63
5 Bangladesh	..	48	..	10	..	1	..	41
6 Ethiopia	69	64	1	10	6	2	24	24
7 Nepal	..	32	..	0	..	0	..	68
8 Somalia	85	17	0	0	(.)	68	15	15
9 Burma	23	31	3	1	(.)	1	74	67
10 Afghanistan	48	42	28	21	0	2	24	35
11 Viet Nam	..	..	..	..	(.)	(.)	..	..
12 Mali	93	68	0	1	..	(.)	7	31
13 Burundi	..	85	..	2	..	(.)	..	13
14 Rwanda	..	93	..	0	..	(.)	..	7
15 Upper Volta	4	86	0	0	0	0	96	14
16 Zaire	89	45	(.)	(.)	(.)	(.)	11	55
17 Malawi	..	82	..	0	..	0	..	18
18 Mozambique	29	49	(.)	(.)	(.)	8	71	43
19 India	66	53	7	17	2	9	25	21
20 Haiti	98	97	(.)	0	0	0	2	3
21 Sri Lanka	75	46	3	5	0	8	22	55
22 Sierra Leone	99	100	0	0	0	0	1	(.)
23 Tanzania	74	62	1	2	0	1	25	35
24 China	14	47	61	0	(.)	3	25	50
25 Guinea	63	80	18	0	(.)	2	19	18
26 Central African Rep.	83	90	0	0	0	0	17	10
27 Pakistan	56	36	4	3	2	14	38	47
28 Uganda	62	78	0	0	0	2	38	20
29 Benin	90	87	2	0	0	0	8	13
30 Niger	74	96	0	0	0	1	26	3

31	Madagascar	79	78	1	4	(.)	0	20	18
32	Sudan	59	42	8	9	4	12	29	37
33	Togo	74	68	0	7	0	0	26	25
	Middle-income Economies	68 w	64 w	7 w	4 w	(.) w	2 w	25 w	30 w
	Oil Exporters	68 w	74 w	4 w	1 w	(.) w	(.) w	28 w	25 w
	Oil Importers	68 w	57 w	9 w	6 w	(.) w	3 w	23 w	34 w
34	Ghana	88	70	7	15	(.)	(.)	5	15
35	Kenya	77	51	0	1	(.)	2	23	46
36	Lesotho								
37	Yemen, PDR	42	61	(.)	(.)	2	8	56	31
38	Indonesia	54	80	11	1	(.)	(.)	42	19
39	Yemen Arab Rep.	46	36	18	2	(.)	13	36	49
40	Mauritania	89	94	0	0	0	1	11	5
41	Senegal	89	70	0	0	0	(.)	11	30
42	Angola	64	51	2	0	0	1	34	48
43	Liberia	100	90	0	(.)	0	(.)	(.)	10
44	Honduras	77	85	0	0	0	(.)	23	15
45	Zambia		79		1		(.)		20
46	Bolivia	88	55	0	0	0	(.)	12	45
47	Egypt	26	73		7	2	1	39	19
48	Zimbabwe			33					
49	El Salvador	88	70	0	(.)	0	0	12	30
50	Cameroon	93	92	1	1	(.)	(.)	6	7
51	Thailand	47	58	2	2	3	4	48	36
52	Philippines	94	76	0	4	(.)	1	6	19
53	Nicaragua	91	66	(.)	1	0	(.)	9	33
54	Papua New Guinea		92		1	(.)	(.)		
55	Congo, People's Rep.	92	72	0	0	0	(.)	7	7
56	Morocco	74	70	3	8	2	2	23	28
57	Mongolia								
58	Albania	1		93				6	20
59	Peru	84	72	(.)	3	0	(.)	16	25
60	Nigeria	95	95	1	(.)	0	(.)	4	5
61	Jamaica	96	82	0	4	0	(.)	4	14
62	Guatemala	94	63	0	0	0	1	6	36
63	Ivory Coast	84	81	0	3	0	(.)	16	16
64	Dominican Rep.	92	90	0	(.)	1	0	7	10
65	Colombia	94	81	1	4	0	(.)	5	15
66	Ecuador	91	64	1	2	0	0	8	34

TABLE 10.1 Destination of Merchandise Exports, 1960 and 1980 (continued)

	Destination of Merchandise Exports (percentage of total)							
	Industrial Market Economies		Nonmarket Industrial Economies		High-income Oil Exporters		Developing Economies	
Origin	1960	1980	1960	1980	1960	1980	1960	1980
67 Paraguay	61	54	0	0	0	0	39	46
68 Tunisia	76	69	3	1	2	3	19	27
69 Korea, Dem. Rep.	..	..	..	..	..	..	..	..
70 Syrian Arab Rep.	39	30	19	15	11	7	31	48
71 Jordan	1	11	11	3	26	23	62	63
72 Lebanon	21	15	8	9	32	47	39	29
73 Turkey	71	60	12	15	(.)	4	17	21
74 Cuba	72	..	19	..	(.)	..	9	..
75 Korea, Rep. of	89	67	0	(.)	0	9	11	23
76 Malaysia	58	61	7	3	0	1	35	35
77 Costa Rica	93	63	(.)	1	(.)	(.)	7	36
78 Panama	99	75	0	(.)	(.)	(.)	1	25
79 Algeria	93	96	0	1	(.)	(.)	7	3
80 Brazil	81	65	6	6	(.)	1	13	28
81 Mexico	93	85	(.)	(.)	(.)	(.)	7	15
82 Chile	91	67	(.)	(.)	(.)	2	9	31
83 South Africa	71	81	1	0	(.)	0	28	19
84 Romania	20	27	66	42	(.)	4	14	27
85 Portugal	56	82	2	2	(.)	(.)	42	16
86 Argentina	75	44	5	17	(.)	1	20	38
87 Yugoslavia	48	34	31	43	1	3	20	20
88 Uruguay	82	48	7	4	0	1	11	47
89 Iran	62	69	3	0	1	1	34	30
90 Iraq	85	61	1	(.)	(.)	(.)	14	39
91 Venezuela	62	64	0	(.)	0	0	38	36
92 Hong Kong	54	65	(.)	(.)	1	3	45	32
93 Trinidad and Tobago	80	77	0	0	(.)	0	20	23
94 Greece	65	59	21	7	1	11	13	23
95 Singapore	38	41	4	2	1	4	57	53
96 Israel	76	80	1	(.)	0	0	23	20
High-Income Oil Exporters	83 w	78 w	(.) w	0 w	0 w	1 w	17 w	21 w
97 Libya	67	84	7	(.)	0	(.)	26	16
98 Saudi Arabia	74	78	0	0	0	(.)	26	22
99 Kuwait	91	78	0	0	0	4	9	18
100 United Arab Emirates	..	78	..	(.)	..	2	..	20

	67 w	69 w	3 w	3 w	( ) w	4 w	30 w	24 w
Industrial Market Economies								
101 Ireland	96	88	( )	1	( )	2	4	9
102 Spain	80	62	2	2	( )	5	18	31
103 Italy	65	67	4	3	2	7	29	23
104 New Zealand	95	67	1	5	( )	1	4	27
105 United Kingdom	57	71	3	2	2	5	38	22
106 Finland	69	68	19	20	( )	1	12	11
107 Australia	75	61	3	6	1	3	21	30
108 Japan	45	48	2	3	2	7	51	42
109 Canada	90	85	1	3	( )	1	9	11
110 Austria	69	71	13	11	( )	2	18	16
111 United States	61	58	1	2	1	4	37	36
112 Netherlands	78	85	1	2	1	2	20	11
113 France	53	68	3	4	( )	3	44	25
114 Belgium	79	85	2	2	1	1	18	12
115 Norway	80	88	4	1	( )	1	16	10
116 Denmark	83	83	4	2	( )	2	13	13
117 Sweden	79	79	4	4	( )	2	17	15
118 Germany, Fed. Rep.	70	75	4	4	( )	3	25	18
119 Switzerland	72	72	3	3	1	3	24	22
Nonmarket Industrial Economies	19 w	..	59 w	..	( ) w	..	22 w	..
120 Poland	29	..	54	..	( )	..	17	..
121 Bulgaria	13	..	80	..	( )	..	7	..
122 Hungary	22	..	61	..	( )	..	17	..
123 USSR	18	..	51	..	( )	..	31	..
124 Czechoslovakia	16	..	67	..	( )	..	17	..
125 German Dem. Rep.	19	..	68	..	( )	..	13	..

Note: w means the average is weighted by merchandise exports.

SOURCE: World Bank, *World Development Report 1982* (New York: Oxford University Press, 1982), Table 11, pp. 130–31. Reprinted by permission.

TABLE 10.2 *Flow of External Capital, 1970 and 1980*

	Public and Publicly Guaranteed Medium- and Long-term Loans (millions of dollars)						Net Direct Private Investment (millions of dollars)	
	Gross Inflow		Repayment of Principal		Net Inflow			
	1970	1980	1970	1980	1970	1980	1970	1980[a]
Low-income Economies								
China and India								
Others								
1 Kampuchea, Dem.	..	..	..	..	..	..	..	..
2 Lao, PDR	..	..	..	..	..	..	..	..
3 Bhutan	..	..	..	..	..	..	..	..
4 Chad	6	9	2	12	4	−3	1	..
5 Bangladesh	..	597	..	40	..	557	..	..
6 Ethiopia	27	132	15	16	12	116	4	..
7 Nepal	1	55	2	2	−1	53	..	..
8 Somalia	4	114	(.)	5	4	109	5	..
9 Burma	16	281	18	64	−2	217	..	..
10 Afghanistan	31	113	15	157	16	−44	..	..
11 Viet Nam	..	..	..	..	..	..	..	..
12 Mali	21	85	(.)	7	21	78	..	4
13 Burundi	1	43	(.)	4	1	39	..	..
14 Rwanda	(.)	34	(.)	1	(.)	33	(.)	..
15 Upper Volta	2	79	2	9	(.)	70	1	20
16 Zaire	31	198	28	155	3	43	42	..
17 Malawi	38	160	3	35	35	125	9	6
18 Mozambique	..	..	..	..	..	..	..	..
19 India	890	2,477	307	636	583	1,841	6	..
20 Haiti	4	55	4	11	(.)	44	3	13
21 Sri Lanka	61	296	27	49	34	247	(.)	43
22 Sierra Leone	8	88	10	34	−2	54	8	12
23 Tanzania	50	210	10	20	40	190	..	..
24 China	..	..	..	..	..	..	..	..
25 Guinea	90	122	10	72	80	50	..	..

26 Central African Rep.	2	43	2	6	()	37	1	21
27 Pakistan	484	1,199	114	363	370	832	31	57
28 Uganda	26	169	4	37	22	132	4	3
29 Benin	2	84	1	4	1	80	7	:
30 Niger	12	177	1	23	11	154	1	:
31 Madagascar	10	438	5	34	5	404	10	−6
32 Sudan	54	749	22	132	32	617	:	:
33 Togo	5	222	2	97	3	125	1	:
Middle-income Economies								
Oil Exporters								
Oil Importers								
34 Ghana	40	129	12	48	28	81	8	10
35 Kenya	30	414	15	79	15	335	14	61
36 Lesotho	()	22	(.)	3	(.)	19	:	:
37 Yemen, PDR	1	101	:	6	1	95	:	:
38 Indonesia	441	2,592	59	953	382	1,639	83	184
39 Yemen Arab Rep.	:	399	:	13	:	386	:	142
40 Mauritania	4	153	3	17	1	136	1	84
41 Senegal	15	283	5	123	10	160	5	:
42 Angola	:	:	:	:	:	:	:	:
43 Liberia	7	90	12	16	−5	74	:	:
44 Honduras	29	180	3	39	26	141	8	5
45 Zambia	351	517	32	237	319	280	:	:
46 Bolivia	54	439	17	117	37	322	:	:
47 Egypt	302	2,982	247	1,246	55	1,736	−76	42
48 Zimbabwe	()	130	5	34	−5	96	:	541
49 El Salvador	8	124	6	17	2	107	4	2
50 Cameroon	28	571	4	79	24	492	16	6
51 Thailand	55	1,329	23	168	32	1,162	43	65
52 Philippines	132	1,390	73	220	59	1,170	−29	186
53 Nicaragua	44	269	17	39	27	230	15	40
54 Papua New Guinea	25	134	(.)	35	25	99	:	3
55 Congo, People's Rep.	35	230	6	58	29	172	:	60
56 Morocco	163	1,567	36	573	127	994	20	46
57 Mongolia	:	:	:	:	:	:	:	90
58 Albania	:	:	:	:	:	:	:	:

TABLE 10.2 Flow of External Capital, 1970 and 1980 (continued)

	Public and Publicly Guaranteed Medium- and Long-term Loans (millions of dollars)						Net Direct Private Investment (millions of dollars)	
	Gross Inflow		Repayment of Principal		Net Inflow			
	1970	1980	1970	1980	1970	1980	1970	1980ᵃ
59 Peru	148	1,231	101	954	47	277	-70	70
60 Nigeria	62	1,526	36	84	26	1,442	205	595
61 Jamaica	15	200	6	82	9	118	161	-12
62 Guatemala	37	93	20	33	17	60	29	111
63 Ivory Coast	77	1,426	27	534	50	892	31	109
64 Dominican Rep.	38	382	7	61	31	321	72	-13
65 Colombia	235	1,005	75	264	160	741	39	233
66 Ecuador	42	749	16	179	26	570	89	81
67 Paraguay	15	158	7	44	8	114	4	31
68 Tunisia	87	431	45	222	42	209	16	234
69 Korea, Dem. Rep.	..		..		..		..	..
70 Syrian Arab Rep.	59	509	30	297	29	212	..	..
71 Jordan	14	307	3	76	11	231	..	31
72 Lebanon	12	109	2	7	10	102	..	..
73 Turkey	328	2,222	128	399	200	1,823	58	89
74 Cuba								
75 Korea, Rep. of	440	3,548	198	1,452	242	2,096	66	-5
76 Malaysia	43	358	45	118	-2	240	94	928
77 Costa Rica	30	398	21	75	9	323	26	13
78 Panama	67	387	24	·210	43	177	33	40
79 Algeria	292	3,401	33	2,405	259	996	45	315
80 Brazil	883	6,039	255	3,769	628	2,270	407	1,568
81 Mexico	772	8,551	476	4,048	296	4,503	323	1,852
82 Chile	397	869	163	915	234	-46	-79	194
83 South Africa	..		..		..		145	-494
84 Romania	..		..		..			
85 Portugal	18	1,371	63	538	-45	833	50	102
86 Argentina	487	2,805	342	1,160	145	1,645	11	741

87 Yugoslavia	180	1,334	168	367	12	967	..	..
88 Uruguay	38	224	47	90	-9	134	..	289
89 Iran	940	..	235	..	705	..	25	..
90 Iraq	63	..	18	..	45	..	24	..
91 Venezuela	224	2,856	42	1,733	182	1,123	-23	55
92 Hong Kong	(.)	131	(.)	36	(.)	95	83	94
93 Trinidad and Tobago	8	106	10	35	-2	71	50	74
94 Greece	164	1,587	61	483	103	1,104	93	1,454
95 Singapore	58	190	6	160	52	30	93	..
96 Israel	410	3,106	25	631	385	2,475	40	-85
High-income Oil Exporters								
97 Libya							139	-319
98 Saudi Arabia							20	-3,367
99 Kuwait							..	-436
100 United Arab Emirates							..	..
Industrial Market Economies								
101 Ireland	..	..	..	..	..	..	32	337
102 Spain	..	..	..	..	..	..	179	1,182
103 Italy	..	..	..	..	..	..	496	-160
104 New Zealand	..	..	..	..	..	..	22	77
105 United Kingdom	..	..	..	..	..	..	-440	-1,221
106 Finland	..	..	..	..	..	..	-34	-102
107 Australia	..	..	..	..	..	..	787	1,641
108 Japan	..	..	..	..	..	..	-261	-2,121
109 Canada	..	..	..	..	..	..	566	-2,373
110 Austria	..	..	..	..	..	..	84	139
111 United States	..	..	..	..	..	..	-6,130	-7,757
112 Netherlands	..	..	..	..	..	..	-14	-1,447
113 France	..	..	..	..	..	..	248	226
114 Belgium	..	..	..	..	..	..	-290	-3,410
115 Norway	..	..	..	..	..	..	32	-194
116 Denmark	..	..	..	..	..	..	75	89
117 Sweden	..	..	..	..	..	..	-105	-368
118 Germany, Fed. Rep.	..	..	..	..	..	..	-290	-3,410
119 Switzerland	..	..	..	..	..	..	..	..

TABLE 10.2 *Flow of External Capital, 1970 and 1980 (continued)*

	Public and Publicly Guaranteed Medium- and Long-term Loans (millions of dollars)						Net Direct Private Investment (millions of dollars)	
	Gross Inflow		Repayment of Principal		Net Inflow			
	1970	*1980*	*1970*	*1980*	*1970*	*1980*	*1970*	*1980*[a]
Nonmarket Industrial Economies								
120 Poland								
121 Bulgaria								
122 Hungary								
123 USSR								
124 Czechoslovakia								
125 German Dem. Rep.								

a. Figures in italics are for 1979, not 1980.

SOURCE: World Bank, *World Development Report 1982* (New York: Oxford University Press, 1982), Table 14, pp. 136–37. Reprinted by permission.

TABLE 10.3 *Official Development Assistance From OECD, OPEC, and Communist Countries*

	Amount								
	1960	*1965*	*1970*	*1975*	*1976*	*1977*	*1978*	*1979*	*1980*
OECD									
ODA (billions of U.S. $ nominal prices)	4.6	6.5	7.0	13.8	13.8	15.7	20.0	22.4	27.3
ODA as percentage of GNP	.51	.49	.34	.36	.33	.33	.35	.35	.38
ODA (billions of U.S. $ constant 1978 prices)	13.1	16.7	14.9	17.9	17.3	18.0	20.0	20.4	22.7
OPEC									
ODA (billions of U.S. $ nominal prices)				5.5	5.6	5.9	4.6	6.1	6.9[a]
ODA as percentage of GNP				2.7	2.2	2.0	1.4	1.5	1.5

Communist Countries Economic Aid to Noncommunist LDCs

	1970	*1972*	*1974*	*1975*	*1976*	*1977*	*1978*	*1979*	*1980*
Extended (billions of U.S. $ at nominal prices)	1.2	2.2	1.9	2.8	1.9	1.0	4.9	2.6	3.3
Drawn	.6	.9	1.2	.9	1.2	1.3	1.1	.9	...

a. Provisional

SOURCE: The World Bank, *World Development Report 1980, World Development Report 1982* (New York: Oxford University Press, 1982). Reprinted by permission. Table 16, pp. 140–41. *Communist Aid Activities in Non-Communist Less Developed Countries, 1979 and 1954–79,* Central Intelligence Agency, 1980, p. 17; *Soviet and East European Aid to the Third World, 1981,* Department of State, Washington, D.C.: February 1983.

TABLE 10.4

Terms of Trade, 1960, 1978 (1970 = 100)

	Terms of Trade (1970 = 100)	
	1960	1978
Low-income Countries	98	98
1 Kampuchea, Dem.	102	136
2 Bangladesh	155	74
3 Lao, PDR	. .	. .
4 Bhutan	. .	. .
5 Ethiopia	75	126
6 Mali	91	93
7 Nepal	. .	. .
8 Somalia	107	72
9 Burundi	. .	. .
10 Chad	106	122
11 Mozambique	103	96
12 Burma	101	83
13 Upper Volta	75	89
14 Viet Nam	. .	. .
15 India	104	80
16 Malawi	116	112
17 Rwanda	89	123
18 Sri Lanka	175	124
19 Guinea	. .	. .
20 Sierra Leone	89	77
21 Zaire	61	61
22 Niger	90	78
23 Benin	89	79
24 Pakistan	93	82
25 Tanzania	96	104
26 Afghanistan	99	133
27 Central African Rep.	93	103
28 Madagascar	118	87
29 Haiti	. .	. .
30 Mauritania	112	68
31 Lesotho	. .	. .
32 Uganda	95	106
33 Angola	89	145
34 Sudan	100	92
35 Togo	95	105
36 Kenya	112	104
37 Senegal	91	100
38 Indonesia	138	225
Middle-income Countries	93	90
39 Egypt	104	92
40 Ghana	92	80
41 Yemen, PDR	. .	. .
42 Cameroon	90	97
43 Liberia	194	85
44 Honduras	91	77
45 Zambia	50	56
46 Zimbabwe	. .	. .
47 Thailand	118	82
48 Bolivia	69	130

	Terms of Trade (1970 = 100)	
	1960	1978
49 Philippines	73	69
50 Yemen Arab Rep.	. .	. .
51 Congo, People's Rep.	98	114
52 Nigeria	97	290
53 Papua New Guinea	. .	. .
54 El Salvador	94	106
55 Morocco	103	86
56 Peru	63	77
57 Ivory Coast	89	94
58 Nicaragua	88	90
59 Colombia	90	107
60 Paraguay	92	107
61 Ecuador	110	129
62 Dominican Rep.	77	62
63 Guatemala	97	100
64 Syrian Arab Rep.	94	139
65 Tunisia	104	133
66 Jordan	99	84
67 Malaysia	139	119
68 Jamaica	100	90
69 Lebanon	78	87
70 Korea, Rep. of	78	81
71 Turkey	. .	71
72 Algeria	115	281
73 Mexico	87	108
74 Panama	89	61
75 Taiwan	79	75
76 Chile	53	50
77 South Africa	100	75
78 Costa Rica	103	81
79 Brazil	88	90
80 Uruguay	99	82
81 Argentina	101	95
82 Portugal	83	86
83 Yugoslavia	96	98
84 Trinidad and Tobago	115	109
85 Venezuela	112	292
86 Hong Kong	. .	97
87 Greece	92	93
88 Singapore	. .	. .
89 Spain	93	68
90 Israel	91	83
Industrialized Countries	99	95
91 Ireland	94	108
92 Italy	104	80
93 New Zealand	115	94
94 United Kingdom	95	94
95 Finland	98	97
96 Austria	100	97
97 Japan	102	88
98 Australia	116	98
99 France	93	96
100 Netherlands	100	92

TABLE 10.4
(continued)

| | | Terms of Trade (1970 = 100) | |
		1960	1978
101	Belgium	110	92
102	Canada	98	102
103	Norway	91	102
104	Germany, Fed. Rep.	90	104
105	United States	93	77
106	Denmark	108	94
107	Sweden	109	94
108	Switzerland	91	112
	Capital-surplus Oil Exporters	107	393
109	Iraq	112	403
110	Iran	108	373
111	Libya	98	280
112	Saudi Arabia	107	396
113	Kuwait	105	393
	Centrally Planned Economies	. .	. .
114	China	. .	. .
115	Korea, Dem. Rep.	. .	. .
116	Albania	. .	. .
117	Cuba	112	66
118	Mongolia	. .	. .
119	Romania	. .	. .
120	Bulgaria	. .	. .
121	Hungary	. .	83
122	Poland	. .	103
123	USSR	. .	. .
124	Czechoslovakia	. .	. .
125	German Dem. Rep.	. .	. .

TABLE 10.4

Terms of Trade, 1960, 1978 (1970 = 100) (continued)

SOURCE: World Bank, *World Development Report 1982* (New York: Oxford University Press, 1982), Table 8, pp. 124–25. Reprinted by permission.

Bauer, P. T. 1965. The Vicious Circle of Poverty. *Weltwirtschafliches Archiv* vol. 95, no. 2, pp. 4–20.

Chenery, Hollis, *et al.* 1974. *Redistribution with Growth.* London: Oxford University Press.

Cohen, Benjamin. 1968. The Less Developed Countries' Exports of Primary Commodities. *Economic Journal* 78 (June): 334–43.

Coppock, J. D. 1962. *International Economic Instability.* New York: McGraw-Hill.

Erb, G. F. and Schiavo-Campo, S. 1969. Export Instability, Level of Development and Economic Size of Less Developed Countries. *Bulletin of the Oxford University Institute of Economics and Statistics* 31 (November).

Frank, André Gunder. 1967. *Capitalism and Underdevelopment in Latin America.* New York: Monthly Review Press.

Glezakos, C. 1973. Export Instability and Economic Growth: A Statistical Verification. *Economic Development and Cultural Change* 21: 670–79.

Griffin, Keith. 1978. *International Inequality and National Poverty.* New York: Holmes and Meier Publishers.

Higgins, Benjamin. 1968. *Economic Development.* Rev. ed. New York: W. W. Norton and Company.

Kindleberger, Charles. 1956. *The Terms of Trade: A European Case Study.* New York: MIT Press–Wiley.

Kravis, Irving. 1970. Trade as a Handmaiden of Growth: Similarities Between the 19th and 20th Centuries. *Economic Journal* 80 (December): 850–72.

Lewis, W. A. 1955. *The Theory of Economic Growth.* London: Allen and Unwin.

MacBean, A. I. 1966. *Export Instability and Economic Development.* Cambridge, MA: Harvard University Press.

Metcalfe, J. S. and Steedman, I. 1974. A Note on the Gain from Trade. *Economic Record* vol. 50, no. 132, pp. 581–95.

Michaely, Michael. 1977. Exports and Growth: An Empirical Investigation. *Journal of Development Economics* 4 (March): 49–73.

Nurkse, Ragner. 1961. Patterns of Trade and Development. In *Equilibrium and Growth in the World Economy,* edited by G. Haberler and R. M. Stern. Cambridge, MA: Harvard University Press.

Palma, Gabriel. 1978. Dependency: A Formal Theory of Underdevelopment or a Methodology for Analysis of Concrete Situations of Underdevelopment. *World Development* 6 (July/August): 881–924.

Prebisch, R. 1962. The Economic Development of Latin America and Its Principal Problems, in U.N., *Economic Bulletin for Latin America* 7 (Feb.) 1–22.

Streeten, Paul. 1979. Development Ideas in Historical Perspective. *Toward a New Strategy for Development.* New York: Pergamon Press.

Vaitsos, C. V. 1974. *Intercountry Income Distribution and Transnational Enterprises.* Oxford: Clarendon Press.

The World Bank. 1978. *World Development Report 1978.* Washington, D.C.

Yeats, Alexander J. 1979. *Trade Barriers Facing Developing Countries.* New York: St. Martin's Press.

Yotopoulos, Pan. A. and Nugent, Jeffrey B. 1976. *Economics of Development, Empirical Investigations.* New York: Harper and Row Publishers.

REFERENCES

Trade and Industrialization

chapter

11

In the 1950s whether or not an LDC specializing in production of agricultural, mineral, or metal commodities should industrialize was a controversial question. The controversy has subsided and now most LDC policymakers concentrate on appropriate approaches to industrialization. This chapter's emphasis is upon the relationship of trade to industrialization. We begin by examining the reasons a country chooses to industrialize.

ROLES OF TRADE IN INDUSTRIALIZATION

The Infant Economy

The preindustrial LDC is occupied to a large degree in feeding its people and providing simple goods and services. Incomes are meager and thus demand for more sophisticated products is limited. Technical absorptive capacity is low and the population's experience and skill levels are highest in agriculture and related areas. Examined at a point in time, the infant economy will be relatively least inefficient in agriculture.

For an extended period agriculture or primary products will serve as this nation's dominant export. Data collected by Chenery and Syrquin show this is the case until the prototype LDC is 60 percent or more through its development growth path (1975). Even when manufactures grow as export earners, these goods may be the kind that utilize heavily agricultural raw materials, or are produced by foreign enclaves that process minerals or metals.

The modernization of agriculture raises incomes and, consequently, the demand for more manufactured goods and new services. There is greater potential for saving and capital formation. But the economy is most inefficient and inexperienced outside of agriculture and simple commerce. Other countries more advanced have a comparative advantage in industrial goods. Should the LDC depend upon imports for these items? Or should it seek to acquire technical knowhow in industry as well as agriculture? And if so, what policies are best for promoting sectoral shift?

Specialization in Agriculture

The answer to these questions will vary with the size and relative resource endowments of an LDC. Economies well endowed with land in proportion to their population and able to grow export crops that earn high incomes for their people, can concentrate upon improving efficiency in agriculture while neglecting diversification into other sectors. Technological change will also generally occur in services and nontraded goods such as construction. So long as agricultural export prices remain high relative to costs and growth in employment opportunities on the land is adequate, this specialization can continue. If the stage of diminishing returns has been reached, then population growth will lead to lower income per capita unless capital growth and/or technological change can offset diminishing returns, or the commodity terms of trade rise. Specialization of this type was seen in countries like Australia, New Zealand, and Denmark in previous development phases. High income earners were mutton and other meats, wool and dairy products.

Diversification of
the Infant Economy

For countries with less favorable resource endowments per capita, the probability is high that diversification into industrial output will lead to a greater potential per capita output once the costs of inexperience and of improving technology have been overcome. This is particularly true for large countries such as India, China, and Brazil, where there are potential gains from scale economies in industry as internal markets grow. Moreover diversification relieves the pressure upon agriculture and the service sector to provide additional job opportunities for a growing population. While the infant economy is experiencing development costs, the nonindustrial sectors must support and subsidize the learning and development—through taxes the government levies, savings that industry can borrow, and export earnings made available to industry. As savings and investment in industry accelerate, ratios of capital to labor and skilled labor to unskilled labor rise. This, along with technological change and economies of scale, leads to higher per capita output per worker.

Diversification out of raising and processing agricultural raw materials, where an important input, land, is relatively scarce and fixed, into other production where dominant inputs such as capital and skilled labor can increase, gives the economy the potential to raise income per capita in both the agricultural and nonagricultural sectors. Put another way, an economy with sectoral diversification continues to improve its efficiency in agriculture, but also develops nonagricultural activities, and as a result specializes less narrowly than an economy with a more abundant endowment of natural resources proportional to labor. The reduced specialization, and domestic demands upon agriculture at this early period, along with the emerging industrial sector's growing needs for machinery and other imports, often create foreign exchange bottlenecks. At this stage, an industrializing economy without strong export earnings can benefit from an inflow of foreign savings while its efficiency improves and it accumulates capital for industry. The analysis of this chapter, however, emphasizes the importance of export earnings during the period of industrial maturation.

Roles of Trade:
Chapter Focus

Trade plays several varying but vital roles under differing economic conditions in LDCs, and is just as important to a country that is diversifying its infant economy as to one specializing more intensely. Some aspects of trade have already been covered in the previous chapter and in the one on risk and uncertainty. The previous chapter pointed out that with trade an economy can consume beyond its domestic potential. The graphic analysis in this chapter places particular emphasis upon the roles of trade in industrialization and its effect on resource employment—two distinct but to some degree related topics. The analysis moves from the static case to consideration of more dynamic options, and from the employment capacity of a specialized agrarian economy to the industrial potential of an import substitution one.

The first topics taken up will be the effect of trade upon resource employment and income distribution, focusing on a preindustrial economy. For such a society specialization in agricultural exports may limit full employment of labor. Agricultural specialization can also skew income distribution. Both conditions can bear upon the LDC's calculation of the dynamic benefits of economic diversification.

Following this will be discussion of infant-industry import substitution; the effects of changing commodity, income, and factor terms of trade upon industrialization; and the development of manufactures exports. Emphasis here is upon analysis of the incipient industrialization process. In such an economy response to changes in variables affecting the export sector is limited and the economy has structural rigidities that help shape its import needs. The analysis is helpful in the next chapter, where policies and programs for the promotion of industry are discussed.

The simple economy in phase 1 agriculture illustrated in chapter 9 had no choice in regard to trade: It had one exportable crop and could either specialize completely in that crop, importing food not grown at home, or, more likely, grow food for domestic needs and trade for other needed imports. For simplicity it was assumed that the LDC had no home demand for the export crop. The need for certain imports resulted in some resources being allocated to exports once food requirements were satisfied. The LDC could not produce these imports, and it had to accept the world price for its export crop because it sold only small amounts of it relative to world supply.

TRADE AND RESOURCE USAGE

Usually the export commodity is land-intensive, utilizing surplus acreage and less labor per acre than the food crop. It may even be grown with off-season labor, or be a "natural product" of the region that needs only to be harvested, for example, certain tree saps and marijuana, a weed. The export crop then becomes an item of surplus relative to domestic use, and trade, in the words of Adam Smith, is a "vent-for-surplus." The economy seeks an export crop that utilizes the least amount of the relatively more scarce resource of labor per unit of imports earned.

In the vent-for-surplus model trade uses under- or unemployed resources. In general, however, there are two possible effects of foreign commerce upon unemployed factors. It may intensify a factor proportions problem of unemployed resources, or it may lead to full employment. In order to show these contrasting possibilities, we turn again to the production possibilities curve reflecting technical limits to factor substitution first introduced in chapter 3. This type curve is shown in figure 11.1 for an agrarian economy that can produce either of two crops, one that is labor intensive or one that is land intensive. With too much specialization in either crop, there is a technical limitation to full factor utilization. Production along the straight-line, constant-cost segment $Q_N B$ of production possibilities curve $Q_N B C Q_\ell$ will result in unemployed labor, while production along the straight-line, constant-cost segment $C Q_\ell$ will lead to unemployed land. Resources are

Trade and the Factor Proportions Problem

FIGURE 11.1

*Incomplete
Specialization*

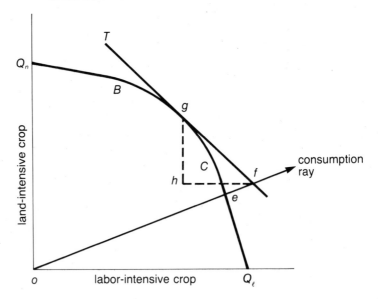

Incomplete specialization with world terms of trade *T*: Production moves from
autarky output at *e* with unemployed land to production at *g* with full employment.
Exports are *gh*, imports *hf*, with consumption at *f*.

fully employed only along the curved segment *BC*. There is a domestic
demand for both crops; and a world market and world prices exist for
both crops.

Assume first that the simple agrarian economy does not trade. Unless the relative demand for goods is along segment *BC*, one or the
other resource will be unemployed as production takes place along
segment $Q_N B$ or segment CQ_ℓ. Here the consumption line indicates
production-consumption is at *e* along segment CQ_ℓ, with specialization
in the labor-intensive crop and unemployed land. Domestic opportunity cost and relative prices in equilibrium are determined by the slope
of CQ_ℓ.

Trade, as will be illustrated, could cause the economy to produce
at Q_N, at Q_ℓ, or along segment *BC*. Thus, trade may (a) create full employment by moving the economy's production to a point along segment *BC*, (b) increase the unemployment of land by moving the economy to complete specialization at Q_ℓ in the labor-intensive good, or (c)
move the economy to complete specialization at Q_N, eliminating the
problem of unemployed land, but creating the problem of unemployed
labor. In all cases, however, consumption is higher with than without
trade.

What determines whether specialization is at Q_ℓ, Q_N, or along segment *BC*? Assume the country does not affect the price paid for its
exports on world markets, but is a price-taker. Assume free trade where
prices in the LDC are allowed to equal world prices, and presuppose

institutions and assumptions that ensure efficiency in production. Given the world terms of trade, efficiency conditions demand that $dQ_N/dQ_\ell = P_\ell/P_N$ = absolute slope of T, where P stands for world prices. World prices are assumed to differ from autarky prices at e. This means production will move to another point on the production frontier. Consumption will shift to a point beyond domestic production capacity. For simplicity we assume that as trade allows greater consumption, the economy moves out a straight-line consumption ray so that *relative* amounts of goods consumed are unchanged with trade.

In the first case considered trade creates full employment. Figure 11.1 contrasts posttrade production-consumption equilibrium with pretrade production-consumption equilibrium at e on segment CQ_ℓ with unemployed land. When trade takes place, production moves to g where $dQ_N/dQ_\ell = P_\ell/P_N$. The amount gh of the land-intensive good is exported in exchange for hf of the labor-intensive good along the world terms of trade line T. This allows consumption outside the production possibilities curve at f and creates full employment.

When the absolute slope of T is less than the absolute slope of $Q_N B$, then $P_N dQ_N > P_\ell dQ_\ell$ and it pays the LDC to specialize completely in Q_N. The optimum trade solution is shown graphically by placing the terms of trade line so that it intercepts the production possibilities curve at Q_N. Complete specialization in the land-intensive good results in unemployed labor. Alternatively, when the absolute slope of T exceeds that of CQ_ℓ, complete specialization in the labor-intensive good occurs and more land is idle. In either case, the terms of trade line will cross the consumption line outside the production possibilities curve allowing greater consumption.

Figure 11.2 shows the case where specialization occurs at Q_N. The LDC exports $Q_N h$ of the land-intensive crop, which has less domestic demand, in exchange for hf imports of the labor-intensive crop. The economy moves from full employment of labor at e to unemployed labor at Q_N, and from a surplus of land to a land constraint upon output.

This analysis provides insights into a possible cause of unemployment with specialization in a land-intensive export crop—a factor proportion problem common to plantation crops. Central American countries that are more heavily populated and have large proportions of their arable land devoted to plantation agriculture, and more densely populated Asian countries during the colonial era, have experienced unemployment or underemployment of labor hours that can be traced to technical limitations of this sort. The terms of trade favor plantation crop exports; but with many people living on limited land there is a technical limit to full absorption of labor. However, where land is relatively abundant, as in many African countries, there is no factor proportions problem in plantation agriculture.

The analysis presents the contrasting possibilities, then, that trade can either worsen or eliminate unemployment of resources caused by technical limitations to factor substitution. Each is empirically relevant. Of the two eventualities, Richard Eckaus emphasized the second—that is, the potential for trade to allow full employment of re-

FIGURE 11.2
*Complete
Specialization*

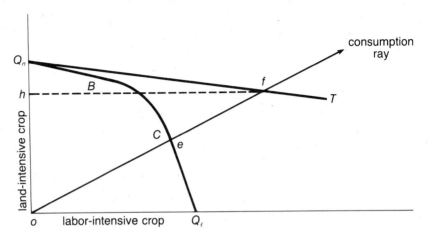

Complete specialization with world terms of trade *T*: Production moves from autarky output at *e* with unemployed land to production at Q_N with unemployed labor and consumption at *f*. $Q_N h$ exports exchange for *hf* imports.

sources by a country faced with a factor proportions problem (1955). This conclusion is more frequently associated with a nonagrarian economy. The graph would show labor-intensive and capital-intensive industrial goods. In autarky the economy would produce relatively more of the capital-intensive item, leaving some labor unemployed. With trade the economy would move to the full employment segment of the production possibilities curve. Recent literature on the attributes of export promotion for labor-intensive manufactured goods, cited later, emphasizes this type of incomplete specialization as a cure for unemployment in nonagrarian economies. In the more agrarian economy specializing in land-intensive crops rather heavily, unemployment can arise because of a factor proportions problem unless the trade is a vent-for-surplus. Agrarian economies with low absorption potential for absorbing labor in farming often seek to expand employment through industrialization. Before turning to this topic, the model's results are applied to the problem of income distribution.

Trade and Relative Factor Prices   As discussed in chapter 3 (and developed more fully in chapter 14), the product mix affects the relative demand for factors of production and their scarcity prices. In the two-crop case shown graphically, trade changes the product proportions, affecting relative factor demand. In figure 11.1 when trade increases demand for the land-intensive good relative to the labor-intensive one, trade also boosts the demand for land relative to labor, raising rents in proportion to wages. In the case of increased output of labor-intensive goods with trade, wages would rise relative to rents. Trade can become a "vent" for surplus resources, raising their prices, or it can create unemployed resources.

By affecting relative factor prices, trade can change family income distribution. Should it increase inequality while maximizing income, then trade may provoke a conflict between goals of maximum output and equitable income distribution. In such cases income redistribution programs can be introduced. As discussed in chapter 14, however, income redistribution is not easily attained in the decentralized economy. On the other hand, trade may contribute to both goals of higher income and lower inequality. Trade mitigates inequality when it increases the demand for resources of lower-income households, in particular lower-skilled labor inputs. For example, labor-intensive manufactures exports from South Korea and Taiwan have helped these countries maintain high employment levels and provide income to poorer households.

Because international commerce is a cause of changed relative factor prices and possibly of unemployed resources, it is important to know whether or not trade for a particular LDC leads to skewed family income distribution, and hence inequality. In particular, when specialization is in the land-intensive crop and these exports are produced entirely or mainly on large plantations, distribution of the income is a question of major importance. In such cases there can be idle labor and a greater demand for land. This creates a higher income for wealthy landowners relative to that of laborers than when the labor-intensive crop is produced.

The export crop may be produced on foreign plantations within the LDC. The presence of foreign managerial resources may raise either productivity of labor and/or land. If so, the production possibilities curve will move outward. It is possible national income will be higher despite foreign ownership, but not necessarily because of the distribution factor. When the land is foreign-owned, the rent is not part of national income.

In sum, trade can increase income and employment levels of resources unemployed because of a factor proportions problem. Yet foreign commerce can also create unemployment while it raises income when there is a factor proportions problem in the production function. By affecting relative demand for resources through its impact on the product mix, trade changes the relative prices and hence the income of factors. Family income distribution may become more or less unequal. When trade creates unemployment and lessens demand for a resource, owners of that resource may be better off without trade unless they share in its national benefits. Examples of unfavorable employment and income distribution effects stemming from specialization in plantation agriculture are often cited in the literature. Recent empirical findings show that for nonagrarian economies, export trade (particularly in manufactures) helps to offset a factor proportions problem rather than creating one. In such cases it raises the relative income of the factor under- or unemployed without trade—typically labor. The effect of *changing* trade conditions on employment is discussed later. We move on now from consideration of trade and resource utilization levels to examine the close relationship between trade and industrialization.

ANALYSIS OF
INDUSTRIAL
DEVELOPMENT

The LDC economy embarking upon domestic production of goods it formerly imported is unable to produce those goods without foreign imports. Some raw material resources may be unavailable domestically. And for an extended period the LDC will not have the technical capacity for domestic production of capital equipment used in the new manufacturing sector. Some of these capital goods will be needed to form infrastructure, such as utilities, that is integral to the establishment of an industrial economy. Here we assume, to begin our analysis, that the LDC must have imported capital it cannot produce for its industrial sector.

Import Substitution

We continue using very simplified graphs as aids in capturing the essence of important interrelations fundamental to the development process studied. The three-sector graph is useful here, and the terms of trade are most helpfully shown as the slope of a line from the origin. Let the scale along the industry axis in figure 11.3 measure quantities of a single good that represents the LDC's industrial output. And let the same axis also have a scale to measure the imported capital needed per unit of the industrial good when the latter is produced domestically. The graph can be assumed to represent domestic output potential of the industrial good for the period of a five-year plan. The capital is assumed to have a production life of five years, and must be paid for during that period.

FIGURE 11.3
Three-sector Economy

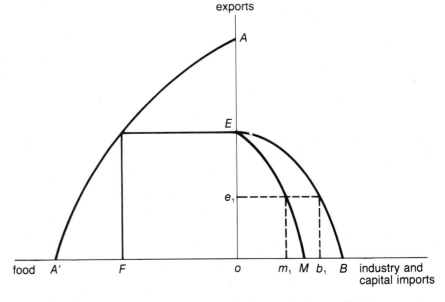

With food consumption and production at F, the production possibilities curve for exports and industrial goods is EB. Curve EM shows units of imports per unit of industrial output. Production of b_1 industrial output is possible so long as e_1 exports earn m_1 imports in trade.

The export and food sectors represent the output potential for the same time frame. Food is a nontraded good, and there is no domestic demand for the export commodity, an agricultural crop sold on world markets. Food needs for the five-year plan are given by the planners and are designated by F on the graph. This allows maximum exports of E. Exports can be used either to import the industrial good or to import the capital equipment so that the industrial good is produced domestically along EB.

For each potential output level of the industrial good along EB, there is a required amount of the imported capital good, M. For example, to produce b_1 output of the industrial good, m_1 capital imports are required. M/B is drawn as constant at all levels of output of B for simplicity, but this is not crucial to the analysis so long as M varies directly with B. The line EM shows this constant relationship of imported capital to industrial output as the latter expands along EB. Thus, EB is no longer a domestic production possibilities curve unless a required amount of imports is available as inputs in the production of industrial output. If e_1 exports exchange for m_1 imports, then b_1 industrial output can be produced.

Food demand is satisfied at F. The economy wishes to maximize output of the industrial good subject to the constraint that food needs are met. What is the optimum allocation of domestic resources to achieve this? The answer depends upon the terms of trade for the industrial good and the capital good. First, consider the maximum output of good B when it is produced within the LDC rather than imported. Given a constant terms of trade for the capital good represented by the slope of T in figure 11.4, the maximum output achievable is b_1, with m_1 imports equal to e_1 exports. (We assume no foreign aid or credit at this point for financing imports in excess of the plan period exports.) A larger output than b_1 would cause a shortage of capital imports, as shown by the dashed line e_2 that crosses T to the left of EM, and thus is not achievable. On the other hand, exports of e_3 would create excess capital imports that could not be utilized because of a shortage of domestic resources. Lower terms of trade for the LDC would increase the slope of T and reduce the maximum industrial output achievable by the infant industry sector to a level below b_1. Higher terms of trade for the capital imports would raise maximum industrial output.

The determination of whether good B truly represents an infant industry calls for a comparison of the maximum amount of B goods that could be produced domestically (output b_1) with the total imports of good B that could be purchased with E exports. If more B goods are obtainable by importing capital goods and producing good B domestically than can be obtained by importing good B, then domestic production should be undertaken. The outcome depends upon the terms of trade for good B. Figure 11.5 outlines the case of a true infant industry. The terms of trade line for capital imports is now labeled T_M to distinguish it from T_B, the terms of trade for good B. Only b_2 units of good B can be imported along T_B, less than b_1 produceable domestically with terms of trade T_M for capital imports.

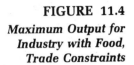

FIGURE 11.4

*Maximum Output for
Industry with Food,
Trade Constraints*

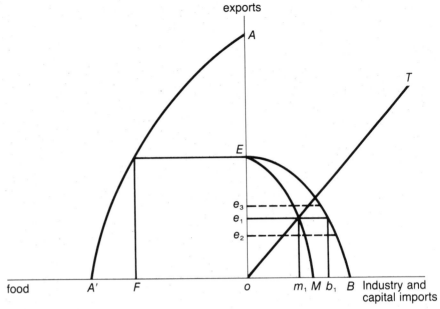

Maximum industry output, given food consumption F and terms of trade for imported capital T, is b_1 with e_1 exports and m_1 imports. Exports of e_2 create a shortage of capital imports; exports of e_3 create a surplus.

Remember this productive capacity is representative of a five-year period. The decision to start up an infant industry requires sacrifices during the initial phases, when learning by doing is taking place. In the early period less of good B will be available than would have been had the country continued to import this good. This loss is more than recouped, however, where the country has a potential efficiency advantage in good B. Import substitution where the country cannot produce more efficiently than it can import would reduce the goods available to the economy.

In sum, a country's ability to replace imports efficiently in an infant industry during its early development when it cannot make capital goods needed in production depends upon (a) its efficiency in production of the export good relative to the import substitute good, and (b) the terms of trade for imported capital inputs relative to the terms for the finished good. Chapter 10 discussed variables affecting the terms of trade faced by an LDC. The LDC often adopts domestic policies such as tariffs and subsidies that affect the development of an infant industry. These are discussed later.

**Growth of Imports
with Import
Substitution**

The static case above shows that exports decline with import substitution from E to e_1 in figure 11.5. This is likely to be a short-lived phenomenon with growth and industrialization because EB (and hence

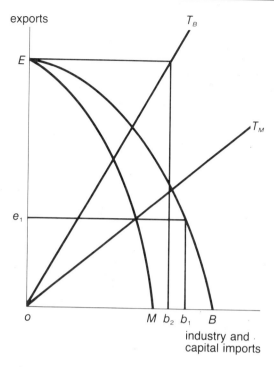

FIGURE 11.5
Infant Industry

Comparative advantage in home production of good B: Exports of e_1 allow imports of capital along T_M for production of b_1 industrial output—more than b_2 imports of good B attainable with exports of E and terms of trade T_B.

EM) will shift outward with growth. The terms of trade line, T_M, will intersect a higher and higher EM curve. Moreover, when industrialization succeeds, manufacturing output and exports expand relative to agricultural output.

In order to consider the dynamics of industrialization, assume an outward shift in the production possibilities curve for food and exports, with population constant. Per capita income increases but food needs do not rise proportionately since food is income-inelastic. We can see this in figure 11.6 where, for simplicity, food output, F, remains constant as the production possibilities curve shifts from A_1A_1' to A_2A_2'. This change in curve AA' allows the EB curve to shift outward. Industrial production and exports can become a larger percentage of total output since food production does not change. As such shifts take place, the T_M line (not shown) and the EM curve will eventually intersect at an export level higher than the old level of E_1, which existed when industrial goods were imported. In this case, then, a rise in the foreign trade sector as a proportion of GNP is caused by increased industrialization where the LDC is dependent upon imports of capital in order to expand its industrial output.

It is even possible that in the real situation, where more than one good is produced, new industrial output becomes more import inten-

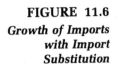

FIGURE 11.6
*Growth of Imports
with Import
Substitution*

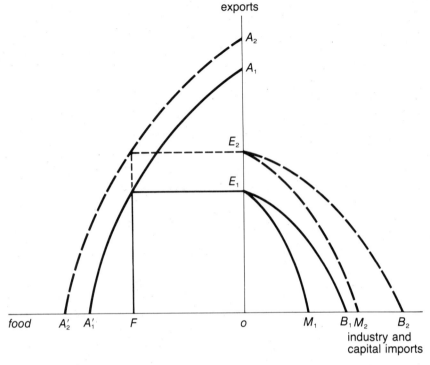

Improved productivity in agriculture shifts A_1A_1' to A_2A_2'. With food consumption
constant at F, E_1B_1 moves outward to E_2B_2. The import curve rises from E_1M_1 to
E_2M_2, indicating greater import needs as industrial potential expands.

sive, in other words, the EM curve is closer to the EB curve. As its
income rises, the LDC moves into production of more-complex products that are more capital intensive. And, of course, this is a simple
model where the country allows no imports of final consumer goods.
With the expanding incomes that industrialization brings, a growing
complement of diversified consumer goods as well as producer goods
are in demand. This too tends to raise imports per capita. Eventually,
as a domestic capital goods sector develops, and industry levels off as
a proportion of total output, imports cease to grow faster than total
output.

Import substitution, then, is not necessarily a process whereby trade
is reduced. It is a process whereby industrialization is begun and so
can lead to greater interdependence and trade. The LDC cannot ignore
its need to increase export earnings to pay for growing capital imports.
And the terms of trade affect how resources should be allocated for
growth. This point is explored next and demonstrated graphically.

Resource Allocation   The effect of the terms of trade upon resource allocation between sec-
for Industrial   tors can be seen by considering alternative shifts in the EB curve. Given
Growth M/B and T, balanced expansion will maximize growth of B only for

some levels of T. This can be seen intuitively in figure 11.7. Assume that the resources available for growth, when placed in the export sector, expand output to $E'B$. When the same resources are devoted to industry, the production possibilities curve is EB'. A division of resources between export expansion and industrial growth will yield production possibilities curve $E''B''$. For simplicity the shifts are assumed to be symmetrical, and just three possible alternatives for allocation are shown.

Given M/B, T determines the level of industrial output and hence the export/industrial output mix on the production possibilities curve, as illustrated earlier in figure 11.4. Only where T crosses curve EM (not shown in figure 11.7) so that optimum production is along xz (as opposed to curve segments xy or yz) would balanced expansion be preferable. In general, the higher the terms of trade, the more resources an LDC can devote to industrial expansion relative to growth in exports. Put another way, a low terms of trade can greatly restrict industrialization, diverting large amounts of resources to exports for each additional unit of industrial output. Conversely, a high terms of trade for the LDC means industrial expansion can be greater since only small increments of resources are needed to earn additional imports for industrial expansion and the larger share of resources can be applied to increased industrial output.

Ironically, the conclusion that the lower the terms of trade, the greater the need for the LDC to increase export potential is a perverse finding in terms of traditional trade theory, which assumes a country

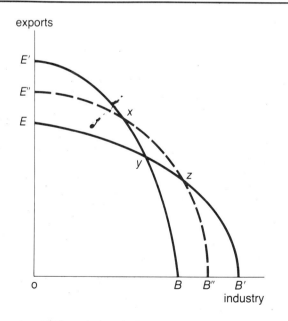

FIGURE 11.7

Resource Allocation to Maximize Industry Expansion

Balanced expansion $E''B''$ maximizes industrial output potential only if $e = m$ along T (not shown) so that output is along segment xz.

can produce the import good domestically. A worsening of the terms of trade in the traditional model results in the affected country's curtailing production for export, boosting domestic production of the import good, and specializing less. The LDC in early development stages does not have this choice, however. Such an economy generally has few consumer imports to cut back and it cannot produce many imports vital to its industrialization process. Thus it has little leeway for reduction of trade.

In sum, industrialization and import substitution do not imply a policy of neglect of exports. When industry grows as a percentage of output, the ratio of imports to output also tends to increase. And when the terms of trade are low, industrial expansion requires large amounts of exports per unit of additional industrial output. Policies aimed at industrial expansion may be self-defeating when they divert resources from export. The LDC at early stages of industrialization has little flexibility in substituting home production for imports. When imports compose a fairly set percentage of output, this prevents the enlargement of industrial output by diversion of resources from exports. There is a delicate balance the LDC must pursue.

Studies indicate LDCs commonly underestimate the export limitation, with the result that their economy operates within its production possibilities curve. The lack of imports such as replacement parts leads to underutilized capacity. This is costly for the LDC with relatively high-priced capital in place. Of course there are other causes of excess capacity, including poor harvests due to weather or pests that shift inward the agricultural, and hence the industrial, output potential. Food from abroad replaces imports for the industrial sector needed to maintain output potential. And India abandoned one five-year plan that coincided with a period of dislocation brought on by war. Another cause of underutilized production potential, discussed next, is instability in the terms of trade.

Instability in the Terms of Trade

It was noted in the previous chapter that LDCs are affected by instability in their terms of trade, and the causes of these fluctuations were discussed. Here, with the graph developed for an LDC in early periods of industrialization, some effects of this instability can be studied.

First, referring back to figure 11.5, identification of a potential infant industry becomes less certain when traditional exports are subject to unpredictable price variations and the level of T_B relative to T_M changes. Also, the level of subsidy needed for the infant industry changes. Second, a shift in T_M changes the feasible level of industrial output for the five-year plan. Planning is made more difficult. Attempts to maintain maximum output levels fail as a change in T_M is reflected in import levels.

Infant Industries and Scale

Market size in an economy is determined by population and per capita income. Often both of these components are small in LDCs, leading to limited markets that can accommodate only a few firms when there are scale economies to firm size. Moreover, the LDC's economy may lack a national market and be broken up into many small localized ones, reducing the potential to achieve economies of scale at the industry level as well as for firms. Fragmentation of an economy's markets is in part related to the supportive infrastructure. The cost and availability of transportation services in particular are important components of market size. Infrastructure also includes utilities and communications, which have strong tie-ins to market size. And, as discussed in chapter 17, financial infrastructure plays a part in determining optimum firm size in LDCs. As markets expand in the LDC, scale economies may determine when an industry becomes efficient enough to be classified as an infant industry.

The interrelation between trade and economies of scale can be illustrated with a simple graphic model. Economies of scale improve the efficiency of resource inputs, in particular capital. Thus the relation between capital imports and output of final good B cannot be constant once production is large enough to achieve scale economies. In fact, M/B declines so long as scale efficiencies exist. In figure 11.8 it is assumed M/B is a constant prior to the onset of scale economies; then line EM shows a declining M/B ratio as output of good B expands beyond X on curve EB. In other words, as B good's production expands after economies of scale come into play, the growth of required imports of capital goods per unit of industrial growth declines.

Because the import bill per unit of industrial output is smaller with scale, and because scale increases the productivity of all resource inputs, economies large enough to experience scale efficiencies have greater potential for industrial development than smaller ones. Not surprisingly, nations at similar levels of per capita GNP vary in their industrial development patterns as a result of differences in population size. India has a broad array of industries not found in other, smaller countries with low per capita GNP.

Notice also in figure 11.8 that the terms of trade affect the ability of the country to achieve scale economies. A lower terms of trade such as T_2 limits output potential for B goods, precluding attainment of scale efficiencies. We return, then, to an important theme of this chapter: that there is a link between the terms of trade and the industrial potential of an LDC. When capital goods are relatively cheap, industrial output can be higher, increasing the incidence of scale efficiencies and thereby the LDC's capacity for industrialization.

Fragmentation of the domestic market among too many competing firms can deter development of the infant industry when scale economies exist. Scale economies for the industry need not imply scale economies for the firm. In LDCs with small markets, however, scale economies often exist at the firm level in manufacturing. This is in contrast to MDC firms, where scale economies are often exhausted due to the relatively large size of all firms. Where markets are small in LDCs and scale economies are found at the firm level, it may be necessary to limit the number of companies in an industry to achieve scale. Otherwise firm efficiency would be below maximum and the economy

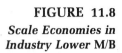

FIGURE 11.8
*Scale Economies in
Industry Lower* M/B

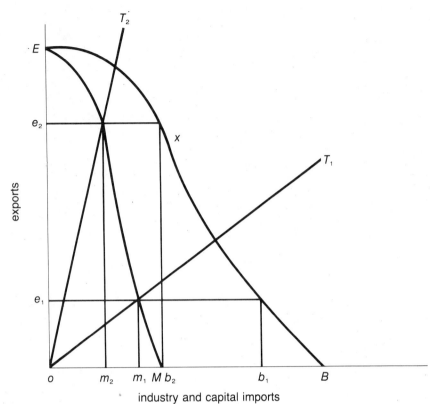

Scale economies in production of good *B* after point *X* cause a continuous drop
in *M/B*, increasing potential production of *B* good per unit of imports as production
of good *B* expands. The terms of trade determine the maximum production of
good *B* and thus affect the efficiency of imports. Terms of trade T_2 preclude scale
economies.

would not operate on its production possibilities curve. The emerging
economy must weigh the distribution cost of monopoly against the
advantages of scale. The failure of the infant industry with scale economies to attain exclusive access to the home market could mean that
it cannot compete with imports.

The following chapter discusses in more detail scale economies as
they relate to industrialization, pointing out that the degree to which
scale accelerates industrialization is affected by production conditions
within the LDC. In particular, the scale efficiencies of modern imported
capital in the less-advanced environment may not duplicate those of
modern technology operating in an MDC. More moderate scale effects,
however, can still be important to efficiency as a traditional economy
enlarges its markets.

Before concluding this section it is important to mention the relationship between exports, industrialization, and scale. Through ex-

porting an economy can achieve scale not attainable when production is for domestic markets only. Thus scale is relevant to both import substitution industries and export industries. The latter are discussed at the end of this chapter.

The analysis used up to this point assumes the commodity terms of trade are a given, unaffected by the amount of exports from the LDC. When this is not true, there is not one T applicable to all levels of output at a given time. Instead, as more exports from the LDC are offered on world markets, the commodity terms of trade for the country fall.

LDC Exports Affect Price

The graphic representation of the terms of trade can be modified to incorporate the case where the LDC affects its own terms of trade. For simplicity assume the LDC is the sole exporter of commodity E. First consider the case where there is a fixed world-demand curve for the export good so that an increase in global supply lowers world price and a drop in this supply raises the price. Assume a constant price for the import good.

When the quantity exported by the LDC affects world supply, export prices change. Exports of e_1 in figure 11.9 will be associated with higher terms of trade than exports of e_2, and so on. Terms of trade line T_1 shows how many exports will exchange for imports only if exports are e_1. Given e_1 exports, import capacity is m_1 as determined by terms of trade line T_1. Each export level and related terms of trade line, T_1, $T_2 \ldots$, will be associated with a different import capacity, m_1, $m_2 \ldots$. Curve T_k traces the loci of all equilibrium export-import points. The terms of trade for any point along T_k is given by the slope of a ray from the origin through that point. The economy with production possibilities curve EB in figure 11.9 will export e_4 and import m_4 in order to maximize output of B. The terms of trade will be T_4.

The shape of the T_k curve in figure 11.9 implies another assumption: The demand for exports is price-elastic. As the price of exports falls, increases in them are large enough to allow more imports. In this case, then, an expanding economy, with import needs growing from m_1 to m_4 as EM shifts out (not shown), encounters lower terms of trade that limit industrial expansion. However, expansion is feasible since export demand is price-elastic.

The relationship between the commodity terms of trade and the quantity exportable is referred to as the *income terms of trade*. Given import prices, the relationship between export quantity and export prices determines foreign exchange earnings and the quantity of goods that can be imported. In figure 11.9 the number of units of imports per unit of exports (m/e) drops with the movement of T from T_1 to T_4. This is caused by a drop in export prices as volume sold abroad rises. When the demand for exports is price-elastic, their volume (e) increases sufficiently so that $m/e \cdot e$ (or imports) rise to m_4. The income terms of trade have improved since there were enough foreign exchange earnings from additional exports to increase imports, despite a drop in export prices relative to import prices.

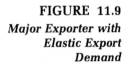

FIGURE 11.9

Major Exporter with
Elastic Export
Demand

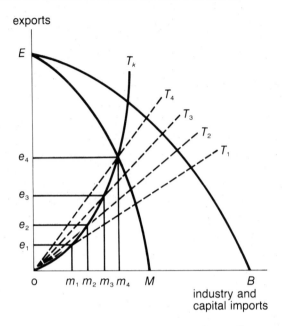

The terms of trade vary with the quantity exported. Curve T_k traces the loci of all points where $e = m$ at varying terms of trade.

Now consider the case of price-inelastic exports over a certain higher range of export volume. To show this clearly, only the curve EM of the previous diagram is used. Since M/B is assumed to be constant, an outward shift of production possibilities curve EB with growth produces the shifts in EM shown in figure 11.10.

In that diagram as the commodity terms of trade continue to drop along T_k with increased exports, the change in imports becomes negative after a certain point and they drop. This is caused by sharper declines in export prices as export quantity rises. The result is that more exports buy less imports, as shown by the backward-bending T_k curve above point x. Given constant world demand for the export good, a growing capacity to export, and increasing import needs, the outcome is that imports cannot grow beyond some maximum. This maximum is shown at point x, where the demand for exports turns from elastic to inelastic. Thus, expansion of EM with growth from E_2M_2 to E_3M_3 is not beneficial to the LDC's industrialization effort because growth in export capacity is associated with an inelastic demand for exports after point x along T_k.

Unfavorable income terms of trade linked to inelastic demand as exports rise can be lessened or even eliminated when over time world demand is growing. Such growth in demand shifts the T_k curve outward to T_k'. The rate of growth in exports relative to that in demand, then, determines whether imports rise or fall. For most goods world

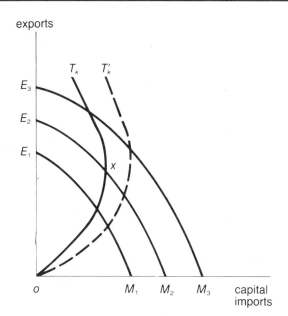

FIGURE 11.10

Major Exporter with Changing Elasticity of Demand for Exports

The volume of LDC exports affects their prices. As LDC exports rise, the demand for them turns from price-elastic to price-inelastic at point x on curve T_k. With growth, *EM* shifts outward, eventually cutting a constant T_k curve in the inelastic range. An increase in world demand for exports shifts T_k outward to T_k', raising import capacity for all levels of exports.

demand grows with world income, although not necessarily proportionately.

A change in the price of the import good will also shift curve T_k. A lower price for the import good pushes T_k outward since each level of exports will reflect higher commodity terms of trade and import capacity. And the T_k curve may fluctuate with the business cycle as the price of imports, world demand for the export good, and world income fluctuate, creating changing commodity and income terms of trade for the LDC. Swings in the income terms of trade pose the same efficiency problems for the large exporter that swings in the commodity terms of trade do for the small exporter.

In sum, this section has demonstrated that improvements in the income terms of trade are limited by demand elasticity when an exporter influences the price of its commodities with supply changes. Once demand turns inelastic, further increases in export volume will lower the income terms of trade. The case illustrated in figure 11.10 shows that with the demand curve given and characterized by inelasticity as exports rise beyond a certain level, industrial expansion can be halted by a foreign exchange bottleneck. Such a blockage is binding with expansion beyond curve E_2M_2, unless M/B is lowered or exports diversified and new export goods developed that improve import potential. This assumes foreign demand is constant. If demand is growing, T_k shifts outward to T_k', reducing the foreign exchange constraint. And of course, a change in the import price affects the constraint.

The Single Factor Terms of Trade Another element must be taken into account when examining the impact upon LDC industrialization of a change in the commodity and/or income terms of trade, and that is whether the origin of export growth is an increase in resource inputs or a change in resource productivity. As efficiency in export production rises, other things remaining constant, the opportunity cost of exports drops and *imports* are cheaper in terms of resource costs. In the case of the large exporter, the increased exports lower price, although not necessarily by the same percentage that resource inputs drop. In order to examine the effect of export cost changes, a third type of terms of trade, the single factor terms of trade, is introduced. This relates imports to the amount of factors contained in export goods. It measures the costs of imports in efficiency units of exports, and can be expressed as:

$$\frac{\text{Units of Imports}}{\text{Factor Inputs per Unit of Exports} \times \text{Units of Exports}}$$

A simultaneous change in the income, commodity, and factor terms of trade is illustrated in figure 11.11. As in the previous graph, only curve EM (here represented as Q_eM) is shown and the associated production possibilities curve EB is omitted. An improvement in factor efficiency in the export sector shifts Q_e (alternatively expressed as $\alpha_e K$ or $\beta_e L$) to Q_e' and again to Q_e'' as α_e and β_e increase. This efficiency improvement leads to higher exports and lower export prices, which reduce the units of imports per export unit; that is, the commodity terms of trade along T_k fall. Each export unit requires fewer resources, but exchanges for fewer imports. Total imports rise, indicating that the decline in the commodity terms of trade did not offset the improvement in factor efficiency. The factor terms of trade have risen.

The income terms of trade have also risen. As explained earlier, imports can increase with a decline in the price of exports so long as the export good is price-elastic. The increase in the quantity of exports when factor productivity improves more than offsets the decline in export price, allowing imports to rise. Thus, when exports are price-elastic, improvements in the factor efficiency coefficient for traded goods will not be completely offset by declines in the commodity terms of trade as exports expand, all else being equal.

An increase in world demand due, say, to growth in world income would move the T_k curve to the right of its present position as shown. Thus, if adequate, an increase in world demand could prevent a deterioration in the commodity terms of trade as exports expand, or even cause them to rise.

Summary of Trade and Infant Industry Development Summarizing, the foreign trade sector limits early industrial expansion even though the LDC begins to produce at home goods formerly imported. In fact, imports needed as inputs into industrial development

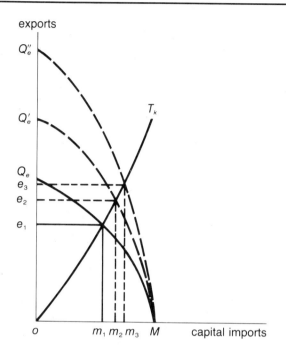

exports

Q''_e

Q'_e

T_k

Q_e
e_3
e_2

e_1

o m_1 m_2 m_3 M capital imports

FIGURE 11.11

Commodity, Income, and Factor Terms of Trade

The factor terms of trade improve as $Q_e = \alpha K = \beta L$ shifts to $Q'_e = \alpha' K = \beta' L$ and to $Q''_e = \alpha'' K = \beta'' L$. Commodity terms of trade decline as m/e falls with expanding exports. The income terms of trade rise as $m/e \cdot e$ rises.

grow as the industrial sector does. Infant industries cannot develop if the export sector is denied sufficient resources. The commodity terms of trade for imported inputs as compared with imports of final goods help determine the import substitution that is efficient. The commodity terms of trade also affect the industrial potential of the country because they influence the quantity of imported inputs that can be paid for by exports.

Higher commodity terms of trade stemming from lower import prices expand the LDC's industrial potential. Higher commodity terms of trade arising from higher export prices benefit industrialization in the small exporting country. The large exporter must take into account the price elasticity of demand for the export good. In the latter case lower commodity terms of trade related to lower export prices may be an aid to industrial expansion when demand for exports is elastic and allows the income terms of trade to improve. And for the large exporter, lower commodity terms of trade may reflect reduced export costs, so that the factor terms of trade need not fall, and may even rise with lower export prices.

When an LDC's income and commodity terms of trade are constrained by both price and income inelasticity of demand, the industrial sector stagnates unless the country can make structural changes and develop new exports. And when there is relatively high instability in the commodity or income terms of trade, whether from internal or external sources, this creates inefficiencies and makes planning more difficult. Diversification of exports is the most hopeful avenue for overcoming foreign exchange shortages and instability. This assumes the LDC has economized on its import needs by planning efficiently, paying close attention to the development of scale economies, identifying infant industries, devising a product mix to reduce import needs, and developing less import-intensive technology. But export diversification is not easily accomplished when the LDC is an infant economy. Export diversification instead often follows the import substitution phase of industrial growth. The next section discusses the role of manufactures exports.

TRADE POTENTIAL FOR INDUSTRY

One hallmark of a true infant industry is that it uses relatively more labor and other cheaper resources and relatively less scarce resources such as imported capital. As these industries develop, their costs drop with their experience in domestic markets. Eventually those whose terms of trade are more favorable become export-earning industries. Alternatively, as an industrial infrastructure develops and industrial know-how improves, specialized export industries can develop that cater mainly to the export markets. Thus while import substitution is not a direct route to reducing foreign exchange limitations to development, it can be an indirect one under appropriate conditions. The lower the terms of trade for agriculture exports, the greater the need for developing a comparative advantage in manufactures exports as industrialization proceeds. But, of course, this industrial export capacity develops more slowly under conditions of low terms of trade for the traditional export crop.

Exports of Manufactures

The country to which development of manufactures exports is most important is the one with limited natural resources and heavy population pressures. Yet, without agricultural transformation so that resources can be diverted from food production and technological change that can offset diminishing returns, such a country cannot generate the foreign exchange earnings important to industrialization. The early development of manufactures exports is a difficult road but the only one open to travel for densely populated countries short of resources. Once achieved, perhaps with the help of foreign aid, its long-run growth effects are relatively favorable, as Japan, Taiwan, and South Korea all illustrate. Among these, Japan was successful without foreign aid.

The infant industry may be in agriculture. Assume that with imported machinery the export crop can be processed or otherwise changed into a product salable abroad. This type of export is preferable to raw-material exports when, net of capital or other imported inputs, it earns more final foreign goods than do raw materials. Early industrialization becomes directly linked to exports rather than import substitution. This may pave the way for subsequent development of import substitutes as demand grows and relative resource endowments favor import substitution. As mentioned previously, processed exports as opposed to raw materials are often excluded from MDC markets by protectionist policies. This can prevent industrial development of this type.

The economy viewed so far has been one without exports from extractive industries and without foreign firms that provide manufactured exports. Foreign capital and managerial skills sometimes combine with local labor and other resources to achieve a comparative advantage in manufactured goods other than processed raw materials. There must be a disciplined work force with adequate skill levels before LDCs are attractive to multinational manufacturing industries engaged in export. With few exceptions, industrial development is begun by nationals, sometimes helped by small-scale immigrant entrepreneurs; and multinationals are attracted mainly to a minimum-sized domestic market enlarged by the nationals.

The foreign firm often plays a key role in earnings from extractive industry exports in early stages of development, however. Under such circumstances, the price paid by the foreign firm for the raw materials tapped is a main determinant (along with the other variables examined in chapter 10) of the LDC's terms of trade. The roles of foreign capital in general and the multinational firm in particular are discussed in chapter 13.

Countries whose high-earning extractive exports lessen pressure to improve productivity and diversify can miss their chance for development. This occurs when the export earnings are used to import food and other consumer goods while insufficient resources are allocated to agricultural and industrial development. When the terms of trade turn less favorable or export minerals or metals are exhausted, such countries can find they've let their development potential slip past them. They must then turn to very stringent consumption denial and try to transform agriculture so that industrialization can take place and eventually produce manufactured exports.

Advantages of Manufactures Exports

As the LDC turns away from the phase of import substitution where exports are traditional commodities and begins to export manufactured goods, the economy is sometimes said to be moving into a phase of export promotion or "outward-looking policies." Empirical work indicates successful transition to manufactures exports is a spur to growth (Chenery 1980, pp. 281–87; Krueger 1978; Balassa 1978, pp. 181–89; and Michaely 1977, pp. 49–53).

The possible impetus to growth from manufactured exports stems from several sources. Already mentioned is the basic idea that as an industrial base and technical know-how are built up, the area of manufactures export may emerge as one with a comparative advantage exceeding the trade gains from specialization in traditional exports. Such an outcome depends on the relative commodity terms of trade and factor terms of trade. With the transfer of resources to manufactures exports, production function relationships allow greater foreign exchange earnings from factors devoted to such exports compared with factors used in traditional exports.

Another possible advantage connected to manufactures exports is that the range of factor substitution between limits could be larger than the factor substitution range for traditional exports, allowing fuller employment of resources. Segments of the production function with a factor proportions problem would be reduced or eliminated. The effect of alleviating or eliminating a factor proportions problem is to move the economy closer to perfect efficiency. It has also been suggested that when the LDC can export manufactured goods, thus ensuring industrial growth, it is less protective of the import substitution sector. An overprotected import substitution sector operates inside the production possibilities curve. Such protection promotes monopoly inefficiencies, excess capacity, and a foreign exchange shortfall. Manufactures exports and a freer trade policy are said to encourage greater efficiency as well as continued industrialization.

Economies of scale may be found in the manufactures export sector, allowing the factor terms of trade to exceed those of the traditional exports. Finally, in a real world situation the introduction of manufactures exports often does not completely replace traditional exports, but diversifies the sector. This can produce greater stability in the commodity terms of trade index.

Trade in Advanced LDCs   Once an economy is past the early stages of industrialization, it has the potential for producing a greater variety of consumer and capital goods, and the import requirements for further growth are less rigidly related to industrial output. The foreign exchange constraint becomes less binding, particularly for larger countries without extremes of population density. When the stock of human and physical capital is larger and more technically advanced, increments to this stock are more readily achieved and they diversify production capacity. Infant industry subsidies can be eliminated gradually and competitive forces strengthened as market size enlarges. Export potential is more diversified, reducing the risks of specialization and trade. This assumes the LDC has avoided policy pitfalls of excessive subsidies and the wrong mix of subsidies that can create dualism and lead to continued rigidity of import constraints. This point is discussed in more detail in chapter 12 on promotion of industry.

REFERENCES   Balassa, B. 1978. Exports and Economic Growth: Further Evidence. *Journal of Development Economics* 5 (June): 181–89.

Chenery, H. B. 1980. Interactions Between Industrialization and Exports. *American Economic Review* (May): 281–87.

———— and Syrquin, M. 1975. *Patterns of Development, 1950–1970*. London: Oxford University Press.

Eckaus, Richard S. 1955. The Factor Proportions Problem in Underdeveloped Areas. *American Economic Review* 45 (September): 539–65.

Krueger, Anne O. 1978. *Foreign Trade Regimes and Economic Development: Liberalization Attempts and Consequences,* Cambridge, MA: Ballinger Publishing Co.

Michaely, M. 1977. Exports and Growth: An Empirical Investigation. *Journal of Development Economics* 4 (March): 49–53.

The Promotion
of Industry

chapter

12

T his chapter focuses upon the appropriate policies for the promotion of industry in LDC environments and within the world trade system. Policy instruments typically available to the mixed economy seeking industrialization include subsidies, domestic taxes, tariffs, quotas, foreign exchange controls, common markets, and government regulation or ownership of selected industries. The chapter tries to identify the best policy instrument under typical conditions or distortions.

INDUSTRY DYNAMICS AND SCALE

We begin with a discussion of the dynamic attributes of industry in the growth process and examine in some detail the relationship of economies of scale to this dynamism. Scale economies are important to the infrastructure that supports industry as well as to the industrial sector itself. This discussion of the dynamics of industry and of the importance of scale economies provides background for a detailed scrutiny of industrial promotion techniques.

Industrial activity based on agriculture, the export sector, or the domestic nonagricultural sector alters the technical foundation of an economy and increases the use of machinery. Production carried on by the family unit must give way and organizational structures develop that can coordinate a mobile labor force. The mobility, specialization, and work discipline of the labor force are important to industrial success. And the necessary technical progress requires a growing stock of human capital, better educated and innovative. Saving and capital formation increase with the rise in productivity, while technological advance is self-reinforcing. Competition acquires a creative dimension as new products and designs become important to success. A more specialized and sophisticated service sector emerges in response to industry's need for financial, legal, transportation, and other infrastructure. Eventually scale economies raise productivity. The input-output matrix is enlarged and diversified.

Dynamics of Industry

Industrial dynamism improves productivity within the firm and for the total economy. Even where internal economies for the firm are lacking, there may be external ones that redound to the economy as a whole. These external economies, or social gains, may offset infant industry costs that are not recouped by the firm as it matures and becomes self-supporting.

An acceleration phase of industrialization can occur once a certain threshold is reached. Savings and investment grow more rapidly, technical advance gains a built-in momentum, resources are used with greater efficiency, and scale economies increase the rate of growth in productivity. Because scale economies are closely associated with manufacturing and economic organization within an industrial society, we explore scale efficiencies in the LDC before taking up industrial promotion.

Economies of scale occur when larger output levels allow changes in organizational features, specialization, and technology that raise factor productivity. When scale in an LDC is discussed from the perspective of the total economy, it is helpful to think of the aggregate production

Scale and Industrialization

function. As the total output of the economy expands, there is greater scope for specialized units and individuals in the production process. Production can be organized differently and scale-related technology that improves productivity can be introduced. With sharpened differentiation of tasks and greater specialization, factor quality improves. Inputs per unit of output drop as scale allows more efficiency in management, finance, marketing, and infrastructure. Manufacturing subunits can grow in size yet still handle more limited tasks. The production of total output is organized into more specialized, interdependent, and complex processes. This growing specialization was described in chapter 5, where it was related to technical capacity and type of goods produceable in the industrial sector. The size of the aggregate economy is an integral part of this transformation.

Such a view of scale on an aggregate level gives insights into the relationship between development and the size of the market. Adam Smith was the first to stress the tie between market size and productivity gains. Writing in the second half of the eighteenth century, he was particularly impressed by the effects upon industrialization of gains from division of labor. Economic historians frequently stress market size in their documentation and explanation of the development process in a particular country. The role of transportation improvements in enlarging markets is an area given great weight in the history of MDC development. Population size is another variable directly related to market size and hence to scale, as was discussed in the chapter on population. And historically, market size has been a major determinant in the development of a capital goods industry that depends upon a broad and diversified industrial economy for scale effects.

In a similar way the production function for a sector, industry, firm, or plant can display economies of scale. Changes of the type described for the aggregate economy occur within its subdivisions. At early levels of development, scale is more important in the industrial sector and its infrastructure. Also, any sector that is engaged in exporting readily achieves scale economies when they exist because of access to world markets. Commerce and agriculture as a whole experience fewer economies of scale in early development.

At the industry, firm, or plant level, scale economies are associated with technology. Historically, as techniques have advanced, the plant size needed to use such techniques efficiently has increased. Economies of scale are considered to exert a strong force on productivity in many industries. Infrastructure industries such as utilities and transportation not only affect market size, but are themselves affected by scale. Thus there is a reinforcing relationship between infrastructure and market size that yields productivity gains. Heavy industry like steel and light industry like food processing are affected by scale economies. It is believed that in advanced countries that are relatively capital intensive, some industries are continuing to improve their efficiencies with larger scale. Evidence is relatively sparse here when referring to the broad range of industries composing a total economy at all possible labor/capital ratios.

Recall that Chenery and Syrquin interpret the differences between small-country and large-country industrialization as attributable to scale.

The large country at an income level of $200 per capita has the same proportion of output generated by industry as a small country with a per capita income of $400. As the smaller country matures, both increased income per capita and manufactures exports can enlarge its potential for achieving scale in the industrial sector. In fact scale is part of the reason a smaller country is relatively more dependent upon trade as a vehicle for raising its income per capita.

Studies of LDC firms measuring the importance of scale in these countries are limited. In MDCs, where modern infrastructure complements industrial activity, analyses indicate an efficiency saving of 40 percent as the norm (see Yotopoulos and Nugent 1976, pp. 150–53 for a summary of these studies). In addition to technical influences upon size, firm size has been associated in MDC empirical studies with economies in finance, management, and marketing, among others. However, in many industries studies show that scale economies are exhausted when plants or firms reach a size that is "moderate" in an economy the size of the United States.

Scale has a space dimension. As a result, economies of scale influence geographic concentration of economic activity as industrialization occurs. A regional area favored in infrastructure can readily acquire scale economies in the labor market that allow development of specialized skills, provision of specialized services, and the emergence of a reinforcing matrix of economic activity that influences firm location and labor force migration. Development can become reinforcing in the region, but such concentration makes it harder for other areas to compete and diversify their economic base. In practice it is difficult to achieve the productivity gains from regional scale economies without some offsetting costs of overconcentration and reduced economic progress in competing regions.

Brazil has struggled with this problem. She even moved her capital city to another location to relieve the overconcentration of economic activity along the coastline. In Africa people come into the cities in part because the infrastructure—water, health facilities, lights, paving, sewage—is so superior to conditions in the bush. Labor allocation can become unbalanced when amenities are subsidized or free. Once a certain region is favored with subsidies of various types and gains momentum, it is very hard to reverse the imbalance. Even a planned economy like that of the Soviet Union has not been able to achieve the geographic dispersion of economic activity she has sought.

Scale economies contribute to productivity gains that arise with industrialization. The dynamics of industrialization are broader than scale economies, however, making industry a common focus of promotional policies. And while manufacturing is an important component of the development process, its promotion must be carefully tailored to the country's potential. We turn now to a closer scrutiny of the costs and benefits of industrialization and a discussion of the conditions and policies appropriate for encouraging industry.

Import substitution that responds to comparative advantage potential as technology and resources change is a gradual process, with new infant industries emerging as time progresses. And, of course, import

Costs and Benefits of Early Infant Industries

substitution is not a route to autarky. The term designates the process of producing at home some goods that were formerly imported. A better description of an LDC's trade as development proceeds than the term "import substitution" would be "changing trade patterns that reflect and support continuous development." And such patterns vary with the individual LDC's size, resource endowments and their changes, population pressures, technical span, and historical variables. As discussed in the chapter on technological change, the supportive web of interrelations of market, government, and socioeconomic forces must develop to allow advances in technical sophistication that industry needs. The increasing complexity and technical absorptive capacity are only gradually acquired.

Since the industrial revolution countries have sought, through government support and indirect policies affecting market decisions, to initiate, encourage, or accelerate infant industries and industrial output along with new technical know-how. The time-consuming nature of the development process has shown itself adjustable to a limited but significant degree to planning spurs, both centralized and decentralized. Policy approaches to agricultural development have already been discussed. Here we concentrate upon trade and industrial evolution, remembering that industrial progress can be directly linked to agricultural exports.

The economic network for internal and international commerce emerges rather spontaneously in LDCs as agriculture improves. Perhaps Adam Smith was right when he assumed that people have an innate tendency to "truck, barter and trade." The evoluation of commerce is aided and abetted by infrastucturo dovelopment that unifies markets. The government often participates in the financing of the relatively capital-intensive, large-scale infrastructure such as internal transportation networks, telecommunications, and port facilities necessary for advances in commerce. Borrowing abroad to finance this framework for industry can lessen the burden on the infant economy with limited savings for acquiring such facilities.

The economic network that supports commerce does not necessarily carry with it the seeds of manufacturing and other industrial activity. The latter are demanding both technically and organizationally. Without a supportive matrix, the risk is high for the initial manufacturing endeavors. With the advent of industry new infrastructure must be developed, and the old expanded. There must usually be a deliberate policy that taxes other sectors in order to subsidize the beginnings of the higher-risk industrial sector. Yet, once success begins to feed upon itself, there is evidence that industrialization produces a reinforcing dynamism. When this develops, the early subsidies are recouped in the expanding prosperity.

There will be, of course, some optimum level and type of subsidy that avoids overtaxing the sectors subsidizing industry and that achieves maximum benefits from the transfer. By now the reader is well aware that resources must be devoted to agricultural as well as industrial development, and that persistent imbalance stalls the whole economy. It is particularly difficult, however, to calculate the return to economic development of resource allocation among sectors over, say, a 20-year plan. This is especially true when, as with infant-industry subsidies, the early costs must be weighed against later benefits to the private sector and the total economy. The infant industries must be identified so that those that do not yield a payoff of internal viability and/or external benefits to economic development are not allowed subsidy status. When five or ten years of subsidies do not produce an industry that can dispense with them, there must be strong external economies that justify resource allocation to such industries rather than to alternative uses.

To begin this discussion we focus on pragmatic methods of identifying infant industries. Next the deficiencies in the supportive network in early development that produce a need for subsidies are discussed. We then examine the appropriate form of subsidy in relation to the respective area of insufficiency. The discussion and examples developed lead to the generalization that subsidies must be connected to the reason a subsidy is needed.

IDENTIFYING INFANT INDUSTRIES

Having discussed the attributes of industry *in general*, we should note that less encompassing statements can be made about the attributes of a particular industry and its chances of being a successful infant for LDCs as a whole. As was explained in earlier discussions of comparative advantage, a number of variables determine a country's efficiency level for imported, exported, and nontraded goods. In the process of beginning industrialization, the planners have the added job of pinpointing areas of potential comparative advantage, and affecting specific variables that must change to ensure successful infancy and growth. In general, the smaller the country, the less scope it has for a diversified industrial base. High levels of specialization and trade are the fate of a small nation seeking to develop.

Pragmatic Methods

The search for budding industries has resulted in various pragmatic identification techniques. The most obvious is a scrutiny of imported goods to see if, for certain ones, import substitution would be viable. It is often said that industry can more readily develop first by serving the home market, where risks of failure are lower. However, under propitious conditions industries can be developed to service export markets. This often is the case where raw materials can be processed.

Generally industries are sought that will require limited amounts of capital, scarce labor skills, or other relatively limited resources. For example, the textile industry is one that can so economize. Industries with limited scale economies may be viable since domestic markets are small. But when an inexpensive, lower-quality, or somewhat differentiated version of an import can satisfy the mass market better than the more expensive foreign product, home manufacture of the cheaper version can expand a market, creating greater scope for scale economies.

Input-output tables, when they exist, are sometimes helpful in anticipating new areas of economic activity for the domestic economy.

Such a table pictures the interrrelations among industries and sectors of an economy at a point in time for a given output level. It reflects how specialized and complex an economy is when the matrix is sufficiently disaggregated. From such a table the reader can trace through, for example, the final use of all steel production, the sources and amounts of all inputs such as iron ore and coal, for a given steel output and use level, and coefficients of production such as labor inputs per unit of steel output.

One way to use input-output tables in identifying infant industries is to study the comparable tables of countries similar to the one in question but more advanced. The presumption is that the more developed country is a picture of the future of the less mature one five or 10 years hence. Differences in the matrix can be analyzed to identify possible new areas of domestic activity for the economy.

Albert Hirschman suggested the use of such tables to identify industries that have high linkages—in other words, need inputs from other industries and in turn are needed as inputs into still other industries. His strategy for development includes selection of high-linkage industries as import substitutes, the rationale being that LDCs have a crucial shortage of decision-making ability. By encouraging infant industries with high backward and forward linkages, governments make the need for further economic activity in the interrelated sectors compelling and facilitate the decision to start up such industries (Hirschman 1958). This strategy of created imbalance, or disequilibrium, designed to elicit decision-making was deemed particularly applicable to South America. Here the costs of imbalance and premature industries are more readily borne than in poorer LDCs, and the political process in many countries precludes the close-knit planning apparatus needed for consistent development programs.

Finally, a common pragmatic approach toward identification of infant industries is the use of a tariff on imports in general, one that is not too high. This controls consumption of imports and allows industries efficient enough to compete behind a tariff wall the opportunity to develop. Ian Little, Tibor Scitovsky, and Maurice Scott suggest a maximum tariff of 20 percent (1970). They also advise forecasting eventual export potential for an industry. They suggest restraint in encouraging infant industries in certain highly competitive areas where other countries already are entrenched in export markets.

The tariff is an indirect subsidy not available to the export industry and nontradeables sectors that do not enjoy protection. Prices rise in the protected economy for goods affected by the tariff. Resources are attracted away from the export and nontradeables sectors that are now relatively less competitive in their ability to bid for and employ resources. These resources are used to expand domestic output of importables where possible.

Remember, however, from the last chapter that there is some optimum division of resources between industry and other sectors to allow industrialization to proceed without a shortage of imported inputs. It is not surprising that studies show this balance has not been achieved in many industrializing LDCs. There is a strong tendency to overprotect industry and transfer too many resources there at the expense of the other sectors. Ultimately this affects industry's ability to expand when imports are a bottleneck and high prices restrict expansion of the domestic market. The economy decreases in efficiency as industries that cannot recoup infant subsidies and become self-supporting require continuous help. Of course the graphic solution shown heretofore is a highly simplified framework to guide our thoughts about real world performance. The criticisms of import substitution do not center upon failure to achieve an exact balance, but upon the degree to which the economy does not perceive the source of its inefficiency. Keeping in mind the tendency for programs of import substitution to become excessive, we turn now to the appropriate policies for promotion of industry.

PROMOTION OF INDUSTRY

There are a minimum set of conditions necessary for industry to develop and grow in an LDC. Once a necessary condition is identified, there is generally a best method for creating or satisfying it, that is, one that costs the least. The degree and type of industrialization depend upon the number and kinds of industries that can achieve internal efficiency and/or create external economies that repay society for their costs. As a general rule the appropriate policy to encourage industry is one that directly subsidizes the minimum condition. Policy needs can vary among different historical settings. Some examples are given here.

Appropriate Policies to Promote Industrial Activity

Skills and human capital needed for industry are different from those for agriculture and commerce. Labor training is a necessary condition for industry growth. There is an impediment to this training when workers are free to change jobs without repaying the firm for the costs of the instruction. Unless these costs are borne by the worker or society as a whole, the labor force may be undertrained.

Some workers finance their own training through borrowing from the family combined with apprenticeship periods. The family partly supports the young worker while he or she earns reduced wages while learning. Workers without family support can remain untrained, however. In Japan it has been traditional for workers out of high school to join a large firm for life. Under such a system the firm will be willing to undertake financing of training more readily. The job security did not deter efficiency because of the unique peer group pressure in Japan that produces high work effort. In addition, however, Japan subsidized education. Generally there are sufficient externalities to labor training to justify some government subsidy.

The financing of industry and the associated assumption of risk may deter sufficiently large industrial activity. Government generally has a role in encouraging savings necessary for growth and in ensuring that financial intermediary activity is adequate, and designed to eliminate unnecessary risks while overcoming the risk aversion of investors. The government may subsidize feasibility studies and improve information about investment opportunities. Some projects necessary to industry, for instance, infrastructure, may require such vast capital that government ownership is the only feasible method of raising the investment funds to begin operations. And some infrastructure, while providing externalities to the economy as a whole, operates at a loss and thus must be government owned or receive subsidies. Transportation services often fall into this category, as do hydroelectric projects that are tied in with flood control and land reclamation.

A final example relates to technical change. Applied research and development may be a necessary condition for infant industry success. The risk, payoff period, and economies of scale can all point to the need for government participation in the financing of this activity.

The approach used to identify the necessary conditions for industry growth at each stage and the efficient method of achieving it should be one that creates a subsidy system designed to aid industry in general, whether it is in the export, nontradeables, or import sectors. In contrast, a tariff only subsidizes the import sector and deters industrial activity in the others. As mentioned earlier, however, a low tariff is often justified on pragmatic grounds. Here we can add the justification that a small tariff accompanied by appropriate subsidies to labor training, infrastructure, and other necessary conditions, may be efficient when the import substitution sector has large external economies that redound to *all* sectors. However, quotas and *high* tariffs at home and abroad are generally harmful to the LDC's industrialization. It is helpful to discuss this in more detail.

LDC Tariffs and Quotas Affecting Imports

As emphasized in the last section, an economywide assessment of industrial infancy will prevent neglect of sectoral interrelations and the total costs, including those for infrastructure, of various development strategies. Such an evaluation promotes the probing of various sectors for development potential. Moreover it helps to avoid diversion of subsidies to a particular sector or industry, or even firm, when such funds would be better utilized to support an area important to the total economy's development. Labor training and improvement in capital markets were mentioned as economywide areas that should take priority over industry-specific subsidies. For this reason tariffs on imports of a particular industry or sector can be a costly form of indirect subsidy that fails to attack and improve the general weakness leading to the need for a tariff.

When tariffs are used, it is preferable, as explained, to impose a general tariff of a fairly low level and see which industries emerge as efficient. A domestic tax to offset the tariff should be placed upon any industry the planners feel can have negative externalities if developed behind tariff walls. Sometimes income distribution is highly skewed and a general tariff could support the emergence of luxury goods production that can have negative externalities. A domestic tax can prevent this. Tariffs are also a tool for offsetting, in part, the effects of an overvalued exchange rate. It is better in general, however, to realign the exchange rate. This point will be explained in a later section.

Quotas on imports are not easily justified since they may have the same effect as a tariff on prices, but yield an unearned profit for the importer, who marks up the price to the higher domestic price that prevails when goods are in short supply. With a tariff, the difference between the import price and domestic price goes to the government as revenue to be used for development. Also, quotas strictly limit imports whereas tariffs do not. Where some flexibility of supply is important, tariffs are superior to quotas.

The allocation of foreign exchange at a government-set price by product quota can have the same effect as a quota on the good itself: It can provide the opportunity to charge a price above the import price that will yield high profits for providers of the scarce item unless the government seeks bids on the foreign exchange. Such bids would drive up the cost of foreign exchange to the purchaser and transfer the excess profits to the government sector.

Special care should be taken to avoid tariffs, quotas, or foreign exchange allocation devices that unnecessarily increase inefficiencies in the infant LDC. Typically LDCs have used differential tariffs or foreign exchange rates to encourage capital imports in an effort to spur industrialization. This has contributed to high capital/labor ratios and underemployment. In labor-abundant India, tractors subsidized in this way were imported to replace farm labor, leading to social and economic costs. More is said about resource distortions and about Indian planning in later sections.

Tariffs designed to control consumption are defensible. When the LDC with an infant economy wishes to encourage savings and reduce consumption in order to free resources for investment, a tariff on imported consumer goods is appropriate so long as it is accompanied by a tax on home production of consumer goods. Without the tax, it becomes profitable to produce the imported consumer goods (although inefficiently) in the LDC. A tariff on a consumer good may also be appropriate when a domestic close substitute could be produced efficiently, but not marketed successfully because consumers have a brand loyalty to the foreign good, perhaps because of advertising or prestige. A lower-quality domestic good is not necessarily to be avoided if it carries a lower price tag, or if the quality difference will disappear when experience develops. Inefficiency of an incipient industry can be in the form of higher costs and/or lower quality.

A tariff designed to reduce imports so that the domestic firm's market size is sufficient to achieve scale economies must be approached with care. Very often markets in LDCs are just large enough to achieve scale economies but not large enough for competitive organization. The tariff can easily be set too high, resulting in inefficiencies and/or monopoly profits. Instead, the levy should raise import prices on competing goods just high enough so that the efficient domestic firm can meet the import price and cover its costs at socially optimum output levels. The threat of potential competition from imports then precludes monopoly profits and forces the LDC's firms to seek out efficient operating procedures. Output levels will be larger than under higher tariffs, producing greater scale economies.

When high tariffs are placed around infant industries and the domestic market is small relative to scale economies, too many imperfectly competitive firms can enter the market. The extra firms compete for the profits induced by the higher prices caused by excessive tariffs; but profits are low or nonexistent when small sales volume drives each firm up its average cost curve to higher-cost, lower-volume production levels. A lower tarifff would reduce the number of firms while raising scale efficiencies for each of the survivors. Government taxes are an additional method for controlling monopoly profits where the number of firms is limited, and can be used to help finance development. With a large number of "tariff factories" operating inefficiently, profits are low and so are taxes.

Since scale potential often leads to prolonged market protection to secure the economies of size, it is important that *premature* protection not be given. It is too costly to protect firms built with excess capacity that will only be fully utilized when the market enlarges. Capital standing idle could have been used elsewhere to increase output. The high import content of the capital adds to the stricture that waste must be avoided. And protected markets with excess capacity can contribute to poor managerial practices and governmental influence to protect vested interests and inefficiencies. There is ample historical evidence of this tendency. France and Ireland are two examples from Europe, while Latin America has many. Moreover, it must be remembered that estimation of the degree to which scale economies exist within the LDC economy is not always clear-cut. Data for MDCs do not automatically establish the existence of scale results in the very different market situation of the LDC.

Sometimes these protected firms find it advantageous to sell abroad below cost to achieve economies of scale. The result is that the LDC is trading in goods with low commodity and factor terms of trade since it cannot produce at world prices and cover costs. Resources are used here rather than in truly efficient export industries that could sell abroad without subsidy in the form of high domestic prices. Thus, when a tariff is applied, it is important that it not be a high one that subsidizes excess capacity in the infant industry.

In summary, protective tariffs do not attack many of the shortcomings of infant economies that need specific attention. Thus they tend to prolong infancy in contrast to a more specific and efficient subsidy approach aimed at eliminating barriers to development. Tariffs and quotas are suspect as tools to help diversify an infant economy more because of their efficiency shortcomings than their consumption effects in an LDC. An economy must impose taxes in order to subsidize industry. In an economy trying to encourage savings, a tax on the consumer is an acceptable method of subsidizing the infant economy when handled correctly. When a portion of this tax falls upon imports, it is called a tariff. Tariffs on products that are not taxed when produced within the LDC allow higher-cost domestic production to develop and thus subsidize certain domestic industry. They are appropriate under specific circumstances, but should usually be fairly low and general in their application. Tariffs to achieve scale economies must not be used to subsidize excess capacity or create monopoly profits.

Export subsidies, usually to manufactured goods, are fairly common in LDCs. Their purpose is to reduce the price of exportable goods. They take the form of tax remission, favorable foreign exchange rates, or use of government funds to reduce input costs. Planners use export subsidies to increase foreign exchange earnings and promote manufacturing; yet often they are not justified by social returns. When they are not, the LDC is subsidizing another economy—an outlay it can ill afford. Moreover, subsidies to labor-training, industrial infrastructure and other areas favorable to export industries, if overdone, can cause a transfer of resources from traditional agricultural or extractive exports and lead to a foreign exchange shortage that limits industrial output.

Another reason for export subsidies is price distortions within the LDC. The general repercussions of this problem are developed in the next section. When price distortions lower exports below optimal levels, an offsetting subsidy is warranted. Usually the subsidy is needed to correct an overpriced resource that causes exports to be too low.

In an effort to promote import substitution industries, export taxes as opposed to subsidies may be used by LDCs to change the international and domestic terms of trade and resource allocation. A tax upon a price-inelastic export can improve the international commodity terms of trade for the large exporter nation, and also its income terms of trade. As explained in the graphic analysis of the last chapter, both improvements will raise industrial output potential. On the other hand, when the country is a price-taker, an export tax cannot affect the international commodity terms of trade; it only changes the domestic cost of production and terms of trade. A tax upon exports raises government revenue and, by reducing the profitability of export production, causes some resources to move out of exports. A policy of industrial promotion may require a tax on exports when commodity export earnings attract too many resources to that sector. The usual warning follows that such a transfer from high earnings must be justified by higher future earnings for the resources in industry.

When export earnings fluctuate, with detrimental effects upon industrial output, alternating subsidies and taxes may be needed to stabilize import capacity. This was mentioned in discussion of the effect of risk and uncertainty upon exports. And finally, subsidies may be necessary to improve productivity in the export sector. Such efficiency improvements can raise export earnings and enlarge industrial potential.

Appropriate plans to promote industry may include policies that correct distortions in factor prices. It is very common in LDCs for the price of factors to reflect not just the influence of scarcity, and hence supply and demand forces, but also the impact of market imperfections, political pressures, and social custom. The price of a relatively abundant resource, labor, is often above its opportunity cost in alternative uses. This contributes to unemployment as capital is substituted for relatively overpaid workers. Labor-intensive goods that could be produced efficiently by the LDC are imported instead.

Consider a labor-intensive industry when labor is overpriced. For simplicity assume this is a constant-cost industry and the long-run supply price is S_d as seen in figure 12.1. World price, P_w, is below domestic costs with high-priced labor. A tariff could raise P_w so that the LDC industry could compete. Thus a tariff is a form of indirect subsidy to industry. In this case it is designed to offset a distortion in labor costs. It also raises prices to the consumer, who pays the subsidy. Note, however, that it does not change the price of labor relative to the price of capital, which is the source of the inefficiency.

In contrast, the effects of a direct subsidy to labor costs are depicted in figure 12.2. Relative costs for capital, P_k, and labor, P_ℓ, are given by the slope of the line between points showing the units of each resource that 120 pesos will buy $\left(\dfrac{120p}{P_k} \div \dfrac{120p}{P_\ell} = P_\ell/P_k\right)$. An output level of 10 units is represented by isoquant Q_1. Before the subsidy, Q_1 output costs 120 pesos to produce. The firm produces at tangency point b using the corresponding amounts of K and L purchasable with 120 pesos. With a subsidy to labor, P_ℓ/P_k (the slope of the relative price line) changes and the amount of labor purchasable with 120 pesos increases to 120 pesos/P_ℓ', further out on the labor axis. A parallel relative price line is tangent to Q_1 (10 units) at c, with a cost for this output now reduced to 100 pesos or 10 pesos per unit. The employment of labor has increased from L to L' and the K/L ratio has decreased to K'/L'.

Since this is a constant-cost industry, all quantities of output will reflect this lower cost. The supply curve in figure 12.1, which reflects the cost per unit, drops and the good is competitive with a P_w of 10 pesos. In contrast to the case where a tariff was used, the consumer does not pay a higher price and reduce consumption.

Note, however, that when technology does not allow factor substitution, and the isoquant is L-shaped, correcting labor costs will lower

FIGURE 12.1

Cost Difference in Domestic and Import Good

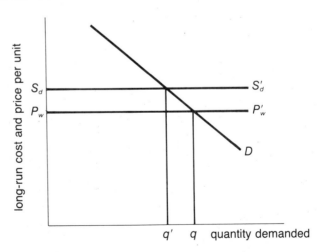

Long-run domestic cost of production is S_d, above the world price and cost of production, P_w.

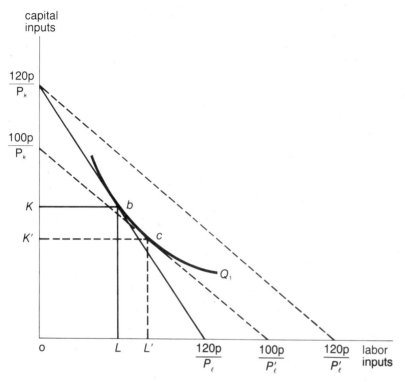

FIGURE 12.2

Efficient Factor Combinations with Varying Wage Rates

Lower labor costs lower K/L. The price of labor falls from P_ℓ to P'_ℓ. This lowers the cost of output Q_1 from 120 pesos at b to 100 pesos at c. K/L falls to K'/L'.

the price by a smaller amount since cheaper labor cannot be substituted for capital and K/L remains the same. Then, even with the correct relative factor prices, LDCs may not be competitive because modern technology does not allow them to substitute their relatively cheap labor for scarce capital.

An alternative to subsidizing labor costs sometimes chosen by LDCs is a change in the exchange rate. The price of imports, P_w, must be translated to pesos from import currency units, which are dollars. Assume the domestic currency, the peso, is currently valued by the monetary authorities in the LDC at 10 pesos/\$1. Thus, the world price of \$1 translates to 10 pesos, and the domestic cost is 12 pesos with the original high labor costs, P_ℓ. Notice that a change in the exchange rate can change the price of imports. Specifically, a depreciation of the peso to 12 pesos/\$1 will raise P_w to 12 pesos, the equivalent of domestic cost with overpriced labor. Thus, without changing domestic labor costs or K/L, the local good is now competitive with imports.

Which is the preferable policy under conditions of distortion? It depends upon the particular situation, for example, whether wages reflect true opportunity costs of labor, whether the foreign exchange rate re-

Best Policy When Distortions Exist

flects its scarcity price, and whether there are other distortions. In some instances it is indeed hard to identify the preferable policy. Here some easier cases are examined.

Assume the only distortion is labor costs. Then the proper policy is a subsidy to labor, or correction of the conditions causing distortions of labor costs so that wage rates reflect labor's true scarcity price. This increases the economy's efficiency by using underutilized labor more heavily through changing the K/L ratio, and through production of labor-intensive goods in which the country has a comparative advantage. The presumption is that the subsidy is financed in a manner that is distortion free or involves less distortion than the tariff.

Now assume capital and labor are priced correctly, but the foreign exchange rate of 10 pesos/$1 overvalues the peso, in other words, the peso buys more dollars than it would if the true scarcity price of foreign exchange, the dollar, were reflected. Put another way, the dollar purchases too few pesos. When this is the case, imports are excessive because they are too cheap and exports are low because they are too expensive. The correct policy is to counteract or eliminate this problem. Either the tariff plus a subsidy to exports or a change in the exchange rate will accomplish this. If capital is imported, a tariff would be needed on it also; otherwise capital would be priced too cheaply relative to labor. In respect to devaluation of the currency, the change in the exchange rate would tend to eliminate distortions on the export side by reducing export prices and thus encouraging exports, while raising import prices.

Countries often promote exports. The question arises as to the optimum policy. Here again the same approach applies. If exports are too low because of an overvalued exchange rate, then that distortion should be corrected. Loss of foreign exchange with devaluation from lower foreign exchange export prices on price-inelastic goods can be overcome by a tax on such exports. If exports are too low because labor or other costs are not priced according to their scarcity price, this can be remedied with a policy designed to change such costs so that prices can be competitive and production efficient in using resources.

A good generalization is that a country should attempt to identify any distortions and seek a policy that corrects the distortions, not merely counteracts them. This will increase efficiency. Tariffs (and quotas too) are ubiquitous in LDCs, and are used for reasons other than offsetting overvalued exchange rates. Studies have shown they tend to be used to excess, causing inefficiencies that can retard development. But there are pragmatic pressures underlying this tendency. Sometimes distortions are so widespread that subsidies cannot be designed to correct them adequately. In such cases there is no general "first-best" policy.

Before leaving the subject of distortions, it is helpful to relate a typical distortion to the economy's development goal of industrialization. The next section examines the effects of a relatively low price for capital upon industrial output.

Underpriced Capital and Industrial Output   LDCs seeking to encourage industrialization have typically subsidized capital with various types of benefits such as tax remission or favorable foreign exchange rates that reduce the domestic price of imported capital. The simple two-sector graph can serve to illustrate why a relatively low price for a resource that does not reflect its scarcity value can retard rather than promote industrialization.

The opportunity cost of imported capital is represented by the slope of the terms of trade line in figure 12.3. EM shows the units of imported capital per unit of industrial output along EB when capital is correctly priced in domestic currency units. Subsidies to capital will lower its domestic price and cause manufacturers to substitute capital for labor in production of good B. This raises m/b to m'/b'. That is, with capital costs below their scarcity value, the K/L ratio used in production will be too high. Since this is an inefficient combination of resources, given their opportunity cost, production cannot take place along curve EB, representing the most efficient combination of resources. The maximum combination of exports and industry output lies inside the production possibilities curve. The attempt to encourage industrial production by making capital relatively cheap will in fact reduce potential industrial output.

The idea that capital intensity should be high was popular in earlier eras of development analysis. The argument was that high capital intensity produced high ratios of profits to wages and high profits promoted high savings and reinventment and this was a major propellant for growth. One problem with that analysis is that it ignores the foreign

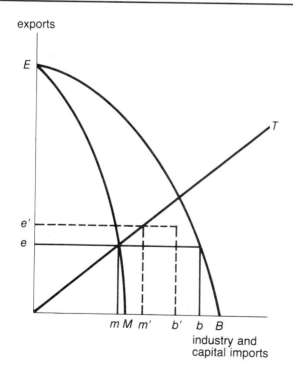

FIGURE 12.3
Underpriced Capital Reduces Industry Output

Relatively low-cost capital that does not reflect the opportunity cost shown by the slope of *T* raises *m/b* to *m'/b'*. An inefficient combination of capital and labor moves production inside the production possibilities curve.

exchange constraint upon investment. The capital stock rises more quickly, but its productivity is lower due to inefficiency, and more capital is needed to attain a given increment to output. Large imported capital needs tighten the foreign exchange constraint upon industrial expansion.

The argument is sometimes made, however, that the lower wages and underemployed labor keep food consumption down. Recall from the three-quadrant graph that a lower food constraint would allow EB to be higher since fewer resources would be needed for food production. This could offset the adverse efficiency effects. The Soviets followed an economic policy of encouraging high capital intensity and simply constricted food consumption via controls in order to obtain a surplus for export after the Bolshevik Revolution. In fact, Stalin rose to power amidst a great debate over the appropriate policy for ensuring export earnings for development. We return to this topic in the last sections on Indian industrialization.

It can also be argued that EB has a constant slope because of a factor proportion problem, and that M/B is fixed at some high level, while labor must be unemployed along EB. Changes in relative factor prices, in such a case, do not affect relative factor use in industry or potential output there. In a multiproduct industrial sector, however, allowance for variation in product mix would permit M/B to vary even in a case of fixed factor proportions if this ratio is not constant across products. And the more recent emphasis has been upon intermediate technology that will improve capital productivity rather than on forced savings to accommodate capital-intensive projects.

Tariffs Abroad on LDC Exports   Sometimes foreign distortions exist over which the LDC has no control, and which can interfere with the promotion of its industry. Consider again the country in early stages of industrialization, which must have imports to allow industrial production and yet has little ability to conserve on them. A tariff abroad on the LDC's exports raises the domestic price in the country buying them. An extensively protected world market with most purchasers imposing tariffs will restrict world demand for LDC exports. At any given price less is demanded on world markets. Put another way, to sell the same amount as could be sold without foreign barriers, export prices must drop.

A case of general protection abroad will lower the terms of trade faced by the LDC whether the LDC affects world price or not. Figure 12.4 illustrates the decline in feasible industrial output as a result of tariffs imposed on LDC exports by the importing countries. As the T_k curve shifts leftward to T'_k, industrial output drops from b to b', and exports rise from e to e'. In the face of falling demand and prices, the LDC must export more, not less, in order to minimize the cutback in its industrial output. A retaliatory tariff is of no help to the LDC. The tariff would keep imports low and/or cause inflation by driving up the import price.

There have been agreements by MDCs to allow LDC exports into their protected markets tariff-free, while retaining the duty on other

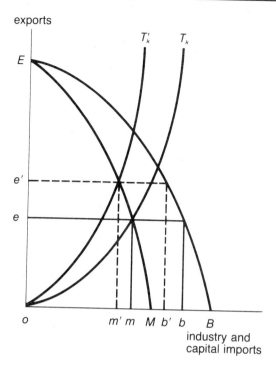

FIGURE 12.4

Tariffs Lower the LDC's Output Potential

Protection abroad shifts T_k to T'_k, and industrial output drops from b to b'. Exports rise from e to e', while imports fall from m to m'.

countries' exports. The European Common Market has done this with selected exports of some former colonial countries. The United States has allowed sugar to enter duty-free by allocating quotas to LDCs and has granted preferences, with restraints, to LDCs on certain manufactured goods.

Such a system of preferential treatment in tariff remission gives the LDC a competitive edge over MDCs in exports to protected MDC markets. However, the list of goods afforded such privileges often excludes items in which LDCs have a comparative advantage. And even for items on the list, there is often a quota that can be triggered by certain growth rates in LDC exports. Moreover, while the volume of LDC exports will expand, the preferential treatment of LDCs need not necessarily improve their terms of trade greatly when the importer has strong bargaining power.

Preferential Trade Among LDCs

Many LDCs are countries with fewer than 20 million people. When small neighboring states allow free movement of goods and even resources among themselves, they enlarge their resource diversity and their market size. The level and diversification of their industrial activity can increase as a result, enabling them to attain the dynamism inherent in industry on a broader scale. This is particularly true when proximity and/or contiguous location reduce transportation costs and allow development of common infrastructure.

The formation of free trading areas among small LDCs helps promote trade in manufactures among members often prevented otherwise by protectionist policies aimed at industry promotion. There are several levels of possible trade integration.

A *free trade area* eliminates tariffs among its members while allowing each country to set its own level of external tariffs. There must be surveillance to prevent nonmembers' goods from entering via a country with a low external tariff and then being sold in other countries with high external tariffs.

A *customs union* avoids the problem of policing goods by agreeing to set up common external tariffs. These are usually adopted at a lower level than that of the highest-tariff country. As with the free trade area, internal tariffs on an agreed set of goods are eliminated, possibly in gradual steps over a specified time period.

A *common market* goes one step beyond a customs union and allows resources to flow among countries that join. Common markets often address institutional differences that can impede trade such as legal structures, currency rules, and capital market structures. Many agreements among LDCs that are called common markets are in reality customs unions. They incorporate a reasonable schedule for implementing a common external tariff, but no realistic provisions for implementing a common market. We will follow popular usage, however, and call LDC customs unions common markets.

The same caveat applies to the common external tariff set for a common market as for an individual external tariff—it should not be high. When it is, the costs of protection outweigh the benefits of increased trade among members.

Common Markets and Shared Costs of Infancy

Common markets among LDCs can allow the costs of infancy to be shared. Assume two LDCs have the same two infant industries. Consider two cases:

Case 1: The two countries have identical relative costs for those two emerging industries. Specialization so that each country has only one infant industry might be beneficial when there are economies of scale or differences in relative demand in the two countries. The costs of early industrialization are reduced even though the countries do not differ in their relative efficiency ratios of production.

Case 2: Relative efficiency ratios differ between the two countries for the infant industries. Four possible sources of gains from a common market exist:

1. There are gains from specialization when each country concentrates on the product in which it has an absolute or comparative advantage.
2. If each country specializes in a good that requires less imports from the rest of the world, then it has a foreign exchange gain. This raises

the potential industrial output above what it could be if each country promoted its own infant industries alone when there is a binding foreign exchange constraint.

3. If the second condition holds and the LDCs export less outside their common market, diverting the resources to additional industrial expansion, then the terms of trade for their traditional exports could be affected. Should the drop in exports raise the terms of trade, this would provide further gains in industrial output potential.

4. This case too can achieve gains from scale effects.

Notice that the subsidy for one country's infant industry may be higher than the subsidy for the second country's. Yet both countries benefit when the gains from specialization are there. The common market is advantageous to both, even though the gains are not shared evenly. This presumes, of course, that both countries have a true potential efficiency advantage in the two industries vis-à-vis the rest of the world.

When one country has a comparative advantage in food, then under a common market arrangement it will not industrialize. This can occur when trade is opened between adjoining countries and food transportation costs are low enough. The LDC is then faced with a decision about remaining primarily agricultural for a longer period of time. Under these conditions it is sometimes feared that the terms of trade will turn against the agrarian economy as development proceeds, and that the transition to industrial growth at some future time will be more difficult because of the head start gained by the common market partner. Worry over such an outcome bothered communist countries in Eastern Europe as they formed a common market. Some countries rejected their comparative advantage in commodities specialization, both agrarian and mineral.

Countries at different levels of development generally do not enter into common market agreements because the lesser-developed one fears being at a competitive disadvantage. There are other problems also. Groups with vested interests can delay rational progress toward specialization. Contention often arises over the costs of subsidization, particularly when, as is commonly the case, industry is oversubsidized and inefficient manufacturers are given long-term underwriting.

The LDCs have experimented with these regional trade arrangements. Countries with histories of high protectionist policies have shown only a limited ability to overcome the opposition of vested interest groups, however. This is true of LAFTA, a trade arrangement among the Spanish and Portuguese-speaking countries of South America plus Mexico. Sometimes the loss of border taxes is too great a cost to pay. Such taxes in areas of Africa, for example, are important revenue sources for the government. And a recent complaint from Latin America is that common markets attract multinationals that profit at the expense of the potential domestic industry they preclude. Political distrust among the member countries has historically been another destabilizing force.

Interestingly measures of regional trade intensity are highest in Asia, where tariffs have not been as high as in Latin America, but where preferential trading arrangements such as free trade areas or common markets are less prevalent. The Central American Common Market nevertheless was reputed to be the most successful common market among LDCs. Composed of El Salvador, Guatemala, Honduras, Nicaragua, and Costa Rica, its earlier period of vibrancy has unfortunately not been sustained. Political tensions among the members caused the turnaround. Mexico, the most advanced economy of Central America, was not a member since she would tend to dominate her smaller, less advanced neighbors. Yet even before the upheavals of the 1980s, there was tension among the more homogeneous members over the relative advantages each received. Similar tensions strained the Andean Common Market, made up of Chile, Peru, Ecuador, Colombia and Venezuela, and Chile eventually dropped out.

Proponents of intermediate technology maintain that more trade among LDCs may promote development of a capital goods industry responsive to specific LDC manufacturing conditions. Simpler machines and goods, they argue, would utilize abundant domestic resources more efficiently. Interestingly India has begun to export such capital goods to other LDCs, and her comparative advantage may be related to scale.

Current Emphasis: Export Promotion

Generally there are growth externalities to be gained by industrialization, especially when population density is high relative to the resource base. The main criticisms of LDC experience with subsidies to infant industries have been that (a) they tend to be excessive and hence lead to imbalances and foreign exchange crises, and (b) they have been the wrong type and poorly administered.

Attention has turned from fostering industry in the area of import substitution to export promotion. This is sometimes referred to as an "outward-looking" industrialization policy. Such a policy tends to minimize the foreign exchange constraint since exports of manufactures help diversify exports and even improve the terms of trade; and the import content of export industries is generally lower than that of the import substitution industry since the LDC is producing a good in which it has a comparative advantage.

Yet experience shows that exports of manufactures tend to require a prior infancy period of growth oriented mainly toward the home market or a common market of LDCs at similar stages of development. When the correct subsidies are used to encourage the necessary infrastructure, human capital development, and technical absorptive capacity, an industrial supportive network develops, allowing the efficiency needed to compete successfully in manufactures exports. A reputable delivery system of sufficient quantity and reliable quality, along with innovative products and accurate cost control are required for success in world trade. Manufactures exports are more apt to be successful when launched from an economy with a beginning industrial base servicing home-market industries (Bhagwati and Srinivason 1979, p. 21).

Export industries based on raw-materials processing are often successful at fairly early stages of an economy's general industrialization.

Sometimes, however, they must depend upon foreign know-how and investment.

The LDC faces protectionist barriers raised against manufactures export products in which it typically has a comparative advantage. As many LDCs enter into competition with each other in producing similar manufactures exports, they may meet deteriorating terms of trade for such manufactures and increased protectionism. However, manufactures exports promise more growth potential than many raw materials; and they help diversify export earnings. Reduced protectionism among LDCs could help their manufactures export potential.

Finally, a policy of export promotion means that at least some of the LDC's industries are selling in the highly competitive markets of world trade. Manufactures exports enable the firm or industry to achieve scale economies while avoiding the noncompetitive market structure associated with scale when domestic markets in LDCs can support only one firm or a few in an industry. Even with a high trade profile, however, monopoly can characterize many areas of a newly industrializing economy, and the allocative inefficiencies of imperfect competition in industry can be large in LDCs.

This concludes our general discussion of industrial promotion. In the remaining sections Indian industrialization experience during earlier planning years serves to illustrate some of the topics presented.

REFERENCES

Bhagwati, J. N. and Desai, Padma. 1970. *India, Planning for Industrialization.* London: Oxford University Press.

———— and Srinivason, T. N. 1979. Trade Policy and Development. In *International Economic Policy,* edited by R. Dornbusch and J. A. Frenkel. Baltimore, MD: The Johns Hopkins University Press.

Bhalla, A. S. 1975. *Technology and Employment in Industry.* International Labour Organization.

Hirschman, Albert. 1958. *The Strategy of Economic Development.* New Haven, CT: Yale University Press.

Little, Ian; Scitovsky, Tibor; and Scott, Maurice. 1970. *Industry and Trade in Some Developing Countries: A Comparative Study.* London: Oxford University Press.

Stewart, F. 1977. *Technology and Underdevelopment.* Boulder, CO: Westview Press.

Yotopoulos, P. A. and Nugent, J. B. 1976. *Economics of Development,* edited by R. Dornbusch and J. A. Frenkel. New York: Harper and Row Publishers.

India's Early Industrial Planning: 1951–66

By her size India dominates the subcontinent of South Asia. She is the second-most populous country of the world, after China, but has only one third China's land area. Along with China, India is among the poorest countries of the globe. Among her greatest achievements is the adoption of a democratic form of government despite a poor population riven by many languages and sects. The seeds for democracy were sown under the country's long British rule. Despite her poverty, India enjoys great political prestige among the family of nations. Now independent and socialist in political outlook, India has received large amounts of foreign aid from both communist and Western powers.

Amidst high illiteracy, India has islands of highly skilled technicians and scientists, some internationally acclaimed. Today the vast majority of her people are still employed in the agricultural sector despite the development since World War II of a broad industrial base. Before turning to particulars of the early development of industry, it is well to note at the outset that it is difficult to judge and compare India's overall economic performance with that of other developing countries for several reasons:

■ The sheer magnitude and diversity of India's underdevelopment and poverty make progress slow.

■ India is a democratic country—a rarity among developing nations. Democratic planning procedures must incorporate innumerable compromises that do not encumber authoritarian planning regimes.

■ India has sought to achieve socialist distribution goals simultaneously with growth. To some degree this may have involved trade-offs, at least in the short turn, although her efforts along these lines have mostly resulted in preventing a worsening of inequality.

Economic performance in India is still highly influenced by agriculture and by foreign exchange constraints. She has experienced increases in per capita GNP in the postwar period of around 1.5 percent—not enough to raise the masses above poverty levels that are severe by international standards.

INDUSTRIALIZATION GOALS UNDER THE FIRST THREE FIVE-YEAR PLANS

India had a nascent industrial base at the time she won independence from Britain, in 1947. Beginning with the first five-year plan in 1951, the government took steps that would greatly enlarge her industrial sector, private and public. The country's planning goals in the period 1951–66 were colored by a particular orientation toward industrialization that, with hindsight, has proven inapplicable to labor surplus economies.

The conventional economic wisdom during the 1950s was that foreign trade could not serve as an engine of growth because of price and income inelasticity of demand for conventional export commodities, that development must be inward-looking, and that for a large economy such as India import substitution should encompass and even emphasize the capital goods and heavy industry sectors. Two reasons for investment in the capital goods or heavy industry sector were given: Scale economies and higher rates of saving were achievable with these capital-intensive industries.

Greater profits both from new state industries and private industry could be a source of new saving. Employment, it was argued, would *eventually* be higher than under a less capital-intensive approach because of a faster rate of capital accumulation. In the interim it was planned that growth in jobs would be adequate to absorb a portion of the increase in the labor force as population grew. The lessons of the Classical economists regarding population pressures on food supplies were downplayed, as were their arguments about comparative advantage.

Some saw potential success for India in achieving rapid growth rates similar to those reached by the Soviet economy, which had invested in capital-intensive industries and raised savings through state profits. The Soviets' growth rate at the time was outstanding, but their economy was very different from the Indian. The USSR was not densely populated. Raw materials were plentiful and labor was actually scarce relative to natural resources. In addition, the Soviet economy had relatively greater export capacity in agricultural and raw materials during its early industrial thrust, in part from centralized control of grains. Furthermore, the planners could ensure savings because they controlled the economy, and did not have to respond to public pressures upon decision-making.

These were among the two countries' major differences ignored in the saving-investment centered planning of the time that caught hold in India. And her performance reflected the limitations of such a growth strategy. More-

over, India had a strong private sector. She used centralized controls to implement her planning in the private and public sectors during this period. Again, there were similarities to the Soviet approach. Both economies suffered from distortions caused by the effect of central controls upon resource allocation. In a society of such profound poverty as India, there was less leeway for inefficiencies. Absolute poverty increased. Eventually she moved away from the worst mistakes of the initial planning approach.

PLANNING DISTORTIONS AND THEIR EFFECTS

Bhagwati and Padma Desai have documented the inefficiencies arising from the early Indian experience with fairly detailed target planning for industry down to the *product* level (1970). The heart of the implementation mechanism to achieve plan goals was a fairly comprehensive industrial licensing system, along with some price controls and curbs on distribution of scarce goods such as iron, steel, and cement. The public sector grew rapidly and was another area for implementing plan goals. In the trade sector, quotas and strict control over foreign exchange were the main methods for guiding industrial growth. Licensing was used to allocate foreign exchange; tariffs were of little consequence. Imports were permitted only if they were essential and not available domestically. Allocation of imports and other scarce items was by industries, and because of the enormity of the task, allotments were granted on the basis of plant capacity, employment, past imports, or other rules-of-thumb. There was pressure upon elected officials to ensure fairness as opposed to efficiency in allocation. Smaller firms tended to lose out, however.

Targets such as increased import substitution in capital goods and consumer goods were set without precise identification of infant industries. These goals guided the licensing and other control schemes. However, private sector investment not targeted was not strictly ruled out if it could overcome the handicap of being outside the allocation controls of scarce inputs. In fact actual investment was quite different from plan targets. And not surprisingly, domestic production of luxury goods no longer imported sprang up.

The subsidies to the industrial sector were excessive because careful identification of infant industries was neglected, and because implementation of targets via the wrong types of direct controls bred inefficiencies. Critics pointed out that excessive or inappropriate subsidies created sectoral imbalances. Disequilibrium conditions showed up in agriculture in the form of food shortfalls and in trade in the lack of foreign exchange. These dificiencies were met to some degree by foreign aid. The aid was insufficient, however, to prevent excess capacity brought on by import inadequacies. Specifically, trade imbalances were related to the following:

■ Industrial output targets greater than import capacity;
■ A high import content per unit of industrial output;
■ Food imports made necessary by inadequate transformation of agriculture;
■ Sluggish performance by traditional commodity exports due in part to the inability of these sectors to bid for resources and in part to inelastic foreign demand;
■ Failure to develop new, labor-intensive export goods;
■ Additional subsidies to the capital-intensive import substitution sector so that it could export goods in which India had a comparative disadvantage in order to absorb excess capacity and achieve scale economies, while earning foreign exchange to pay for the high import content of this sector;
■ An overvalued exchange rate.

As executed the plan was not supportive of equity and even worked against fair distribution. The licensing system for industry production and imports combined with import quotas created wealth in the private sector from monopoly advantages. Licenses for expanding existing industrial capacity were more easily obtained than for new plants. Once a firm received authorization for import substitution, it could expand more readily than new competitors could enter the industry. Protection from imports through quotas ensured survival and even profitability. The lack of competition contributed to the slow growth in factor productivity experienced in the industrial sector.

Quotas on imported inputs instead of tariffs means that those with import licenses had access to an input good with a domestic scarcity price higher than the import price. When final goods prices reflected the domestic scarcity value of all inputs, there was a gain for the producer from the license to import needed materials at world prices. If a tariff had been used instead of quotas to achieve development goals, the outcome would have been less distorting and revenue would have been generated for the state to help finance development. Not surprisingly, the licenses for foreign exchange themselves had a price when sold to other firms in the industry so that some firms could make profits just from gaining a license. And the bureaucratic inefficiencies and pressures were such that corruption arose in allocation of licenses, compounding the system's economic inefficiencies.

In sum, India's early planning approach encountered sectoral imbalances leading to crises in agriculture and foreign exchange, and limited employment opportunities outside of farming. The indiscriminate promotion of heavy industry and manufacturing through overly protectionist policies and poorly conceived central controls created distortions. These and the lack of competition behind tariff walls fostered inefficiencies India could ill afford. And the planning procedures had many aspects that contributed to inequality in a country politically committed to limiting inequality.

Planning mistakes of the period between 1951 and 1966 were a costly lesson for such a poor country. Yet the task of organizing economic activity with inadequate information within the milieu of Indian social institutions and preexisting distortions was enormous. Eventually India corrected some of its more damaging policies, moving toward more labor-intensive industry and a more outward-looking approach. Despite the shortcomings of the early plan's procedures and strategy, India overcame the historical tendency for its per capita income to stagnate or even fall. And some of the groundwork of the early planning provided a springboard for improved performance in the decades ahead.

Foreign Savings as a Supplement to National Savings

chapter

13

ountries such as Japan, Russia, and China have chosen development paths using relatively small savings inflows. In the case of the United Kingdom, economic evolution was accompanied by net savings outflows. And interestingly, countries that historically have received similar rates of *per capita* savings inflows have had markedly differing development rates (Hughes 1979, p. 106). In some cases savings inflows have exerted a seemingly strong positive influence on growth for some of today's LDCs and for a number of MDCs when they were emerging. On the other hand, certain forms of foreign capital inflow are viewed today by LDCs with apprehension and considered to be a mixed blessing. In this chapter we seek to identify the potentially positive and negative sides of foreign savings inflow.

FORMS AND IMPACT OF SAVINGS INFLOWS

Potential Impact of Long-Term Capital Inflow: An Overview of Basics

Before examining the exact form of the foreign savings inflow, it is helpful to use the framework of the aggregate production function to highlight the capacity that savings inflow has to affect aggregate growth variables and the scarcity value of resource inputs. In this highly simplified abstraction of an economy, the stream of foreign savings has the potential for increasing the rate of capital formation, raising labor productivity, and accelerating the rate of technical change. Consumption may rise at a faster rate with foreign capital because output also does, yielding greater income growth. Consumption may also expand as a percentage of national income because less national savings are needed to support a given growth rate.

It is quite possible that a greater rate of capital formation accompanying foreign savings inflow will raise the scarcity value of labor relative to capital. When this happens and resources reflect their scarcity value, the ratio of wages to profits increases. Or, in cases where the labor force grows faster than capital financed with national savings, foreign savings inflow may prevent a fall in per worker capital and output. The ratio of wages to profits, then, would fall in the absence of foreign capital inflow.

When there are diminishing returns to capital, it is possible that profits decline absolutely as well as relatively as a result of foreign capital inflow. With shrinking profits, payment for savings inflows from past periods falls, raising national income. Technical change may interfere with these results, however, when the technological progress accompanying external capital inflow is capital using and laborsaving.

The exact impact of foreign savings is actually more complex than these potential effects identified from the aggregate production function. To understand more fully the impact of this inflow upon development, we must expand our framework of analysis. We begin by noting that the proportion of the increment to output that goes to national resources relative to payment for the foreign capital varies with the form that the capital inflow takes and with the market conditions or other contractual arrangements that set returns to the foreign savings. The chapter now delves into these areas in more detail.

Forms of Long-Term Capital Inflow

Developing countries may use foreign savings to supplement or substitute for domestic savings in their development. There are several conduits through which the savings in MDCs can be made available to LDCs for the long term. The private sector of MDCs may make savings available through purchase of LDC bonds (private or government), acquisition of stock, and direct investment, that is, the operations in the LDC of a foreign-controlled firm that are financed in part or totally by MDC savings.

Governments through their taxing power make MDC savings available to LDCs directly and indirectly via international agencies such as regional development banks or the World Bank. Some of this savings is made available on a concessionary basis and is called foreign aid. A mixture of loans and grants compose foreign aid. The loans generally have at least a 25 percent grant element.

Some MDC savings made available to LDCs are from foreign income arising in the LDC, usually as a result of previous inflows from abroad. Profits earned on foreign investment may remain in the country and be reinvested. Interest payments on past loans may be offered to borrowers rather than spent or repatriated.

Foreign savings made accessible to the LDC allow real output to increase by yielding foreign exchange that can purchase imports to supplement domestic goods and resources. This is true of both savings that enter the country from abroad and savings of foreigners arising in the LDC. Savings from income earned by foreign resources in LDCs are potential claims against LDC foreign exchange earnings since foreign income that is repatriated must be in the form of MDC currency. Thus, as the next section illustrates, when foreign savings enter from abroad, imports can exceed exports. When foreign earnings in the LDC are lent, the developing country avoids the need to cut imports to allow repatriation of foreign earnings. When the original investment is repatriated or amortized through repayment of loans or sale of foreign assets to locals, claims on export earnings arise.

For today's LDCs the form that long-term capital inflow takes varies with the level of the immature economy's development. At early stages the country with natural resources sought on world markets will be able to borrow to develop them and/or attract investment by foreign firms into their export sectors. When export earnings per capita are high and royalties paid for resources ample, the country at this stage has no need of further capital inflows since its absorptive capacity is limited. (The absorptive capacity of an LDC is discussed in more detail in a subsequent section.) Poor countries without resources that can command high amounts of foreign exchange relative to domestic absorptive capacity generally must depend upon foreign aid to supplement domestic savings. LDCs without strong export earnings at early stages of economic evolution tend to be considered poor credit risks on international capital markets, and their governments cannot float bonds to raise financial capital. Without foreign aid they are thrown back on their own domestic savings capacity.

An LDC must develop a domestic manufacturing sector and a minimum of human capital before *sizable* amounts of direct foreign investment stream into manufacturing. When this happens the LDC is beyond early stages of development, and some have the capacity to enter world capital markets and sell bonds. For example, by far the dominant portion of United States manufacturing investment abroad is in wealthier Latin American countries. Foreign aid available at this stage is connected typically to political rationale for the aid or to foreign exchange shortfalls. These wealthier Latin American countries have established a domestic savings capacity. It is at this stage of development that foreign direct investment may replace potential domestic investment if bottlenecks limit the total investment the LDC markets can support and there is a strong proclivity for national and foreign investment. On the other hand, the foreign direct investment could clear out domestic bottlenecks, allowing larger realized savings and investment. Before discussing in greater depth each form of long-term capital inflow and the impact it may have upon LDC development, it is helpful to consider patterns of savings inflow as a whole over time and their impact upon foreign exchange.

For the aggregate economy net capital inflow exists when earnings reinvested and new capital from abroad exceed any repayment of loans or repatriation of capital stock owned by foreigners. As mentioned, the absorptive capacity and borrowing capacity of LDCs at early stages of development are low. Foreign savings entering the LDC generally averages 20 percent of total savings. With national growth, reinvested earnings and new capital inflows expand, but at a slower rate than repayment of loans and repatriation of capital abroad. National savings expand with growth and net savings coming in tend to fall as a percentage of GNP and total savings (see table 1.1, chapter 1).

Aggregate Net Capital Flows

The length of the period over which there is a net capital inflow depends upon the inflow's expansion rate relative to the inevitable outflows in the form of debt repayment that follow past investment from abroad. Continuous foreign direct investment can prolong a period of net capital inflow. In fact, if continuous foreign direct investment is large enough, the LDC could achieve MDC status before entering a period of net capital outflow where new savings inflow and reinvested earnings are exceeded by repatriation of capital from past investment plus repayment of loans.

When there is a net flow of capital outward, the LDC is no longer a nation where foreign savings are available to supplement domestic capital formation, and so must export part of its current savings abroad. In contrast to repatriation of earnings, there is no exchange of domestic product for the export earnings, and output available to the national economy falls. LDCs further along the development path that nationalize foreign investment often have such a net capital outflow; so do LDCs that have borrowed, need to repay the loans, and are unable to borrow additional savings above the repayment. And net capital outflow typically occurs in periods of political instability. The LDC cannot arrange further foreign borrowings because of high risk.

Data by country for public and private capital flows and aid were presented in tables 10.2 and 10.3 in chapter 10. Communist China is a well-known example of a country with an outflow of capital at a time of extremely low per capita income. In the 1950s Russia severed relations with the Mainland Chinese and demanded repayment of its loans. This created a net capital outflow since there were no other outside sources of capital at the time. Communist countries are averse to foreign ownership and have no sizable foreign direct investment. More currently, debt repayment problems deepened for many LDCs as a result of the worldwide dislocations in trade and finance of the 1970s. This was in part the outcome of increased short-term debt servicing problems.

Capital Flows and the Balance-of-Payments Accounts

Note that net capital flows do not include repatriated earnings, only reinvested earnings. Earnings repatriated must be kept distinct from a capital outflow, both in their effects upon output available to the domestic economy and, hence, investment and consumption, and in their effects upon a country's balance-of-payments accounts and its foreign exchange. A capital outflow is a debit entry in the *capital* account of the balance of payments. It must be offset by an excess of exports (credit entry) over imports (debit entry) in the *current* account of the balance of payments as the economy frees foreign exchange to accommodate the capital outflow. In this way national savings are made available to foreign countries. (Analogously, during the period a country experiences a net capital inflow, imports exceed exports.)

In contrast, when foreign earnings arise they are treated in the national accounting as imported services of foreign capital, an item entered as a debit with other imports in the current account. When the earnings are repatriated, no surplus in the balance of payments is required to accommodate the foreign exchange transfers. Moreover, the repatriated earnings, while they absorb foreign exchange from exports, free claims over an equal value of national product generated by the foreign firm while it is creating earnings so that domestic output available to the LDC does not drop. In contrast, when there is a net savings outflow, output available to the economy declines as export earnings are sent abroad and potential imports are forgone.

Summing up, new capital inflows bring in additional foreign exchange and require a deficit in the current account of the balance of payments; that is, these inflows require a current account with imports in excess of exports and a balancing credit entry in the capital account of foreign capital inflow. Table 13.1 shows the balance of payments for a country with net capital inflows. Net capital outflows absorb foreign exchange and thus require a surplus of exports over imports in the current account of the balance of payments, with a balancing debit entry in the capital account of foreign capital outflows. Foreign earnings are treated as payment for the import of the services of foreign resources. Repatriated earnings create claims upon export income, and reinvested earnings are part of capital inflow and reduce claims upon foreign exchange.

Debit		(millions of pesos)	Credit	
Current Account				
Merchandise Imports	1,000	Merchandise Exports	1,100	
Services of Foreign Capital (earnings plus interest)	250			
Total (current a/c)	1,250		1,100	
Capital Account				
Debt Payment	15	Foreign Loans	20	
Nationalization of Foreign Firm	10	Purchase of Stock by Foreigners	5	
		Foreign Direct Investment		
		(a) reinvested earnings	100	
		(b) new capital inflow	50	
Total (capital a/c)	25		175	
Overall total	1,275		1,275	

TABLE 13.1
Balance of Payments of LDC with Net Capital Inflow

Notes:
1. New capital inflow: 150 = (exports − imports)
2. Net foreign exchange absorption associated with capital flows: (275 − 175) = 100 = (merchandise exports − merchandise imports)

Foreign Exchange Absorption: Direct and Indirect Effects

The direct effects of these flows upon foreign exchange needs should be considered. Consider first the LDC experiencing net capital inflows and repatriated earnings. Since these have opposite effects upon the need for foreign exchange, we must establish which is larger. A situation where new capital inflow exceeds repatriated earnings in the LDC is short-lived. Prolonged foreign direct investment in an LDC results in an accumulation of foreign-owned capital stock that yields earnings. These foreign earnings create claims upon foreign exchange that are lowered by reinvested earnings. Even with such reductions from earnings reinvested, claims from repatriated earnings upon foreign exchange soon exceed new capital inflows and the net effect is absorption of foreign exchange earnings. This too is illustrated in table 13.1. Debit entries of 250 million pesos exceed credit entries showing foreign capital flows of 175 million pesos.

The case of a net capital outflow with repatriated earnings is straightforward since both increase the need for foreign exchange. Overall, then, tracing the direct (versus indirect) effects upon foreign exchange earnings of aggregate capital flows reveals a possible foreign exchange absorption even under conditions of net capital inflow from new outside funds.

There are additional trace effects from foreign investment upon foreign exchange earnings. We rather arbitrarily refer to these as indirect or secondary effects. Foreign investment allows greater physical capital formation, which changes an economy's input-output matrix. It can thereby affect exports and imports through the production activity of other economic units in the economy. More information than is available in a consolidated balance-of-payments account would be needed to identify these indirect effects.

Foreign exchange absorption, should it result from foreign investment, sometimes makes it difficult for the LDC to accelerate industrial output. A situation of net capital outflow or repatriated earnings larger than net capital inflow requires adjustments in resource allocation that tend to hold back the growth of national and total industrial output and to require increased exports. These effects can be offset when, as a result of indirect effects, the foreign investment increases exports, reduces the need for imports, or raises the productivity of national resources. To analyze these effects and others, we turn to further discussion of each form of savings inflow.

Stocks, Bonds, and Long-Term Loans

The LDC may sell stocks and/or bonds to foreigners. Over time such transactions have savings-inflow and earnings-repatriation effects. When stocks are sold back to nationals or bonds mature, there is a savings outflow. These financial instruments are often referred to as portfolio investment. This type of investment was large during the period 1870–1913. The funds came from private sources in more advanced countries and went in large part to private borrowers in various parts of the globe, including America, Australia, and other countries now developed. The largest demand was for long-term borrowings for infrastructure, particularly railways and utilities.

Portfolio investment can be more risky for the foreign investor than direct foreign investment when the LDC does not have colonial ties or similar legal systems, and when LDC securities markets are underdeveloped. Today, partly because of the risk, financial intermediaries are the main participants in portfolio investment; and LDC governments or their agencies are very often the issuers of securities, especially bonds, or the applicants for loans. Thus the government of an LDC or its agency may sell bonds in world capital markets (New York, London, or the Eurocurrency market), borrow directly from MDC banks, or negotiate a loan from The World Bank. The loan from The World Bank may be "hard" or "soft." In a "hard" loan the LDC is financially strong enough to pay the going price for money in world markets and amortize the debt over a commercially acceptable period. On the other hand, the poorer LDCs that cannot raise money on world capital markets may borrow from The World Bank's International Development Association, which makes "soft" loans. Such loans, given to countries unable to compete for international capital, include grant elements in the form of interest costs below market rates, extended repayment periods, and a grace period before repayment begins. MDC governments contribute funds for soft loans.

The World Bank raises its money from MDC governments and private capital markets of the world. Thus it helps to channel global savings to LDCs. Unlike commercial banks it is specifically constituted to carry on long-term lending and the global redistribution of world savings. The bank's portfolio is constituted so that enough hard loans enable it to operate commercially yet perform the important development role of transferring savings to poorer countries. One subdivision of The World Bank, the International Financial Corporation, invests in equities and seeks to stimulate private investment. Regional development banks also obtain funds from MDC governments and lend for longer-term development needs.

Foreign aid began in the period following World War II with the United States Marshall Plan. The aid was extended to war-ravaged nations to help them rebuild world prosperity and trade. It was offered to friend and foe, and was historically a most generous outpouring of funds. The aid went to advanced countries with high absorptive capacity, and was used successfully to rebuild these developed economies. Their reviving prosperity soon led to a change in aid focus to the needs of LDCs and a program under the Truman administration of technical assistance. From the very beginning foreign aid was a part of United States government policy. The precepts upon which it was based stemmed from national defense, economic relations, the urge to spread Western social institutions, and humanitarianism.

Foreign Aid

American aid to LDCs soon expanded beyond mere technical assistance; and with the breakup of colonialism and the rise of East-West tensions, industrialized countries over the globe began to participate in bilateral aid. The main sources of both trade and aid for the LDCs are the countries of the West, although individual states have received large amounts of communist help and preferential trade relations, often linked to aid projects. Many critics have felt that funds would be better allocated if more aid were channeled through multinational agencies such as the United Nations, The World Bank, and regional development banks. This would, they argue, diminish, if not eliminate, the influence of national self-interest among donor countries.

The emphasis of Western assistance has vacillated between loans and grants. Growth targets in programs for economic progress generally are ambitious, and development is time-consuming when compared with postwar reconstruction of advanced countries. During the postwar years, foreign aid to LDCs continued, leading to an accumulation of loan repayment and servicing charges. Some aid recipients were unable to meet these payments and yet were still in need of net aid inflows. These LDCs had to seek help in refinancing their debt to avoid defaulting on loan repayments and debt servicing. Some loans were forgiven, in other words, turned into grants.

Over the postwar period the United States has dominated aid flows in terms of aggregate amounts given. Much of the American aid is military, and it is difficult to disentangle the economic from the military. In later years the United States has not been a front-runner measured by ability to pay. That is, the United States is not a top donor when aid is calculated as a proportion of GNP. Lower world prosperity and historically high inflation diminished real aid flows to LDCs in the 1970s.

EFFICIENT ABSORPTION OF AID

LDCs that are least developed are often described as having limited power to absorb foreign aid. This does not mean the poorer people could not use the aid to increase their consumption. It means that complementary domestic resources are limited, so that the foreign aid would be used on marginal investment projects of high risk, high import content, and low return. The payoff in greater productivity would be low, and in the case of loans, the aid might not increase output enough to cover even subsidized loan costs. This limited absorptive power means that the very poorest peoples in Africa, for example, may receive less assistance per capita than somewhat more advanced countries that can absorb more aid productively.

The classic case of limited absorptive capacity is the OPEC countries, with their high oil earnings per capita. The oil funds are used for consumption and many low-return projects, and foreign technicians are imported to raise the absorptive capacity.

The Two-Gap Model

Some economists, concentrating upon explaining the need for aid, point out that the LDC at various stages of development can encounter both a savings and/or a foreign exchange constraint that limit its growth potential. Hollis Chenery and Alan Strout in their "two-gap" model emphasize the role foreign aid plays in alleviating both shortages (1966). Foreign aid is emphasized as opposed to other forms of savings inflow since the debt service burden is lower, and other forms of savings may not be available (or acceptable) to the LDC.

Assume an LDC has established a target growth rate that will generate an increase in income per capita of 2 percent a year, given the economy's expected rate of population growth. Assume also that the economy has structural rigidities that prevent it from raising savings enough to achieve the target growth rate, and/or structural or resource limitations that prevent it from increasing exports or lowering imports enough to fulfill its plan goals. Foreign aid inflows can fill both gaps since foreign savings flow into the LDC in the form of currency exchange. The amount of aid needed is then determined by an identification of the larger gap—savings or foreign exchange. We now consider each gap in turn.

Assume industry is the sector whose growth the planners wish to maximize, once food needs are met. This is the sector that needs savings in the form of exports to acquire capital imports. The foreign exchange gap can be illustrated by assuming a target industrial output. This is shown as output b_t in figure 13.1. Given a terms of trade of T, import potential falls short of target growth needs by $m_t - m'$. This is the foreign exchange gap.

Notice that an improvement in the terms of trade could solve the problem as readily as foreign aid. In fact, LDCs tend to prefer com-

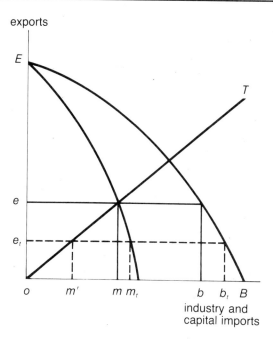

FIGURE 13.1

Foreign Exchange Gap

With a target industrial output of b_t and exports of e_t, there is an import shortfall of $(m_t - m')$.

modity agreements or other preferential trade arrangements that improve their terms of trade as a solution in lieu of aid. Recall from the three-sector presentation of this graph that a reduction in food needs (increase in savings) or improved technology could also dissolve this constraint, assuming resources are mobile.

The foreign exchange constraint may be related to an inelastic demand for export goods. Figure 13.2 illustrates the ability of the LDC to save by restricting food consumption to F. The resources freed for industrialization, however, will not achieve target industry output at coordinate point k. Exports of e' cause a drop in the terms of trade, and hence imports, by raising exports above level e, after which demand is inelastic. Even with exports of e and imports of m, the maximum industrial output that the LDC is capable of is below b_t, given the shape of T_k. The foreign exchange gap in this case is $(y - z)$.

The country maximizing industrial output without foreign aid will shift resources over to food output, lowering EB and EM so that EM crosses T_k at point z. Consumption is high here not because of an inability to save but because of a foreign exchange constraint traceable to declining terms of trade along T_k. Improving productivity, and thus AA' and EB shifting outward, allows higher consumption but no increase in industrial output. Only with foreign aid or the ability to diversify exports into areas with better terms of trade can the LDC overcome a foreign exchange constraint of this type. The foreign subsidies should be designed to aid the country in finding new exports.

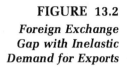

FIGURE 13.2

*Foreign Exchange
Gap with Inelastic
Demand for Exports*

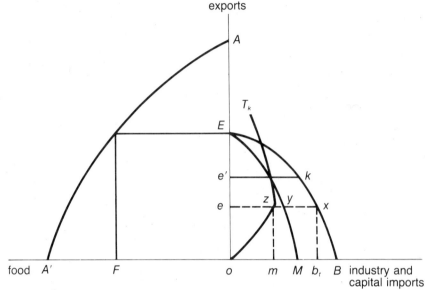

With target industrial output of b_t, there is a foreign exchange shortfall of $(y-z)$. Exports are at their maximum level at point z.

The savings constraint is illustrated in figure 13.3. Again industrial sector growth is the residual sector, limited by the food (consumption) needs of the populace. Targeted output is b_t, a level beyond curve EB. Output b_t and the needed imports (m_t) require an outward shift in EB to $E'B'$, and can only be reached with less food consumption (more saving), and the use of freed resources for industrial expansion. The savings gap $(F - F_t)$ can be filled by importing either food or resources that industry can use. Alternatively, the foreign aid could be used to finance technical change that would raise productivity so that b_t was achievable. This technical improvement could require more foreign aid than food subsidy, but would yield a higher long-term growth effect.

When the LDC calculates its foreign aid needs, they would reflect the larger gap—savings versus foreign exchange. Of course it is rare, if not unprecedented, that a country can continuously fill its aid gaps. Moreover, the need for foreign assistance can be reduced by an inflow of savings in other forms that close the gaps.

Tied Aid   Specifying what foreign aid must be spent on can lower its efficiency. For example, in the past aid has been tied in the sense that it took the form of actual shipment of food or required that the aid money be spent in the country proffering it. Sometimes food imports are inferior to other imports an LDC needs for increasing output. The inferiority can derive from disincentive effects on the food sector when increased food supplies depress prices rather than freeing resources from agriculture.

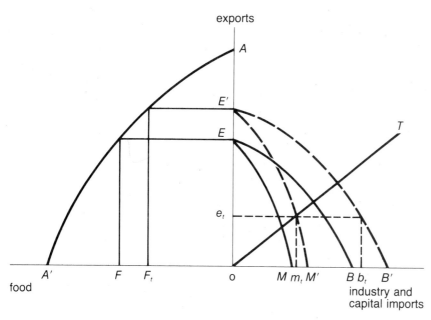

FIGURE 13.3
Saving Gap

To achieve a target output level for industrial production of b_t, food production must be F_t. The saving gap of $(F - F_t)$ shows the shortfall in the country's ability to forgo consumption to achieve the target industrial output.

Moreover, imports to raise agricultural productivity may have a higher long-run pay-off per unit of aid expenditure than food from abroad. And when aid must be spent in the country of origin, the LDC is not free to purchase the input with the highest return. Instead it buys more expensive or less productive inputs. This not only lowers the effectiveness of the aid expenditure, it also burdens the LDC in that output expansion per unit of aid currency is lower. When aid is in the form of a loan, the LDC is less able to repay the loan because of inefficient purchases with aid money.

The inflow of private funds to LDCs exceeds official aid funds. Foreign direct investment dominates these private sources and is an important, if highly controversial, form of savings inflow. For this reason we discuss the economic implications of foreign direct investment in some detail.

There is no clear agreement in the literature on just what is the dominant motivating force in foreign direct investment, given conditions of imperfect competition. The firm may be seeking the location of highest expected returns. It may be looking for firm growth or diversification of risk. It may need outlets for internally generated funds when home markets are suffering from excess capacity. It may be responding to tariff walls blocking exports from the home country, or

ANALYSIS OF FOREIGN DIRECT INVESTMENT

investing abroad to protect its share of world markets. Or it could be seeking new sources of increasingly scarce raw materials or lower-cost labor. Generally profits, risk, markets, and growth are important variables to the multinational or transnational corporation moving into the LDC.

In contrast to loans that assure the lender a fixed interest payment, and require repayment of the loan principal at a set time, equity investment shares in a firm's on-going earnings after all contractual commitments and costs have been deducted from earnings. The investor in equity assumes more risk. For the LDC, this means that it must pay more on the average for foreign savings in equity form. Yet it does not pay for a specific project when the investment yields losses except to the degree that contractual payments for local inputs are not paid in times of insufficient earnings. In contrast, when savings inflow is in loan form, the LDC is obligated to pay interest and repay the principal even when the project undertaken with the funds fails. But there is a contractual limit on payments. The transfer of savings, however, is only one aspect of foreign direct investment.

The Foreign Firm as a Set of Imported Inputs

The foreign firm can be viewed as a set of imported inputs—inputs of capital, technology, entrepreneurship, marketing skills, and the like. The identical set or a substitute set may be available to the LDC as direct imports without foreign ownership. Management contracts are available to supply foreign human capital, foreign savings can be raised on international financial markets to purchase imports of machinery and other capital imports, licensing contracts permit the use of technology protected by patents, and some private firms contract for project development and technical assistance.

If there were an integrated world economy with perfect competition, perfect information, and complete mobility of resources, and a world financial market unrestricted by national governments, world savings would be allocated to all economies so that this resource's return at the margin was the same in any investment in any economy. And with small firms, perfect competition, profit maximization, free entry, and no technical monopolies, resource inputs acquired domestically and abroad would cost the same to each firm, whether foreign or nationally owned. The point is that for there to be important differences in costs of the set of imports provided by the foreign firm compared with the costs available to the national firm, these conditions must be violated, as indeed they are.

Generally there are imperfect competition, economies of scale, technological monopolies, uncertainty and risk, restricted capital markets and savings flows; and resources available to the foreign firm for which there are no close substitutes may not be available to the national firm. In addition, under conditions of imperfect competition the amount of foreign savings inflow will vary depending upon its form— direct foreign investment in wholly owned branches or subsidiaries, joint ventures involving national and foreign ownership, or foreign portfolio investment that provides additional capital to nationally run firms. Thus, in the real world situation the foreign firm may provide some inputs at higher cost and some at lower cost; it may also provide some inputs not available to domestic operations and for which there are no substitutes.

The differential cost of the set of imported inputs with foreign versus national ownership can vary over time. Foreign direct investment may provide imported inputs at lower cost upon initial entry but the cost may rise at a later point in time, perhaps because of changed domestic potential or increased monopoly conditions exploited by the foreign firm. Under these conditions there is an inclination to nationalize the foreign operations to lower their cost to the LDC. A problem with a policy of planned nationalization to minimize costs of imported inputs is that such a policy may discourage foreign investment in areas where it is desired.

Foreign direct investment in an LDC can produce externalities, both positive and negative. The positive dynamics of foreign direct investment are centered around the net additions to national capital formation traceable to such firms, their impact upon the rate of technological change, and how much they contribute to a reduction of foreign exchange constraints. Negative externalities can be linked to the same general areas. If positive externalities exist, the LDC receives gains for which it does not pay. When the externalities are negative, the LDC encounters a cost caused by the presence of the foreign enterprise that is not internalized into the firm's cost structure. Comments upon the various areas of expected externalities are in order.

Externalities and Foreign Direct Investment

The problems surrounding the use of modern technology were explained in chapter 5. The foreign firm generally transfers modern technology into the LDC with little modification. This can be efficient for the foreign company when the price it pays for capital is relatively low and the capital replaces skilled labor that is relatively expensive in the LDC. Generally there is limited financial advantage to the foreign firm from modifying either the product or the process. However, such technology transfer can curtail linkage effects and domestic employment. Both the product mix and the production process in the foreign sector may contribute to dualism and inequality in the LDC (Helleiner 1975).

The foreign firm must have linkages with the domestic economy for there to be strong positive technical externalities not paid for through royalties and the firm's profits. When linkages exist, the foreign firm can foster efficient technology transfer in a particular sector; or it may create externalities that redound to the total economy. Cases have occurred where foreign infrastructure investment lowered costs for LDC industries and created technical efficiencies shared with the LDC. In another example the foreign firm supports technical change in agriculture by producing and successfully marketing low-cost fertilizer needed for the introduction of higher-yield hybrids. And labor training is often mentioned as a positive externality of foreign firms.

The foreign exchange impact of the foreign firm can be complex to trace. A graphic presentation appears in the next section. Here we note the basic areas of potential reaction. Foreign direct investment creates income in the LDC using resources from abroad combined with local ones. The income generated is equivalent to expenditures by the firm on its output less taxes, if any. Part of this income is a return to foreign resources. When the income earned by foreign resources is spent on output in the LDC, it places claims on output equivalent to the share of foreign earnings. When the foreign income is saved but *remains* in the LDC, it lays no claims on current (as opposed to future) output, thus freeing resources to form capital. When the savings are repatriated, claims arise on export earnings because foreign exchange must be made available for repatriation to take place.

In sum, while the foreign resources create output that determines the value of their income, they also place demands upon export earnings rather than on domestic goods when the earnings are repatriated. If the foreign firm, through its activities in the LDC, increases foreign exchange earnings or reduces imports, then there may not be a negative foreign exchange impact, depending on the net effect. Or, if new inflows of savings equal in the aggregate repatriated earnings and there are no secondary consequences, there will be no net claim upon the export earnings of the LDC. Should new inflows minus repatriated earnings be positive, the foreign exchange constraint will be reduced, again assuming no secondary absorption of foreign exchange by the foreign firm.

Other externality effects associated with foreign exchange are often seen. For example, capital flows and earnings repatriation related to foreign direct investment can fluctuate, and are especially sensitive to investment profitability and security and even to business swings in the home country. Variations in such streams mean that foreign exchange availability is less predictable. Foreign firms can add to risk and uncertainty for the LDC when they contribute to increased fluctuations in foreign exchange availability.

A country's terms of trade can be affected by the supply and demand for foreign exchange. Foreign firms affect foreign exchange through influencing exports, imports, and capital flows, directly or indirectly. A foreign firm may, for example, use no imported inputs in its production process; yet, it could instigate the manufacture by local firms of intermediate goods for its use, goods that could have high import content. An example might be the extension of a national telecommunications network to the foreign firm's production site. And other examples could be developed where the foreign firm indirectly stimulates exports. These effects can be difficult to trace and thus it is not always easy to determine empirically the net balance-of-payments result of foreign investment, or its impact upon the terms of trade. The fact that such effects occur warrants mentioning, however, since, as was shown in chapter 11, changes in the terms of trade or availability of foreign exchange have an impact upon an LDC's development.

A net inflow of foreign direct investment may stimulate national saving and capital formation or substitute for national saving, allowing greater current consumption in the LDC. If the foreign firm has linkages with the domestic economy, it may encourage supplier or related industries downstream to accelerate their investment by channeling more profits into new output capacity, perhaps employing underutilized resources for new construction or other capital goods. When idle resources are employed, GNP and hence saving and investment can rise. In cases where the foreign direct investment is supportive of national capital formation and avoids negative externalities, development can be accelerated. The additional capital raises labor productivity; and any advances in technology or scale economies that accompany the additional capital will also improve efficiency.

On the other hand, when foreign direct investment substitutes for national investment, it tends to reduce or retard the growth in national (as opposed to domestic) income and leave the LDC economy with less nationally owned productive wealth from which to generate income to service or repay foreign capital. Foreign firms can be more aggressive than national firms, in part because they operate with a more complete information set in areas such as engineering, management, and marketing, reflecting their superiority in human capital in these areas. The substitution effect will be more likely to happen when there are shortages in domestically generated resources needed for investment. The foreign firm then may bid such resources away from national investment.

Substitution can also take place when a foreign firm purchases an existing national firm. S. Lall notes that takeover activity in LDCs in recent years has been at a fairly high level and that there has been a tendency toward market dominance in manufacturing by multinational corporations (MNCs) in some sectors. He cautions, however, that more empirical work is needed before categorical statements can be made about the effects of MNCs on industrial structure in LDCs (Lall 1978).

Still and all, the economic analysis does not deal with the sensitive area of foreign firms' political influences in LDCs. Even under conditions removed from colonialism, the large multinationals, some of which generate global sales that exceed the GNP of small LDCs, may present the LDC governments with pressures for economic concessions or make decisions not in line wth national welfare as conceived by the governments involved. Multinationals have even been used as fronts for political intrigue by their home governments. Another sensitive area is the foreign firm's control of limited domestic resources under liberal property rights. Instances of the latter, however, are becoming more rare as LDCs have moved to gain greater control of their natural resources.

As indicated, the effect of foreign direct investment upon an LDC's GNP and industrialization depends upon the exact conditions surrounding the investment such as the sector of investment, the use of domestic resources, the rate of new investment inflow relative to repatriation and/or reinvestment of earnings, mobility of domestic re-

A Graphic Analysis of Foreign Direct Investment[1]

---

1. This section provides further depth of analysis for the interested reader. It may be omitted along with the short section following on factor immobility.

sources, competitive conditions, and the effect upon productivity, among other variables. There are effects on both growth and the balance of payments. Such complex and interrelated economic variables are difficult to assess with finality.

Here we try to gain insights into the multiple results that can flow from foreign direct investment by examining individual effects within the context of the simple graph of a three-sector economy. You will recall that this graph illustrates maximum output under conditions of full employment, mobile resources that are readily reallocated, perfect factor allocation, and maximum LDC technical efficiency. We assume that the economy wishes to maximize industrial output, given a certain level of food consumption. Exports are a route to obtaining imports required for industrial output; and imports, which cannot be produced domestically by the LDC, are needed in some constant proportion to industrial output. GNP increases when, for example, the terms of trade improve, raising imports per unit of exports, thus allowing industrial output to increase.

The simple model is one with foreign exchange limitations upon development and is a starting point in that it can be used to examine some of the important effects of foreign direct investment and establish conditions under which such investment is potentially beneficial or harmful to industrial transformation. Then, suppositions such as perfect mobility and allocation of resources are relaxed, and the foreign firm is assumed to possess monopoly pricing power in order to consider how this would affect the results obtained when assuming competitive returns to foreign firms. Although the analysis is incomplete, given the complex ramifications of foreign direct investment, it sorts out important strands, ties them together, and presents a guiding framework for thought.

The approach here concerns itself with foreign direct investment in new facilities as opposed to "take-over" investment. Takeover investment, while it may free national financial capital to invest in a new project, is generally viewed as having a potential for reducing GNP. This occurs when the foreign direct investment neither raises productivity of domestic resources nor results in reinvested national capital. As a result, domestic assets owned by nationals from which income is generated are reduced. Takeovers may also reduce competition and create monopoly income for the foreign firm.

The Simple Model with Foreign Investment

Using graphic analysis it is easily shown that the foreign firm does not simply add to output the marginal product of the foreign resources. The graphic approach pinpoints how foreign direct investment can affect national resource allocation and productivity and the foreign exchange constraint, among other things. The simple model illustrates the potential benefits of foreign direct investment upon an economy with a foreign exchange constraint that is seeking to transfer resources into industrial production. These advantages arise when foreign direct investment increases import potential and raises national factor productivity. The graphic analysis also shows that foreign direct investment can reduce employment or productivity of national resources when it absorbs foreign exchange or carries negative externalities. In such cases national output declines despite a rise in domestic industrial output. When foreign direct investment in the export sector brings a decline in the terms of trade, curtailing foreign exchange availability, the LDC may be worse off as a result of foreign investment in the export sector.

The simple graph illustrates how foreign direct investment that makes foreign exchange availability less predictable increases the need for greater mobility of domestic resources. In the absence of such mobility, the investment from abroad can worsen a short-run foreign exchange bottleneck and cause unemployment. Graphic presentation also shows clearly that foreign direct investment affects sectoral employment of national resources. Such investment in the industrial sector may reduce the proportion of *national* resources employed in that sector, while foreign direct investment in the export sector is more likely to increase the proportion of national resources in industry.

In demonstrating these areas of potential impact, the common assumption is that foreign direct investment is sector-specific while national resources are assumed to be mobile between sectors (Batra and Ramachandran 1980). The assumption that national resources are mobile between sectors can then be dropped and the effects of immobility examined. To simplify the analysis, we omit the food sector from the graph and consider only foreign investment in the industrial and export sectors. It is also helpful to assume that foreign-owned resources reflecting investment in a previous period are located in the LDC and that in the period under study new investment inflow and/or repatriation of investment and earnings are possible. New investment can come from profits originating in the LDC or can flow into the country from abroad.

We begin the analysis by presupposing that foreign direct investment does not shift out the production possibilities curve for LDC resources. The additional income created by foreign resources located in the LDC is a return to these resources. When the income remains in the LDC, it places claims upon gross domestic product; and when it leaves the country, it absorbs foreign exchange earnings that otherwise would have gone for imports.

Foreign Investment Specific to Industry

First consider the case where foreign direct investment is specific to the industrial sector. Figure 13.4 depicts industry output produced by foreign-owned resources located in the LDC of $b_f o$ on the vertical axis to the left of the origin. Will foreign investment in this case change the amount of domestic exports and national output originating in the industrial sector? This depends on the effect upon foreign exchange needs. Three possibilities exist: Foreign direct investment can raise, lower, or leave unchanged the need for foreign exchange, and hence exports.

Foreign investment could lower the need for national resources to generate foreign exchange. This takes place when there is an inflow of capital in excess of foreign exchange absorption from imports related to foreign investment, and repatriation of earnings and investment from the previous period. In such a case exports drop from e to e', yet imports can rise to m'. National industrial output and income rise to b'. Foreign direct investment loosens the foreign currency bottleneck by supplying savings from abroad in the form of foreign exchange.

The case where imports and repatriation of earnings, and/or capital exceed foreign capital inflow is also shown in figure 13.4. Exports move to e". Imports are cut to m", allowing exports to move ahead of potential imports by xz. This creates a surplus of export earnings to cover the foreign exchange needs of foreign firms. National industrial output drops to b". In the case of earnings repatriation or imports, the foreign firm must exchange industrial output for the foreign exchange. In the case of repatriation of capital, national savings are exchanged for foreign resources or capital used up in production (depreciation funds).

Now consider what would happen in the above case if national resources were immobile. A failure of national resources to move into the export sector and increase exports would cause a foreign exchange shortfall of xz, forcing unemployment of resources.

Foreign Investment Specific to Exports   The case where foreign direct investment is specific to the export sector is shown in figure 13.5. Foreign resources raise export output by e_fo. The terms of trade line is dropped from T to T' so that it originates at

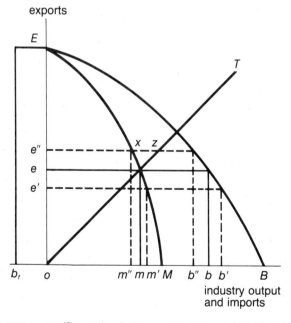

FIGURE 13.4

Foreign Investment in Industry

Foreign resources specific to the industrial sector add b_fo to industrial output. Industrial output produced with national resources can vary (as illustrated by b' and b''), depending upon the net addition or absorption of foreign exchange by the foreign firms.

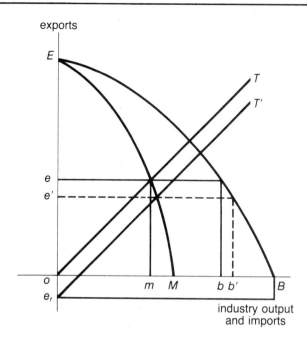

FIGURE 13.5
Foreign Investment in Exports

Foreign resources produce *e,o* exports. When foreign firms absorb none of the export earnings, industrial output can rise to *b'*.

e_f. The new level of industrial output is now dependent upon the ratio of additional export earnings not drained off by the foreign firm as imports, repatriation of profits, or repatriation of capital. When the foreign firm does not absorb any of the foreign exchange it generates, industrial output rises to *b'*. Foreign export earnings are saved or exchanged for industrial output of equivalent value.

In this case, however, the proportion of national resources in the industrial sector will not fall and is more likely to rise than where foreign direct investment is in the industrial sector. In both situations, however, the availability of foreign exchange becomes less predictable than in the absence of foreign investment because repatriation of earnings and capital flows can vary. The foreign investment requires mobility of domestic resources to maintain full employment and maximize industrial output.[2]

These conclusions depend upon the terms of trade remaining constant or improving. However, a foreign firm that increases exports and thereby lowers the terms of trade may not support an LDC's industrial growth. In fact, foreign direct investment under conditions of inelastic demand for the export good can be detrimental to the LDC. This case

---

2. All in all, however, this case illustrates why LDCs are most receptive to foreign direct investment when it locates in the export sector. The exceptions here are when the foreign firm locates in an extractive industry that is depleting national resource endowments or in plantation agriculture that creates dualism in agriculture.

is examined in the appendix at the end of the chapter. Here we move on to consider the cases where foreign firms affect the productivity of national resources. To do this we return to the assumption that the foreign direct investment is specific to the industrial sector.

Foreign Investment Affects Productivity of National Resources

In figure 13.6 the foreign firm located in the industrial sector raises the productivity of national resources when they are employed in that sector. Thus curve EB shifts outward to EB'. National income will be higher. However, just as in the case without productivity improvement, industrial output produced by national resources (b) can rise, fall, or remain the same, depending upon the effect of the outside firm upon foreign exchange availability. Because of improved productivity in the industrial sector, however, b is less likely to decline. If improved productivity takes the form of fewer imports per unit of industrial output so that the curve EM is unchanged (as illustrated), this lessens the probability that the proportion of national resources in the export sector will rise. With zero net inflow and outflow of capital and no repatriation of earnings for the period, a shift in EB to EB' and a constant EM would raise industrial output produced by national resources to b'.

Should the foreign firm create negative externalities, national resource output potential, rather than rising to EB', would drop below

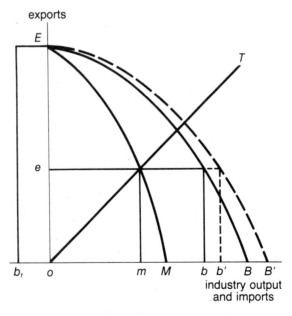

FIGURE 13.6

Foreign Investment with Externalities

Foreign resources specific to the industry sector produce output $b_r o$, and, by affecting productivity of national resources, raise EB to EB'. Foreign direct investment also lowers M/B. Industrial output can expand to b'.

the level of EB, even though there need be no unemployment. Negative externalities could arise, for instance, from differences in technology that lead to a high demand for relatively scarce national resources. Absorption of these resources by the foreign sector could lower the efficiency of the remaining national resources. It is common to find charges in the literature that the foreign firm creates negative externalities when juxtaposed with the less modern national economy. The causes of negative externalities can vary and, according to some, even include the transmission of attitudes and behavior patterns associated with modern economies that are not compatible with locally oriented, broad-gauged development. The tendency to copy the foreign firm's technology even though national costs of capital are higher is one example.

In sum, the foreign firm locating in the industrial sector raises *domestic* industrial output. However, even where it increases the productivity of national resources in the industrial sector, it can reduce the proportion of national resources there. This happens when foreign exchange is absorbed by the foreign firm or where improved productivity of resources in national industrial production and a constant M/B result in a need to allocate more resources to the export sector so that b can increase. In fact, there is a greater probability that the proportion of national resources allocated to industry will rise when the foreign firm invests in the traditional export sector rather than the industrial sector. *Total* industrial expansion is not as great, however.

A drop in the proportion of national resources in the industrial sector can lead to foreign domination of the country's industrial wealth. With industrialization, assets and hence wealth in the industrial sector expand rapidly. R. S. Newfarmer and W. R. Mueller find that in Mexico and Brazil, two rapidly industrializing nations, foreign firms own a large and growing portion of the expanding industrial wealth (1975, cited in S. Lall, 1978). Foreign domination of this wealth as it grows can irritate sensitive political nerves within an LDC. Even a country as wealthy as Canada has found outside control of industrial wealth to be of considerable political-economic significance.

Foreign Investment and Unutilized Resources

Assume now that the foreign firm employs surplus resources that would remain idle in the absence of outside investment. Assume also these are renewable resources as opposed to national resource mineral deposits. National income rises as a result of the increase in efficiency. Even when there is no net inflow of foreign savings in the period examined, national income can rise so long as the foreign sector employs idle resources.

The impact is less straightforward when, as a result of foreign investment in the export sector, deposits of natural resources are depleted by exports at a rate determined by foreign firms. In such cases e_f will gradually shrink as natural resources are depleted, leaving the country with less potential output in this sector at a later period. In other words, national wealth is being sold. The LDC must be sure that as a result of such sales, greater national wealth is created. When resources are used up faster than national absorptive power can utilize the export earnings to form new assets, then the country will be reducing its potential for development. This is the problem faced by lightly populated countries such as Saudi Arabia and the oil emirate countries of North Africa, with vast deposits of valuable natural resources sought in world markets. Mexico is also facing a decision on the optimum rate of depletion of newly discovered oil. The problem is complicated by the risk that new technology and discoveries will reduce the value of oil deposits or other depletable natural resources that are being conserved for later exploitation.

Factor Immobility   For beneficial effects to flow from foreign direct investment, national factor mobility may have to increase. In the cases shown, the acceleration of industrial output and constancy or increase in national output accompanying foreign direct investment hinged upon factor mobility of national resources. Short-run or even long-run immobility of resources under conditions of uncertainty is not uncommon in LDCs and can mean lost potential gains and/or greater declines in national industrial output associated with foreign direct investment. For example, in figure 13.4, where there is a favorable impact from foreign savings inflow and an increase in national resources employed in the industrial sector from b to b', immobile resources could mean unchanged exports and industrial output. Again, in figure 13.4, when the foreign firm absorbs foreign currency equal to xz imports, the failure of the LDC to divert resources to exports could result in foreign firms bidding away limited foreign exchange from national corporations, reducing the latter's output. GNP would drop.

Going one step further, the foreign investment may affect the degree of mobility of domestic resources. It has been mentioned that the flow of capital into a country and the flow of repatriated earnings often fluctuate, making the impact of foreign direct investment upon the balance of payments unpredictable. Uncertainties surrounding foreign exchange availability then rise, heightening risk, and risk can reduce mobility of resources. In such cases the LDC's resource allocation problems are compounded by the foreign investment.

Immobility problems could exist without foreign investment. The point is that in many cases the need for mobility rises with foreign direct investment. Moreover, changes causing dislocations and requiring factor movement would create income for domestic as opposed to foreign resources and thus offset somewhat the unemployment and other dislocation effects.

Critics of foreign direct investment emphasize that substitution effects appear when factors are immobile and foreign firms usurp limited domestic supplies. Proponents, on the other hand, point out that over time the foreign firm may help eliminate bottlenecks by accelerating the rate of growth of inadequate national resources such as foreign exchange, skilled labor, or entrepreneurship. Which impact dominates is an empirical question, and could vary among LDCs. However, our limited knowledge at present prevents any categorical statements about these countervailing forces.

This section points to several general conclusions regarding policies LDCs are likely to adopt in regard to foreign direct investment. To mitigate fluctuations in the availability of foreign exchange related to foreign direct investment, policies designed to reduce uncertainty here are often followed. Control of the timing and rate of earnings and capital repatriation is typical. Policies that regulate the ownership share of assets in the industrial sector and the rate of depletion of natural resources are also more and more prevalent today. The exact programs pursued will vary with the individual country and its specific needs and structure. Policies along these lines, however, have a trade-off in that they can cut down the inflow of foreign savings.

Generally the multinational firm operates under conditions of imperfect competition in national and international markets. The LDC with small domestic markets and few competing firms may provide monopoly pricing advantages to the foreign firm. The effects of this can be illustrated intuitively from the simple cases used. **Monopoly**

Recall, for example, that as illustrated in figure 13.4, the foreign firm exchanges industrial output for an equivalent value of export earnings in order to repatriate foreign earnings. Assume that the foreign company's price of industrial output exceeds the competitive price of national manufacturing firms because of a segmented domestic market in which the foreign firm has a monopoly. This means the foreign firm exchanges less industrial output per unit of export earnings because of its monopoly prices. The LDC's claim over units of industrial output would have declined. Or, where the foreign firm exports, as in figure 13.5, and manipulates these prices through internal transfer pricing to a parent company, the foreign exchange acquired by the LDC is affected, as is the amount of domestic output the multinational can claim by selling its foreign exchange to the LDC.

Monopoly rents and profits can raise the cost of foreign resources to the LDC over what they would cost if acquired without direct foreign investment. This presumes the foreign monopolist operates a healthy, prosperous firm where revenues are high relative to costs and risks. Monopolies tend to restrict output below what would be produced by competitive suppliers. This can accentuate shortages and factor dislocation problems.

Often monopoly rents are the price exacted for technology not obtainable otherwise because of patents. The LDC must be sure productivity gains are not wiped out or even exceeded by payments for the technology in such form as royalties or profits. Generally modern technology is not as efficient in the LDC environment as in the MDC, raising the possibility that more will be paid for the technology than is warranted by economic gains to the LDC.

Monopoly bargaining power in foreign companies' negotiations with LDC governments over prices for extractive resources such as minerals and metals affects the royalties or rents received from these resources. In very poor LDCs where land and natural resources are the main productive assets other than labor, the price received for natural resources extracted by foreign firms can have a profound effect upon the country's development.

Surveys find that the foreign firm, in particular a manufacturer, pays more for national labor than local firms. Thus, assuming the labor is homogeneous, some of the monopoly profits may be shared with locals. The foreign firm has access to cheaper capital and usually employs more of it per worker than local firms. This raises labor's productivity and hence its value to the firm. It is often profitable for the foreign employer to pay somewhat more than prevailing local wages to attract a better quality, more stable work force. In this case the additional wages are not all at the expense of the remaining local populace since the foreign firm raises labor productivity and this is the source of some, if not all, of the additional output shared with the local workers. Also, when the industrial labor force is organized, union wages may force the outside corporation to share some of its monopoly profits with native workers, reducing the loss to the LDC from monopoly pricing.

Having analyzed the various forms of foreign capital inflow, we now turn to a brief discussion of criteria for assessing optimal foreign savings inflow.

OPTIMAL SAVINGS INFLOWS

In regard to net savings inflows, two questions are pertinent: What is the optimum amount of savings inflow and what is the optimum mix in terms of the form of savings inflow? The LDC may not be able to achieve either, but the concept of optimality is difficult to ignore. Should this concept be identifiable, it would provide a useful framework for assessing foreign capital inflow.

Consider the optimum mix first. For a given level of inflow above foreign aid, how much should be loans and how much foreign direct investment? As mentioned, the outside firm can be viewed as a set of imported inputs with price tags attached, plus a charge for risk assumption. The LDC can compare costs of these inputs, including capital, the cost of lower efficiency if any from national control, and what it is willing to pay for risk assumption. It can then borrow abroad and make the investment itself or allow the foreign firm to invest, depending upon the relative cost of the two options.

Problems exist. These relative costs are not easily known, and if foreign direct investment is discouraged in one area, other foreign firms will hesitate to locate in other areas. Externalities, positive and negative, are ignored in this approach. Policies to attract more foreign direct investment can be expensive, and are not always successful. Yet most LDCs today have some policy vis-à-vis foreign direct investment, promotional and/or restrictive. This presumes a desired mix although the optimum may be influenced by noneconomic as well as economic criteria. Many place great weight upon perceived, but not necessarily measurable, externalities. In the Republic of Ireland, for example, an active promotional campaign to attract foreign investment, plus a generous tax holiday, has increased capital inflow. The incentives are extended to foreign firms that will export as opposed to firms interested in the home market (Donaldson 1965). Brazil was an openly attractive country for foreign investors in the 1970s, while the Andean Common Market countries became more inaccessible.

When considering the optimum foreign savings inflow, the foreign savings are viewed as a supplement or substitute for domestic savings and "optimum" describes the domestic-plus-foreign savings needed to acheive the most desirable growth rate. Borrowing affects the amount of savings necessary from national income to support a given growth rate. It allows the economy at earlier stages of growth to sacrifice less in forgone consumption or achieve higher growth per level of national saving. And by doing so, the repayment of the debt at later stages of growth results in a need for higher savings in that period. Thus the LDC reallocates its national savings needs for capital formation and technical change along the growth path. This can lessen the burden on earlier generations to forgo consumption while requiring later generations to bear some of the cost of the higher income made possible by the previous accumulation of capital. This presumes that the economy allocates adequate resources to capital formation and technical progress so that the debt servicing and repayment can be financed from higher income. When capital formation just keeps abreast of population growth and there is no gain in productivity, consumption drops as later generations repay savings borrowed earlier.

Previous discussion on optimum savings-growth rates made it clear that the concept in welfare terms is illusive and that value judgments must be made in accepting a target growth rate. Once the target growth rate is accepted, planners confront the same type of welfare problems in choosing an inflow of savings in early years that must be repaid by later generations. A commonly accepted judgment is that some redistribution of the savings to finance development over the growth path is equitable.

The amount of foreign savings available to the LDC may be below desired levels based on the country's growth targets and time path preferences. Foreign borrowing is often limited by the foreign exchange constraint faced by LDCs rather than by the return to the investment earnable and the desired level of capital inflow. Foreign direct investment may also be restricted by the foreign exchange constraint when this limits repatriation of earnings. Unless adequate foreign aid is available, the capital inflow may be below desired levels based on growth targets. The two-gap model calculates the foreign aid based on foreign exchange needs as well as savings needs to achieve a target growth rate.

We turn now to the Republic of Ireland, which began to reverse policies restricting foreign direct investment in the 1950s. Ireland presents an interesting example where both internal and external conditions created a unique role for foreign direct investment in the country's development strategy.

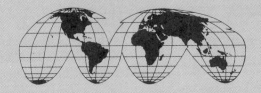

Foreign Direct Investment in Ireland: A Key to Manufactures Export

Today the Republic of Ireland is grouped among developed nations by The World Bank. A small nation with low population density, the republic occupies about two-fifths of the island it shares with Northern Ireland, which is a part of the United Kingdom. Ireland has limited natural resources. She is a highly trade-dependent small country with domestic markets too small in many cases to support economies of scale. In the 1950s as an economy highly dependent upon agricultural exports, she sought to stem the outflow of her educated population seeking jobs abroad. Trade and job creation were the keys to survival of her economic kingdom.

The Republic of Ireland was then at a crossroads, forced to choose between an inward-looking versus an outward-looking development policy. Approximately 40 percent of the population in the mid 1950s was still employed in agriculture, which produced approximately 30 percent of GNP. Industrialization had been fostered by a policy of increased protection during the 1930s. By the mid-1950s 16 percent of the population worked in industry. However, growth from import substitution seemed to have exhausted itself. Several factors were at work here, among the more important being,

■ A small domestic market not supportive of scale economies,
■ Some inefficiencies in agriculture that affected the size of the domestic market for goods,
■ A lack of competition in small, protected domestic markets,
■ A lack of managerial sophistication and technical know-how, and
■ A deficiency in marketing skills needed to penetrate competitive export markets.

The consequence of stagnation was ever-higher rates of emigration from the Emerald Isle. Indeed, Ireland faced the specter of becoming a "vanishing nation." Population was down to below 3 million people (compared with 8 million in 1841, before the potato famine of 1845–47). Ireland was in a rather unique and disadvantaged position as a result of her declining population. The out-migration drained off people of working age, leading to a loss of labor resources and an increased dependency ratio per work-force member.

In addition to the danger to national survival posed by a population seeking higher living standards abroad, Ireland's import substitution policies, including protective tariffs, were threatened by the planned entry of her major trading partner, Britain, into the European Economic Community (EEC). In 1952 a total of 86 percent by value of exports went to the United Kingdom, composed mainly of agricultural goods, predominately livestock. If Ireland did not enter the EEC with Britain, her exports to that market would be adversely affected by the common external tariffs applied to nonmembers by the European Community. Moreover, European Community external tariffs were especially high for agricultural goods, Ireland's main exports. Entry, however, required lowering and eventual elimination of tariffs among member countries, that is, an end to protection of home industries from competition.

Ireland chose the road of an outward-looking policy and eventual entry into the European Economic Community. To stem outmigration and avoid becoming an agricultural adjunct of the Community, as she had been to the United Kingdom during her years as a colony, she needed to strengthen her industrial sector before joining the common market by developing manufactures exports. Pressed for time in this regard and faced with an inexperienced, domestically oriented industrial sector, Ireland relied upon foreign direct investment as the keystone of her export promotion phase of development. It turned out to be a highly successful strategy, free of most of the shortcomings that can arise from foreign direct investment. In great part this was because of the conditions in Ireland and the fact that foreign direct investment was directed toward export sales as opposed to the home market.

Why would multinational firms come to Ireland when the home market was small and GNP stagnant? Ireland was in a unique position. She already had duty-free entry for exports into the United Kingdom market and she was well located for exporting to the European markets. Moreover, at the time there was a labor shortage in Europe. Irish labor was less expensive than British and more skilled than Portuguese or Spanish workers. But most importantly, Ireland competed for foreign firms by giving tax holidays of 10 to 25 years on profits from export sales along with subsidies on plant and equipment. Thus subsidies, proximity to European markets, and an abun-

dant labor supply attracted firms to Ireland (Donaldson 1965).

Products of multinational firms were exported and thus did not compete for the domestic market. In order to provide incentives for foreign firms, Ireland had to reverse a law limiting foreign ownership on the Isle. From 1958–64, during the first five-year plan, 133 new firms with foreign participation located in Ireland, contributing 85 percent of new industrial investment and 77 percent of new employment. Most firms produced goods that were not expensive to transport. Ireland continued to court foreign corporations successfully in the 1970s and entered the European Economic Community along with Britain during that decade without loss of her competitive position and industrial momentum.

The period between 1960 and 1979 showed a growth in per capita GNP averaging 3.2 percent, and an enlarged population of 3.3 million in 1979. The proportion of the labor force in industry rose from 25 percent in 1960 to 37 percent in 1979 while the proportion in agriculture was almost halved, dropping from 36 percent to 19 percent over the same period. And most importantly, manufacturers exports nearly doubled, soaring from 28 percent of total merchandise exports in 1960 to 54 percent in 1978, while merchandise exports of primary commodities dropped from 72 percent to 46 percent. Among manufactured exports, traditional exports—textiles, food, drink and tobacco products—accounted for a shrinking proportion while new exports such as chemicals and allied products, metal and engineering products, and electrical equipment and electronics accounted for a growing proportion. Moreover, while Britain remained an important export market, manufactured exports greatly diversified the destination of Irish exports compared with the 1950s. In fact, Ireland felt independent enough of Britain by the 1980s to cut the Irish currency loose from the British pound.

CONCLUSIONS

The main contributions of foreign investment in Ireland, starting in the late 1950s, were:

- Increased productivity in the industrial sector through the introduction of new technology, managerial know-how, marketing skills, and achievement of scale economies,
- Job provision and a sectoral shift of jobs into industry where productivity is higher than in agriculture,
- Improved efficiency of resource allocation through trade creation, and,
- Higher and more stable foreign exchange earnings as a result of exports diversified in both product and geographic destination.

These contributions helped to stem emigration and strengthen Ireland prior to her entry into the European Economic Community.

Because Ireland is stable politically, and because of the success of the development program, capital repatriation has not been a problem as in some other less stable countries that are semiindustrialized when foreign capital enters. There is an inevitable buildup of profits from investment inflows; however, there have been a continuous stream of foreign direct investment and a positive contribution to the balance of payments from export earnings.

There have, of course, been costs involved as a result of foreign direct investment. Subsidies were necessary to compete with Northern Ireland and other countries of Europe where multinational firms might choose to locate. And as labor markets tightened in Ireland and skilled workers were attracted to foreign firms, local businesses were strapped. Interestingly, Ireland did not suffer from a saving constraint and thus foreign firms neither dissolved a saving bottleneck nor tightened short-term credit markets precipitously by competing for funds. Nevertheless, despite concentration in export sales, foreign firms in Ireland have come in for their share of resentment from the local business populace and even some public servants. Most government personnel argue, however, that the strategy devised in the 1950s by Ireland for attracting foreign firms also channeled their activity so that a good return was received on subsidies given.

The trade theorist Jagdish Bhagwati noted that a large exporter country expanding its export potential under conditions of inelastic demand for the export good could encounter a deterioration in well-being. This occurs when such a country's terms of trade decline so much that despite greater export capacity, it can import less goods than prior to growth. Bhagwati called this "immiserizing growth" (1958, pp. 201–5). Here we assume the growth in exports is related to foreign investment. This enables us to show a classic case of a foreign enclave that expands exports, improving its home-country terms of trade but causing a weakening in the host country's terms of trade. We assume first that the LDC will reduce its own resources used in the export sector so as to limit the rise in exports in the face of inelastic foreign demand. We concentrate upon the effect of foreign direct investment upon in-industrialization. It is shown that immiserizing growth is most likely when foreign exchange earnings are repatriated.

We assume the simple model where M/B is constant, indicative of a foreign exchange constraint. The foreign export enclave can affect national resource allocation and well-being through its effect upon the terms of trade and foreign exchange availability even though it has no other linkages with the domestic economy. Two cases are shown: one where the foreign firm repatriates all the foreign exchange it earns, and another where the foreign firm absorbs none of its foreign exchange. Whether the foreign currency earned by the outside firm is made available to the LDC affects its optimal terms of trade and hence its optimal export level. When currency exchange earnings of the foreign firm are repatriated, the LDC will export more and receive lower terms of trade. It cannot avoid reduced industrial output. Both cases can create a foreign exchange gap. These results are most readily seen by graphing the two situations separately.

Figure 13.7(a) shows the case of repatriated earnings and immiserizing growth. T_k is the locus of the terms of trade with changing export levels. Prior to foreign direct investment, exports are e and industrial output b. With export production by foreign firms that are sector specific of $e_f o$, T_k shifts to point e_f, as shown in frame (b) of figure 13.7. Import capacity of the LDC does not move along this curve, however, when foreign currency earnings generated by foreign resources are absorbed by the firm.

From the terms of trade generated along T_{k_2} in frame (b) as exports rise from e_f, we can derive curve T'_k originating at o in frame (a). This curve shows changes in import capacity with changes in *national* exports, given foreign firm exports of $e_f o$. (It is derived by drawing the terms of trade ray in frame (b) for each export level above o from origin e_f. National exports and imports will be measured by the side and the base of a triangle formed by moving along the terms of trade ray above axis oB up to its intersection with T_{k_2}.) Curve T'_k in frame (a) then originates at o and shows the import capacity of *national* exports as the terms of trade vary with *total* exports (national plus foreign firm exports), as indicated by movement along T_{k_2} above axis oB in figure 13.7(b). T'_k is elastic up to point e', where the quantity of national exports is high enough to encounter lessened import capacity with further exports. (Recall that the formula for elasticity is $\Delta Q/Q \div \Delta P/P$.

**FOREIGN
DIRECT
INVESTMENT
AND
IMMISERIZING
GROWTH**

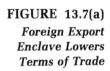

FIGURE 13.7(a)

*Foreign Export
Enclave Lowers
Terms of Trade*

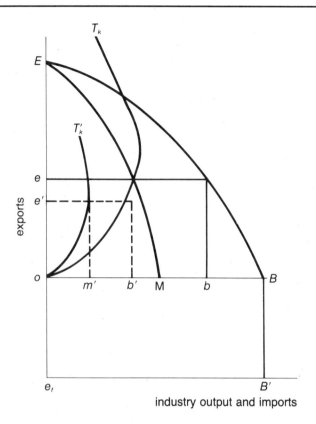

The foreign export enclave absorbs all the foreign exchange it creates. The terms of trade of the LDC drop and national import capacity is along curve T'_k.

Q refers to national exports along T'_k, a smaller amount than total exports. Thus T'_k is elastic beyond the point where T_{k_2} become inelastic.)

Optimum exports for the LDC are now oe' in frame (a). This allows imports sufficient to produce b' industrial output. A foreign exchange gap arises even though total exports ($e_f e'$) have risen. Resources must be relocated in food production (not shown) or left unemployed. The export enclave has caused a deterioration in the growth potential of the LDC.

The case of foreign direct investment without repatriation of earnings or other absorption of foreign exchange is shown in Figure 13.7(b). The optimal export point along T_{k_2} to maximize industrial output is e''. With mobile resources, national resources are reallocated to the industrial sector to achieve output b''. There is a foreign exchange gap so that some national resources must be allocated to the food sector.

Without mobility of resources, industrial output would drop as the terms of trade fall along T_{k_2} past the export level e''. A higher level of foreign exports could also lower the terms of trade to the degree that the T_{k_2} line crosses the industry-import axis oB below import levels associated with output level b. The economy becomes highly export-centered with reduced industrial capacity.

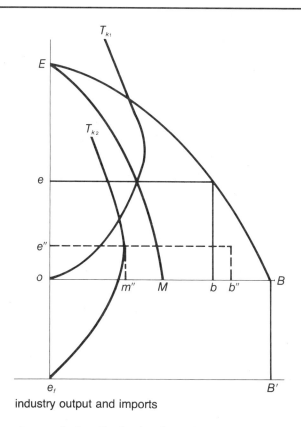

FIGURE 13.7(b)

Foreign Export Enclave Lowers Terms of Trade

industry output and imports

Optimum exports are *e″* when the foreign firms do not absorb foreign exchange. National industrial capacity output rises to *b″* where there is a foreign exchange gap.

REFERENCES

Batra, R. N. and Ramachandran, R. 1980. Multinational Firms and the Theory of International Trade and Investment. *American Economic Review* 70 (June): 278–90.

Bhagwati, J. 1958. Immiserizing Growth: A Geometric Note. *Review of Economic Studies.* 25:201–5.

Chenery, Hollis B. and Strout, Alan M. 1966. Foreign Assistance and Economic Development. *American Economic Review* 50 (September): 679–733.

Donaldson, L. 1965. *Development Planning in Ireland.* New York: Frederick A. Praeger Publishers.

Helleiner, G. K. 1975. The Role of Multinational Corporations in the Less Developed Countries' Trade in Technology. *World Development* 3, 4 (April): 161–89.

Hughes, Helen. 1979. Debt and Development: The Role of Foreign Capital in Economic Development. *World Development* 7 (February): 95–112.

Lall, S. 1978. Transnationals, Domestic Enterprises, and Industrial Structure in Host LDC: A Survey. *Oxford Economic Papers* 30: 217–48.

Newfarmer, R. S. and Mueller, W. R. 1975. *Multinational Corporations in Brazil and Mexico: Structural Sources of Economic and Non-Economic Power.* U.S. Senate Subcommittee on Multinational Corporations. Cited in Lall (1978).

Inequality: National

chapter

14

tudy of inequality deals with the relative distribution of income and with differences in absolute income levels. Examination of this phenomenon may also focus on the distribution of wealth, in other words, income-earning assets. Among many observers, concern over inequality in LDCs is in part at least related to the absolute income level of the poorest. They are concerned that growth has benefited only those in the higher-income deciles, and has not trickled down to the people barely surviving at subsistence. They are concerned that the poor have actually suffered a decline in their already marginal well-being as growth has benefited others. And they are concerned that even where the poorest have shared in a proportionate gain in income, the gap in absolute income between them and the rich has widened.

The absolute differences in living standards between the very rich and the poor within LDCs can be as great or greater than that between the affluent in more advanced countries and the poor in LDCs. And when relative income inequality is measured within countries before taxes, most underdeveloped nations show markedly greater relative inequality than MDCs. The difference would be even larger if there were adjustment for tax expenditures and incidence. Compared with nonsocialist LDCs tax systems tend to be more progressive in MDCs, where there is more welfare-type spending from tax monies to benefit the poor.

The work on income distribution and growth is still in its exploratory stages and awaits a better data base, more refined indices of inequality, and explanatory models identifying the major determinants of income distribution. The results of studies cited here should be taken only as preliminary evidence bearing upon the topic.

The chapter begins with a brief discussion of the implications of relatively high inequality for LDCs and their development.

The literature on economic development today is typically critical of a growth process where large segments of the population share relatively less in the society's progress. As already mentioned, conditions of inequality can mean the lowest 40 percent of the populace live in extreme deprivation on meager income. In addition, countries that have high inequality by international standards exhibit certain social and market distortions that affect the type of growth they experience. We now review the main criticisms of this type of growth.

Development entails social as well as economic costs, and requires commitment by all socioeconomic groups in support of important economic goals. Successful development is typically accompanied by a spirit of nationalism that unifies the people behind a common effort. Such dedication is more easily generated under conditions where inequality, both relative and absolute, is not intensifying, and all groups can feel they have a stake in a common cause of mutual benefit. Lack of such a spirit can lead to stagnation or destabilizing social change.

In contrast to the era of Western economic development, ideas of social justice weight material inequality more heavily in today's world.

IMPLICATIONS OF INCOME DISTRIBUTION

Implications of Relatively High Inequality

One of the more popular "isms" among LDC social reformers is socialism. This is a vague term with a kaleidoscope of meanings among various users of the phrase. But a common denominator of the term is a connection between limited ranges of inequality and social justice. Ironically many countries that call themselves socialist (India) or have had socialist revolutions (Mexico) exhibit greater inequality than so-called capitalist systems such as the United States has. However, the tension between reality and ideology can breed social and political unrest when there is high and/or growing inequality in LDCs. Periods of political instability rooted in this kind of imbalance can create greater poverty and divert resources from development.

High inequality has led the wealthy to levels of consumption luxurious even by Western standards, intensifying the shortage of savings and foreign exchange. It has contributed to dualism by channeling the limited capital into production of Western-type consumer goods demanding high skill and import content. These goods are consumed mainly by the rich, possibly restricting the stimulus of market growth and scale economies. Production of mass consumption items of different type and quality is limited by shortages of capital and other resources and inhibited by the low purchasing power of the masses. Yet, some economists argue, production of simpler goods of varying quality could contribute to higher demand for unskilled labor and so reduce inequality.

Wide income differences usually mean that both governmental and economic power is controlled by the rich for their own purposes, hampering government action to improve the material conditions of the masses. For example, it can interfere with the channeling of foreign aid inflows to the development needs of the poor since the government is the main conduit of funds for the eradication of poverty.

Inequality can reflect a backward agricultural sector with low labor productivity. The rural poor usually have the greatest number of destitute and the lowest income of all a nation's poor. Inequality then can reflect a failure to attack the problems of agriculture. And that, as emphasized elsewhere, will limit development efforts. Sharp disparities in income between rural and urban dwellers can also create high migration rates from the countryside to the cities that lead to urban unemployment.

All in all, there is a presumption that extremes of inequality are not viable conditions for continued development. There is, however, no model that shows the causal network here.

Implications of Egalitarian Distribution

Since World War II arguments like those presented above against high levels of inequality in LDCs have surfaced in response to the development experiences in some LDCs. Predating the concern over high inequality and its effects upon development are arguments that equality promoted by government conflicts with growth. Proponents of this viewpoint focus on the disincentive effect that highly egalitarian government policies have upon work effort and saving-investment levels.

This analysis points to the possible positive effects of market-determined income distribution.

The planned economy without private ownership of assets can set the level of saving-investment through resource control. However, such an economy must be concerned about the effect of planned income distribution upon work effort, based upon the assumption that this effort is related to wages. The planners of a centrally controlled economy that ensures basic needs and very equal pay may find that workers prefer more leisure than they do under conditions of less security and where pay rewards depend strictly upon effort.

The mixed economy seeking high growth is concerned with private savings plus work effort. Such an economy can use the tax system for redistribution purposes and combine that with central regulation such as a minimum wage or land reform. When the income distribution achieved is highly egalitarian, then work effort can be adversely affected. And for the market-oriented economy there is an often-presented line of thought that egalitarian redistribution reduces profits, savings, and growth. This has been encountered in some of the ideas presented in earlier chapters.

The usual assumption is that higher-income recipients of profits in a market economy (that is, the competitive return to capital, entrepreneurship, and risk) tend to plow them back into investment and that with reduced inequality and profits, savings and capital accumulation are lower. Moreover, the funding and the incentive for technological change would be jeopardized with reduced profits. Profits are assumed to be the main source of savings in LDCs.

The capitalist class is assumed to contain the main savers. Entrepreneurs are motivated by profits and the innovation dependent upon them. Risk assumption is said to demand reward, and inevitably contributes to inequality. As capital grows relative to labor and the capitalist class expands relative to the total population, inequality can lessen. Even where wage earners save, the presumption is that the marginal propensity to consume out of wages is very high so that redistribution from the entrepreneurial class, with its high marginal propensity to save, to wage earners will reduce growth. As to this last point, a Brookings Institution study on income distribution and growth notes that recent empirical studies cast doubt on the existence of large differences in the marginal savings rates between the rich and poor in LDCs (Frank and Webb, eds. 1977, p. 48).

Few LDCs have highly egalitarian income distribution. And for those with policies aimed at this result, such as China, Tanzania, and Cuba, the data base is not sufficient to determine the effects upon work effort or savings. On the other hand, LDCs with market distortions and high inequality of income distribution are not uncommon. The inequality reflects many variables and is inadequately explained by the scarcity value of labor and capital in competitive markets. Because of the predominance of high inequality in many LDCs, this chapter concentrates upon measurement, causes, and cures of the problem within developing countries.

EMPIRICAL
INVESTIGA-
TIONS

Measurements of relative inequality in LDCs are not clear-cut. First, the data are politically sensitive and thus suspect. Next, recall all the problems connected with GNP data in terms of conception, accuracy, and so forth, outlined in chapter 1. GNP measures, in fact, are not comprehensive enough for a statistical profile identifying such variables as the income unit of sharing, the age of recipients, and income in kind. The logical unit for establishing income is the family. In many LDCs the family unit will be larger than the nuclear family of the West. In Africa, where incidentally inequality is lowest among all LDCs, the unit may be the tribe. The family often supports one or more unemployed members migrating to other areas in search of work and betterment. Success in the endeavor is shared with the family unit. The sick and the elderly also share in the family income. Since family sizes differ, the income to the unit would need to be converted to a per capita figure for comparison purposes. Despite data limitations, visual observation alone indicates the vast gaps between the living standard of the rich and the poor in LDCs.

Measurement of
Income Distribution

Two methods are commonly used to measure inequality, although neither is completely satisfactory for answering all questions of interest concerning inequality. The Lorenz curve is a convenient tool for comparing (1) income inequality with a situation of perfect equality and (2) relative inequality among countries. The vertical axis represents income on a percentage scale. The horizontal one depicts income recipients also on a percentage scale. Thus both axes total to 100 percent each and in figure 14.1 are subdivided into deciles. Along the diagonal, income of each percentage of recipients is equal to the same percentage of income. That is, 10 percent of income recipients receive 10 percent of the income, 20 percent receive 20 percent, and so on. This is a reference line of absolute equality. With inequality, the lower-income groups will receive cumulatively less than their percentage weight in the total population of recipients. Thus the Lorenz curve for a country with inequality is convex and rises back toward the equality line as the income of the higher deciles adds proportionately more to the cumulative income percentile. Figure 14.1 illustrates Lorenz curves for two countries, A and B, with B having more inequality. Notice that Lorenz curves could cross, giving an ambiguous representation.

Another method of comparing relative inequality of income among countries is the GINI coefficient. In figure 14.1 the GINI coefficient is a ratio of the area between the Lorenz curve and the diagonal equality line divided by the area of the triangle formed by the 45-degree line. The GINI coefficient for Lorenz curve A in figure 14.1 is the shaded area divided by the triangle CDE.

The smaller the GINI coefficient, the more equal the income distribution. Countries with relatively equitable income distribution tend to have coefficients in the .20 to .35 range, while those with more inequality can have coefficients in the high 60s. Notice, though, that countries with the same GINI coefficient can have different shapes to

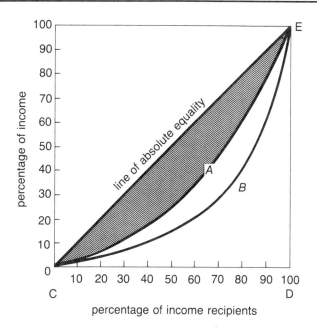

FIGURE 14.1

Lorenz Curves and GINI Coefficient

Moving along Lorenz curves *A* or *B*, lower-decile income recipients receive a smaller percentage of income than higher-decile recipients. Income in country *B* is more unequally distributed than in country *A*. The GINI coefficient for country *A* is the shaded area as a percentage of triangle CDE.

their Lorenz curves. This allows different inequality levels when the lowest decile or quintile is compared with the proportion of income received by those in the highest decile. Remember, also, such relative comparisons say nothing about absolute poverty.

M. S. Ahluwalia, working with World Bank data, makes several generalizations about relative inequality among nations. Certain socialist countries have the least inequality. The income share of the lowest 40 percent amounts to approximately one quarter of total income. This can be seen as a benchmark of the limits to equality in the real world.

Developed countries average about 16 percent of income for the bottom 40 percent and individually show low to moderate degrees of disparity. And these are pretax data, and thus do not account for transfer payments and subsidies in kind.

In LDCs the average income share for the lowest 40 percent is 12.5 percent; but there is considerable variation around this average. Half of these nations show income shares of 9 percent for the lowest two-fifths of their people and so fall in the high inequality range (Ahluwalia, chap. 1 in Chenery *et al.*, 1974). Table 14.1 shows countries ranked according to relative inequality.

TABLE 14.1   *Cross-classification of Countries by Income Level and Equality*

High Inequality
Share of Lowest 40% less than 12%

Country (year)	Per Capita GNP US$	Lowest 40%	Middle 40%	Top 20%
Kenya (1969)	136	10.0	22.0	68.0
Sierra Leone (1968)	159	9.6	22.4	68.0
Philippines (1971)	239	11.6	34.6	53.8
Iraq (1956)	200	6.8	25.2	68.0
Senegal (1960)	245	10.0	26.0	64.0
Ivory Coast (1970)	247	10.8	32.1	57.1
Rhodesia (1968)	252	8.2	22.8	69.0
Tunisia (1970)	255	11.4	33.6	55.0
Honduras (1968)	265	6.5	28.5	65.0
Ecuador (1970)	277	6.5	20.0	73.5
Malaysia (1970)	330	11.6	32.4	56.0
Colombia (1970)	358	9.0	30.0	61.0
Brazil (1970)	390	10.0	28.4	61.5
Peru (1971)	480	6.5	33.5	60.0
Gabon (1968)	497	8.8	23.7	67.5
Jamaica (1958)	510	8.2	30.3	61.5
Costa Rica (1971)	521	11.5	30.0	58.5
Mexico (1969)	645	10.5	25.5	64.0
South Africa (1965)	669	6.2	35.8	58.0
Panama (1969)	692	9.4	31.2	59.4
Venezuela (1970)	1004	7.9	27.1	65.0
Finland (1962)	1599	11.1	39.6	49.3
France (1962)	1913	9.5	36.8	53.7

Moderate Inequality
Share of Lowest 40% between 12% and 17%

Country (year)	Per Capita GNP US$	Lowest 40%	Middle 40%	Top 20%
El Salvador (1969)	295	11.2	36.4	52.4
Turkey (1968)	282	9.3	29.9	60.8
Burma (1958)	82	16.5	38.7	44.8
Dahomey (1959)	87	15.5	34.5	50.0
Tanzania (1967)	89	13.0	26.0	61.0
India (1964)	99	16.0	32.0	52.0
Madagascar (1960)	120	13.5	25.5	61.0
Zambia (1959)	230	14.5	28.5	57.0
Dominican Republic (1969)	323	12.2	30.3	57.5
Iran (1968)	332	12.5	33.0	54.5
Guyana (1956)	550	14.0	40.3	45.7
Lebanon (1960)	508	13.0	26.0	61.0
Uruguay (1968)	618	16.5	35.5	48.0
Chile (1968)	744	13.0	30.2	56.8
Argentina (1970)	1079	16.5	36.1	47.4
Puerto Rico (1968)	1100	13.7	35.7	50.6
Netherlands (1967)	1990	13.6	37.9	48.5
Norway (1968)	2010	16.6	42.9	40.5
Germany, Fed. Rep. (1964)	2144	15.4	31.7	52.9
Denmark (1968)	2563	13.6	38.8	47.6
New Zealand (1969)	2859	15.5	42.5	42.0
Sweden (1963)	2949	14.0	42.0	44.0

Low Inequality
Share of Lowest 40%, 17% and above

Country (year)	Per Capita GNP US$	Lowest 40%	Middle 40%	Top 20%
Chad (1958)	78	18.0	39.0	43.0
Sri Lanka (1969)	95	17.0	37.0	46.0
Niger (1960)	97	18.0	40.0	42.0
Pakistan (1964)	100	17.5	37.5	45.0
Uganda (1970)	126	17.1	35.8	47.1
Thailand (1970)	180	17.0	37.5	45.5
Korea (1970)	235	18.0	37.0	45.0
Taiwan (1964)	241	20.4	39.5	40.1
Surinam (1962)	394	21.7	35.7	42.6
Greece (1957)	500	21.0	29.5	49.5
Yugoslavia (1968)	529	18.5	40.0	41.5
Bulgaria (1962)	530	26.8	40.0	33.2
Spain (1965)	750	17.6	36.7	45.7
Poland (1964)	850	23.4	40.6	36.0
Japan (1963)	950	20.7	39.3	40.0
United Kingdom (1968)	2015	18.8	42.2	39.0
Hungary (1969)	1140	24.0	42.5	33.5
Czechoslovakia (1964)	1150	27.6	41.4	31.0
Australia (1968)	2509	20.0	41.2	38.8
Canada (1965)	2920	20.0	39.8	40.2
United States (1970)	4850	19.7	41.5	38.8

SOURCE: From *Redistribution with Growth* by Hollis Chenery et al. Copyright © 1974 by International Bank for Reconstruction and Development. Reprinted by permission of Oxford University Press, Inc. Table 1.1, pp. 8–9.

The following questions concerning income distribution recur in development literature:

1. As countries begin development, does growth bring an inevitable worsening of income inequality prior to a lessening of it?
2. Do the poorest groups suffer an absolute decline in income with growth?
3. Is inequality heightened by more rapid development?
4. Does inequality differ among sectors or regions of LDCs?

Question 1—whether or not growth in LDCs increases relative income inequality—is of keen interest. There are insufficient time series data from LDCs to answer it categorically. A rough estimate for countries with data available at more than one point in time gives an uneven picture, and there is no correlation between growth rates and changes in the distribution of income. Studies on Mexico, Argentina, the Philippines, and Brazil support a positive answer to question 1 (Fishlow 1972; Ranis 1974; and Weisskoff 1970). Exceptions are Taiwan and South Korea, some socialist economies, and communist economies.

William Loehr notes that inequality need not worsen with growth. He warns that the GINI index might be misleading "since income gains by middle income groups seem to come at the expense of *both* upper and lower income groups" (in Loehr and Powelson, eds. 1977, p. 16). Studies by the World Bank also conclude that a worsening of inequality with growth is not inevitable.

Another approach to analyzing the relation of growth to inequality in the absence of country time series data is to look at societies with different income and development levels and see if there is a systematic variation within each country in the relative inequality and the level of per capita income. Studies using this approach find distribution worsens between the poorest and the middle-income countries and then improves in the advanced countries. The share of the middle 40 percent does not vary significantly with income levels. The cross-country data suggest the worsening inequality may continue for three to six generations if mitigating forces are absent.

In regard to question 2, Kuznets was among the first to suspect from data available to him in the early 1960s that income among the poorest groups could decline despite growth in per capita income for the country. In regard to both questions 2 and 3, I. Adelman and C. T. Morris looked at 24 countries experiencing development in the year 1850. These were societies that underwent strong economic changes over the last half of the nineteenth century. The authors emphasize that structural changes that inevitably accompany growth affect income distribution and the income of the poorest. They conclude that the obsolescence and displacements that accompany growth tend to lower living standards of the most deprived. Moreover, rapid change inhibits absorption and reallocation of displaced labor in new areas, further worsening the living standards of the poorest (summarized in Adelman, Morris, and Robinson 1976, pp. 561–82).

More currently, rapid growth in Iran under the shah and Brazil was accompanied by growing inequality. Korea, Taiwan and, some suspect, Japan (although data are not available for Japan) are unusual in that rapid growth was accompanied by unusually *favorable* trends in income distribution (Ranis, in Loehr and Powelson, eds. 1977, p. 45). Ahluwalia concludes, however, ". . . there is little firm, empirical basis for the view that higher growth rates inevitably generate inequality." (1974, p. 13).

Regional inequities in income in LDCs are often noted. Such inequities are related to sectoral inequality and immobility of the population.

Question 4, on sectoral inequality, was answered by Kuznets in 1963 and supported in studies by R. Weisskoff (1970) and S. Swamy (1967). The general conclusion is that inequality is less severe in the rural-agricultural sector than in the urban-industrial. Thus as the economy shifts toward industry, inequality can rise.

The identification of the industrial sector as the cause of growing inequality has led to closer scrutiny of forces there conducive to inequality. Other studies to be mentioned concentrate upon the rural sector as having the greatest incidence of low-income recipients as well as the lowest incomes. These studies emphasize conditions necessary to raise agricultural income relative to that of the industrial sector.

DETERMINANTS OF INCOME DISTRIBUTION

The four questions in the previous section could be more readily answered if the following were also answered: What are the major variables that affect income distribution in LDCs? A theoretical and empirical response to this question that sorts out from the many variables the major determining ones does not exist. Variables suggested as important to income division can be grouped under three headings:

A. Basic economic variables determined by the structure of an LDC.
B. Sociohistorical variables.
C. Variables associated with or defining the economic system.

Structural Variables

Variables determined by the structure of LDCs include the size of the agricultural sector relative to the industrial and the terms of trade between the two. Because agricultural goods are price- and income-inelastic, the commodity and income terms of trade tend to move in favor of the industrial sector during growth as agricultural productivity improves. Adelman, Morris, and Robinson emphasize that the agricultural terms of trade, along with rural-urban migration, are important to inequality. Out-migration raises income per capita in the rural sector closer to that of the urban sector, but is not sufficient to equalize it.

Population growth is another structural variable associated since the time of the Classical economists with income distribution. They noted population growth affects what is now called the functional distribution of income: the income share going to wages, rents, and profits. Labor's scarcity value relative to that of land and capital is lower with larger population. Moreover, population growth, by holding incomes down, perpetuates high fertility rates among the poor. This in turn perpetuates the poverty of lower-income groups by leaving them with less land, capital, and education as well as poorer health—all of which contribute to inequality.

Studies have identified another structural variable as closely related to inequality, dualism (Adelman and Morris 1973; Oshima 1970, p. 24; and Weisskoff 1970). Dualistic development can vary in degree. High degrees of dualism are often associated with growing inequality and little or no trickle-down or spread effect to the poorer people. It is helpful here to review certain aspects of the dual economy from the standpoint of income distribution.

First consider basic economic forces affecting inequality where dualism may or may not be present. Market forces often play a more important role in income determination in LDCs outside of agriculture, particularly in industry. Thus it is useful as a starting point to think in terms of asset ownership and the market-determined price of income-earning assets. The market is unlikely to be competitive, and a monopoly model may be needed to explain returns in many industries and even in labor markets. Nevertheless, it can be assumed the demand for factors of production is a derived demand related to the marginal product of the factor, although imprecisely.

In the LDC capital and skilled labor are scarce relative to unskilled labor, which generally has a negative income elasticity of demand with growth. This scarcity of skill specialties reflects a limited supply relative to a growing demand for new skills. Price of the factors, and hence income, will tend to vary with relative scarcity. The greater the relative abundance of unskilled labor, the lower its relative income and the higher inequality. Human capital (a function of training and education) and ownership rights to physical capital are very unequally distributed in many LDCs.

The industrial sector is typically dual in nature, at least to some degree. It is composed of companies applying modern technology and small, family-run firms using traditional techniques. For those using modern methods, the elasticity of substitution between capital and unskilled labor can be very low.[1] In other words, the isoquant between factor limits is narrow in range and highly convex. In the short run the point at which the marginal product of labor drops to zero may be relatively high because of the high K/L ratio for the relatively fixed coefficients of production. This is shown in figure 14.2. The result is there are jobs for a limited number of workers in modern industry, which has a relatively high K/L ratio and consequently a high marginal product of labor.

Institutional pressures such as government and union intervention in market price-setting lead to high wages for these jobs. This prevents

---

1. The elasticity of substitution measures the extent to which labor can be substituted for capital with a change in their relative prices, (P_K/P_L). Notationally it is:

$$\frac{\Delta(K/L)}{K/L} \div \frac{\Delta(P_K/P_L)}{P_K/P_L}$$

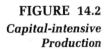

FIGURE 14.2
Capital-intensive Production

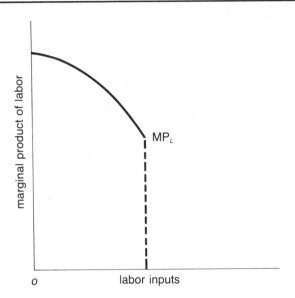

The marginal product of labor drops to zero once the *K/L* limit is reached.

firms from paying scarcity prices in relatively more abundant labor categories and reaping high profits in imperfectly competitive markets. Those able to acquire these jobs through luck, mobility, education, nepotism, or political influence join the ranks of the relatively well-off.[2] There is a surplus of workers seeking these jobs. On the other hand, qualified workers in some skill groups, including those with managerial skills, are in short supply. The size of the firm and its modern nature create a demand for scarce skills. This results in high incomes for those with such know-how, reflecting their scarcity price in the dual economy (Bacha and Taylor 1978).

Labor productivity is lower in the traditional sector. Ownership of capital assets and access to financial capital are below levels in the modern sector. For the family firm with many members to employ, the marginal product can be well below that in the modern corporation. All family members share in the average product, as on the family farm.

Government tax policies, trade policies, and other programs tend to reinforce dualism. In the absence of a progressive tax system, the return to risk assumption, capital, innovation, and monopoly can be high in the industrializing LDC and intensify inequality. Usually tax systems are not progressive in LDCs. In fact, The World Bank has found that the fiscal system in these countries tends to be regressive (Chenery, in Loehr and Powelson, eds. 1977, p. 34).

Import substitution is often a contributor to high incomes in the industrializing LDC since this is a protected, subsidized sector with

2. A Latin American study found employment in such modern firms to account for only 7.7 percent of urban jobs (Turnham and Jaeger 1971).

monopoly conditions. Moreover, protection can be excessive, and warp production away from a more labor-intensive—particularly unskilled labor-intensive—output mix. As will be explained in a later section, the more labor-intensive product mix could reduce inequality. Thus, as LDCs support their infant industries for development purposes, inequality can develop as a spin-off. A Brookings Institution study identifies various other subsidy and tax policies and their administration as contributors to inequality in many LDCs (Frank and Webb, eds. 1977).

The government sector itself often contributes to inequality because of the high salaries paid to the upper echelons of the bureaucracy. Job access here is determined by education as a screening device (that is, the designated education level is not needed for the work but is an accepted method of job allocation), by nepotism, political influence, luck, and sometimes skills.

The idea of social dualism was introduced in chapter 1. Sociologists and anthropologists have explored the claim that understanding and being able to operate successfully within a set of socioeconomic institutions associated with a modernizing economy can only happen gradually (see e.g., Inkeles and Smith 1974). Such assimilation takes more than a generation for most, and can take many generations for less exposed groups.

John Powelson relates social dualism to inequality (in Loehr and Powelson, eds. 1977, pp. 113–43). The poorer groups operate under a different set of socioeconomic institutions that make it difficult for them to achieve equality. They have neither the experience nor the sophistication to handle conditions in the complex modern economy. The elites, by contrast, readily adopt policies and structures that omit the poor, in part because the social dualism creates a gap in cultures.

Social dualism combines aspects of both economic structural variables and sociohistorical variables. Of course, this latter category opens up the whole context of individual historical conditions that have bearing upon an LDC's particular situation.

Variables that are specific to a country's culture and history can play an important role in income distribution. These include the extended family with its mutual obligations of income sharing, the caste system, land ownership, tenancy and acquisition rights, tribal rights, social and geographic mobility, minority rights, political organization and patronage, labor unions, nepotism, price controls, and a host of other social and economic institutions that have a part in income distribution in a country. Moreover, market forces are much less likely to play a dominant role in income distribution in the agricultural sector of an LDC than in the industrial sector.

Sociohistorical Variables

It is estimated that 70 percent of the impoverished live and work in the agricultural sector. Not surprisingly, the division of land and the income it generates has been a focus of analysts seeking the causes of poverty. When the poor have land ownership rights, their holdings are typically between one-half and five hectares. Sometimes such small holdings are made even smaller by subdivision of parcels among children. Population growth differentials between the poor and higher-income groups can affect these landholdings. Unequal land distribution often goes back centuries in origin, being connected with such factors as tribal dominance, foreign conquerors, colonial policies, and population growth. For owners of small plots savings and access to capital for land improvement are less than those available to wealthier landholders. Access to government distributed inputs is also uneven.

Tenants or serfs are locked into poverty intertwined with the laws and social customs determining the division of the crop revenues. Where there is an excess of unskilled labor as in surplus labor economies, tenancy rights can be weakened and attempts to improve them undermined by the labor surplus.

A peripheral point is worth noting here. In very poor countries (such as China after the end of the civil war and the ascension to power of the Maoist Communists), land and wealth redistribution can mean that the few who did not suffer from poverty before now join the masses who do. Relative inequality is reduced, but the country still faces the problem of destitution. The productivity of the redistributed land must increase in order to overcome the absolute poverty. Land redistribution or better tenancy rights may be steps in the right direction, but these cannot eliminate poverty.

Migrant farm laborers are usually the poorest of the poor with little surety in food deficient countries of an income yielding adequate nutrition. Their survival depends upon their ability to withstand harsh physical conditions without adequate calories. Tinkerers and the small-scale self-employed in rural areas can also be among the destitute landless.

As a sector agriculture often has the greatest absolute poverty but less inequality than other parts of the economy. Thus Kuznets noted that a sectoral shift away from farming can exacerbate the total economy's inequality. Morever, agriculture's total income and hence, the amount to be divided among inputs, is often influenced by government policies and their administration such as price controls, marketing boards, foreign exchange rates, and taxation. The industrial sector typically seeks low food prices. As it gains economic and political dominance national inequality can increase because of the constrictions upon the net income available to agriculture for division among the large population remaining there. There are then sociohistorical influences on the agricultural-industrial terms of trade, as well as economic structural influences. Government constriction of income available to agriculture contributed to inequality in Soviet Russia, despite the absence of surplus labor there and the state's egalitarian ideology.

In LDCs the majority of the poor work at some task. Unemployment as opposed to underemployment is a route to starvation unless you are supported by your family. Poorer economies generally have a cultural system for absorbing workers that avoids widespread joblessness and starvation. The newly emerging industrial sector typically is more impersonal, and lacks some of these sociohistorical traditions. As a result, the nonindustrial sector absorbs more workers when jobs are limited in industry. This heightens both equality in the nonindustrial sector and inequality between the nonindustrial and the industrial sectors. Thus the sectoral aspect of job expansion with growth affects the relationship between growth and inequality.

In some countries studies show that many of the unemployed in the modern sector are from wealthier families and have above-average education. They are awaiting "suitable" jobs. For this reason, unemployment figures in LDCs must be examined with care. They may reflect cultural attitudes about "appropriate" work, especially in urban areas. On the other hand, unemployment related to ethnic or other social causes of labor market segmentation can contribute to inequality.

Economic Systems

The third category of variables affecting income distribution is economic systems. The World Bank data (the most complete data source on inequality) identify the type of economic system that sets a lower limit on inequality. It cannot eclipse the structural variables that affect a developing economy or overcome completely sociohistorical variables. Yet it is generally recognized that an effective socialist or communist system can moderate inequality of income within the LDC environment. The question of greatest interest is whether fairly high inequality over the middle level of development is inevitable in mixed economies. Such economies encompass a broad and extremely diverse group of LDCs, including some that refer to themselves as socialist but do not have effective redistribution measures or extensive nationalization of production.

I. Adelman and S. Robinson develop a model used to explore the effects of different policies on inequality in mixed systems, using the South Korean economy as a source of basic data. Their findings cast doubt upon the usual approach to income distribution of single-policy intervention that leaves intact the basic structure responsible for the inequality. On the other hand, their simulations point to success for a mixed economy with built-in policies geared to the control of inequality. The mixed economy could tilt toward export promotion of labor-intensive goods instead of emphasizing import substitution. And marketing boards, cooperatives, and programs to improve agricultural productivity could substitute for extensive redistribution of land. But the economy would need a strong set of policies fostering social development, rural and urban public works, cooperatives, and industrial decentralization to withstand the strong forces in LDCs that rapidly erode the effects of piecemeal programs to redistribute income or wealth.

The authors conclude: "On the whole, our results underscore the difficulties of attempting to use effective policy intervention to improve the distribution of income. . . . [T]he implementation of a successful antipoverty program would entail either a change in the ideology of the ruling classes toward explicit egalitarian concerns or a certain degree of centralization of authority in order to overcome resistance by the rich, or, most likely, a combination of both. The problem would then remain of reducing the power of the centralized authority once its basic job is done" (in Loehr and Powelson 1977, pp. 22–23).

The fairly pessimistic conclusion of the Adelman-Robinson work is that there must be a systemwide approach to inequality that restructures the mixed economy; and such a reorganization carries with it the strong chance of overcentralization that can erode income growth. A more optimistic outlook on the chances of reducing inequality in mixed systems without excessive centralization can be found in a review of the Taiwan experience by Gustav Ranis (1977, pp. 41–59). Taiwan is a particularly important case study since it represents a surplus labor economy with high growth and favorable trends in income distribution. Thus population pressures toward inequality have been overcome.

Ranis argues that two conditions are necessary for results similar to those of Taiwan: Assets in all sectors must not be distributed very unequally as growth takes hold, and relative prices must reflect resource scarcities. Because these two requirements seldom have been met in the postwar growth experience, he states, the conclusion has arisen that there is inevitable conflict between distribution, employment, and output objectives in mixed economies.

Radical economists claim that the experience of the past decades has led to such great inequality that neither condition set out by Ranis can be satisfied short of a revolution. The radical economists give equity high priority and thus find the conclusion that drastic social change is needed is fairly straightforward. They would move to a socialist or communist system.

Once the topic of economic systems is broached, it should be noted that there are economic and political implications other than income distribution that affect comparisons among economic systems. The degree of inequality is one important element. The degree of centralization of economic decision-making is another element with far-reaching ramifications. Economic growth performance is a third important element. Moreover, political organization and the extent to which individual political and civil rights are protected vary more among mixed than centrally planned systems. This is because a centrally planned system must maintain control and must have a political organization that guarantees such control.

Here we note that mixed systems have higher levels and variance in measures of inequality than those that are centrally planned. The mixed economy with more-equal income distribution is often judged superior in social welfare to mixed economies with greater inequality. We return to the criterion of social welfare choice in a later section. The welfare criteria examined, however, concentrate upon income distribution, and are not designed for comparing simultaneously other important variables that affect well-being in different economic systems.

The Product Mix and Relative Factor Prices   The product mix affects the relative price of factors, P_L/P_K, and hence the functional distribution of income. This can be shown by considering first an economy producing only one good, good A. The economy has K capital and L labor, as shown in figure 14.3. There will be an

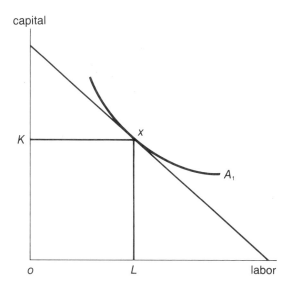

FIGURE 14.3

Efficient Relative Resource Prices

An economy with *K* capital and *L* labor producing efficiently can produce output represented by isoquant *A₁* at point *x*. The price of labor relative to the price of capital will equal the slope of *A₁* at *x* under scarcity pricing.

isoquant for good A that exhausts the total factors and provides maximum output under efficiency conditions. This is isoquant A_1, tangent to the point of intersection of the K and L coordinates at x. What will be the slope of a price line representing P_L/P_K that is consistent with full utilization of both resources? Only a P_LP_K line tangent to A_1 at x is consistent with cost-minimizing production at point x on isoquant A_1, as explained in chapter 12.

Now consider an economy that can produce either good A or good B, the latter a labor-intensive good. That is, for any given set of factor prices and output levels, good A uses less labor per unit of capital in production than good B. Thus the isoquants for good B are skewed toward the capital axis.

Figure 14.4 shows the isoquants for goods A and B that would fully employ all labor and capital when only one of the goods is produced. Notice that the absolute slope of isoquant A_1 at x is less than the absolute slope of isoquant B_1. If only good A is produced, then a P_L/P_K consistent with efficiency conditions is lower than if only good B is produced. This makes sense since good A is capital intensive, and the relative demand for resources will reflect the relative factor intensity. The slopes of isoquants A_1 and B_1 at x set the upper and lower limits for P_L/P_K. An economy producing both goods would have relative factor prices between these limits. The more of good A that is produced relative to good B, the lower P_L/P_K and vice versa.

Thus, the product mix affects the distribution of income between wages and profits when the return to factors reflect their relative scarc-

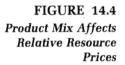

FIGURE 14.4
*Product Mix Affects
Relative Resource
Prices*

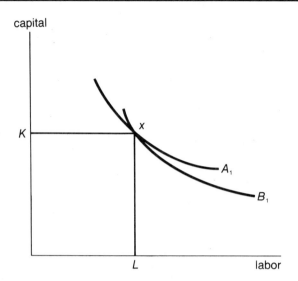

An economy with *K* capital and *L* labor can produce at *x* on isoquant A_1 or on isoquant B_1. The slope of B_1 in absolute terms is greater than the slope of A_1 at *x*. Production of only the labor-intensive good, good B, will result in P_L/P_K greater than production of only the capital-intensive good, good A.

ity in production. In an economy with an abundance of workers producing labor-intensive goods, income will still be very unequally distributed between recipients of profits and wages unless the limited capital is extremely widely held. The product mix cannot easily offset the effect upon inequality of limited capital held by a few in an economy with surplus labor. A supposition often made about labor-intensive production is that it will be of relatively smaller scale and allow widespread ownership of productive assets, thus limiting inequality.

Relative factor intensities among products reflect technical limitations of the production function and the design and quality of the product. Development literature has varied in its emphasis upon a more self-sufficient capital-intensive product mix as being a positive factor in development compared with a more trade-oriented, labor-intensive product mix. And very recently it has been suggested that deliberate changes in technology and product design are conducive to development when they increase demand for relatively abundant factors. These ideas were discussed in previous chapters. Here we emphasize that income distribution is affected by scarcity pricing of resources, which in turn is influenced by the product mix.

After this introduction to the topic of income inequality in LDCs, it is helpful to discuss problems of identifying guidelines for optimal income distribution.

There is no accepted principle for distribution of income that is intellectually satisfying in the sense that, given reasonable assumptions, logic shows welfare to be maximized with a certain distribution of income. To assess the community's well-being requires interpersonal comparisons about the distribution of income. And herein lies the problem. There is no way to speak precisely about the welfare received from 100 units of goods by Jane and compare that with Joe's welfare from the same goods, even though both received the same amount of the same item. There is no unit of measurement for the imprecise term "welfare."

CRITERIA FOR INCOME DISTRIBUTION

A person's welfare function is often assumed to be concave and to depend upon absolute but not relative income. That is, as individual income or consumption rises, welfare also does, but at a decreasing rate. However, in a very poor economy enjoyment of goods may rise at an increasing rate over certain income levels as higher income provides a minimum of accompanying health and other benefits that raise enjoyment potential. Even if the shape of the function were known, no two functions need be the same or increase at the same rate. With no certain knowledge of the welfare function and no unit for measuring it, the well-being of individuals cannot be compared.

Problems of Interpersonal Welfare Comparison

Because interpersonal welfare comparisons are subjective in nature, the discipline of Western economics shies away from them. The question of what income distribution maximizes welfare is left unanswered. Yet Western economics is a social science concerned with maximizing welfare from consumption through choice. Maximization of output is a route to maximization of consumption. To achieve the highest welfare possible, demand patterns must be known. These patterns are related to initial income distribution, which in turn depend on resource ownership. At this point, Western economics makes distribution of the ownership of resources an exogenous variable, a given. Under perfect competition functional income distribution is determined by the marginal product of each resource in its highest use. These returns include rents and quasi-rents on resources in fixed or inelastic supply in the short run.

In the competitive model the welfare level attainable by the individual, then, is a function of wealth and work, and reflects the scarcity value of the resources each individual owns, including human ones. The social welfare level is accepted if there is no change that would make someone better off without making someone else worse off—a criterion referred to as Pareto optimality. The distribution of income is in essence taken as given since there are many distributions that can satisfy Pareto optimality (Sen 1973, pp. 6–7).

Distribution is a vitally important, sometimes explosive topic. It cannot be ignored because of a lack of precise criteria for solving an optimum distribution. Discussion has proceeded by appealing to ideas of justice, ideas in part universal, in part cultural. Normative arguments about

Normative Criteria of Income Distribution

income distribution generally include needs and/or just deserts in developing an idea of "appropriate" distribution. Equal distribution of income is generally not the highest preference since it ignores "needs and deserts." Both of these terms, however, carry ambiguities.

There is a strong tradition defining appropriate inequality as the distribution associated with equal opportunity in a competitive market system. Everyone takes off from the same starting line and the race goes to the swift, so to speak. This idea of deserts ignores need but tries to eliminate differences in inherited wealth or power and differences in human capital caused by lack of income. It would not eliminate return to natural ability, which is unevenly distributed. Equal opportunity can be combined with an appropriate adjustment of the results to accommodate needs. This criterion, then, calls for establishing competitive markets. Moreover, we have intervened in a strong reason for saving according to some: the desire to secure family income. Would such saving be forthcoming without inheritance?

In economies that allow private ownership of capital, saving-investment is not determined by the state. Individuals save and invest. Returns from capital then become a source of inequality. The private mixed economy depends upon private decisions plus taxes to ensure adequate savings. What is the "appropriate" reward for saving-investment where there is private choice between consumption and saving? Can we assume that saving is a way of reallocating consumption over time, and will be preferred to consumption in some amount? Is the amount independent of the return to saving and the ability to pass on accumulated saving to heirs? (Recall from chapter 4 that income is an important determinant of saving, but that it is difficult to identify with confidence other determinants.) Where incomes are low, savings are limited and their scarcity value high. They are important to the size and growth of output.

Traditionally the need to elicit voluntary savings from the people has been a justification for greater inequality in market economies than is found in centrally planned economies. The saver in early paradigms of capitalism was a folk hero, sanctioned by the concept of religious stewardship over the assets arising from self-imposed thrift. While the income of the capitalist was high, it was used predominately to maintain and increase business activity rather than for personal consumption. Certainly this was the concept of the wages fund of the Classical economists. In such models the capitalist performs the role of the state in the planned economy in ensuring savings and capital formation.

The normative distribution sanctioned by Karl Marx was "from each according to his ability, to each according to his needs." (1875). This principle, however, required prior conditioning of human beings to remove their selfish proclivities unleashed by capitalism. Reward according to work effort was sanctioned for transition phases of communism (socialism in Marx's terminology). There has been experimentation by the communist Chinese in introducing the late-communism principle in early stages of precapitalist development. The Great Leap Forward, a grand design for simultaneous development of industry and agriculture begun in the late 1950s, and the Cultural Revolution of

1966–76 brought on by Mao and his wife in part to return the country to the basic principles of communism, both pleaded for adherence to the idealistic principle of Marx. These periods were marked by lowered output and great social tension for the Chinese. Certain egalitarian changes were subsequently rescinded.

The Chinese and the Russians—indeed most societies—have been faced with the need to acknowledge work effort in defining appropriate distribution. (Where there is no private income from ownership of physical capital assets or natural resources, then inequality reflects innate talent, human capital, and work effort in the perfectly functioning reward system.) Those who work harder and longer receive more. However, this introduces the problem of comparing work effort in different jobs. How do you gauge such effort objectively when each individual has different subjective utility and disutility in different jobs? And how do you weight the occupations of greater responsibility and implications for total economic performance? Does a scientist deserve the same pay per time period for effort as the coal miner, except for a differential reflecting income forgone during longer years of training?

Defining needs can be as challenging as defining equal work effort. The United Nations speaks of "basic" human needs like food, shelter, and health. But, for a poor society, what is the type and amount of shelter that is basic, that everyone should have? What diet is basic—a nutritional minimum (which can be very simple and cheap) or a desired diet? Poor societies generally have vastly inadequate health systems for the masses by MDC standards. How much of GNP should be devoted to health care as opposed to education or capital formation? Do so-called basic needs change as income per capita rises? Here, as with the concept of work effort, goals are imprecise and there is leeway for disagreement. Yet the general idea that need and effort should influence income distribution tends to be accepted, and capriciously determined income distribution is not widely held to be desirable.[3]

One other approach is of interest in relation to seeking justification for distribution guidelines. This one implies that when individuals are not encumbered by a known position of absolute and relative income, they will be objective in that their vested positions cannot influence their preferences. They are asked to rank by preference different income distributions under the assumption that probability determines the income they will have. The choices expressed can be assumed to reflect the individual's risk preferences and attitudes (innate or acquired) toward social justice.

This approach would rule out complete equality and high inequality, and establish a preferred set of social welfare choices in the intermediate inequality range. Only gamblers with no altruistic leanings would prefer high inequality unrelated to needs or deserts. They

---

3. Interestingly, many Third World economies reject the idea of private property rights over valuable national resource deposits as capricious distribution of income rights. Resources deposited under ground or water are viewed as belonging to all the people. Even with national ownership of the rights to income from natural resource deposits, however, income channeled through the government for resource depletion often ends up being a source of income inequality in LDCs.

would, as risk-lovers, gamble on being the high-income recipients. Most people would be risk-averse and would not choose complete equality or high inequality over a system that established reward for effort and needs.[4]

Concentration upon extremes leaves unanswered the questions surrounding the ambiguities of appropriate reward for effort and definitions of needs. The discussion brings us back, however, to the concern over high inequality (both observed firsthand and as measured by the Lorenz curve and GINI coefficient) that has emerged out of the historical context of development in LDCs, and provides philosophical grounds for moving away from high inequality. The problem still remains of how a society with existing high levels of inequality overcomes vested interests to reduce the disparities and establish a more equitable allocation of income. It is a telling point that the philosophical approach presumes individuals must be removed from their known income before a meaningful preference ranking emerges.

Conclusions   This chapter has explored causes or sources of high levels of inequality in some LDCs today. Problems of measurement of inequality and current empirical findings on this topic were presented. The issue in general is a difficult but important one that exceeds the boundaries of economics. Current knowledge leaves many unsettled areas, and offers no clear guidelines for assessing optimum income distribution.

Policies designed to deal with high levels of inequality have in general been integrated into discussions of technological change, agricultural transformation, promotion of industry, human resource use, and the like presented in other chapters. Additional areas for policy intervention are suggested in this chapter. Since our understanding of the forces determining inequality in LDCs is relatively rudimentary at this stage, the confidence with which policy can be proposed is tenuous. The reader interested in more detailed exploration of policy design is referred to The World Bank study, *Redistribution with Growth* (Chenery et al., 1974). In general, the focus is upon policies to equip the poor in mixed economies with more income-earning assets, including human capital (especially primary education), to provide them with better access to infrastructure and complementary government services, and to reduce their fertility rate. We turn now to consideration of income distribution in Brazil, which gave inadequate attention to these policy measures during the postwar period.

REFERENCES   Adelman, I. and Morris, C. T. 1973. *Economic Growth and Social Equity in Developing Countries.* Stanford, CA: Stanford University Press.

Adelman, I.; Morris, C.T.; and Robinson, S. 1976. Policies for Equitable Growth. *World Development* 4 (July): 561–82.

---

4. The principle may dissolve if it could be shown that the total income to be divided were a positive function of inequality. Then it is possible that higher income is attainable even for lower-income groups under conditions of high inequality. Thus we return to the importance of question 3 about the relationship between rapid growth and inequality.

Ahluwalia, Montek S. 1974. Income Inequality: Some Dimensions of the Problem. In Hollis Chenery, et al., *Redistribution with Growth*. London: Oxford University Press, chap. 1.

Bacha, E. L. and Taylor, L. 1978. Brazilian Income Distribution in the 1960s. *The Journal of Development Studies* 14 (April): 271–95.

Chenery, Hollis; Ahluwalia, M.; Bell, C. L. G.; Duloy, J. H.; and Jolly, R. 1974. *Redistribution with Growth*. London: Oxford University Press.

Chenery, Hollis. 1977. The World Bank and World Poverty. In *Economic Development, Poverty and Income Distribution*, edited by W. Loehr and J. P. Powelson. Boulder, CO: Westview Press.

Fields, Gary. 1980. *Poverty, Inequality and Development*. Cambridge, England: Cambridge University Press.

Fishlow, I. 1972. Brazilian Size Distribution of Income. *American Economic Review* 62 (May) 391–402.

Frank, Charles R. and Webb, R.C. (eds.) 1977. *Income Distribution and Growth in the Less Developed Countries*. Washington, D.C.: The Brookings Institution.

Inkeles, A. and Smith, D. H. 1974. *Becoming Modern*. Cambridge, MA: Harvard University Press.

Kuznets, S. 1963. Quantitative Aspects of the Economic Growth of Nations: Distribution of Income by Size. *Economic Development and Cultural Change* 11 (January): 1–80.

Lee, Teng-hui and Chen, Yueh-eh. 1979. Agricultural Growth in Taiwan, 1911–1972. In *Agricultural Growth in Japan, Taiwan, Korea and the Philippines*, edited by Yuiro Hayami et al. Honolulu: The University Press of Hawaii.

Loehr, William. 1977. Economic Underdevelopment and Income Distribution: A Survey of the Literature. In *Economic Development, Poverty and Income Distribution*, edited by W. Loehr and J. P. Powelson. Boulder, CO: Westview Press.

Marx, Karl. 1875. *Critique of the Gotha Programme*. 1938. Rev. translation edited by C. P. Dutton. New York: International Publishers.

Oshima, H. T. 1970. Income Inequality and Economic Growth: The Postwar Experience of Asian Countries. *Malayan Economic Review* 15 (October): 7–41.

Powelson, J. 1977. Operating in a Complex Society. In *Economic Development, Poverty and Income Distribution*, edited by W. Loehr and J. P. Powelson. Boulder, CO: Westview Press: pp. 113–43.

Ranis, Gustav. 1974. Employment, Equity and Growth: Lessons from the Philippine Employment Mission. *International Labor Review* 110 (July): 17–28.

———1977. Growth and Distribution: Trade Offs or Complements? In *Economic Development, Poverty and Income Distribution*, edited by W. Loehr and J. P. Powelson. Boulder, CO: Westview Press: pp. 41–59.

Sen, A. 1973. *On Economic Inequality*. Oxford: Clarendon Press.

Swamy, S. 1967. Structural Change in the Distribution of Income by Size: The Case of India. *Review of Income and Wealth* 13 (June): 155–76.

Syvrud, Donald E. 1974. *Foundations of Brazilian Economic Growth*. Washington, D.C.: Hoover Institution Press.

Turnham, David and Jaeger, I. 1971. *The Employment Problem in Less Developed Countries: A Review of Evidence*. Paris: Organization of Economic Cooperation and Development (OECD).

Weisskoff, R. 1970. Income Distribution and Economic Growth in Puerto Rico, Argentina and Mexico. *Review of Income and Wealth*, vol. 16, no. 4, pp. 303–32.

Brazil: Rapid Growth and Growing Inequality

Brazil is the largest country in Latin America in both geographic area and population. Her income per capita is similar to that of Mexico or Costa Rica. Brazil is a country with broad opportunity for capitalist free enterprise, including foreign direct investment. She has an excellent endowment of resources per capita, although she lacks oil reserves. Much of the resource base is in the rugged interior of the country and so is underexplored.

Brazil has long been characterized by its political limitations to balanced development and the plague of high inflation. She had two periods of strong growth between World War II and 1975, bounded by interim intervals of slower growth. The 1950s saw relatively rapid development. And in the period 1967–74 Brazil was one of the world's fastest-growing economies, averaging an annual growth rate in GNP of 10 percent. She is a country where rapid growth has gone hand in hand with high inflation, rising income, and sectoral inequality stemming from dualism. The political change in 1964 to military rule did not eliminate the income and sectoral imbalance or the inflation, but it demonstrated that authoritarian rule could achieve certain economic reforms and produce high growth in Brazil. The military regime's official policy on in-

come inequality alternated between neglect and weak, ineffectual efforts to halt the trend toward growing imbalance.

Brazil's growth experience illustrates the economic and political limits to controlling inequality once it has become very high. Another lesson from her performance is that reducing absolute poverty under the dual approach to development can require very high growth rates. Failure to achieve such growth can result in very little trickle-down effect and considerable political instability. Yet rapid industrial growth accompanied by intensifying sectoral inequality can be self-limiting.

POLITICAL POWER AND THE POOR

Brazil's governing oligarchy was dominated before World War II by the coffee barons; after the war, the coffee interests were still protected, but industrial wealth came to the fore and achieved political dominance. Gradually coffee became less important to Brazil's foreign trade and economic prosperity. Policies beneficial to these sectors were costly to the poorest segment of society, traditional agriculture, where the majority of the people earned their living as late as the mid-1960s. Reforms inaugurated by the military government that took over in 1964 corrected many of the previously created market distortions designed to spur industrial growth through import substitution. However, the reforms lacked the added thrust of assertive government programs to prevent further deterioration of relative income. The period of rapid economic growth in the late 1960s and early 1970s reduced absolute poverty to some degree, but relative inequality deepened. Perhaps in no country in the world are the contrasts in living standards between rich urbanites and poor peasants so stark.

AGRICULTURE AND POVERTY

Since the worst poverty exists in traditional agriculture, it is important to review Brazil's policies that led to stagnation for this sector. First, land distribution was very uneven and there was no effective effort to reallocate it. In the mid-1960s for instance, 3.4 percent of the farm establishments controlled 62 percent of the land; 35 percent of the farms operated with only 1.3 percent of the land. Large tracts were left idle or committed to land-intensive uses such as cattle raising, while poor farmers crowded onto small tracts. The land tenure system in Brazil is not progressive by international standards.

Second, there was a lack of supportive services needed to raise the traditional farmer's productivity. Programs like rural extension services, cooperatives, education, and research did not receive investment funds. The main solution to land shortage for the poor was to open up the interior. Peasants moved onto these lands with their same primitive techniques of farming. Thus farm output rose as population and land under cultivation increased, but agricultural productivity has lagged considerably behind gains made in other LDCs. Movement to new lands eventually slowed, while transportation, storage, and other costs rose as a result of increased distances from farm to market. The peasant was still locked into low-productivity agriculture, although labor density on the land fell somewhat.

The policies launched in the 1950s with the push toward import substitution and rapid industrialization greatly aggravated sectoral inequality and agricultural poverty. Specifically, agriculture was starved of investment credits to the benefit of industry. The exchange rate was overvalued, subsidizing imports to industry and penalizing agricultural exports except for coffee, which faced inelastic demand conditions and was given favorable treatment in the exchange rate. Inflation was high and continually raised domestic prices, squeezing the farmer between low export earnings and rising costs.

By 1953 the domestic terms of trade had turned against agriculture and in favor of industry. Food output lagged behind demand as a result of disincentives. The growing scarcity of food for the urban workers led to price controls and export restrictions for agricultural products. Not surprisingly, industrial wages in the 1950s were four times those in agriculture and workers fled the rural sector to live in city slums for the chance at an urban job. Most, ill-trained and uneducated, were employed in the service sector rather than in industry. The government also provided some with work (Syvrud 1974).

Stagnation of its agricultural sector deprived Brazil of a growing domestic market and exports needed for further industrial growth. Industrial output languished in the early 1960s. The military regime's solution was to correct relative price distortions and install credit and tax incentives—that is, to spur market forces in agriculture.

The removal of export restrictions, price controls, and devaluation of the exchange rate along with improved credit helped to diversify and increase agricultural exports. The market incentives, however, benefited the more advanced farmers—about 5 percent of the agricultural sector. Most traditional farmers were not touched by the program. Dualism *within* agriculture deepened as a result. Donald Syvrud concludes: "For the majority of Brazilian farmers market incentives are not sufficient; they must be supplemented with rural extension services, education, research, and in some areas, changes in the land tenure system." (1974, p. 236).

INDUSTRIAL WAGES AND INEQUALITY

Brazil's highest intrasectoral inequality is within industry. The sector has limited competition among firms in many areas but strong market pressures on wages. Certain pincers related to past inefficiencies and policy failures caught the military regime and limited the options for wage increases in the 1960s.

First, past inflation rates had been high, resulting in a negative interest rate. This, along with protectionist policies and subsidies for capital related to import substitution, left capital underpriced relative to labor. The industrial sector expanded behind tariff walls, absorbing a limited amount of labor. Industrial labor's marginal product was relatively high because of the capital intensity of production. Along with the neglect of agriculture, this meant that there was a gap in marginal productivity and wages between agriculture and industry and ample labor migrating to keep pressure on wages. Labor unions were kept under control by the government so that the wage earner's share of the industrial pie was subject to market forces. Yet the minimum wage rate was above the opportunity cost of migrating labor. And since interest rates were negative, labor was considerably overpriced in proportion to capital.

There were hard choices to be made in the 1960s to turn the economy around. The profitability and growth impetus from import substitution began to falter. Scale economies anticipated for a country as large as Brazil were not fully realized, due in part to the sharp inequality that limited the growth of mass markets. Foreign exchange constraints brought on by inefficient industrial expansion also appeared. The regime was faced with excess industrial capacity and a high inflation rate.

Failure to control wages in these circumstances would have (a) aggravated inflation in a period of slow growth, (b) increased migration rates, (c) offset the regime's attempt to raise the price of capital relative to labor by tightening credit and creating a positive real interest rate, and (d) made it difficult to improve the terms of trade between agriculture and industry. Limiting industrial wages was viewed by the regime as central to their effort to reduce the rate of inflation and allow market forces greater play. Not surprisingly, the policy of the military government was to let the real wage fall from 1964 to 1967 by keeping the increment below the inflation rate. This helped to control inflation in a time of currency devaluation, which is often inflationary.

The control of wages was also central to the thrust toward exports and away from import substitution. It was hoped that exports would be relatively labor intensive, increasing industrial employment opportunities, and that holding wages down would help to make the country's exports competitive. In fact, Brazil's export thrust proved quite successful. Wage control, however, allowed inequality to worsen.

EFFECTS OF RAPID GROWTH ON INEQUALITY: 1967–74

Gary Fields points out the absolute gains of the poor between 1967 and 1974. During these years of rapid growth, income in each decile rose. Those remaining below the poverty demarcation line experienced a marked percentage increase in income, sometimes as much as two thirds higher. This percentage exceeded that for those above the poverty line. These aggregates mask sectoral and occupational disparities in the gains of growth, however. Earnings of landless laborers did not increase at all, and the real minimum wage fell by 25 percent between 1964 and 1970. Areas of the economy such as the perennially povertystricken Northeast achieved very little progress (Fields 1980, pp. 210–18).

And as Fields, Fishlow, and others have pointed out, Brazil's relative income distribution worsened amidst rapid growth and under a government immune from democratic pressures to alleviate poverty. The GINI coefficient rose from .59 to .63 in the economically active population, and the income share of the top 3.2 percent rose from 27 percent to 33 percent (Fields 1980, p. 212). Regions such as that around São Paulo greatly increased their productive capacity of sophisticated goods and services, deepening the regional dualism of Brazil. They also attracted labor from rural regions, where inequality was lower. Thus the sectoral shift affected inequality.

The increase in relative inequality was reflected in greater wage disparity among occupational groups. Rapid expansion of the relatively modern, skill-intensive sector raised the demand for highly trained labor relative to the growth in supply. Yet that growth was quite impressive. College graduates increased by 79 percent compared with a population growth rate over the period of 33 percent (Fields 1980, p. 213). School enrollments increased dramatically. This demand for high skills took place despite a change in policy toward labor-intensive exports. Brazil turned away from a policy of import substitution where capital is subsidized. She controlled labor costs among lower-skilled groups, however, helping to raise occupational differences.

Critics of the Brazilian economy point out that the highly unequal income distribution promotes a product mix that brings high returns to modern skills, placing them at a premium under conditions of rapid growth. They maintain that multinationals share in the largesse while helping to spread tastes for consumer durables common to wealthier countries. This benefits workers able to transfer to the advanced sector and obtain the necessary skills; but their number is limited by the relative capital-intensity (human plus physical) of the modern sector. Supporters of the market-oriented development pattern note that any period of rapid growth in a country as resource-rich as Brazil can create rental returns to scarce factors that are quite high. They emphasize that income has trickled down to the masses and that all have shared to some degree in the growth. This, they point out, is preferred to more equal income distribution combined with negligible increase in earnings.

Yet most observers feel that the government's combination of the wrong policies and lack of policies allowed, or even caused to some degree, the rising income dualism in Brazil in the 1967–74 period, thus compounding an already highly skewed distribution of income. They point out that a different set of education policies favoring disadvantaged groups, coupled with attention to raising productivity in traditional agriculture in particular, would have been more conducive to balanced growth, would not have reduced the economy's momentum, and would have contained the growing inequality. And finally, there are the uncertainties over political stability in the absence of high growth rates and sufficient trickle-down effects to raise incomes of the bottom layer. Nationalism was used by the military regime to unite the population behind the government and gain acceptance of the sacrifices needed for growth. Brazil faces the threat, however, that nationalism can lose its appeal in the face of flagrant inequality and slow growth.

Human Resources and Their Use

chapter

15

The whole focus of development is to improve the well-being of people, many of whom lead lives of dehumanizing poverty. The other side of the coin is that the human condition ultimately is changed by people in their capacity as productive resources. The utilization level of human resources along with labor force allocation plays a central role in the determination of output. And additions to human capital via education, skill formation, and better health are vital to the long-run dynamics of development. Some aspects of the growth, deployment, and development of human resources have already been touched upon and integrated into the analysis of economic development. In this chapter these topics are pursued in somewhat more detail.

The chapter focuses upon dual labor markets, where some of the labor force work for themselves or their families and some work as hired labor. In order to explore labor supply of the self-employed, we emphasize allocation of labor hours by the household. (This approach is developed in depth in the following chapter.) The interrelation between household income for the self-employed and market supply of labor and wage rates is developed. Determinants of the long-run supply of labor and human capital formation are discussed. And finally, various explanations of unemployment in LDCs are presented. (A precise definition of unemployment as well as underemployment is developed in the next chapter.)

This introductory section describes in a very general way gradual changes that occur over the time span of development in the pattern of labor usage and production for the market. Time allocation analysis is helpful in discussing human resource responses in the absence of forced labor, and in interpreting empirical data on labor force behavior patterns with development. One particular trend of interest is the increased number of hours devoted to market production-consumption with development. Another significant trend, illustrated in table 15.1, is the rise in the percentage of the labor force in wage employment. To discuss these and other aspects of labor hours and their allocation, it is helpful to begin by describing an LCD household without market production, in an economy of self-sufficient farms and no labor market.

The technology used by such a household is primitive, workers' health is poor, and work conditions are harsh. The family whose consumption patterns are simple, produces both goods and services. A food crop is cultivated, water is hauled from a river, firewood is collected, food is prepared and stored, garments are made, entertainment is provided by ceremonies, child-care services are performed. Production and consumption both utilize time. Production-consumption activity is one category of time utilization; and the other is rest. Given production function constraints, the worker is free to allocate hours among activities so that the utility from time-consuming activities is maximized.

Constraints, especially those of farming, can force the worker to give up needed rest or endure seasonal idleness. The lack of a market

LABOR TIME USE IN DUAL MARKETS

Labor Hours and Allocation with Development

	Percentage of Labor Force in Wage Employment in:				
	Industrialized Countries		Middle-income Countries		Low-income Countries

TABLE 15.1
Percentage of the Labor Force in Wage Employment for Selected Countries circa 1970

Industrialized Countries		Middle-income Countries		Low-income Countries	
Sweden	91	Spain	74	Sri Lanka	54
USA	90	Argentina	71	Mozambique	40
UK	88	Portugal	70	Indonesia	33
Canada	87	Chile	70	Sudan	25
Switzerland	89	Mexico	62	Pakistan	22
Australia	85	Algeria	60	India	17
Germany	84	Venezuela	59	Tanzania	9
Norway	83	Brazil	55		
Denmark	80	Egypt	54		
Austria	79	Tunisia	54		
Belgium	79	Yugoslavia	50		
Finland	78	Ecuador	49		
Italy	70	Guatemala	48		
Ireland	66	Peru	47		
		Iran	44		
		Greece	42		
		Syria	42		
		Philippines	40		
		Paraguay	39		
		Korea	38		
		Morocco	37		
		Turkey	28		
		Thailand	15		

SOURCE: Lyn Squire, *Employment Policy in Developing Countries: A Survey of Issues and Evidence* (New York: Oxford University Press, 1981), Table 17, p. 58 and ILO primary sources listed there. Reprinted by permission.

for crops affects how many labor hours are allocated to farming. The amount of land per worker, work conditions, and worker health affect the level of utility (disutility) from production, consumption, and hours of rest relative to work. A time study for Cameroon illustrates how both males and females divide the hours of a twelve-hour day.

Development brings changes in labor resource allocation of the self-sufficient farming community. Continuous technical change in farming will raise the household's food supply and eventually lead to fewer hours farmed per worker unless the new technology involves elements that shift upward net utility from work or consumption. New crops, better work conditions, and so on could be elements of technological change that shift upward the marginal utility from farm production-consumption hours. However, it is the development of a market for output that can bring the greatest changes in allocation of labor hours.

The introduction of a market for crops increases the efficiency of farming through specialization. The gains from exchange will shift utility curves. It is quite likely that the substitution effect (where work hours that earn more substitute for hours of rest) predominates in agrarian LDCs as trade materializes, raising hours worked per worker in

	Males	Females
Farm Work	17	14
Nonfarm Work	22	9
Domestic Work	11	15
Illness	18	17
Social Activities	12	27
Rest	10	18

TABLE 15.2

Division of 12-Hour Day Among Activities (%) in Cameroon

SOURCE: Lyn Squire, *Labor Force, Employment and Labor Markets in the Course of Economic Development,* World Bank Staff Working Paper No. 336 (New York: Oxford University Press, 1979). Table 23, p. 46. Reprinted by permission.

farming. This is particularly true where the health of the household is improved by a more varied diet with trade. Better health reduces the disutility of work.

Cottage industries can also generate gains from exchange and specialization. Specialization emerges in clothing, utensils, tools, and other home-produced goods. Hours are now divided among home production-consumption, market production-consumption, and rest. Even with local and regional markets, however, the household at early stages of development allocates a large percentage of its time to goods and services produced and consumed at home. Transportation is time-intensive, limiting the size of the market and the gains from trade. The technical level of cottage industries is low and efficiency gains from specialization do not offset transportation costs for many items or services. Low incomes and small markets prevent scale economies.

Production away from the home eventually replaces cottage industries. Technical progress and growth of the market allow small manufacturing and service companies with hired labor to develop and operate independent of the household. Such firms gradually drive out cottage industries since they provide similar goods and services at a cost of fewer labor hours. The household shifts labor hours away from home production-consumption into market production-consumption. However, dualism can thwart a smooth transition here. Under conditions of dualism consumer goods production is geared toward upper-income markets. In the absence of an array of goods at prices competitive with home production, the household allots fewer work hours to farm or other labor for the market. The motivation for the household to supply labor hours to market production is the core of the Kilby-Johnston incentive effect of simple, labor-intensive consumption goods upon development (see chapter 9). Such goods provide a carrot lure, additional to the stick of taxation, that will ensure more hours for market output. When strong enough, this carrot incentive will offset any rise in disutility associated with market work as freedoms are lost and work conditions change.

Once the movement toward market organization gains momentum, constraints increase. They reduce the degree to which the household producing for market can approximate equilibrium in the allocation of its labor hours between home and market production-consumption.

Producing for the market requires greater regimentation and hence changed organization of production to meet delivery schedules, quantity and quality minima, and cost competition. Labor markets allocate relatively more labor and entail uncertainties and indivisibilities. The workday becomes prescribed by socioeconomic pressures. The pace and organization of tasks are not controlled by the worker to as great a degree.

The market reduces the interdependence of the extended family and scatters the family geographically as labor mobility needs rise. The reduced household size results in diseconomies of small scale in home production-consumption of goods and services. It makes social observances less feasible. The market worker tends to substitute material goods earned through market labor for social ceremonies and other activities carried on in the extended family.

**Growth Effects of
Labor Hour Shifts**

Market production-consumption has greater potential than home production-consumption for labor productivity gains arising from specialization and scale, technical progress, and capital formation. Growth, then, can be accelerated by a shift in labor hours from home production-consumption to market production-consumption. The movement of labor hours occurs as farm crops and cottage industries specialize for the market and as workers are absorbed into hired labor jobs. Growth is also accelerated by a reduction in hours of rest or leisure. The switch of labor from home to market production generally raises the hours of work per worker. Two forces bring this about: First, as mentioned, market production-consumption usually has a high marginal utility as against home production-consumption or rest, increasing the hours devoted to work. And second, the organization and regimentation of the work schedule intensify under market constraints, raising the workday hours.

The value of market output (GNP) is increased by the rise in labor hours and by the fact that productivity of labor hours spent in market work exceeds the productivity of home labor. Measured output grows by more than actual output, however. Labor hours formerly spent in nonmarket work that was not a part of GNP are now devoted to market work and included in GNP. Thus, the shift of labor hours from home to market production raises growth rates but confounds an accurate measurement of the increment.

The rise in labor hours devoted to market production is not inevitable. Recall that productivity gains may lower the numbers of hours voluntarily offered for market production-consumption when the income effect dominates. This dominance is not usually evident in early development unless the rise in utility from new goods is limited. We return to the point that the income effect is more likely to dominate under conditions of dualism where new consumer goods for the masses are not produced. Thus where development raises the marginal utility curve for market production-consumption, more hours are voluntarily devoted to work for the market. In the absence of such a shift, diversion of more hours to production for the market as a growth strategy would require that in some way such hours be "forced" upon the worker.

Growth gains from the shift effect as labor hours are reallocated is limited to the initial phases of development. In the long run, the increase in each worker's labor hours available for market production-consumption in most historical settings reaches a peak and eventually declines. That is, over an extended time span the income effect wins out, partly because once a large segment of the work force provides hours for hire and incomes rise significantly, the standard market work-week declines. The United States, for example, had a standard work-week in 1890 of 66 hours, dropping to 57 hours in 1910, then to 52 hours in 1930, and 40 hours in 1950. The reduced number of work hours are not all allocated to rest. When, with growth, the income elasticity of demand for market consumer goods and services favors those products that require more time to consume, fewer hours are available for production or rest. Time-consuming goods and services, including leisure activities, are curtailed in early development and then expand as affluence is achieved.

There is a policy problem related to the shift to market production, however. Undue emphasis on measured growth can lead to a neglect of opportunities to raise labor productivity in home production. As mentioned, home production-consumption remains an important part of their welfare for households in poor countries. Women perform much of the work for home consumption needs as the market absorbs relatively more males in off-farm work. Improved productivity in home production can make important contributions to the family's well-being, even though the productivity gains may be lower than those for market output. Home extension services can play a role in changing household production functions. The knowledge they provide is also vital to health improvements and population planning. Too little attention is given to the traditional areas of female work by male planners.

We conclude this section with a tangential point. Sometimes observers have been interested in the workday in LDCs measured against an international norm, usually an 8 to 10 hour workday. The workday of individuals, groups, and categories of labor in specific LDCs is observed to be less or more than the international norm. When an LDC is seen to have a shorter than normal workday, there are several possible explanatory variables. The observer may not have considered home production as part of the workday or may not be able to make comparisons in this category of work because of lack of data. Disutility from work may be relatively high because of low productivity, harsh working conditions, or poor health. The utility from work may be relatively low due to organizational features, tastes of the populace, or the absence of a variety of goods to motivate the worker. And finally, there may be constraints that limit the workday. Care must be taken not to make the hasty assumption that differences in tastes for work must account for the differential. Such international comparisons are a separate issue, of course, from the observation that over an LDC's long-run growth path labor hours per worker available for market production increase and eventually decrease, although the same variables will influence this outcome.

Dual Labor Markets   In very poor economies family production units share income among workers, so that the earnings of each approximate the average product of labor. This occurs in agriculture, commerce, and trades and even small family manufacturing operations. Social obligations require support of the extended family to a greater or lesser degree in such societies. Family members are given jobs and share in income. The family adjusts each worker's hours to maximize satisfaction from work and rest. When the economy has few complementary resources and low technology, the marginal product of one laborer working the standard ·workday or week is below subsistence. Withdrawal of such a person from family employ would reduce output by the labor hours lost minus output from any hours made up by the remaining workers.

When some production units experience technical change and/or resource augmentation, labor productivity rises. And with sufficient productivity growth, a laborer can be hired away from a less-efficient family operation. The value of the marginal product in such operations will exceed somewhat the value of the average product in family work of lower productivity. The former family worker is willing to toil for someone else when the net utility of the new work and consumption hours adjusted for their uncertainty exceeds the net utility of the work, consumption, and rest hours forgone. Work hours for hire grow with development, and labor markets allocate an increasing proportion of the work force.

Labor markets in LDCs have many variables affecting job allocation and wages. The supply of labor and a demand curve related to its marginal product may or may not influence greatly the wage rate. Assume for discussion purposes that labor markets evolving with development feature wages that approximate the marginal product of labor and that these wages reflect labor income outside the market for hired labor. The market wage does not equal the opportunity cost of labor from the family production units that have a low marginal product of labor but whose members share in the average product. That is, the value of the output lost as labor moves from jobs with low value of marginal product is less than the value added by the laborer in the higher-productivity job where the marginal product approximates the average income in the worker's former job.

The situation where some workers receive their average product and some their marginal product is described as dual labor markets. At a point in time a snapshot view of an LDC with part of the work force employed in jobs with higher value of marginal product than the remaining workers presents a picture of inefficiency. The value of total output could be expanded if labor were allocated so that its value of marginal product were the same in all production units of the economy. But if additional labor were to be added to sectors with higher productivity, the value of the marginal product would decline. Labor will not leave family employ for an income less than its value of average product there. Yet the more efficient units have no incentive to hire outside family members for more than the value to them of their marginal product. As a result, the family unit of shared income and employment remains strong during early development. It is eventually undercut by efficiency advantages in the hired-labor firms and changing demand patterns that emerge with growth. Moreover, it is more difficult for children of market hired-labor to be employed in a family firm since they must start such an operation. The risk of unemployment is higher for such labor force entrants.

The description of dual labor markets points to an interrelation between the market supply curve for hired labor and the self- or family-employed sector, which is a potential source of additional market workers when labor is mobile. In a country such as India where most workers are self- or family-employed, there is the seeming potential for the market supply curve for hired labor to be very elastic over a given range of wage rates. Before drawing this conclusion, however, we need to ask just how the self-employed sector influences the shape of the short-run supply curve for hired labor.

STRUCTURAL PROBLEMS AND POLICY GOALS

The alternative to working in the hired labor market is to work for oneself or one's family. Thus while the income for the self-employed does not reflect the opportunity cost of labor, it reflects the income forgone by the worker employed in the labor market and thus influences his/her willingness to leave self-employment. In order to predict how elastic the supply curve for market labor is, we must predict any changes in the income of the self-employed as labor is withdrawn from that sector.

The Short-Run Market Supply Curve for Labor

What effect will the withdrawal of labor from work for its own account have upon the value of the average product of remaining workers? This depends upon the production function of the self-employed, the sector-specific resources used, and the terms of trade for market-produced goods as labor leaves.

Income and hours of labor are determined simultaneously in the self-employment sector as workers seek to get the most utility from time available. Production functions and constraints vary among households engaged in family occupations. This means incomes will vary among the self-employed. We need to know, then, the particular type of self-employment from which labor is drawn to the hired labor market. Moreover, the households supplying market labor need not be the lowest-income households when mobility varies among the self-employed. In the absence of specific details on a particular LDC labor force, it is helpful to compare supplier households where labor is combined with a productive resource such as land with supplier households where labor utilizes very few complementary resources.

The transfer of workers from what W. Arthur Lewis calls marginal jobs such as bootblacks, messengers, servants, and petty trade, using only a few simple tools, will at most improve income for those remaining in such jobs because of reduced supply. The effect on income will be slight where workers were underemployed and good substitutes exist for the products and services provided. Workers may leave cottage industry for jobs in manufacturing firms turning out goods similar to the home manufactures. When this occurs, incomes of the remaining cottage workers often decline as manufactured counterparts are produced more efficiently and the supply of such goods grows.

On the other hand, when workers leave agriculture with its sector-specific resources, this withdrawal has a stronger effect upon the income of those remaining. The laborers staying on the farms have more resources per capita, and so the average product of labor rises. Total food output, however, will usually decline. There can be constraints in the production function such as peak-season labor needs that affect output as workers are lost by the agricultural sector. Even where underemployment exists, the additional labor hours put in by the workers who stay usually will not replace fully the hours lost when workers leave. Moreover, the demand for food is both price- and income-inelastic. Reduced supply raises prices sharply. In the absence of technical progress that improves labor and land productivity, or price controls, the terms of trade favor agriculture, increasing the value of the average product there, and the income of farm families. And even with constant terms of trade, the average income can rise because of the effect of the changed factor proportions of labor relative to other resources. Not surprisingly, estimates of short-run labor supply curves drawing upon rural households show an inelastic response to wage rate changes. (See World Bank studies by Pranab K. Bardhan [1977] and Lyn Squire [1981] and references there.)

Other factors influence the elasticity of the market supply curve for labor. The relative return to labor among sectors is often affected by taxation differentials. The use of some peasant earnings in agrarian economies to finance industrialization is not uncommon. When there are no large landlords the "surplus" income resides with the affluent farms where the average income per family member is above subsistence. Governments, either by taxation or state controls, have commandeered such income. This lowers the average farm income, reduces sectoral differentials, and raises the supply of labor to the industrial sector. The labor hours may also be hired by the government to raise investment and improve technology.

The job-related disutility of self-employment relative to wage employment will influence the supply curve for hired labor. Working for an employer often forces the worker to commit more hours to work than he or she considers optimal. Workers may consider the location and working conditions of the market job more or less desirable. Such a job may change the worker's productivity at home due, for example, to time commitment to the job under the standard workday or the lack of a vegetable garden plot in the city.

Where the self-employed live in relation to where the opportunities for wage employment are affects the elasticity of market labor supply curves. Hired labor jobs tend to be concentrated near urban areas in

LDCs. Migration rates from countryside to city reflect an imbalance in economic opportunities and job utilities. Some of the laborers relocating in the city become self-employed; some remain jobless. Studies of migrants show that economic betterment is the driving thrust behind their desire to relocate (Yap 1977). Many LDCs have experienced very high migration rates, especially where population growth enlarges the labor force at a rapid pace. The ability of the migrant to survive with minimum shelter in warmer climes also affects rates of population shifts. This relocation of the self-employed in urban areas and the existence of a pool of idle workers raises the elasticity of the supply curve for hired labor jobs.

Where workers are highly immobile, labor markets are segmented by caste or other barriers, tradition dictates job categories for women, or other impediments to labor transfer exist, then the supply curve will be inelastic. However, factors that make the short-run labor supply curve less elastic are often relaxed the longer the time period considered.

The wage rate for hired labor reflects institutional and market elements affecting variables of demand as well as of supply. The fact that in the absence of distortions, a given number of workers would be available at a series of possible wage rates may have only a limited effect upon the actual rate paid when disequilibrating forces are at work. Wages negotiated by labor unions in response to monopoly profits, or set by government edict and influenced by organized civil servants often create a disequilibrium wage rate so that too many workers are seeking these types of jobs. Where economic dualism exists, the duality of labor markets is intensified. The hired-labor market generally has dual wages for labor. Smaller operations using hired labor pay close to the income earnable in the self-employment sector, while large, capital-intensive operations and the government pay more. When the supply curve is relatively elastic, however, institutional forces must be very strong to overcome the basic market pressures toward lower wages in the face of excess job applicants at the going wage.

Wage Determination and Distortions

Labor force reallocation is fundamental to structural change and broad-based development in LDCs. And the shape of the short-run supply curve affects wage costs, profits, and savings. Labor supply is related to the impact of wage inflation upon the economy as demand for workers rises. Policies that encourage efficient labor force allocation and improve supply elasticity can also be those that promote broad distribution of the gains of development. They include programs that:

Policy Goals for Labor Markets

■ Motivate the self- or family-employed to allocate more labor hours for market relative to home production. Consumer goods for the masses are important to this policy goal.
■ Encourage action to raise the productivity of workers with the lowest marginal product in dual labor markets. As discussed subsequently in the chapter, primary education can be important here.

- Raise productivity on the farms through technical advances so that farm prices do not rise as labor leaves farm work.
- Locate industry regionally so that diseconomies of excess urbanization and migration are avoided, and labor supply pools develop near regional job opportunities.
- Overcome labor market distortions that segment labor markets and intensify dualism.
- Raise productivity of workers in home production. This frees labor for market production and improves living standards.

The need for some of these goals is underscored in the last part of the chapter by discussion of unemployment, and in the next chapter by in-depth analysis of the household's allocation of labor hours. Additional policy needs are discussed in these sections.

Supply of Labor: Long-Run

The chapter up to this point has concentrated upon the short-run supply of labor and shifts in the short-run supply curve with growth. We discussed labor hours supplied by the self- or family-employed and labor hours supplied to the hired labor market. Now we turn to the concept of a long-run supply curve of labor and its determinants.

By far the most important variables affecting the long-run supply curve of labor in LDCs are fertility and mortality rates (Stolnitz in E. O. Edwards, ed. 1974). As explained in chapter 7, these variables influence the growth rate and age composition of the population. The age composition affects the percentage of the population in the labor force.

The long-run supply curve for market labor is affected by changes in labor force participation rates. Durand, using data from the 1960s, finds labor force participation rates by those between 15 and 19 years of age are 61.6 percent in MDCs and 75.5 percent in the least-developed countries. A dramatic difference marks the labor force participation rate of those over 65. Only 29.5 percent have jobs in advanced countries whereas 63.4 percent are working in the poorer countries (Durand 1975, Appendix H). Lyn Squire reports that women's labor force participation rates vary markedly in different regions of the world. Arab countries have low participation rates, Southeast Asia's are high; in India and Africa rural rates are high but urban rates there are low, while in Latin America it is the reverse (Squire 1979, p. 17). Male labor force participation rates for those between 25 and 55 are high in all countries.

Various factors influence participation rates in addition to demographics. These include:

- Changes in education qualifications for labor force entry. Secondary and college education delays labor force entry.
- Differences in mores governing women's participation in the work force. Religion, tradition, family organization affect these rates.
- Structural change away from agricultural production. Activity levels for males in the age groups 15–19 and 65 and over decline as the agricultural labor force relative to the total labor force shrinks with industrialization.

The population growth rate, however, is the variable expected to have the largest impact upon labor supply in the LDCs into the year 2000. Already LDCs have experienced growth rates in their labor force almost twice as high as those realized by MDCs during their period of industrialization (Squire 1979, p. 4).

In both the long and short run, it is meaningful to talk of supply curves for different types of labor, even though there is a high elasticity of substitution among workers. While unskilled labor is a large category in poorer economies, labor training take's place and produces workers in skilled categories. Development of labor skills is both costly and vital to an LDC's progress. The next section explains the importance of investment in human capital and identifies policy options for the LDC.

HUMAN CAPITAL FORMATION

Education can be in large part an end in itself or, in economic terms, expenditures for it can be treated as consumption. Education also affects growth. Certain aspects of education have the characteristics of investment. That is, education can be viewed as a produced input that, once resources have been devoted to it, affects output over a given period of time. Like physical capital, human capital can depreciate over time and become obsolete.

An LDC oriented toward development will need to improve the quality of its human capital stock gradually, raising the level of training and education. Countries that have been successful in their development efforts and have avoided dualism have upgraded the skills and training of the total labor force, including those people outside the organized labor market. Rural workers and self-employed women are especially important in this context.

Yet there is a limit as to how fast human capital can be accumulated. Education must compete with other uses for savings. Just as with physical investment, resources are used in a current period to increase future output. When schooling is treated strictly as investment and not consumption, efficiency demands that savings be allocated to the investment areas of education and physical capital based on a review of all investment opportunities in these areas and comparison of their expected increment to output less cost. Output expansion may include education's external effects beyond its specific impact upon the worker's productivity. The costs of education must include forgone output students would have produced if they were not in school. The time flow of costs and output increments differs among projects and must be discounted. These expected increments in net earnings from investment opportunities can be expressed as a compound rate of return on the investment. Tax money would then be allocated to projects with the highest expected return.

Types of Labor Force Investment

Informal education in LDCs can compose an important and large part of total training. Formal education interacts with informal training, upgrading it. For example, studies indicate learning that can affect human capital formation begins at a very early (preschool) age. Upgrading of parents' skills and knowledge carries over into child training, improving the labor force quality in later periods. Training of the work force in LDCs is to a large degree a learning-by-doing process. Here, too, formal education can play a supportive role, improving on-the-job training, whether structured or unstructured. An example of such supportive formal education is government-sponsored agricultural and home extension service designed to reach into the hinterland. Skills developed here, including those related to housing, health, and nourishment as well as farming, are vital to the economy.

Primary education has received increasing emphasis of late for its potential contribution to labor force competence. Basic education skills attainable in primary education are integral to the gradual upgrading of mass labor skills. In fact, the expected return to primary education in the form of development impact is generally greater than the expected return to higher education. In part this reflects the relative costs of the two. Thus even though increased output from investment in primary education does not begin until labor force entry, the expected rate of return, including both direct and indirect returns to the economy from basic education, is large. It is impossible to measure some of these returns. For example, the inculcation of discipline and study habits leads to continuous learning and self-improvement applicable to the economic sphere. This receptiveness to learning is among the most important products of a fledgling education system because it is prerequisite to technical change. The economic planner cannot calculate the value of such intangibles. Yet their presence leads to a strong conclusion: When the society fails to maintain and improve the skill levels and learning process of the masses, including those of women in the home, the economy cannot experience broad-based development. Successes like Japan, the Soviet-Union, and Taiwan all testify to the productivity of broadly disseminated education. Table 15.3 shows the progress made between 1960 and 1975 in LDCs in advancing the level of formal education.

In addition to stressing basic education and the upgrading of work skills and learning, the economy must enlarge the percentage of the labor force with more advanced technical skills. Mechanical, business, science, engineering and similar industry-oriented skills must be provided to a growing proportion of the work force, and the level of such skills upgraded. The ability to absorb and adapt modern technology depends upon these capabilities along with the more basic ones of the mass labor force. Training for technical careers will require secondary education plus some postsecondary schooling, along with on-the-job training.

More advanced formal training must be carefully weighed against alternative returns to savings invested in physical rather than human capital. The two can be complements but they are also in part substitutes. The costliness of more advanced formal learning in labor hours forgone and appropriation of scarce savings dictates the need for frugality and efficiency in offering such services. The fact that an economy efficiently allocating human capital funds can only afford to develop

Educational Level and Year	Country Income Group				All Developing Countries
	Low[a]	Low Middle[b]	Inter- mediate Middle[c]	Upper Middle[d]	
Primary[e]					
1960	42	47	53	72	47
1965	50	53	63	76	54
1970	52	55	70	80	58
1975	56	58	75	85	62
Secondary[f]					
1960	15	8	11	20	14
1965	21	13	15	27	19
1970	23	16	20	33	22
1975	25	21	28	45	26
Tertiary[g]					
1960	0.9	2.3	1.8	4.5	1.5
1965	1.4	3.4	2.7	5.7	2.2
1970	2.3	4.0	4.3	6.7	3.2
1975	2.4	4.8	7.6	11.3	4.4

TABLE 15.3

Enrollment Ratios by Levels of Education and Country Income Group

a. Less than US$265 per capita in 1975.
b. Between US$265 and US$520 per capita in 1975.
c. Between US$520 and US$1,075 per capita in 1975.
d. Between US$1,075 and US$2,000 per capita in 1975.
e. Proportion of group aged 6–11 years enrolled in primary schools.
f. Proportion of group aged 12–17 years enrolled in secondary schools.
g. Proportion of group aged 18–23 years enrolled in higher education.
SOURCE: Lyn Squire, *Employment Policy in Developing Countries: A Survey of Issues and Evidence* (New York: Oxford University Press, 1981), Table 13, p. 50. Reprinted by permission.

a limited supply of these advanced skills means such labor will have high earning power because of a rental return to the human capital.

Two extremes can occur in misallocation of education funds. In the first attention is paid only to training an elite in advanced skills. This limits broad-based development and conditions necessary for steady upgrading of the labor force. The incomes of the elite are high compared with the illiterate masses. Another approach has been to spend too much on higher education relative to physical capital, primary education, and supportive job training. The rental value of the educated is reduced by their unemployment so that savings spent on a portion of education gives a negative return. Migration abroad and thus permanent loss is common as the educated jobless seek work in economies with sufficient complementary capital and advanced technical requirements to make use of their skills. Or the unemployed migrate to urban areas within the country. There they often foment political unrest while awaiting jobs they judge suitable to their expectation levels based on their education.

Public support of education in addition to private inputs is warranted for two reasons. First, education brings benefits external to the firm. The firm cannot capture the full return to its educational process. In

Public Support and Social Responsibility

particular, companies that train workers cannot recoup the training costs when workers leave to work for other enterprises. As a result firms consider investment in workers risky and limit training to types and levels that yield a higher internal return. In the absence of state support, this results in underinvestment in worker training.

Second, the individual or family is often unable to finance the amount of education that would be optimal from the economy's standpoint because of poverty, risk, and capital market limitations. The individual faces uncertainties about the return to investment in education. Risk aversion on the part of the individual, the family, or the financial institution lending funds (if any) for education will affect the education level. The private lender demands a premium for assuming risk, especially in the absence of collateral. Private financing of formal education would only be available to the very rich in LDCs because of the poverty of the masses. Financial markets generally do not make loans for human capital. State-supported education reduces the risk premium and risk-aversion factors. It allows schooling to be made available to the most talented regardless of financial status, or at least permits a closer approach to using the best talent available. Attention to women's education increases the talent pool.

The population in LDCs usually exhibits strong demand for subsidized education. The state generally finances a large proportion of it, and does not charge full price for it. This can create excess demand and give rise to the need for rationing. In particular the private as opposed to the social return to education may include access to jobs with higher status or less disutility. Moreover, compared with primary education, higher learning can be more heavily weighted toward private gains than social returns. The earnings potential is then very high for such human capital, and education is avidly sought. Because the economy is poor, criteria for limiting access to education are required when the government provides it free or at highly subsidized rates. Academic potential is generally the recommended criterion to ensure the highest return to the investment in public schools.

Many writers on development feel care should be taken to establish the social responsibilities of the few educated elite during periods of development when the LDC cannot afford to finance a large supply of individuals with more advanced education. The foreign exchange costs for those sent abroad can weigh heavily upon some LDCs; and the students abroad who fail to return abrogate their social obligations to their native land. Failure to return may be to avoid heavy taxes or other devices to limit high incomes of the educated and control national inequality. Yet the poor LDC simply cannot afford to educate its best talent to be sent abroad in a world of self-interested nation-states, where reciprocity for this gift is not forthcoming. Few situations illustrate more vividly the dilemma of unbridled self-interest and freedoms in conflict with national welfare.

Investment in Health   The allocation of savings to public health expenditures is also considered to be a form of human capital investment. Both productive life span and labor productivity can be affected by health. Moreover, the loss of children before their productive years is reduced when health improves.

As with education, investment in the health of the masses has returns to the society as a whole and warrants state subsidy. Areas of high return for tax monies spent are health education and preventive medicine. Examples are nutrition, hygiene, prenatal and postnatal care, eradication of disease-carrying hosts, identification of symptoms and simple home remedies for common infections, and regimens for health promotion such as dental care. Also, training personnel in these areas is not inordinately costly relative to health benefits it confers.

The majority of the populace remains in the countryside for a prolonged period over the development process. Geographic dispersion of health services to the hinterland is vital therefore to maintenance of the health of the masses. And of course, one of the most basic health requisites is adequate food intake for the total population. This in turn is connected to agricultural organization. Thus part of food consumption, if not all, is human capital formation.

The United Nations has stressed the importance in development of providing "basic human needs" such as adequate food, decent housing, safe water supplies, modern medical care, and clothing for the masses as priority areas for resource allocation. While such emphasis can result in slower physical capital formation for the economy when it raises consumption levels, elements of such basic consumption contribute to improved health, and thereby can raise productivity. Such gains are generally not sufficient for choosing a basics-oriented development on economic growth grounds alone; rather the approach of meeting primary human needs must reflect social goals. But the basics approach properly handled has an aspect of economic health that can help to offset the effects of reduced investment in directly productive capital.

UNEMPLOYMENT IN LDCs

The return to the existing stock of human capital from investment in health and education is affected by the allocation and level of employment of these stronger, more capable people. Analysis of unemployment and its causes in LDCs has produced various explanations. We turn now to a discussion of this topic.

Measurement of Unemployment

Classification schemes used in MDCs for counting the unemployed are often misleading or just not applicable to LDCs (Bruton 1978). Self-employment is much greater in LDCs than MDCs. In India less than 20 percent of the labor force are classified as "employees" compared with over 90 percent in the United States. Even in middle-income LDCs it is common to find fewer than 50 percent of the labor force receiving wages. The farm family, the shopkeeper's family, the cottage weaver, the fisherman, the tinkerer, the child shepherd are all working, even though often erratically, during a year. Tribal leaders who arbitrate disputes or the elderly who supervise children are engaged in activities that would demand pay as judges or day-care workers in advanced societies. Much of women's work in LDCs, like food processing, farm labor, weaving, sewing, and cooking are activities that provide paid jobs for workers in advanced countries. It becomes difficult with such widespread self-employment to identify the labor force and define employment and unemployment, In fact, the term "unemployment" may not be in the vocabulary of the population in general. Yet, economists proceed to transfer this advanced economy classification, albeit with some modification, to LDCs and seek to measure unemployment and trace its causes in this type of society.

Determinants of Unemployment

Unemployment relative to underemployment tends to rise with specialization, industrialization, and accompanying labor markets, as well as with urbanization. The specific causes of unemployment vary among LDCs. Data are poor and economists are not sure which causes are most important or how extensive joblessness is. Estimates vary by regions. One study shows Latin America had unemployment rates of 5.1 percent in the 1970s while the figures were 7.2 percent for Asia excluding communist China and 9.6 percent for Africa (Sabolo 1975). Unemployment is estimated to have grown more rapidly than employment since the 1960s. The stituation is expected to worsen into the 1990s (Todaro 1977, pp. 166–67). We turn now to a survey of various explanations of unemployment in LDCs.

The Factor Proportions Problem

Table 1.3 in chapter 1 shows that labor force allocation proportions and the proportion of GNP generated in the primary, industry, and service sectors are far from equivalent. The primary sector absorbs a much larger percentage of the labor force than its percentage of GNP, while industry's share of GNP exceeds its share of the labor force. The same is true of the service sector until late in the development process. And that sector accounts for a larger share of labor force absorption at all levels of per capita GNP than the industrial sector.

Proportionality between GNP and labor force percentages cannot be expected since there can be consistent technical differences in production functions within each sector that limit the profitability of labor absorption in the aggregate and make one sector more labor intensive. However, the limited absorption of labor by the industrial sector with GNP expansion in LDCs has caused observers to examine closely the causes of this sector's relatively low labor absorption.

The idea that there has been a historical bias in technology development toward capital-intensive technology was discussed in chapter 5. Such a bias may lead to technological unemployment; and it implies that countries with little capital relative to labor are at a disadvantage in utilizing more advanced technology to raise factor productivity compared with countries that have higher capital/labor ratios.

One of the first hypotheses relating technical bias to unemployment was developed by R. S. Eckaus and was illustrated in figure 3.8 of chapter 3. The argument divides the economy into industrial, agricultural, and export sectors. It is assumed that the production functions for the latter two sectors are relatively labor-intensive, while that for industry is relatively capital intensive. As explained in the Kelley-Williamson-Cheetham model (chapter 8), differing factor intensities in the production functions affect the allocation of labor among sectors. The idea that all production functions over time have experienced technical change making them more capital-intensive means that there are limits to labor absorption. These limits are more readily encountered when demand patterns favor industry output over that of other sectors. With development, Eckaus posited a factor proportions problem in a closed economy; that is, technical rigidities in the production function for all industrial goods prevent labor absorption at full employment with a declining role for agricultural labor. He noted that foreign trade involving specialization in labor-intensive goods could allow an LDC to overcome this type of unemployment. Sen and Marglin, as shown in figure 4.3 of chapter 4, emphasize that a retreat to traditional technology when there is a factor proportions problem will reduce output and savings.

Whether or not there is a factor proportions problem traceable to technical rigidities is an empirical question. However, it is an extremely large empirical question since it requires examination of the mix of industrial output in regard to the technical limitations of absorbing labor at various relative prices of capital and labor. Not only is the size of the empirical needs intimidating, but testing of the hypothesis from available data has to date proved intractable as well (Morawetz 1974, p. 516).

The factor proportions problem will be aggravated by high rates of population growth. Fast expansion of population makes it difficult to maintain and add to the human and physical capital per worker. The rate of absorption of new job seekers can be slower than their rate of increase when population growth expands the younger age group in relation to the total population. When labor absorption limits are reached, unemployment ensues. Unemployment among youth is especially high in LDCs and is traced to high population growth rates in some countries.

The higher labor force growth relative to growth in capital results in a need to raise capital productivity if full employment is to be achieved and per capita income increased. Labor productivity growth cannot depend upon increased capital per unit of labor to as great a degree as when labor force growth is lower relative to capital. We are back then to the need for intermediate technolocy that raises both capital and labor productivity with growth and eliminates technical limitations to labor force absorption.

Chapter 5 discussed intermediate technology as a potential cure for low productivity in labor-intensive methods of production and for unemployment associated with modern technical bias. Some economists argue that vintage equipment is a currently viable alternative to modern technolocy and any unemployment it may cause. Here again the empirical base for this argument is limited.

Relative Prices   Evidence has grown that LDCs' resource prices often do not reflect the scarcity value of the resources. It has been noted that capital costs are frequently subsidized by overvalued or preferential exchange rates, tax subsidies, controlled interest rates, and other devices. These lower capital costs relative to labor costs, particularly less-skilled labor. Firms then substitute capital for labor.

Some students of development deny the existence of a factor proportions problem and trace unemployment to policy distortions in LDCs. Others acknowledge these price distortions probably play some part, but hold that other rigidities and constraints, in particular socioeconomic variables, play a part also. For example, studies show labor markets in some LDCs are segmented along ethnic lines, leading to very uneven responses to demand shifts and/or increases.

The Product Mix   If some products are more labor-intensive than others, then the product mix can affect unemployment. Specialization and trade in more labor-intensive goods, as mentioned, could raise employment levels. The effect of domestic demand patterns upon employment has also been noted. Tastes, perhaps due to exposure to consumption patterns in affluent countries, may favor goods and services requiring relatively more capital to produce. Thus even when labor is correctly priced so that labor-intensive items are relatively cheap, the quantity demanded may not be very large because of tastes. A different product mix in this situation would require a change in tastes toward more labor-intensive goods or controls.

Some economists have explored income redistribution as a method of shifting the product mix toward more labor-intensive goods. The assumption here is that the type, quality, and amount of products consumed vary with income. While some studies indicate that such a change would increase employment, others note that the countries with unequal income distribution consume large amounts of labor-intensive services. The rich hire servants, buy custom-tailored clothes, and make use of labor-intensive tourist services. Income redistribution in such cases would add little to employment, although it would change the type of job available to a portion of the work force (Cline 1975; Chinn 1977; Morley and Williamson 1974; and Berry 1981).

Another approach emphasizes the effect of the product range upon labor requirements. The definition of a product or an industry is not unambiguous. Goods with varying characteristics can serve the same need. Some economists note that goods that are simpler to make and considered of lower quality often require greater amounts of unskilled labor. Studies show that once the product is fully specified, resource substitution potentials are greatly limited (Morawetz 1974, p. 530). It is pointed out that mimicking products of the advanced countries to fulfill various needs has unnecessarily constricted labor absorption in industry. Foreign firms may play a part in this pattern. Moreover, since they face lower capital costs, they have less incentive to change the product so that it absorbs more labor.

Products of lower quality can often be produced by smaller-scale operations. There is scattered evidence that smaller firms are more efficient in their use of capital and are more labor-intensive. They may also, however, face lower labor costs than larger firms in some LDCs.

Excessive import substitution is often associated with product mix distortions, and has been cited as a cause of unemployment. Importables are often high quality, technically advanced products that tend to use greater amounts of relatively scarce resources when made within the LDC. Excessive home production of importables due to overprotection absorbs relatively scarce resources into production marked by low absorption of labor.

Ironically, education has led to unemployment problems. In LDCs highly short of many modern skills, the schooling process has often contributed to investment in the wrong type of human capital, or overinvestment in specific types. This can be connected to poor planning for human capital formation, income distribution and elitism that lead to education of upper-income people for status occupations, acquisition of inappropriate education abroad, and unrealistic expectations about suitable jobs for attained levels of education. Unemployment connected to urban migration, discussed below, is associated with the level of education.

Education

Education of the right type and quantity can facilitate substitution of human for physical capital in manufacturing while raising productivity of labor. Employment rather than unemployment is such a situation is promoted by education.

Unemployment is often concentrated in urban areas, especially industrial centers. Many of the unemployed are migrants attracted to cities. Why do migrant numbers exceed job opportunities in urban areas? In the time allocation framework used previously to discuss labor supply, work is assumed to provide both utility and disutility. The utility of various types of work (urban versus rural) includes location factors.

Urban Migration

The younger, more educated seek jobs commensurate with their education level. Such jobs carry status and have a distinct utility-disutility set. They tend to be located in cities in the government or industrial sectors or the professional sector serving these segments. Migration can be a prerequisite to attaining such jobs. The less educated also seek better jobs than they can find in rural areas. And location factors affect consumption available, particularly leisure consumption. Some consumption items such as water from a public spigot (versus water carried from a river), streets, and public health, are provided free or are subsidized in urban areas. In many LDCs the difference in consumption choice and hence utility can be large. And the distance from health facilities can be lifesaving.

Information costs are high in LDCs, and migrants are uncertain about the number of openings for them. Even where unemployment rates in urban areas are known, migrants must make decisions based on the probability of obtaining a higher net utility position than they can achieve in rural areas. Information costs, plus transportation costs, are lower for migrants from nearby. Thus studies show distance is a factor influencing migration.

Michael Todaro emphasizes that the potential migrants compare their *expected* utility for a given time horizon in the urban sector with the rural utility to be given up over that same time period, adjusted for time flow. Under conditions of uncertainty about that utility, percep- tions of the unemployment rate greatly influence migrants' expecta- tions (Todaro 1968). Migrants often spend time in jobs in the informal sector that generate lower income and job utility before locating pre- ferred work in the modern sector, and this also affects total utility expected. With a high urban unemployment rate, the probability of finding the type of job sought is low and this affects the expected utility from work in the urban sector and thereby migration rates. But when unemployment is perceived to be low, the expected utility from mi- gration adjusted for time flow is high. The migration rate induced by more employment tends to raise unemployment. This lowers expected income and the flow of migrants. In this scenario there must be con- straints in the expansion of "plum" jobs sought by migrants relative to those with qualifications for such jobs. The unemployed generally need some help from their families to survive. Supportive relatives then share in the job lottery benefits that come, if they come.

Governments can increase unemployment in this model by raising the rural-urban differential in amenities, or by expanding the number of jobs in the cities, which increases the probability of migrants' lo- cating work. Planners can decrease unemployment by paying attention to the causes of dual labor markets and the need for balanced geo- graphic development, encouraging smaller urban centers than those currently emerging. LDCs today have many more cities, and those they have are larger, than today's MDCs experienced at comparable levels in their development. The cities in many cases have encountered dis- economies of scale and exhibit negative externalities when their effect upon total development is considered. Unemployment is one of those diseconomies. A shortage of food with excess migration is another.

In addition governments can correct policies that spread the lim- ited scarce resources poorly, concentrating them in sophisticated prod- ucts and advanced technology projects so that for each unit of scarce resource only a limited number of jobs for unskilled or less-skilled workers is created. Policies that encourage work sharing and second shifts to utilize scarce capital can be instituted. Such programs reduce the rural-urban wage differential and help expand job opportunities.

Aggregate Demand Output changes in important activities such as agriculture and trade can cause a shortfall of aggregate demand, leading to unemployment in various sectors. Bad weather or a drop in the terms of trade can produce income-related employment dislocations. Uncertainties caused by political tensions can also reduce aggregate demand.

The applicability of Keynesian-type stimulus of aggregate demand to the problem of unemployment in LDCs is limited by distortions and by general response problems in underdeveloped market systems. Prices often fail to give accurate information guidelines, markets are segmented, and in some cases resources are not highly responsive to relocation incentives. In particular, generalized deficit spending and unselective taxation policies may have very limited impact upon the level of unemployment. Programs to activate idle resources must be carefully tailored to the economy at hand. The Keynesian framework as it applies to the use of monetary policy to activate idle resources is discussed in chapter 17. As explained there, Keynesian policy is more appropriate to the counteraction of cyclical forces in MDCs than the type of unemployment generated in earlier stages of growth in LDCs.

How high is the cost of unemployment? This question is fairly complex. First, it is generally assumed that the jobless are maintained in some way but at a lower consumption level because of unemployment. Recall from chapter 4 that Sen and Marglin argued that unemployment can be a cost paid for higher growth. Growth can be faster with unemployment when there are technical rigidities causing the marginal product of labor to be low. Employment of idle labor when wages exceed their marginal product, and workers' marginal propensity to consume from wages is one, results in less saving and capital formation. More employment in these circumstances means less employment growth as capital expands at a slower pace. Utility, measured by a discounted time stream of consumption, could be less with the maximization of current employment. Again we note that the degree of such technical rigidities is unknown. There is also the difficult problem of comparing utility between generations. Finally, there are other costs of unemployment in addition to forgone consumption.

The Cost of Unemployment

Consumption is not the only utility created by work. Work itself generates both utility and disutility. Transfer payments to the unemployed can replace part of the lost consumption but cannot provide work that hones human capital to sharper skills and may create greater disutility by its absence than its presence. While rest and some home production-consumption are gained by the unemployed, the utility of marginal hours spent in such pursuits may be low when they are available in large quantities. By the same token, the absence of market work implies forgone creativity and social status, and increased uncertainty. Low transfer payments to the unemployed plus the discontent over their lack of access to market jobs by those without possible family employment can lead to political instability. And the economy suffers from the deterioration of human capital.

There are other losses as well. Concentration of capital in a few capital-intensive projects can reduce total labor hours supplied. Such projects restrict by design labor hours per unit of capital. The remaining labor force has less capital and hence lower productivity. This can decrease the labor hours offered when low-productivity, low-income jobs attract fewer hours before the marginal utility of work is exceeded by the marginal utility of rest. The loss of output from fewer labor hours must be offset against the gains of technically advanced, capital-intensive equipment.

Another cost may accompany concentration of capital in highly capital-intensive modern equipment. There may exist a range of more labor-intensive production technology that is not used because, given the scarcity prices of capital and labor in LDCs, the most advanced equipment that has a lower L/K is more efficient so that by using it costs are less. This is an efficient micro criterion. However, it ignores the sectoral shift effect that can be achieved when an overall approach · of capital-spreading is applied in the modern sector, using the vintage equipment with a higher L/K ratio. Both the latest equipment and the vintage equipment raise the productivity of labor transferred from the traditional sector. The latest advanced machines raise labor productivity more but draw fewer workers from traditional work; that is, the sectoral shift effect is lower. Viewed from the vantage point of the aggregate economy, then, the vintage equipment may raise efficiency as much as the most modern. This occurs when the sectoral shift effect outweighs the efficiency differential between vintage and advanced equipment (Donaldson 1981). When it does, policies such as a penalty for capital intensity would be appropriate to ensure the use of vintage equipment.

In sum, when there is a trade-off between unemployment and growth, care must be taken to identify and weigh all the costs of unemployment against the gains of growth. Innovative but efficient work sharing to help workers maximize their time allocation, and support of greater labor intensity in the modern sector are two avenues that promise less unemployment with minimum trade-off, if any, in growth. For example, in Japan access to jobs in the modern sector was spread by a policy of early retirement without retirement income from such jobs, as well as adaptation of technology. When unemployment arises from some of the distortions discussed earlier, then income and work are forgone unnecessarily, compounding poverty. Remember, however, that with the socioeconomic conditions of poverty, policy distortions are not always easy to correct.

Centrally planned economies, while they lack efficiency related to the flexibility of decentralized systems, usually are effective in minimizing unemployment. By commanding labor hours they avoid in general the costs of joblessness unless the planning is inept. Any costs of work sharing are paid by the state, and the laborer's disequilibrium in time allocation is more likely to be on the side of overemployment, largely because of limited market consumer goods purchasable from wages. However, state regimes that demand labor hours from the populace do not necessarily try to control completely the individual's job choice or education choice. Even in planned economies wage differentials often play an important role in allocating labor. Reward through status and prestige is relatively more important where consumer goods are limited, however.

REFERENCES

Bardhan, Pranab K. 1977. Wages and Unemployment in a Poor Agrarian Economy: A Theoretical and Empirical Analysis. World Bank Working Paper. Washington, D.C.

Berry, Roger. 1981. Redistribution, Demand Structure and Factor Requirements: The Case of India. *World Development*, vol. 9, no. 7, pp. 621–35.

Bruton, Henry J. 1978. Unemployment Problems and Policies in Less Developed Countries. *American Economic Review*, vol. 68, no. 2, pp. 51–55.

Chinn, Dennis. 1977. Distribution, Equality and Economic Growth: The Case of Taiwan. *Economic Development and Cultural Change*, vol. 26, no. 1, pp. 65–79.

Cline, William. 1975. Distribution and Development: A Survey of the Literature. *Journal of Development Economics*, vol. 1, no. 4, pp. 359–400.

Dasgupta, Biplab; Laishley, Roy; Lucas, Henry; and Mitchell, Brian. 1977. *Village Society and Labor Use*. Delhi: Oxford University Press.

Donaldson, L. 1981. Efficiency Ranges for Intermediate Technology: A General Equilibrium Approach. *Greek Economic Review*, vol. 3, no. 1, pp. 59–70.

Durand, John D. 1975. *The Labor Force in Economic Development*. Princeton, NJ: Princeton University Press.

Hart, Keith. 1973. Informal Income Opportunities and Urban Employment in Ghana. *The Journal of Modern African Studies*, vol. 2, no. 1: 61–69. Reprinted in *Development Economics and Policy*, edited by Ian Livingstone. London: George Allen and Unwin, 1981, pp. 75–84.

Morawetz, David. 1974. Employment Implications of Industrialization in Developing Countries. *The Economic Journal*, vol. 84, pp. 491–542.

Morley, Samuel and Williamson, Jeffrey. 1974. Demand, Distribution and Employment: The Case of Brazil. *Economic Development and Cultural Change*, vol. 23, no. 1, pp. 33–60.

Sabolo, Yves. 1975. Employment and Unemployment 1960–70, *International Labour Review*, vol. 112, no. 6, pp. 401–17.

Squire, Lyn. 1979. *Labor Force, Employment and Labor Markets in the Course of Economic Development*. World Bank Staff Working Paper No. 336. Washington, D.C.

———. 1981. *Employment Policy in Developing Countries*. London: Oxford University Press.

Stolnitz, George. 1974. Population and Labor Force in Less Developed Regions: Some Main Facts, Theory and Research Needs. In *Employment in Developing Nations*, edited by E. O. Edwards. New York: Columbia University Press.

Todaro, Michael P. 1968. An Analysis of Industrialization: Employment and Unemployment in LDCs. *Yale Economic Essays*, vol. 8, no. 2.

————. 1977. *Economic Development in the Third World*. New York: Longman.

Yap, Lorene Y. L. 1977. The Attraction of Cities: A Review of Migration Literature. *Journal of Development Economics*, vol. 4, no. 3, pp. 239–64.

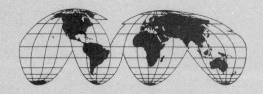

Ghana: The Effect of High Urban Migration on Employment Patterns

The many types of self-employment that emerge in the "informal" sector of urban areas illustrate how migration affects overall labor force allocation, as well as allocation between the formal and informal sectors. It is from the informal sector that most additional urban wage earners are drawn; and thus the opportunity cost of employment here affects the short-run supply curve of labor. This sector also teems with activity not found in the rural villages from which migrants come. There is a differential in work hours supplied per laborer between the rural and urban areas. Generalizing about this informal urban employment is not easy. It can vary among cities within the same country and there are insufficient data and descriptions of this portion of the urban economy. Here we rely upon Keith Hart's study of one city in Ghana, Accra, in the 1960s for an illustration of the informal urban labor market and its implications for efficient labor allocation (1973, pp. 61–89).

Ghana is a country of 11 million people in West Africa, roughly half the size of Kenya and with about the same per capita income. Like most African nations she has a high birth rate (about 49 per 1,000 population) and a sharply declining death rate, resulting in rapid population growth. A smaller proportion of the population is in agriculture than in Kenya

and a much higher proportion is in urban areas—approximately 36 percent in 1980 compared with 14 percent for Kenya. Population in the cities climbed by 5.1 percent between 1970 and 1980 versus an overall growth in population of 3 percent. Accra, the capital, is one of two cities with more than 500,000 people. Life expectancy at birth in 1980 was 49 years. The adult literacy rate in 1960 was 27 percent; however, school enrollment has risen dramatically since then; 80 percent of males and 61 percent of females were enrolled in primary school in 1978. Secondary school enrollment stood at 32 percent while approximately 1 percent pursued higher education.

Ghana has a very small industrial sector, concentrated in the cities. In 1960, 14 percent of the population was employed there and this grew to 20 percent in 1979. She is an exporter of agricultural and other primary commodities and an importer of food and manufactured goods. The high migration to the cities affects her sectoral output and was accompanied by decreases in the urban real wage in the 1960s. We now take a detailed look at employment and unemployment patterns in Accra.

Table 15.4 shows that over a third of Accra's labor force in the year 1960 was employed in the informal or self-employment sector. Nima

		Percentage				
	Males		Females		Total	
Economic Situation	Accra	Nima	Accra	Nima	Accra	Nima
Public-sector Employee	30.3	29.3	6.9	2.6	22.4	22.9
Private-sector Employee	31.6	31.2	6.3	2.7	23.0	24.6
Employer/Self-Employed	21.5	18.2	67.5	81.6	37.1	32.9
Other Nonwage Earning	4.2	2.7	3.9	2.4	4.1	2.7
Unemployed	12.4	18.7	15.5	10.8	13.5	16.9
Total Economically Active	100	100	100	100	100	100
Not Economically Active (as % of working-age population)	15.1	6.3	42.0	52.0	26.6	23.3

TABLE 15.4
Economic Situation of Working-Age Population in Accra and Nima, 1960

SOURCE: Keith Hart, Informal Income Opportunities and Urban Employment in Ghana. *The Journal of Modern African Studies*, vol. 2, no. 1, p. 76, 1973. Reprinted with permission of Cambridge University Press.

is the center of one slum on the city's northern outskirts. The 26.6 percent of the work-age population that is "inactive" are mainly housewives, students, or disabled persons. Thus the category of self-employed, as defined here, omits activities not sold in the market. Notice the large proportion of women who are self-employed.

Unemployment in Nima is relatively high among men compared with Accra. The small number of educated elite in Accra, often exposed to Western education, typically look down on many occupations and seek bureaucratic careers. However, those who leave middle school often have to settle for blue-collar work. Educated youths awaiting suitable jobs compose a good proportion of the unemployed.

Employment in Accra's formal sector labor market is mainly in sales jobs for women and some tailoring. Male employment in the formal job market is mainly in manual work, with white-collar jobs composing only 8 percent of the occupations. Wages are low and workers may double up on shift work if possible or supplement earnings in the informal sector, or even hold more than one job. Migrants seeking formal sector jobs must stay in the informal sector for more than one season to gain employment because of the competion for these jobs.

The self-employed range in scope from prosperous entrepreneurs to those pursuing petty endeavors to sustain themselves. They include truck farmers on the city's outskirts; artisans with small tools like sewing machines, cobbler tools, and furniture-making tools, who often work outside under a tree or in their living quarters; barbers; washerwomen; brewers of homemade beer; transport operators; commodity speculators; traders in food and handicrafts; wholesale merchants; millowners; landlords; and brokers in many areas of distribution. While those carrying on these occupations are often illiterate, informal training and knowledge are essential. Artisans, for example, typically undergo an extended apprenticeship with scanty pay to acquire their skills. In addition to legitimate activity, there is also a high incidence of illegal activity in the informal sector, such as black-market operations, fencing of stolen goods, and prostitution.

In addition to education, family environment, ability, training, and location, ethnic factors determine access to jobs. Tribal and regional loyalties are strong in Ghana, as in many countries in sub-Sahara Africa. This results in segmentation of labor markets. Many workers only apply for a job if the kin group is able to smooth the way. It is quite common for migrants from the same village to be clustered in an occupation.

One of the most striking outcomes of the job mix and wage scale open to the mass of workers in Accra is the fact that most workers have more than one job. This can be a mixture of formal-informal work or more than one job in either sector. This holds for the individual as well as the family. Hart writes: "This preference for diversity of income streams has its roots in the traditional risk-aversion of peasants under conditions of extreme uncertainty, and is justified by the insecurity of urban workers today" (in Livingston 1981, p. 80). The informal sector is highly risky and workers will seek even a badly paid formal sector job when it adds to the security of their income and when the opportunity cost of their time in the informal sector is not too high. Of course, the worker prefers a better-paying, secure job in the formal sector. Since the marginal product for most in the informal sector is low and the insecurity high, wage employ is highly prized. The short-run supply curve of labor to the formal sector as a result is highly elastic in Accra.

What can be said about underemployment in Accra? First, full-time workers employed at the government minimum wage are often as underemployed because of poor management as many in the informal sector without formal wage employment. Second, many migrants hold more than one job, and some have built up their self-employment into prosperous undertakings, legitimate or illegitimate. Their hours of work certainly exceed those in the agricultural villages from which they migrated. There technology was primitive and only one crop a year was eked out from poor land. With a higher marginal product in the city, they have traded rural leisure for urban work.

The informal sector is rife with petty capitalism and urban cottage industry. But a few amass enough capital in the very saving-deficient economy of Ghana to build thriving small businesses and even hire workers away from self-employ. The productivity of such capital can even far exceed that of endeavors such as the capital-intensive brewery operated by the inexperienced government trying to increase employment. In other words, there is often an unevenness to slum activity around cities attractive to illiterate migrants in developing economies. Some of this activity can be quite dynamic. And a few make it out of the slums by husbanding scarce capital until they can build a prospering small-scale firm providing attractive goods or services. Services tend to dominate the activity in value terms. Many of the goods providers must struggle to compete once more efficiently produced manufactured items become available, especially where these goods are of a quality and type attractive to the same market served by artisans and urban cottage industry.

The Household Time Allocation Model*

chapter

16

G enerally labor supply curves for the MDC market economy are composed mostly of workers who are employed by others. In a less-developed economy populated by small landholders or tenants, by cottage industry and family businesses in the main, the predominate portion of the work force does not enter the labor market. The workday and workweek are not uniform as in a market for labor. In agriculture weather and seasonal factors play a large role in determining the flow of work and shape of the workyear. In many areas of self-employment, there is greater leeway for the laborer to adjust hours on the job than under a regimented market workday, week and year.

This chapter develops a model useful in explaining and predicting optimal time allocation by the household member. The model yields insights into labor supply and allocation where tradition is not all-controlling, and workers are not in bondage or serfdom. The analysis serves to explain a backward-bending supply curve of labor hours, the amount of such hours devoted to market as opposed to home production by the self-employed, the effect of land distribution and taxes upon farm output, and allocation of time to investment. Definitions of unemployment, overemployment, and underemployment are derived within the framework and then used to clarify the concepts of surplus labor and "forced growth." This last topic is related to the type of economic system a society has.

The Household Time Allocation Model

The task here is to analyze the short-run utilization level and allocation of labor resources in an LDC, and see how the short-run labor supply can vary at different levels of development. It is helpful to begin by viewing the household as the labor supply unit and by assuming it is a self-sufficient production unit free of outside forces or constraints affecting its behavior. In LDCs the household may encompass the extended family. Each potential worker in the household faces a time constraint; that is, a given number of hours are available to each worker over a time period, say a year. We speak of a representative worker as a helpful fiction in various discussions that follow.

The household production function is known and, in the short-run, labor is the only variable input. Thus, we might think of land as the fixed input to which labor hours are added. When all workers toil an extra hour, the change in output is the marginal product of an extra hour of work of the representative worker times the number of household workers. Assume momentarily that the workers produce only one good (which is consumed within the time period studied) and that there are constant returns to additional labor hours.

Since the reason for production is consumption, these two activities are treated as one time-consuming activity. Time available to the household can be divided between production-consumption activity

---

*This chapter is designed to give the interested reader a framework for analyzing specific topics related to human resource use. To a certain degree it is like an appendix to chapter 15.

and rest. The *net* satisfaction rendered by production-consumption hours is determined by physical and psychic responses to:

1. Disutility of work
   (a) fatigue
   (b) work conditions
   (c) health of the worker
2. Utility of work
   (a) status
   (b) social interaction
   (c) satisfaction of creating
   (d) security
3. Utility of consumption
   (a) tastes
   (b) survival needs
   (c) level of consumption
   (d) variety of consumer goods

Variables listed under 1, 2, and 3 suggest factors influencing the utility-disutility set.

Each hour worked produces the same output under constant returns. However, each does not produce the same utility or disutility from production-consumption activity over a given time period. Given work conditions and the health of the worker, as more hours are worked per time period, fatigue sets in and incremental hours yield increasing levels of disutility.

The utility from additional hours spent at work (utility from both consumption and work) also varies with hours worked. It is common to assume that an activity that produces utility produces less of it for each additional unit. Diminishing marginal utility is encountered as more and more time is allotted to production-consumption.

The *net* utility from production-consumption per time block is the utility of work and consumption minus the disutility of work. Even when the output per work hour does not vary with the number of hours put in, the net utility from production-consumption hours increases at a decreasing rate and eventually declines when the disutility of additional work hours becomes high enough.

The worker wishes to maximize utility from production-consumption and rest to the degree that constraints allow. Here the only constraint is assumed to be that of time. The net utility from production-consumption time must be compared with the utility from hours spent at rest, the only alternative use for them, when determining the allocation of total available time. The satisfaction received from additional hours of rest will also exhibit diminishing marginal utility.[1]

---

1. The analysis can be cast into a more sophisticated theoretical framework where the assumption of diminishing marginal utility is not needed. The findings based on diminishing marginal utility are consistent with those of the more sophisticated approach. Moreover, the marginal utility curve for production-consumption can be expressed in calculus notation as:

$$dU/dt = dQ/dt \cdot dU/dQ$$

Consider how the representative household member in the absence of any constraints except that of time allocates total time between production-consumption activity and rest over a given period in order to maximize utility. Because the marginal utility of each activity is falling, the household member can maximize utility by dividing time between rest and production-consumption so that the marginal utility from the last hour spent on one equals that of the last hour spent on the other. Figure 16.1 illustrates this. The marginal utility curve for production-consumption as the time allocated to this activity increases is read from left to right, while the marginal utility curve for rest is read from right to left. Total utility is the area under the marginal utility curves. On either side of t, the shaded areas show the utility loss compared with allocation at t.

The household's net marginal utility curve from production-consumption depends upon the production function that determines the output per hour worked, the utility from consumption and work, and the disutility from work. Modifications in variables affecting any of these will shift the net marginal utility curve. For example, changes in the tastes of the family that affect the satisfaction received from work-consumption or rest will shift the affected marginal utility curve and change the equilibrium time allocation for the worker. Changes in work conditions, and hence the utility-disutility from work, will also shift the net marginal utility curve of production-consumption.

Generalizing, when there is more than one consumption good upon which production time can be spent, the same principle holds: The last hour in production-consumption for each good and the last hour for rest must yield equal utility in order for the household to maximize total utility. The graph is two-dimensional and cannot handle multiple goods deftly.

The assumption of constant returns to additional hours or work can be dropped without difficulty. Assume now that because of diminishing returns, the output of a good falls with additional hours of work. The change in net marginal utility from production-consumption time is a function of the change in output per time period and the change in utility associated with consumption of the additional units of output. Since the rate of production per hour of work is declining, this will tend to lower net marginal utility; however, the slower rate of consumption per time period will tend to keep the utility from ad-

---

where U = utility, Q = output, and t = time. In addition, assuming all inputs but labor constant:

$$dQ/dt = dQ/dL \cdot dL/dt$$

Since the input of one laborer's work per hour is considered, dQ/dt is the marginal product of the representative worker. There is also a production function for rest. The marginal utility curve for rest for the representative worker is straightforward. The price of rest is the forgone output and vice versa. In equilibrium:

$$dQ_r/dt \cdot dU_r/dQ_r = dQ_c/dt \cdot dU_c/dQ_c$$

or

$$dU_r/dt = dU_c/dt$$

where t is the proxy for opportunity cost, and the subscripts r and c stand for rest and production-consumption, respectively.

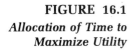

FIGURE 16.1
Allocation of Time to
Maximize Utility

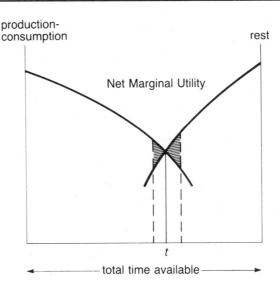

Utility from time allocated between production-consumption and rest is maximized at point *t*. Hatched areas show utility that would be lost if time were allocated either side of point *t*, where marginal utilities are not equal.

ditional consumption per time period (that is, marginal utility) higher than when the rate of consumption is faster. Net marginal utility still declines, although at a different rate.

Constraints other than that of time affect the household's ability to maximize utility by allocating available time among various production-consumption goods and rest so that the last hour spent on each yields equal utility. Examples are the uncertainties of weather and technical rigidities of the production function. When rainfall is uneven, planting and certain other farm tasks may demand long workdays or workweeks that cannot be avoided without crop loss or severe damage to the harvest. Or, the production function may involve technical rigidities so that a block of time is necessary to turn out a particular good or none will be made.

The conceptual framework can be adapted to incorporate the situation where the good produced is sold on the market, and items for consumption are purchased with the proceeds. Here we must know the terms of trade for the producer—the price of the good sold relative to the price of purchased goods. Given the utility function, the production function, and the terms of trade, it is possible to speak of the consumption utility each production hour generates. The terms of trade, then, become an additional variable that can shift the net marginal utility curve of the self-employed worker.

MODEL
APPLICATIONS:
AGRICULTURE,
EMPLOYMENT

Agricultural output is of particular interest in LDCs because even when it makes up less than half of GNP, it accounts for a large percentage of household expenditures, and contributes directly to wage rate increases that affect prices, costs, profits, and output in nonagricultural sectors. Given the labor-intensity of agriculture in early stages of development, the number of hours worked per laborer on the farm producing a crop for market is vitally relevant to the LDC's development potential. The household time allocation model can be applied to allocation of labor hours on the farm. Here we work through several examples to illustrate the usefulness of the model, and begin by examining what effect the number of family workers has upon the hours each works.

Let the one good of our model be a crop produced on a self-sufficient farm. The effect of household size on a given farm upon hours worked per representative worker is indeterminate. This can be shown by simplifying the original graph and showing the net marginal utility curve for production-consumption as a straight line, AB in figure 16.2, which implies a constant rate of decline of marginal utility. Now let line CD be the net marginal utility line for a representative worker on the same farm when the household size is smaller. More land per worker raises his or her productivity so that there is more output and hence total utility the first hour worked. However, because more consumption is available each succeeding hour worked, the marginal utility declines more rapidly along CD than when there is less output and consumption per consecutive hour worked.

Family Size, Income, and Work Hours Per Worker

Whether the representative worker in the smaller household works more, less, or the same number of hours as his or her counterpart in a larger household depends upon the marginal utility of rest relative to the marginal utility of production-consumption. When the marginal utility of rest cuts the two lines at E, time allocation does not change. To the left of E, the representative worker in the larger household works fewer hours; and to the right of E, he or she works more hours.

Since income per capita is lower in a larger household, other things being the same, why don't workers always work more hours and thus raise their income? The answer lies with the satisfaction received from rest relative to income, and with diminishing returns. Because of diminishing returns, the extra work produces less additional consumption for the representative worker in the larger household than in the smaller household with more land per laborer. The marginal utility of rest may outweigh the marginal utility from longer hours that generate small additional output for the poorer household members. This is shown in figure 16.2. A relatively high marginal utility curve for rest, MU_r, for both households results in the representative worker from the larger one devoting a hours to production-consumption, compared with c hours for the representative worker from the smaller.

Income and Substitution Effects

However, when the marginal utility curve for rest is relatively low, as shown by MU_r' in the same figure, a representative worker achieving equilibrium in a larger, poorer household will work longer hours than one in a smaller household, the difference being $a' - c'$. In the larger household the typical member receives more utility from additional hours in the neighborhood of a', c' than in the smaller one, despite

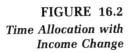

FIGURE 16.2
Time Allocation with Income Change

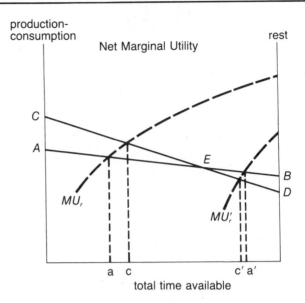

A representative worker with net marginal utility line *AB* may work more or less hours than such a worker with net marginal utility line *CD*. When the marginal utility of rest intersects *AB* and *CD* at *E*, both representative workers allot the same hours to work and rest.

producing less per hour. The reason lies in the greater number of hours both large and small households work when the marginal utility of rest is relatively low. While there is diminshing marginal utility in both size households, a representative worker in the smaller one produces and consumes more per time period than such a worker does in a larger household. As a result, the marginal utility curve declines more rapidly for the small-household member. After point E, the marginal utility of an additional hour's work is lower for the smaller-household member than the larger household member even though output from the additional hour is greater. In this vicinity the marginal utility curve for production-consumption is lower for the member of the smaller household because of the dominance of diminishing marginal utility of consumption as more hours are worked. The smaller household member then allocates fewer hours to work than the larger household member.

　The effect of income upon hours worked has been illustrated in figure 16.2, since *AB* is the net marginal utility of the representative worker at lower income and *CD* is the net marginal utility for the same worker at higher income. A rise in the representative worker's income may increase or decrease the hours worked, depending upon the marginal utility of rest. When the representative worker puts in fewer hours at a higher income level, as at c' compared with a', the *income effect* is said to dominate as the more affluent worker substitutes leisure for work.

Alternately, should the representative worker move from a to c as income rises, there is a substitution of production-consumption hours for hours of rest. The rest hours are relatively more costly to the affluent worker since he or she loses more income per hour of rest. This, considered alone, will lead to a *substitution effect* as hours are shifted away from rest into production-consumption. And while income is higher and therefore more rest is affordable, the substitution effect is relatively more important than the income effect in this case.

The effect of land redistribution upon total farm output depends upon the relative production efficiency of estate versus smallholder agriculture, the allocation of resources prior to redistribution and their relative quality, and the effect of redistribution upon total labor hours available to agriculture. In order to concentrate on the effect of land redistribution upon total labor hours, let us assume that all land and labor are homogeneous, that the production function technology is the same for estate and smallholder agriculture, and that prior to land redistribution smallholders and estates each have, in aggregate, half of the total farmland.

Land Redistribution and Farm Output

Estates have fewer laborers and labor hours available to them. Smallholders do not work for the estates part-time either because of transportation costs or because of the disutility associated with working for someone else. Smallholders work their acreage until the marginal product of labor is below that of estate land. Their incomes do not depend upon the marginal product, but instead they receive the average product of their labor. In contrast, labor markets for hired workers establish a wage reflective of labor's marginal product or its opportunity cost and the disutility of estate work.

Consider first the effect of land redistribution upon the hours of farm work of the smallholder receiving land. Land redistribution from large estates with hired farm labor to the self-employed farmers may either raise or lower the hours worked by the representative farmers, depending upon their MU_r curve and the amount of land they acquire. The line CD in figure 16.2 now represents marginal utility after land reform. The acquisition of *enough* land will raise the slope of CD so that E is to the left of the MU_r curve. When this occurs, fewer hours of work per worker are forthcoming. However, it is quite possible that land acquired from redistribution is of a size that results in a movement from a to c, indicating the worker toils more hours.

Redistribution also affects the number of hours offered by hired workers. As estate land is cultivated more intensively, the marginal product of labor on it is lowered; and as less labor is crowded upon the portion of land originally held by the smallholders, the marginal product rises there. This means that if the wage rate reflects the marginal product of a hired worker's labor hours, then wages fall. At a lower rate of pay, hired workers offer fewer labor hours.

Figure 16.3 shows the results of the case where there are fewer total labor hours available from both farmers and hired workers after land redistribution. Prior to land reform total hours offered are OO'.

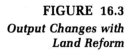

FIGURE 16.3

Output Changes with
Land Reform

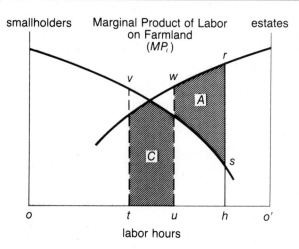

Prior to land reform total output is the area under the smallholders' MP_ℓ curve from
O to h. Estate output is the area under the MP_ℓ curve for estate land from h to O'.
Maximum possible output with the same labor hours is the total area under the two
intersecting MP_ℓ curves. When land reform reduces labor hours by tu labor hours,
total output changes by the net gain area A minus the net loss area C.

Oh hours of labor are applied to the half of total farmland cultivated
by smallholders. Hired workers supply *hO'* hours at a wage rate of *r*
per hour.

The MP_ℓ curve for hired workers on estate land exceeds the MP_ℓ
on smallholders' land by *rs*. After land redistribution, *tu* labor hours
are lost. *Ot* labor hours are on the smallholders' original acreage after
land redistribution, and *uO'* on the former estate land. The marginal
product of labor is now equal (*v* or *w*) on all land. Whether or not total
output rises, falls, or remains the same depends upon the loss of labor
hours, and will be determined by the gain in output on estate land
now farmed more intensively (area *uwrh*) compared with the loss on
small farms now worked less intensively (area *tvsh*) or:

$$\text{Net Gain (Loss)} = \text{Area } A - \text{Area } C$$

In the case where smallholders supply more labor hours, offsetting any
diminution from hired labor as wages fall, then output expands.

What are the consequences for total output when land is given to
the hired workers? Here again we concentrate upon just the effect on
labor hours. The marginal utility from production-consumption hours
of the hired farm labor depends upon the wage rate. Also, the disutility
and utility of hired work differ from those of self-employment, and
this affects hours of labor offered at a given wage rate. Generally the
marginal utility curve of workers is flatter and lower than that of the
self-employed due to less income per hour and the disutility of hired
work.

Giving acreage to the landless hired worker will raise his or her hours offered as the marginal utility curve rises markedly from increased income that was formerly part of estate income from land. Thus the more heavily land reform is weighted toward the landless, the more likely labor hours of farm workers will rise. This, in turn, raises the yield per acre, assuming efficiency is not inferior to that of estate farming.

Where technology and productivity differ between estate and smallholder farming, then the MP_ℓ curves will differ. The MP_ℓ curve for estate land will shift as land is transferred to smallholders, including former hired workers. Nonhomogeneous resources may also affect relative productivity. Some underutilized estate land may be relatively infertile. And there are other factors that determine the exact outcome of land reform. For example, supportive services are often disproportionately supplied in favor of estates. When, with reform, these are shifted to smallholders, productivity differences will decline. Here we have concentrated upon the effect of land redistribution upon work hours, and found it hard to predict the effect on the original smallholders. And as discussed below, taxation affects the outcome (Gersovitz 1976).

Institutional arrangements that affect the income of the farmer will also influence hours worked. Let CD in figure 16.2 represent the farm household without a landlord relationship, while AB depicts the situation where the landlord taxes away a percentage of the same household's crop. The outcome as to hours worked is indeterminate, as explained. Either the income effect or the substitution effect may dominate.

The Effect of Taxes Upon Work Hours Per Worker

On the other hand, a lump-sum tax will mean the peasant receives no income for the first hours worked and must work those hours to have access to any earnings at all. The hours available for producing consumption utility are reduced. Line AB will begin above and to the right of line CD, starting after taxes are produced. After output is equivalent to taxes, all additional output is available to the household for consumption. The marginal output from aftertax hours of work will be the first available for consumption and will have greater marginal utility than the corresponding hours along CD where no taxes are paid. The household paying a lump-sum tax will work longer hours than one that is untaxed. Total farm output will be greater, but the farmer's income and utility are lower since the first hours worked produce disutility and no income.

What is the effect of technical change upon hours worked? A change in output per worker will shift the net marginal utility curve AB to CD, as shown in figure 16.2. C is above A because more output is available per hour. D is below B because net marginal utility along CD will fall more rapidly due to diminishing utility as more output is consumed per time period. Hours worked may rise or fall, as explained previously. Continuous technical change will increase the slope of CD

Technical Change and Work Hours

and move E to the left, so that CD eventually cuts the curve of marginal utility of rest below and to the left of AB, reducing hours worked, other things remaining constant.

The Terms of Trade and Work Hours Per Worker   The last outcome noted above is less predictable when instead of sustaining a self-sufficient family, the crop is sold in the market, and technical change influences the supply and hence the crop price. A fall in the terms of trade tends to lower the position and slope of the net marginal utility curve for production-consumption. In fact, it is helpful now to drop the assumption of self-sufficient farming.

Assume all the farms produce one of two crops and farms producing a different crop barter with each other. The marginal utility of production-consumption time will be affected by the gains to be had from exchange. Each hour worked now brings different satisfaction from production-consumption than it did without trade. The effect on hours worked depends upon whether the new marginal utility curve for production-consumption cuts the marginal utility curve for rest to the left or right of its pretrade equilibrium. Note, however, that the total utility from production-consumption time (in other words, the area under the net marginal utility curve) will be larger after barter, or exchange would not have taken place.

Another graphic variation is helpful in furthering insight into allocation of the farm household's time in early development, and in particular the effects of the terms of trade upon time allocation. Let the time span be allocated to production-consumption only (ignoring rest hours), and let the two vertical axes represent production for home consumption and production for the market. The division of labor hours between the two types of production-consumption will depend upon the production functions and utility functions for each and the terms of trade for market production.

A lower terms of trade for market production can shift more hours to such production. However, as figure 16.4 shows, there is a limit to the positive effect of a lower terms of trade upon hours worked for market production. Once the marginal utility curve for market production-consumption shifts down far enough, it will intersect the marginal utility curve for home production-consumption to the left of E.

Looked at from a carrot and stick standpoint, as planners hoping to increase market production hours might do, a change in the terms of trade is an unpredictable carrot or stick. Also, as explained previously, an improvement in productivity for market output may raise or lower hours allocated to market production. And even new goods and services shift the marginal utility curve in an unpredictable way, depending upon their utility function and terms of trade.

Increases in Market Production Hours   Now assume the good produced for home consumption is available in the market for fewer hours. This ensures an increase in production for

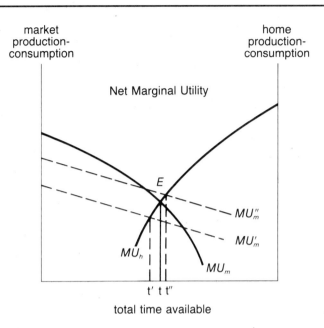

FIGURE 16.4

Lower Terms of Trade and Market Production

Lower terms of trade may increase or reduce hours worked for the market (MU_m), depending upon size and shift in net marginal utility (MU'_m compared with MU''_m).

the market.[2] A fall in the disutility or a rise in the utility function of market production relative to that for the home will also ensure greater output for the market. Such shifts in utility functions plus the provision of home-produced goods by the market for less hours of work are predictable in their positive impact upon hours spent in market production. Recall, also, the effects of a lump-sum tax upon the marginal utility curve. Such a tax upon market output would shift hours away from home production-consumption to production for the market.

Allocation of Time to Investment

Needed resources that will raise labor productivity can be made available. New land can be cleared, physical capital can be produced, and human capital can be increased. This demands the allocation of labor hours to resource augmentation, a possibility ignored up to this point. The same time allocation framework can account for the allotment of labor hours to add to other resource inputs. A simple example can be given for the farm.

A farmer can spend hours clearing and improving land rather than resting or producing-consuming. Such investment of time will raise

2. Notice though that a technically more efficient production function for home consumption may or may not raise the hours allocated for the market output. Yet it could give the same increment to total utility.

next season's output, but means giving up present consumption and rest. The question then becomes, will the additional future consumption and rest compensate the peasant for what he or she forgoes at present? The answer depends upon the increment to future consumption attained as a result of giving up an hour of current consumption and rest, and upon the peasant's preference for present over future consumption. Depending, then, upon the worker's time preference for consumption and rest, and the techniques available for raising future consumption, time may be spent now to raise future consumption. The amount spent will depend upon how highly the peasant values current consumption and rest relative to future consumption and rest.

Investment in human capital requires diversion of hours from production-consumption and rest to education and training. Future earnings are larger as a result of increased hourly productivity or the value of scarce skills. Theoretically the individual will allocate time to human capital formation up to the point that the forgone current consumption is compensated for by greater future consumption. Education is also attractive to workers when it changes the job utility-disutility set so that there is greater status, less fatigue, and so on associated with work. Tastes, and thus utility from consumption, may also change as a result of education.

Underemployment, Overemployment, Unemployment

A definition of underemployment of labor can be developed within the time allocation framework. When the worker's marginal utility from production exceeds that gained from rest, then he or she is working fewer than the desired number of hours. Assume that given technology and nonlabor resources, the utility of a set number of marginal hours allocated to rest by the labor force is below the utility those hours would have when spent on work and consumption. Additional hours allotted to production-consumption by the total labor force would raise worker utility. The labor force is underemployed in either market and/or home production-consumption.[3]

There may be limits that prevent optimum allocation of labor hours. On the farm, seasonal constraints, tenancy requirements, or caste barriers may produce underemployment. Examples of such constraints for market labor might be a law setting a minimum wage that results in fewer work hours than desired at that wage, labor unions that accomplish the same result, a minimum workweek, prohibition of night shifts, early retirement laws, or a hierarchical social system that allocates labor without maximizing utility. Inadequate demand relative to productive capacity, a factor proportions problem, or immobility of resources could all result in underemployment. Lack of entrepreneurial talents and information can also contribute.

Analogously, overemployment is also a state of disequilibrium in time allocation. The effect is the opposite of underemployment; over-

---

3. The term underemployment is sometimes used in a different sense in the literature to refer to workers earning a very low income because of low productivity and sporadic unemployment.

employment can be defined as a situation where rigidities require diversion of hours from rest to production-consumption when the utility of the hours diverted from rest was higher than their utility when devoted to production-consumption. The household strives for optimal allocation of its hours, but will invariably experience disequilibrium in the form of underemployment and/or overemployment among members.

Blocked from achieving an optimal pattern of time utilization, the household seeks its "second best" solution under constraints and distortions. The basic idea of an equilibrium solution, however, identifies the direction toward which the members strive. This enables the policymaker to predict household reaction to policy stimuli.

Indivisibilities of the workday, week or year could leave some workers underemployed, others overemployed. Technical constraints of the production function can make some types of work sharing inefficient, particularly in specialized market work conditions. The employed worker may have to allocate more hours to market production-consumption and fewer to rest and home production-consumption than are optimal. The less-desirable disequilibrium for the worker would be no market production-consumption. When employers depress wages so that the worker would desire only eight hours of market production-consumption but must work 10 hours at lower wages to keep the job, the worker prefers a job to no job, and works the extra hours. When weather and seasonal constraints demand longer workdays on the farm at the expense of rest, the peasant can be overemployed over specific time periods. Again, rigidities prevent achieving optimal labor hour allocation, and failure to work the necessary additional hours would result in large losses exceeding that of forgone rest.

The African experience with migrant workers illustrates tensions that surface as workers seek to avoid overemployment in market production-consumption. Certain mining jobs have high levels of disutility because of harsh working conditions, including separation from family. The labor force available for mining jobs in Africa is in short supply and the job turnover rate high. African migrant workers often leave their jobs after a given period of time since they can generally get another as other workers leave. Job switching becomes an adjustment mechanism for approximating an optimal time allocation. Mining companies, seeking to avoid the cost of high turnover, try to impose a minimum work period of one year. Their methods of doing this include holding back part of the miner's wages and making them contingent upon a year's work.

Foreign or colonial companies often view such a labor force as undisciplined and "lazy." The firms either cannot or will not change the disutility of the work or raise wages. Moreover, when companies raise wages, the increase in income affects the workers' desire to offer labor hours. Given the worker's tastes for home production-consumption and rest, the higher income can lead to a reduction in market labor hours offered. The worker can attain the optimal amount of market utility with fewer hours since wages are higher, and so diverts his time to other areas. This is said to be a common response of migrants who have left their families behind in seeking market work. They are anxious to devote time to pursuits located in another geographic region and must return home for an extended period of time to do so. Their supply curve for market labor hours is backward bending at a wage rate that is low by international comparison.

Historically many economies have increased their GNP growth rate by institutional arrangements that result in overemployment for the work force. Long workdays legally enforced, sweatshop conditions, forced labor including that of slaves and children, are all historically documented. Overemployment may not increase growth, however. Labor productivity can be affected by the disutility of work under disequilibrium systems for labor with prescribed working hours. The worker must put in the regular workdays but, in the case of set hourly pay, the worker may adjust for the disutility of work by lowered effort. The output from extra hours of work must exceed the drop in labor productivity for the growth rate to be increased.

Another example of overemployment that does not increase output is certain types of work sharing. Assume two workers perform the tasks of one worker, but both stay on the job a full workday to do the job. Assume both could improve their lot by working efficiently a half day and spending the remaining hours in other pursuits, including home production-consumption. The job is so organized, however, as to prevent this. Such overemployment involves inefficient work sharing arrangements often found in government jobs in LDCs. Growth is not increased and may be blocked by the general tenor of outlook and attitudes toward work developed by such an organization.

Unemployment is a specific type of underemployment for workers in the labor market. Rather than a shortened workday or other period of too few work hours, the worker has a period with no contractual work hours and usually no contractual relationship with an employer. Institutional settings are such that when underemployment occurs in agriculture, it is not accompanied by widespread unemployment. Instead workers share shortened workdays.

In extremely poor economies, unemployment means starvation. The socioeconomic network generally provides some jobs for most people, and family obligations here are heavy since there are few state commitments. Industrial production with its attendant labor markets breaks down the family employment network. In early development there may be little to replace the family system and the social institutions providing work in preindustrial societies. The state in poor LDCs is generally short of taxing capacity to support the unemployed. Social tensions rise as nascent labor markets emerge and unemployment is more prevalent.

Economic Systems and Time Allocation Constraints   The time allocation model used analyzes the implications of the individual's desire to allocate time between work-consumption and rest. Preferences are not questioned. While such preferences may be formed or influenced by the social network, they are presumed to be acted upon by the individual or household so as to optimize utility from such actions. The expected income from work hours must be known as well as the prices of goods purchased with earnings from market production-consumption. In the absence of constraints the maximization of utility is possible; but social and economic constraints affect the outcome. The individual can only approach equilibrium in allocation of time. The effort of the individual or household to approximate equilibrium, given constraints, helps to explain and predict labor force behavior.

Constraints upon the worker that prevent optimum allocation of time are found in all economic systems. Such limits may deter or promote growth. It is not surprising that development has been associated with economic systems that ensure increased work hours during beginning stages of evolution. Both the labor market that emerges in market systems and the labor employment policies in planned systems dictate labor hours so that more work time is offered per work year than in the traditional economy with flexible self-employment. Constraints that produce underemployment are reduced while those that promote overemployment may become dominant in economic systems that promote growth.

The relative decline of agriculture works hand in hand with the economic system to reduce the forces leading to underemployment. As industrialization takes place and the proportion of the labor force in agriculture dwindles, seasonal constraints on the work year lessen. Even when a fairly large proportion of the work force remains in agriculture, a more diversified economy that is more advanced technically can increase the yearly harvests while providing supplemental off-seasonal employment.

When the state commands the allocation of labor hours and is oriented to development, the laborers generally find their time tightly committed to state production for growth. Time for production and consumption of consumer goods and home production is highly restricted. State control of an agrarian economy means state control over land and labor hours along with a few tools and improvements in land. Augmentation of land is limited. Thus, the government's main growth input is control over labor hours. Such hours will be devoted to capital formation and technology transfers to raise growth rates.

When the worker prefers to allocate less time than the state desires to investment, productivity can be affected and resistance aroused. For that reason the state determined to attain growth is faced with the need to change the people's tastes and preferences. State-led growth is generally accompanied by propaganda campaigns to increase the satisfaction level from hours spent in production that yield only limited present consumption. The term "forced growth" is sometimes used to refer to state-induced overemployment geared to rapid development.

Recent social unrest in Poland illustrates a reaction to state-led growth. An independent labor union movement (Solidarity) challenged the state-determined workweek and the state allocation of resources to consumer goods. In a direct challenge to state control of the economy and state-led growth, the workers demanded Saturdays off and more meat, among other consumer goods. Not surprisingly, the free labor union movement in Poland was sharply criticized by other governments in centrally controlled communist states.

In mixed economies the government influences both directly and indirectly labor hours spent on investment and market production. Labor hours of the unemployed can be purchased by the government and used for such projects as building dams and roads. In some LDCs taxes are paid in labor hours devoted to government-sponsored local development projects. Taxation of consumption and use of tax monies for infrastructure investment is another way that government policy allocates labor hours toward growth in the mixed economy. The tax itself, as explained earlier, may result in the self-employed allocating more hours to production for the market and less to home production-consumption.

Surplus Labor Once More   Poorer LDCs have limited resources to combine with labor hours and low technology. The consensus is that more hours devoted to investment and technical change and away from time-intensive consumption and rest will promote growth. And in LDCs with poor organization of work hours that creates constraints leading to underemployment, an improvement in organization can aid growth without a reduction in satisfaction from rest or consumption.

Deployment of labor to industry to raise investment was discussed in the description of the Lewis-Fei-Ranis model where labor in agriculture is said to be surplus, that is, when labor is withdrawn from agriculture there is no drop in agricultural output. Consider the necessary assumptions for this to occur in the time-allocation framework. Assume that the allocation of farm labor hours is in equilibrium. The drop in labor hours as workers are removed raises the output at the margin of the remaining farm labor hours under the assumption of diminishing returns to labor hours. Assume it does not change output at the margin for home production, which uses very little in the way of complementary resources. The net marginal utility curve for market production-consumption will shift upward and have a steeper slope. Remaining workers may devote more, less, or the same number of hours to farm work relative to home production-consumption and rest, as explained previously.

If the workers who stay put in the same or fewer hours, output falls. It will also fall if the remaining workers increase their time on the job but by fewer hours than those lost by workers leaving. For surplus labor to exist, then, the remaining workers must increase their labor hours enough to offset the work hours of their former colleagues. Is that a likely outcome?

Based on the time allocation model, the answer is no. Diversion of time from home production to market production increases the value of the last hours spent on home production. Moreover, a reduction in the number of workers raises the amount of land per worker and output per labor hour. This can result in more hours worked. However, it also results in a higher rate of consumption of market goods per time period and thus a more rapidly falling marginal utility curve per time increment. The diminishing utility of higher market consumption levels and the rising marginal utility of home production-consumption as fewer hours are devoted there make it unlikely that the remaining workers will increase their market production-consumption enough to offset completely the hours lost as workers move to other sectors (Zarembka 1972; and Berry and Seligo 1968).

Remember, however, that the surplus labor model assumes that food formerly consumed by migrating farm workers is made available to them in the city. This requires a tax on farm output. It is possible that with the proper tax policy, market output remains constant on the farm with fewer workers. A lump-sum tax on market production could raise the hours spent farming enough to offset the loss in output when the number of workers declines somewhat. However, continuous withdrawal of labor must lead to a drop in farm output unless there is technological change since there is a limit to the lengthening of the workday and workweek per worker.

REFERENCES

Berry, R. A. and Seligo, R. 1968. Rural-Urban Migration, Agricultural Output and the Supply Price of Labor in a Labor Surplus Economy. *Oxford Economic Papers* 20 (July): 230–49.

Gersovitz, Mark. 1976. Land Reform: Some Theoretical Considerations. *Journal of Development Studies* vol. 13, no. 1, pp. 79–91.

Zarembka, Paul. 1972. *Toward a Theory of Economic Development.* San Francisco: Holden-Day.

Monetary Policy: National

chapter

17

Most LDCs today have a national currency and central bank, yet the economy may not be "monetized." That is, the use of money and banking services may be limited to a small portion of the society. The hinterland is essentially a barter economy, one where the national currency is not used as a unit of account or denominator of value. Commodities that are relatively scarce such as cattle, rare shells, or precious metals typically serve as denominators for measuring the value of items exchanged or held as wealth. Where there are dowries, either the bride or groom has a price so denominated. Even in the more advanced sector, the financial services are fairly limited, and foreign banks may provide imported skills needed to finance foreign trade.

This rudimentary system changes with development. The organization and evolution of the financial structure have important implications for development. In this chapter we begin by discussing the basic role and functions of the financial system in development. The central role of money and banking are explained. Once the functions of the financial structure have been developed, the chapter focuses upon the appropriate monetary policy within the context of economic evolution. The Classical, Keynesian, Structuralist, and Monetarist approaches to monetary policy in LDCs are discussed and contrasted. Special emphasis is given to inflationary pressures accompanying the development process.

The Roles of Money

Money serves as a medium of exchange and store of value. A well-managed money supply consisting of demand deposits and currency reduces the inefficiencies of barter and the use of commodities as a store of value. Barter is a time-consuming method of executing exchange, depending upon a coincidence of wants. Thus money is sometimes referred to as the lubricant for market exchange transactions. It also can be held for future transactions. The use of a commodity like gold, rice, or coffee as a store of value in an economy requires resources whereas money is "costless" in that the cost of producing modern money is very low. And commodity money does not expand in the correct proportion to satisfy the liquidity needs of a growing economy.

Money, in other words, demand deposits and currency, is more liquid than other forms of financial assets, and so provides flexibility to the asset holder seeking to exchange assets for goods. The basic unit in which money is denominated is the *numeraire* in which all goods, services, and resources are valued. As a medium of payment, money exchanges directly for goods, services and resources. Other forms of financial assets such as ownership claims to productive wealth, bonds, and life insurance policies must go through market transactions where they are sold for money in order to acquire general purchasing power over goods and services or other assets.

An economy's supply of money can affect its value and the level of production. The value of money is a composite of the prices of all the goods and services it buys. This means the value of money varies inversely with the general price level. And the supply of money affects its own worth by changing the prices of all goods and services. In a very simplified way the process whereby money affects it own value and the level of production works as follows: Should the authorities who control the money supply issue more when there is no increase in demand for it for transactions purposes or as a store of value, then the return for holding money and the cost of borrowing it fall, and the additional money supply raises spending in the economy. The only impact of new spending will be to drive up prices when the economy is at full employment. When the economy is below full employment, the increased spending can raise output and the greater production boosts the demand for money while supplying goods to absorb the additional money flows, until full employment is approached or bottlenecks limit further expansion. These unique aspects of money endow it with avenues of more general economic impact than other financial assets. Much more will be said about the role of money as the chapter unfolds.

Functions of the Financial System

Market economies typically have a variety of private institutions specializing in particular financial services such as investment or commercial banking services, foreign exchange transactions, stock and bond transactions, or insurance. Taken together with the central bank and other public financial structures, such institutions compose the financial system of the economy. The functions of a financial system are varied and pervasive:

- It provides for the monetary needs of a growing economy.
- It allocates savings among competing uses and spreads risks that accompany investment.
- Financial services help households and businesses allocate expenditures optimally over time.
- The financial system intermediates between the saver and investor. This allows savers to share in the returns generated by their savings without being directly involved with investment of the funds in real productive wealth.
- Financial institutions concerned with credit allocation increase information flows and serve an educational function, improving financial management practices in the economy.

In the absence of the services of financial intermediaries, savings are likely to take forms that are less supportive of growth and to be allocated less efficiently. These functions are elaborated upon in the next section.

The introduction of basic modern financial services into an LDC constitutes a change in technology that raises both productivity and consumer welfare. Consider the effect upon consumer satisfaction. Modern forms of money offer convenience and reduce the cost of exchange. New financial services raise the utility of the consumer's savings. Savings accounts, commercial paper, bonds, stocks, insurance, and the like, increase the satisfaction attainable from a given quantity of savings by allowing the saver a choice of instruments for his or her reserves that satisfy various needs. The next section brings out the effect of financial services upon productivity, that is, how resources devoted to financial services can raise household and business efficiency levels and improve resource allocation in the total economy.

The role of financial intermediation is less important in planned economies. Where private ownership of business is banned or highly circumscribed, there is less scope for financial services. Financing in centrally planned economies is essentially internal, and savings are determined by state profits and control of resources. The financial structure develops along a different route, being essentially the planners' accounting and control system for transfers between firms and cash outflows, mainly in the form of wages. In a market economy where government is less pervasive, specialized financial services, although in part regulated and provided by the state in many cases, have typically played an important role in the decentralized savings-investment process.

An LDC will not replicate an MDC's financial structure. The appropriate depth and character of financial institutions vary with the level of development so that there is an optimal evolution of the formal financial structure. LDCs in early development stages possess fairly rudimentary and largely informal financial structures of different degrees of efficiency. With some adaptation, the technology of more sophisticated financial structures can be gradually transferred from market economy MDCs. The technology has some scale economies in addition to absorption limitations arising from the development level of the economy. In general, the potential for productivity gains stemming from financial deepening varies with business organization and personal wealth, both of which are to a great degree determined by the level of development. A description of important elements of financial deepening is helpful at this point in understanding the potential effect of the financial system upon productivity growth.

The Process of Financial Deepening

Rural credit needs dominate private sector financing in a country's early development. Internal financing by the landlord is a common source of rural funds for agriculture. Many rural credit markets operate on a personal basis, with wealthier individuals lending to borrowers whom the lender knows. Supplier credits are frequent sources of loans. Even though bank credit is available, the small farmer may be unable to obtain bank credit because of risk and banks' avoidance of the higher costs associated with small loans. Credit cooperatives for smaller farmers, sometimes organized by the government, are another approach. Some investment by small as well as large farm units is self-financed. When surplus labor hours are available in the off-season, farmers mobilize their families and friends to clear land, dig ditches for irrigation, build storage bins, and so on.

In early stages of development, private investment in industry and commerce is in large part self-financed. The personal wealth of the owners is invested in the firm and augmented by reinvested profits and loans from family and associates. The corporate form of ownership is limited and stock and bond markets nonexistent or very meager. Outside financing is mainly bank credit composed of short or intermediate-term loans.

The cost of searching for new investment opportunities and financial backing can be high for the individual investor, who thus stops well short of an exhaustive exploration of alternative investment opportunities. At some stage of industrial development, it becomes economic to establish stock and bond exchanges, markets for bills and notes, and other forms of financial intermediation. When these specialized market services have evolved, the search costs will be lowered since one of their prime functions is to facilitate optimal allocation of investment by accumulating and disseminating information about business opportunities. While search costs are high, however, and information limited, the allocation of savings among alternative uses takes place in fragmented markets that function relatively imperfectly. The inability to diversify adds to the risks of investment. The matrix of projects among which segmented savings are allocated (arranged according to risk and return) is incomplete. The result is that some lower-return projects are undertaken in one segment while higher-return projects in another suffer for lack of financing; and risks associated with self-financing influence the allocation of funds.

The "unorganized," or informal, credit markets are generally high-interest sources of credit because of diseconomies of small-scale lending, higher risk, and monopoly pricing advantages. They operate with varying degrees of efficiency, responding to the demands of smaller units. Organized credit markets ideally should replace these unorganized markets whenever this will increase GNP or reduce the cost of credit allocation to the economy. But as unattractive as the proverbial moneylenders may be to those dependent upon them, they are sometimes able to provide credit at a cost less than those of the formal markets. (The rapacious moneylender is not uncommon, on the other hand.) Attempts to regulate informal markets can result in reduced credit availability. Many forms of interest rate limitations lead to this.

The affluence of the economy affects the mix of financial services demanded and hence the marketing, insurance, and diversification costs the economy is willing to pay for those services. As income per capita rises along with savings, the society becomes increasingly competent at allocating consumption over longer time periods for larger segments of the economy. With the growth of the corporate form of organization and of total savings available, financial institutions such as stock and bond markets become both feasible and efficient. Self-financing of physical and working capital, which dominates in early periods, diminishes in importance. Public demand grows for life insurance, retirement funds, and other sophisticated financial services.

There are costs involved in modernizing financial markets. As mentioned, scale affects the cost of financial intermediation and the industry structure. Even when externalities exist in LDCs and offset some of the cost of geographically dispersed financial intermediaries, it is generally uneconomic to organize a ubiquitous, formal financial system with diversified services capable of allocating savings efficiently throughout the economy. Moreover, scale is not the only variable that must be considered in calculating the cost of formal financial systems. Modern financial industry demands high skills and places claims upon an economy's stock of skilled labor. Admittedly resources devoted to financial intermediation, by responding to growth needs, facilitate resource allocation and growth in the total economy. But since there is a cost involved in committing additional resources to achieve more sophisticated financial services, optimal expansion of such services will occur as the cost is repaid. Otherwise, the cost of financial expansion under scarcity pricing would exceed its benefits, and the LDC would be transferring financial technology into the economy at a rate above the optimum. Also, there may be a cost advantage to the importation of some financial services at various levels of development.

Financial systems in LDCs may be more in need of reform than of sophisticated technology to improve their performance. Reform needs can reflect corruption and weak financial organization. A poorly designed financial system can impede the achievement of growth goals. Oftentimes inefficient financial intermediation reflects and reinforces distortions in the private and/or public sectors of an LDC. Where large production units dominate the economy and small units coexist, dualism in credit allocation can readily reinforce the production dualism. Financial institutions favor large production units with advantages of scale and risk. The reinforcement of industrial monopoly by the financial structure can have far-reaching distortion effects upon development.

Development literature is replete with examples where the financial structure is not responsive to the credit allocation needs of a broad-based development path. Banks may be forced to finance deficit spending by a corrupt government. Power groups with strong economic influence, such as landed or corporate elites, can dominate the channels of financial flows, further enhancing their economic hegemony but distorting the allocation of savings. Governments intent upon fostering development may dictate a financial policy that keeps interest rates lower than optimum, thus distorting the price of funds for investment. This encourages capital-intensive production beyond that supportable on the basis of scarcity pricing and requires a rationing process open to distortions.

Several important points are worth summarizing here. As the market size and level of development allow absorption of the technology of financial deepening, efficiencies ensue from specialization, scale, risk reduction, and organization. The financial system is a vital component of a decentralized process of savings and investment. It affects consumer satisfaction and efficiency of households as well as businesses. Financial deepening is no panacea for market distortions, concentrated economic power, or poorly conceived government policies that affect the allocation and returns of savings. The expansion of the financial system at an optimum rate, however, can prevent the development of financial distortions such as those created by dominant groups under conditions of dualism.

The Banking System: Importance and Organization

Prior to the development of stock and bond markets, bank credit plays a central role in satisfying credit needs for working capital and physical capital. Banks, with some infusion of government savings and guarantees, often handle longer-term financing. Such financing can be dispensed under the aegis of specialized institutions called development banks. These in turn may serve only particular sectors or even industries.

The banking system gives the small saver an alternative, liquid form in which to hold wealth. The liquidity afforded is helpful to financial management and flexibility in the household and production unit, and reduces the need for commodities to be tied up unnecessarily as a store of wealth. A common alternative to money is gold, which demands resources for production or import, earns no interest, and does not promote investment. Its attractiveness lies in the belief that it is a hedge against inflation when the money supply is mismanaged. Other alternatives are commodities readily stored and salable. Studies of LDC firms often uncover high inventories as a form of business savings when the banking system is inadequate or managed so that it fails to give a scarcity reward for funds.

The banking system facilitates the short-term financing of both national and international trade. In achieving a smooth flow of international commerce, national banking systems with national currency units must provide for the interchange of currencies needed for exports and imports. The exporter earns currency of another country but wishes to transfer funds to local currency. The importer must arrange for payments to be translated from local to foreign currency units. Either national or foreign banking can handle the conversion. But the national government must decide what policy it will follow in regard to the flow of foreign exchange, including not just flows related to trade but also those related to financial investment capital. International monetary flows can affect the domestic money supply as discussed below.

The need for money and banks in the LDC economy rises as growth increases the number of transactions, and nonmonetized areas become monetized. Some studies show an income elasticity of demand for money greater than one in LDCs. That is, in a growing LDC the ratio of money to national income needed to carry out transactions increases.

The banking system is generally set up with fractional reserve banking. There is a government central bank with which the associated banks must deposit reserves. The amount required as backing for demand deposits is set by law. Bank deposits, then, cannot exceed reserves by more than a set multiple. These reserves provide security behind deposits, and are composed of money and other assets freely accepted by the central bank in exchange for money.

The government can increase the money supply by reducing the reserve ratio. Banks are then free to create new deposits by making loans to customers since they have excess reserves. The banking system will expand its demand deposits until the excess reserves are exhausted. Since the excess reserves will support a multiple in demand deposits, this is a powerful tool for increasing the money supply. There must be a commensurate demand for loans, however.

A government deficit may also expand the money supply when banks are required to purchase the government debt and there is no corresponding reduction in loans to the private sector. Should government bonds be counted as reserves, this would allow a multiple expansion of the money supply.

In many LDCs foreign exchange serves as reserves with money expansion potential. Consider an emerging country where there is an excess of foreign currency inflows over outflows of local currency. This foreign currency surplus could be eliminated if the excess demand in foreign exchange markets for local currency were allowed to decrease the amount of local currency exchanged for a unit of foreign currency. That is, supply and demand could be allowed to set a price on foreign exchange that would clear the market. Assume, however, that the foreign exchange rate is not permitted to change. Recipients of the foreign exchange have turned in an excess to their commercial banks to be exchanged for local currency. The banks in turn must by law hand the surplus over to the central bank. The central bank must pay the commercial banks for the foreign exchange, and does so by increasing bank reserve deposits which then allow a multiple expansion of the money supply. A net inflow of foreign exchange, then, increases the domestic money supply; analogously a net outflow depletes foreign exchange and reserves and leads to a multiple decline in the money supply.

Seldom does an excess supply of foreign exchange fail to produce a full expansion of the money supply. Domestic loan demand tends to be high in periods of high exports as the foreign exchange constraint is reduced and prosperity in the export sector leads to new spending for domestic goods. Moreover, when a small economy with a high level of trade experiences surpluses, it is hard for the central bank to offset the money supply increase without creating overly tight money markets that can disrupt economic expansion because of the uneven impact of credit restraints.

As banks experience an excess demand for foreign exchange, they purchase it from the central bank, drawing down their reserves to pay for it. This has potential for shrinking the money supply as banks must by law reduce the deposits outstanding to align them with the new lower reserve level. The central bank can offset this effect, however, when tight money is not the appropriate policy for domestic economic conditions.

LDCs can be expected to run seasonal and even cyclical deficits in their balance of payments under a system of fixed exchange rates. In periods of surplus, the central bank can retain foreign exchange, which is fed out in periods of shortage so that the excess demand is reduced.

Of course, the holding of foreign exchange means domestic savings are made available to foreigners and this is costly when required holdings are high. To avoid tying up too much savings this way, the LDC often uses some of the foreign exchange to purchase development inputs and relies in part on compensatory borrowing to even out seasonal and cyclical shortfalls.

The Relative Return to Money and Development

In earlier stages of financial deepening, bank credit and money (including time or savings deposits) dominate the debt-asset entries of the nation's financial balance sheet. This fact, according to E. S. Shaw (1973) and R. I. McKinnon (1973) creates a pressing urgency for the nation seeking development to promote and firmly establish a well-functioning monetary system. The failure to do so, they contend, will severely retard economic development. The well-functioning monetary system ensures an optimal stock of money and optimal changes in that stock so that growth is financed and high rates of inflation are avoided. Distortions of the relative return to money or absolute price levels are also avoided. Such a smoothly operating system prevents what Shaw and McKinnon consider to be undue reliance on fiscal policies to promote savings and on foreign aid or foreign private savings.

First, consider how households apportion their income over time. Families wishing to allocate consumption over time can hold money; acquire other financial assets; and invest in storable commodities, land, or physical capital. These assets have differing characteristics for satisfying the households' needs and varying risks. Whenever the expected return of any asset, adjusted for utility and risk, is below the expected return from other assets, then that asset will not be competitive in attracting savings.

McKinnon and Shaw go one step further when discussing LDCs where there are limited forms of financial assets as outlets for savings. They argue that when the return to money relative to other investments is low, either because the government has set an interest ceiling on money deposits or because inflation erodes the return to money relative to other assets, savings and investment will be reduced. They contend that when the return to money is too low, savings will take alternative forms such as gold or excess commodity inventories in LDCs with shallow financial offerings. These are inefficient forms for savings to take, as we have mentioned. Inefficiencies cut output below potential, and savings are reduced because income is lower. Moreover, savings in commodities as opposed to banks do not make short-term loans available to business. These short-term loans, they emphasize, can be a complement to capital formation in LDCs. As borrowers seek savings to form new firms or expand physical productive capacity, they must also expand their working capital and goods inventories. They need ongoing short-term loans from banks to achieve capital expansion and the banking system must be adequate to satisfy such loans. It will only be adequate when the public holds savings in monetary form (broadly defined to include savings or time deposits along with demand deposits).

Of course, if the return to money exceeds the return to other forms of financial assets, with adjustment for risk and utility, then capital formation would be hindered. Thus too high or too low a return to money can deter capital formation. The former limits financial intermediation in the area of short-term business loans needed for expansion of capital and business size. The latter causes too much preference for short-term money among savers and denies longer-term financial intermediation for capital formation.

The LDC, then, needs not only to monetize and achieve efficiencies from reduced barter and increased financial specialization, that is, to deepen its financial capability as growth proceeds, but it also must pay close attention to *relative* returns on assets since this can affect capital formation and development. The optimal amount of monetization and financial deepening is the one that covers the scarcity value of resources used to expand financial services. The optimal rate of return on money is a return equal to the return on other investments adjusted for risk and utility of liquidity.

Shaw gives symptoms of financial repression in a situation of shallow financial development relative to LDC needs for financial deepening. These include:

- Inflation and low, regulated real interest rates on savings that discourage savings;
- Distortion of rates among financial assets that leads to poor allocation of savings and inadequate monetary deepening stemming from low monetary returns to savings;
- High unemployment traceable to capital intensity spurred by low interest rates;
- Too much reliance on unorganized money markets as individuals try to avoid extensive controls in regulated markets;
- Higher risk;
- Capital flight and overvalued exchange rates;
- And "overdependence" on government finance and foreign aid.

MONETARY POLICY: FOUR APPROACHES

An economy's adjustment to an inappropriately managed money supply generally causes economic dislocations and affects the distribution of income. If all prices were perfectly flexible and the economy could adapt to changes in the value of money with costless ease, there would be no need to be concerned for achieving the right amount of money. All prices would adjust so that the economy would have the right amount.

Prices in the real world are not perfectly flexible and changes in their general level can occur through a process that affects resource allocation, output, income distribution, employment, and risk. When there is a shortage of money, people hold on to it (to build back their money holdings) rather than spend it. This cuts spending on goods and services. Inventories accumulate, interest rates rise and cut off some investment spending, labor is let go, income drops, some prices fall, and profits are squeezed as costs lag behind price declines. Debtors are penalized since they must repay loans in currency that is appreciating in value, and creditors gain. Uncertainty develops about future prices, leading investors to borrow and invest less. All of this ends the shortage of money, but at a cost of depressed economic activity. As a result of these negative repercussions from too little money, we speak of the liquidity growth needs of an economy so that deflation will not occur.

If there is too much money relative to the demand for it at current interest and income levels, people spend it and banks lend it at reduced rates of return to investors. When there are underemployed resources, investment can be spurred by the increased spending, and output and employment expand. The growth in the money supply should not only avoid deflation but also be adequate to help maintain a full-employment growth rate. A controversial issue arises, however, in connection with this last proviso: Are a full-employment growth path and the money supply adequate to attain it inevitably characterized by inflation? If so, what rate of inflation should be tolerated? Here we look at several schools of thought that vary in emphasis in regard to monetary policy, inflation, and growth. There is the Classical approach, older and updated by McKinnon and Shaw, the Keynesian, the Structuralist, and the Monetarist approaches. Each school assigns a somewhat different role to monetary policy in the context of development.

The Classical Approach

A. P. Thirwall calls Shaw and McKinnon's a Classical approach (1976). It brings out strongly the importance to development of a well-designed financial structure, growing as development proceeds. The Classical approach finds no large role for the monetary authorities in creating credit (and thereby savings for growth) by activating idle resources or diverting resources to savings via inflation. Their emphasis is upon prior savings for self-finance and a saving function that responds to changes in interest rates. The financial system with competitive interest rates on all financial assets promotes thrift. It cannot directly discourage or encourage investment perceptibly by the level of interest rates because the investment function is assumed to be interest-inelastic. The investment function is responsive to the large array of investment opportunities in LDCs and is limited only by savings. There are only two roles for the monetary system: (1) to provide an appropriate stock of money for functional purposes without inflation, and (2) to allocate limited savings among the many alternative investment opportunities.

The level of the interest rate affects saving, according to the Classical school. Inflation can distort the level of the interest rate and have harmful effects upon saving. To understand this we need to probe further into the relation between inflation and the interest rate.

Interest is a cost to the investor. The scarcity value of savings is reflected in the interest rate. Since debt has a time component and generally is a promise to repay a specified sum at a future date, change in the aggregate price level over time will change the purchasing power of the savings at the time of repayment. The effect of the shift in the price level is to change the earnings from the loan. Inflation lowers the interest earned on previously issued debt while deflation raises it. Under inflation, the interest rate can become negative when the losses in purchasing power exceed the interest charged for the loan. This interest rate adjusted for price level is referred to as the "real" interest rate, meaning it is adjusted for changes in real purchasing power as money flows are spread out over time. The unadjusted rate is the nominal interest rate. When the term "interest rate" is used without a modifier, the presumption is that there is a stable price level so that the distinction is moot.

Failure of the financial system to raise the nominal interest rates under conditions of inflation lowers the real interest rate. This warps the allocation of funds because it leads to excess demand for loans that requires rationing of credit by methods other than prices. And, by making the cost of borrowing to the investor relatively cheap compared with inflated labor costs, it encourages too much use of physical capital and too little use of labor, leading to unemployment.

The above analysis is non-Keynesian in the sense that low real interest rates do not spur investment undertaken with surplus resources, and thereby create new savings out of expanded income equal to the change in investment. The presumption is that the savings supply is at capacity levels when the monetary structure is functioning correctly. Surplus resources are surplus because of the wrong relative price rather than a shortfall of aggregate demand. The lowering of real interest rates by inflation leads to lower, not higher, savings.

In the Classical approach, the allocative role of the monetary system takes precedence over any stimulative role it might play. Efficiencies developed in the allocative role will, however, yield some gains to output and thereby savings. Attempts to use monetary policy as a stimulus can result in a retreat from holding money (especially savings deposits) if inflation lowers the real interest rate. Since money is an important component of financial intermediation in LDCs, inefficiencies result when an inflation tax is placed upon money. The stimulative role to be played by money is the one fulfilled when the optimum money supply is attained as opposed to one that is lower than optimum.

The Keynesian Approach

In the Keynesian paradigm presented in current textbooks, the savings rate in the economy may be considered inadequate because it is below potential full employment saving, or because full employment saving is insufficient to support growth. The monetary system, through credit creation, provides the investment funds to activate idle resources and thereby generate higher levels of income and saving; or it provides the investment funds to enable investors to attract resources away from consumers by creating inflation, which reduces the ability of certain groups to bid on resources.

Unemployment is caused by insufficient aggregate demand. With too little stimulus from monetary and fiscal policies, the economy can remain at output levels that are below full employment. When income is less than the level attainable at full employment, saving, which is a function of income, will also be below full-employment potential. The interest rate will reflect the scarcity value of the lower savings level.

Monetary policy can affect employment and output through increasing the money supply and thereby lowering the interest rate charged for borrowing investment funds. With cheaper loan costs, business finds additional investments profitable. The new spending puts idle resources to work, creating income that is partly spent and partly saved. The additional spending spurs a respending flow that causes a multiple expansion of GNP arising from the money injection and investment increment. With adequate stimulus the economy utilizes all its idle resources and achieves full employment.

A new interest rate reflective of full employment saving, the new money supply, the demand for investment funds at capacity income levels, and the demand for money at full employment income levels establishes itself. This interest rate may be lower than, higher than, or equal to the initial interest rate prevailing prior to full employment. But at the beginning of expansion, the money supply increased, lowering the interest rate and spurring investment. Had interest rates not been lowered, and in the absence of fiscal policy to stimulate aggregate demand, output would not have expanded. Over a growth path, governments hoping to stimulate investment and maintain full employment would maintain "easy-money" policies. Taxes would be used as needed to control consumption and inflationary pressures.

Should full employment saving be considered too low, inflation could be deliberately induced by feeding money into the economy to divert resources from consumption to investment. The preferable approach, of course, is to tax consumption. The inflation tax is used as a substitute when the political capacity to tax consumption directly does not exist.

Inflation can emerge as the economy expands prior to full employment. This type of inflation is caused by diminishing returns and rigidities and impediments to competitive market adjustments. And while the reduction of rigidities would be preferable to inflation, in many cases this may not be achievable—especially in LDCs, in the short term, where foreign exchange constraints or vested interests are the source of the inflexibility.

Applicability of Keynesian Analysis to LDCs

Keynes was not writing with LDCs in mind. He assumed the financial system and the market institutions were highly developed and that rigidities were moderate. Keynesian expansion is characterized by smooth respending paths for new money income arising from the initial investment injection. This spending generates equilibrium responses in labor, bond, and commodity markets. More deep-seated structural rigidities and market inadequacies in LDCs can prevent smooth expansionary spending in response to monetary policy. Unemployed resources may be sector-specific and not very reactive to cheaper credit.

It can be argued that the Keynesian model is not very applicable to LDCs, at least without modification, as a tool of analysis. Careful examination of the specific effects of credit creation upon employment and growth is mandatory case by case in the nonoptimal conditions of LDCs. Yet the potential for credit creation to activate idle resources and support development policy under responsive conditions is an important tool monetary authorities can use. Moreover, the Keynesian approach that minimizes inflation associated with expansion does not call for continuously low interest rates; it allows for rising interest rates with economic expansion. The use of credit creation that entails inflation to raise saving is more controversial and demands closer attention in subsequent discussion.

Theories are tools for the applied economist, who must possess an astute sense of which one to select from the tool kit to aid in constructing the policy for a specific development context. There is no general theory of economic development. And theories available from models of developed economies cannot easily be used for drafting policy blueprints without allowing for their design limitations under conditions of underdevelopment. Both the Classical and Keynesian models identify an appropriate monetary policy in terms of growth needs. They differ in their emphasis and their tolerance levels for inflation. The advantage of having both tools is that they enable the planner to build in safeguards against a disregard of either the importance of financial deepening and relative returns to assets or the importance of credit creation. In addition, planners can calculate the cost of favoring one approach over the other in areas where they conflict. It should be noted that the Keynesian and Classical approaches are compatible in some respects, and the Keynesian approach does not call for interest rate controls to encourage investment. As discussed in chapter 4, the Keynesian saving function has empirical support for LDCs while the Classical saving function does not.

Inflation and Saving at Full Employment

Before leaving Keynesian analysis, we stop to mention a hybrid Keynesian-Classical idea about how monetary policy alone, without the use of fiscal policy, can redirect resources to savings in an economy with full employment. Monetary policy has been viewed both theoretically and empirically as capable of influencing saving when, by creating inflation, it redistributes functional income shares toward profits and away from wages. If, as in the Classical Growth Model, the propensity to save from wages is zero, then no loss of savings occurs as the inflationary monetary policy reduces the purchasing power of wages. A large portion of the income transferred to profits will be saved, and investment is thereby stimulated.

The Classical Growth Model is too simple to apply to today's LDCs. More realistically, some of wages are saved and the difference between the ratio of saving to wages and that of saving to profits is not as large as in the Classical Growth Model. Workers are organized in the industrial sector to escalate their wages to avoid some of the impact of inflation. The rural nonmonetized sector escapes income transfer through inflation. The result is that using inflationary monetary policy alone to effect an increase in savings can require high inflation rates to attain small increments to savings.

The Structuralist Approach

Return to the "important" question: Could an LDC using its credit creation capacities as a development aid activate idle resources and promote growth without inflation? The answer, not unlike the answer in MDCs, is that even the activation of idle resources unleashes inflationary forces prior to full employment of resources, and the inflationary impact of monetary expansion accelerates as full employment is approached. Contrary to the full employment case, however, the rate of inflation required to implement a change in saving and investment is less when the economy is below full employment because total output expands as unemployed resources are brought into play. Thus growth with some slack in the employment of resources is less inflationary than a full employment growth path.

In LDCs, inflation that is not traceable to excess demand at full employment is referred to as structural inflation because it is considered to stem from immobility of resources in the short-run, bottleneck scarcities that cannot be overcome because of technical limitations, instability in foreign exchange earnings, and other like impediments. The simple model that has been used previously can give insight into some forces that cause inflation when the LDC attempts to operate at full employment and maximize the industrial output of its infant industries.

Assume the economy was operating at levels F of food and b of industrial output in figure 17.1, and exporting e. A poor harvest reduces the food supply to F'. The shortfall of food is made up by a reduction in imports for industrial output from m to m', and the foreign exchange thus freed is used to buy food abroad. Industrial output must drop to b'. Similarly, a drop in b could be caused by a deterioration in the terms of trade. Real income attainable has declined until the next harvest is brought in or the terms of trade improve.

In an economy without a deep financial sector or smooth adjustments to changes in the money supply, it is difficult to shrink the money supply to compensate exactly for the decline in rural income. Food prices rise rapidly, affecting rural and urban wages. As demand is diverted to food from other goods, some of these goods have sticky prices and output drops to match the shrunken demand as well as import shortages. A curtailment of the money supply by monetary authorities prevents credit creation needed to allow farmers to recoup and replant. If the terms of trade fluctuate, credit restraint prevents borrowing for imports that could offset a temporary shortfall in export earnings.

Viewed another way and more dynamically, the dashed curve in figure 17.2 showing an outward shift in curve AA' represents expected productivity gains in agriculture that will free resources for industrial

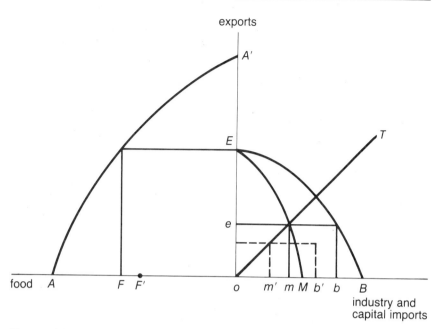

FIGURE 17.1

Effects of Harvest Failure

Harvest failure diverts imports from capital goods to food. Food output drops from
F to *F'*. Food imports result in a drop in capital imports from *m* top *m'*. Industrial
output drops to *b'*.

expansion to b_t over the five-year plan. Immobilities of such resources
can reduce the plan's output level. The planner may feel that a continued expansion of the money supply in accordance with target levels
will increase resource mobility by allowing somewhat higher wages
and other prices on resources used in industry to attract them from
agriculture, or by allowing inflation to reduce consumption, especially
food consumption, somewhat more than plan targets estimated. As
food prices rise, new money is supplied to allow resources to continue
to transfer along target lines. The inflation arising out of the growth is
not high but limited, based on the assumption that immobilities associated with resource transfers from agriculture are not large and only
lag somewhat behind the timing of the plan.

Now notice that the diagram shows export prices relative to import
prices fall with increased output. This means the scarcity price of imports rises. There are no domestic substitutes for imports and their
higher prices tend to cause inflation in the industrial sector even without agricultural shortfalls. Oligopolies follow a markup pricing technique in protected markets. The type of inflation the MDCs learned
about when OPEC raised oil prices is said to be endemic to LDCs.

More importantly, tight credit and depressed demand in response
to each structural complication could retard growth by blocking productivity changes associated with new investment. Monetary policy

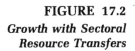

FIGURE 17.2
Growth with Sectoral
Resource Transfers

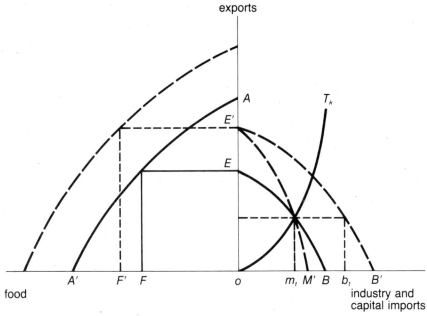

Productivity increase in agriculture with transfer of resources to industry and exports allows output b_t of B goods.

would serve price stability instead of growth since, according to Structuralists, there must be a trade-off. The structural problems have multiple roots such as population growth that creates diminishing returns in agriculture and thus puts pressures on short-run food prices until technology improves; shifting expenditure patterns as development proceeds and resources are attracted to new areas by higher prices; an inelastic tax system relative to growth needs; and migration patterns. The scenario, then, is one of inevitable inflation accompanying development.

The inflation rate accompanying growth, however, can be moderate, that is, below 10 percent, with a well-functioning monetary system that continues to feed credit to the economy for development needs but stops short of fueling soaring inflation. A favorable international climate in regard to inflation can also be a requisite for controlling domestic inflation. Postwar Mexico would be a case in point, with a well-developed monetary sector and credit creation oriented toward growth needs, but controlled inflation up until the eruption of high international inflation in the 1970s. Countries with very high inflation, for example, Argentina, Chile, Brazil, and Indonesia, would not be cases of structural inflation in the sense used above.

Tight money, the Structuralists argue, could contain the inflation, but would not correct or change its cause, and for that reason is not the best policy. Growth with toleration of moderate inflation and pol-

icies to minimize recurring structural dislocations are the correct policies. The market cannot eliminate the inflation because it is underdeveloped, and even when functioning well, can only deal with marginal
adjustments, not large dislocations. The Structuralist position is compatible with Keynesian ideas of activating idle resources through the
use of credit. A well-designed financial system can pinpoint potential
growth areas in need of credit expansion.

The Monetarist model is helpful in examining high inflation rates in **The Monetarist**
LDCs where structural factors embedded in the economic framework **Approach**
do not account for the *high* growth rate of the price level. Monetarists
use an equation of exchange to gain insight into the relationship between the price level and the money supply. Instead of structural rigidities prior to full employment, the Monetarists assume perfectly mobile resources and an adjustment process that, through markets and
prices, can achieve full employment without structural price pressures.
Financial markets are well developed and integrated. The Monetarist
view aggregates the economy into an index of total physical output
exchanged over a given time period, (Q); a price index, (P), measuring
the *general* price level associated with exchange transactions of the
total output mix at a set of unit prices; the total money supply, (M_s);
and its velocity or rate of turnover, (V), as output is exchanged over a
given time period. Thus:

$$M_sV = PQ$$

or, the value of total output exchanged during a given time period is
equal to the money supply times the velocity of money.

This truism emphasizes that when V and Q are constant, changes
in the money supply result in price level changes. The inverse of V is
the demand for money per unit of expenditure. Recall that the Classical
approach emphasized that over a development path $1/V$ is not constant.
Thus as the economy demands more money per unit of total expenditure, velocity slackens and an increase in the money supply need
not change PQ, the value of total output exchanged. The growth of
money is absorbed by an increase in its use throughout the economy.

For growth in the monetary value of aggregate output to take place
without deflation, the money supply must expand enough to offset the
fall in velocity associated with early development and allow for the
additional output to be sold at the same prices. When the money supply grows faster than this, prices are driven up, and P rises.

The Structuralists posit exogenous influences upon P that would
cause physical output to decline if the money supply were not expanded to offset the price rises. It is impossible to eliminate the exogenous forces, at least in the short term. In the Monetarist model as
opposed to the Structuralist, the causal network relating to price changes
inherent in development is to be found in changes in the variables of
the equation of exchange, in other words, in changes in M_s, V, and Q,
but not in structural immobilities. When structural immobilities do

exist they are the result of poor government policies that create inelasticities such as price controls (including interest rate limits) or exchange rate allocations, and are not an inevitable by-product of growth. Repealing the poor policies, according to the Monetarists, removes the inelasticities as the market responds again to scarcity price signals. Control of the money supply can control price changes. And as in the Keynesian approach, credit creation can activate idle resources when output is below the level it would reach with full employment. On the other hand, Monetarists hold that inflation is readily controlled by the money supply without retardation of growth.

In their *theoretical* model, the Monetarists assume frictionless adjustment of markets and prices so that when the monetary authorities create an excess supply of money, prices converge efficiently to a price-multiple of their previous level in the long run. That is, an economy with too much money lowers the price of money by a proportionate erosion of its purchasing power over all goods, services, financial assets, and resources, thereby eliminating the excess supply without economic repercussions. In their policy analysis, however, Monetarists, while assuming an absence of structural inflation caused by irreducible impediments to adjustment of resources, markets, and prices, make the asymmetrical assumption that important and costly imperfections surface when a market economy must adjust to inflation caused by excess money.

INFLATION POLICY

Both the Classical and Monetarist schools maintain that inflation is costly and reduces growth, while the Structuralists contend that (a) some inflation is an inevitable by-product of growth and/or underdevelopment, (b) attempts to control it completely will have a cost in forgone growth, and (c) any costs attached to *moderate* inflation rates are exceeded by the gains in growth. These are certainly incompatible positions. It is important to examine the costs of inflation, given these opposing assessments.

The Costs of Inflation

The effects of inflation vary with its degree, the accuracy with which it is anticipated, and the adjustment process. Since inflation is a tax on money, if affects the demand for money. In extreme cases, inflation deters the use of money as a medium of exchange as well as a store of value and standard of deferred payment. The economy reverts to barter and incurs the accompanying costs of a loss in financial services that money and financial intermediation provide. According to the Classical arguments, even a milder inflation that lowers the return to holding money interferes with monetizing the economy and financial intermediation.

When inflation is not predictable, it increases the risk level in an economy, assuming the degree of inflation is of import. The return to investment outlays must be high enough to compensate for uncertainties regarding rates of return created by the price instability. This can reduce the level of investment in an economy. Examples of unpredictable inflation can be found in some countries in Latin America that have vacillated between high and lower inflation rates. Brazil, Chile, Argentina, and Uruguay are cases in point. The risk effect also encourages a flight of savings abroad.

Inflation in the real world is not a proportionate change in all prices. Some price increases are above the mean, others below it, and some can fall so long as the general price level rises. This changes price incentives that determine resource allocation. People try to hedge against price changes. Hedging can change the timing and type of consumer purchases and the kinds of investments chosen. While relative price changes can differ in various conditions, critics contend there is a stimulus produced by inflation that channels funds to nonproductive assets or commodities that have a history of being a good inflation hedge in LDCs such as gold and other storable commodities and real estate, including housing. Others contend costs tend to lag behind prices and stimulate profits in general at the expense of wages, and thereby consumption. This would promote growth, but, as discussed earlier, it is a doubtful contention in most LDCs today.

Because relative prices change, income redistribution accompanies inflation. What groups are affected varies with the relative price changes and the recoupment process as people struggle to avoid the impact of the inflation. Those with less scope for substitution among market basket items and less bargaining power for avoiding income erosion lose income, while those with earnings that benefit from inflation gain. If, out of this struggle over income redistribution, a system of indexing arises, the resulting automatic adjustments avoid a large portion of the income redistribution effects, depending upon how effective and extensive the indexing is. Indexing of debt instruments in some LDCs has allowed for continuation of debt issues where money is a standard of deferred payment. Critics contend that indexing can accelerate inflation.

The income distribution effects of inflation may either favor or deter growth. When the source of the inflation is a monetized government debt, income is diverted toward the public sector. If the loss in saving-investment from the private sector is exceeded by government investment, then investment will expand, promoting growth. An inflation favoring the entrepreneurial class could promote growth, depending upon their consumption function. When income redistribution favors groups that consume most of their income, saving and investment can be deterred; and when the marginal propensity to save is the same among various groups receiving and losing income, then saving levels are unaffected.

When the income redistribution effects are large, social unrest can flare. This generally happens when lower-income groups are taxed by the inflation. Food inflation has toppled governments even in totalitarian countries, including communist states. In underdeveloped countries, food costs absorb half of the income of the poorer groups.

Monetarists contend that governments react to the social and reallocation effects of inflation by imposing price controls. As interest rates rise to offset inflation, governments fear this will deter investment, so they place limits on interest rates. This cheapens capital relative to labor, leading to its substitution for labor in production, and so causing unemployment. Controlled interest rates also deter indexing, and creditors are unwilling to lend. Food price controls prevent investment in agriculture to raise supplies of food; and other price controls similarly distort allocation and thereby growth. Without inflation (caused by too much money, according to the Monetarists) and controls, markets function efficiently, thus promoting growth.

The foreign trade sector, important in the promotion of successful growth, is adversely affected by inflation when exchange rates are fixed. As domestic prices rise, exports are priced out of world markets and imports become more attractive. A deficit in the trade account is likely. This generally is dealt with by imposing controls, although some LDCs have indexed the exchange rate to the rate of inflation, devaluing monthly where inflation rates are high.

Information costs, already high in LDCs, rise with inflation because price changes are more frequent and uncertain, thus requiring more resources to monitor them. When the outcome is poorer information, economic decisions are less efficient.

The Inflation of the 1970s

The 1970s were a period of relatively high inflation worldwide in response to supply-side dislocations and monetary shocks. The decade began with devaluation of the dollar, which was then allowed to fluctuate in purchasing power vis-à-vis other countries' currencies and gold. The demand for dollars as a reserve currency dropped, and countries sometimes spent their surplus dollars speculatively upon commodities, raising prices of commodities on world commodity markets.

Worldwide harvest failures in the first half of the decade were the worst in 30 years, raising food prices sharply. The commodities inflation was fueled to new heights by OPEC's decisions to reduce oil shipments and raise oil prices. Petroleum prices leaped 400 percent in one bound, followed by repeated smaller increases during the decade. The short-run price elasticity for oil and other commodities was very low. Oil and basic food grains in particular have no close substitutes. Supply-side shocks led to higher prices and/or reduced employment and GNP in one country after another. Structuralists pointed out that in this period advanced economies faced some of the same structural dislocations that were typically pervasive in LDCs. Monetarists emphasized the failure to control money supply growth, both national and international.

Inflation rates rose to double-digit levels in many advanced and less-advanced countries, and output growth for the decade was extremely sluggish. Recessions following the oil shock were the largest suffered since the 1930s in some advanced countries. The stagflation proved to be persistent. Balance of payments problems became acute for many LDCs and MDCs. The impact of world inflation and instability was felt in countries of both greater and less trade dependency.

Stabilization policies to deal with the dislocations of the seventies were no more successful in developed than underdeveloped countries. In fact, the fall in GNP growth was greater for the decade in MDCs than LDCs as a whole. Balance of payments adjustment was more difficult for LDCs however. More advanced LDCs went heavily into debt to finance their higher-priced imports. Among LDCs those of Asia were the only ones that succeeded in reducing their inflation rate below double-digit levels by the second half of the decade. As table 17.1 shows, Africa, Latin America, and the Middle East continued to suffer high and rising inflation rates. Stabilization policies do not easily succeed in the face of rising food prices or deterioration in the terms of trade (Krueger in William R. Cline and Sidney Weintraub, eds. 1981, p. 104).

Studies of the Latin American cone countries—Argentina, Chile, Uruguay, and Brazil—show that stabilization policies improved their balance of payments but led to stagflation. Optimal stabilization policies can differ in different historical settings. Preexisting conditions in the cone countries were not conducive to lowering the inflation rate in the face of international price rises.

Typically, stabilization policies for the cone countries in the 1970s were compatible with Monetarist tenets. They included (1) monetary and fiscal restraint, (2) higher prices for subsidized utilities, (3) wage repression, (4) freeing of prices from controls, (5) gradual elimination of import restrictions, (6) devaluation, (7) reducing public employment, (8) sale of public enterprises to the private sector, and (9) decontrolling interest rates. The general result of these programs was improvement in the balance of payments as exports responded to devaluation, but poor domestic performance and persistent inflation (Cline and Weintraub 1981, p. 16). Cline and Weintraub note: "One major factor underlying the greater difficulty in reducing inflation seems to

	Change in Consumer Price Index (annual average percentage)					
Group	1967–72	1973	1974	1975	1976	1977
Industrial Countries	4.5	7.5	12.6	10.7	7.7	7.8
Oil-Exporting Countries	8.0	11.3	17.0	19.0	16.2	15.0
Non-oil Exporting Developing Countries	10.1	22.1	33.0	32.9	32.3	31.5
Africa	4.8	9.3	18.6	16.4	18.8	25.0
Asia	5.4	14.9	27.8	11.5	1.5	8.8
Latin America	15.9	30.8	40.9	54.6	62.7	51.6
Middle East	4.3	12.7	21.8	20.3	17.4	24.2

TABLE 17.1

Inflation Rates in Industrial and Developing Countries, 1967–77

SOURCE: *World Inflation and the Developing Countries*, William R. Cline and Associates. Copyright © 1981 by The Brookings Institution, Washington, D.C., Table 1–1, p. 3.

be the higher background level of international inflation than in the past." (*ibid.*, p. 31).

Monetarists argue that in countries with high inflation such as that experienced in the cone countries, correction of past policies will require short-term adjustment costs as poor resource allocation is rectified. This occurs when prices are freed, regulations relaxed, and so on. Monetarists generally support free movement of trade and capital flows and a greatly reduced role for government as policies conducive to reduce inflation in the long run.

Structuralists weight more heavily the short-to-medium term costs of stabilization in the cone countries in terms of forgone growth, express concern over worsening income distribution from the Monetarist approach, and point out that export elasticity in response to devaluation can be low for many less-advanced countries dependent upon commodities as export earners. They suggest an active role for government in maintaining investment, employment, and acceptable income distribution in the cone countries while pursuing stabilization of prices. Structuralists recommend directing Latin American economies toward long-run development goals. Noting that inflation is often of external as well as internal origin, they feel short-run price stability should not be a high priority goal when it entails trade-offs that are too costly.

In the case of the cone countries, Carlos Diaz-Alejandro concludes: "The success achieved in the fight against inflation, modest though it may be, is to be credited to a large extent to the wage-repressing incomes policy, while the balance of payments success derives support from the sagging real aggregate demand." (Diaz-Alejandro 1981, p. 127). He warns that "too simple a diagnosis of inflation leads to an excessively sharp reduction in aggregate demand, credit use, and fiscal and incomes policies. A doctrinaire faith in private, as compared with public, investment contributes to these costs." (*ibid.*, p. 134).

The Empirical Record and Some Conclusions

The empirical record of inflation in LDCs prior to 1973 is mixed. While Latin America is often singled out as an area where it is high, only a handful of countries—Brazil, Chile, Argentina, and Uruguay—have records of high inflation and high variance in its rates. LDCs have also experienced high war-related and oil-related, inflation. Many have had inflation rates no greater than those in developed countries in the postwar periods, and most have had *average* rates below 10 percent (Cole, chap. 7 in McKinnon, ed. 1976).

High inflation rates in the wake of war or warlike dislocations such as worldwide harvest failures or cartel operations are not limited to LDCs. In order to delve behind the high rates of inflation in the handful of Latin American countries prior to the dislocations of the 1970s, Hagen has developed an explanation of the forces that cause high growth rates in the money supply in the absence of military conflict. Once some inflation exists in the economy, bargaining and contention begin as affected groups seek to recoup their original positions. According to Hagen, in some Latin American countries the groups fighting over the pie distrust each other so deeply that the bargaining turns into internecine economic warfare. The government sector is under pressure to acquiesce to power groups and employment demands by increasing the money supply. Since the income increases sought in the bargaining war exceed greatly the actual product available for division, prices spiral. The origin of the class struggle and group distrust is traced to the domestication of colonialism where Spanish and Portugese conquerors ruled the ethnic groups of "lesser origin." Not surprisingly even military governments have been unable to deal with the inflation successfully without threat to their rule (Hagen 1975, pp. 381–82).

The conflicting views on the costs of inflation are not easily resolved by empirical testing. E. S. Shaw has been influential in the institution of Classical policies in some LDCs, notably South Korea. Interest rates were adjusted for inflation and hiked to reflect the scarcity value of savings. Monetization of the economy was pushed, as was the control of inflation. Monetarists have been influential in some LDCs while Structuralists have prevailed in others. The difficulty with comparing various cases lies with the multitude of variables that can influence growth in an LDC and the differences in country-specific variables that affect the growth process.

The data in table 17.2 show both high growth and low growth accompanying inflation in various countries. The data also show countries can attain high growth with moderate inflation rates. Given the fact that none of the analyses of inflation presented denies a cost to inflation that probably intensifies with its rate, and that the

	Average Annual Growth Rate of GDP		Average Annual Rate of Inflation	
Country	1960[a]–70[a]	1970–79[b]	1960–70[a]	1970–79
Low-Income Countries	4.5 w	4.7 w	3.0 m	10.8 m
China and India	4.5 w	4.9 w	. .	. .
Others	4.3 w	3.8 w	3.0 m	10.9 m
1 Kampuchea, Dem.	3.1	. .	3.8	. .
2 Lao PDR	. .	. .	. .	. .
3 Bhutan	. .	. .	. .	. .
4 Bangladesh	3.6	3.3	3.7	15.8
5 Chad	0.5	−0.2	4.6	7.9
6 Ethiopia	4.4	1.9	2.1	4.3
7 Nepal	2.5	2.7	7.7	8.7
8 Somalia	1.0	3.1	4.5	11.3
9 Mali	3.3	5.0	5.0	9.7
10 Burma	2.6	4.3	2.7	12.1
11 Afghanistan	2.0	4.5	11.9	4.4
12 Viet Nam	. .	. .	. .	. .
13 Burundi	4.4	3.0	2.8	11.2
14 Upper Volta	3.0	−0.1	1.3	9.8
15 India	3.4	3.4	7.1	7.8

TABLE 17.2

Growth of GDP, Inflation Rate (Percent) 1960–70, 1970–79

TABLE 17.2

Growth of GDP,
Inflation Rate
(Percent) 1960–70,
1970–79 (continued)

Country	Average Annual Growth Rate of GDP		Average Annual Rate of Inflation	
	1960[a]–70[a]	1970–79[b]	1960–70[a]	1970–79
16 Malawi	4.9	6.3	2.4	9.1
17 Rwanda	2.7	4.1	13.1	14.6
18 Sri Lanka	4.6	3.8	1.8	12.3
19 Benin	2.6	3.3	1.9	9.2
20 Mozambique	4.6	−2.9	2.8	11.0
21 Sierra Leone	4.3	1.6	2.9	11.3
22 China	5.2	5.8	. .	. .
23 Haiti	−0.2	4.0	4.1	10.9
24 Pakistan	6.7	4.5	3.3	13.9
25 Tanzania	6.0	4.9	1.8	13.0
26 Zaire	3.6	−0.7	29.9	31.4
27 Niger	2.9	3.7	2.1	10.8
28 Guinea	3.5	3.6	1.5	4.4
29 Central African Rep.	1.9	3.3	4.1	9.1
30 Madagascar	2.7	0.3	3.2	10.1
31 Uganda	5.9	−0.4	3.0	28.3
32 Mauritania	. .	1.8	1.6	10.1
33 Lesotho	4.6	7.0	2.5	11.6
34 Togo	8.5	3.6	1.1	10.3
35 Indonesia	3.9	7.6	. .	20.1
36 Sudan	1.3	4.3	3.7	6.8
Middle-Income Countries	6.1 w	5.5 w	3.0 m	13.3 m
Oil Exporters	6.5 w	5.5 w	3.0 m	14.0 m
Oil Importers	5.9 w	5.5 w	3.0 m	12.2 m
37 Kenya	6.0	6.5	1.5	11.1
38 Ghana	2.1	−0.1	7.6	32.4
39 Yemen Arab Rep.	. .	8.4	. .	17.8
40 Senegal	2.5	2.5	1.7	7.6
41 Angola	4.8	−9.2	3.3	21.6
42 Zimbabwe	4.3	1.6	1.3	8.4
43 Egypt	4.2	7.6	2.7	8.0
44 Yemen, PDR	. .	. .	. .	. .
45 Liberia	5.1	1.8	1.9	9.4
46 Zambia	5.0	1.5	7.6	6.8
47 Honduras	5.3	3.5	2.9	8.4
48 Bolivia	5.2	5.2	3.5	32.4
49 Cameroon	3.7	5.4	4.2	10.3
50 Thailand	8.2	7.7	1.8	9.5
51 Philippines	5.1	6.2	5.8	13.3
52 Congo, People's Rep.	2.7	2.9	5.4	10.9
53 Nicaragua	7.2	2.6	1.9	12.2
54 Papua New Guinea	6.5	2.2	3.6	9.5
55 El Salvador	5.9	4.9	0.5	10.8
56 Nigeria	3.1	7.5	2.6	19.0
57 Peru	4.9	3.1	10.4	26.8
58 Morocco	4.2	6.1	2.0	7.3
59 Mongolia	2.8	6.0	. .	. .
60 Albania	7.3	6.8	. .	. .
61 Dominican Rep.	4.5	7.5	2.1	8.4
62 Colombia	5.1	6.0	11.9	21.5
63 Guatemala	5.6	5.9	0.1	10.6
64 Syrian Arab Rep.	5.7	9.0	1.9	12.7

Country	Average Annual Growth Rate of GDP		Average Annual Rate of Inflation	
	1960[a]–70[a]	1970–79[b]	1960–70[a]	1970–79
65 Ivory Coast	8.0	6.7	2.8	13.5
66 Ecuador	. .	8.3	. .	14.7
67 Paraguay	4.2	8.3	3.1	9.3
68 Tunisia	4.7	7.6	3.7	7.5
69 Korea, Dem. Rep.	7.8	6.2	. .	. .
70 Jordan	. .	. .	. .	. .
71 Lebanon	4.9	. .	1.4	. .
72 Jamaica	4.5	−0.9	3.9	17.4
73 Turkey	6.0	6.6	5.6	24.6
74 Malaysia	6.5	7.9	−0.3	7.3
75 Panama	7.8	3.4	1.6	7.4
76 Cuba	1.1	6.0	. .	. .
77 Korea, Rep. of	8.6	10.3	17.5	19.5
78 Algeria	4.6	5.8	2.3	13.3
79 Mexico	7.2	5.1	3.6	18.3
80 Chile	4.5	1.9	32.9	242.6
81 South Africa	6.4	3.6	3.0	11.8
82 Brazil	5.4	8.7	46.1	32.4
83 Costa Rica	6.5	6.0	1.9	15.4
84 Romania	8.6	10.6	−0.2	0.8
85 Uruguay	1.2	2.5	51.1	64.0
86 Iran	11.3	. .	−0.5	. .
87 Portugal	6.2	4.5	3.0	16.1
88 Argentina	4.2	2.5	21.7	128.2
89 Yugoslavia	5.8	5.9	12.6	17.8
90 Venezuela	6.0	5.5	1.3	10.4
91 Trinidad and Tobago	3.9	5.2	3.2	19.5
92 Hong Kong	10.0	9.4	2.4	7.9
93 Singapore	8.8	8.4	1.1	5.5
94 Greece	6.9	4.9	3.2	14.1
95 Israel	8.1	4.6	6.2	34.3
96 Spain	7.1	4.4	8.2	15.9
Industrial Market Economies	5.1 w	3.2 w	4.3 m	9.4 m
97 Ireland	4.2	3.7	5.2	14.6
98 Italy	5.3	2.9	4.4	15.6
99 New Zealand	3.9	2.4	3.3	12.3
100 United Kingdom	2.9	2.1	4.1	13.9
101 Finland	4.6	2.8	5.6	12.9
102 Austria	4.5	3.7	3.7	6.5
103 Japan	10.5	5.2	4.9	8.2
104 Australia	5.5	3.2	3.1	11.7
105 Canada	5.6	3.2	3.1	9.1
106 France	5.7	3.7	4.2	9.6
107 Netherlands	5.5	3.1	5.4	8.3
108 United States	4.3	3.1	2.8	6.9
109 Norway	4.9	4.8	4.3	8.2
110 Belgium	4.8	3.2	3.6	8.1
111 Germany, Fed. Rep.	4.4	2.6	3.2	5.3
112 Denmark	4.7	2.8	5.5	9.8
113 Sweden	4.4	2.0	4.4	9.8
114 Switzerland	4.3	0.2	4.4	5.4

TABLE 17.2
(continued)

	Average Annual Growth Rate of GDP		Average Annual Rate of Inflation	
Country	1960[a]–70[a]	1970–79[b]	1960–70[a]	1970–79
Capital-surplus Oil Exporters	. .	6.5 w	1.7 m	18.2 m
115 Iraq	6.1	10.5	1.7	14.1
116 Saudi Arabia	. .	11.1	. .	25.2
117 Libya	24.4	1.9	5.2	18.7
118 Kuwait	5.7	2.0	0.6	17.7

TABLE 17.2

Growth of GDP, Inflation Rate (Percent) 1960–70, 1970–79 (continued)

a. Figures in italics are for 1961–70, not 1960–70.
b. Figures in italics are for 1970–78, not 1970–79.

Note: Country groups are weighted by population (*w*) or GDP in 1970 dollars (*m*).

SOURCE: World Bank, *World Development Report 1981* (New York: Oxford University Press, 1981), Tables 1, 2, pp. 134–37. Reprinted with permission.

Structuralist arguments for the toleration of inflation costs do not support undertaking the costs of prolonged *high* inflation rates, it seems prudent to avoid if at all possible high rates of inflation, that is, annual rates averaging above 10 percent over a plan period.

As for lower rates of inflation, the evidence is inconclusive. An LDC attempting to approximate price stability usually cannot achieve target results, and can prudently err on the side of inflation rather than deflation under the assumptions that structural inflation is a reality, deflation retards growth, and credit creation is important to the activation of idle resources and achievement of plan targets. Such policies can be accompanied by attention to a well-functioning financial system emphasized as so important to development by those writing in the Classical vein. The policy for long-run growth, moreover, requires alleviation of structural dislocations to the degree possible. And finally, avoidance of high inflation and the inevitable controls that accompany it lessens the incidence of distortions that reduce growth. Whether or not such a goal to control inflation is achievable depends in part upon international variables. The next chapter explores the international monetary flows and their impact.

REFERENCES   Cline, William R. and Weintraub, Sidney, eds. 1981. *Economic Stabilization in Developing Countries*. Washington, D.C.: The Brookings Institution.

Cline, William R. and Associates. 1981. *World Inflation and the Developing Countries*. Washington, D.C.: The Brookings Institution.

Cole, David D. 1976. Concepts, Causes, and Cures of Instability in Less Developed Countries. In *Money and Finance in Economic Growth and Development*, edited by R. I. McKinnon. New York: Marcel Dekker.

Diaz-Alejandro, C. 1981. Southern Cone Stabilization Plans. In *Economic Stabilization in Developing Countries*, edited by W. R. Cline and S. Weintraub. Washington, D.C.: The Brookings Institution.

Hagen, E. E. 1975. *The Economics of Development*. Homewood, IL: Richard D. Irwin.

McKinnon, R. I. 1973. *Money and Capital in Economic Development*. Washington, D.C.: The Brookings Institution.

Krueger, Anne. 1981. Interactions Between Inflation and Trade Regime Objectives in Stabilization Programs. In *Economic Stabilization in Developing Countries*, edited by W. R. Cline nad S. Weintraub. Washington, D.C.: The Brookings Institution.

Shaw, E. S. 1973. *Financial Deepening in Economic Development*. New York: Oxford University Press.

Thirwall, A. P. 1976. *Financing Economic Development*. London: McMillan Press.

World Bank. 1981. *World Bank Development Report 1981*. Washington, D.C.: The World Bank.

Monetary Policy: International

chapter

18

Trade and investment across national borders require financial
accommodations. Policymakers in the LDC often find that the
problems of international finance stalk them relentlessly. Failure to respond to these problems in a timely and constructive
manner can lead to ever-deepening balance-of-payments crises. There
are no simple hard-and-fast rules to guide the policymaker in each and
every case. Experience, knowledge of the particular situation, and luck
are all ingredients in policy success. Job security is not high for the
finance minister.

In this chapter we dip a toe, so to speak, into the waters of international monetary policy. We review the relationship between the foreign exchange rate and domestic prices, and explore the idea of an
equilibrium exchange rate that clears the market for foreign exchange.
This requires the development of the relationships among exports, imports, nontraded goods, and the exchange rate. Policy options in regard
to fixed as compared with flexible exchange rates are discussed in some
detail. Some qualified conclusions are presented.

The foreign exchange rate is simply the number of units of the currency
of a foreign country that exchange for a unit of the home currency.
There is an exchange rate for each foreign currency the LDC has occasion to convert. For simplicity we speak of the exchange rate as
though there were only one other currency, or more realistically as a
composite rate for all other countries' currencies.

Through its foreign exchange rate, the economy of the LDC is tied
to the international financial system that serves world trade and investment. Policies affecting outflows of domestic money from the economy and inflows of foreign money to the economy have repercussions
upon resource allocation, domestic prices and price levels, and investment, both national and foreign. The only way for an LDC to avoid
a monetary relation with the world economy is to pursue barter trade
arrangements. Even communist countries with highly controlled economies supplement barter arrangements with a financial relationship.

The international financial system is a complex set of institutions
providing a wide diversity of financial services worldwide. Prominent
among these institutions are the foreign exchange markets for spot and
forward sales of currencies. Here specialized dealers located in various
world financial centers transact currency exchanges almost instanta-
neously via modern communication networks. In the spot market, currencies bought are made available immediately as an account at a bank
designated by the purchaser; and the seller delivers the foreign exchange—a bank account denominated in the currency—at the time of
sale.

In the forward market, buyers and sellers are covering future needs
for foreign exchange. They agree to make foreign exchange available
or to purchase it at a date in the future. The price at which the currency
will be sold or bought on the future day specified is agreed upon at
the time of the contract, which predates the delivery of the currency
by anywhere from a month to a year. The purpose of forward contracts

TRADE AND MONETARY RELATIONS

The World Monetary System and the LDC

is to allow business decisions that require foreign exchange to be based on known prices, thus reducing the risk in foreign transactions and facilitating trade. The forward market is also a convenient market for the extension of trade credits.

The world financial markets, their relationships with each other and with national central banks are structured by international agreements among nations, through their membership in the International Monetary Fund (IMF) and through mutually accepted behavior patterns. The network of world financial markets, central banks, IMF, and rules and agreements governing their relationships is known as the international monetary system.

The world financial system has evolved historically. Different eras have been characterized by differing rules. Both the Gold Standard era of the mid-to-late nineteenth century and the Bretton Woods era following World War II were characterized by great rigidity of exchange rates. Less rigidity prevails under the current rules that evolved in the 1970s, when the Bretton Woods system was superseded. The current system, marked by relatively frequent movement in exchange rates of many currencies including reserve currencies such as the dollar, is in something of a state of flux. It has been referred to as a system of managed floating, meaning market forces influence the exchange rate, but central banks intervene to influence or manage the degree of flexibility in the rates. With major currencies frequently changing in value, it is difficult for any one country to maintain a constant exchange rate in the sense of the fixity attainable in previous systems.

Even with flexibility among world currencies, the LDC can retain some control of its exchange rates by pegging its currency to a key world currency or a weighted average of a bundle of currencies. As G. M. Meier notes, LDCs prefer a greater fixity to world currencies than the current system offers (1976, p. 365). Reasons for this preference will be explained subsequently. The approach taken involves a discussion of flexible rates as compared with an adjustable peg as they affect the LDC. Keep in mind, however, that the current system precludes attainment of either in its pure form, although approximations are possible.

LDCs generally constrict the degree to which their respective national financial systems are integrated with the world financial system. Not unlike many MDCs, they limit the free flow of national funds to other countries for investment purposes. Placing of funds abroad on either a short- or long-term basis denies savings to the domestic economy.

LDCs experience recurrent foreign exchange pressures and shortfalls during the development process, and their governments often enact controls to deal with such pressures. This affects the value and/or availability of their currency. As a result, LDCs with "weak" currencies find their money is traded infrequently on world markets. Invoices for exports and imports are generally denominated in a major financial currency used in world trade, or in that of the country traded with. There is no forward market for the weak currency. The term applied to such a currency is "inconvertible." Inconvertible currencies often have more than one price placed upon them by LDC governments, depending upon usage. Typically there is also a black market for the currency.

The value of domestic money is reflected in the price level. The foreign exchange rate reflects domestic prices to foreigners when currencies are convertible and controls absent. It is a two-way mirror, in addition, reflecting foreign prices into the LDC. For example, assume the ratio of local currency to foreign currency is 1/10 and the price of a domestic good exported is 5 units of domestic currency. The price of that good in foreign currency units is 50. Now let the exchange rate change to 1/15. The domestic currency has appreciated vis-à-vis the foreign currency; and the foreign currency has depreciated against the domestic currency. The price to foreigners of the item costing 5 domestic currency units has now risen from 50 to 75 units of foreign currency. Analogously, items imported are now less expensive in the domestic currency.

The Foreign Exchange Rate and Domestic Prices

When the domestic currency appreciates vis-à-vis the foreign and prices in each country in their own currency remain the same, export prices expressed in foreign currency rise. This is because with appreciation export purchases require more units of the foreigner's currency. On the other hand, foreign goods are cheaper for the appreciating country since the domestic currency can acquire more foreign currency. This outcome assumes, as mentioned, there are no offsetting domestic price changes as the currency rates change, or distortions from inconvertible currencies.

A higher foreign exchange rate for domestic currency, then, encourages imports by making them cheaper but discourages exports by making them dearer. A lower foreign exchange rate has the opposite effect. And the foreign exchange rate and changes in it can affect the commodity or net barter terms of trade. Since this whole topic is complex, it is helpful to begin with an analysis of the basic economic variables that determine an equilibrium exchange rate, which is a monetary datum reflective of trade and investment flows. After exploring the important fundamental forces at work through the help of a naïve model, we will return to a discussion of real-world options for the LDC in the area of international monetary policy.

THE EQUILIBRIUM EXCHANGE RATE

An equilibrium exchange rate is a theoretical construct that helps to identify disequilibrium forces found in the real world that can lead to inefficient or unsustainable conditions in the balance of payments. Given world prices for exports and imports and the rate of net long-run capital inflow, if any, an equilibrium exchange rate is one that is consistent with relative costs of production at full employment with a balanced foreign account. The concept of an equilibrium exchange rate under conditions of import constraints combined with development

The Simple Model

goals can be examined within the simple model, used previously, of a country at early stages of development. There is an infant industry sector operating with capital imports that are not produceable by the LDC. We assume the government sets the exchange rate.

Small Exporter Case   In the first case considered the LDC's proportion of total world trade is small, and the country is a price-taker. Its currency is weak, and prices are expressed in the major world trading currency. No matter what foreign exchange rate the LDC sets, a given quantity of exports earns a given amount of foreign exchange, which in turn can purchase a set number of units of capital equipment imports. With world prices denominated in the world trading currency given and constant, the barter terms of trade are known and are shown by the slope of T in the diagram. The barter terms of trade are not affected by the number of units of domestic currency exchanged for a unit of world currency. Exports and imports, however, are affected by the foreign exchange rate because it influences the price in domestic currency received for exports and the production cost of industrial goods and their profitability.

Figure 18.1 shows the diagram for an LDC economy with trade. One slight change has been made from earlier presentations of the diagram: The import curve (EM) showing imports required for varying production levels of good B over a 5-year plan, and the international commodity terms of trade line (T) have been "flipped over" to the northwest quadrant. This is a simple maneuver that allows us to show the domestic terms of trade between exports and the domestic content of industrial goods (T_D) more clearly.

Movement along the curve EB from E toward B means that local resources are freed from export production and, combined with imports, can provide an additional amount of B goods. The slope of EB depicts increasing costs as resources are transferred from exports to industrial production. Curve EB will reflect a feasible trade-off of exports for B goods only if there is no binding trade constraint—that is, imports in adequate amounts can be financed.

The assumptions of the model are that there is a development goal of maximization of B goods and a constraint that, over the 5-year plan, exports equal imports in barter or value terms. Given the international terms of trade, there is only one point on curve EB where exports produced will earn the required imports per level of B goods as shown along curve EM in the northwest quadrant. This is point x, with output of b industrial goods and e exports. Imports of equivalent value to e exports are shown at m in the northwest quadrant. Thus b is the maximum quantity of industrial goods that can be produced given the constraint $E = M$. Larger quantities of B goods are feasible only where imports in excess of exports are allowed.

The slope of curve EB reflects the opportunity cost of B goods *excluding* import costs, and is expressed as $dE/d\hat{B}$. Equilibrium relative prices at production point x expressed in domestic currency must reflect opportunity cost so that $dE/d\hat{B} = (P_B - P_M)/P_E$. This price ratio

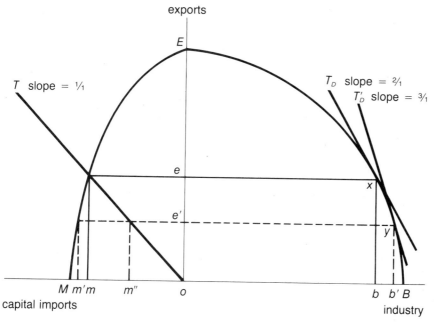

exports

E

T slope = ⅟₁

T_D slope = ²⁄₁
T'_D slope = ³⁄₁

e

x

e'

y

M m'm   m"   o   b b' B

capital imports   industry

FIGURE 18.1

Appreciation of the Domestic Currency, Price-taker Case

An overvalued foreign exchange rate changes relative prices in domestic currency from T_D to T'_D. Producers respond to price signals and reduce export production from e to e' while expanding industrial output from b to b'. This leads to an excess of imports over exports equal to (m' − m"). The industrial expansion cannot be maintained unless the current account deficit can be financed with foreign savings inflow.

is shown in Figure 18.1 as the slope of T_D tangent to EB in the northeast quadrant.

Since the ratio of international prices, P_M/P_E, is given by the slope of T in the northwest quadrant, P_B/P_M can be derived by dividing the ratio P_B/P_E by P_M/P_E. Alternatively we can say that the exchange ratio of B goods and imports can be expressed in units of exports, so that we know barter exchange ratios in equilibrium. In sum, when an economy is maximizing output of B goods for a plan period and all costs are covered, there will be a set of barter exchange ratios for exports, imports and B goods reflective of their opportunity costs, and a set of relative prices consistent with these barter exchange rates.

The barter terms of trade reflecting equilibrium costs shown in figure 18.1 are summarized in table 18.1. The domestic content of good B is worth two units of exports (T_D). One unit of exports exchanges for one unit of imports (T); therefore, including import costs B = 3E and one unit of either imports or exports exchanges for 1/3 unit of good B. Whatever the existing absolute price level, *relative* prices that reflect

A Numerical Example

TABLE 18.1
Equilibrium Prices and Barter Ratios

Good	(1) Foreign Unit Prices	(2) Domestic Barter Terms	(3) Domestic Unit Prices	(4) Quantity Exported Imported	(5) Exchange Rate
Exports	10F	1 unit	100D	500 units	
Imports	10F	1 unit	100D	500 units	10D/1F
B Goods	n.a.*	1/3 units	300D	0	n.a.

* Not applicable.

the scarcity value of resources would maintain these barter ratios among imports, exports and industrial goods, and clear markets without excess demand or supply at these relative prices. In table 18.1 a set of domestic and foreign unit prices consistent with these relative costs of goods is given in columns one and three. The *absolute* level of domestic prices reflects the money supply.

The relationship between absolute prices and the equilibrium exchange rate is also illustrated by the numerical example in table 18.1. given foreign unit prices of 10F each for exports and imports that cannot be affected by the LDC, and given the domestic prices of 100D for exports and imports, the equilibrium exchange rate must be 10D/1F. This will ensure that the values of both the export good and the import good in domestic and foreign currency are equivalent. Another exchange rate, such as 1D/1F, would translate into domestic import and export prices per unit of 10D instead of 100D. Only if domestic prices were 10 percent of their current level would 1D/1F be a consistent foreign exchange rate. As discussion proceeds, it becomes apparent that the foreign exchange rate both affects and reflects the absolute level of domestic prices.

An Overvalued Exchange Rate: A Graphic Illustration

An overvalued exchange rate creates a current account deficit in the balance of payments and expands production of *B* goods beyond long-run capacity. This can be seen with the help of the numerical example above, and can be illustrated graphically.

Assume in the numerical example given that the exchange rate changes to 7.5D/1F from 10D/1F, with export and import prices fixed in foreign currency at 10F. The domestic unit price of exports and imports each drops to 75D. When exports and imports were priced at 100D they were worth 1/3 unit of *B* goods. Put another way, one-third of the cost of a unit of *B* goods priced at 300D was the 100D cost of imports. With appreciation of the currency both export and import prices drop by 25D. Assuming the price of good *B* remains 300D, the slope of T_D is now:

$$(P_B - P_M)/P_E = \frac{(300 - 75)}{(75)} = \frac{225D}{75D} = 3/1$$

Expressed in domestic currency, exports have become cheaper relative to good *B*. The repercussions of this are best shown graphically.

Consider again equilibrium conditions shown in figure 18.1. Relative prices P_M/P_E are shown by the slope of T. Relative prices for domestic resource production, $(P_B - P_M)/P_E$, are shown by the slope of T_D. These ratios are 1/1 and 2/1, respectively, when production is at equilibrium point x. This is the same set of relative prices shown in table 18.1 when the exchange rate is 10D/1F.

Appreciation of the currency to 7.5D/1F raises the relative price ratio $(P_B - P_M)/P_E$ from 2/1 to 3/1. This means that when production is at the general equilibrium point of x in figure 18.1, $dE/d\hat{B} < (P_B - P_M)/P_E$ with the new exchange rate. In value terms domestic resources earn less at the margin in export compared to B goods production. Following price signals, producers will expand output of the now relatively profitable industrial good to where $dE/d\hat{B} = 3/1 =$ slope of T'_D. Exports drop to e' and import demand is at m'. When financing is available from abroad to purchase the excess imports $(m' - m'')$, industrial output expands to b'. This expansion of industrial production cannot be maintained, however, in the absence of independent long-term foreign savings inflow, since the borrowings cannot be repaid without an increase in exports or reduction in imports.

Assume that foreign financing of the import surplus is not available and that the exchange rate remains overvalued, so that exports relative to B goods are priced too low. Exports remain at e' with imports at m''. The economy's capacity for production of B goods drops. Output would be inside the production possibilities curve with unemployed resources. Note that an attempt to overcome unemployment problems and raise output by expanding the money supply would exacerbate the difficulty. Industrial output cannot expand without more exports and imports. This requires correction of *relative* prices. More money in circulation with output constant would simply raise domestic prices, creating inflation and thereby a greater overvaluation of the exchange rate. This would push the demand for imports higher while reducing incentives for exports.

Analogously an undervalued exchange rate would produce a surplus in the trade account and reduce industrialization below plan goals. The surplus represents a savings outflow from the LDC. Experience indicates it will usually set up pressures to increase spending leading to higher imports of consumer goods. In sum, an over- or undervalued exchange rate will divert resources away from development goals.

The Major Exporter Case

Appreciation in the case of a major exporter can create a foreign exchange shortfall just as with a small exporter. There is a difference in the adjustment to a new currency ratio, however, in that both foreign and domestic relative prices can change. And in the case of the major exporter, an improvement in the international terms of trade with appreciation of the exchange rate encourages excess supplies of the export good amidst import shortfalls. We can view this possibility graphically.

For simplicity, assume the LDC is the sole exporter. The immediate effect of an appreciation of the exchange rate to, let us say, 5D/1F from

10D/1F upon the numerical example of table 18.1 is to change export prices in foreign currency since the LDC is the only supplier. With a domestic price of 100D, the price of exports in foreign currency is now 20F. Import prices are fixed at 10F. The barter or commodity terms of trade rise to 1E/2M.

Figure 18.2 shows the result of this change in the exchange rate under a case of elastic demand for the export good. Prior to appreciation, equilibrium production is at b industrial goods, e exports and m imports. The shape of T_k shows the loci of coordinate points where $E = M$ as the terms of trade vary with the level of exports. The terms of trade where T_k crosses EM are the slope of T (1/1). The domestic opportunity cost in equilibrium is shown by the slope of T_D (2/1).

With appreciation to 5D/1F, export prices are 20F (100D), import price 10F, and the slope of T changes from 1/1 to 1/2, i.e., from T to T'. Such high-priced exports can only be sold if the quantity exported drops to e'. Imports of equivalent value are at m''. Thus while the immediate effect of appreciation is to improve the commodity terms of trade, this lowers the income terms of trade when the demand for exports is elastic. With e' exports full employment production is b' industrial goods. The import shortfall for production at b' and e' with

FIGURE 18.2

Appreciation of the Domestic Currency, Major Exporter Case

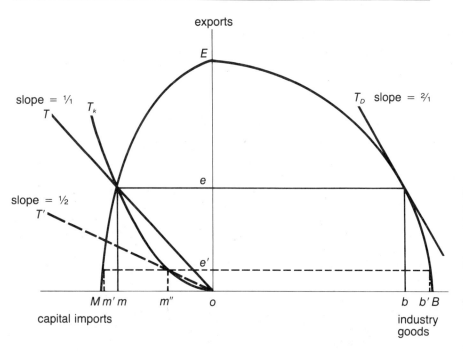

A rise in the value of the domestic currency increases the price of export goods in foreign currency. This improves the commodity terms of trade from the slope of T to the slope of T'. The higher export prices cannot hold unless exports fall to e'. This causes a drop in the income terms of trade as the value of exports in importables drops to m''. Full employment production at b' creates a foreign exchange shortfall of $(m' - m'')$ that is not sustainable without foreign savings inflow.

the new terms of trade is $(m' - m'')$. This production combination is not attainable without reallocation of domestic resources and foreign savings inflow. In this case, then, a foreign savings inflow will allow the LDC to improve its terms of trade.

Sticky domestic prices will turn the domestic terms of trade in favor of B goods, but need not reduce exports enough to maintain the higher terms of trade. In the absence of controls export production will exceed demand, leading to a fall in export prices in both domestic and foreign currency. In fact, if domestic prices are completely flexible, they will return to the equilibrium relative prices prior to the change in the exchange rate, re-establishing the old terms of trade, but with absolute prices consistent with the new exchange rate. This assumes no foreign savings inflow.

If prices are not flexible, and usually they are not completely so, distortions and unemployment can result. Thus attempts to set a disequilibrium foreign exchange rate cause dislocations that must be dealt with by changes in domestic output and employment and, if available, foreign savings inflows. Not surprisingly, an LDC with a disequilibrium exchange rate often has excess supplies of exports because of the combination of an overvalued exchange rate and the wrong export incentive price, and yet may suffer from foreign exchange shortfalls! Output losses can offset any gains from a more favorable commodity terms of trade. Such conditions indicate the LDC is a major exporter. Recall that in the small exporter case the overvalued exchange rate did not improve the terms of trade and yet, in the absence of foreign savings inflows, led to output shortfalls stemming from insufficient export production.

Devaluation and Inflation

In the cases of the small and large exporters, appreciation lowered import prices in domestic currency, potentially lowering the price of B goods. Thus if prices are flexible downward appreciation can be deflationary on first impact. Analogously, devaluation can be inflationary. As the units of domestic currency needed to purchase a unit of foreign currency rise, import prices in domestic currency increase. When imports are intermediate goods, such as equipment or oil, their prices affect an array of domestically produced goods. Moreover, prices move upward more easily than downward, especially where demand for goods with import content remains strong. A country with an over-valued exchange rate seeking to correct the problem with devaluation, then, can encounter inflationary pressures as a result. Sometimes this perpetuates disequilibrium. We will return to this point.

Inelastic Demand and Appreciation

One final example is of interest here because it portrays the case for exporters of commodities such as oil that have inelastic demand for their exports at certain export levels. In such cases an appreciation of the exchange rate can improve both the income and commodity terms of trade and move the exporter to a new higher-income equilibrium level. This is shown in figure 18.3 where the original equilibrium level

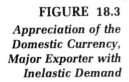

FIGURE 18.3

Appreciation of the Domestic Currency, Major Exporter with Inelastic Demand

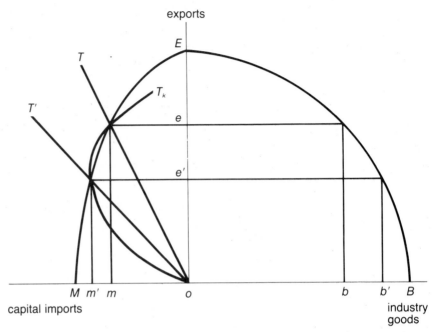

An appreciation of the exchange rate improves the commodity terms of trade, moving T to T'. Because demand is inelastic along T_k between e and e', the income terms of trade also improve as exports drop. The economy moves to a new, higher equilibrium income level with b' industrial goods and m' imports.

is production of b industrial goods and e exports. A foreign exchange rate consistent with terms of trade T places exports along the inelastic portion of the equilibrium balance of trade line T_k. In contrast to the case where demand was elastic, appreciation that raises the terms of trade to the slope of T' allows a new trade equilibrium with higher imports (m') and B goods (b') while exporting less. Exports must drop for these terms of trade to hold.

Sometimes the LDC is seeking to diversify out of a major commodity export such as oil. Indeed the oil exporters are attempting to export "downstream" products such as petrochemicals. In such cases the exchange rate that will maximize the terms of trade for a good with inelastic demand such as oil may leave other goods overpriced in export markets. An alternative to appreciation of the domestic currency in these situations can be a tax on the exported commodity combined with a lower exchange rate that will induce specialization and trade in a greater variety of products.

Changes in the Equilibrium Exchange Rate

Any change in world prices modifies the terms of trade, creating both an income effect and a relative price effect so that the equilibrium rate of foreign exchange is modified. A change in the terms of trade transfers income into or out of the LDC, raising or lowering the industrial output as exports are dearer or cheaper relative to imports. The new relative prices for exports compared with imports affect the domestic prices consistent with coverage of costs for exports and industrial goods. Thus, there will be a different equilibrium exchange rate for each set of world prices and associated terms of trade.

Needless to say, a change in world prices requires resource reallocations, changes in relative prices, and exchange rate adjustment to maintain equilibrium. Foreign credit as opposed to domestic credit may be required to ease the transition period; and when the terms of trade are lower, income is transferred abroad rather than among domestic income earners.

Growth also affects the equilibrium foreign exchange rate. With growth *EB* shifts outward; and with nonproportionate shifts, the slope of *EB* is altered, meaning that the real costs of production of exports relative to industrial output will have changed. Absolute and relative prices will be realigned in domestic currency. The exchange rate consistent with optimal allocation of resources between exports and industrial output at full employment will be different from the rate prior to growth.

Inflation at home with prices steady abroad induces disequilibrium. If growth or excess expansion of the money supply brings inflation, then domestic prices rise. At the preinflation equilibrium exchange rate, exports are now priced too high while imports are attractively cheap. Without a devaluation of the currency to a lower equilibrium exchange rate, trade imbalance will occur in the form of a monetary deficit.

Finally, a shift in the rate of inflow of long-term capital will modify the equilibrium exchange rate. Imbalance in the current account is possible when there is long-term investment from abroad. A change in the rate of inflow alters the equilibrium export level. A new exchange rate and export level are needed to reestablish general equilibrium.

Equilibrium conditions are presented as known in an analysis of this type. Such conditions, however, are far from self-evident in the real world. Those guiding the development process must grope for equilibrium amidst poor data, inadequate information, distortions, and other hindrances. Not surprisingly, real-world discussion of the appropriate exchange rate for an LDC can be complicated by disagreement over what constitutes a feasible development goal and sustainable international financing for the development plan. Setting development targets is at best an art within the LDC environment.

An Introduction to Policy Problems

Even the extremely simple numerical and graphic examples illustrate the complexity of system requirements that relative prices, absolute prices, and the exchange rate be in simultaneous or general equilibrium. There are many reasons in the real world why disequilibrium is a common occurrence. Relative prices can be distorted by resource prices unrelated to their scarcity value. It may be politically impossible to allow food prices to reflect their scarcity value. Prices may be distorted by monopoly, taxes, credit allocation, or inflation. In

a situation of multiple distortions, optimum policies are hard to identify, let alone execute.

LDCs often want faster industrialization than (with hindsight) may
be achievable, given the level of foreign savings inflow. When this is
the case, the foreign lender, seeking assurances of repayment of loans,
views the exchange rate as overvalued and urges control of the money
supply and depreciation of the currency. Along the lines presented in
the analysis, lenders argue that once distortions are corrected output
will be higher. The LDC sees such actions as "belt tightening," and is
greatly concerned about the short-term consequences of adjustment to
tight money and higher-cost imports. Emerging nations note that in the
short run export sales may not expand with devaluation and a change
in relative prices, because of inelasticities in either supply or demand.
The LDC is more likely to identify the problem as poor terms of trade,
inelastic demand for exports, or insufficient international lending provisions. That is, the problem originates abroad, not at home; therefore
the solution lies abroad, not at home.

We will return to this discussion of policy implications after further analysis. Here it is sufficient to note that a policy that does not
allow adjustment of the exchange rate removes an important equili-
brating variable for the policymaker. Fixity of exchange rates can result
in poor resource allocation and bring on the need for direct controls
on exports and imports. Foreign exchange shortfalls can easily occur
when the exchange rate is immobile. The adjustment process falls more
heavily upon output and adjustments in absolute and relative prices
in the domestic economy. The economy often retreats inside its production possibilities curve because of distortions and unemployed resources.

In sum, the policymaker must be aware of the mounting costs as
the economy moves further from equilibrium. Large distortions in exchange rates (above or below equilibrium) and in relative prices, or
high rates of change in absolute prices, can be costly, and are not easily
contained or offset with a system of controls. This is true for centrally
planned economies as well as the more decentralized ones.

Yet, as discussed subsequently, the economy with large distortions
in its exchange rate cannot move toward equilibrium without encountering short-run costs. Due to the economic and political costs that arise
in the near term, movement toward equilibrium may require careful
execution and phasing. Such adjustments are among the most difficult
dealt with by LDC policymakers. Ironically, where a country is heavily
dependent upon trade for a large proportion of its GNP, currency changes
can be self-defeating because of inflationary pressures. This topic was
introduced in the model, and is returned to below. (Note that a country
that provides either a large or small proportion of the world supply of
a good need not be heavily trade dependent for its GNP. Often countries
that are relatively small in population and area are heavily trade dependent.)

EXCHANGE   In the simple model we identified an exchange rate consistent with
RATE POLICY   development goals and balance-of-payments equilibrium at full em-

ployment, indicating the fundamental variables determining the equilibrium rate, and how changes in these variables would cause a change in the equilibrium exchange rate. Consider now an actual LDC producing many goods and services and importing and exporting a variety of products; and allow for conditions of less than full employment so that supply elasticities vary. The government of such an economy can at a point in time set its exchange rate at a level that reflects consistency with fundamental variables at full employment and keep the rate constant despite cyclical, seasonal, or minor factors that can impinge on the balance of payments. Such an approach is effective, and under the Bretton Woods System was commonly used in the more complex, real-world situation. The exchange rate under the Bretton Woods System could be changed to accommodate shifts in the fundamental full employment equilibrium variables. Of course, uncertainties arose about how fundamental the symptoms of disequilibria were.

Another approach, less commonly used, is for the LDC to identify development needs and establish any necessary policies vis-à-vis exports or imports and then let the international currency markets set the foreign exchange rate daily based on supply and demand as affected by exports, imports, and financial flows of savings into or out of the LDC. The country could expect feedback effects upon the domestic economy from the changes in the exchange rate that would influence resource utilization and allocation, assuming the resources move responsively and price signals are not blocked by planners. In such a situation the exchange rate fluctuates constantly (although not necessarily by large amounts), and not just in response to shifts in basic variables affecting equilibrium. Such fluctuations are allowed to affect the domestic economy rather than being offset by taxes, domestic price manipulation, or subsidies. Domestic aggregate spending and, it is hoped, inflation are controlled to allow the domestic economy to respond to balance-of-payments needs.

The Market-Determined Foreign Exchange Rate

More specific discussion will be helpful here. With completely flexible exchange rates, the demand for foreign exchange and its supply determine the foreign exchange rate. The supply of foreign exchange is a function of export sales, which can be assumed to be responsive to market forces, including risk. Usually, however, the quantity of exports will also indicate resource allocations related to development planning. The demand for foreign exchange reflects the demand for imports. It too is responsive to market forces, but most often there are constraints placed upon it by LDC governments. Part of the constraints placed upon imports may be related to tariffs to encourage infant industry (see chapter 12). In addition, LDCs with a foreign exchange constraint generally rely upon quantitative controls when they wish to accelerate savings and investment for development. Quotas may be set for consumer goods not produceable at home that are attractive imports for richer citizens. And plans sometimes call for priority allocations of foreign exchange to development-related imports, especially when such imports yield growth externalities that would not be reflected in market bidding for the foreign exchange.

Economists generally admonish against reliance upon quotas and tariffs because of their capacity for distortion. Using them to a limited degree, however, especially in the economic environment of LDCs, finds acceptance among many economists and among most planners. Judicious use of such tools has been discussed in the chapter on promoting industrialization. The point of the discussion here is that the demand for foreign exchange in an LDC generally reflects development goals, and market forces are subject to restraint. This fact moves attention away from identification of an equilibrium exchange rate reflective of unfettered supply and demand. Rather we must speak of a development-related demand for foreign exchange that reflects, at the minimum, some priority allocations and import restrictions. In cases of severe foreign exchange constraint, the demand and supply of foreign exchange are closely interrelated.

Once the priorities are established, and allowing for variation in the degree of constraint, we can identify the shapes of the demand and supply curves for foreign exchange by asking how the quantity imported and the quantity exported rise or fall when prices shift *as a result of* a change in the foreign exchange rate *only*. As imports and exports change with a movement in the foreign exchange rate, the quantity of foreign exchange demanded and the quantity supplied by foreign buyers vary. Over a *range* of possible foreign exchange rates, then, we can identify a demand curve and a supply curve for foreign exchange. These curves will have a time dimension; and generally their elasticities will be higher when the period considered is longer.

Consider the supply curve for foreign exchange for an LDC that affects its own terms of trade according to the quantity it exports. Assume the LDC faces an inelastic demand for its exports over a given price range, above and below which the exports are price elastic. In the inelastic portion of the export demand curve, let a depreciation of the domestic currency lower prices expressed in foreign exchange. This must result in a loss of foreign exchange because the additional quantity of exports salable is insufficient to offset the loss in foreign exchange earned per unit of exports. In this range, then, the quantity of foreign exchange falls with depreciation. For example, the data in table 18.2 show a 50 percent devaluation of the domestic currency (D) relative to the foreign currency (F). The quantity exportable rises, but foreign exchange earnings fall. In contrast, over price ranges where the demand for exports is elastic, the quantity exportable expands with depreciation by enough to increase the quantity of foreign exchange. A change in the foreign exchange rate, then, may raise or lower the

	Foreign Exchange Rate	Quantity Exportable	Price Per Unit Exported	Supply of Foreign Exchange
TABLE 18.2 *Inelastic Demand for Exports*	IF/1D	100	1F or 1D	100F
	IF/2D	140	.5F or 1D	70F

amount of foreign currency earned, depending upon the elasticity of demand for exports.

Export supply elasticities also affect the quantity exportable and hence the supply of foreign exchange. Countries exporting, say, rubber or coffee cannot expand their exports of these commodities until new trees mature, a period of several years. Unless other goods or commodities are exportable as relative prices change, the devaluation will not raise exports from current capacity levels in the short run.

Consider now the demand for foreign exchange. A depreciation of the LDC currency, other things remaining the same, raises the price of imports in domestic currency and will reduce the quantity of foreign exchange demanded to buy imports because, even with a highly inelastic demand, fewer units are bought when the price goes up. And while it takes more domestic currency to buy the total quantity of imports when demand is inelastic, with fewer units bought it takes less foreign currency, assuming the foreign price per unit has not changed. The demand for foreign exchange, then, varies inversely with the price of foreign currency.[1]

Elasticities of demand for the export good affect stability in the market for a currency. Figure 18.4 illustrates the case where export demand varies from elastic to inelastic and back again. Such an export demand curve will trace out a supply curve for foreign exchange that first is positively sloped with devaluation, then negatively sloped, and finally, when the units of domestic to foreign currency are high enough, rises again. Depending upon the position of the foreign exchange demand curve, there may be more than one foreign exchange rate where demand equals supply. More importantly, should the foreign exchange rate be at k in figure 18.4, a disturbance of this rate would initiate a continuous movement away from k toward x or z since below k supply exceeds demand and the price of foreign exchange falls, while above k demand exceeds supply and the price will rise.

Unstable Foreign Exchange Rates

Both x and z are stable equilibria; that is, when demand exceeds supply, prices rise toward equilibrium and when supply exceeds demand, they fall toward equilibrium, as opposed to moving away from it. Seeking to pinpoint an equilibrium exchange rate reflecting supply and demand, we have identified *two* stable rates on either side of an unstable one. And should S slope downward throughout, stability would not exist.

Unstable supply and demand curves for foreign exchange are applicable to some LDCs, especially at the stage of their development when they have essentially only one or two export commodities and no capacity to turn out manufacturers to supplement exports with inelastic demand, Moreover, most LDCs have very inelastic demand for

---

1. The demand for foreign exchange in the limiting case where the demand for imports has zero elasticity is a constant and no savings of foreign exchange are achieved on the import side with depreciation of the currency. The demand curve for imports would be a rectangular hyperbola.

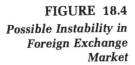

FIGURE 18.4
*Possible Instability in
Foreign Exchange
Market*

Foreign exchange demand and supply with stable equilibria at *x* and *z*, unstable at *k*.

imports. It is common to find they have pared down their import list to products required for the development program. In such cases, when there is excess demand for foreign exchange, devaluation of the currency can be destabilizing. It can leave the LDC with little change in its imports and with less foreign exchange earnings from exports facing inelastic demand, even where export *supply* elasticities are favorable.

Not all LDCs face inelasticity of demand for exports. Even when the LDC markets a commodity for which total world demand is price-inelastic, the LDC may face an elastic demand for its exports if it is not a large supplier of the commodity. This occurs when the LDC can erode the market of other suppliers by cutting price. And LDCs with few natural resources to sell abroad tend to develop manufacturers exports earlier. They are less dependent on one or two export commodities. When the currency is depreciated, some exports are price-elastic; and new goods become competitive with the new exchange rate. Under such stable conditions, the LDC's supply curve for foreign exchange is always positively sloped. Such LDCs, as well as those more developed, may have less inelastic import demand also. And as the demand curve shifts outward with growth, it intersects the supply curve at a lower, stable exchange rate with higher imports and exports. Such stable conditions require resource mobility and output responsiveness to trade advantages.

Flexible Exchange   We have now seen that the equilibrium exchange rate for an LDC is
Rates: not always a unique rate, and it changes with development. As re-
Disadvantages   sources, relative prices, productivity, government policies, price elas-

ticities for traded goods, and the price level all change, the position and shape of the demand and supply curves for foreign exchange also change. Failure to allow adjustments in the foreign exchange rate over the development path can create balance-of-payments problems and poor resource allocation.

Yet seldom does an LDC permit its exchange rate to vary daily without limits; that is, completely flexible exchange rates are not generally allowed. When frequent fluctuations are orchestrated by the government, the procedure is usually designed to adjust to high inflation rates by a prescribed formula devaluation; it is not a free market float. Several problems or costs of flexible exchange rates make LDCs shy away from them.

Destabilizing Elasticities First, assume an LDC's supply-demand curves are as shown in figure 18.4. The S-shaped supply curve for foreign exchange can present difficulties for uncontrolled flexibility. When equilibrium is unstable, the foreign exchange rate could gyrate unpredictably, destabilizing an LDC economy unable to respond easily to sharp exchange rate changes. Destabilizing speculation in the currency can readily develop in a market of this type. The risks in foreign trade would worsen, deterring the trade effort required for development. The range and frequency of foreign exchange rate swings can be great when the market for the LDC's currency is "thin" because of a limited volume of exchange transactions, and when speculation in the currency is triggered by uncertainty.

Destabilizing factors are also apt to be at work. Commodities sold by LDCs suffer demand changes over the business cycle and supply distruptions as well. A change in supply or demand for price-inelastic goods causes a relatively large change in price. The domestic and foreign prices of such commodities are then unstable. This disturbs the equilibrium foreign exchange rate, and destabilizing speculation may emerge. Flexible exchange rates under conditions of very inelastic supply and demand for foreign exchange can engender more instability rather than correcting trade imbalance.

Inflation Second, as McKinnon has pointed out (1963 and 1981), devaluations are inflationary for small countries when a large percentage of their GNP flows through trade channels. Imports are more expensive in domestic currency. Assuming resources are mobile, the higher prices attract resources from other domestic goods to import substitution production. Export prices in foreign currency are lower. Domestic producers in the export sector expand output as foreign demand increases with devaluation. Resources must be bid away from other sectors. Domestic prices of exports rise when this sector encounters increasing costs, reversing to some degree the export price incentive associated with devaluation.

The turnaround in the trade imbalance under conditions of full employment and favorable supply and demand elasticities requires that national consumption, investment, and government spending decline so that more goods may go abroad. Failure to curb spending would further fuel inflation. Even with such controls, the price rises for imports and exports connected directly to the change in the exchange rate affects such a large portion of the country's output that the general price level must move up. Some small countries have 50 percent of their GNP flowing through trade as exports or imports. As inflation erodes some of the effects of devaluation, the currency's value falls further in repeating sequences of devaluation and induced inflation.

Structuralists would also note that LDCs without such a high trade dependency can easily experience inflation from devaluation. When imports are intermediate goods for which there are no close substitutes so that they affect the general price structure, and imperfect competition leads to price markups to cover costs, then inflationary pressures build. Oil imports, wage-related food imports, and imported capital goods could all cause such inflation accompanying devaluation. And savings are not easily raised in LDCs to dampen spending.

Structuralists, drawing upon experience in Latin America, point out that control of the money supply with devaluation may exacerbate rather than ameliorate inflation. The problem is the potential for a fairly sharp rise in the cost of working capital when interest rates respond to tight money in segmented financial markets. Even where legal restrictions on banks hold interest rates down, tight money forces firms into borrowing at sharply rising rates outside regulated official sources. Where interest rates are free to rise, they will have to reach higher nominal levels the higher inflationary expectations are in the economy (Foxley in Cline and Weintraub, eds. 1981; and Diaz-Alejandro, *ibid*).

Excess Short-Term Changes   Third, when unpredictable events of short-term impact are the source of instability, fixed exchange rates provide an interval for corrections without the immediate stimulus to resource reallocation that occurs with flexible rates. Should harvest failure caused by weather conditions boost imports higher than exports, depreciating the foreign exchange rate will not correct the imbalance since agricultural exports cannot be spurred during the current growing season by a transfer of resources from the other sectors of the economy; and with the rise in food prices further inflationary effects from devaluation would exacerbate conditions while not cutting the import bill.

Of course, with high instability there is no steadying capability from either fixed or flexible rates that can offset the unpredictable dislocations. Typically trade is retrenched via controls when such conditions prevail. Uncertainties surrounding a change in government by force or conditions of famine can easily spark violent swings in currency markets. Capital flight can be especially destabilizing under conditions of political uncertainty.

Absence of Forward Market   Fourth, LDCs with small trade volume in world markets, restrictions on foreign exchange usage, and weak or problem balance-of-payments cannot expect that flexible exchange rates will create a convertible currency where there are adequate forward markets to hedge against changes in the value of the currency. Under inadequate hedging conditions, flexible exchange rates can increase the risks of trade greatly, deterring participation in trade.

All in all, individual LDCs could face formidable problems under conditions of completely flexible exchange rates. Yet, as discussed next, the alternative to flexible exchange rates is not without drawbacks.

The problems associated with fixed exchange rates center around the incidence and degree of disequilibrium exchange rates. We concentrate here on the adequacy of adjustments needed to accommodate disequilibrium of greater or lesser degree and duration that inevitably arises under a system of pegged rates. The first problem concerns the adequacy of compensatory financing needed to accommodate seasonal, cyclical, or other temporary deficits in the current account of the balance of payments. The credit creation capacities for LDCs can be well below that of MDCs for this type of credit.

Problems of Disequilibrium with Pegged Exchange Rates

Credit Problems Inflows of financial capital, short-term and long-term, allow imbalance between the value of exports and imports in the trade account, as explained in chapter 12. Ideally under fixed exchange rates, short-term inflows of financial capital are a cushion for offsetting fluctuations in foreign exchange earnings that will be self-correcting. Higher interest rates can be used to attract foreign capital and force traders to seek short-term financing abroad. IMF loans may be available.

Compensatory credit flows, however, do not operate smoothly when the foreign exchange rate of an LDC fluctuates too far from equilibrium. Creditors fear direct controls, or that devaluation will be forthcoming to contain the inevitable imbalance. Given such anxieties, the risks of restricted reverse flows or repayment in cheaper currency are judged to outweigh the higher interest rate. Foreign saving inflows are inadequate to offset short-run disequilibria in the current account. Destabilizing speculation can take place, forcing a change in the exchange rate or controls.

Rationing Problems When the exchange rate is fixed and excess demand for foreign currency arises, if credit is not available to fill the gap, then the available foreign exchange must be rationed among those seeking it at the fixed price. The LDC may have identified some areas or industries of high priority to be favored by banks as a precautionary measure in a country prone to foreign exchange shortages. However, when demand pressures on foreign exchange are high relative to supplies, more stringent measures such as rationing are required. And rationing can cause distortions in the economy that decrease efficiency.

A common solution in such predicaments is a set of multiple exchange rates that replace the single disequilibrium rate. Such rates are set according to expenditure categories for the foreign exchange, plus other criteria. In essence, then, the disequilibrium rate is adjusted; and rationing criteria are used to set the multiple rates. Politics and patronage can also enter the picture, to the undoing of efficiency criteria.

Theoretically, an overvalued exchange rate that produces foreign exchange shortages can be counteracted by tariffs on imports and a subsidy on exports, since the effect is the same as devaluation—higher import prices and lower export prices. Practically, however, when exchange rates are far enough from equilibrium to create a need for high tariffs and subsidies, tariffs become rigidified and subject to political manipulation because of their great economic impact, while subsidies suffer from inadequate funds and sometimes political neglect if the sector needing assistance is without political leverage. Subsidies too are subject to political abuse. Moreover, a high return awaits the entrepreneur willing to undertake the risks of smuggling or black market operations in foreign currency.

Currency Speculation Problems   Traditionally, fixed exchange rates have been maintained in the face of fundamental changes in equilibrium variables. The pegged rate is adjusted too infrequently and speculative forces build up. When foreign exchange reserves are depleted, anticipation of devaluation escalates. The forward market or a black market rate may signal the inevitability of devaluation, spurring a flight from the currency and increasing the risks and uncertainty of foreign exchange dealings.

Speculative buildup under fixed rates is not easily prevented. Nor does control of capital flows prevent such buildups. Trade payments flows can produce similar effects upon the exchange rate. Any timing changes that lead to a bunching or new pattern of payments for exports or imports can evoke pressures for exchange rate changes. Increased inflows per time period can push the exchange rate upward; acceleration of outflows can exert devaluation pressures on the pegged rate.

Interdependence Problems   Generally LDCs trade most heavily with one or two MDCs. It is well established that under the situation of fixed exchange rates, instability in a partner's economy is felt in the home country. Thus the LDC with a pegged rate may experience sharp repercussions upon their imports, exports, and price level from the trade partner's output fluctuations and inflation. Flexibility of the exchange rate could alleviate this interdependence to some degree. However, a highly interdependent country simply cannot insulate itself from trade sector repercussions either by fixed or flexible rates. Nor can it withdraw from trade without high cost.

Adjustable Peg Most Acceptable, with Exceptions   In general, the LDC faces difficult and important policy formulations in the area of foreign exchange rates, their degree of flexibility, or conditions of change. These rates affect allocation of resources between exports and imports; but they must also reflect resource allocation needs for development. The policy that is best can vary with specific conditions in an LDC and between that country and its trading partners. Flexible exchange rates are inappropriate in many cases. Pegged rates that are not adjusted for changes in fundamental factors affecting equilibrium are also undersirable. An adjustable peg is the best path in many cases. When an LDC has high inflation rates and consequent adjustments to the exchange rates, the term "crawling peg" is more appropriate. Brazil has had a fairly successful experience with the crawling peg.

In some cases, when most world currencies float, a pegged rate vis-à-vis a major trading partner whose currency is flexible against other currencies achieves a useful marriage of policies. This can be particularly appropriate for small countries with high trade dependency. An exchange rate pegged to that of the LDC's major trading partner or partners can reduce the inflationary impact of changing currency values yet retain some flexibility of international monetary ratios for adjustment purposes. Rates with lesser trading partners are allowed to fluctuate while the pegged rate with the major partner is changed (presumably rather infrequently) as disequilibrium forces affect trade flows with that partner. Many LDCs have pursued such a policy.

Three results, then, flow from this type of selective pegging. It allows more flexible adjustment of exchange rates with nonpeg countries, it mitigates the inflationary repercussions of exchange rate changes, and it prevents being priced out of the major export market *because of* appreciation of the LDC currency vis-à-vis the peg currency. However, it does not prevent being priced out of the major export market. When the peg currency appreciates, the LDC currency moves with it and appreciates against those that are not pegged. The LDC will face competitive pressures from these nonpeg countries in world markets, including its major export customer.

A country whose invoices for exports and imports are denominated in a major world trading currency such as the dollar will face competitive pressures when the dollar appreciates in world markets. South Korea and Thailand have experienced this situation. Large changes in the value of the dollar such as were seen in 1981 affected those countries' competitive positions considerably.

While foreign exchange operations are complex and at times distorting, international financial relations are important to the transaction of trade. Retreat to barter arrangements is an extremely costly alternative to international finance. Such arrangements restrict trade. Two of the first reconstruction tasks after World War II were the implementation of the Bretton Woods Agreement, setting the rules of international finance, and the formation of the European Payments Union, designed to pool dollar reserves and resuscitate trade devastated by the disruptions of war. The world financial system does not work perfectly and LDCs have criticized many aspects of its current state such as IMF criteria for lending, the role of multinational banks, and refinancing terms. Yet the barter-based alternative is much less attractive.

Once the best financial policy for a nation is chosen, the difficult task of implementing that policy must be tackled. Implementation is especially difficult where poor policy choices have operated for a long time. The transition to a well-designed policy carries costs. Some LDCs with overvalued exchange rates that have borne these costs and moved from a situation of tight rationing, multiple rates, and other controls to greater reliance upon adjustable pegged rates have seen improvement in their balance of payments and distortions reduced. Brazil, South Korea, and Taiwan are three examples predating the 1980s. Export price elasticities in response to devaluation proved favorable in these countries (Krueger 1978).

Political Aspects of International Monetary Policy

Policies followed to regain balance of payments health are not always politically palatable. When the income terms of trade deteriorate, real output potential is stunted. The economy is poorer, less able to finance imports either through exports or borrowing. Both devaluation and restrictive domestic policies may be needed if the trade account deficit is to remain manageable.

Assume an LDC that is a major exporter of a commodity suffers a decline in the commodity and income terms of trade for all export levels because of a drop in foreign demand. More goods must be sent abroad to maintain a given import level. The change leaves the country with an overvalued exchange rate and a current account deficit. In order to balance the trade account after the commodity and income terms of trade deteriorate, national consumption must be cut.

The regime in power is faced with the need to reduce spending and devalue. Exporters are perhaps the only group in the country in support of the policy, and their prosperity can be short-lived as higher import prices raise the cost of living and perhaps wages. The balance of trade will be responsive in this case to devaluation if we assume favorable price elasticities for exports and the economy's ability to redirect resources from other goods to exports. The external imbalance will not be corrected, however, if consumption of imported goods remains high. The government must restrict the money available for financing production and tax the populace to control aggregate demand and inflation.

Should the government expect the drop in world demand for the LDC's exports to be temporary, it may seek short-term funding of the imbalance through the IMF. Once funds are available to continue imports at a high level and avoid decreased national consumption, the government will usually prefer to assume that the current slump will soon improve. It postpones devaluation and restrictive policies indefinitely. The IMF, on the other hand, will assess conditions differently. Their concern is to ensure repayment of the loan and balance-of-payments conditions that are self-financing in the long-run. They are prone to take the position that devaluation cannot be postponed and that more conservative, restrictive policies are appropriate for the hard-pressed LDC. Loans are offered to ease the adjustment period. Generally the IMF is unwilling to extend the loan unless the government pursues devaluation and restrictive policies. Critics contend that IMF focus is on balance-of-payments equilibrium more than long-term growth goals.

The LDC government generally walks a tightrope between maintaining political power at home and satisfying IMF conditions for lending. Growth conditions with and without the loan are estimated. Acceptance of IMF conditions are often politically astute only if the LDC government protests and condemns the conditions. This diverts public blame for the inevitable belt-tightening away from the LDC government and toward the IMF. On the other hand, growth considerations may induce the LDC government to reject the loan and seek some other short-term solution. Should the condition prove to be permanent rather than temporary, however, cutbacks in growth are imperative.

The next section discusses Mexico, a country with a currency pegged to that of her major trading partner, that has had to agree to IMF conditions on two occasions when the currency was devalued. In 1976 she was favorably situated to handle a change in the peg and satisfy IMF conditions for loans. In 1982 she faced a far-reaching economic crisis as a result of devaluation, a loss in international credit standing, and the need to satisfy IMF conditions.

REFERENCES

Cline, William R. and Weintraub, Sidney. 1981. *Economic Stabilization in Developing Countries.* Washington, D.C.: The Brookings Institution.

Diaz-Alejandro, Carlos F. 1981. Southern Cone Stabilization Plans. In *Economic Stabilization in Developing Countries*, edited by William R. Cline and Sidney Weintraub. Washington, D.C.: The Brookings Institute, pp. 119–41.

Foxley, Alejandro. 1981. Stabilization Policies and Their Effects on Employment and Income Distribution: A Latin American Perspective. In *Economic Stabilization in Developing Countries*, edited by William R. Cline and Sidney Weintraub. Washington, D.C.: The Brookings Institution, pp. 191–225.

Krueger, Anne. 1978. *Liberalization Attempts and Consequences.* Cambridge, MA: Ballinger Publishing Company.

McKinnon, R. I. 1963. Optimum Currency Areas. *American Economic Review*, September: 717–25.

———. 1981. The Exchange Rate and Macroeconomic Policy: Changing Postwar Perceptions. *Journal of Economic Literature* 19 (June): 531–57.

Meier, G. M. 1976. *Leading Issues in Economic Development.* 3d ed. New York: Oxford University Press.

Weintraub, Sidney. 1981. Case Study of Economic Stabilization: Mexico. In *Economic Stabilization in Developing Countries*, edited by William R. Cline and Sidney Weintraub. Washington, D.C.: The Brookings Institution: 271–91.

Mexico: Fundamental Disequilibrium of a Pegged Rate with a Major Trading Partner

Mexico today, as a result of postwar growth, has a semiindustrialized economy that reflects many successes in her development performance. Prospects for her future prosperity were greatly improved by the discovery in the 1970s of large oil deposits. Yet Mexico is a country of great contrasts in wealth and poverty, that is, a country suffering to some degree from dualism. Currently many of her 72 million people live in poverty. The poor tend to have low literacy, high unemployment, and high fertility rates.

Mexico is the largest country in Central America, with a land area over three times that of France and roughly 20 percent that of the United States. She is the second-most populous country of Latin America after Brazil. Her size and per capita GNP ($2,090 in 1980) provide a large internal market compared with other LDCs. It also means that foreign trade does not dominate the economy. Yet, as with most LDCs, trade is vital to her economic health.

Mexico's border with the United States is one of her great trade advantages. Exports and imports of goods and financial capital flow quite freely from one country to the other. Approximately 60 percent of Mexico's trade is with the affluent United States economy. Not surprisingly, the Mexican currency has been pegged to the currency of her major trading partner. From 1954 to 1976 the peso was pegged at 12.5 to the dollar.

The post-World War II history of the Mexican peso until the 1970s was that of a relatively strong convertible LDC currency. This reflected Mexico's development progress in the postwar period, her relatively advanced financial structure, and her political stability. GNP per capita grew at about 3 percent a year despite high population growth, and her international financial standing was first among LDCs seeking capital on world markets. Inflation was modest until the 1970s by LDC standards despite a steady GDP growth rate, in the range of 6 percent and over per annum. Her ability to borrow on world financial markets also reflected a good balance-of-payments position.

MEXICO'S SUCCESSFUL DEVALUATION OF 1976

In the 1970s, however, the peso became overvalued, resulting in a crisis situation for a nation that historically had declared defense of the 12.5 peso exchange rate for the dollar as vital to the national interest. The peso proved indefensible and was devalued on August 31, 1976, to between 22 and 23 to the dollar. The devaluation reflected a fundamental disequilibrium that dictated adjustment of the peg. What were the causes of the overvaluation of the peso in the 1970s?

In part they were external; but to a great degree they were internal, and had been building over the previous development decades. The external aspects were the trade dislocations of the 1970 decade related to oil and other commodity price fluctuations that contributed to slowed global growth, high inflation, and unprecedented postwar recessions. The United States recession of 1974 hit Mexico fairly hard by 1975. However, a great deal of Mexico's problems lay on the import side. And once the current account became severely unbalanced, there was a speculative reversal of capital flows that left Mexico with a severely overvalued exchange rate. The advantage of foreign credit inflow became a disadvantage since it increased the adjustments needed to achieve a new equilibrium.

The domestic roots of the fundamental disequilibrium can be found in the development strategy and the inflation acceleration of the 1970s. In regard to the latter, Mexico experienced a higher rate of inflation for tradable goods than many of her trade partners during the dislocations of the 1970s. This, combined with the cumulative influence of past inflation rates somewhat in excess of the United States rate contributed to the disequilibrium vis-à-vis the dollar.

The effects of the development strategy are more complex and difficult to assess fully. When the peso was pegged in 1954, there was greater dependence upon agricultural and other commodities to earn foreign exchange. The pegged rate was an equilibrium one within the earlier trade pattern. But Mexico's structural transformation left the exchange rate too high to allow continued expansion of new exports from the growing industrial sector. Industrial production advanced strongly in Mexico in the postwar period. Its growth relative to that of other sectors changed the opportunity cost of industrial goods relative to agriculture and other sectors. (Such forces affecting the crisis of 1976 predate the discovery of oil in large quantity; and the oil export prospects did not

reverse them during the crisis period.) Devaluation was needed to sustain growing diversity in Mexican exports and increased exports of manufactures with greater price elasticity of demand than commodities exports.

Distortions also contributed to her problems. The industrial sector was given incentives to import fairly capital-intensive equipment and became relatively import-intensive. Such encouragement came partly from the ease of financing capital imports with low-cost loans from abroad and partly from subsidies to the industrial sector that created distortions. Foreign direct investment also contributed to this trend. Thus Mexico became increasingly dependent upon the industrial sector, which in turn was very import-intensive. Traditional exports could not support the sector and were somewhat discriminated against by domestic policies. New manufactures exports were deterred by inflation and their relative capital intensity. Mexico's comparative advantage, given her high rate of population growth, was instead in relatively labor-intensive exports, not favored in development policies. An increasingly overvalued exchange rate reinforced these distortions.

Once the current account worsened, speculative flight from the peso and the precipitous drop in financial inflows made devaluation inevitable. It also brought in help from the IMF and the United States to cushion the short-run costs of the devaluation. Conditions of the IMF loan were imposition of an export tax on price-inelastic commodities, suspension of many export incentives and import licenses now that the currency was devalued, control over public sector debt and the money supply, and policies to raise the saving rate and restore international reserves.

Mexico lived up to these demands to the satisfaction of lenders. There was a period of economic stagnation associated with the transition during which real wages declined. Economic growth, however, had slowed prior to devaluation because of the disequilibrium conditions. Moreover, the adjustment costs were eased somewhat by the beginnings of increased earnings from oil exports. And as estimates of the oil reserves rose, Mexico again became the favorite of creditors. The favorable conditions of renewed foreign capital inflow, increased export potential, and improved terms of trade lessened Mexico's adjustment costs. In the 1982 devaluation these conditions did not hold and were actually reversed.

MEXICO'S FOREIGN EXCHANGE CRISIS OF 1982

By 1982 oil prices were depressed because of conservation measures taken by oil importing countries and falling demand related to a world recession. In part weakened demand for oil was also a reaction to a substantial rise in the cartel price of oil in 1979. Mexico does not belong to OPEC, but is affected by the cartel's pricing-output decisions.

In the heady days of strong demand for oil and firm prices, Mexico borrowed heavily at relatively high interest rates to finance expansion. Creditors lined up to lend to her and she easily maintained her position along with Brazil as the LDCs with the highest credit inflow. Her economy was viewed by international lenders as one of high absorptive capacity and growth potential. The government and the private sector both floated large loans abroad. There was no close government monitoring of debt growth.

As oil prices fell with the world recession and the glut of crude in 1982, Mexico's ability to service her debt was affected. Prices of other commodity exports such as silver, cotton, and sugar also dropped. Her terms of trade and export capacity weakened, while inflation accelerated. The exchange rate was again overvalued. Speculative pressures built up. Devaluation was accompanied again by capital flight and further devaluation. These devaluations led to inflation rates of 100 percent in 1982 and further speculation against the peso.

Figure 18.5 gives insight into the disequilibrium conditions faced by Mexico in the 1982 crisis. The T_k curves sum up her export-import potential under higher and lower demand conditions. Sizable exports by Mexico from her relatively large oil deposits could depress spot prices for oil. Yet, by cutting her price she could sell more at the expense of cartel sales. Thus her T_k curves are elastic over

a given range of increased exports despite an inelastic world demand for oil.

Prior to the drop in world demand, industrial output was at b, imports at m, and exports at e. Capital inflow was xy, allowing a deficit in the current account of the balance of payments. The drop in demand for exports worldwide shifts the T_k curve to T'_k. This lowers Mexico's terms of trade and creates the need for yz additional credit inflow. But the worsening trade position leads to the conclusion that the peso is overvalued, precipitating a credit flight. Mexico is forced to export more, which lowers her terms of trade further in weak commodity markets.

Without IMF loans, Mexico would actually need a surplus to meet her debt service obligations in the face of credit flight. This would require exports of e', imports of m' and a surplus of rs, with domestic production dropping to b'. Such increased exports would require time to achieve. Moreover prior to reallocation of resources, domestic output would be well within the production possibilities curve as import shortfalls occurred.

A surplus of rs would require a greatly devalued foreign exchange rate to spur export production and limit imports. With lower terms of trade and less foreign credit, real income would drop with the decline in B goods production. A more likely outcome would be default on the debt since time is needed to reallocate resources and change domestic policies oriented toward B goods production. Because of the political ramifications of greatly recessed output to achieve a balance-of-payments surplus, default on the debt would be an attractive alternative to the politicians.

Under these conditions the IMF and the United States government felt too large a drop in domestic income would destabilize Mexico politically. Mexico was extended credit so that a transition deficit was possible, although the deficit was well below xz. Moreover, private banks were more willing to renegotiate loan repayments once IMF credit was available and belt-tightening conditions were established by the IMF.

Even with the rescue credit from the IMF and United States support, devaluation carried with it two handicaps—inflation accel-

FIGURE 18.5 *Capital Flight with Drop in the Terms of Trade*

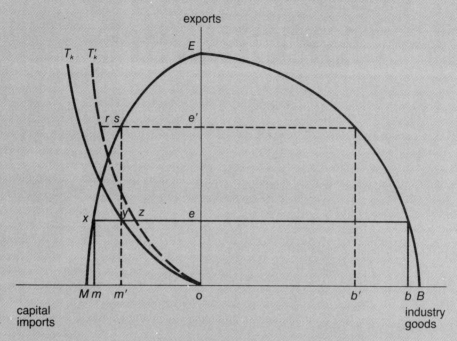

With *e* exports and capital inflow of *xy*, imports are *m* and industry output *b*. A drop in the T_k curve to T'_k lowers the terms of trade, raises the deficit by *yz* and creates a flight of capital. Now a surplus of *rs* is needed to repay prior loans in the face of no new capital inflow. The terms of trade drop further as exports rise to *e'*. With imports of *m'*, industry output must drop to *b'*.

erated with shortages and rising import prices, and debt servicing became more costly to borrowers as the devalued exchange rate echoed the drop in the commodity terms of trade. Under the uncertainty speculative pressure was so great that exchange controls were enacted. Unemployment and bankruptcies rose in the midst of import shortfalls and increased debt burden. Mexican banks were nationalized in an effort to gain domestic support for the needed sacrifices. All in all, commentators called the devaluation of 1982 the worst crisis faced by Mexico since her revolution. Politicians shifted part of the blame onto the restrictive IMF loan conditions.

In retrospect, it is apparent that Mexico's attractiveness to foreign lenders and investors, combined with a dramatic turnaround in market conditions for oil, was destabilizing for the Mexican economy and the peso. Her new-found oil wealth brought mixed blessings. It helped stabilize conditions after the 1976 devaluation, only to prepare the way for a very destabilizing disequilibrium in 1982. One lesson from the experience is the need to monitor the size, term structure, and origin of foreign capital inflow so that the stream of funds is not easily transformed to capital flight as conditions of trade change. Another lesson is the need to consider the dollar/peso peg as adjustable and to recognize conditions of disequilibrium earlier. Yet, the severe conditions of the 1982 devaluation show how difficult it is to execute a successful devaluation under circumstances such as those experienced by Mexico in 1982.

Fiscal Policies for Growth

chapter

19

This chapter focuses upon principles and techniques of government fiscal action (taxation and spending) to promote development in the private and public sectors. The introductory sections point out that the role of government has varied historically, and is highly circumscribed by the political-economic conditions the policymaker faces within a given LDC. Next the economically optimum level of government employment is discussed, followed by a review of policies designed to improve private sector performance. The remaining sections take up techniques of government planning. In particular, the uses of input-output techniques and principles of project selection are explained.

The leadership role of the government sector in the development process has varied among nations and between historical eras. In the last 30 years the prescribed role for government in LDCs has been to provide leadership in promoting and supporting modernization of the economy. Where such leadership is forthcoming, there is usually a development plan setting longer-range goals, both general and specific, that dovetail into planning targets for the near term. Plan goals such as increased income and jobs, equitable distribution of both, expanded literacy, and better health care are translated into specific objectives: a quantified growth rate target, a specified rise in the savings rate, a given percentage increase in jobs in specific sectors, a specified number of new schools, and a percentage rise in the proportion of income received by the lowest fifth of income recipients. Policy instruments that will achieve these politically determined plan objectives are then identified.

The government seeks to implement the targets by both direct and indirect intervention in the economy. There is generally a planning budget that develops tax and expenditure proposals consistent with plan objectives. Typically the government in a mixed economy sets up a commission or bureau to work within the political structure to design and coordinate the planning effort. The planning bureau is generally faced with the difficult task of galvanizing an entrenched bureaucracy into rethinking its role and purpose so that the plan goals are served.

Politics, in conjunction with the government's bureaucratic structure, has an overriding influence upon any role the government plays in the development process—positive or negative. Politically determined government policies will reflect the social tensions, power structure, cultural patterns, and foreign influences within a country. Political tensions can render a government impotent or gear it toward self-destructive strife. And even where political organization is supportive of growth, the sheer enormity of the task and the limited experience of the leadership in conceiving and implementing the policy needs of development ensure that mistakes and shortcomings will abound. In addition, the pressures of poverty and dislocations of change associated with development lay stress upon relatively stable governments, periodically toppling even charismatic leaders from power. It is not uncommon, then, to hear the statement that much of an LDC's devel-

opment potential is lost through government inaction, unsuitable public policies, or poorly implemented plans. Even the better plans of the
better LDC governments go astray.

How can economics guide the policymaker tossed by the waves of
LDC politics and dragged by the undertow of poverty? Some political
economists have reached beyond economics to identify the optimum
political structure and associated economic system for development.
Modern Marxian economics proceeds in this vein. Most economists
shy from such a comprehensive attempt at social engineering and set
their sights lower. The less ambitious development literature seeks out
policy guidance techniques and principles that have a general validity
for the developing economy—before or after a revolution. Policies to
influence the private sector and policies to guide government planning
are identified. Because the majority of LDCs have mixed economies,
government activity conducive to growth in such economies is emphasized.

The analysis and policy planning techniques described emphasize
the most efficient, or optimum, policy. There is general acknowledg-
ment that the optimal policy may serve mainly as a starting point for
identifying the best workable policy for the particular political-economic conditions. Principles and techniques provide an important beginning or framework. However, the real world moves to its own rhythms.
A policymaker who doesn't select a tune in the right time can't expect
the economy to march in cadence.

**Tax Limits to
Government
Investment**
It is not unusual for government revenue sources to limit the scope of
a plan. In such cases, the planners are able to calculate a rate of return
on an array of investment projects above the scarcity price of capital,
especially when risk and externalities are considered. However, the
investment potential is limited by the political-economic realities of
taxing capacity. Thus, instead of the plan dictating the tax levels, tax
levels control the size of the government's development program. Here
we have another example of how optimality is thwarted.

Table 19.1 gives historical data on tax ratios and income elasticities
for total tax revenue for selected LDCs for two periods. Revenues from
taxes varied from a low of 5 percent for Paraguay in the period 1953–
55 to a high of 23.4 percent for Congo in 1966–68. Column 3 shows
that the marginal tax rate, that is, the change in tax revenue divided
by the change in GNP, exceeded the average tax rate for most countries,
and thus tax revenues as a percentage of GNP rose between the two
periods. Exceptions were Colombia, China, Ecuador, Trinidad and Tobago, Ceylon, and Ghana. The income elasticity of total tax revenue
for these countries is one or below one, less than half of that for India,
Morocco, Korea, Honduras, and Paraguay. However, the latter countries had much lower tax revenues as a percentage of GNP from 1953
to 1955. Their ability to finance government development programs
increased considerably over the period. Other countries with relatively
low tax ratios such as Indonesia and Guatemala did not raise their tax
revenues very much. Raja Chelliah traces the difference in large part

| Country[2] | Ratio of tax revenue to GNP | | Marginal tax rate[3] | Income elasticity of total tax revenue[4] |
	1953–55 (1)	1966–68 (2)	(3)	(4)
India	6.3	11.6	15.1	2.4
Morocco	10.0	16.5	22.2	2.2
Korea	5.7	11.8	12.2	2.2
Honduras	6.7	10.5	14.2	2.1
Paraguay	5.0	9.5	10.5	2.1
Chile	10.1	19.4	19.6	1.9
Tunisia	15.5	20.7	25.6	1.7
Philippines	7.0	9.8	11.2	1.6
Pakistan	6.2	8.3	9.5	1.5
Jamaica	12.6	16.9	19.2	1.5
Congo, Dem. Rep. of	16.2	23.4	24.4	1.5
Guyana	16.7	20.6	24.2	1.5
Brazil	15.3	20.6	20.6	1.3
Thailand	10.8	12.8	13.8	1.3
Turkey	11.7	14.1	14.6	1.3
Indonesia	6.2	7.5	7.5	1.2
Peru	12.2	13.7	14.0	1.2
Kenya	13.1	13.9	14.3	1.1
Guatemala	7.6	7.9	8.2	1.1
Lebanon	10.4	10.7	10.8	1.0
Colombia	10.3	10.3	10.3	1.0
China	14.9	14.9	14.9	1.0
Ecuador	12.8	12.6	12.4	0.97
Trinidad and Tobago	15.5	15.2	15.0	0.97
Costa Rica	11.5	11.0	10.6	0.92
Ceylon	16.3	15.7	14.9	0.91
Ghana	18.2	13.3	12.4	0.69

TABLE 19.1

Selected Developing Countries: Ratios of Tax Revenue to Gross National Product, Marginal Tax Rates, and Income Elasticities of Total Tax Revenue, 1953–55 and 1966–68[1]

1. Relate to total taxes excluding social security contributions.
2. The countries are ranked according to the income elasticity of total tax revenue.
3. Absolute change in tax revenue divided by absolute change in GNP.
4. Percentage change in tax revenue divided by percentage change in GNP. This measure, it may be noted, has been calculated by relating changes in actual tax revenues to changes in income, and hence differs from the coefficient of built-in elasticity, which is calculated with respect only to the "automatic" increase in tax revenue in response to economic growth or increase in income. Here the interest is more in the total relative increase in tax revenue, whether owing to economic growth, or changes in the tax structure and rates, or improvements in compliance and enforcement.

SOURCE: Raja J. Chelliah, "Trends in Taxation in Developing Countries" in *Readings on Taxation in Developing Countries*, 3d ed., R. M. Bird and Oliver Oldman, eds. (Baltimore, MD: The Johns Hopkins University Press, 1975), p. 107.

to concerted government effort (Chelliah in Bird and Oldman, eds. 1975, p. 112).

The country's taxing capacity can vary with its tax sources. Tax sources are sometimes categorized as direct, meaning the levy applies to the individual or household, and indirect, meaning the tax is collected from a source other than the household or individual. Examples of direct levies are income taxes, poll or personal taxes, and property taxes. Among indirect taxes are tariffs or customs duties, taxes on exports, and taxes on production such as sales and excise taxes and license fees.

Most LDCs lean heavily upon indirect taxes as sources of revenue particularly at earlier stages of development. Border taxes are a main source of revenue in many African states. Even countries as developed as Chile and Brazil depend on production taxes for much of their revenue. In contrast, income taxes are a dominant source of revenue in Mexico, Trinidad and Tobago, Venezuela, Iran, and Zambia (Chelliah, Bass, and Kelly 1975). Despite the accounting and administrative requirements of an income tax, some poorer LDCs have successfully instituted simplified levies upon income. One attribute of an income tax important to the tax-deficient country is that it has a potentially high income elasticity of tax revenue. Another advantage is that it is the most direct approach to equalizing income distribution.

Given the scarcity of government revenues relative to the great pressures for government investment in many LDCs, analysts stress the importance of choosing carefully the projects funded with scarce tax monies. Literature on this subject is referred to as "project selection criteria" or "project appraisal citeria." In the last sections of the chapter we take up this important topic.

Government Sector Employment

The government sector, a provider of services, is generally relatively labor-intensive. Clerical work, administration, jobs implementing law and legislation, education, public health, social work, and the like require relatively high labor inputs. There are exceptions such as government owned utilities or transportation services, which tend to be relatively capital intensive.

Government sector employment may play a role in raising overall labor productivity. This takes place when (a) productivity of labor transferred to the government sector exceeds its productivity in its former occupation, (b) labor productivity in the government sector adjusted for externalities has a marginal social benefit that exceeds the marginal contribution of the labor outside government employment, and (c) government puts unemployed labor to work.

A word of caution is in order. These sources of gains from the reallocation of labor to the government sector imply that the labor is transferred from sectors of lower productivity. In fact, government employees are often more highly skilled and better paid. Administrative or managerial abilities are in short supply in LDCs. The gains from government versus private employment can be more difficult to compare in such cases.

One other aspect of government employment is important to assessing its contribution. Whether the government hires the unskilled or the skilled, wages paid to civil servants are often above their opportunity cost. When this is the case, either government employment is below its optimum level, or there is a transfer of income from other sectors to accommodate the higher wages. Figure 19.1 illustrates a case of optimum labor allocation but excess wages in the government sector.

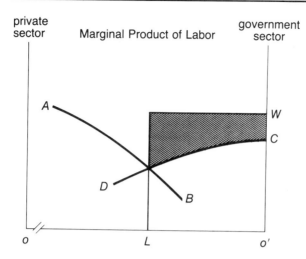

FIGURE 19.1
*Effect of Excess
Government Wages*

Optimum labor allocation is at *L* with *OL* labor in the private sector and *LO'* labor in the public sector. Wages equal to *W* in the government sector require a transfer of income from the private sector equivalent to the hatched area over and above the contribution of resources in the public sector.

The marginal product of labor in the private sector from which the government labor supply is drawn is shown by curve *AB* in figure 19.1. Curve *CD* represents labor's marginal product in the government sector. This latter curve includes any externalities associated with government employment, and can be referred to as the marginal social product generated by additional employment in the public sector. The optimal employment level is *LO'* for the government sector, with *OL* labor in the private sector.

Assume government sector wages are *W*, above the opportunity cost of labor. Should *LO'* labor be employed in the public sector, the private sector must transfer an amount equivalent to the hatched area to the government sector over and above what resources in the latter sector contribute to output. Alternately, if government employment is less than optimum due to high wages and limited taxes, then the transfer is less. However, output for the economy is below what it would be with optimum government employment as labor remains in work of lower productivity in the private sector.

The efficiency level of labor employed in the government compared with the private sector, and hence the intersection of their respective marginal product curves, varies greatly among LDCs. Governments able to appropriate sufficient tax monies may extend employment past the optimum level so that output is lost, a situation illustrated in figure 19.2. The hatched area *E* shows the output lost when excess labor of *L'L* is occupied in the public sector. The minimum wage needed to attract people to government jobs will be the equivalent of the marginal product of labor in the private sector, which is *W*. Thus there must be an uncompensated transfer from the private to the public sector equivalent to the entire hatched area even when the government

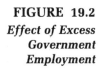

FIGURE 19.2

Effect of Excess Government Employment

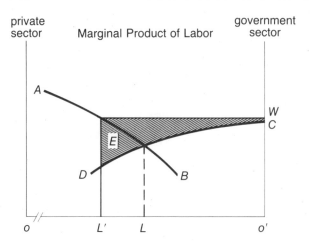

With excess government employment of *L'L*, output equivalent to area *E* is lost. With wages of *W*, the government sector receives an uncompensated transfer from the private sector equal to the total hatched area.

pays the equivalent of the opportunity cost of the labor. This arises because of excess government sector employment beyond the optimum level where the marginal products of both private and public labor are the same. Should the government pay wages above the opportunity cost of labor, the transfer would be larger.

High government wages and excess government employment then can reduce output, taxing the people heavily for the benefit of those receiving the high government wages. We might characterize this as dualism arising from government power as opposed to dualism rooted in distortions from the private sector. When the marginal propensity to consume from government wages exceeds that from private sector incomes that finance the wages, then savings decline.

The relative productivity of labor in public as compared with private employment may vary over the development path. Growth externalities from employment in government can be relatively high at certain stages when the government acts as a catalyst. This occurs when early infrastructure investment is called for to spur industrialization and agricultural transformation. The need to spread risk is another source of social externalities. In addition to its stage of development, a country's historical evolution greatly affects the contributions of government compared with private sector employment in the course of economic evolution.

GOVERNMENT POLICIES IN THE MIXED ECONOMY   LDC political leaders characteristically adopt a policy perspective that emphasizes development promotion and guidance. The mixed economy entails direct government participation and indirect policies aimed at motivating the private sector. Public policies designed to increase growth by affecting the private sector can be grouped under three headings:

- Incentive policies
- Stabilization policies
- Policies to correct or offset distortions in the market

Incentive policies include tax concessions to encourage exports, regional development, or employment; preferential tax rates for reinvested profits; and penalty levies upon idle land. Stabilization policies are often concerned with manipulation of aggregate demand not so much for controlling unemployment as for managing the balance of payments. Harvest failures, shifts in the terms of trade, inflation, or debt servicing are typical causes of balance-of-payments stress demanding government action. Moreover, changes in the government deficit or surplus are not the only or even the main tool for stabilization. Government marketing boards that stabilize export earnings to the producer, government stockpiling to avoid deficits of food and fluctuations in its price, selective price controls, foreign exchange restrictions, and a battery of other policies may be aimed at dealing with major variables contributing to instability in LDC economies. **Policy Instruments**

Steps to correct distortions include income redistribution policies, subsidies in the form of tax concessions to compensate for overvalued labor, expenditures to capture growth externalities, regulations of monopolies, and so on. Unfortunately there may be a need to institute policies to deal with distortions in the private sector stemming from poorly designed or executed government policies. An example is a set of tax levies to curb inflation caused by unsuitable government monetary policies. Such taxes may be necessary to counteract the tendency for inflation to divert savings into less productive investment such as speculation in land, buildings, inventories, or commodities.

Policy tools used in the examples given are taxation and regulations, the major instruments for affecting the private sector. Optimally these should be designed so that they achieve the development goal as efficiently as possible. This generally means adopting policies that attack the source of the problem. For example, if the level of inequality is judged to be a distortion that interferes with balanced development, then the most efficient means for reducing inequality in the private sector are progressive income taxes and subsidies. A much less efficient route for achieving this goal is a policy controlling the importation of "luxury goods" or taxing domestic consumption of them. Or, policies designed to develop infant industries, as explained in chapter 12, are most effective when they can correct the cause of inefficiency such as poor labor training, fragmented capital markets, or overvalued exchange rates. A tariff is a "second best" policy since it does not attack the cause of infancy and is treating the problem more indirectly and hence less efficiently.

There is a qualification to the rule of seeking the most efficient policy for the objective. The most efficient policy is of no use whatever if it cannot be administered in the milieu of LDC politics and social constraints. A tax that requires complicated record-keeping by the firm or household may have to be passed over and a less efficient impost adopted for administrative reasons. Again we make use of the concept of the optimum as a way of focusing upon maximum potential, a beginning point, a guidance framework.

Government Deficit Spending

Deficit spending by the government sector is a major stabilization tool utilized in MDCs. Its purpose is to increase aggregate demand in affluent economies with large productive capacity and high propensities to save. Development economists do not agree unequivocally about the use and purpose of deficit spending within an LDC economy, particularly one at early stages of development where markets are regional and the input-output matrix is sparsely filled in. The more advanced developing country, on the other hand, is more likely to suffer from periodic shortfalls in aggregate demand and lean toward some government deficit spending for stability reasons. In some emerging nations the deficit is restricted to financing of a capital budget, and ongoing government services and administration are funded without borrowing. The rationale, borrowed from principles of private finance, is that the capital spending will generate increased productive capacity and thereby government income and/or taxes to repay the debt.

Critics do not accept even financing the capital budget as a justification for government deficit spending. Arguments against such spending are that the deficit's impact can be limited and/or distorting. Seldom, it is asserted, is there a broad productive base underutilized as a result of insufficient aggregate demand. Where there is a small modern sector, limited monetization of an economy, segmented and poorly functioning financial markets, regional goods markets, and unemployment rooted mainly in a factor proportions problem or other structural components, deficits may contribute little to correcting the causes of instability. They can even destabilize by aggravating inflation and balance-of-payments problems.

Critics of deficit spending in LDCs argue, in other words, that it is unlikely that deficits can contribute to stability. They emphasize the improbability of demand shortfalls in an economy generally suffering from lack of saving (as opposed to consumption). Even if there were a need for deficit spending, they point out that a capital budget deficit would not necessarily contribute the right amount of increased aggregate demand at the appropriate time. On the other hand, a balanced budget is viewed by its proponents as fiscally responsible in a poor economy and is said to serve as a limit upon wasteful spending arising from political corruption in an emerging nation.

Proponents of deficit spending point out, however, that there are two important rationales for government deficits at earlier stages of development. The deficit may be foreign-financed. This means the savings of other countries are used by the LDC to promote development. Servicing the foreign loans requires reduced national consumption or investment at the time of repayment to allow exports to exceed imports. Thus, foreign borrowing to finance a deficit can be used as a device to redistribute the tax burden related to financing development among generations, letting those enjoying the eventual benefits from projects financed with foreign savings pay some proportion of the costs.

Secondly, a deficit may be required to allow adequate growth of the money supply. Increases in the money supply require debt creation—public or private. In many LDCs there are no markets for bonds or shorter-term debt. It may be important for the government to supplement private sector debt by issuing bonds to be purchased by the banking system. Just as with bank loans to the private sector, bank lending to the public sector leads to an increased money supply. In some cases, government debt serves as reserves in the banking system and the rise in reserves reflects the government deficit.

The need for government debt to expand the money supply can occur because of internal or external factors. Internally there is a need for the money supply to expand enough to support a growth path of full employment. When private sector debt does not lead to an adequate growth rate in the money supply, then a government deficit can make up the shortfall. Externally, when imports exceed exports, more money is spent abroad than returns via export demand. Aggregate spending in the private sector is depressed and demand for loans by that sector drops off. Thus when there is a deficit in the balance of payments, government deficit spending may be necessary to prevent a decline in the money supply if private sector borrowing is inadequate.

Government Surpluses

Government surpluses for stabilization purposes, as opposed to government deficits, are less likely to encounter criticism. A typical example of the use of surpluses to stabilize the economy is the taxation of exports when earnings fluctuate. The export tax may stabilize production in the export sector and provide the government with a surplus in the form of foreign exchange. These reserves are then fed out in years of foreign exchange deficits so that development plans are not disrupted. Moreover, the inflow of foreign exchange generally serves as reserves in the banking system from which a multiple expansion of the money supply can be launched. Government withdrawal of some of the foreign exchange inflow from the banking system can control growth of the money supply in boom periods when export earnings are high, and thus curb inflation.

A shortcoming of a government surplus held in the form of foreign exchange, however, is that the capital-shy LDC is in effect lending abroad during the period of overage. Government surpluses generated in the form of domestic currency, on the other hand, encourage savings and investment in the national economy. The surplus keeps consumption under control when there is a need to free resources for investment purposes. Which form the surplus is held in will depend upon the stabilization needs of the economy.

Government Spending and Development

In addition to influencing the private sector, the government plays a direct role in development through its spending priorities. These are established through a political process and identified in a development plan. A common denominator in all plans is a projected growth rate for GNP. The overall GNP target is determined by making estimates of resource growth over the plan period and productivity growth. Recall that GNP can be expressed as labor force inputs times labor productivity. Thus if the labor force is expected to grow by 2 percent a year over the plan period and, as a result of capital formation, technical change, and shift in the labor force among sectors, labor productivity is expected to grow by 4 percent per annum, then annual planned growth will be 6 percent.

These global figures may be generated from sectoral growth paths estimated by reference to past sectoral performance and expected changes in each sector that will influence plan performance. Expressed algebraically, the growth rate in year t (G_t) is:

$$G_t = \ell_a p_a + \ell_i p_i + \ell_s p_s + \ell_g p_g + \frac{L_t - L_{t-1}}{L_{t-1}} \qquad (1)$$

where ℓ_k = percentage of the labor force in sector k in year t,

p_k = growth rate of labor productivity in sector k for year t,

and subscript k refers to any of four sectors of the economy; agriculture (a), industry (i), services (s), and government (g). Over the plan period, then, the growth rate will be:

$$G_n = \sum_{t=1}^{n} G_t = \sum_{t=1}^{n} \left[(\ell_k p_k)_t + \frac{\Delta L_t}{L_{t-1}} \right] \qquad (2)$$

The sectoral changes in labor productivity will reflect supply-side changes. Sectoral changes in labor force allocation will reflect income elasticities of demand and biased technical change, among other variables.

Note that when 50 percent or more of the labor force is in agriculture, growth will be highly influenced by the increase in productivity in that sector. As productivity rises in agriculture, the proportion of the labor force employed there declines since the income elasticity of demand for food is less than one. The industry sector, on the other hand, has an income elasticity of demand greater than one until late development. When capital-intensive technology is used in industry, labor productivity (p_i) may climb dramatically while the proportion of the labor force in this sector (ℓ_i) rises more slowly. Labor absorption in the remaining sectors is then relatively larger. As labor seeks employment outside industry, this influences the growth in labor productivity in these sectors since they perforce become relatively more labor intensive. Eventualities like these, then, influence the planner's estimates of sectoral productivity growth.

TOOLS OF GOVERNMENT PLANNING

There are techniques to help the planner calculate changes in sectoral output levels. Once the GNP target is established, initial estimates of sectoral output implied by the target GNP can be generated by the use of an input-output table and a coefficient matrix derived from it. They are preliminary estimates since, in calculating sectoral output levels, this technique assumes unchanged technology and fixed factor proportions. The associated resource levels needed by each sector for the target GNP are then adjusted for anticipated technological change and factor substitution. Alternately, these calculations may be used to check on the feasibility of independent estimates of sectoral targets.

Sectoral performance, in turn, is predicated in part upon government spending on development projects and other government activity. In the remaining part of this chapter the uses of the input-output table in development planning and the methodology of project appraisal are explained. Project appraisal in particular has received increasing emphasis of late as an aid to improving the government's contribution to development goals.

A development plan should reflect fundamental knowledge about the economics of development. Such a base provides a framework, a perspective for planning. Once important variables and their interrelations are understood, general policy options can be presented. More detailed planning strategy must be rooted in the specific historical conditions of the country. Plan conception and implementation will reflect political constraints and leadership. Economic analysis points out policy options, trade-offs, and efficiency criteria. And while planning is the art of the possible, not the optimal, it is helpful to have an understanding of optimal performance as a gauge to guide the planners as they move toward their policy formulations.

From Optimality to Reality: Planning and Input-Output Tables

The idea of optimality for a plan has already been broached with the use of the three-sector economy diagram. In that diagram we sketched a highly simplified economy and very limited five-year plan goals, expressed in physical units of food, exports, and industry output. The planners wish to maximize industrial output subject to two constraints: Food output must equal that set by the plan target and the value of exports must cover the value of needed imports. Moreover, the industrial production function is one where each unit of industrial output requires a given number of imported capital units. We noted that anywhere along the terms-of-trade line (a given), the value of exports equaled that of imports. However, there was only one export-import point that maximized industrial output, allowing the needed ratio of imported to industrial goods. Moreover, output would not be on the production frontier unless resources were combined efficiently. This requires scarcity prices on resources and a combination of resources by planners or the market economy minimizing costs. We assume that relative prices reflect relative costs.

The simple plan outlined above can be cast in the form of an input-output table, often referred to as a flow matrix. This has been done in table 19.2, and illustrates what a simplified economy we have modeled. Planning is unwieldy when expressed exclusively in physical units, as was done on the graphs; thus output is given in monetary units in the table. This requires adopting efficiency prices on output.

The first two rows of the matrix list the output or supply from agriculture and industry that will be either consumed domestically, exported, or used as intermediate inputs. Since imports are an additional source of supply, an import row appears. The columns repeat the same sector subdivisions. Reading across, sector output is absorbed as an input into the same or other sectors and into final uses—consumption or exports in our simple table. Thus, agricultural output is used either for food or exports, and appears in the appropriate columns under "final uses." Industry output is consumed. Imports are an intermediate input into the industry sector. The row labeled "value added" gives the value of resources employed directly in all sectors.

When the sector columns are read, they trace all inputs employed in producing that sector's output. Since in our simple economy agriculture uses no inputs other than resources directly applied, only the value-added column shows an entry. Industry, on the other hand, makes use of imported capital and combines that with domestic resources. The last rows and columns show the total value of output for the industrial and agricultural sectors, added either across or down.

Once we transfer the graphic economy into an input-output table, we eliminate the dimensional limitations of flat-surfaced graphs and can achieve a more realistic depiction of intersectoral relations in an economy for a given output level, produced efficiently. We can divide the economy into as many sectors as seem helpful (or as data and computer limitations allow). A sector or industry is an arbitrary subdivision of total production, aggregating related subgroups of production into one production function. Table 19.3 remains highly schematic, but illustrates a more fleshed-out flow for an economy for a given time period. The table data are assumed to reflect potential output under efficiency conditions. The table is a snapshot of interindustry flows on a monetary basis, and of the monetary flow of imports by industry.

This schematic view of the economy is aggregated and static. A simple permutation must be made in order to create a tool for dynamic calculations. A coefficient matrix is derived from input-output table 19.3 to develop a planner's tool. That is, a matrix showing the input required from each sector per monetary unit of total output from each is calculated in table 19.4. For example, for one monetary unit of agricultural output shown in table 19.3 the input coefficient is .10 for

TABLE 19.2

Input-Output Table for Three-Sector Graph (value units)

Outputs →	Sectors		Final Use		(5)
Inputs ↓	(1) Agriculture	(2) Industry	(3) Exports	(4) Consumption	Total Use
1. Agriculture			50	50	100
2. Industry				100	100
3. Imports		50			
4. Total Purchases		50			
5. Value Added	100	50		150	
6. Total Output	100	100			200

TABLE 19.3 *Input-Output Table for Simplified Economy (value units)*

Outputs →	Sectors				Final Use (demand)			
	(1)	(2)	(3)	(4)	(5)	(6) Private	(7) Government	(8) Total
Inputs ↓	Agriculture	Construction	Industry	Services	Exports	Sector	Sector	Use
1. Agriculture	10				30	60		100
2. Construction	5		5			1	10	21
3. Industry	5	10	40			40	10	105
4. Services	10	5	20			40	10	85
5. Imports	5		15	10				
6. Total Purchases	35	15	80	10				
7. Value Added	65	6	25	75		171 GNP		
8. Total Output	100	21	105	85				311

agriculture, .05 for industry and construction, .10 for services, and .05 for imports.

Now let us make the simplifying assumptions that the coefficient matrix is independent of time and of the value of total output, admittedly large assumptions. Then, the planners may project a new higher level of GNP for a selected time period and, using the coefficient matrix, compute the associated input-output table data. More realistically, in projecting new levels of GNP and associated sectoral output, adjustments can be made in the coefficients where it is known that technology, relative resources available, the terms of trade, types of industries, and so forth will change over time.

The projection of plan output by sectors can be expressed more formally. The intermediate flow of output from sector i (row) to sector j (column) is noted as X_{ij}. X_{ij} is derived by multiplying the total use for sector j, (X_j), by the input coefficient of sector i to sector j, (a_{ij}). Thus:

$$X_{ij} = a_{ij}X_j \qquad (3)$$

This calculation is made for all sectors and the subscripts i and j are generalized to refer to any sector. We use matrix notation to denote

	Agriculture	Construction	Industry	Services
Agriculture	.10			
Construction	.05		.05	
Industry	.05	.49	.38	
Services	.10	.24	.19	
Imports	.05		.14	.11
Total Purchases	.35	.71	.76	.11
Value Added	.65	.29	.24	.89
Total Output	1.00	1.00	1.00	1.00

TABLE 19.4
Coefficient Matrix for Input-Output Table 19.3

the input-output table with all sectors plus final demand usage as

$$AX + FD = X \tag{4}$$

where A is the coefficient matrix, X is the total use vector, and FD is the final demand matrix. Noted in terms of final demand, the equation is:

$$FD = X - AX \quad \text{or} \tag{5}$$
$$FD = (I - A)X$$

where I is the identity matrix. Solving for X from equation (3) we get:

$$X = (I - A)^{-1} FD \tag{6}$$

where $(I - A)^{-1}$ is obtained by the process of matrix inversion. $(I - A)^{-1}$ is called the Leontief inverse after the father of the input-output table, W. W. Leontief, a Russian-born economist who emigrated to the United States and won a Nobel Prize in economics. The Leontief inverse allows us to calculate the total resources required to support a unit of final demand projected by the plan targets.

This type of exercise, when the underlying data are robust, allows the planners to check for consistency of the plan. By comparing the projected input-output table data with industry planned capacity for the plan period, sectors with bottlenecks may be identified. Bottlenecks reflect target output levels inconsistent with resource constraints. In particular, import needs may exceed expected export earnings, given that sector's expansion path and expected terms of trade. Planners then adjust output to capacity potential. Care must be taken, however, in using the input-output projections since the coefficients are based on historical data that can be misleading when dynamic elements influence the coefficients. This is an approximate, not a precise tool for planners.

In addition to checking planning targets for consistency, the input-output matrix can be used in various other ways. For example, it may aid in designing policies of import substitution or export diversification by identifying industries of potential comparative advantage, or in anticipating labor training needs. And, with the help of a computerized technique known as linear programming, the input-output table data can be used to generate a set of scarcity or shadow prices that reflect the planners' objective function such as output maximization. Shadow prices are useful in project selection, and are discussed in the next section.

Specific assumptions of input-output analysis can affect the accuracy of the projections. These are:

1. Each sector has a production function characterized by constant returns to scale and fixed technical coefficients of production. Thus, the level of output uniquely determines input requirements.
2. The coefficient matrix reflects efficiency conditions.
3. Technology is given and constant.
4. There are no new industries over time.

Needless to say, input-output data and the associated coefficient matrix are quickly dated, and this affects the accuracy of the projections from them. Even when the coefficient matrix is based on perfect information, it need not calculate correctly data for another period of time, or for another output level, since the assumptions realistically do not hold over time or for another level of output.

Other problems can affect the reliability of projections. Obviously a coefficient matrix based on perfect information regarding efficiency conditions of an aggregate production function for each sector cannot be the basis for the actual coefficient matrix utilized by planners. Planners will begin with input-output data for aggregated sectors from national income accounts and other available sources. The data will reflect actual, not optimal, output and the coefficient matrix will be representative of an actual level of efficiency for a given time period. That is, it will show real output flows to the degree that the input-output data are accurate. Generally data in LDCs are poor and are inadequate for more than a limited industry breakdown. In sum, the coefficient matrix most often is derived from data reflecting less than optimal conditions, and therefore does not indicate capacity potential; and the matrix is based upon data of varying degrees of accuracy, which affects its usefulness.

Project Appraisal

Project appraisal is a technique for project selection in the government sector. General development goals identified in the political planning documents are reduced to more concrete objectives, and the projects that will make the greatest contribution to these goals are pinpointed. There are two very similar but not identical sets of guidelines for project appraisal that are commonly referred to—one developed by the United Nations Industrial Development Organization (UNIDO) and the other by the Organization for Economic Cooperation and Development (OECD) (Das Gupta, Marglin, and Sen 1972; and Little and Mirrlees 1974).

A prime criterion or objective function of project selection is the maximization of output from the limited resources available to the government sector. This demands examination of the projects for (a) output contribution, (b) resource usage, (c) externalities, and (d) dynamic growth effects. Consider first the calculation of output contribution and resource cost.

The planner first computes the financial values of a project—expected output, costs, profit or losses—based on existing prices in the economy. This identifies expected financial flows over the project's lifetime and its expected budgetary impact. Financial values, however, do not identify a project's economic value in efficiency terms, that is the project's contribution to maximizing the plan goal of output.

Financial data reflect the many distortions in an LDC economy that cause actual values to deviate from scarcity values. Even where financial flows are expressed in constant prices, distortions arise from monopoly, tariffs, controls on imports, minimum wages, union wages, over- or undervalued exchange rates, resource immobility, and subsidies. The planner must accommodate to the fact that ranking projects by financial values will not satisfy efficiency criteria of output maximization. A closer approximation to economic values must be sought.

The planner is more likely to raise efficiency in the economy as a whole when government projects are selected according to economic, not financial, values, even though economic activity in the rest of the society is determined by financial flows. In such cases, the government sector is seeking a "second-best" solution for an economy with distortions by utilizing economic values in the government sector. The assumption is that distortions in the nongovernment sector will not warp the outcome when economic values are used as a guide to selecting the optimum project in the government sector.

The economic values calculated are not exact; they are approximations to scarcity prices. When data are sufficient and reliable, the complex mathematical technique of linear programming may be used to generate economic values out of a general equilibrium solution. Values so generated are called *shadow prices*. However, most often data are not sufficient for using this technique. Adjustment to financial values then must proceed on an ad hoc basis, often requiring creative calculations to attain some of the adjustments discussed below. Approximations to scarcity prices are sought for important inputs such as foreign exchange and unskilled labor and for any input that composes a significant proportion of total costs. Generally project spending by the government is presumed to be small enough relative to total spending so that the projects themselves will not influence scarcity prices. We discuss now typical adjustments that must be made to financial values to generate economic values.

Foreign Exchange Calculations must be expressed in one *numeraire*. Thus prices denominated in foreign exchange must be converted to domestic prices or vice versa. So as not to distort values with price conversion, the correct ratio of foreign to domestic currency units must be used. This scarcity value for foreign exchange is the equilibrium exchange rate discussed in chapter 18. Very often domestic currency is overvalued in terms of its foreign currency equivalency in LDCs. The balance of payments reflects open or repressed deficits as exports lag and import demand is high. An overvalued exchange rate will understate the import component of the project, leading planners to select projects with excessively high import content.

Labor Costs Unskilled labor's wages may deviate considerably from such workers' economic value, especially where there is surplus labor, minimum wage legislation, or unemployment. The economic cost of unemployed labor is the cost of additional resources like food or housing necessary to make the worker employable at a given location. If there are no such costs, the economic cost is zero, not the wage the worker is paid.

The economic cost of employed labor is the marginal product lost from transferring the laborer and, where the worker transferred or those remaining behind work longer hours as a result, the cost of forgone leisure. Where the worker moves out of agriculture and receives the average as opposed to the marginal product, then the financial value will overstate worker cost. Even if the unskilled worker is transferred from urban employment, the wage there may reflect the average as opposed to the marginal product of labor in agriculture, the ultimate source of urban workers.

When skilled labor is an important component of project costs, there may have to be some adjustment to the financial prices it commands. This is true when skilled workers have increased their salaries beyond their scarcity value through political or economic strength. The government sector itself may be causing the overpricing of skilled labor by overpaying civil servants. Skilled workers from abroad are generally assumed to be priced according to their economic value.

Capital Costs

Capital's scarcity price is related to the economy's capacity to save, freeing resources from consumption for capital formation, and thus to how the community values present as compared with future consumption. The cost of capital is reflected in the discount rate used to calculate the net present value of output from a project. The rate should be the interest rate needed to get savers to forgo consumption voluntarily when the funds for the project come from additional savings. When the funds are diverted from alternative investment opportunities, then the discount rate should reflect the marginal product in shadow prices when invested in the last project that would be undertaken, adjusted for any risk differential between the private and government sectors.

Pragmatically, the cost of capital in these terms is difficult to generate. The UNIDO *Guide to Practical Project Evaluation* recommends exploring the sensitivity of a project's net present value to higher and lower discount rates. The rate chosen may well reflect budgetary limitations or a "ball-park" figure of 10 to 15 percent as reflecting the "true" economic interest rate (1978, p. 42).

The Use of International Prices

A helpful shortcut for estimating scarcity values for goods is to divide them according to whether they are nontradable, traded, or potentially tradable. If they fall into the last two categories, then they may be valued according to international prices. Two assumptions are implicit here. First it is assumed that international prices approximate scarcity prices; that is, international prices are considered to be free of distortions or essentially so. Second, it is assumed that the goods characterized as tradable or potentially tradable for the LDC would be so under conditions of full employment general equilibrium so that their value to the LDC economy is truly reflected in the international price. The OECD Manual emphasizes the use of international prices and recommends denominating the calculations for a project in foreign exchange equivalency units. The UNIDO *Guide* cautions against assuming that goods that are potentially traded will, under development policies of the LDC, be traded in the future (1978). It is common to restrict trade with development planning.

Demand-Side Valuation

In some cases economic values are estimated according to consumption value rather than cost-side value. Of course, in equilibrium the marginal value to the consumer and the marginal cost of supply are equivalent. In cases of distortions such as import quotas and subsidized goods, the two prices differ. When this occurs and the planner is seeking a scarcity price for an intermediate input or final good whose total availability for consumption over time is affected by the project, the marginal value to the consumer is the appropriate estimate for scarcity value.

Valuation Over Time

Output prices and costs can change over the project's lifetime. In part this can be due to inflation. This is adjusted for by valuing output and costs in constant prices. The expected scarcity values of inputs and outputs expressed in constant prices, however, can change over the project's lifetime. As a first approximation under conditions of uncertainty, unchanging scarcity values in constant prices are often assumed. For some projects, however, the planner may generate more than one set of economic values reflecting expected changes over time.

Externalities

Project valuation may entail adjustments for externalities, positive or negative, which are often important in LDCs. When they exist, the social and private benefits or costs of goods or services diverge. An efficiently functioning market, equating private benefit and cost, would produce a different amount of a good than is socially optimal. Externalities can arise from interactions between the utility functions of individuals (for example, health externalities) or the production function of firms (such as labor training) or between the production function of firms and the utility function of individuals (industrial pollution, for instance). The first type are called consumption externalities, the latter production externalities.

When consumption patterns of one or more individuals affect the welfare of one or more other individuals, consumption externalities exist. In general this does not mean that utility from consumption depends upon relative income—that is utility from consumption for individual A depends upon his or her relative consumption level compared with individual B's. Rather it refers to direct side effects from individual B's consumption that affect individual A's welfare. An example of a negative externality is cigarette smoke. Positive externalities exist when, for example, preventive health care is used to control diseases.

Production externalities exist when the production by firm A creates costs or benefits that affect production by firm B or by members of society, but are not reflected in prices. Infrastructure is often identified as providing externalities. Transportation improvements lower the time spent in travel, allow specialization and scale economies for industries located nearby, and affect real estate values. Dams eliminate flooding, create recreational areas, provide water for irrigation and power. Builders typically cannot charge so that they capture full benefits. Telecommunications unify the country, increase information flows, facilitate education, and reduce risk, all of which raise productivity. Water and sewage treatment prevents illness. Education raises the technical capacity of the economy and its ability to manage modernization. Public benefits exceed private ones for which individuals would be willing to pay. Development of a banking system can raise productivity and reduce risk, yielding benefits beyond its private costs.

Projects involving physical and human infrastructure are generally justified by estimating economic costs and benefits, including expected net positive externalities. It is often presumed that the present value based on direct returns to such projects greatly understate their true economic worth. As a result, priority is given to infrastructure projects.

Outside the area of infrastructure, however, it can be dangerous to assume highly positive production externalities without close documentation. Research, for example, may be an area of potentially high externalities but high risk. Urban housing projects may increase migration and fail to reduce overcrowding. The project evaluator must proceed with caution in estimating externalities when they are not so widely recognized as those of infrastructure. Moreover, infrastructure externalities can easily be estimated too high so that premature or excessive development occurs in areas such as capital-intensive dams, railroads, airlines, skill-intensive communication, or financial networks.

Growth Dynamics

One last adjustment is relevant to the objective function of output maximization and that is adjustment for variables related to the dynamics of growth. The national plan may select growth areas for emphasis that are expected to have dynamic impact within the particular context of an individual country's development. Small-scale agriculture or regional development may receive emphasis for both their political and economic repercussions upon growth potential. Dynamic externalities can be related to behavior changes that accompany the market and technical changes of industrialization or common market formation. Externalities reflecting growth repercussions beyond the plan period as a result of current projects may be present. Adjustments would then be needed so that such externalities are given weight in project appraisal.

Often it is argued that the main contribution to the dynamics of development of the government sector is to increase the economy's marginal saving rate—the change in saving with an incremental change in income. This is particularly true where the government diverts income away from consumption by the affluent and towards government investment for development. When the rate of saving is below the social optimum, the government may use tax and monetary policy to raise the saving rate. Assuming this direct approach is not adequately implemented, then projects may be selected that will raise the saving rate. Along these lines, the impact of the government project upon savings is calculated.

How can project appraisal be adjusted for its impact upon savings? Income generated by an undertaking may go to consumption or saving.

Project appraisal guidelines suggest weighting such income differently, giving greater weight to savings so that projects generating more savings will have a greater chance for selection because of the weights. Often projects that generate greater savings are more capital-intensive; and the income may favor high-income groups whose marginal propensity to save is above the average for the economy. The weighting of the savings impact of a project can be criticized on the basis of such effects. On the other hand, the defense of such weighting rests on the importance of savings to the dynamics of growth in the particular LDC's circumstances. Both the UNIDO and OECD guidelines for project selection suggest weighting the consumption generated by a project less than the savings.

Sensitivity Analysis
The project's viability in terms of economic or shadow prices is directly related to the discount rate used. As the following table illustrates, a unit of currency received 15 years in the future and discounted at 10 percent is worth only .239 units of currency in the current period (year zero), and only .065 units when discounted at 20 percent. The formula for calculating the net present value of a stream of future payments can be expressed as:

$$PV = \frac{R_1}{(1+i)} + \frac{R_2}{(1+i)^2} + \frac{R_3}{(1+i)^3} \cdots + \frac{R_n}{(1+i)^n} \qquad (7)$$

where

PV = expected net present value of a discounted stream of income arising over time
R_n = expected future net payments in years 1, . . . n
i = social discount rate

The social discount rate is the rate chosen by the planners to reflect the economic value of capital. When, using this discount rate, the present value is zero, the community will receive enough in future consumption to offset exactly the value of forgone present consumption necessary for saving and investment to take place. Thus any project with a present value of zero or above is acceptable. When funds are limited, projects must be ranked and those with lower present value excluded.

Only perchance will the present value of a project at a particular social discount rate equal zero. The current value of a project changes from positive to negative when the discount rate increases by a sufficient amount. It can be helpful to ask, What discount rate would yield a zero present value for a project? This rate is called the *internal rate of return*. It is the upper boundary for the social discount rate when projects that fail to compensate the saver for forgone consumption are avoided.

The graph in figure 19.3 shows the net present value for a project calculated at various discount rates, including zero. The project's net

Year of Receipt	Discount Factor	
	10%	20%
1	0.909	0.833
2	0.826	0.694
3	0.751	0.579
4	0.683	0.482
5	0.621	0.402
6	0.564	0.335
7	0.513	0.279
8	0.467	0.233
9	0.424	0.194
10	0.386	0.162
11	0.350	0.135
12	0.319	0.112
13	0.290	0.093
14	0.263	0.078
15	0.239	0.065

TABLE 19.5

Values in Year Zero of One Unit of Currency Received in the Future Discounted at 10% and 20%

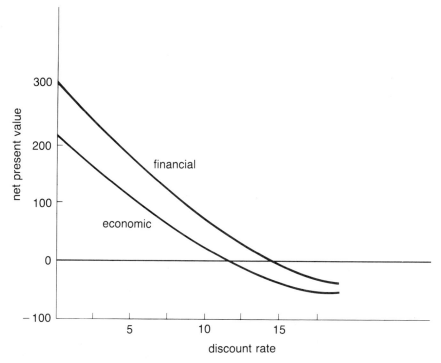

FIGURE 19.3

Financial, Economic Net Present Values

Divergence of net present value calculated according to financial and economic values at varying discount rates.

present value is figured using, alternatively, financial and economic prices. At any social discount rate up to 12 percent the project is economically profitable. Such curves may be drawn freehand by calculating the present value of a high and intermediate discount rate and connecting the two points and the axis point. The slope of a project's curve will vary with the time flow of returns.

Higher discount rates reduce the present value more on projects with delayed returns. Figure 19.4 represents the economic value of two projects, A and B. Assume the social discount rate is 10 percent. The selection of projects according to the highest internal rate of return would lead to a different choice than one based upon the highest net present value, our criterion for selection. However, because the social discount rate is usually not known with confidence, the crossover discount rate may be examined for relevance in determining project acceptability. The crossover rate is the discount rate at which the present value of two projects calculated at varying discount rates change their relative ranking.

Here we have examined the sensitivity of the undertaking to the social discount rate. Sensitivity analysis can also be useful when uncertainty about the project's expected net returns is high due to high variability levels for important components of net returns. Upper and lower bounds for sensitive variables can be utilized to show the range of net present value that can be expected. Projects with higher ranges and uncertainties would be considered riskier.

Another Goal:
Income Distribution Static and dynamic output maximization may not be the only plan goal. Some plans aim for income distribution. Income taxation combined with subsidies to the poor is the most direct route to income redistribution in mixed economies. And other types of legislation also affect income flows among groups. However, with the increasing concern about the income distribution effects in developing LDCs in the postwar period, attention has turned to the impact of government spending upon inequality (UNIDO 1978; and Mirrlees 1978). In part this is because of the failure in so many cases of tax legislation in this connection. Even where progressive tax laws are enacted, they seldom are effectively implemented. The wealthy and those with high incomes tend to be politically powerful and thus capable of thwarting income redistribution via taxation.

Adjustment of project evaluation to accommodate income redistribution goals calls for identification of income groups and their gains and losses from the project. In practice there are generally just two groups identified: the poor and everyone else. Ideally both primary and secondary income effects should be traced. Thus a fertilizer project may raise income mainly for wealthier farmers whose holdings are irrigated; but lower food prices may help the poorer groups who spend a larger percentage of their income on food than do richer groups. Or a factory that produces cheap rubber thong sandals may drive many relatively poor cobblers out of business. In actuality it is difficult to

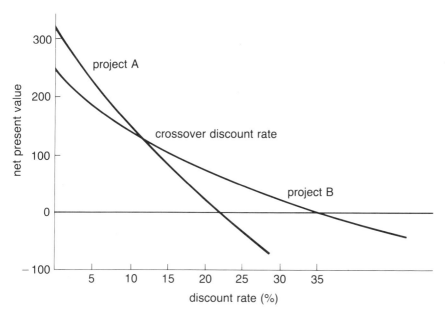

FIGURE 19.4

Comparison of Project Net Present Values

Net present value for two different projects, A and B, at varying discount rates showing the crossover discount rate at which projects A and B change their relative ranking.

identify even the first-round effects; the second-round effects are generally ignored unless very important and measurable.

Once income distribution flows are identified, then differential weights are assigned to the project's income flows depending upon the group receiving them. Income going to poorer groups is weighted more heavily.

The income received is traced as financial flows arising from project selection, not flows valued in economic or shadow prices. It would be an enormous task to adjust economic values according to income distribution. In order to avoid this work, the economic values can be adjusted for the project's distribution impact by a premium or penalty reflecting the distribution of financial flows. Such weights are not easily established. They reflect political priorities about income distribution. Thus in economies with social unrest from unemployment, projects favoring the unemployed may receive enough political support to warrant selection even though their net present value is lower relative to other projects with less capacity for job creation. The difference between the present value of the last project selected after adjustment for income distribution and the present value of the last project that would be selected without such adjustment, expressed as a percentage of project cost, is the premium that politicians attach to income for the poor. This concrete measure of priority by political decision guides the planners in selecting the appropriate weight to be assigned to distribution effects.

Further Adjustment: Merit and Demerit Goods

Merit goods are defined as goods whose social value exceeds their economic value; a demerit good has a social value below its economic worth. Examples of merit goods are defense expenditures, export products that reduce fluctuations in foreign exchange when the politicians or populace are risk averse, or products that satisfy "basic needs" and thereby are considered more valuable than their economic price because of ethical judgments. Examples of demerit goods are opium or alcohol where the populace uses them in a manner that creates social or domestic unrest, "luxury items" considered to have negative ethical value amidst conditions of poverty, or goods that replace artistic craftsmanship associated with a national heritage.

Valuation adjustment for merit or demerit goods proceeds by assigning a premium or penalty factor to such products in the same way as the adjustment for income distribution. Thus the net present value in economic prices of a road project may gain a 20 percent upward valuation when it contributes to border defense.

Summary of Project Appraisal

Project appraisal for government expenditures is not a science. Guidelines developed by UNIDO and OECD, however, provide a carefully thought-out approach that promises more thorough documentation and estimation of the actual value of a project to the development goals of an LDC than simple financial evaluation or political persuasion. These guidelines concentrate upon the adjustment of financial values to reflect economic values in order to achieve efficiency in project selection. This involves estimating the opportunity cost or shadow prices of resources and output. It also includes calculation of some externalities so that social costs and benefits are internalized.

Growth goals and social goals can be incorporated into a project appraisal by establishing adjustment factors or weights, which are then used to adjust the net present economic value of a project. Premiums are attached most often to the project's saving flows, to income redistribution flows, and to merit goods. Figure 19.5 summarizes the various adjustments with a graph showing net present value at various discount rates.

A difficult part of project appraisal is the selection of the social discount rate. This determines the value of future consumption relative to present consumption that is influenced by the project. The welfare criterion generally accepted is that the stream of future output should be discounted according to the consumption time preference of the present community, which must forgo current consumption so that investment may take place. Theoretically, this discount rate is the interest rate needed to attract the last unit of saving from the economy. When the economy is in equilibrium, this will equal the return to the marginal investment project.

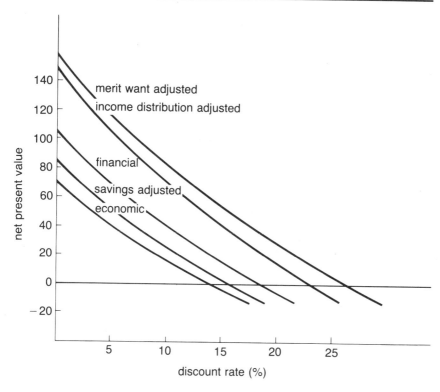

FIGURE 19.5

Adjustments to Net Present Value

Project summary graph showing possible adjustments to the calculation of net present values.

SOURCE: UNIDO, *Guide to Practical Project Appraisal.* New York: United Nations, 1978, p. 79.

Two problems arise here—one theoretical, one mechanical. Concerning the latter, the LDC economy diverges from equilibrium to the degree that estimating a community time preference from interest rates in the economy is fraught with difficulty. Distortions in all markets, including financial ones, confound the selection of a scarcity price for savings. The theoretical problem is equally intractable. It raises the question of intergenerational income distribution, a welfare question. The time preference of the community under current income levels and distribution may not allow adequate savings to raise the growth rate so that future generations endure less poverty. An adjustment for the project's savings flows indicates the government is increasing the importance of future over present consumption. The normative argument for such adjustment is that the government has a role to play in raising the marginal saving ratio of the economy for growth purposes.

The practical solutions to these problems vary. Techniques for selecting the discount rate can be fairly rudimentary. Sensitivity analysis, political feedback to planners, and use of "ball park" rates of 10–15 percent commonly suggested in guidelines are all possibilities. Adjustment for the savings (growth) impact of projects is fairly common.

The degree of adjustment can be somewhat arbitrary. Yet despite problems with the discount rate, with estimating economic values, and with setting premiums for selected goals, project appraisal as an aid to planning is itself considered to have a positive net present value and an internal rate of return high enough to warrant its absorption of government funds.

REFERENCES   Chelliah, Raja J. 1975. Trends in Taxation in Developing Countries. In *Readings on Taxation in Developing Countries*, edited by R. M. Bird and Oliver Oldman. Baltimore, MD: Johns Hopkins University Press: 105–27.

Chelliah, R. J.; Bass, H. J.; and Kelly, M. R. 1975. Tax Ratios and Tax Effort in Developing Countries, 1969–71. *IMF Staff Papers* 22 (March): 187–205.

Das Gupta, P.; Marglin, S.; and Sen, A. 1972. *Guidelines for Project Evaluation.* New York: United Nations.

Little, I.M.D. and Mirrlees, J. A. 1974. *Project Appraisal and Planning for Developing Countries.* New York: Basic Books.

Mirrlees, J. A. 1978. Social Cost-Benefit Analysis and the Distribution of Income. *World Development* 6 (February): 131—38.

UNIDO, 1978. *Guide to Practical Project Evaluation.* New York: United Nations.

Index